MANAGING IN THE
INFORMATION ECONOMY
Current Research Issues

Edited by

Uday Apte
And
Uday Karmarkar

 Springer

Uday Apte
Naval Postgraduate School
Monterey, CA, USA

Uday Karmarkar
University of California
Los Angeles, CA, USA

Library of Congress Control Number: 2006930393

ISBN-10: 0-387-34214-1 (HB)   ISBN-10: 0-387-36892-2 (e-book)
ISBN-13: 978-0387-34214-6 (HB)   ISBN-13: 978-0387-36892-4 (e-book)

Printed on acid-free paper.

Printed in the United States of America.

9 8 7 6 5 4 3 2 1

springer.com

TABLE OF CONTENTS

CURRENT RESEARCH ON MANAGING IN THE INFORMATION ECONOMY
Introductory Note

Uday S. Karmarkar[a] and Uday M. Apte[b]

[a]*UCLA Anderson Graduate School of Management, 110 Westwood Plaza, PO Box 951481, Los Angeles, CA 90095-1481;* [b]*Graduate School of Business and Public Policy, Naval Postgraduate School, 555 Dyer Road, Monterey, CA 93943*

There are two major trends visible in economies all over the world. The first trend, far along in developed countries, is the shift to a service economy. The second, also quite advanced in some countries, but barely visible in others, is the shift to an information economy. By the "information economy" we mean those sectors in the economy that are concerned with the production of information goods and services, including the creation of assets and technologies for processing and distributing information.

Several researchers have followed the progress of this trend in the US economy over some decades. One of the most recent of such studies is the paper by Apte and Nath in this volume that uses data from 1997 for the US economy. They show that the information economy now comprises over 60% of private industry in the US in terms of GNP value added. What is also apparent is that information services make up the major part of the information economy.

While Apte and Nath give us a broad and comprehensive look at changes in the economy over three decades, these economic changes have come about due to many underlying changes at the operation, task, process, firm and sector levels. As these changes have occurred in firms, managers have had to adapt to the need to manage the changes and to learn to manage in the changed environment. This is an ongoing process that we expect to take perhaps a couple of decades. Some of the changes underway have been compared to the industrial revolution, and the process of adaptation will not occur overnight.

This volume presents a collection of recent research directions that address the issue of management in this economy. The contributors include leading researchers with interests in a diverse set of topics. Indeed the subject is so vast, that this collection cannot pretend to do more than provide a sample of the research that is being conducted. So the purpose of the volume cannot be to give a complete and comprehensive picture, but rather to provide introductions to important areas, and a few pointers to some important topics for future research. So the book begins with perspectives at the level of the economy as a whole and then progressively addresses industrial structure, sectors, functions (ecommerce) and business practice. We provide brief introductions to the main sections and the papers in each section.

1.1.   The Information Economy

The paper by Uday Apte and Hiranya Nath, establishes that the US economy is indeed in the middle of a shift to an information economy. Using the Benchmark Input–Output (I-O) tables for 1992 and 1997 as compiled by the Bureau of Economic Analysis (BEA) of the US Department of Commerce (the latest Benchmark data available as of 2006), they show that the US private sector is already dominated by information intensive firms and processes. The accompanying paper in the first section by Dale Jorgenson, entitled "Information Technology and the G7 Economies", presents comparison of economic growth among the G7 nations. These comparisons focus on the impact of investment in information technology (IT) equipment and software over the period 1980–2001. The paper concludes that surge in investment in IT equipment and software contributed substantially to economic growth in all G7 countries including the United States.

1.2.   Structure and Organization of the Information Economy

The economics of information intensive industries are of course far different from those of physical products. In addition market structures and mechanisms can also be very different. Uday Apte and Uday Karmarkar analyze the role that information technology plays in globalizing information-intensive services to discuss a theoretical framework that identifies the criteria and guidelines for successfully selecting service activities that can be globally outsourced. Applying this theoretical framework to year 2000 data for the US economy they estimate that about 10.5 million service jobs hold the potential for global outsourcing. The paper also analyzes the geographic distribution of language clusters and presents a conjecture concerning the emerging pattern of global trade in information-intensive services. The paper by Vijay Gurbaxani develops a model for the structure of contracts for outsourced information services and tests it against ten examples. Hamid Ekbia's paper looks at the mechanisms and driving forces behind network organizations. Finally Eric Clemons argues that new technologies are creating a much higher level of product and service differentiation in the economy. This notion is complementary to the idea that technologies are permitting higher levels of de-integration and vertical specialization in information chains. In other words, there is in a sense both a horizontal and vertical fragmentation visible in information intensive businesses.

1.3.   Marketing and Ecommerce

Ecommerce was one of the earliest visible effects of the Internet and web on industry structure. Lee Cooper describes the application of advanced technologies in marketing and sales over the Internet. Mohanbir Sawhney and Eleonora Di Maria, turn their attention to B2B transactions, and posit that the real value of new technologies for B2B markets lies in the interaction and knowledge sharing that is enabled, and not just in efficiency in the sales transaction. Haim Mendelson and Tunay Tunca turn their attention to the specific case of B2B exchanges, and ask for whom they create value.

1.4.   Emerging Issues in the Information Economy

There are a number of major areas in which information technology has impacted market structure, company conduct and the nature of competition. Apart from some of these major issues dealing with operational costs, transactions, and structure, there are a number of other management issues that arise. Stephen Cohen and Cinzia Dal Zotto address the concept of organizational absorptive capacity in a world in which there is much more to absorb. Richard Mason introduces the complex issues surrounding ethics in the new world of the Internet. De Liu, Xianjun Geng, and Andrew Whinston discuss the emerging phenomenon of on-line communities, and the role of status seeking in these new social structures.

1.5.   Information and Transaction Based Services

This section presents analytical studies of three industry sectors that have been hugely affected by technological change. Bashyam Anant and Uday Karmarkar analyze business data services, keying on Aspect Development as an example. They use this sector to illustrate several basic ideas, including the effect of technologies on access and hence on market segmentation, and the connection between technology, process economics, and competition. Reynolds Byers and Phillip Lederer study consumer (retail) banking and analyze how different banking channels compete for market share. Both of these papers also illustrate the fragmentation of markets that occurs with the appearance of a new technology that competes with existing processes. Finally, Uday Apte and S. Viswanathan study the emerging opportunities available to e-Commerce retailers in proactively managing inventory. The web-based buying process allows the e-retailer to adjust the display prominence of a product and thereby exercise better influence over the demand level for its products. This makes it possible for the e-retailer to link its inventory policy decisions to the display prominence actions and lower its overall inventory related costs. Apte and Viswanathan develop optimization models to investigate these issues and derive closed form equations for the optimal parameter values for implementing proactive demand management for controlling e-retailer inventory.

1.6.   Empirical Studies of Business Practice

In the final section we present three papers based on surveys of business practice in three countries at different levels of technology penetration and adoption and with different patterns of technology use. These surveys were all pilot studies for the Business and Information Technologies (BIT) project centered at the UCLA Anderson School. The paper by Uday Karmarkar and Vandana Mangal presents an overview of the BIT project and documents the information technology driven changes occurring in a wide range of industry sectors in the United States and Canada. Atanu Ghosh and T. N. Seshadri present a pilot study of information and communication technology in India and its impact on business sectors. Finally, the paper by Demattè, Biffi, Mandelli and Parolini present a study of digital technologies and e-business in Italy.

The BIT project is now in its third year and includes studies of industry sectors and economies, in addition to the practice survey. More information about the project can be found at www.anderson.ucla.edu/bit.xml. In the second year of the project, five countries conducted the survey, and the project has since expanded to over ten research teams. On the one hand, these surveys show that the actual pace of adoption of new technologies is not quite as rapid as the popular press might lead one to believe. However, the surveys also show some significant trends and evolutionary changes. For example, the US survey shows a marked degree of real shifts in organizational structure, including flattening of structures, increase in the average span of control, and a higher level of geographical distribution and cross firm interaction. On the other hand, the Italian survey suggests that in Italy technology adoption has primarily been a matter of using the technologies to strengthen existing networks and interrelationships, rather than changing internal organizational structure.

Chapter 1

SIZE, STRUCTURE AND GROWTH OF THE U.S. INFORMATION ECONOMY

Uday M. Apte [a] and Hiranya K. Nath [b]

[a]*Graduate School of Business and Public Policy, Naval Postgraduate School, 555 Dyer Road, Monterey, CA 93943;* [b]*Department of Economics and Intl. Business, Sam Houston State University, Huntsville, TX 77341-2118*

Abstract   This paper presents the results of our empirical research in measuring the size and structure of the U.S. information economy in 1992 and 1997, and in assessing the growth experienced by different industries and sectors since Porat's research on the U.S. information economy in 1967. The study indicates that the share of the information economy in total GNP grew from about 46 percent in 1967 to about 56 percent in 1992, and to 63 percent in 1997. The study further indicates that during this time period the share of service sector information activities in total GNP increased substantially, while the shares of non-service sectors declined correspondingly. The industries displaying the highest growth rates include business services, and medical and educational services. The paper also provides a critical assessment of Porat's methodology and suggests specific improvements that may be made to obtain a more plausible measure of the size and structure of the information economy.

Keywords: information economy, primary information sector, secondary information sector, input–output analysis, information services, information workers, information occupations

1.   INTRODUCTION

That we live today in an information economy is a frequently encountered assertion that few people would have any disagreement with. However, to our knowledge, in the past few decades since the pioneering research work of Machlup (1962) and Porat (1977),[1] comprehensive studies concerning the size

---

[1]   Porat started this study and Rubin joined him later. We will refer to this study as Porat (1977).

and structure of the information related activities in the U.S. have been few and far in between.[2] Hence, the current research is specifically aimed at measuring the size and structure of the U.S. information economy based on the latest available data. Other main objective of the research is to compare the results of the current study with those of Porat's study so as to identify the sector/s and industries that may have experienced the fastest growth in their information related activities. It is expected that the results of the current research will unveil new directions for future fruitful research in today's information economy.

In developed economies today, information has come to play an important role in almost every walk of life. For example, consumers can make more informed decisions today in their purchasing activities. Producers, on the other hand, can now decide more easily on what to produce, how to produce, and for whom to produce. The unprecedented progress of computers and communications technology in last few decades has increased the information intensity of most activities in value chains (Apte and Mason, 1995). In brief, information is increasingly holding 'the key to growth, output, and employment' (Martin, 1988), a role that was played in the past by traditional factors of production such as land, labor and capital in the industrial society. The all-pervasive impact of information revolution also has important implications for the economy at macro level in terms of the increasing share of information activities in national income. Hence, we believe that it is important to measure the size, structure and growth of the information economy in the US.

As we have already mentioned, there exist two well-known studies, which have tried to define and measure the so-called information economy. Fritz Machlup's 1962 study is one of the first attempts to conceptualize what he calls the 'knowledge industry' and to present a comprehensive statistical profile of this industry. This study provides a conceptual framework for research into quantitative as well as qualitative aspects of knowledge-based information activities. It identifies the components of the 'knowledge industry' and measures its contribution to Gross National Product (GNP). According to Machlup, 29 percent of the U.S. GNP was generated by the knowledge industry in 1958.

In 1977, Marc Porat undertook an extensive study of information based activities in the U.S. economy on behalf of the U.S. Department of Commerce. Using a conceptual framework similar to that of Machlup, he measures the size and structure of the U.S. information economy in 1967. However, to define and measure the information economy, Porat adopts an approach that is quite distinct from the one used by Machlup. He strictly follows the national income

---

[2]   Recently, the U.S. Census Bureau, in their 1997 Economic Census, has created a new 'Information Sector'. However, as we will discuss, the scope and size of this new sector is much smaller than most earlier studies suggest.

accounting framework. Machlup, on the other hand, includes a number of economic activities that are not part of the national income accounts. The difference was about a choice between orthodoxy and completeness. Machlup's approach would require a new system of national accounting if one wants to analyze the information sector ('knowledge industry' à la Machlup) within the broader concept of the national economy. Porat recognizes Machlup's innovation and its novelty but justifies his stance in using conventional national income accounting framework: "the concept of an information sector was sufficiently new that a simultaneous overhaul of the GNP scheme would confuse and obfuscate more than it would help" (Porat, 1977, vol. 1, p. 45). Moreover, the compilation and manipulation of data is significantly easier using Porat's method that makes use of the Bureau of Economic Analysis (BEA) National Income and Product Accounts data that already exist. However, it has its limitations. Because the BEA data are collected largely at the four-digit SIC level many of the information activities which can only be identified at a high level of disaggregation are not included in Porat's method.

Moreover, Porat in his study distinguishes between "primary" and "secondary" information sectors whereas Machlup does not make any such distinction. The primary information sector includes industries that produce information goods and services for the market. The secondary information sector, on the other hand, includes information activities that are used as inputs in the production of other goods and services. The measurement of the secondary information sector requires dividing 'noninformation' firms and industries into two parts: one involves 'pure' non-information activities and the other involves 'pure' information activities. Machlup argues that this approach "mixes information inputs in industries outside the information sector with outputs of industries in the information sector" (Machlup, 1980, p. 240).

Finally, Machlup uses "final demand" whereas Porat uses "value added" as the measure of GNP.[3] Thus, Machlup's method is based on measuring GNP by product sales and Porat's method is based on measuring GNP by income. Although the total for each of these measures will be the same for the entire economy the total for individual industries can vary substantially. Porat justifies the use of 'value added' on the following grounds. "First, it allows the researcher to measure the cost of the secondary information services directly. Second, value added is a more accurate measure of wealth and income originating in the economy since it is insensitive to the cost of goods sold. An item with costly intermediate purchases will "sell" more to final demand since its output price will be correspondingly higher. Two goods with identical wealth-generating attributes could have very different final demand sales, depending on the use of the item" (Porat, 1977, vol. 1, p. 47). However, as Huber and

---

[3] For a detailed discussion on the differences see Huber and Rubin (1986, Chapter II).

Rubin (1986) later concede, 'the depth of detail is substantially greater when the Machlup method is used ...' although it '... could overstate the size of the knowledge industries compared to GNP, if care is not taken'.

The methodology developed by Porat is subsequently employed by the Organization for Economic Cooperation and Development (OECD), to study the information sectors in nine of its member nations in 1978 and 1979. The results were published in 1981 under the title *Information Activities, Electronics and Telecommunications Technologies: Impact on Employment, Growth and Trade*. This study shows that the share of the primary information sector in the U.S. GNP increases from 19.6 percent in 1958 to 24.8 percent in 1972 (OECD, 1981, Table I.8). The contribution of the secondary information sector, on the other hand, increases from 23.1 percent in 1958 to 24.4 percent in 1972 (OECD, 1981, Table I.10).[4]

Machlup planned an ambitious project of bringing out the series *Knowledge: Its Creation, Distribution and Economic Significance* with ten volumes highlighting different aspects of knowledge industry. However, because of his untimely demise this project remained unfinished with only three volumes having been published. Nevertheless, as a sequel to his unfinished work, Michael Rubin and Mary Huber brought out a volume in 1986 entitled *The Knowledge Industry in the United States: 1960–1980*. Following Machlup's methodology, this study presents measurements of knowledge industry for the years when the U.S. Bureau of the Census conducted economic censuses. These 'census years' include 1963, 1967, 1972, 1977 and 1980. Contrary to expectations of high growth of the knowledge industry as documented by Machlup in his 1962 study, they find that its contribution to the U.S. GNP increased from 29 percent in 1958 to only about 34 percent in 1980.

In this paper, following Porat's definitions and methodology as closely as possible, we estimate GNP accrued to the information related activities in the U.S. in 1992 and 1997. Our results confirm the findings of the OECD 1986 study: the primary information sector is growing faster than the secondary sector.[5] We also examine in detail the contributions of various sectors, particularly of the service sector, to the rapidly growing information activities. Discussion of the analysis we conduct and the results we find are the main subject matter of this paper.

The rest of the paper is organized as follows. The second section discusses the main concepts and definitions. The sources of data and the computational methodology are described in section three. The fourth section presents the measures of the size and structure of the U.S. information economy in 1992

---

4   See Appendix Table 1-A.1.

5   During 1992–97 this does not seem to be the case. However, as we will discuss, it may have
    to do with the recent reclassification of industries.

and 1997. It includes a comparison of these measures with the measures for 1967 as reported by Porat (1977), and a discussion on the growth of various sectors of the economy during the 1967–1992 and 1992–1997 time periods. It also analyzes in detail the growth of the information components of the service sector between 1967 and 1992, and between 1992 and 1997. In section five, we include a discussion on the 'information sector' as defined and measured by the U.S. Census Bureau. Section six critically evaluates Porat's approach and suggests certain improvements for arriving at more plausible measures of the information economy. The last section briefly indicates the direction of future research and makes a few concluding remarks.

2.   CONCEPTS AND DEFINITIONS

In order to measure the information economy, Porat (1977) divides the economy into two distinct but inseparable domains: one 'involved in the transformation of matter and energy from one form into another' and the other 'in transforming information from one pattern into another' (Porat, 1977, vol. 1). The second domain is referred to as information economy. The notion of information economy rests on the concepts of 'information' and 'information activity'. Porat defines information as the 'data that have been organized and communicated', while his operational definition of information activity encompasses 'all workers, machinery, goods and services that are employed in processing, manipulating and transmitting information' (Porat, 1977, vol. 1, p. 2).

He then divides the information economy into two sectors: 'primary information sector' and 'secondary information sector' (PRIS and SIS respectively hereafter). The PRIS is defined as one that includes all industries which produce goods and services which intrinsically convey information or are directly used in producing, processing or distributing information for an established market. The broad categories of PRIS industries are: (1) knowledge production and invention: private R&D and private information services; (2) information distribution and communication: education, public information services, telecommunications etc.; (3) risk management: insurance and finance industries and others; (4) search and coordination: brokerage industries, advertising etc.; (5) information processing and transmission services: computer based information processing, telecommunications infrastructure etc.; (6) information goods: calculators, semiconductors, computers; (7) selected government activities: education and postal service; (8) support facilities: buildings, office furniture etc.; (9) wholesale and retail trade in information goods and services. These major categories, in turn, are composed of hundreds of industries.

The SIS, on the other hand, is defined to 'include all information services produced for internal consumption by government and non-information firms'

(Porat, 1977, vol. 1, p. 4). It comprises 'most of the public bureaucracy and all of the private bureaucracy. It includes the costs of organizing firms, maintaining and regulating markets, developing and transmitting prices, monitoring the firm's behavior and making and enforcing rules' (Porat, 1977, vol. 1, pp. 15–16). The public bureaucracy comprises all the informational functions of the federal, state and local governments. Governments perform planning, coordinating, deciding, monitoring, regulating and evaluating activities. Those portions of public bureaucracy which have direct analogs in the primary information sector—such as printing, law and accounting—are, however, included in the primary sector for accounting purposes. It should also be noted that education is one of the largest components of public bureaucracy that is included in the primary sector.

The private bureaucracy, on the other hand, is that portion of every non-information firm that engages in purely informational activities. It produces information services similar to those in the PRIS, such as data processing and library services. Conceptually, they are the informational costs of providing a non-information good. However, these information services are not sold in the market and hence are included in SIS.

3.   DATA SOURCES AND COMPUTATIONAL METHODOLOGY

The main source of data for this study is Benchmark Input–Output (I-O) Tables for 1992 and 1997 as compiled by the Bureau of Economic Analysis (BEA) of the U.S. Department of Commerce. Note that the 1997 I-O table is the most up-to-date complete table available as of 2006 (although as this manuscript goes to the press, a few preliminary tables from 2002 Benchmark Input Output estimates are available on the website http://www.bea.gov). The BEA compiles the underlying statistics for the construction of the benchmark I-O tables at 5-year intervals. This compilation takes several years and that is why the 1997 I-O table was released only in 2002. Other important data sources include (1) 'National Income and Product Accounts' (NIPA) detailed tables on 'Income, Employment and Product by Industry' as compiled by BEA; (2) Occupational Outlook Handbook, 1994–1995, and Occupational Employment Statistics for 1992 and 1998, both published by the Bureau of Labor Statistics (BLS), U.S. Department of Labor; (3) 1997 Economic Census: Summary Statistics for United States (1997 NAICS Basis) and 1997 Economic Census: Information—United States, as available on the Census Bureau's website (www.census.gov).

3.1.　　Measuring Primary Information Sector

In order to measure the PRIS, Porat identified 25 major 2-digit I-O industries[6] and aggregated them into four broad categories of construction, manufacturing, service and government sectors. Following Porat, we identify the 6-digit information industries within each of these 2-digit I-O categories. Out of 480 6-digit industries included in the detailed I-O table in 1992, we identify 87 industries as belonging to the PRIS. We then obtain value-added figures from 1992 Benchmark Detailed I-O Use Table for each of these 6-digit information industries. Aggregating over 6-digit industries we obtain the information value added at the corresponding 2-digit industry levels.

In the 1997 Benchmark I-O Tables, the I-O industry classification system is, however, based on the new North American Industrial Classification System (NAICS)[7] and therefore, different from the 1992 I-O industry classification. We use Appendix A of Lawson et al. (2002) to obtain the 1997 NAICS industries corresponding to the 6-digit 1997 I-O industries, which are then mapped to 1987 SIC industries using a detailed matching between these two different classification systems as available from www.naics.com/files/sic2naics.htm. This exercise helps us identify 63 of 1997 6-digit I-O industries as belonging to the PRIS.

In case of a few industries at 2-digit level, such as communications, office, computing and accounting machines, radio, television and communication equipment, and electronic equipment, the entire industries are identified as belonging to the PRIS. More often, however, only a part of an industry's value added is identified as being information-based.

3.2.　　Measuring Secondary Information Sector

As we discussed in the previous section, the SIS accounts for the resources devoted to the production of information services for the in-house consumption of private and public bureaucracies. In order to measure the SIS, non-PRIS firms and public bureaucracies are taken apart, in an accounting sense, into an information division and a non-information division. To measure the non-marketed services of the SIS, Porat uses a rather restrictive definition of value added. According to this definition, value-added of an SIS industry includes (1) employee compensation of information workers, (2) part of proprietors' income and corporate profits earned for performing informational tasks,

---

[6]　I-O classification of industries is different from more familiar Standard Industrial Classification (SIC).

[7]　Under NAICS, establishments are grouped according to the similarities of their production processes rather than the similarities of their products. For detailed discussion on the changes, see Lawson et al. (2002).

and (3) capital consumption allowances on information machines. To calculate compensation of information workers, Porat uses a BLS matrix[8] (unpublished) that shows detailed occupational structure of all U.S. industries, together with wages and salaries for various occupations. He imputes the value of proprietors' income earned for performing informational tasks by matching them with information workers in similar occupations and using their salaries as the value of compensation for proprietors for informational activities. Similarly, he uses an unpublished BEA matrix that shows the detailed capital flows of all industries to calculate depreciation allowances on information capital goods.

Our study, however, is mainly based on published data, and hence of necessity, we make a few modifications to the methodology. The most important one is that since most data are available at the 2-digit level of Standard Industrial Classification (SIC), we use those data for the subsequent quantitative calculations. In order to be consistent with the use of I-O industry classification in our calculation for the PRIS, we also make a few minor adjustments, which are discussed later in this section.

3.2.1.   Measuring employee compensation of information workers

To calculate employee compensation of information workers in 1992 a matrix of occupations versus 2-digit SIC industries is compiled from the *Occupational Employment Statistics* for 1992. This matrix consists of 181 information occupations and 41 2-digit SIC industries in 1992. In identifying the information occupations we strictly follow the scheme developed by Porat. This matrix represents the distribution of information workers over all occupations in all industries. Average/median salaries of information workers are obtained from the *Occupational Outlook Handbook*, and then each entry in the above matrix is multiplied by the average/median salary for the corresponding occupation to calculate the total employee compensation by industry. As noted earlier, a few exceptions have been made in implementing this methodology. For 'agriculture, forestry and fishing', 'finance, insurance and real estate', 'government enterprises' (federal, state and local) and 'general governments', the data by occupational categories, unfortunately, are not available for 1992. For these industries the shares of the SIS in total employee compensation for 1967 are taken from Table 9.2 of volume I of Porat (1977, pp. 155–156) study, and are applied to the BEA-compiled total compensation of employees in these industries in 1992.

For 1997, we create a matrix of 232 information occupations and 70 2-digit SIC industries from the 1998 Occupational Employment Statistics that also

---

[8]   Vol. 6 and vol. 7 of Porat (1977) contain two matrices showing the employee compensation paid to 422 occupations in the 108 industries by I-O classification for 1967 and 1970 respectively.

reports the mean hourly wages in different occupations. The survey uses fourth quarter of 1998 as the reference period and adjusts the wage data for inflation accordingly. In order to make them comparable with other components, after calculating the compensation of information workers for each industry group we adjust them back to 1997 values by applying industry-wise GDP deflator calculated from the Bureau of Economic Analysis.

3.2.2.   Measuring proprietors' income and depreciation allowances

Data on proprietors' income and depreciation allowances by broad industry groups for 1992 are obtained from the Bureau of Economic Analysis. We need to calculate the shares of these two categories respectively as accounted for by the information activities and information capital. We apply the percentage shares of the SIS in total proprietors' income, and percentage shares of the SIS in total depreciation allowances by industries, as reported in Table 9.2 of volume 1 of Porat (1977) study, to 1992 figures.

Since these proportions are available for aggregate industries (roughly at 1-digit level of SIC), applying them to 2-digit level industry data would ignore the fact that there could be some variations among 2-digit industries within each of these aggregate industries. To get around this problem, we first calculate proprietors' income for informational activities and depreciation allowances on information capital at aggregate levels (at 1-digit level) and they are apportioned according to the shares of corresponding 2-digit industries in aggregate (1-digit level) employee compensation of information workers, as obtained in the previous subsection. However, we want to make it clear that the procedure we use does not take into account the possibility that over the years the informational activities of the proprietors or relative use of information capital goods may have increased. However, we also want to point out that by using the above-mentioned procedure, we arrive at very conservative estimates of proprietors' income for informational activities and for depreciation of information capital goods. In any case, these two items represent only a very small part of the total SIS, and therefore this method presumably has a negligible impact on the overall accuracy of estimation.

For 1997, however, we use a slightly different approach. The 1997 Benchmark I-O Tables report three components of gross value added for each I-O industry: 'Compensation of Employees', 'Indirect Business Tax and Nontax liability' and 'Other Value Added'. The component 'Other Value Added' mainly includes proprietors' income and depreciation allowances. We use the mapping between 1997 NAICS and 1987 SIC to calculate other value added for each of the 2-digit SIC industry. We then calculate the shares of proprietors' income and depreciation allowances accounted for by information activities in total for 1992, and apply them to the 1997 'other value added' to obtain corresponding components of SIS value added.

As we mentioned earlier, in measuring the SIS we use SIC rather than I-O classification as used by Porat. It is important to recognize that while calculating the value added contributions of different 2-digit SIC industries to the SIS using the procedure described above, we carefully make suitable adjustments for those disaggregated industries, which have already been entirely or partially allocated to the PRIS. Otherwise, it would lead to double counting of parts of value added of PRIS industries. To prevent double counting, we calculate the shares of the 6-digit I-O industries included in PRIS, in total value added of corresponding 2-digit SIC industries. We then apply these proportions to the SIS value added as calculated above, to purge out the pure contributions of the 2-digit SIC industries to the SIS.

By carrying out the above-described computational methodology we arrive at the estimation of the size and structure of the U.S. information economy in 1992 and 1997. The results are then compared with Porat's results for 1967 to compute the growth rates experienced by different industries. The results are presented and discussed in the next section.

4.   SIZE, STRUCTURE AND GROWTH OF THE INFORMATION ECONOMY

Table 1-1 below presents the value added contributions of primary and secondary information sectors to the U.S. GNP in 1967, 1992 and 1997.[9] As seen in Table 1-1, 55.9 percent of the total U.S. GNP in 1992 was generated in the information sector. About three-fifth of this—or 33.0 percent of total GNP—was generated in the PRIS and the rest was contributed by the SIS. In 1997, the share of the information sector in the total U.S. GNP rose to 63 percent, of which the larger part: 35.2 percent, was accounted for by the PRIS. In comparison, the share of the information sector in the total GNP was about 46.2

---

[9]   For comparison, we also append a table (Appendix, Table 1-A.1) that presents the size and broad structures of the U.S. information economy for 1958, 1967 and 1972 as measured by the OECD (1981). Although OECD study follows Porat's methodology, the size of the primary information sector is smaller and that of the secondary sector is larger as compared to Porat's estimates for 1967. Overall, OECD measure of the U.S. information sector is larger than Porat's. Note that OECD study calculates percentage shares in GDP at factor cost whereas Porat (1977) uses GNP. As we can see from the table, the information sector accounted for about 43 percent of GDP in 1958. Between 1967 and 1972 the size grew from 48.5 percent to 49.2 percent of GDP. Interestingly, Rubin and Taylor (1981) find that the primary information sector accounted for 24.8 percent of GNP (same number as the OECD study) in 1972, a decline from Porat's estimate for 1967, and observe that while the 'information service industries outpaced the economy as a whole, ... the growth in these industries was offset by a contraction in many of the manufacturing elements of the sector' ...However, in real terms, 'virtually every industry in the information sector lagged behind the economy as a whole' (Rubin and Taylor, 1981, p. 164).

Table 1-1. Value Added Contribution of Primary and Secondary Information Sector to GNP in 1967, 1992 and 1997. (Values in millions of current dollars)

Sector	1967	1992	1997
Primary	200,025	2,055,950	2,940,121
	(25.1%)	(33.0%)	(35.2%)
Secondary	168,073	1,427,119	2,317,419
	(21.1%)	(22.9%)	(27.8%)
Information	368,098	3,483,069	5,257,540
[Total value added]	(46.3%)	(55.9%)	(63.0%)
Non-information	427,290	2,750,836	3,088,106
[Total value added]	(53.7%)	(44.1%)	(37.0%)
Total GNP	795,388	6,233,905	8,345,646
	(100.0%)	(100.0%)	(100.0%)

Note: Numbers in parentheses represent percentage shares in total GNP.

percent in 1967. Moreover, the share of PRIS in the total GNP in 1967 was only about 25.1 percent. Thus, it is evident that the PRIS has shown a substantial growth in the 30 years since 1967. During 1992–1997, the SIS registered much faster growth.

Tables 1-2 and 1-3 show value added contributions of major industries to the primary and secondary information sectors and to the total information economy. Consider first the broad categories of 'agriculture, forestry and fishing', 'mining', 'construction', 'manufacturing', 'services', and 'government'. As we can see from Table 3, the shares of service sector industries in both PRIS and SIS increased substantially over the past 30 years. We observe that the share of service industries was 59.05 percent of total value added generated in the PRIS in 1967 and this share rose to 68.52 percent in 1992, and then to 72.37 percent in 1997. Similarly, the share of service industries in the SIS increased from 45.05 percent in 1967 to 66.64 percent in 1992, and to 72.60 percent in 1997. A part of these increases can be ascribed to the growth of the information components of the service industries. The emergence of new information services may also have contributed to the faster growth of services in the information economy. However, further research is needed to gain a more complete understanding of the newly emerging information services. The size, structure and growth of information activities in service industries have been discussed in further detail in Apte and Nath (1999).

At a more detailed level of individual industries within the manufacturing and services categories, we can see that in 1967, 'finance and insurance' made the largest contribution (13.01 percent) to PRIS. This was followed by the contributions of 'business services' (11.44 percent) and 'communications services' (8.80 percent). In contrast, in 1992 and 1997, 'business services'

Table 1-2. Value Added of Information Economy by Major Industries: 1967, 1992 and 1997. (Values in millions of current dollars)

Year/Sector Industry	1967			1992			1997		
	Primary	Secondary	Total	Primary	Secondary	Total	Primary	Secondary	Total
Agriculture, Forestry and Fishing	0	467	467	0	3401	3401	0	9969	9969
Mining	0	1512	1512	0	13242	13242	0	22556	22556
Construction	8527	13243	21770	58752	72781	131533	94550	72692	167242
Manufacturing	32693	57879	90572	229434	234393	463827	267649	360365	628014
Food and kindred products	0	5248	5248	0	17448	17448	0	25724	25724
Tobacco products	0	254	254	0	692	692	0	1625	1625
Textile mill products	0	1373	1373	0	6677	6677	0	7410	7410
Apparel and other textile products	0	2670	2670	0	8748	8748	0	10062	10062
Lumber and wood products	0	1069	1069	0	6811	6811	0	9506	9506
Furniture and fixtures	528	777	1305	4384	3651	8035	6497	5512	12009
Paper and allied products	1539	2109	3648	2399	7707	10106	2520	12758	15278
Printing and publishing	10224	565	10789	83868	9743	93611	91137	0	91137
Chemicals and allied products	0	5266	5266	0	26469	26469	0	44405	44405
Petroleum and coal products	0	1337	1337	0	3270	3270	0	4661	4661
Rubber and miscellaneous products	0	1702	1702	0	11104	11104	0	21102	21102
Leather and leather products	0	520	520	0	1197	1197	0	1243	1243
Stone, clay, and glass products	0	2035	2035	0	6880	6880	0	11313	11313
Primary metal products	0	4350	4350	0	8535	8535	0	15075	15075
Fabricated metal products	0	4681	4681	0	18709	18709	0	32300	32300
Industrial machinery and equipment	3198	7259	10457	19319	30539	49858	20317	58353	78670
Electronic & other electric equipment	12235	3273	15508	61779	8700	70479	101492	27557	129049
Transportation equipment	0	11887	11887	0	36752	36752	0	55722	55722

Table 1-2. (Continued)

Year/Sector Industry	1967			1992			1997		
	Primary	Secondary	Total	Primary	Secondary	Total	Primary	Secondary	Total
Instruments and related products	4198	365	4563	53391	16448	69839	39589	9768	49357
Miscellaneous manufacturing	771	1140	1911	4294	4312	8606	6097	6269	12366
Service	118108	75719	193827	1408826	951088	2359914	2127727	1682535	3810262
Transportation	0	8115	8115	0	53038	53038	0	82452	82452
Communications	17609	0	17609	132370	0	132370	198517	0	198517
Electric, gas and sanitary service	0	2612	2612	0	20602	20602	0	34835	34835
Wholesale and Retail Trade	16053	42447	58500	115462	446004	561466	145234	478952	624186
Finance and Insurance	26031	577	26608	341571	3907	345478	598575	18894	617469
Real Estate and Rental	15394	2764	18158	153516	4595	158111	158051	171366	329417
Hotels, Personal repair services except auto	853	3740	4593	1389	37757	39146	2007	60051	62058
Business Services	22886	6535	29421	463925	169185	633110	734216	186273	920489
Amusements	2010	780	2790	25669	18364	44033	34515	19710	54225
Medical, Education & Non-profit organization	17272	6773	24045	174924	182516	357440	256612	613053	869665
Other services	0	1376	1376	0	15120	15120	0	16951	16951
Government	40699	18735	59434	358938	151046	509984	450195	169136	619331
Rest of the World	0	517	517	0	1168	1168	0	166	166
Total	200027	168072	368099	2055950	1427121	3483071	2940121	2317419	5257540

Sources: Porat (1977) and Authors' Calculation.

Table 1-3. Shares of Different Industries in PRIS and SIS Value Added. (Values in percentages)

Year/Industry	1967			1992			1997		
	Primary Info Sector	Secondary Info Sector	Total	Primary Info Sector	Secondary Info Sector	Total	Primary Info Sector	Secondary Info Sector	Total
Agriculture, Forestry and Fishing	0.00	0.28	0.13	0.00	0.24	0.10	0.00	0.43	0.19
Mining	0.00	0.90	0.41	0.00	0.93	0.38	0.00	0.97	0.43
Construction	4.26	7.88	5.91	2.86	5.10	3.78	3.22	3.14	3.18
Manufacturing	16.34	34.44	24.61	11.16	16.42	13.32	9.10	15.55	11.95
Food and kindred products	0.00	3.12	1.43	0.00	1.22	0.50	0.00	1.11	0.49
Tobacco manufactures	0.00	0.15	0.07	0.00	0.05	0.02	0.00	0.07	0.03
Textile mill products	0.00	0.82	0.37	0.00	0.47	0.19	0.00	0.32	0.14
Apparel and other textile products	0.00	1.59	0.73	0.00	0.61	0.25	0.00	0.43	0.19
Lumber and wood products	0.00	0.64	0.29	0.00	0.48	0.20	0.00	0.41	0.18
Furniture and fixtures	0.26	0.46	0.35	0.21	0.26	0.23	0.22	0.24	0.23
Paper and allied products	0.77	1.25	0.99	0.12	0.54	0.29	0.09	0.55	0.29
Printing and publishing	5.11	0.34	2.93	4.08	0.68	2.69	3.10	0.00	1.73
Chemicals and allied products	0.00	3.13	1.43	0.00	1.85	0.76	0.00	1.92	0.84
Petroleum and coal products	0.00	0.80	0.36	0.00	0.23	0.09	0.00	0.20	0.09
Rubber and misc. plastics products	0.00	1.01	0.46	0.00	0.78	0.32	0.00	0.91	0.40
Leather and leather products	0.00	0.31	0.14	0.00	0.08	0.03	0.00	0.05	0.02
Stone, clay, glass, and concrete products	0.00	1.21	0.55	0.00	0.48	0.20	0.00	0.49	0.22
Primary metal industries	0.00	2.59	1.18	0.00	0.60	0.25	0.00	0.65	0.29
Fabricated metal products	0.00	2.79	1.27	0.00	1.31	0.54	0.00	1.39	0.61
Industrial machinery and equipment	1.60	4.32	2.84	0.94	2.14	1.43	0.69	2.52	1.50
Electrical and electronic equipment	6.12	1.95	4.21	3.00	0.61	2.02	3.45	1.19	2.45
Transportation equipment	0.00	7.07	3.23	0.00	2.58	1.06	0.00	2.40	1.06
Instruments and related products	2.10	0.22	1.24	2.60	1.15	2.01	1.35	0.42	0.94
Misc. manufacturing industries	0.39	0.68	0.52	0.21	0.30	0.25	0.21	0.27	0.24

Table 1-3. (Continued)

Year/Industry	1967			1992			1997		
	Primary Info Sector	Secondary Info Sector	Total	Primary Info Sector	Secondary Info Sector	Total	Primary Info Sector	Secondary Info Sector	Total
Service	59.05	45.05	52.66	68.52	66.64	67.75	72.37	72.60	72.47
Transportation	0.00	4.83	2.20	0.00	3.72	1.52	0.00	3.56	1.57
Communications	8.80	0.00	4.78	6.44	0.00	3.80	6.75	0.00	3.78
Electric, gas and sanitary service	0.00	1.55	0.71	0.00	1.44	0.59	0.00	1.50	0.66
Wholesale and retail trade	8.03	25.26	15.89	5.62	31.25	16.12	4.94	20.67	11.87
Finance and Insurance	13.01	0.34	7.23	16.61	0.27	9.92	20.36	0.82	11.74
Real estate and rental	7.70	1.64	4.93	7.47	0.32	4.54	5.38	7.39	6.27
Hotels, personal repair services, except auto	0.43	2.23	1.25	0.07	2.65	1.12	0.07	2.59	1.18
Business services	11.44	3.89	7.99	22.56	11.85	18.18	24.97	8.04	17.51
Amusement	1.00	0.46	0.76	1.25	1.29	1.26	1.17	0.85	1.03
Medical, education & non-profit	8.63	4.03	6.53	8.51	12.79	10.26	8.73	26.45	16.54
Other services	0.00	0.82	0.37	0.00	1.06	0.43	0.00	0.73	0.32
Government	20.35	11.15	16.15	17.46	10.58	14.64	15.31	7.30	11.78
Rest of the World	0.00	0.31	0.14	0.00	0.08	0.03	0.00	0.01	0.00
Total	100	100	100	100	100	100	100	100	100

constituted the largest component (22.56 percent in 1992 and 24.97 percent in 1997) of the PRIS, followed by 'finance and insurance' (16.61 percent in 1992 and 20.36 percent in 1997) and 'medical, educational and non-profit organizations' (8.51 percent in 1992 and 8.73 in 1997). Evidently, 'business services' have shown a high rate of growth during the 1967–1992 time frame.

Within the SIS, the changes over the span of same 30 years were more dramatic. In 1967, 'wholesale and retail trade' was the largest contributor (25.26 percent), followed by 'transportation equipment' (7.07 percent) and 'transportation services' (4.83 percent). In 1992, the 'wholesale and retail trade' retained its position with 31.25 percent of total SIS value added. However, 'medical, educational and non-profit organizations' (12.79 percent) and 'business services' (11.85 percent) took the second and third positions respectively. Interestingly, in 1997 'medical, educational and non-profit organizations' with 26.45 percent of total SIS value added had the largest contribution, followed by 'wholesale and retail trade' with 20.36 percent. This can partly be explained by changes in I-O industry classification system. As Lawson et al. (2002) point out, "... In the 1997 benchmark accounts, 3.1 percent of total value added is moved into these industries, mostly from manufacturing and from wholesale and retail trade" (p. 20).

For the information economy as a whole, in 1967, the 'wholesale and retail trade' was the largest contributor (15.89 percent) followed by 'business services' (7.99 percent) and 'finance and insurance' (7.23 percent) respectively. In comparison, in 1992, 'business services' had the largest contribution (18.18 percent), followed by 'wholesale and retail trade' (16.12 percent) and 'medical, educational and non-profit organizations' (10.26 percent). In 1997, 'business services retains its position at the top (17.51 percent of total information value added), closely followed by 'medical, educational and non-profit organizations' with 16.54 percent. 'Wholesale and retail trade' finishes a distant third with 11.87 percent.

In addition to analyzing the shares of different industries in the information value added, it is also interesting and important to estimate and analyze the growth rates experienced by these industries. For this purpose, we first converted the 1967 value added measures from current dollars to 1996 constant dollars by using GDP implicit deflators by industries with 1996 as the base year. We then compared the 1967, 1992 and 1997 measures, all stated at 1996 prices, to estimate the average annual growth rates for different industries. The results are shown in Table 1-4.

We can see from Table 1-4 that the U.S. information economy, in constant 1996 dollars, grew at an average annual growth rate of 3.82 percent during the 25 years between 1967 and 1992 and at an even faster rate of 5.91 percent between 1992 and 1997. Among the broad industry categories, information activities in services were growing at 4.83 percent per year between 1967 and 1992

Table 1-4. Growth of the Information Economy between 1967 and 1992 and between 1992 and 1997

Year/Sector Industry	Information value added in 1996 constant dollar			Average annual growth rates	
	1967	1992	1997	1967–1992	1992–1997
Agriculture, Forestry and Fishing	2064	3981	11015	2.66	22.57
Mining	6233	14460	22186	3.42	8.94
Construction	95262	152462	160527	1.90	1.04
Manufacturing	362688	500889	614038	1.30	4.16
Food and kindred products	24259	21364	24697	−0.51	2.94
Tobacco products	1068	772	1584	−1.29	15.46
Textile mill products	5840	7523	7296	1.02	−0.61
Apparel and other textile products	11128	9658	10078	−0.56	0.85
Lumber and wood products	4194	7078	9366	2.12	5.76
Furniture and fixtures	4001	6526	13281	1.98	15.27
Paper and allied products	9380	6884	16781	−1.23	19.51
Printing and publishing	47568	109329	91634	3.38	−3.47
Chemicals and allied products	24540	32674	41248	1.15	4.77
Petroleum and coal products	5308	3438	4592	−1.72	5.96
Rubber and misc. products	6760	11683	20234	2.21	11.61
Leather and leather products	1357	828	1119	−1.96	6.22
Stone, clay, and glass products	7662	6861	10965	−0.44	9.83
Primary metal products	16614	8636	15025	−2.58	11.71
Fabricated metal products	21376	22630	34965	0.23	9.09
Industrial machinery & equip.	48300	61000	74566	0.94	4.10
Electronic & other elec. equip.	65249	78549	128645	0.74	10.37
Transportation equipment	33457	27400	45403	−0.80	10.63
Instruments & related products	17010	68970	50429	5.76	−6.07
Misc. manufacturing	7618	9087	12130	0.71	5.95

Continued on next page

and at 7.43 percent between 1992 and 1997, rates considerably higher than the average for the information economy. Within the service sector, value added of 'business services', 'amusements', 'medical, educational services and non-profit organization' and 'finance and insurance' were each growing at a rate higher than 5 percent annually between 1967 and 1992. During 1992–1997, on the other hand, 'medical, educational and non-profit organizations' and 'real

Table 1-4. (Continued)

Year/Sector Industry	Information value added in 1996 constant dollar			Average annual growth rates	
	1967	1992	1997	1967–1992	1992–1997
Service	803051	2612956	3739352	4.83	7.43
Transportation	30664	53088	78407	2.22	8.11
Communications	68666	136729	195792	2.79	7.45
Electric, gas & sanitary service	10516	21971	34181	2.99	9.24
Wholesale and retail trade	237006	602548	643212	3.80	1.31
Finance and insurance	114224	392852	598172	5.07	8.77
Real estate and rental	75556	174273	323564	3.40	13.17
Hotels, personal repair services, except auto	18929	42734	56998	3.31	5.93
Business services	123296	702807	893878	7.21	4.93
Amusements	12019	50245	52560	5.89	0.91
Medical, education & non-profit organization	106327	418685	846265	5.64	15.11
Other services	5849	17023	16323	4.37	−0.84
Government	254703	578922	602298	3.34	0.79
Rest of the world	2125	1272	163	−2.03	−33.71
Total	1513037	3864942	5149579	3.82	5.91

Note: The growth rates are average annual compound growth rates calculated from real value added at 1996 constant prices.

estate and rental' registered growth rates higher than 10 percent. In the manufacturing sector, 'instruments and related products' was the fastest growing industry during 1967–1992. However, information activities in several manufacturing industries experienced a decline during this period. Among them, 'tobacco products', 'paper and allied products', 'petroleum and coal products', 'leather and leather products' and 'primary metal products' were declining at an annual average rate of more than 1 percent. These declines may reflect two factors. First, there could have been substantial outsourcing of information activities in the manufacturing industries to outside vendors. That is, industries are possibly relying more and more on marketed information services provided by vendors rather than on in-house production. The growth in the contribution of service industries to the information value added indicates that this may, in fact, be the case. However, it needs further investigation to fully substantiate this argument. Secondly, the estimation methodology we use for the SIS may have caused an underestimation of actual contribution of the manufacturing industries to the information economy. It is our belief that the first possibility, i.e. outsourcing of information services, is the most likely cause of declining contribution of manufacturing industries to the information economy.

Table 1-5. Growth of Total GDP and of Value Added in Broad Sectors between 1967 and 1992 and between 1992 and 1997.

Sectors	Values in billions of 1996 constant dollar			Average annual growth rates	
	1967	1992	1997	1967–1992	1992–1997
Total GDP	3428	6880	8160	2.83	3.47
Agriculture, forestry & fishing	110	131	144	0.69	1.91
Mining	63	96	117	1.67	4.10
Construction	172	272	325	1.84	3.62
Manufacturing	838	1085	1387	1.04	5.04
Services	1708	4259	5151	3.72	3.88
Government	508	1015	1036	2.81	0.39

Between 1992 and 1997, 'paper and allied products' seems to be the fastest growing industry. However, one needs to be careful in interpreting the growth rates by industries during this period. Because of the new industry classification system, many industries have been reclassified and therefore it does not make much sense to compare the growth performances of the disaggregate industries in this period with those during the earlier period. The growth performances are more reasonable only when we compare them by broad categories such as 'manufacturing', 'services' etc.

In order to assess the growth performance of the information economy we now consider the overall performance of the U.S. economy during the 25 years between 1967 and 1992, and between 1992 and 1997. As we can see from Table 1-5, the U.S. GDP was growing at an average annual growth rate of 2.83 percent between 1967 and 1992, and at a faster rate of 3.47 between 1992 and 1997. Among the broad sectors, the service sector was growing at 3.72 percent, which is higher than the average for the economy during the 25 years between 1967 and 1992. The manufacturing sector on the other hand was growing merely at 1.84 percent annually during the same period. This is not surprising if we consider the productivity slowdown of the manufacturing industries during the 1970s. All the other sectors were growing at rates slower than that for the aggregate economy. Between 1992 and 1997, on the other hand, the manufacturing sector was growing the fastest. According to our calculations, the service sector was growing at a rate higher than the average annual growth rate for the overall economy. The high growth rate might have been driven by the unprecedented growth of the high-tech sector. Since the data are based on the old SIC classification, value added accrued to many of the auxiliary services may have been included in manufacturing value added.

It is interesting to note that information value-added of all these broad sectors were growing faster than total value added of the respective sectors between 1967 and 1992. During 1992–1997, the information manufacturing sector was growing slower than overall manufacturing and the information service sector was growing much faster than the overall service sector. One has to be cautious in interpreting these results. These differences between the recent period (1992–1997) and earlier period (1967–1992) may partly be explained by redefinition and reclassification of some of the industries that we use in our calculation of 1997 information economy. The patterns of growth of information components within broad sectors, however, reinforce our finding that the share of the information economy in the U.S. GNP has grown from 46 percent to 56 percent in 1992, and to 63 percent in 1997.

From the above analysis, we can draw several important conclusions about the size, structure and growth of the U.S. information economy. First, more than half of total GNP in 1992 and in 1997 was generated by information related activities. Second, growth of the primary information sector was much higher than that of the secondary sectors during 1967–1992 whereas the secondary information sector seemed to grow faster during 1992–1997. Third, within the information economy the shares of the service industries increased by leaps and bounds. Until 1992 business services registered the highest growth while during the 5 year period between 1992 and 1997, 'medical, education and non-profit organization' witnessed the fastest growth in its information component. Finally, information activities in a number of manufacturing industries experienced decline during 1967–1992. That possibly had its origin in the increased outsourcing of information services by these industries.[10]

Given the increasing prominence and high growth of 'business services' and 'medical, educational and non-profit organizations', it would be important to gain a better understanding of the specific services that have been included in these two broad categories. The I-O category of 'business services' includes four 2-digit SIC industries: business services (73), legal services (81), engineering and management services (87) and services not elsewhere counted (89). Details are provided in Chart A.1, with a listing of all 4-digit SIC industries included in this I-O 'business services' category. We would like to point out that in 1992, the SIC industry of business services (73) accounted for more than half of the value added of this category. For the reasons of brevity, the detailed calculation of this number hasn't been shown in any of the tables. It can also be seen in Chart A.1 that the I-O category 'medical

---

[10] The extraordinary growth of some of the manufacturing industries, such as 'paper and allied products', 'tobacco products', 'furniture and fixtures' should be interpreted with care as they may simply be the consequences of reclassification of industries.

and educational services, and non-profit organizations' consists of the following SIC industries: health services (80), educational services (82), social services (83), museums, botanical and zoological gardens (84) and membership organizations (86). More than two-third of the value added of this category in 1992 was accounted for by health services (80).

5. INFORMATION SECTOR AS DEFINED BY THE CENSUS BUREAU AND THE BEA

In its 1997 Economic Census, the U.S. Census Bureau creates a new 'Information Sector' that is also added in 1997 benchmark I-O table under a separate I-O industry category which corresponds to a new NAICS industry. This new sector is "created by combining industries from manufacturing, services, and transportation, communication, and utilities" (Lawson et al., 2002, p. 23). The information sector is formally defined to include "establishments engaged in producing and distributing information and cultural products, providing the means to transmit or distribute these products and data, or communications services" (Lawson et al., 2002, p. 25). Table 1-6 shows the detailed break-up at 6-digit I-O level of the information sector and corresponding value added.

As we can see from the definition and the table, the scope of the information sector is very narrow and substantially different from Porat's conceptualization and measurement of the information economy. According to BEA's estimate the information sector accounts for only 4.22 percent of the total GNP which is substantially lower than our calculation.

6. CRITICAL ASSESSMENT OF PORAT'S APPROACH TO INFORMATION ECONOMY

Porat's conceptual framework and the computational methodology provide a reasonable, interesting and useful way of looking at the structural aspects of the national economy using the conventional national income accounting framework. Also, use of 'the I-O framework enables analysts to investigate the intersectoral relationships between the information economy and the rest of the economy' (Engelbrecht, 1997).[11] However, Porat's study has been criticized on various grounds.

For example, although the decomposition of the information economy into PRIS and SIS is conceptually appealing, the methods of measuring them may

---

[11] Also see Carter (1989) for discussion on use of I-O tables in measuring information economy.

Table 1-6. Value Added by the Industries in the BEA's New Information Sector, 1997. (Values in millions of current dollar)

I-O Code	Description of the Industry	Value Added
511110	Newspaper publishers	25808
511120	Periodical publishers	15940
511130	Book publishers	10122
5111A0	Database, directory, and other publishers	12975
511200	Software publishers	40881
512100	Motion picture and video industries	18796
512200	Sound recording industries	6744
513100	Radio and television broadcasting	13807
513200	Cable networks and program distribution	21217
513300	Telecommunications	154946
514100	Information services	6987
514200	Data processing services	23559
	Total (Information Sector)	351782
	Total GNP	8345646
	As share of Total GNP	4.22%

lead to inconsistency. As Machlup (1980) argues, the integration of the PRIS and SIS in one approach is perhaps inappropriate as it mixes information inputs in non-PRIS industries with outputs of PRIS industries. Furthermore, this method of aggregation may lead to an overstatement of the size of the information economy as it fails to exclude the non-information activities in the PRIS.

The scheme developed by Porat for identifying and classifying information workers is used to assess the GNP contribution of the secondary information sector. But as he himself admits, every occupation has an informational component. Thus, it is possible to argue that his identification scheme, to some extent, is arbitrary and ad-hoc. Even if we accept Porat's scheme of designating information occupation, the facts that new information occupations have been continually emerging with the advent of new technology, and that the nature of occupations has been continually changing make it imperative that the list of information occupations be updated regularly.

In order to measure the information economy, Porat uses various concepts of the national income accounting. It should be noted that the size of the information economy was measured in terms of its contribution to GNP. At the sectoral level the term 'value added' has been used to represent GNP, as they are equivalent concepts. Porat uses detailed Input–Output table to measure information value added at disaggregated levels. By concentrating on value added he puts more emphasis on the production side of the information economy. On the contrary, Machlup uses 'final demand' to measure the contribution of knowledge industries. Since they represent two distinct methods of measuring GNP, the total for each of these measures will be the same for the entire economy. However, the total for individual industries can substantially vary. Therefore the methodologies used by Machlup (1962) and Porat (1977) may lead to different measures of the information economy at industry levels. Hence, care must be taken in comparing and interpreting the results of these two methodologies.

Perhaps, the most vehement criticism of Porat's study is that it lacks the foundation of a theory (see Wellenius, 1988; Miles, 1990, and Engelbrecht, 1997). As these critics argue, Porat's information economy includes very diverse activities whose growth cannot be explained by unitary theory, that Porat's concept of information economy does not provide a theory to explain the development of advanced capitalist economy, and finally, that there are no theories to explain the different components making up the information economy.

We believe that Porat's methodology can benefit from several improvements, the principal ones of which are identified next. In order to exclude the non-information activities in the PRIS, we would propose that the employee compensation of information workers, part of proprietors' income earned for performing informational tasks, and capital consumption allowances on information machines in the PRIS be calculated to measure their contribution to value added. It may be noted that Engelbrecht (1997) has already advocated this approach and in one specific case it has already been put to use (see Rabeau, 1990).

As we discussed earlier, new information services have emerged to cater to the needs of the society that is increasingly becoming more information-intensive. To capture this phenomenon we need to study newly emerging as well as older information services more carefully and in more detail. For better accuracy, the categorization of information occupation should be revised in the light of the facts that industries such as computers and communications have grown substantially over the last few years, and so have various occupations related to these industries. A detailed study of these industries and related occupations would therefore be useful. In other words, the growth of new information-based industries should be studied separately in all their varied dimensions. Furthermore, their linkages with other sectors of the economy should be examined using the input–output matrix.

7.   CONCLUSIONS

The main contribution of this research is not only in confirming our intuitive understanding about the growth of information economy, but also in quantifying its current size and structure, and its growth during the past 30 years. Following the concepts and methodology developed by Porat (1977), we calculate the contribution of the information activities to the U.S. GNP in 1992 and 1997. A two-way classification into primary and secondary information sectors suggests that marketed information goods and services, i.e., the primary information sector, accounted for a third of the total GNP in 1992 and more than a third in 1997. The primary information sector also registered a higher growth rate during 1967–1992. The information services produced for internal consumption of non-information firms, i.e., the secondary information sector, on the other hand, contributed about one-fifth of total GNP in 1992 and more than one-fourth in 1997, thus registering a faster growth during the later period.

The results indicate that on the whole the information economy is growing faster than the aggregate economy. Within the information economy, it is the service category that is growing at the highest rate; and among the service industries, the most dynamic industries are the 'business services', and 'medical, educational, and non-profit organizations'. Information activities in a number of manufacturing industries, on the other hand, declined during the period between 1967 and 1992. This indicates that the manufacturing industries are possibly outsourcing information services to outside vendors. Higher growth in the information components of the business services also lends support to this hypothesis. However, this conjecture needs further investigation which we intend to carry out in future.

REFERENCES

Apte, Uday M. and Mason, R. O., 1995, "Global Disaggregation of Information-Intensive Services", Management Science 41(7), 1250–1262.

Apte, Uday M. and Nath, Hiranya K., 1999, "Service Sector in Today's Information Economy", Proceedings of the Service Operations Management Association, 106–111.

Carter, Anne P., 1989, "Input-Output Recipes in an Information Economy", Economic Systems Research 1(1), 27–43.

Engelbrecht, H.-J., 1997, "A comparison and critical assessment of Porat and Rubin's information economy and Wallis and North's transaction sector", Information Economics and Policy 9, 271–290.

Huber, M. T. and Rubin, M. R., 1986, The Knowledge Industry in the United States: 1960–1980 (Princeton University Press, Princeton, NJ).

Lawson, A. M., Bersani, K. S., Fahim-Nader, M. and Guo, J., 2002, "Benchmark Input-Output Accounts of the United States, 1997", Survey of Current Business, 19–109.

Machlup, F., 1962, The Production and Distribution of Knowledge in the United States (Princeton University Press, Princeton, NJ).

Machlup, F., 1980, Knowledge: Its Creation, Distribution and Economic Significance, Volume 1: Knowledge and Knowledge Production (Princeton University Press, Princeton, NJ).

Martin, W. J., 1988, The Information Society (Aslib, London).

Miles, I., 1990, Mapping and measuring the information economy, Library and Information Research Report 77 (British Library Board).

OECD, 1981, Information Activities, Electronics and Telecommunications Technologies: Impact on Employment, Growth and Trade, volumes I and II (Paris).

OECD, 1986, Trends in The Information Economy (Paris).

Porat, M. U. and Rubin, M. R., 1977, The Information Economy (9 volumes), Office of Telecommunications Special Publication 77-12 (US Department of Commerce, Washington, DC).

Rabeau, Y., 1990, The information economy in Canada: An 'input–output' approach (Department of Communications of Canada, Laval).

Rubin, M. R. and Taylor, E., 1981, "The U.S. information sector and GNP: An input–output study". Information Processing and Management 17(4), 163–194.

U.S. Census Bureau, 1997 Economic Census: Summary Statistics for United States (1997 NAICS Basis) and 1997 Economic Census: Information, United States, http://www.census.gov.

U.S. Department of Commerce: Bureau of Economic Analysis, 1997, "Benchmark Input–Output Accounts for the U.S. Economy, 1992; Detailed Use Table". Diskette.

U.S. Department of Labor: Bureau of Labor Statistics, 1994–1995, Occupational Outlook Handbook (U.S. Department of Labor, Washington, DC).

U.S. Department of Labor: Bureau of Labor Statistics, Occupational Employment in Manufacturing, 1992 (U.S. Department of Labor, Washington, DC).

U.S. Department of Labor: Bureau of Labor Statistics, Occupational Employment in Mining, Construction, Finance, and Services, 1993 (U.S. Department of Labor, Washington, DC).

U.S. Department of Labor: Bureau of Labor Statistics, Occupational Employment Statistics, 1998, http://www.bls.gov.

Wellenius, B., 1988, "Foreword: Concepts and issues on information sector measurement" in: Jussawalla, M., Lamberton, D., and Karunaratne, N. (eds.), The Cost of Thinking: Information Economies of Ten Pacific Countries (Ablex, Norwood, NJ).

ACKNOWLEDGEMENT

The authors would like to thank Dr. Khawaja A. Mamun for his excellent research assistance.

Appendix

Table 1-A.1. Size of PRIS, SIS and the Information Economy in 1958, 1967 and 1972: OECD Study. (Percentage share in GDP at factor cost)

	1958	1967	1972
Primary Information Sector	19.6	23.8	24.8
Secondary Information Sector	23.1	24.7	24.4
Information Economy	42.7	48.5	49.2

Source: Table I.8 and I.10, OECD (1981).

Chart 1-A.1. Detailed SIC Industries included in I-O Categories of 'Business Services' and 'Medical and Educational Services, and Non-profit Organizations'

SIC Code	Industry Description

Industries included in 'Business Services'

73 Business Services

7311	Advertising agencies
7312	Outdoor advertising agencies
7313	Radio, TV, publisher representatives
7319	Advertising, not elsewhere classified (nec)
7322	Adjustment and collection services
7323	Credit reporting services
7331	Direct mail advertising services
7334	Photocopying and duplicating services
7335	Commercial photography
7336	Commercial art and graphic design
7338	Secretarial and court reporting
7342	Disinfecting and pest control services
7349	Building maintenance services, nec
7352	Medical equipment rental
7353	Heavy construction equipment rental
7359	Equipment rental and leasing, nec
7361	Employment agencies
7363	Help supply services
7371	Computer programming services
7372	Prepackaged software
7373	Computer integrated systems design
7374	Data processing and preparation
7375	Information retrieval services
7376	Computer facilities management
7377	Computer rental and leasing

Chart 1-A.1. (Continued)

SIC Code	Industry Description
7378	Computer maintenance and repair
7379	Computer related services, nec
7381	Detective & armored car services
7382	Security systems services
7383	News syndicates
7384	Photofinishing laboratories
7389	Business services, nec

81 Legal Services
| 8111 | Legal services |

87 Engineering and Management Services
8711	Engineering Services
8712	Architectural services
8713	Surveying Services
8721	Accounting, auditing & bookkeeping
8731	Commercial physical research
8732	Commercial nonphysical research
8733	Noncommercial research organizations
8734	Testing laboratories
8741	Management services
8742	Management consulting services
8743	Public relations services
8744	Facilities support services
8748	Business consulting, nec

89 Services, not elsewhere counted
| 8999 | Services, nec |

Industries included in 'Medical, Educational Services and Non-profit Organizations'

80 Health Services
8011	Offices and clinics of medical doctors
8021	Offices and clinics of dentists
8031	Offices of osteopathic physicians
8041	Offices and clinics of chiropractors
8042	Offices and clinics of optometrists
8043	Offices and clinics of podiatrists
8049	Offices of health practitioners, nec
8051	Skilled nursing care facilities
8052	Intermediate care facilities
8059	Nursing and personal care, nec
8062	General medical & surgical hospitals
8063	Psychiatric hospitals
8069	Specialty hospitals exc. Psychiatric
8071	Medical laboratories
8072	Dental laboratories

Chart 1-A.1. (Continued)

SIC Code	Industry Description
8082	Home health care services
8092	Kidney dialysis centers
8093	Specialty outpatient clinics, nec
8099	Health and allied services, nec
82 Educational Services	
8211	Elementary and secondary schools
8221	Colleges and universities
8222	Junior colleges
8231	Libraries
8243	Data processing schools
8244	Business and secretarial schools
8249	Vocational schools, nec
8299	Schools & educational services, nec
83 Social services	
8322	Individual and family services
8331	Job training and related services
8351	Child day care services
8361	Residential care
8399	Social services, nec
84 Museums, Botanical, Zoological Gardens	
8412	Museums and art galleries
8422	Botanical and zoological gardens
86 Membership organizations	
8611	Business associations
8621	Professional organizations
8631	Labor organizations
8641	Civic and social associations
8651	Political organizations
8661	Religious organizations
8699	Membership organizations, nec

Source: http://weber.u.washington.edu/~dev/sic.html.

Chapter 2

INFORMATION TECHNOLOGY AND THE G7 ECONOMIES

Dale W. Jorgenson

Department of Economics, Harvard University, 122 Littauer Center, Cambridge, MA 02138-3001

1. INTRODUCTION

In this paper I present international comparisons of economic growth among the G7 nations—Canada, France, Germany, Italy, Japan, the U.K., and the U.S. These comparisons focus on the impact of investment in information technology (IT) equipment and software over the period 1980–2001. In 1998 the G7 nations accounted for nearly sixty percent of world output[1] and a much larger proportion of world investment in IT. Economic growth in the G7 has experienced a strong revival since 1995, driven by a powerful surge in IT investment.

The resurgence of economic growth in the United States during the 1990's and the crucial role of IT investment has been thoroughly documented and widely discussed.[2] Similar trends in the other G7 economies have been more difficult to detect, partly because of discrepancies among official price indexes for IT equipment and software identified by Andrew Wyckoff.[3] Paul Schreyer has constructed "internationally harmonized" IT prices that eliminate many of these discrepancies.[4]

Using internationally harmonized prices, I have analyzed the role of investment and productivity as sources of growth in the G7 countries over the period 1980–2001. I have subdivided the period in 1989 and 1995 in order to focus on the most recent experience. I have decomposed growth of output for each country between growth of input and productivity. Finally, I have allocated the

---

[1] See Angus Maddison (2001) for 1998 data for world GDP and the GDP of each of the G7 countries.

[2] See Dale Jorgenson and Kevin Stiroh (2000) and Stephen Oliner and Daniel Sichel (2000).

[3] See Wyckoff (1995).

[4] See Schreyer (2000). Alessandra Colecchia and Schreyer (2002) have employed these internationally harmonized prices in measuring the impact of IT investment.

growth of input between investments in tangible assets, especially information technology and software, and human capital.

Growth in IT capital input per capita jumped to double-digit levels in the G7 nations after 1995. This can be traced to acceleration in the rate of decline of IT prices, analyzed in my Presidential Address to the American Economic Association.[5] The powerful surge in investment was most pronounced in Canada, but capital input growth in Japan, the U.S., and the U.K. was only slightly lower. France, Germany, and Italy also experienced double-digit growth, but lagged considerably behind the leaders.

During the 1980's productivity played a minor role as a source of growth for the G7 countries except Japan, where productivity accounted for twenty five percent of economic growth. Productivity accounted for only fifteen percent of growth in the U.S., thirteen percent in France and the U.K, and twelve percent in Germany; only two percent of growth in Canada was due to productivity, while the decline of productivity retarded growth by fourteen percent in Italy. Between 1989 and 1995 productivity growth declined further in the G7 nations, except for Italy and Germany. Productivity declined for France and the U.K. but remained positive for the U.S., Canada, and Japan.

Productivity growth revived in all the G7 countries after 1995, again with the exception of Germany and Italy. The resurgence was most dramatic in Canada, The U.K., and France, partly offsetting years of dismal productivity growth. Japan exhibited the highest growth in output per capita among the G7 nations from 1980 to 1995. Japan's level of output per capita rose from the lowest in the G7 to the middle of the group. Although this advance owed more to input per capita than productivity, Japan's productivity growth far outstripped the other members of the G7. Nonetheless, Japan's productivity remained the lowest among the G7 nations.

The U.S. led the G7 in output per capita for the period 1989–2001. Canada's edge in output per capita in 1980 had disappeared by 1989. The U.S. led the G7 countries in input per capita during 1980–2001, but U.S. productivity languished below the levels of Canada, France, and Italy.

In Section 2 I outline the methodology for this study, based on my Presidential Address. I have revised and updated the U.S. data presented there through 2001. Comparable data on investment in information technology have been have been constructed for Canada by Statistics Canada.[6] Data on IT for France, Germany, Italy, and the U.K. have been developed for the European Commission by Bart Van Ark, et al.[7] Finally, data for Japan have been assembled by me and Kazuyuki Motohashi for the Research Institute on Economy, Trade,

---

5   See Jorgenson (2001).
6   See John Baldwin and Tarek Harchaoui (2002).
7   See Van Ark, Johanna Melka, Nanno Mulder, Marcel Timmer, and Gerard Ypma (2002).

and Industry.[8] I have linked these data by means of the OECD's purchasing power parities for 1999.[9]

In Section 3 I consider the impact of IT investment and the relative importance of investment and productivity in accounting for economic growth among the G7 nations. Investments in human capital and tangible assets, especially IT equipment and software, account for the overwhelming proportion of growth. Differences in the composition of capital and labor inputs are essential for identifying persistent international differences in output and accounting for the impact of IT investment.

In Section 4 I consider alternative approaches to international comparisons. The great revival of interest in economic growth among economists dates from Maddison's (1982) updating and extension of Simon Kuznets' (1971) long-term estimates of the growth of national product and population for fourteen industrialized countries, including the G7 nations. Maddison (1982, 1991) added Austria and Finland to Kuznets' list and presented growth rates covering periods beginning as early as 1820 and extending through 1989.

Maddison (1987, 1991) also generated growth accounts for major industrialized countries, but did not make level comparisons like those presented in Section 2 below. As a consequence, productivity differences were omitted from the canonical formulation of "growth regressions" by William Baumol (1986). This proved to be a fatal flaw in Baumol's regression model, remedied by Nazrul Islam's (1995) panel data model. Section 5 concludes the paper.

2. INVESTMENT AND PRODUCTIVITY

My papers with Laurits Christensen and Dianne Cummings (1980, 1981) developed growth accounts for the United States and its major trading partners—Canada, France, Germany, Italy, Japan, Korea, The Netherlands, and the United Kingdom for 1947–1973. We employed GNP as a measure of output and incorporated constant quality indices of capital and labor input for each country. Our 1981 paper compared levels of output, inputs, and productivity for all nine nations.

I have updated the estimates for the G7—Canada, France, Germany, Italy, Japan, the United Kingdom, and the United States—through 1995 in earlier work. The updated estimates are presented in my papers with Chrys Dougherty (Dougherty and Jorgenson, 1996, 1997) and Eric Yip (Jorgenson and Yip, 2000). We have shown that productivity accounted for only eleven percent of economic growth in Canada and the United States over the period 1960–1995.

---

[8] See Jorgenson and Motohashi (2003).
[9] See OECD (2002). Current data on purchasing power parities are available from the OECD website: http://www.sourceoecd.org.

My paper with Yip (Jorgenson and Yip, 2000) attributed forty-seven percent of Japanese economic growth during the period 1960–1995 to productivity growth. The proportion attributable to productivity approximated forty percent of growth for the four European countries—France (.38), Germany (.42), Italy (.43), and the United Kingdom (.36). Input growth predominated over productivity growth for all the G7 nations.

I have now incorporated new data on investment in information technology equipment and software for the G7. I have also employed internationally harmonized prices like those constructed by Schreyer (2000). As a consequence, I have been able to separate the contribution of capital input to economic growth into IT and Non-IT components. While IT investment follows similar patterns in all the G7 nations, Non-IT investment varies considerably and helps to explain important differences in growth rates among the G7.

2.1.   Comparisons of Output, Input, and Productivity

My first objective is to extend my estimates for the G7 nations with Christensen, Cummings, Dougherty, and Yip to the year 2001. Following the methodology of my Presidential Address, I have chosen GDP as a measure of output. I have included imputations for the services of consumers' durables as well as land, buildings, and equipment owned by nonprofit institutions. I have also distinguished between investments in information technology equipment and software and investments in other forms of tangible assets.

A constant quality index of capital input is based on weights that reflect differences in capital consumption, tax treatment, and the rate of decline of asset prices. I have derived estimates of capital input and property income from national accounting data. Similarly, a constant quality index of labor input is based on weights by age, sex, educational attainment, and employment status. I have constructed estimates of hours worked and labor compensation from labor force surveys for each country.

In Table 1 I present output per capita for the G7 nations from 1980 to 2001, taking the U.S. as 100.0 in 2000. Output and population are given separately in Tables 2 and 3. I use 1999 purchasing power parities from the OECD to convert output from domestic prices for each country into U.S. dollars. The U.S. maintained its lead among the G7 countries in output per capita after 1989. Canada led the U.S. in 1980, but fell behind during the 1980's. The U.S.–Canada gap widened considerably during the 1990's.

The four major European nations—the U.K., France, Germany, and Italy—had very similar levels of output per capita throughout the period 1980–2001. Japan rose from last place in 1980 to fifth among the G7 in 2001, lagging considerably behind the U.S. and Canada, but only slightly behind France in 2001. Japan led the G7 in the growth of output per capita from 1980–1995, but fell behind the U.S., Canada, the U.K., France, and Italy after 1995.

Table 2-1. Levels of Output and Input Per Capita and Total Factor Productivity

Year	U.S.	Canada	U.K.	France	Germany	Italy	Japan
Output Per Capita							
1980	63.9	67.6	45.0	45.9	49.3	45.9	37.5
1989	79.7	78.8	56.5	54.1	58.6	57.3	50.9
1995	85.6	79.6	61.4	57.0	65.0	62.1	57.5
2001	100.3	91.9	71.3	64.0	69.2	68.8	63.6
Input Per Capita							
1980	70.5	64.2	50.2	46.5	61.0	43.1	52.3
1989	83.9	74.4	61.2	53.3	71.1	55.5	64.8
1995	88.8	75.2	67.0	57.0	73.7	58.8	69.8
2001	100.8	83.7	73.6	61.7	79.0	67.2	73.3
Total Factor Productivity							
1980	90.6	105.4	89.5	98.6	80.8	106.6	71.7
1989	94.9	105.9	92.3	101.5	82.4	103.2	78.5
1995	96.4	105.9	91.7	99.9	88.1	105.6	82.5
2001	99.5	109.7	96.9	103.6	87.6	102.5	86.8

Note: U.S. = 100.0 in 2000, Canada data begins in 1981.

In Table 1 I present input per capita for the G7 over the period 1980–2001, taking the U.S. as 100.0 in 2000. I express input per capita in U.S. dollars, using purchasing power parities constructed for this study.[10] The U.S. was the leader among the G7 in input per capita throughout the period. In 2001 Canada ranked next to the U.S. with Germany third and the U.K. fourth. France and Italy started at the bottom of the ranking and remained there throughout the period.

In Table 1 I also present productivity levels for the G7 over the period 1980–2001. Productivity is defined as the ratio of output to input, including both capital and labor inputs. Canada was the productivity leader throughout the period 1980–2001 with France and Italy close behind, despite the drop in productivity in Italy! Only Japan made substantial gains in productivity during the period, while there were modest increases in the U.S., Canada, the U.K., France, and Germany.

I summarize growth in output and input per capita and productivity for the G7 nations in Table 4. I present growth rates of output and population for the

---

[10] The purchasing power parities for outputs are based on OECD (2002). Purchasing power parities for inputs follow the methodology described in detail by Jorgenson and Yip (2001).

Table 2-2. Growth Rate and Level of Output

Year	U.S.	Canada	U.K.	France	Germany	Italy	Japan
Growth Rate (percentage)							
1980–1989	3.38	3.10	2.69	2.38	1.99	2.51	3.98
1989–1995	2.43	1.39	1.62	1.30	2.34	1.52	2.39
1995–2001	3.76	3.34	2.74	2.34	1.18	1.90	1.89
Level (billions of 2000 U.S. Dollars)							
1980	5361.2	618.4	934.0	932.0	1421.7	955.7	1612.9
1989	7264.2	792.6	1190.3	1154.3	1700.2	1197.4	2308.3
1995	8403.3	861.4	1311.8	1247.8	1956.3	1311.5	2663.7
2001	10530.4	1052.3	1545.9	1436.0	2099.8	1470.1	2983.3
Level (U.S. = 100.0 in 2000)							
1980	51.6	5.9	9.0	9.0	13.7	9.2	15.5
1989	69.9	7.6	11.4	11.1	16.3	11.5	22.2
1995	80.8	8.3	12.6	12.0	18.8	12.6	25.6
2001	101.3	10.1	14.9	13.8	20.2	14.1	28.7

Note: Canada data begins in 1981.

Table 2-3. Growth Rate and Level in Population

Year	U.S.	Canada	U.K.	France	Germany	Italy	Japan
Growth Rate							
1980–1989	0.92	1.18	0.16	0.54	0.05	0.05	0.59
1989–1995	1.23	1.22	0.24	0.45	0.62	0.18	0.33
1995–2001	1.12	0.95	0.24	0.41	0.14	0.18	0.22
Level (millions)							
1980	227.7	24.8	56.3	55.1	78.3	56.4	116.8
1989	247.4	27.3	57.1	57.9	78.7	56.7	123.1
1995	266.3	29.4	58.0	59.4	81.7	57.3	125.6
2001	284.8	31.1	58.8	60.9	82.3	57.9	127.2
Level (U.S. = 100.0 in 2000)							
1980	80.7	8.8	20.0	19.5	27.8	20.0	41.4
1989	87.7	9.7	20.3	20.5	27.9	20.1	43.6
1995	94.4	10.4	20.5	21.1	28.9	20.3	44.5
2001	101.0	11.0	20.8	21.6	29.2	20.5	45.1

Note: Percentage, Canada data begins in 1981.

Table 2-4. Growth in Output and Input Per Capita and Total Factor Productivity

Year	U.S.	Canada	U.K.	France	Germany	Italy	Japan
Output per capita							
1980–1989	2.46	1.92	2.54	1.84	1.93	2.46	3.40
1989–1995	1.20	0.17	1.38	0.85	1.72	1.33	2.06
1995–2001	2.64	2.38	2.50	1.93	1.04	1.72	1.67
Input Per Capita							
1980–1989	1.94	1.86	2.20	1.52	1.71	2.82	2.38
1989–1995	0.94	0.17	1.49	1.11	0.60	0.96	1.23
1995–2001	2.10	1.80	1.59	1.33	1.14	2.21	0.83
Total Factor Productivity							
1980–1989	0.52	0.06	0.34	0.32	0.23	−0.36	1.01
1989–1995	0.26	0.00	−0.11	−0.26	1.12	0.37	0.83
1995–2001	0.54	0.58	0.91	0.60	−0.10	−0.49	0.85

Note: Percentage, Canada data begins in 1981.

period 1980–2001 in Tables 2 and 3. Output growth slowed in the G7 after 1989, but revived for all nations except Japan and Germany after 1995. Output per capita followed a similar pattern with Canada barely expanding during the period 1990–1995.

Japan led in growth of output and output per capita through 1995, but fell to the lower echelon of the G7 after 1995. Japan also led in productivity growth throughout the period 1980–2001. For all countries and all time periods, except for Germany during the period 1989–1995 and Japan after 1995, the growth of input per capita exceeded growth of productivity by a substantial margin. Productivity growth in the G7 slowed during the period 1989–1995, except for Germany and Italy, where productivity slumped after 1995.

Italy led the G7 in growth of input per capita for the periods 1980–1989 and 1995–2001, but relinquished leadership to the U.K. for the period 1989–1995. Differences among input growth rates are smaller than differences among output growth rates, but there was a slowdown in input growth during 1989–1995 throughout the G7. After 1995 growth of input per capita increased in every G7 nation except Japan.

2.2. Comparisons of Capital and Labor Quality

A constant quality index of capital input weights capital inputs by property compensation per unit of capital. By contrast an index of capital stock weights different types of capital by asset prices. The ratio of capital input to capital stock measures the average quality of a unit of capital. This represents the difference between the constant quality index of capital input and the index of capital stock employed, for example, by Kuznets (1971) and Robert Solow (1970).

In Table 5 I present capital input per capita for the G7 countries over the period 1980–2001 relative to the U.S. in 2000. The U.S. was the leader in capital input per capita throughout the period, while Japan was the laggard. Canada led the remaining six countries in 1980, but was overtaken by Germany and Italy in 1995. Italy led the rest of the G7 through 2001, but lagged considerably behind the United States.

The picture for capital stock per capita has some similarities to capital input, but there are important differences. Capital stock levels do not accurately reflect the substitutions among capital inputs that accompany investments in tangible assets, especially investments in IT equipment and software. The U.S. led the G7 in capital stock per capita as well as capital input in 2001, while Japan led in earlier periods. The U.K. lagged the remaining countries of the G7 throughout the period.

The behavior of capital quality highlights the differences between the constant quality index of capital input and capital stock. There are important changes in capital quality over time and persistent differences among coun-

Table 2-5. Levels of Capital Input and Capital Stock Per Capita and Capital Quality

Year	U.S.	Canada	U.K.	France	Germany	Italy	Japan
Capital Input Per Capita							
1980	57.7	56.0	25.8	36.3	44.6	35.6	25.2
1989	73.7	67.1	37.9	48.3	62.1	62.4	35.0
1995	81.6	68.3	50.0	52.7	72.3	73.1	43.2
2001	103.9	78.0	56.1	58.1	83.5	89.4	52.4
Capital Stock Per Capita							
1980	76.8	40.7	24.1	36.2	60.2	36.0	85.6
1989	88.4	48.5	31.2	42.4	67.9	52.4	91.5
1995	92.2	50.8	35.9	47.0	77.0	62.3	97.0
2001	101.7	55.1	44.5	52.0	85.5	72.3	100.2
Capital Quality							
1980	75.1	137.5	107.0	100.1	74.0	98.8	29.4
1989	83.4	138.2	121.7	114.0	91.5	119.1	38.3
1995	88.5	134.6	139.3	112.2	94.0	117.4	44.5
2001	102.2	141.5	126.1	111.9	97.7	123.6	52.3

Note: U.S. = 100.0 in 2000, Canada data begins in 1981.

tries, so that heterogeneity in capital input must be taken into account in international comparisons of economic performance. Canada was the international leader in capital quality throughout the period 1980–2001, while Japan ranked at the bottom of the G7.

I summarize growth in capital input and capital stock per capita, as well as capital quality for the G7 nations in Table 8. Italy was the international leader in capital input growth from 1980–1989, while the Canada was the laggard. The U.K. led from 1989–1995, while Canada lagged considerably behind the rest of the G7. The U.S. took the lead after 1995. There was a slowdown in capital input growth throughout the G7 after 1989, except for the U.K., and a revival after 1995 in the U.S., Canada, France, and Italy.

A constant quality index of labor input weights hours worked for different categories by labor compensation per hour. An index of hours worked fails to take quality differences into account. The ratio of labor input to hours worked measures the average quality of an hour of labor, as reflected in its marginal product. This represents the difference between the constant quality index of labor input and the index of hours worked employed, for example, by Kuznets (1971) and Solow (1970).

In Table 11 I present labor input per capita for the G7 nations for the period 1980–2001 relative to the U.S. in 2000. Japan was the international leader through 1995, but the U.S. took the lead by 2001. Labor input in Japan was nearly double that of Italy. The U.S. led the remaining G7 nations for the period 1980–1995. The U.K. ranked third among the G7 through 1995. Italy and France lagged behind the rest of the G7 for the entire period.

The picture for hours worked per capita has some similarities to labor input, but there are important differences. Japan was the international leader in hours worked per capita. The U.S., Canada, and the U.K. moved roughly in parallel. The U.K. ranked second in 1980 and 1989, while the U.S. ranked second in 1995 and 2001. France and Italy lagged the rest of the G7 from 1980–2001.

The behavior of labor quality highlights the differences between labor input and hours worked. Germany was the leader in labor quality throughout the period 1980–2001. The U.S. ranked second in labor quality, but Canada, France, the U.K, and Japan approached U.S. levels in 2001. Labor quality levels in these four countries moved in parallel throughout the period. Italy was the laggard among the G7 in labor quality as well as hours worked.

I summarize growth in labor input and hours worked per capita, as well as labor quality for the period 1980–2001 in Table 12. Canada and Japan led the G7 nations in labor input growth during the 1980's, France led from 1989–1995 but relinquished its leadership to Italy after 1995. Labor input growth was negative for France during the 1980's, for the U.K., Germany, Italy, and Japan during the period 1989–1995, and for Japan after 1995.

Hours worked per capita fell continuously through the 1989–2001 period for Japan and declined for all the G7 nations during the period 1989–1995. Growth in labor quality was positive for the G7 nations in all time periods. Japan was the leader during the 1980's, relinquishing its lead to France during the early 1990's, but regaining its lead in the 1995–2001 period. Growth in labor quality and hours worked are equally important as sources of growth in labor input for the G7.

3. INVESTMENT IN INFORMATION TECHNOLOGY

Using data from Tables 1 and 2, I can assess the relative importance of investment and productivity as sources of economic growth for the G7 nations. Investments in tangible assets and human capital greatly predominated over productivity during the period 1980–2001. While productivity fell in Italy during this period, the remaining G7 countries had positive productivity growth.

Similarly, using data from Table 5 I can assess the relative importance of growth in capital stock and capital quality. Capital input growth was positive for all countries for the period 1980–2001 and all three sub-periods. Capital quality growth was positive for the period as a whole for all G7 countries. Although capital stock predominated in capital input growth, capital quality was also quantitatively significant, especially after 1995.

Finally, using data from Table 11 I can assess the relative importance of growth in hours worked and labor quality. Hours worked per capita declined for France, Germany, and Japan, while labor quality rose in these nations during the period 1980–2001. For the U.S., Canada, the U.K., and Italy, both hours worked per capita and labor quality rose. I conclude that labor quality growth is essential to the analysis of growth in labor input.

3.1. Investment in IT Equipment and Software

The final step in the comparison of patterns of economic growth among the G7 nations is to analyze the impact of investment in information technology equipment and software. In Table 6 I present levels of IT capital input per capita for the G7 for the period 1980–2001, relative to the U.S. in 2000. The U.S. overtook Germany in 1989 and remained the leader through 2001. Canada lagged behind the rest of the G7 through 1995, but France fell into last place in 2001.

Table 6 reveals substantial differences between IT capital stock and IT capital input. The G7 nations began with very modest stocks of IT equipment and software per capita in 1980. These stocks expanded rapidly during the period 1980–2001. The U.S. led in IT capital stock throughout the period, while Japan moved from the fourth highest level in 1980 to the second highest in 2001.

Table 2-6. Levels of IT Capital Input and IT Capital Stock per capita and IT Capital Quality

Year	U.S.	Canada	U.K.	France	Germany	Italy	Japan
IT Capital Input Per Capita							
1980	4.5	1.0	3.0	4.2	7.1	6.7	2.3
1989	19.3	3.9	10.9	11.9	18.7	18.8	12.1
1995	38.1	11.2	20.9	19.1	31.1	31.2	21.9
2001	115.3	45.6	53.6	38.1	59.7	60.3	55.5
IT Capital Stock Per Capita							
1980	9.8	0.8	2.5	3.5	6.1	4.6	4.5
1989	27.4	3.7	9.6	9.9	15.5	13.1	17.5
1995	46.8	9.7	19.2	18.0	28.2	23.8	28.7
2001	110.7	31.8	44.9	33.4	49.7	44.1	73.1
IT Capital Quality							
1980	46.4	118.4	118.5	117.5	117.4	146.8	51.7
1989	70.4	107.4	112.7	119.7	120.4	143.2	69.1
1995	81.3	115.0	108.9	106.2	110.1	131.0	76.2
2001	104.1	143.4	119.3	114.1	120.2	136.6	75.9

Note: U.S. = 100.0 in 2000, Canada data begins in 1981.

IT capital quality reflects differences in the composition of IT capital input, relative to IT capital stock. A rising level of capital quality indicates a shift toward short-lived assets, such as computers and software. This shift is particularly dramatic for the U.S., Canada, and Japan, while the composition of IT capital stock changed relatively less for the U.K., France, Germany, and Italy. Patterns for Non-IT capital input, capital stock, and capital quality largely reflect those for capital as a whole, presented in Table 5.

I give growth rates for IT capital input per capita, capital stock per capita, and capital quality in Table 9. The G7 nations have exhibited double-digit growth in IT capital input per capita since 1995. Canada was the international leader during this period with the U.S. close behind. Japan was the leader in growth of IT capital input during the 1980's, another period of double-digit growth in the G7. However, Japanese IT growth slowed substantially during 1989–1995 and Canada gained the lead.

Patterns of growth for IT capital stock per capita are similar to those for IT capital input for the four European countries. Changes in the composition of IT capital stock per capita were important sources of growth of IT capital input per capita for the U.S., Canada, and Japan. IT capital stock also followed the pattern of IT capital input with substantial growth during the 1980's, followed by a pronounced lull during the period 1989–1995. After 1995 the growth rates of IT capital stock surged in all the G7 countries, but exceeded the rates of the 1980's only for the U.S., Canada, and Japan.

Finally, growth rates for IT capital quality reflect the rates at which shorter-lived IT assets are substituted for longer-lived assets.

Japan led in the growth of capital quality during the 1980's, but relinquished its lead to the U.S. in 1989. IT capital quality growth for the U.S., Canada, and Japan outstripped that for the four European countries for most of the period 1980–2001. Patterns of growth in Non-IT capital input per capita, Non-IT capital stock per capita, and Non-IT capital quality given in Table 10 largely reflect those for capital as a whole presented in Table 8.

Table 13 and Figure 1 present the contribution of capital input to economic growth for the G7 nations, divided between IT and Non-IT. The powerful surge of IT investment in the U.S. after 1995 is mirrored in similar jumps in growth rates of the contribution of IT capital through the G7. The contribution of IT capital input was similar during the 1980's and the period 1989–1995 for all the G7 nations, despite the dip in rates of economic growth after 1989. Japan is an exception to this general pattern with a contribution of IT capital comparable to that of the U.S. during the 1980's, followed by a decline in this contribution from 1989–1995, reflecting the sharp downturn in Japanese economic growth.

The contribution of Non-IT capital input to economic growth after 1995 exceeded that for IT capital input for four of the G7 nations; the exceptions were Canada, the U.K., and Japan. The U.S. stands out in the magnitude of the contribution of capital input after 1995. Both IT and Non-IT capital input contributed to the U.S. economic resurgence of the last half of the 1990's. Despite the strong performance of IT investment in Japan after 1995, the contribution of capital input declined substantially; the pattern for the U.K. is similar.

3.2.   The Relative Importance of Investment and Productivity

Table 14 and Figure 2 present contributions to economic growth from productivity, divided between the IT-producing and Non-IT-producing industries. The methodology for this division follows Triplett (1996). The contribution of IT-producing industries is positive throughout the period 1980–2001 and jumps substantially after 1995. Since the level of productivity in Italy is higher in 1980 than in 2001, it is not surprising that the contribution of productivity growth in the Non-IT industries was negative throughout the period. Productivity in these industries declined during the period 1989–1995 in the U.K., France, and Germany as well as Italy, and in Germany and Italy from 1995–2001.

Table 15 and Figure 3 give a comprehensive view of the sources of economic growth for the G7. The contribution of capital input alone exceeds that

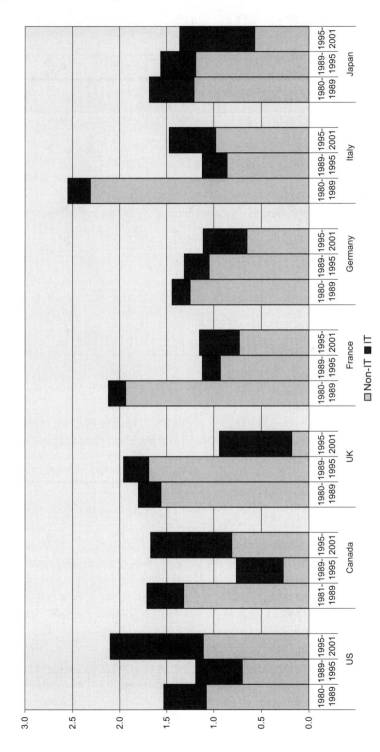

Figure 2-1. Capital Input Contribution by Country.

Table 2-7. Levels of Non-IT Capital Input and Capital Stock Per Capita and Non-IT Capital Quality

Year	U.S.	Canada	U.K.	France	Germany	Italy	Japan
Non-IT Capital Input Per Capita							
1980	73.8	73.1	30.7	41.3	51.9	41.6	31.3
1989	87.0	83.1	43.4	53.9	70.3	71.3	39.9
1995	90.7	79.9	55.9	57.9	79.7	81.2	47.4
2001	102.2	84.0	56.4	62.6	87.3	94.7	48.3
Non-IT Capital Stock Per Capita							
1980	82.5	44.1	25.7	38.0	63.4	38.2	91.6
1989	92.5	51.5	32.6	44.0	70.6	54.8	96.6
1995	94.8	53.0	36.9	48.3	79.3	64.4	101.6
2001	101.4	57.4	44.5	54.1	87.2	75.1	102.5
Non-IT Capital Quality							
1980	89.5	165.7	119.2	108.5	81.9	109.2	34.2
1989	94.1	161.2	133.2	122.6	99.5	130.0	41.3
1995	95.6	150.7	151.5	119.9	100.5	126.0	46.6
2001	100.8	146.5	126.7	115.8	100.1	126.1	47.1

Note: U.S. = 100.0 in 2000, Canada data begins in 1981.

Table 2-8. Growth in Capital Input and Capital Stock Per Capita and Capital Quality

Year	U.S.	Canada	U.K.	France	Germany	Italy	Japan
Capital Input Per Capita							
1980–1989	2.72	2.26	4.28	3.19	3.70	6.25	3.67
1989–1995	1.70	0.31	4.61	1.46	2.53	2.63	3.49
1995–2001	4.03	2.20	1.92	1.63	2.40	3.35	3.21
Capital Stock Per Capita							
1980–1989	1.56	2.19	2.85	1.74	1.34	4.18	0.74
1989–1995	0.70	1.05	2.36	1.74	2.09	2.87	0.97
1995–2001	1.63	1.36	3.57	1.67	1.75	2.49	0.53
Capital Quality							
1980–1989	1.17	0.07	1.43	1.45	2.36	2.07	2.93
1989–1995	0.99	−0.74	2.25	−0.27	0.44	−0.24	2.51
1995–2001	2.40	0.84	−1.65	−0.04	0.65	0.86	2.68

Note: Percentage, Canada data begins in 1981.

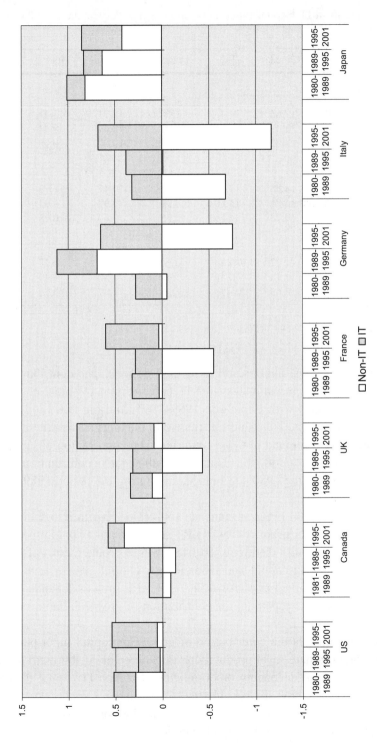

Figure 2-2. Sources of Total Factor Productivity Growth by Country.

Table 2-9. Growth in IT Capital Input and Capital Stock Per Capita and IT Capital Quality

Year	U.S.	Canada	U.K.	France	Germany	Italy	Japan
IT Capital Input Per Capita							
1980–1989	16.09	17.66	14.43	11.66	10.71	11.44	18.33
1989–1995	11.35	17.42	10.91	7.92	8.47	8.44	9.92
1995–2001	18.47	23.42	15.69	11.55	10.87	10.98	15.49
IT Capital Stock Per Capita							
1980–1989	11.47	18.88	14.98	11.46	10.43	11.72	15.10
1989–1995	8.94	16.28	11.50	9.91	9.97	9.94	8.29
1995–2001	14.34	19.73	14.16	10.35	9.40	10.28	15.55
IT Capital Quality							
1980–1989	4.63	−1.22	−0.56	0.20	0.28	−0.27	3.23
1989–1995	2.41	1.14	−0.58	−1.99	−1.50	−1.49	1.63
1995–2001	4.12	3.69	1.53	1.20	1.47	0.70	−0.06

Note: Percentage, Canada data begins in 1981.

of productivity for most nations and most time periods. The contribution of Non-IT capital input predominates over IT capital input for most countries and most time periods with Canada in 1989–1995, and the U.K. and Japan after 1995 as exceptions. This can be attributed to the unusual weakness in the growth of aggregate demand in these countries. The contribution of labor input varies considerably among the G7 nations with negative contributions after 1995 in Japan, during the 1980's in France, and during the period 1989–1995 in the U.K. and Germany.

Finally, Table 16 and Figure 4 translate sources of growth into sources of growth in average labor productivity (ALP). ALP, defined as output per hour worked, must be carefully distinguished from overall productivity, defined as output per unit of both capital and labor inputs. Output growth is the sum of growth in hours worked and growth in ALP. ALP growth depends on the contribution of capital deepening, the contribution of growth in labor quality, and productivity growth.

Capital deepening is the contribution of growth in capital input per hour worked and predominates over productivity as a source of ALP growth for the G7 nations. IT capital deepening predominates over Non-IT capital deepening in the U.S. throughout the period 1980–2001 and in Canada after 1989, the U.K., and France after 1995. Finally, the contribution of labor quality is positive for all the G7 nations through the period.

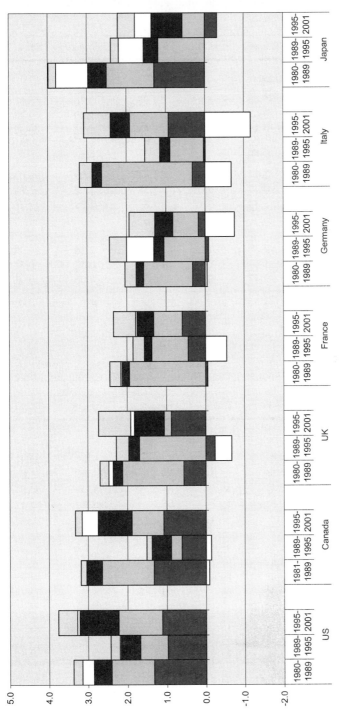

Figure 2-3. Sources of Economic Growth by Country.

Table 2-10. Growth in Non-IT Capital Input and Capital Stock Per Capita and Non-IT Capital Quality

Year	U.S.	Canada	U.K.	France	Germany	Italy	Japan
Non-IT Capital Input Per Capita							
1980–1989	1.83	1.60	3.85	2.97	3.36	5.97	2.69
1989–1995	0.68	−0.66	4.22	1.20	2.09	2.17	2.85
1995–2001	2.00	0.85	0.15	1.30	1.52	2.57	0.33
Non-IT Capital Stock Per Capita							
1980–1989	1.27	1.94	2.62	1.61	1.20	4.03	0.59
1989–1995	0.41	0.47	2.07	1.58	1.92	2.68	0.84
1995–2001	1.11	1.32	3.12	1.87	1.59	2.56	0.15
Non-IT Capital Quality							
1980–1989	0.56	−0.35	1.23	1.36	2.16	1.94	2.10
1989–1995	0.27	−1.13	2.15	−0.38	0.17	−0.51	2.01
1995–2001	0.88	−0.47	−2.97	−0.57	−0.06	0.01	0.18

Note: Percentage, Canada data begins in 1981.

Table 2-11. Levels of Labor Input and Hours Worked Per Capita and Labor Quality

Year	U.S.	Canada	U.K.	France	Germany	Italy	Japan
Labor Input Per Capita							
1980	81.1	73.0	78.9	63.0	75.4	48.8	84.8
1989	91.9	82.1	85.4	59.4	78.7	51.0	97.4
1995	94.2	82.3	82.4	61.7	75.2	50.6	95.6
2001	98.8	89.3	89.2	65.3	75.9	55.1	91.4
Hours Worked Per Capita							
1980	89.7	91.4	92.0	79.3	82.3	71.4	111.9
1989	97.1	96.6	97.7	71.2	82.7	72.1	115.6
1995	95.9	90.9	89.8	67.6	76.4	68.9	109.9
2001	98.3	96.3	94.2	69.7	75.3	72.3	101.3
Labor Quality							
1980	90.4	79.9	85.7	79.5	91.6	68.3	75.8
1989	94.7	85.0	87.4	83.5	95.2	70.7	84.3
1995	98.2	90.6	91.7	91.2	98.4	73.5	87.0
2001	100.5	92.7	94.7	93.7	100.9	76.1	90.3

Note: U.S. = 100.0 in 2000, Canada data begins in 1981.

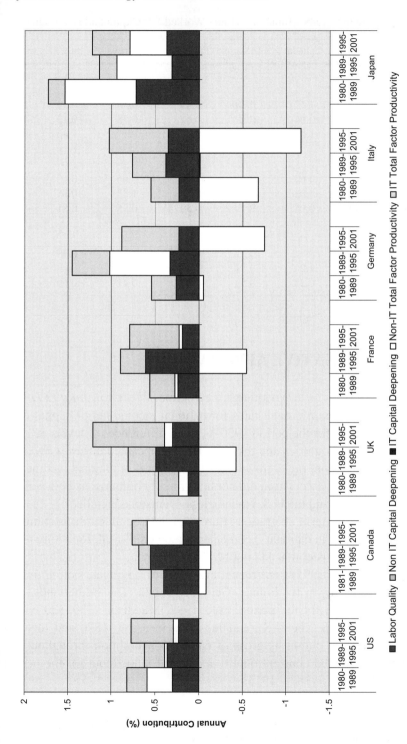

Figure 2-4. Sources of Labor Productivity Growth by Country.

Table 2-12. Growth in Labor Input and Hours Worked Per Capita and Labor Quality

Year	U.S.	Canada	U.K.	France	Germany	Italy	Japan
Labor Input Per Capita							
1980–1989	1.38	1.47	0.88	−0.65	0.48	0.49	1.53
1989–1995	0.41	0.04	−0.59	0.61	−0.78	−0.13	−0.31
1995–2001	0.79	1.35	1.32	0.95	0.17	1.40	−0.74
Hours Worked Per Capita							
1980–1989	0.87	0.69	0.67	−1.20	0.06	0.10	0.36
1989–1995	−0.21	−1.02	−1.41	−0.86	−1.33	−0.75	−0.84
1995–2001	0.41	0.98	0.79	0.50	−0.25	0.81	−1.36
Labor Quality							
1980–1989	0.51	0.78	0.21	0.55	0.42	0.39	1.18
1989–1995	0.61	1.06	0.81	1.47	0.55	0.63	0.52
1995–2001	0.38	0.38	0.53	0.45	0.41	0.60	0.62

Note: Percentage, Canada data begins in 1981.

4.   ALTERNATIVE APPROACHES

Edward Denison's (1967) pathbreaking volume, *Why Growth Rates Differ*, compared differences in growth rates for national income net of capital consumption per capita for the period 1950–62 with differences of levels in 1960 for eight European countries and the U.S. The European countries were characterized by much more rapid growth and a lower level of national income per capita. However, this association did not hold for all comparisons between the individual countries and the U.S. Nonetheless, Denison concluded:[11]

Aside from short-term aberrations Europe should be able to report higher growth rates, at least in national income per person employed, for a long time. Americans should expect this and not be disturbed by it.

Maddison (1987, 1991) constructed estimates of aggregate output, input, and productivity growth for France, Germany, Japan, The Netherlands, and the United Kingdom for the period 1870–1987. Maddison (1995) extended estimates for the U.S., the U.K., and Japan backward to 1820 and forward to 1992. He defined output as gross of capital consumption throughout the period and constructed constant quality indices of labor input for the period 1913–1984, but not for 1870–1913.

---

[11]   See Denison (1967), especially Chapter 21, "The Sources of Growth and the Contrast between Europe and the United States", pp. 296–348.

Table 2-13. Contribution of Total Capital, IT Capital and Non-IT Capital to Output Growth

Year	U.S.	Canada	U.K.	France	Germany	Italy	Japan
Total Capital							
1980–1989	1.53	1.71	1.80	2.12	1.44	2.55	1.68
1989–1995	1.19	0.76	1.96	1.12	1.31	1.12	1.56
1995–2001	2.10	1.67	0.94	1.15	1.11	1.47	1.36
IT Capital							
1980–1989	0.45	0.39	0.24	0.18	0.19	0.24	0.47
1989–1995	0.49	0.49	0.27	0.19	0.26	0.26	0.37
1995–2001	0.99	0.86	0.76	0.42	0.46	0.49	0.79
Non-IT Capital							
1980–1989	1.08	1.32	1.56	1.94	1.25	2.31	1.21
1989–1995	0.70	0.27	1.69	0.93	1.05	0.86	1.19
1995–2001	1.11	0.81	0.18	0.73	0.65	0.98	0.57

Note: Percentage. Contribution is growth rate times value share. Canada data begins in 1981.

Maddison employed capital stock as a measure of the input of capital, ignoring the changes in the composition of capital stock that are such an important source of growth for the G7 nations. This omission is especially critical in assessing the impact of investment in information technology. Finally, he reduced the growth rate of the price index for investment by one percent per year for all countries and all time periods to correct for biases like those identified by Wyckoff (1995).

4.1. Comparisons without Growth Accounts

Kuznets (1971) provided elaborate comparisons of growth rates for fourteen industrialized countries. Unlike Denison (1967), he did not provide level comparisons. Maddison (1982) filled this lacuna by comparing levels of national product for sixteen countries. These comparisons used estimates of purchasing power parities by Irving Kravis, Alan Heston, and Robert Summers (1978).[12]

Maddison (1995) extended his long-term estimates of the growth of national product and population to 56 countries, covering the period 1820–1992. Maddison (2001) updated these estimates to 1998 in his magisterial volume, *The World Economy: A Millennial Perspective.* He provided estimates for 134

---

[12] For details see Maddison (1982), pp. 159–168.

Table 2-14. Contributions of Productivity from IT and Non-IT Production to Output Growth

Year	U.S.	Canada	U.K.	France	Germany	Italy	Japan
Productivity							
1980–1989	0.52	0.06	0.34	0.32	0.23	−0.36	1.01
1989–1995	0.26	0.00	−0.11	−0.26	1.12	0.37	0.83
1995–2001	0.54	0.58	0.91	0.60	−0.10	−0.49	0.85
Productivity from IT Production							
1980–1989	0.23	0.14	0.23	0.29	0.28	0.32	0.19
1989–1995	0.23	0.14	0.32	0.29	0.43	0.38	0.20
1995–2001	0.48	0.17	0.82	0.56	0.65	0.68	0.43
Productivity from Non-IT Production							
1980–1989	0.29	−0.08	0.11	0.03	−0.05	−0.68	0.82
1989–1995	0.03	−0.14	−0.43	−0.55	0.69	−0.01	0.63
1995–2001	0.06	0.41	0.09	0.04	−0.75	−1.17	0.42

Note: Percentage. Canada data begins in 1981.

countries, as well as seven regions of the world—Western Europe, Western Offshoots (Australia, Canada, New Zealand, and the United States), Eastern Europe, Former USSR, Latin America, Asia, and Africa.

Purchasing power parities have been updated by successive versions of the Penn World Table. A complete list of these tables through Mark 5 is given by Summers and Heston (1991). The current version of the Penn World Table is available on the Center for International Comparisons website at the University of Pennsylvania (CICUP). This covers 168 countries for the period 1950–2000 and represents one of the most significant achievements in economic measurement of the postwar period.[13]

4.2. Convergence

Data presented by Kuznets (1971), Maddison, and successive versions of the Penn World Table have made it possible to reconsider the issue of convergence raised by Denison (1967). Moses Abramovitz (1986) was the first to take up the challenge by analyzing convergence of output per capita among Maddison's (2001) sixteen countries. He found that convergence characterized the postwar period, while there was no tendency toward convergence before 1914

---

[13] See Heston, Summers, and Aten (2002). The CICUP website is at: http://pwt.econ. upenn.edu/aboutpwt.html.

Table 2-15. Sources of Output Growth

Year	U.S.	Canada	U.K.	France	Germany	Italy	Japan
Output							
1980–1989	3.38	3.10	2.69	2.38	1.99	2.51	3.98
1989–1995	2.43	1.39	1.62	1.30	2.34	1.52	2.39
1995–2001	3.76	3.34	2.74	2.34	1.18	1.90	1.89
Labor							
1980–1989	1.33	1.33	0.56	−0.06	0.32	0.32	1.29
1989–1995	0.98	0.62	−0.24	0.44	−0.09	0.03	0.00
1995–2001	1.12	1.08	0.88	0.59	0.17	0.93	−0.32
IT Capital							
1980–1989	0.45	0.39	0.24	0.18	0.19	0.24	0.47
1989–1995	0.49	0.49	0.27	0.19	0.26	0.26	0.37
1995–2001	0.99	0.86	0.76	0.42	0.46	0.49	0.79
Non-IT Capital							
1980–1989	1.08	1.32	1.56	1.94	1.25	2.31	1.21
1989–1995	0.70	0.27	1.69	0.93	1.05	0.86	1.19
1995–2001	1.11	0.81	0.18	0.73	0.65	0.98	0.57
Productivity from IT Production							
1980–1989	0.23	0.14	0.23	0.29	0.28	0.32	0.19
1989–1995	0.23	0.14	0.32	0.29	0.43	0.38	0.20
1995–2001	0.48	0.17	0.82	0.56	0.65	0.68	0.43
Productivity from Non-IT Production							
1980–1989	0.29	−0.08	0.11	0.03	−0.05	−0.68	0.82
1989–1995	0.03	−0.14	−0.43	−0.55	0.69	−0.01	0.63
1995–2001	0.06	0.41	0.09	0.04	−0.75	−1.17	0.42

Note: Percentage Contributions. Canada data begins in 1981.

and during the interwar period. Baumol (1986) formalized these results by running a regression of growth rate of GDP per capita over the period 1870–1979 on the 1870 level of GDP per capita.[14]

In a highly innovative paper on "Crazy Explanations for the Productivity Slowdown" Paul Romer (1987) derived Baumol's "growth regression"

---

[14] Baumol's "growth regression" has spawned a vast literature, recently summarized by Steven Durlauf and Danny Quah (1999), Ellen McGrattan and James Schmitz (1999), and Islam (2003). Much of this literature is based on data from successive versions of the Penn World Table.

from Solow's (1970) growth model with a Cobb-Douglas production function. Romer's empirical contribution was to extend the growth regressions from Maddison's (1982) sixteen advanced countries to the 115 countries in the Penn World Table (Mark 3). Romer's key finding was an estimate of the elasticity of output with respect to capital close to three-quarters. The share of capital in GNP implied by Solow's model was less than half as great.

Gregory Mankiw, David Romer, and David Weil (1992) defended the traditional framework of Kuznets (1971) and Solow (1970). The empirical part of their study is based on data for 98 countries from the Penn World Table (Mark 4). Like Paul Romer (1987), Mankiw, David Romer, and Weil derived a growth regression from the Solow (1970) model; however, they augmented this by allowing for investment in human capital.

The results of Mankiw, David Romer, and Weil (1992) provided empirical support for the augmented Solow model. There was clear evidence of the convergence predicted by the model; in addition, the estimated elasticity of output with respect to capital was in line with the share of capital in the value of output. The rate of convergence of output per capita was too slow to be consistent with 1970 version of the Solow model, but supported the augmented version.

4.3.   Modeling Productivity Differences

Finally, Islam (1995) exploited an important feature of the Penn World Table overlooked in prior studies. This panel data set contains benchmark comparisons of levels of the national product at five year intervals, beginning in 1960. This made it possible to test an assumption maintained in growth regressions. These regressions had assumed identical levels of productivity for all countries included in the Penn World Table.

Substantial differences in levels of productivity among countries have been documented by Denison (1967), by my papers with Christensen and Cummings (1981), Dougherty (1996, 1997), and Yip (Jorgenson and Yip, 2000) and in Section 2 above. By introducing econometric methods for panel data Islam (1995) was able to allow for these differences. He corroborated the finding of Mankiw, David Romer, and Weil (1992) that the elasticity of output with respect to capital input coincided with the share of capital in the value of output.

In addition, Islam (1995) found that the rate of convergence of output per capita among countries in the Penn World Table substantiated the *unaugmented* version of the Solow (1970) growth model. In short, "crazy explanations" for the productivity slowdown, like those propounded by Paul Romer (1987), were unnecessary. Moreover, the model did not require augmentation by endogenous investment in human capital, as proposed by Mankiw, David Romer, and Weil (1992).

Table 2-16. Sources of Labor Productivity Growth

Year	U.S.	Canada	U.K.	France	Germany	Italy	Japan
Output							
1980–1989	3.38	3.10	2.69	2.38	1.99	2.51	3.98
1989–1995	2.43	1.39	1.62	1.30	2.34	1.52	2.39
1995–2001	3.76	3.34	2.74	2.34	1.18	1.90	1.89
Hours							
1980–1989	1.79	1.87	0.82	−0.66	0.11	0.15	0.95
1989–1995	1.02	0.20	−1.17	−0.41	−0.71	−0.57	−0.51
1995–2001	1.53	1.93	1.03	0.91	−0.11	0.99	−1.14
Labor Productivity							
1980–1989	1.58	1.23	1.87	3.04	1.88	2.36	3.04
1989–1995	1.40	1.19	2.79	1.71	3.05	2.09	2.90
1995–2001	2.23	1.41	1.71	1.43	1.29	0.92	3.03
IT Capital Deepening							
1980–1989	0.40	0.35	0.22	0.19	0.19	0.23	0.45
1989–1995	0.44	0.48	0.29	0.20	0.28	0.28	0.39
1995–2001	0.92	0.79	0.71	0.39	0.46	0.45	0.85
Non-IT Capital Deepening							
1980–1989	0.37	0.42	1.20	2.29	1.20	2.25	0.86
1989–1995	0.34	0.16	2.11	1.15	1.33	1.06	1.37
1995–2001	0.55	−0.14	−0.21	0.25	0.70	0.61	0.96
Labor Quality							
1980–1989	0.30	0.40	0.12	0.24	0.26	0.23	0.72
1989–1995	0.36	0.55	0.49	0.61	0.33	0.38	0.31
1995–2001	0.23	0.18	0.30	0.19	0.23	0.35	0.37
Productivity from IT Production							
1980–1989	0.23	0.14	0.23	0.29	0.28	0.32	0.19
1989–1995	0.23	0.14	0.32	0.29	0.43	0.38	0.20
1995–2001	0.48	0.17	0.82	0.56	0.65	0.68	0.43
Productivity from Non-IT Production							
1980–1989	0.29	−0.08	0.11	0.03	−0.05	−0.68	0.82
1989–1995	0.03	−0.14	−0.43	−0.55	0.69	−0.01	0.63
1995–2001	0.06	0.41	0.09	0.04	−0.75	−1.17	0.42

Note: Percentage. Contributions. Canada data begins in 1981.

Islam concluded that differences in technology among countries must be included in econometric models of growth rates. This requires econometric techniques for panel data, like those originated by Gary Chamberlain (1984), rather than the regression methods of Baumol, Paul Romer, and Mankiw, David Romer, and Weil. Panel data techniques have now superseded regression methods in modeling differences in output per capita.

5.   CONCLUSIONS

I conclude that a powerful surge in investment in information technology and equipment after 1995 characterizes all of the G7 economies. This accounts for a large portion of the resurgence in U.S. economic growth, but contributes substantially to economic growth in the remaining G7 economies as well. Another significant source of the G7 growth resurgence after 1995 is a jump in productivity growth in IT-producing industries.

For Japan the dramatic upward leap in the impact of IT investment after 1995 was insufficient to overcome downward pressures from deficient growth of aggregate demand. This manifests itself in declining contributions of Non-IT capital and labor inputs. Similar downturns are visible in Non-IT capital input in France, Germany, and especially the U.K. after 1995.

These findings are based on new data and new methodology for analyzing the sources of economic growth. Internationally harmonized prices for information technology equipment and software are essential for capturing differences among the G7 nations. Constant quality indices of capital and labor inputs are necessary to incorporate the impacts of investments in information technology and human capital.

Exploiting the new data and methodology, I have been able to show that investment in tangible assets is the most important source of economic growth in the G7 nations. The contribution of capital input exceeds that of productivity for all countries for all periods. The relative importance of productivity growth is far less than suggested by the traditional methodology of Kuznets (1971) and Solow (1970), which is now obsolete.

The conclusion from Islam's (1995) research is that the Solow (1970) model is appropriate for modeling the endogenous accumulation of tangible assets. It is unnecessary to endogenize human capital accumulation as well. The transition path to balanced growth equilibrium after a change in policies that affects investment in tangible assets requires decades, while the transition after a change affecting investment in human capital requires as much as a century.

REFERENCES

Abramovitz, Moses (1986), "Catching Up, Forging Ahead, and Falling Behind", Journal of Economic History, Vol. 46, No. 2, June, pp. 385–406.

Baldwin, John R. and Tarek M. Harchaoui (2002), Productivity Growth in Canada—2002, Ottawa, Statistics Canada.

Baumol, William J. (1986), "Productivity Growth, Convergence, and Welfare", American Economic Review, Vol. 76, No. 5, December, pp. 1072–1085.

Chamberlain, Gary (1984), "Panel Data", in Zvi Griliches and Michael Intriligator, eds., Handbook of Econometrics, Vol. 2, pp. 1247–1318.

Christensen, Laurits R., Dianne Cummings, and Dale W. Jorgenson (1980), "Economic Growth, 1947–1973: An International Comparison", in John W. Kendrick and Beatrice Vaccara, eds., New Developments in Productivity Measurement and Analysis, Chicago, University of Chicago Press, pp. 595–698.

Christensen, Laurits R., Dianne Cummings, and Dale W. Jorgenson (1981), "Relative Productivity Levels, 1947–1973", European Economic Review, Vol. 16, No. 1, May, pp. 61–94.

Colecchia, Alessandra and Paul Schreyer (2002), "ICT Investment and Economic Growth in the 1990s: Is the United States a Unique Case? A Comparative Study of Nine OECD Countries", Review of Economic Dynamics, Vol. 5, No. 2, April, pp. 408–442.

Denison, Edward F. (1967), Why Growth Rates Differ, Washington, The Brookings Institution.

Dougherty, Chrys and Dale W. Jorgenson (1996), "International Comparisons of the Sources of Economic Growth", American Economic Review, Vol. 86, No. 2, May, pp. 25–29.

Dougherty, Chrys and Dale W. Jorgenson (1997), "There Is No Silver Bullet: Investment and Growth in the G7", National Institute Economic Review, No. 162, October, pp. 57–74.

Durlauf, Steven N. and Danny T. Quah (1999), "The New Empirics of Economic Growth", in Taylor and Woodford, eds., pp. 235–310.

Heston, Alan, Robert Summers, and Bettina Aten (2002), Penn World Table Version 6.1, Philadelphia, Center for International Comparisons at the University of Pennsylvania (CICUP), October.

Islam, Nasrul (1995), "Growth Empirics", Quarterly Journal of Economics, Vol. 110, No. 4, November, pp. 1127–1170.

Islam, Nasrul (2003), "What Have We Learned from the Convergence Debate?" Journal of Economic Surveys, Vol. 17, No. 3, July, pp. 309–362.

Jorgenson, Dale W. (2001), "Information Technology and the U.S. Economy", American Economic Review, Vol. 91, No. 1, March, pp. 1–32.

Jorgenson, Dale W. (2003), "Information Technology and the G7 Economies", World Economics, Vol. 4, No. 4, October–December, pp. 139–170.

Jorgenson, Dale W. and Kazuyuki Motohashi (2003), "Economic Growth of Japan and the U.S. in the Information Age", Tokyo, Research Institute of Economy, Trade, and Industry, July.

Jorgenson, Dale W. and Kevin J. Stiroh (2000), "Raising the Speed Limit: U.S. Economic Growth in the Information Age", Brookings Papers on Economic Activity, 1, pp. 125–211.

Jorgenson, Dale W. and Eric Yip (2000), "Whatever Happened to Productivity Growth?" in Charles R. Hulten, Edwin R. Dean, and Michael J. Harper, eds., New Developments in Productivity Analysis, Chicago, University of Chicago Press, pp. 509–540.

Kravis, Irving B., Alan Heston, and Robert Summers (1978), International Comparisons of Real Product and Purchasing Power, Baltimore, Johns Hopkins University Press.

Kuznets, Simon (1971), Economic Growth of Nations, Cambridge, Harvard University Press.

Maddison, Angus (1982), Phases of Capitalist Development, Oxford, Oxford University Press.

Maddison, Angus (1987), "Growth and Slowdown in Advanced Capitalist Economies: Techniques of Quantitative Assessment", Journal of Economic Literature, Vol. 25, No. 2, June, pp. 649–698.

Maddison, Angus (1991), Dynamic Forces in Capitalist Development, Oxford, Oxford University Press.

Maddison, Angus (1995), Monitoring the World Economy, Paris, Organisation for Economic Co-operation and Development.

Maddison, Angus (2001), The World Economy: A Millenial Perspective, Paris, Organisation for Economic Co-operation and Development.

Mankiw, N. Gregory, David Romer, and David Weil (1992), "A Contribution to the Empirics of Economic Growth", Quarterly Journal of Economics, Vol. 107, No. 2, May, pp. 407–437.

McGrattan, Ellen and James Schmitz (1999), "Explaining Cross-Country Income Differences", in Taylor and Woodford, eds., pp. 669–737.

Organization for Economic Co-operation and Development (2002), Purchasing Power Parities and Real Expenditures, 1999 Benchmark Year, Paris, Organization for Economic Co-operation and Development.

Oliner, Stephen D. and Daniel J. Sichel (2000), "The Resurgence of Growth in the Late 1990's: Is Information Technology the Story?" Journal of Economic Perspectives, Vol. 14, No. 4, Fall, pp. 3–22.

Romer, Paul (1987), "Crazy Explanations for the Productivity Slowdown", in Stanley Fischer, ed., NBER Macroeconomics Annual, Cambridge, The MIT Press, pp. 163–201.

Schreyer, Paul (2000), "The Contribution of Information and Communication Technology to Output Growth: A Study of the G7 Countries", Paris, Organisation for Economic Co-operation and Development, May 23.

Solow, Robert M. (1970), Growth Theory: An Exposition, New York, Oxford University Press.

Summers, Robert and Alan Heston (1991), "The Penn World Table (Mark 5): An Expanded Set of International Comparisons, 1950–1988", Quarterly Journal of Economics, Vol. 106, No. 2, May, pp. 327–368.

Taylor, John B. and Michael Woodford, eds., (1999), Handbook of Macroeconomics, Vol. 1A, Amsterdam, North-Holland.

Triplett, Jack (1996), "High-Tech Industry Productivity and Hedonic Price Indices", in Organization for Economic Co-operation and Development, Industry Productivity, Paris, Organization for Economic Co-operation and Development, pp. 119–142.

Van Ark, Bart, Johanna Melka, Nanno Mulder, Marcel Timmer, and Gerard Ypma (2002), ICT Investment and Growth Accounts for the European Union, 1980–2000, Brussels, European Commission, June.

Wyckoff, Andrew W. (1995), "The Impact of Computer Prices on International Comparisons of Productivity", Economics of Innovation and New Technology, Vol. 3, Nos. 3–4, pp. 277–93.

ACKNOWLEDGEMENTS

The Economic and Social Research Institute provided financial support from its program on international collaboration through the Nomura Research Institute. I am very grateful to Jon Samuels for excellent research assistance. Alessandra Colecchia, Mun S. Ho, Kazuyuki Motohashi, Koji Nomura, Kevin J. Stiroh, Marcel Timmer, and Bart Van Ark provided valuable data. The Bureau of Economic Analysis and the Bureau of Labor Statistics assisted with data for the U.S. and Statistics Canada contributed the data for Canada. I am grateful to all of them but retain sole responsibility for any remaining deficiencies. An earlier version of this paper was published under the same title in *World Economics* for 2003.

Chapter 3

BUSINESS PROCESS OUTSOURCING AND "OFF-SHORING": THE GLOBALIZATION OF INFORMATION-INTENSIVE SERVICES

Uday M. Apte[a] and Uday Karmarkar[b]

[a]*Graduate School of Business and Public Policy, Naval Postgraduate School, 555 Dyer Road, Monterey, CA 93943, e-mail: umapte@nps.edu;* [b]*UCLA Anderson School of Management, UCLA, Los Angeles, CA 90095-1481, e-mail: ukarmark@anderson.ucla.edu*

Abstract   Information-intensive services are being globalized as corporations take advantage of the opportunities made available by the progress of information technology and respond to the challenge of increasing global competition. After analyzing the role that information technology plays in globalizing information-intensive services, the paper reviews a wide range of illustrative examples where information-intensive services have been globalized. Based on this analysis, the paper proposes a theoretical framework that identifies the criteria and guidelines for successfully selecting service activities to be globalized, and presents guidelines to managers for choosing the appropriate country location. By applying this theoretical framework to the U.S. economy the paper provides a rough estimate of the potential impact of globalized information-intensive services on the labor market in the U.S. The paper also analyzes the geographic distribution of language clusters and presents a conjecture concerning the emerging pattern of global trade in information-intensive services. The paper ends with a brief discussion on the opportunity for conducting further research into this growing and important phenomenon.

1.   INTRODUCTION

Services have traditionally been characterized by the intangibility of outputs, co-production requiring inputs from both the producer and the customer, and simultaneity of production and consumption demanding direct interaction between the producer and the customer. These characteristics have meant that services are inherently more location-bound and are consequently less tradable as compared to manufactured goods. However, information intensive services display tradability characteristics that make them behave more like manufacturing, especially due to advances in information technologies. While services may still need to be "produced" in response to demand, and while the eventual output may still be intangible, the co-location of customers and providers is no longer a rule. Information and communications technologies have made it feasible to de-integrate services processes, and to deliver services remotely, even when there is a significant degree of interaction between provider and customer. The explosive growth of the Internet and other digital networks is fueling a revolution in the way commerce is conducted. Increasingly, firms are using networks and information technology to electronically design, produce, market, buy, sell and deliver information products and services throughout the world. The progress in IT is making it possible to unbundle the production and consumption of information-intensive service sectors such as banking and insurance, entertainment, publishing/media, education, professional and technical services, research and development, and some aspects of health care. Thus, with the use of IT, information-intensive services can potentially be produced in one place and consumed in another either simultaneously or at a later point in time.

Electronic banking transactions, such as making payment on a future day to a pre-designated merchant, are every-day examples where a customer can access the service at a place far removed from the location of the customer's bank. Even services in which the consumer-provider interaction has traditionally been high (as in education and health) are now becoming amenable to unbundling and eventually to cross-border trade. Distance education is a familiar example in the field of professional and university-level education. Experiment in telemedics, where hospitals in Saudi Arabia are linked to the radiology and pathology departments for consultations with health care experts in Massachusetts General Hospital (Houlder, 1994) is another example. In essence, information technology has improved the transportability and tradability of services, particularly that of the information intensive services. Advances in telecommunications have been particularly useful in moving information intensive tasks away from the office, domestically or globally. These developments represent at once both an opportunity and a challenge to the managers of service enterprises and national economies. O'Reilly (1992) was one of the early observers who concluded that there is a growing migration of white-collar service jobs to overseas locations. This migration of service jobs has been taking place in a number of different ways. In some cases, it is a result of competitive strength of foreign-owned companies based abroad. In other cases, it is due to American-owned companies' decisions to perform selected service activities overseas. In either case, this is simply the result of market forces at work—in a free market economy an activity will be performed wherever it makes the most economic sense.

In effect, the pressures of increasing global competition, the emerging global work force, and the opportunities made available by the advances in information technology are forcing corporations to reevaluate the performance and cost of their value chains in the creation and consumption of services. Corporations are struggling with several key questions: (1) how to perform service activities within a given value chain? (2) whether or not to carry out a service activity within the organization? and (3) where to locate the activity?

Following Quinn (1992), we call this phenomenon the *disaggregation of services.* It occurs when one or more components of a value chain of service activities, that have been traditionally carried out within an organization at a single location, are disaggregated (i.e. decomposed or dispersed) in a manner that transcends both the organizational and geographic bounds. Faced with cost reduction and performance improvement pressures, a growing number of U.S. companies are finding the option of global disaggregation of services quite attractive since it not only allows them to take advantage of relatively lower wages in other parts of the world, but also makes it possible to access a skill that is perhaps in a short supply, and deliver a service at a level that is the "best in class."

Global disaggregation (i.e., globalization) of services offers enormous challenges and opportunities for corporate managers in today's increasingly global economy. In this paper we discuss the rationale underlying the disaggregation of services and the resulting patterns of globalization, In the next section we analyze the role information technology plays in globalizing information-intensive services and provide examples to illustrate the nature, scope, and increasing pace of the globalization of such services. In the third section we present a theoretical framework that identifies the criteria and guidelines for selecting service activities to be successfully globalized. This framework is then used to estimate the potential size of the market for globalized information-intensive services in the United States. This section also provides guidelines to managers for choosing the appropriate country location. The fourth section discusses the emerging picture of the global disaggregation of services. The final section concludes the paper with a summary and some thoughts on further research.

2. IT AND GLOBALIZATION OF INFORMATION-INTENSIVE SERVICES

The ability to distribute manufacturing activity across large geographies is clearly facilitated by the physical and tangible nature of products at all levels of manufacture. Parts and components can be manufactured in one location and shipped to another easily. It is not uncommon for parts to be sent outside a firm for a single operation or process that happens to be performed efficiently elsewhere. The intangible nature of service outputs have historically made this infeasible. As a result, it was common to find large co-located service processes in the form of hospitals, universities, banks and the like. It has been advances in information technology that have changed this picture. The first step was the appearance of telecommunications, which created the potential for low cost transportation of information along with instantaneity in interaction. Other logistical means included the technologies of broadcasting as with radio and television. The development of the modern computer complemented developments in transportation, by providing processing power. Oddly though, the factories (boxes) and transportation channels (wires) remained unconnected for a long time. The change came with the development of networked communications, and finally with the implementation of data networks and the TCP/IP protocol that allowed computers to communicate with swiches and networks. That development provided end to end connectivity across information chains, The development of the world-wide web and browser functionality extended the connectivity to human users who did not need to be experts to access these vast resources. The developments in hardware and communications protocols were further complemented by the development of the object oriented paradigm in software. This fundamentally different way of thinking about software, permitted the distribution of information processing functionality across different locations, first in the form of client-server architecture, then multitier designs, and finally as distributed computing across wide area networks with very little need for a formal computing architecture. At the same time, advances in the representation of data and information types, and in encryption, made it feasible to transfer very rich and very large data files between processes, without loss of information, with security, as batches or flows and at very low cost.

This flexible distributed information processing and computing structure, enabled by concurrent and complementary developments in hardware, software, data standards, and communication technologies (including wireless), have created an information processing "shop floor" where work processes can be broken down into very fine granularity, executed anywhere, dis-assembled and transported through packet switched, store and forward, data networks, and then reassembled for human use, all with manageable latencies, and very low costs. This "shop floor" picture has now enabled the same characteristics to hold for so-called business processes, and further, to hold for information intensive services as well.

The impact of the technological substrate on services is taking place in at least two major ways: first, by allowing electronic capture and subsequent transmission of outputs of certain specific types of information-based services, and second, by removing or reducing the constraints of space and time on information-intensive service activities. Technological innovations of the first kind have expanded the opportunities for creation of services that used to be traditionally embodied in goods — print media such as newspapers, magazines and books, software in diskettes, video games and films on videotapes, and music in compact discs. Due to capture in digital forms and due to the convergence in the transportation of digital information, these goods can now be transported rapidly to the point where many goods are morphing into services. Most forms of entertainment and media are being affected by this transformation to some extent.

In the second type of technological innovation, IT is used to facilitate the disaggregation and recombination of information-intensive activities without regard to their location in space or time. These information-intensive activities include research and development, computing, inventory management, payroll, accounting, personnel administration, secretarial, marketing, advertising, and legal services. It should be noted that these activities are performed in all economic sectors. They play a fundamental role not only in service industries, but also in manufacturing and primary industries. In the United States, for example, as much as 65 to 75 percent of employment in manufacturing has been attributed to such service activities (Quinn, 1992). With progress in information technology, outsourcing of these activities has become increasingly common. IT-based linkages now allow managers to separate out many information-intensive service activities from their core operations, procure them from outside suppliers, and still integrate them with core activities that continue to be performed internally. With continuing decline of communications costs, the globalization of information-intensive services in the form of cross-border trade has seen significant growth.

Schuknecht and Pérez-Esteve (1999) determined that the trade in potentially digitizable media goods amounted to about $44 billion in 1996, or less than one percent of total world trade. Electronic delivery already plays an important economic and trade role in many services sectors. It has been crucial for the development of cross-border trade in services. Legal advice is given by telephone, news services are transmitted by fax, payments are settled via electronic networks, not to mention that telephone, fax, etc. constitute communication services. Communication services, computer and information services, and a number of financial services and insurance services, as well as other business services are frequently conducted over telecommunication networks. Cross-border trade in these sectors amounted to about US$ 370 billion in 1995, or 6 per cent of total world trade, and it is much more important than trade in the digitizable media products discussed above. Thus, we will focus our attention on the latter category in discussing illustrative examples in the next sub-section.

2.1. Past and Recent Experience in the Globalization of Information-intensive Services

Data entry was one of the earliest information technology-based tasks to be *globally outsourced*. For example, Pacific Data Services has been contracting data entry services to China since 1961 (Noble, 1986). Data entry has been one of the easiest service activities to be globally outsourced, since, it requires only a low level of computer literacy and very little interaction between the customer and the vendor. The customer mails paper-based data forms, or electronically sends scanned images of data forms, to the vendor for data entry. The vendor, in turn, sends the computerized data back via telecommunication links. In Jamaica, about 3,500 people work in office parks linked to the U.S. by satellite dishes. They do data entry, handle calls to toll-free numbers and perform other clerical duties (O'Reilly, 1992).

With the growing need for information technology applications in all facets of business life, there is an increasing trend toward globalization in the $200 billion software industry (Economist, 1996). The case of semi-conductor giant, Texas Instruments (TI) and its Indian subsidiary, TI, India, is an interesting example where the Indian subsidiary in Bangalore is entrusted with the design and development of software for computer aided design (CAD) of integrated circuits (Apte and Mason, 1992). All designs are communicated to other global locations electronically. As one TI executive explained, TI's move to India in 1985 was caused by the fact that TI could not hire enough engineers knowledgeable in both software and semiconductor chip design in the U.S. or in Europe, while India was training more such engineers than it could gainfully employ. Even after accounting for the fact that TI had to install its own satellite dish and electricity generators, the salaries in India have been low enough that work gets done for less than half of what it costs in the U.S. Software programming generally accounts for a third of the R&D budgets of many high tech companies. Hence, as TI's manager in India commented, as chip designs and software development become more complex, the cost advantage of locating in such places as India can become even greater. Several well-known American companies, including Microsoft, Hewlett-Packard, and IBM, have recently set up operations in the cities of Bangalore, Delhi, Hyderabad, and Mumbai in India.

Back-office clerical tasks and various corporate staff functions including accounting services have become attractive candidates today for global disaggregation. These globalized services, other than software related services, are also referred to by the term "remote services." An interesting characterization of remote services is that they entail using software rather than writing it (Economist, 1996). The work in remote services can range from typing in telephone-directory entries, to reconciling account statements, to call centers, to conducting basic research. Generally, it involves activities that are considered too routine for expensive western workers who could be serving customers directly; but not so repetitive that a computer can be programmed to do them.

Western companies with big back offices are setting up operations, or hiring outsourcing vendors, in Ireland, India, or other developing countries such as Barbados. For example, the back-office tasks of sorting, data entry and filing of thousands of tickets and boarding passes collected by American Airlines in cities around the world are handled by Barbados-based Caribbean Data Services, a sister company of American Airlines (Yearwood, 1993). Speed in processing tickets and boarding passes is crucial to the success of CDS, since, the faster it can verify the travel to the credit card companies and other airlines, the faster American Airlines collects the cash. As an official of the government owned investment and development corporation said, "In Barbados, the wages rate is lower and the quality of work is higher than in the U.S., where similarly qualified people simply don't want to do the data entry work." Selectronic, a two-year-old firm in Delhi, India, retrieves doctors' dictation from a toll-free number, transcribes the recordings and sends the results back as text to an American HMO (Economist, 1999). At Selectronic, a six-month training course in American medical terminology is provided to all employees. To assure quality, the company has also instituted a procedure that examines every one of the 1.3 million lines of transcription the company produces monthly.

Other past examples of remote services include, medical claims processing operations of New York Life Insurance and Cigna Corporation (Lohr, 1988 and Wysocki, 1991) and Metropolitan Life's underwriting and claims processing operations in Ireland (O'Reilly, 1992). In Fremoy, Ireland, Metropolitan Life employs claims analysts to evaluate medical insurance claims to determine if they are eligible for payment and the amount to be paid if they are eligible. This is no low skill clerical work. Required are the knowledge of insurance business, the American medical system and practices, and even some familiarity with medical science. Metropolitan's Irish staff also reviews new policies being sold by salesmen in the U.S. for errors and omissions. The operational set-up for this work involves over-night shipment of forms by air, and on-line access to Metropolitan's system in the U.S. by the staff in Ireland. As managers of these facilities explain, low operating costs (about 30% less than the U.S. costs) and financial incentives offered by the Irish governments are only part of the reasons for global disaggregation. Even more important are the availability of well-educated staff, a strong work ethic, and the low turnover rates induced by the high unemployment levels in Ireland.

As the above examples illustrate, back-office work makes up the bulk of the remote services business, but the range goes beyond that. Bechtel, an American company, has a team of engineers near Delhi, India, working on construction projects worldwide. Delhi is also the home of McKinsey's "knowledge center", which does research for the rest of the company. Pfizer and Quintiles, two health-care firms, find India an ideal place for conducting inexpensive trials of new drugs (Economist, 1999).

In manufacturing companies, service activities such as product design work and logistics management, and in some cases even R&D activities, are being globalized. National Semiconductor Corporation provides an example of a company that is using the Internet to create a truly global laboratory (Pollack, 1992). The company operates integrated circuit design laboratories in Santa Clara, California and in Tel Aviv and Tokyo. It uses its global network of computers in an innovative way to speed the task of simulation—a time-consuming but critical task in IC circuit designs. At the end of a day, researchers in Santa Clara hand off simulation analysis to their colleagues in Tel Aviv who in turn, after a full day of work, pass it on to researchers in Tokyo, so that by the beginning of the next day, the results of simulation come back to the Santa Clara staff. Thus, the Internet is being used to conduct research around the world, and around the clock.

Numerous other examples of the globalization of information-intensive services can be found in trade literature. They include Quarterdeck Software's customer service function, Hewlett-Packard's portable ink-jet printer business being run from its subsidiary in Singapore which is responsible for design and manufacturing, and Microsoft and Motorola conducting selected R&D projects in Southeast Asia, just to name a few.

Economic factors, such as costs, benefits and the associated risks are undoubtedly the most important considerations in the global disaggregation of services. In addition, all the above examples are characterized by the effective use of information technology. Information, unlike products such as automobiles or televisions, can be transported quickly, reliably and cheaply using modern communications and computer technology. Thus, many information intensive tasks can be moved halfway across the world whenever it is operationally feasible and economically desirable to do so. Order of magnitude improvements in the performance and the benefit-to-cost ratio of information technology have been critical enablers in this regard.

The experience of globally disaggregated services cited earlier can be used to identify the advantages and disadvantages of global disaggregation. Global disaggregation can have substantial benefits: significant cost savings, access to a large pool of skilled labor, foothold in foreign markets with large growth potential, and faster cycle time for design and development. These benefits are the primary reasons why a number of large and small corporations have actively considered the option to globalize information intensive services. In pursuing this option, however, one must keep in mind certain pitfalls. These drawbacks include: difficulties with communication and coordination, possible violations of intellectual property rights, the loss of control over quality and timetable, difficulties in managing cultural diversity, overcoming governmental bureaucracy and controls, and unstable social, political and economic systems. Apte and Mason (1995a) provide a detailed discussion of advantages and disadvantages of globalizing services.

3.   THE DISAGGREGATION OF SERVICES

The patterns of disaggregation of information intensive services depend first of all on the potential of service activities to be dis-aggregated and re-located, and then on the appropriate location for any given activity. Apte and Mason (1995b) addressed the first issue at length by proposing taxonomy of disaggregation, and developing a theoretical framework for analyzing service activities and for identifying the criteria and guidelines for successfully selecting service activities to be disaggregated and relocated. We begin with a short description of that framework, and employ the framework to estimate the potential market size for the disaggregation of information-intensive services in the U.S.

3.1.   Analyzing Service Activities

Although it is perhaps easier to evaluate information technology's impact on services at the enterprise level by considering the effect on a firm's profitability or its market share performance, a deeper understanding of the impact of IT can be obtained by examining its role in specific activities within the enterprise (National Research Council, 1994). Examining the use of IT at the activity level allows more penetrating insight into why and how IT has been associated with major changes in individual activities and in the overall value chain of a service. Thus, we analyze the fundamental characteristics of service activities that determine the feasibility and desirability of globalizing a service. Apte and Mason (1995a) proposed that a service activity be viewed as a combination of four types of actions:

1. *Physical* actions that involve manipulation of physical objects. The purpose here is to move, transform, or create physical objects. Cooking, delivering a package, and repairing an automobile are some examples.
2. *Informational* actions that involve manipulation of symbols, i.e., collection, processing and dissemination of symbols—data, information and decisions. Actions such as developing a computer program, designing a chemical process, or analyzing an income statement all fall in this category. These actions are the building blocks of today's growing information economy.

3. *Interpersonal* actions that involve dealing with customers and others. The term customer is to be understood here as both the external customers, i.e. the ultimate beneficiaries of services, as well as the internal customers, i.e., the next person in the value-added chain who is the recipient of the service. Examples of interpersonal actions include giving a haircut, providing therapy, or greeting a visitor to the facility.

4. Other *indirect and non-value-adding* actions that do not belong to any of the above categories. Examples of such actions include doing unnecessary paperwork, or taking avoidable long coffee breaks.

Clearly, the above action types are not mutually exclusive. In a given activity, one may be collecting information while also interacting with a customer. To operationalize the proposed concept, the framework suggests that a service activity be studied and analyzed to understand the type of actions being performed under that activity. For example, an activity such as data entry will have large component of informational actions, and small proportions of interpersonal actions and physical actions respectively. This activity can therefore be characterized by its high "information intensity," a very low "customer contact need," and also a very low "physical presence need". The potential for the application of information technology is evident, but as discussed earlier, this activity can be located practically anywhere in the world. Thus, data entry shows a very high potential for globalization.

Analyzing a service activity using the above concepts and methodology is useful in answering a number of important questions. Apart for the potential for disaggregation and globalization, it is also useful for answering broader questions such as *reengineering*, or re-designing, an activity using information technology. Consider again the example of telemedicine involving the hospital in Saudi Arabia and the Mass General Hospital. In effect, the original radiology job was reengineered using data communications and computer imaging technologies to create two new jobs: (1) on-site job of a radiology technician in Saudi Arabia dealing with customer contact, physical presence and collection of radiological information, and (2) the remote job of an expert radiologist at the Mass General performing symbolic manipulation and diagnosis.

We now discuss the application of these concepts to the estimation of the potential for globalization and disaggregation of jobs.

Information intensity is an intuitively appealing and powerful concept. Operationalizing this concept, however, is very challenging. Porter and Millar (1985) proposed assessing *information intensity* for identifying opportunities for the competitive use of information technology. However, they did not provide a concrete, measurable definition of the concept. The framework defines *information intensity of an activity as the ratio of time spent in dealing with informational actions to the total time spent in that activity.* This measure also relates directly to Chase's (1981) measure of customer contact.

In the context of the proposed information intensity measure, it can be seen that the higher the information intensity of a service activity, the easier it can be to use information technology for performing that activity at a time and location that is more suitable for achieving lower cost and for higher quality outcome. Thus, the higher the information intensity of a service activity, the easier it is to globalize the service activity, i.e., disaggregate the activity and perform it at an overseas location.

Chase (1981) proposed a theory based on the customer contact approach to services. Following Chase, the framework defines *the degree of customer contact as the ratio of time during which a customer is in direct contact with the service facility to the total time required for the creation of the service.* This has implications for the use of information technology in reengineering a service activity. In general, the lower the need for customer contact, the easier it is to globalize the service activity.

The physical presence need arises primarily from the requirement to perform the physical object manipulation, i.e., the movement, transformation or creation of physical objects. The essential characteristic of physical object manipulation is that it must take place within the confines of specific time and space constraints. The subject of physical object manipulation has been studied extensively by industrial and manufacturing engineering disciplines where the time and motion studies are used as the primary means of analysis for finding improvements in physical object manipulation process. Following the rationale of earlier definitions, the framework defines *physical presence need as the ratio of time spent in physical actions to the total time spent in a service activity.* In general, the lower the physical presence need, the easier it is to globalize the service activity.

3.2.   Selecting Candidate Service Activities for Globalization

The analysis of service activities, in terms of action types and information-intensity, can be used as the basis for selecting candidate service activities for globalization. Apte and Mason (1995b) hypothesized that service activities that are good candidates for globalization generally satisfy the following necessary conditions:

1. The activity is information intensive. The need for physical presence is low. The customer contact need is also low. Moreover, within customer contact time, the ratio of symbolic contact time to in-person contact time is high.
2. The symbolic manipulation component of the activity is separable. It can be isolated and disembodied from the customer contact component and the physical object manipulation component of the activity.

A three dimensional model for estimating global disaggregation potential of a given service activity using the first criterion is shown in Figure 1. Based

Table 3-1.

Legend	Occupation	Information Intensity	Customer Contact Need	Physical Presence Need	Disaggregation Potential
1	Actuary	H	L	L	H
2	Marketing Manager	H	M	L	M
3	Civil Engineer	H	L	M	M
4	Comm. Eqpt. Operator	M	L	L	M
5	Cleaning	L	L	H	L
6	Food Service Manager	L	H	H	L
7	Secretary	M	H	H	L
8	Registered Nurse	H	H	H	L

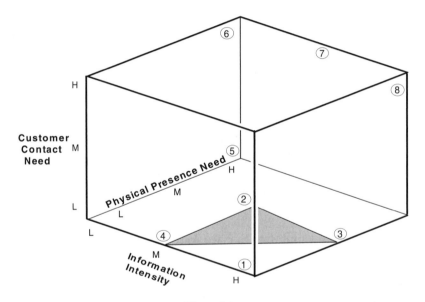

Figure 3-1.

on this criteria identified above, the disaggregation potential of an activity is assumed to be high when its information intensity, its customer contact need, and physical presence need are respectively high, low, low, or (H, L, L). The disaggregation potential is assumed to be medium (M) when the values of three respective characteristics are (H, M, L), or (H, L, M), or (M, L, L). In all other cases, the disaggregation potential is assumed to be low. To illustrate the use of this framework, eight selected service activities and assessment of their globalization potential are analyzed in Table 1. These activities are also plotted in Figure 1.

Table 3-2.

	1990	2000
Service Job Disaggregation potential (millions of jobs)	8.85	10.54
Total Service Jobs (millions)	87.70	98.54
Percent of Jobs with Disaggregation potential	10.1	10.7

As Bell (1979) noted in the coming of post-industrial society, and for which Porat and Rubin (1977) and Apte and Nath (2006) have provided evidence, the number and importance of information intensive jobs is increasing throughout the global economy. The number of jobs vulnerable to global disaggregation is therefore expected to grow further in the future.

3.3. Estimating the Potential for Disaggregation of Services

The methodology described in the last section was used by Apte and Mason (1995b) to estimate the total number of service jobs in the U.S. that could be vulnerable to global disaggregation. Their study used U.S. job classification data for 1990 as published by Bureau of Labor (1992). They considered the nature of work involved in each occupation to assess its level of information intensity, customer contact need and physical presence need, and its potential for global disaggregation. These assessments were further used to estimate the total number of service jobs in the U.S. that were vulnerable to global disaggregation. We have repeated this study for employment data for 711 occupations in the U.S. in 2000 as published by the U.S. Department of labor. Both studies suggest that over 10% of the total number of service jobs in the U.S. is vulnerable to disaggregation in the form of outsourcing, reengineering, and possibly off-shore provision. Of course, since the total number of service jobs has increased, so has the absolute number of jobs that could be affected. The figures from the two studies are summarized in Table 2

The data can also be analyzed to show which industry sectors exhibit the largest potential effects. Some of this analysis for the year 2000 data is summarized in Table 3.

In order to further examine the nature of the offshore sourcing phenomenon, we studied the activities being outsourced to 83 third party and 15 captive service providers in India and the Philippines. Some of the tasks and jobs that are being outsourced to these locations are shown in Table 4.

3.4. Patterns of Location and Globalization

India provides an illustrative and comprehensive study of a country where disaggregated service activities are being increasingly located (Economist, 1999). With a vast population, low wages, and a pool of high-quality labor that

Table 3-3.

SIC Code	Sector	No. of Jobs ('000)
48	Communications	274
60	Depository Institutions	362
61	Non-Depository Credit Institutions	158
62	Security and Commodity Brokers, Dealers, Exchanges, and Services	150
63	Insurance Carriers	367
64	Insurance Agents, Brokers, and Service	166
67	Holding and Other Investment Offices	48
73	Business Services	1489
78	Motion Pictures	55
87	Engineering, Accounting, Research, Management, and Related Services	690
	Selected Sectors Total	3758
	Other Sectors	6778
	Total	10536

Table 3-4.

Category	Offerings
Customer Care	Technical Support/Help Desk, Tele-Marketing, Inbound/Outbound Sales, Voice-Email-Chat Support, Customer Management, Customer Acquisition
Payment Services	Billing, Account Receivable/Payable Services, Collection Services
Administration	Claim Processing, Form Processing, Back Office Administration/Operations, Network & Security Management, Medical Transcription, Content/Data Management
Finance & Banking	Payroll Services, Taxation, Banking Services, Transaction Processing, Financial Research, Project Feasibility & Research Support
Human Resource	Payroll and Benefits Management, PF and other retirement benefits management, HR Staffing Services, Consulting and Training, Specialized Staffing and Recruitment Services, Corporate Secretarial Services
Content Development	eCRM Solutions, Software Design & Development, Product Design, Project Quotation & Development, Graphic Design for media & entertainment

has a good grasp of English, India has the potential to excel in exporting remote services to the developed countries. Recognizing this potential the Indian government has introduced a number of incentives including exemption from corporate taxes for export-oriented service industries. Although half of India's population is illiterate, Indian universities produce roughly 2 million degree-holders every year, most of whom have some facility in English. Many of those employed in the remote-services business would be deemed overqualified in the West. Consider for example the GE Capital's "international services" division near Delhi. This division deals with mortgage and credit card services and has on its payroll about 700 employees. A certified public accountant working on account reconciliation costs GE Capital about $15,000–20,000 a year. In contrast, in the US, a less qualified worker doing the same job can cost up to three times as much. GE Capital expects that its Indian operation can save the company some $10 million per year.

As estimated by India's National Association of Software and Service Companies, in 1998, about 25,000 Indians were employed in businesses geared to providing remote services. McKinsey, a consultancy company, estimates that this number can rise to about 3 million people within the next decade and that the remote services business can be worth as much as $50 billion by 2010.

What are some of the major obstacles that a company faces in locating remote services to India? India's inadequate infrastructure (telecommunications, transport and electric power) and high prices of telecommunications services are seen as the principle obstacles. Another major hurdle is India's stifling bureaucracy and regulation, especially labor laws that can make it hard to fire workers. A number of firms have failed because their workforces became bloated and inflexible. Automation may look like a threat to the remote services in general as the businesses in developed countries may choose to use automation in place of remote services. But computer automation is also proving to be a blessing, at least for the time being. As more information gets collected and processed by computers, the higher becomes the chances for errors that need human intervention for correction. For example, British Airways' World Network Services, based in Mumbai, India, handles an array of back-office jobs for its parent and other airlines, for dealing with errors in automatic reservation systems, accounting, and for keeping track of frequent-flier miles. British Airways had found in the past that its customers were offended by machine-generated letters. Now it customizes them in India.

In general, the important factors related to the choice of a specific country can be identified as follows:

- Cost
  - Savings
  - Change Mgt.
  - Switching
  - Value Add
- Capability
  - Experience
  - Scalability

Table 3-5.

	Cost	Capability	Provider Value	Culture	Climate	Country Risk
Australia	5	8	6.5	9	8	8.5
Canada	4	8	6	9	9	9
China	9	8	8.5	5	7	6
India	9	8	8.5	8	6	7
Ireland	6	8	7	9	7	8
Philippines	7	8	7.5	8	6	7

- – Training
- – Skills
- – Processes
- – Management Team
- – Integrity
- • Culture
  - – Language
  - – Expatriate Manager Comfort
  - – Power Distance
  - – Uncertainty Avoidance
  - – Individualism / Collectivism
  - – Masculinity / Femininity
- • Climate
  - – Political Stability
  - – Social Acceptance
  - – Government Support
  - – Security in trade of data
  - – Market Maturity
  - – Knowledge Worker Pool

It is generally the case that all these factors are not found to apply for any given location. In fact, there are some negative correlations across these factors. To illustrate the relative attractiveness of locations for outsourcing based on these factors, we make subjective estimates of scores for these factors on a scale of 1 to 10, for 6 countries. The score are shown in Table 5. We emphasize that these score are indeed subjective, and more for the purposes of illustration than defensible analysis; however they are not unreasonable either. In order to compare the locations, we compare the cost plus capability scores versus the culture and climate scores for these countries.

The results are plotted in Figure 2. The figure suggests that there are two major types of locations preferable for outsourcing—those that are superior in terms of culture and climate, and those that dominate on low costs while

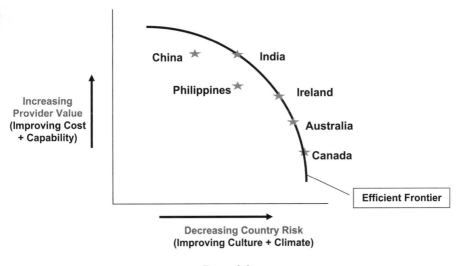

Figure 3-2.

possessing adequate performance capabilities. In fact in our subjective scores, capability is not a differentiating element.

3.5. The Topography of Outsourcing

Over the centuries, supply chains have evolved substantially. The early pattern was simple trading involving high value, low weight or volume goods (such as silk and gems) or unique agricultural products (such as tea or chocolates). These patterns evolved into trading networks, and over time into complex supply chains with elaborate patterns of manufacturing with movement of goods through several countries before assembly of the final product. Service chains or information chains for information intensive industries are showing similar evolution, from simple transfer of information goods, to complex chains of production, processing and delivery. However, the nature of information gives rise to some characteristics for these chains that are quite different from supply chains for physical products. Physical product chains today are dominated by the factors of cost, quality and capability. However, service and information chains show a pronounced effect of culture and language. When one thinks back further into the causes for particular patterns of distribution with respect to language and culture, it is clear that colonial histories have played a large part in determining the current distribution of languages around the world. Furthermore one can see that language not only affects the topography of service and information chains, but is also likely to determine major distinct markets for consumer services.

Table 6 shows the largest linguistic grouping in the world, in terms of the number of people in each group. Since the way in which languages are identi-

Table 3-6.

Language	Approximate Number of Speakers
1. Chinese (Mandarin)	1,075,000,000
2. English	514,000,000
3. Hindi	496,000,000
4. Spanish	425,000,000
5. Russian	275,000,000
6. Arabic	256,000,000
7. Bengali	215,000,000
8. Portuguese	194,000,000
9. Malay-Indonesian	176,000,000
10. French	129,000,000

Source: Ethnologue, 13th Edition, and other sources.

fied is not completely determined, this table should be taken as being broadly indicative rather than definitive.

There are several qualifications that need to be made about these numbers—too many to do a thorough job here. But we might note that many of these grouping contain dialects and variants that are different enough that they cannot really be understood by others in the group. This is true for Hindustani and Malay-Indonesian. On the other hand, languages like English, French and Spanish are relatively homogenous and understandable (though not everyone would agree with that statement either).

The size of the population speaking a language is roughly indicative of the size of the potential market for information intensive goods and services. To this we might add considerations of geographic distribution, to understand what trade patterns might result across countries, and how markets are likely to spread across physical geographies. Clearly the patterns of geographic distributions for different languages are very different, and they give strong indications of how the markets for information intensive services might look from a trade and outsourcing perspective. We may evaluate some of the most obvious features of these patterns. First of all the Chinese group is largely confined to the Asian land mass. The reason of course is that Chinese kingdoms never made a serious attempt to colonize other countries. The same is true of Hindi and other Indian languages (not shown). Of course, this does not mean that these languages did not spread. In case of both Chinese and Indian languages there was a dispersion due to emigration, and due to the transport of indentured labor to other countries by colonial powers. Nevertheless, by and large these languages are geographically fairly localized. A very different picture is visible for English and Spanish. In both cases (especially English), colonialism led to a very widespread distribution of these languages. Other European languages also display this colonial pattern (French, German, Swedish) though

Table 3-7.

GNP Range ($/Capita)	Spanish	English	French	Arabic	German
⩽3000	154.3	1070.6	35.4	253	21.6
3000–6000	149.6	70.4	0	32.2	54.2
6000–9000	36.9	0	0	0	0
9000–12000	0	0	0	3.9	0
12000–15000	41.3	0	0	0	0
15000–18000	0	14.7	0	0	0
18000–21000	0	110.7	0	0	0
>21000	0	295.7	70.2	0	989.1

perhaps not to as significant an extent. Arabic languages present a different picture; the spread is more complex, over a longer period, due to many different kingdoms, dynasties and conquests, and as a result is much less homogenous.

Based on the understanding of the patters of geographic dispersion of languages we may conjecture that the patterns of trade in informative intensive services are likely to mimic the same patterns as that for the languages. For example, consider the English language block. The service trade in this block of countries is likely to originate from such places as India, Philippines, and Ireland and end at destinations in North America, United Kingdom and Australia.

We can further our understanding of service and information chains and global trade, by considering one other factor: the distribution of wealth for a language group. Table 7 shows the population for five language groups broken down into ranges of GNP measured in $ per capita. This data is plotted as a histogram in Figure 3.

It should be noted that the way the data has been computed is to record the population for each language group by adding the populations of all countries which have that language as an official national language. Now of course, this does not mean that everyone in that country speaks the language. In addition, a person may speak several languages sufficiently well in many of these countries. The corrections for all these factors have not been made. However again, this data is adequate for illustrative purposes. In particular, the data shows certain striking features. English is unique in that it is the one language with a pronounced U-shaped distribution, in that it includes a number of fairly large wealthy countries, large poor populations, and very little in the mid-range. Even correcting for the overestimates on the side of the poor populations, this is clearly a unique pattern. It implies a significant economic driving force for service trade along linguistic lines. No other linguistic group displays these characteristics. Spanish in contrast has only about 40 million people (in Spain)

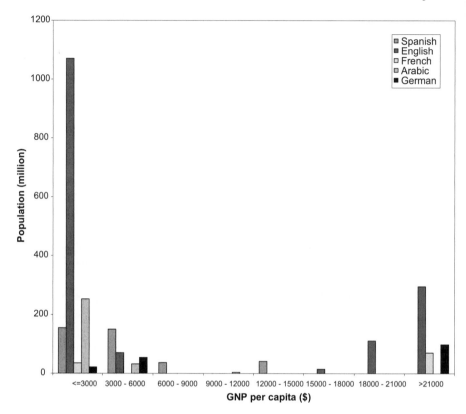

Figure 3-3.

with an average GNP in the mid-range, and has a very large number (over 300 million) at the lower end of the distribution.

This discussion leads us to certain broad conclusions about service markets and patterns of service and information chains across the world. First we reiterate that for consumer services which are information intensive, the topography of the world trade and outsourcing will be strongly colored by language, culture and colonial history. In short the defining feature of topography is language and not mountains and oceans, and the language barrier may well be the hard thing to cross. One can conclude that the world English market in consumer services is unique in its size, geographic distribution and potential for trade. It is also one of the most open markets. Spanish shares some of these features, but the distribution being less extreme offers less opportunities for those in poorer countries. China will be the largest market, and will be a largely closed market where the suppliers are also Chinese for the most part. Other trading groups will form, but they will be much smaller with specific matchups. For example, the French will look to North Africa, the Germans to

Poland and the Czech Republic, and the Swedes to Estonia. Some countries may be rather isolated linguistically. Greece and Turkey might be examples. This might well prove to be a boon for those engaged in services in those countries, since they will not be subject to the intense competition seen due to outsourcing and offshoring, in the English and perhaps the Spanish worlds.

3.6.   Evolution of Service and Information Chains

The language groups described above present a picture of B2C (business to consumers) information intensive services. However, the best locations for B2B (business to business) services could take a very different pattern. In the provision of software services, and computer based platforms, the languages that are relevant are Java and C++ and not necessarily English and Chinese. It is clearly the case that the suppliers of these services need not be in the same language group. Secondly, some kinds of information are not that dependent on language. Graphics are a major example. So the development of graphics and animation need not go to an English speaking country. For example, the Simpson's animation production appears to be done in Korea and Thailand, probably with Thai labor. It is in fact likely that there will be clusters which specialize in certain types of information goods and services provision, much like we see specialization in manufactured products in many parts of the world.

As far as evolution of service outsourcing within the English world goes, there has been a tendency over time for low costs to overtake culture and fit factors as key choice determinants. For example, till 2002, Canada and Australia were major call center locations for the U.S. market. Today they have been overtaken by India. Till 2004, Ireland was the biggest supplier of content management services to the U.S. It is safe to predict that India will take over that segment as well. In short, over time, as information diffuses, low cost will tend to overwhelm cultural similarity whenever the linguistic factors are not hugely important. Of course, culturally rich products and services may still tend to go to the countries that are closest on those attributes; for the U.S. those are the UK, Ireland, and Australia. But in higher volume commodity areas, India, Pakistan, Bangladesh, Sri Lanka and the Philippines will probably play a major role.

4.   SUMMARY AND CONCLUSIONS

The pressures of increasing global competition and the opportunities made available by the progress in information technology are forcing corporations to evaluate the value-added chains involved in the production and consumption of services. The central issues are how best to disaggregate a service delivery system, and where in the world to locate it, within or outside the geographic boundary of a nation. As was seen from examples of the past two decades, both in manufacturing and in services, the value-added chains are being reformulated and geographically dispersed around the world.

In managing global disaggregation, a corporate manager should analyze each service activity to assess its level of information intensity, customer contact need, and the physical presence need. The activities that rate high, low and low respectively on these three characteristics are likely to have a high potential for global disaggregation. To further evaluate the feasibility and desirability of globally disaggregating a service activity, five additional factors should be taken into account: separability of symbolic manipulation component of the activity, the structuredness and specificity of the activity, its strategic importance, the relative efficiency with which the company can perform that activity, and the legal and cultural feasibility of disaggregating the activity.

The proposed methodology was applied using 2000 data on the economy and labor situation in the U.S. to estimate the potential market size of globalized information-intensive services. Our analysis indicated that a total of about 10.5 million jobs are vulnerable to global disaggregation in the U.S. It should be kept in mind that these estimates are broad approximations at best, but they do serve to bring out the enormous size of emerging opportunities in cross-border trade of information-intensive services.

In choosing the country where the disaggregated service activity may be located, a manager should analyze the following country-specific factors: salary level and size of the pool of skilled workers, telecommunications and other infrastructure, the size and growth potential of the market, governmental incentives including foreign currency restrictions, and the stability of the economic, political and social environment.

In summary, the emerging phenomenon of globalization of information-intensive services offers enormous challenges and opportunities for managers in today's increasingly Internet-based and global economy. At a more general level, the national policy implications raised by the phenomenon are equally significant and pressing. Globalization of services can lead to the loss of certain types of jobs in one country while creating new jobs in another country. Thus, serving as an engine of export-led employment growth, the phenomenon represents an enormous opportunity for economic development for developing countries. This raises important questions related to education, trade, fiscal, and infrastructure development policy for both developing and developed nations. These and a range of other socio-economic issues must be researched and addressed before the structural transformation triggered by the global disaggregation of services can be better understood and harnessed.

REFERENCES

Apte, U. M. and R. O. Mason, 1992. "Texas Instruments (India) Private Limited," *Working paper of the Cox School of Business*, Southern Methodist University, Dallas, TX 75275.

Apte, U. M. and R. O. Mason, 1995a. "Global Outsourcing of Information Processing Services," in P. T. Harker, ed., *The Service Productivity and Quality Challenge*, Kluwer Academic Publishers, Norwell, MA, pp. 169–202.

Apte, U. M. and R. O. Mason, 1995b. "Global disaggregation of Information-Intensive Services," *Management Science*, vol. 41, no. 7, pp. 1250–1262.

Apte, U. M. and Hiranya Nath, 2006. "Size, Structure and Growth of the US Information Economy," Chapter 1, in U. S. Karmarkar and U. M. Apte (eds.), *Current Research on Managing in the Information Economy*, Springer, Norwell, MA.

Bell, D., 1979. *The Coming of Post-Industrial Society: A Venture in Social Forecasting*, Basic Books, New York, NY.

Bureau of Labor, 1992. *Occupational Projection and Training Data,* Bulletin 2401, Department of Statistics, Washington, DC, May.

Chase, R., 1981. "The Customer Contact Approach to Services: Theoretical Bases and Practical Extensions," *Operations Research*, vol. 21, no. 4, pp. 698–705.

Economist, 1996. "A Survey of the Software Industry," *The Economist*, May 25.

Economist, 1999. "Indian Business: Spice Up Your Services," *The Economist*, January 16.

Hayes, R. and S. C. Wheelwright, 1984. *Restoring Our Competitive Edge: Competing Through Manufacturing*, J. Wiley & Sons, New York, NY.

Houlder, V., 1994. "Specialists Come to the Patient," *Financial Times,* November 10.

Karmarkar, U. S., 2004. "Will You Survive the Services Revolution", *Harvard Business Review*, vol. 82, no. 6, June, pp. 100–110.

Lohr, S., 1988. "The Growth of the Global Office," *The New York Times*, October 18.

National Research Council, 1994, Information Technology in the Service Society, National Academy Press, Washington, DC, pp. 14–15.

O'Reilly, B., 1992. "Your New Global Workforce," *Fortune*, December 14.

Pollack, A., 1992. "Technology Transcends Borders, Raising Tough Questions in U.S.," *The New York Times*, Jan. 1.

Porat, M. V. and M. R. Rubin, 1977. *The Information Economy*, 9 Volumes, U.S. Department of Commerce, Office of Telecommunications Special Publication 77-121(1) through 77-12(9), U.S. Government Printing Office, Washington, DC.

Porter, M. E. and V. Millar, 1985. "How Information Gives you Competitive Advantage," *Harvard Business Review*, July–August.

Quinn, J. B., 1992. *Intelligent Enterprise: A Knowledge and Service Based Paradigm for Industry*, The Free Press, New York, NY.

Schuknecht, L. and R. Pérez-Esteve, 1999. "A Quantitative Assessment of Electronic Commerce," Staff Working Paper ERAD-99-01, Economic Research and Analysis Division, World Trade Organization, Genéve, Switzerland.

Wysocki, B., 1991. "Overseas Calling," *The Wall Street Journal*, August 14.

Yearwood, J., 1993. "A Ticket to Pride: Barbados Unit of AMR Excels at Data Entry," *The Dallas Morning News*, pp. 1H, August 15.

Chapter 4

INFORMATION SYSTEMS OUTSOURCING CONTRACTS: THEORY AND EVIDENCE

Vijay Gurbaxani

The Paul Merage School of Business, University of California, Irvine, CA 92697-3125

Abstract   The information systems outsourcing market has seen rapid growth. Companies are increasingly choosing to outsource many of their information systems activities to services firms rather than sourcing them internally. This trend is inconsistent with the predictions of some of the published literature which point to the high costs of using an outside market. These articles, based on transaction cost economics, point out the difficulty of writing efficient contracts in the face of high transaction costs which result from the considerable technological and business uncertainty in a typical outsourcing arrangement. Yet, the growth in the outsourcing market clearly indicates that the economics of external provision are dominating these contractual concerns. Given that companies are outsourcing information systems services through multi-year contracts, economic theory suggests that outsourcing contracts will seek to minimize the associated transaction costs. I propose a framework for the analysis of information systems outsourcing contracts based on transaction cost theory and the economics of production of information systems services. Based on this framework I develop propositions related to the contractual elements likely to be observed in outsourcing contracts. I test the predictions of the model by studying ten outsourcing contracts in detail. The results indicate that contracts are designed to mitigate transaction costs, and that transaction cost economics is a useful lens with which to analyze an IT services sourcing arrangement.

1.   INTRODUCTION

In recent years, companies have increasingly opted to source many of their information systems (IS) activities from external services firms rather than sourcing them internally as was their practice. Companies cite a variety of goals in their decision to outsource including the intent to reduce costs or improve the quality of IS services, to acquire new technological capabilities, to increase the business impact of their information systems, and to focus on their core competencies (DiRomualdo and Gurbaxani, 1998). As a result, the IS out-sourcing industry grew very rapidly in the nineties, and continues to grow at a significant rate today. The Gartner Group estimates global revenues of the IT outsourcing industry at $316 billion in 2004 and predicts an annual growth rate of 8–9% for the next 5 years (Young, 2004).

The term "outsourcing" has been interpreted in a variety of ways in the IS context. I define an IS outsourcing arrangement as a long-term contractual arrangement in which one or more service providers are assigned the responsi-bility of managing all or part of a client's IS infrastructure and operations. This is consistent with the definition of most leading market research firms such as the Gartner Group (Gartner, 2003) and other academics (Lacity and Hirscheim, 1993, Grover et al., 1996). The term is sometimes used to describe the sourc-ing of discrete projects such as a software development or integration project from a services firm. My focus is on time-based multi-year relationships[1] (e.g. maintain legacy applications for 10 years) wherein significant decision rights are allocated to the provider, rather than on discrete tasks (build and implement an application program).

While the trend toward outsourcing IT services has become commonplace, both practitioners (Strassmann 1995, 2004) and academics (e.g. Lacity and Hirscheim, 1993, Kern and Willcocks, 2001) have pointed out the associated risks and called for companies to comprehensively assess how best to leverage the global IT sourcing market (Lacity, 2003). In academia, the arguments are frequently derived from transaction cost economics (Coase, 1937, Williamson, 1985) which posits that internal provision should be preferred when the trans-action costs of securing a product or a service from an external source are high. Specifically, these researchers point to the difficulty of writing efficient con-tracts that align the interests of client and vendor in the face of considerable technological and business uncertainty (Kern and Willcocks, 2001). These ob-servers argue that the external sourcing of information services is likely to be characterized by high transaction costs (Kern and Willcocks, 1996, Poppo and Zenger, 2002) which may outweigh the savings in production costs that accrue from specialized providers. Yet, the growth in the outsourcing industry seems to indicate that the economics of external provision are dominating these con-tractual concerns. In a study of U.S. banks, Ang and Straub (1998) find that

---

[1] Some market research firms, such as the International Data Corporation (Tapper, 2004), adopt an even more restrictive definition requiring it to include infrastructure-related oper-ations and not including the outsourcing of selective services such as network outsourcing, desktop outsourcing or application outsourcing unless these are included in a larger out-sourcing deal that includes infrastructure. None of the major market research firms use the term to mean supply arrangements that are project-based, though some academic studies do use the term to describe these arrangements.

managers believe that production cost advantages from outsourcing tend to outweigh transaction cost factors.

When one observes empirical trends, it is clear that an increasing number of companies look to external service providers for the appropriate supply relationship. The Gartner Group (Young, 2004) estimates that in 2004, 55% of corporate IT spending will be externally sourced, of which a little more than half (29% of total spending) will be on outsourced services, and the remainder (26%) on discrete project-based services. Interestingly, they predict no further growth in the internal IT budget with all growth accruing in externally sourced services. Indeed, many recent contracts tend to be for a larger array of IS activities, not just data centers, but also applications, desktop and distributed computing services, and networks (Grover et al., 1996). Some companies have expanded the scope of their outsourcing contracts after a few years and many have renewed their outsourcing contracts. Moreover, there are only a few failures that have resulted in contract termination. Accordingly, this preliminary evaluation suggests that managers have found ways of mitigating the impact of potential transaction costs so that they can exploit the production cost advantages that can accrue from the external sourcing of IS services.

The intensity of the discussion and debate on IS outsourcing amidst its increasing popularity raises some very interesting research questions. Given that we are observing a high volume of IS outsourcing contracts, and that transaction costs are likely to be high, it must be the case that profit-maximizing companies attempt to minimize these transaction costs. In this paper, I focus on the role of contract and the use of specialized contractual features to mitigate the impact of transaction costs and improve the performance of these exchange relationships. Clearly, mechanisms such as relational governance can also be used to mitigate these costs. Poppo and Zenger (2002) argue in the context of IS outsourcing that contracts and relational governance are complementary approaches, concluding that "well-specified contracts may actually promote more cooperative, long-term, trusting relationships." Kern and Willcocks (2001) point out that "a major finding in research has been that, if an organization outsources IT, the outsourcing contract is the only certain way to ensure that expectations are realized." Kern and Willcocks (2000) conclude that "research and industry best practice has clearly shown that a central focus has to remain on the contract and hence its enforcement in the post-contract management stage."

This paper focuses on analyzing the role of contract in order to assess how this mechanism can be utilized to promote economic efficiency in the context of IS outsourcing. I examine the following research questions: What are the features of IS sourcing contracts? Do these contracts promote economic efficiency by reducing transaction costs and by enabling the supply relationship, and if so, how do they achieve this? My goals are to simultaneously test the validity of transactions cost economics as the appropriate theoretical framework for understanding IS outsourcing contracts, and to further our understanding of how best to design and manage these external supply relationships, which have come to be the predominant form of sourcing information services. I propose a transaction cost economics framework for the analysis of outsourcing contracts. Based on this framework I develop predictions related to contractual elements likely to be observed in outsourcing contracts. I test the predictions of my model by studying ten outsourcing contracts in detail. The results indicate that the predictions of the model are supported, indicating the appropriateness of transactions cost economics as the theoretical basis, and resulting in the development of guidelines for managing the supply relationship.

This paper is in the tradition of, and follows the approach of, Joskow (1985), who conducted an empirical analysis of contracts between coal-burning electric generating plants and their coal suppliers. In particular, Joskow (1985) develops a theoretical framework based on transaction cost economics, and develops normative implications for contractual provisions that attempt to mitigate these transaction costs.

The outline of this paper is as follows: In the next section, I outline the theoretical foundations for the transaction cost approach and present a few key illustrations of how the theory has been applied empirically. Then, I present a review of the relevant empirical literature in IS outsourcing. Next, I describe the IS outsourcing industry. This is followed by a description of the essential characteristics of the production of information services as viewed from a transaction cost economics perspective. I then develop propositions for how IS outsourcing contracts mitigate the impact of transaction costs. Next, I present the results of the empirical examination of the data and find evidence in support of the propositions. I close with a discussion of the findings.

2. THEORY: AN OVERVIEW OF TRANSACTIONS COST ECONOMICS

Williamson (1985) developed a comprehensive framework for the analysis of the vertical arrangement between two parties based on identifying the characteristics of transactions, industries and markets that have a significant effect on the magnitude of transaction costs. He observed, among other factors, that the existence of a durable, transaction-specific asset is often the source of large market transaction costs since special arrangements, typically long-term contracts, are necessary to prevent the other party from acting in an opportunistic manner after one firm makes an investment in a specific asset. In particular, when there is a high degree of uncertainty in supply or demand, such a contract must attempt to account for future contingencies. Given the high level of uncertainty, it is difficult to predict future contingencies. However, if a contract is incompletely specified (Hart and Moore, 1999), the occurrence of an event that is unaccounted for in the contract may provide one party with an opportunity to exploit the other. In many cases, the intractability of developing an efficient contractual solution implies that it is optimal to source the product or service internally.

The focus of much of the transaction cost literature has been on understanding the relationship between the characteristics of exchange and the optimal governance structure (Boerner and Macher, 2001, Masten, 1996, Shelanski and Klein, 1995). The literature has traditionally focused on markets versus hierarchies or stylized representations of governance structures. In practice, of course, the choice of governance structures is vast, ranging from vertical integration on the one hand to spot markets on the other, with a variety of specialized contractual options in between. These specialized contracts have emerged as a result of firms seeking to minimize the costs of external sourcing with the features of the contract aimed at minimizing the transaction costs of the specific production situation. There is also an emerging literature (Adler, 2001) that focuses on the relationship between social and economic institutions in producing optimal governance performance. This literature looks at how relational norms such as trust complement or substitute for elements of formal contracts. In the IS outsourcing realm, Poppo and Zenger (2002) have found that relational governance and contracts function as complements.

The underlying premise of this literature is that economic institutions emerge to minimize the costs of organization. These costs are typically categorized as production costs and transactions costs. Production costs are those costs directly associated with the operations of a firm and include such input factors as labor, capital, energy and materials, and can be thought of as those elements that would typically be included in a neoclassical cost function. Transaction costs, on the other hand, are the costs associated with developing and managing a supply relationship with an external supplier of goods or services. In this framework, firms will seek to minimize the sum of their production and transaction costs over a planning horizon.

As Coase (1937), Klein et al. (1978), Williamson (1985), Joskow (1985, 1988) and others have argued, there are at least three major characteristics of transactions that determine the nature and magnitude of transaction costs. These include

1. durable transaction-specific investments,
2. uncertainty and complexity,
3. reputation.

Williamson identifies four types of durable transaction-specific investments. These are site specificity, physical asset specificity, human capital specificity, and dedicated assets. Site specificity refers to the importance of the geographical location of the investment, physical asset specificity refers to the degree of customization of the physical asset for the specific exchange, human capital specificity refers to the importance of specialized knowledge, and dedicated assets refers to the need to make a substantial investment in an asset to support the specific transaction. In all cases, the implication of asset specificity is that the value of the asset in its next best use is substantially below its value in its use to support the current transaction.

As discussed above, when there is considerable uncertainty about future demand, about factor prices, and about the technology, and therefore supply, it becomes extremely difficult to adequately specify terms of exchange under all possible future states of nature. In the presence of a transaction-specific asset, an implication of incomplete contracts (Hart and Moore, 1999) is that when an event occurs that is unaccounted for, one party may have the opportunity to extract rents from the other. Reputation may serve as a constraint on behavior if a supplier perceives that it might lead to a loss of future business from other customers.

While there has been a large volume of work on providing a theoretical and conceptual understanding of the appropriate supply relationship, there has been a limited but growing empirical literature, much of it focused on the relationship between governance form and transaction characteristics (Shelanski and Klein, 1995, Masten, 1996, Boerner and Macher, 2001). There are fewer studies that conduct an empirical analysis of contracts due largely to the difficulty of obtaining such data (Coase, 1992). These include studies that examine the decision to contract as well as studies that examine the contract terms. Lyons (1994) studies the impact of asset specificity on engineering firms' decisions to contract to subcontractors and on optimal contract duration finding a preference for formal contracts over flexible agreements where relation-specific assets left the sub-contractor vulnerable to post-contractual opportunism. Joskow (1985) conducted a comprehensive case study of coal contracts, explaining differences in contractual features—both pricing and other provisions—based on differences in asset specificity conditions in different arrangements. Joskow (1987) showed that when relation-specific investments are more important, buyers and sellers engage in longer contract durations. Masten and Crocker (1985) study minimum purchase requirements in the case of natural gas contracts finding that contract designs were sensitive to efficiency considerations. Goldberg and Erickson (1987) study the duration and minimum quantity requirements of petroleum coke contracts in response to site specificity of production facilities as well as price adjustment provisions which they conclude are aimed primarily at reducing post-agreement negotiating over the terms of trade and pre-contract search costs.

3. COST ECONOMICS AND CONTRACTS IN THE IS OUTSOURCING LITERATURE

Unsurprisingly, the outsourcing of IS services has also received considerable attention from a transaction cost perspective. As discussed earlier, there is a point of view which holds that the sourcing of IS services is in fact often characterized by significant transaction costs (Lacity and Hirschheim, 1993, Alpar and Saharia, 1995, Grover et al., 1996, Nam et al., 1996, Ang and Cummings, 1997, Ang and Straub, 1998). It is noted that there are considerable uncertainties in information technology supply trends. In particular, there is uncertainty about future technologies, and about factor price trends. It is further argued that there is a high degree of uncertainty on the demand side, and in user requirements as well (Kern and Willcocks, 2001, Wholey et al., 2001). Business environments are increasingly volatile, new technologies lead to new solutions and services, and companies grow or shrink. Moreover, there is often a need to make transaction-specific investments to support an IS outsourcing relationship (Grover et al., 1996). Outsourcing vendors usually make significant investments in capital assets such as equipment and structures, and in firm-specific human capital to provide IT services to a client.

Given the inherent complexity of contracts dealing with the sourcing of IS services, it is then argued that in the presence of asset specificity and uncertainty, IS outsourcing contracts are costly, in a transaction cost sense, to write, and will necessarily be incomplete (Kern and Willcocks, 2001). This can give rise frequently to situations where the likelihood of post-contractual opportunistic behavior increases (Ang and Cummings, 1997, Clemons et al., 2000, Saunders et al., 1997). With the ever-increasing dependence of organizations on their information systems, the economic rents that a supplier could potentially extract from a customer are very high.[2] This often results from the considerable switching costs that buyers face in transferring an outsourced service to a new supplier or in bringing the service back in-house. Likewise, given the supplier's considerable investment in transaction-specific assets, an opportunistic customer can also seek to extract rents from the provider. Therefore, some observers conclude that the track record of contractual arrangements is likely to be mixed at best (Kern and Willcocks, 2001).

Indeed, Wholey et al. (2001) find that an increase in asset-specificity results in a lower likelihood of outsourcing. Poppo and Zenger (2002) show that

---

[2] It is important to note that while the typical assumption is that external service providers have incentives to extract rents from a customer, it is also the case that internal service providers as agents of the owners of the firm, also have incentives to extract rents from the principals of the firm. One major difference is that disputes with internal agents can be resolved administratively; those with external providers are likely to require arbitration or litigation, and are much more costly.

as asset specificity increases, IS outsourcing contracts are more customized. Grover et al. (1996) find that while overall outsourcing of IS functions, and in particular that of less asset-specific transactions such as data center and network management, is positively related with success, outsourcing of more asset-specific interactions like applications development leads to less satisfactory results.

In the IS outsourcing realm as defined here, Kern and Willcocks (2001) is the only study that I am aware of that broadly examines the existence and role of contractual features. They focus on understanding the purposes of a contract beyond its legal nature, and in particular, on the management control dimensions that both parties aim to enforce. They identify key elements of a post-contract management agenda, and specify seven categories of contractual issues that facilitate management control of the outsourcing relationship. These include service description and exchanges, service enforcement and monitoring, financial exchanges, financial control and monitoring, key vendor personnel, dispute resolution, and change control and management. They conclude that there are five main ways in which contractual terms influence management of the client-vendor relationship. The contract has a legal function, attempts to specify future service levels in the present, provides a client with control over the venture, gives structure to the relationship, and imparts essential guidance to key managers on both sides.

In addition, there are a few papers that have examined discrete service contracts in the context of externally sourced software development projects. Ang and Beath (1993) examine the role of contractual elements that are essentially hierarchical control mechanisms in contracts for externally sourced discrete software development projects. These include features such as authority relations, incentive systems, standard operating procedures, pricing systems and dispute resolution mechanisms. They propose that the use of hierarchical elements will vary with transaction characteristics. They find empirical support for their propositions based on a content analysis of actual software contracts. In particular, hierarchical elements of contracts are seen to be important in facilitating the governance of outsourced activities. Gopal et al. (2003) examine the determinants of contract structure—fixed price or time and materials—and its impact on vendor profitability in the context of discrete offshore software development contracts. Specifically, they find that transaction characteristics such as higher requirement uncertainty, larger projects and potential resource shortages which increase riskiness of a project are more likely to lead to time and material contracts. Similarly, Kalnins and Mayer (2004) find that uncertainty, measurement issues and prior relationship between parties influence the type of contract selected, and conclude that time and material contracts are preferred when it is difficult to estimate costs ex ante or difficult to measure quality ex post. In a study of the Indian software industry, Banerjee and Duflo

(2000) find that vendor reputation determines contractual outcomes, wherein ex ante pricing provisions vary with vendor firm characteristics, plausibly associated with reputation.

Another set of arguments brought to bear on this issue focuses on the strategic value of information systems (Ang and Straub, 1998, Huber, 1993). This perspective holds that many IS services are strategic to the company and should therefore be provided internally. At the very least, it is argued, these services are idiosyncratic or specific to the firm. From a transaction cost perspective, effective provision of idiosyncratic services requires firm-specific business and process knowledge usually embodied in human capital. Given the co-specialized nature of these specific business and IT assets, these assets should be owned by the same entity, the client firm. This observation may also imply that there are few vendor economies of scale or specialization that would make it effective to procure these services externally. This raises the question of whether outsourced IS services are commodities or idiosyncratic. Specifically, while the use of information that results from information systems can be of strategic importance, it is not clear that the same can be said for the production processes for IS services. Does it matter who owns and manages the production process for IS services? Is it possible to outsource the production processes for information services, while maintaining the competitive advantage that accrues from the use of information?

4.   THE INFORMATION SYSTEMS OUTSOURCING INDUSTRY

In this section, I first describe the structure of the IS outsourcing marketplace and then discuss the dominant sourcing strategies. On the provider side, there are a few large players such as Accenture, Computer Sciences Corporation, Electronic Data Systems, and IBM that dominate the marketplace. There are numerous other players including second tier-providers (who may be quite large) with growth ambitions, larger players such as Hewlett-Packard that are recent entrants, and offshore providers (Apte, 1990). There are smaller providers as well. On the buy side, there are of course, numerous customers. Our focus is on large customers in the Fortune 1000. It is important to note that while the marketplace is often characterized as experienced sellers and inexperienced buyers—because providers engage in many such deals while buyers engage in one or at most, a few, IS outsourcing deals—the reality is that most customers retain experienced consultants and attorneys who provide expert advice on structuring the outsourcing relationship. As we can see, the evidence is consistent with the theory, which typically assumes that markets are *ex ante* competitive.

The service offerings in this marketplace include the set of activities that comprise the production of information services.[3] These activities include data center services, application services (both maintenance and new development), network services, distributed and desktop computing, help desk and so on. Recall that my focus is on time-based deals wherein a vendor manages a set of technology assets to deliver IS services for a specified duration. Companies outsource in a variety of ways—they may contract for the external provision of services with multiple vendors with each service sourced separately from a unique vendor (selective sourcing), or they may contract with a single provider or an alliance of providers for a set of multiple services (total outsourcing). The determinants of the choice between selective sourcing and total (or at least multifunctional) outsourcing have led different companies to different strategies. On the one hand, selective sourcing provides the opportunity to work with a best-of-breed supplier for each service offering but raises the transaction costs associated with working with multiple suppliers and may not allow for synergies between co-specialized assets. Total outsourcing to a single vendor, on the other hand, does not allow for best-of-breed selection, but reduces transaction costs. Total outsourcing to an alliance of suppliers is an attempt to find the middle ground. In this paper, we examine both selective and total outsourcing arrangements.

5.   A TRANSACTIONS COSTS VIEW OF INFORMATION SYSTEMS SERVICES DELIVERY

In this paper, I focus on data center services and application services, which are the two largest components of a typical IS budget. In order to understand the implications of the theory, it is useful to assess the transaction cost and the production cost characteristics of these service offerings. I arrived at my conclusions based on my prior research of the economics of the production process (Gurbaxani, 1990), the literature review above, and on numerous discussions with client and vendor personnel. Before proceeding, I should point out that the following discussion attempts to characterize a wide variety of IS environments, but it is not difficult to imagine other settings. Furthermore, there is no well-defined methodology for developing and measuring these characteristics; rather I simply categorize them as low, medium, or high using an experiential approach.

---

[3]   More recently, business process outsourcing has emerged as a new type of service offering, which rather than being based on horizontal IS services, provides the operations of a business process as a service, together with all the underlying technology services that support this process.

Table 4-1. Durable Transaction-Specific Investments

Determinant	Data center	Applications
Site specificity	Low	Low/medium
Physical asset specificity	Low/medium	Low/medium
Human-capital specificity	Low/medium	High
Dedicated assets	High	High

There are two categories of transaction costs—contractual costs and operational costs (Gurbaxani and Whang, 1991). Contractual costs include the costs of such activities as negotiating contracts, writing contracts, ongoing monitoring of a supplier, enforcing contractual agreements, legal costs, and the opportunity costs resulting from inefficient or opportunistic behavior. An important element of opportunistic behavior is the actions that result when events occur that aren't accounted for in the contract, presenting a party with an opportunity to extract rents from the other party. The operational costs associated with external sourcing are the one-time costs related to the vendor selection process, and ongoing costs such as communications costs (e.g. for service requests), making payments and so on.

5.1.   Transaction Cost Characteristics

In the case of *data center services*, I argue that these are characterized by high levels of investment in dedicated assets, low levels of site specificity, low to medium levels of physical asset specificity, and low to medium levels of human capital specificity (see Table 1). I discuss each in turn. Note that the largest IT cost component of providing data center services is hardware, followed by hardware personnel who operate and maintain the system, and system software licenses (Gurbaxani, 1990). To provide outsourcing services to a large customer, a service provider must make substantial investments in hardware, software and facilities.[4] While having noted that IT investments are often general purpose, it is still the case that it is difficult to re-deploy assets to other customers given the specific software solutions and architecture of a company, and the fact that potential clients will already have substantial capacity of their own. Finally, given the rapid price decline in hardware, and the rate of technological obsolescence, the investment in durable hardware assets made for a specific transaction are largely sunk.

Further, given the low costs of communications, and specifically the observation that the marginal costs of communication are fast approaching zero, the

---

[4]   It is not uncommon for an outsourcing company to invest one to two hundred million dollars to acquire the IT assets of a Fortune 500 client.

location of a service facility is becoming irrelevant resulting in low site specificity. Likewise, physical asset specificity is characterized as low to medium, largely because many computing assets are general purpose, though there may be some assets that are specific to a given customer (Grover et al., 1996, Ang and Straub, 1998, Wholey et al., 2001). Human capital specificity is categorized as low to medium because many aspects of data center services are standard across organizations but some of the work practices that an organization employs are usually idiosyncratic and have evolved over many years. In the case of data center services, because of the commodity nature of many of the activities involved with running a data center, it is usually relatively easy to acquire proficient human capital.

Accordingly, the potential for holdup occurs as follows. From the perspective of the buyer, the potential threat from the service provider is one of withholding or not being able to deliver services that are critical to the operations of the firm which would of course have serious consequences. A second concern is that of the service provider transferring knowledge assets in the form of employees who understand the idiosyncratic nature of the client's business, to other accounts. From the perspective of the provider, the main concern is the threat of early contract termination or withholding of payment, which would leave a provider with a large transaction-specific sunk investment.

Next, I consider the case of *application services*, comprising both legacy systems maintenance and new systems development. Note that the largest cost component of providing application services is software personnel, followed by the hardware environments to support software development and maintenance, and software licenses (Gurbaxani, 1990). Software environments consist of custom software, packaged software and software tools. Correspondingly, the human capital necessary to provide these services requires both firm-specific and technology-specific knowledge (Grover et al., 1996, Wholey et al., 2001). Therefore, I argue that site specificity can be categorized as low to medium, physical asset specificity as low to medium, human capital specificity as high, and dedicated assets as high (see Table 1).

Site specificity is characterized as low because a majority of systems development personnel can be located anywhere, with only a small percentage of them required to be co-located with the client. Even in the latter case, these personnel can be reassigned at reasonable cost to other clients. Physical asset specificity is categorized as low to medium because the hardware environments used to generate and service software are largely general purpose, but sometimes tailored to the needs of the business. Examples of this are graphical and engineering workstations. On the other hand, human capital specificity is high because a firm's portfolio of legacy systems software is usually the dominant portion of its installed base of software, and requires knowledge of a firm's specific implementations of custom software, and of older proprietary languages that are less commonly used in new software development today. In the case of new software development projects, the languages used are more current and there is a trend toward software packages which are more generalizable, but still require knowledge of a firm's specific processes and domain-specific expertise. Finally, the investment in dedicated assets is high because providing these services requires large investment in human capital, not just in hiring programmers and analysts, but in training them in systems and programming methodologies and in the acquisition of domain specific knowledge.

In the case of application services, the buyer's potential for hold up occurs primarily for two reasons. First, a client may lose valuable knowledge assets if software professionals who are domain experts or have idiosyncratic knowledge of the firm's software and processes are shifted to a provider's other customers. This risk can be very serious given the highly idiosyncratic nature of a firm's software assets relative to the case of data center services in which knowledge assets are much less idiosyncratic. Further, as in the case of data center services, a provider has the ability to impose significant costs on the buyer by withholding or inadequately delivering services. These costs may be less critical than in the case of data center services since delays in software maintenance will not typically affect daily or critical operations, though of course, they may do so in the case of software errors that shut down a system. Similarly, new applications development can be a source of value for a client, but given that these benefits will accrue in the future the immediate threat may be lower. A provider's concern is one of early contract termination or withholding of payment given the transaction-specific investment. In this case however, the risk to a provider is lower because human assets can be redeployed or their services terminated, which is much more difficult to achieve for hardware assets.

Next, we consider the impacts of uncertainty and complexity in the presence of transaction-specific investments. It is difficult to conceptualize or define measures of these characteristics. As has been articulated in the transaction cost economics literature, the importance of these factors is that as uncertainty and complexity increase, it becomes ever more difficult to write unambiguous and easily enforceable contingent claims contracts. In particular, it becomes difficult to specify all future states of nature, making it impossible to write complete contracts. When contracts are incomplete, it becomes possible for one party to engage in post-contractual opportunistic behavior and attempt to extract economic rents from the other.

I argue that the technology and business contexts for IS services are characterized by high degrees of uncertainty and complexity (Ang and Beath, 1993). Focusing on the technology aspects first, there is considerable uncertainty about the future costs of technology, particularly hardware. Even in the case of software, there is wide variability in the costs of programming labor (Gopal et al., 2003) when there is a sudden demand for a new technology (e.g. ERP, Internet). In addition, it is difficult to predict future technology developments and their subsequent adoption by corporations.[5] Most observers would agree that information services involve highly complex technological environments. The business environment today is highly competitive and dynamic. Companies frequently encounter the effects of business cycles, resulting in variations in the demand for IS services. In many cases, companies are unsure of the value of IT investments, adding further to the uncertainty of their future demand for these services. The difficulty associated with defining the output of information system services also contributes to the uncertainty. Moreover, business developments such as acquisitions and divestitures introduce additional uncertainty into a company's demand predictions.

Reputational considerations are important in the IS outsourcing industry (Lacity and Hirscheim, 1993, Bannerjee and Duflo, 2000). The marketplace is highly competitive and it is dominated by a small number of suppliers. There are also a small number of high-profile consulting, law and market research firms that provide information about the reliability and capabilities of suppliers. Companies typically engage in reference checking before entering into a relationship with a provider. Yet, in the face of confidentiality agreements, and given the complexities of the business and technology environments, it is difficult to obtain reliable information on the underlying causes of performance issues in any given arrangement. While supplier performance is clearly a cause of failure, it is also understood that many arrangements fail due to poor performance on the part of the buyer of services. Indeed, given the competitive nature of the marketplace, provider firms recognize the important role of reputation in vendor selection criteria and often act accordingly, but buyers have few such constraints.

5.2.   Production Cost Characteristics

The main benefits of external sourcing derive from the economies of scale and specialization that can potentially accrue to provider firms. In the case of data center services, the argument is that large providers have economies of scale in operations that allow them to achieve cost savings relative to their customers. Given that large companies are predominantly customers in outsourcing arrangement, it is important to note that while economies of scale may accrue to these clients, the scale of a viable external service provider is much larger. Moreover, external providers continue to grow their customer base and are likely to gain additional economies in the future.

---

[5] For example, most IS outsourcing contracts written before 1995 in my sample did not plan for adoption of Internet-based systems.

In the case of application services, it is argued that there are economies of specialization and learning. Providers who are in the business of developing and managing applications have stronger incentives to invest in developing and deploying new proprietary software methodologies, acquiring software development tools and best practice databases, and to benefit from the learning that they acquire from the experience base resulting from working with multiple customers. They are also able to achieve higher utilization rates for labor by pooling demand over a large client base. Of course, the economies available for both data center and application services will depend on the client's scale and sophistication in the production of IS services. In general, in the cases where outsourcing arrangements are entered into, external providers typically offer prices to customers that result in forecasts of significant cost savings.[6]

5.3.   Summary

It is clear from the above discussion that while there may be significant production cost advantages to IS outsourcing arrangements, it is also likely that transaction costs may inhibit these arrangements. Given uncertainty, technological complexity and difficult performance measurement, it is reasonable to assume that IS outsourcing contracts are incomplete. It is also the case that durable transaction-specific investments are required on the part of the seller to support the outsourcing arrangement. From the buyer's perspective, the delivery of agreed-upon IS services is critical to successful ongoing operations of the company. Accordingly, the costs of inadequate service delivery can be considerable. Moreover, with the considerable costs in time and money of switching to another supplier or bringing service back in-house, it is clear that the buyer is also vulnerable to post-contractual opportunistic behavior. It is reasonable to conclude then that there is significant potential for either party to engage in post-contractual opportunistic behavior and attempt to engage rents from the other party. While reputational constraints may mitigate these impacts, they are an inadequate substitute for an effective contract. In summary, when internal sourcing is not economical due to diseconomies of internal provision, either in production or in coordination, contractual arrangements that emerge between a company and its IS service provider will attempt to economize on transaction costs. The structure of the contract will reflect efforts to

---

[6] One limitation of this study is that it focuses only on outsourcing arrangements; we have no data on how many companies declined to pursue such an arrangement after receiving bids from suppliers. It should be noted that a majority of the Fortune 500 firms, who are both the largest and the most experienced, have outsourced significant components of their IS organizations.

create incentives and penalties that account for anticipated performance problems.[7]

6.   INFORMATION SYSTEMS OUTSOURCING CONTRACTS

In this section, I first present the general objectives of an IS outsourcing contract, and then discuss the specific features and provisions of a contract that are implied by transaction cost considerations.

6.1.   Overview

In the current business context, an IS outsourcing arrangement occurs within a rapidly changing technology and business environment. In an outsourcing relationship, key decision rights pertaining to the provision of IS services are allocated to an outsourcing service provider. In any situation where consequential decision rights are allocated to parties that have objectives that are different from a client's objectives, it is important to ensure that the decisions that these parties make and the actions that result are in the client's interests. As the role of information technology becomes more critical to the profitable functioning of a company, it is imperative that technology investment and operating decisions that are the responsibility of the outsourcing vendor are made appropriately.

The contract provides the detailed blueprint for the outsourcing relationship. It is critical because it specifies the "rules of the game." These rules include an articulation of the allocation of decision rights between the client and the vendor, the performance measurement and evaluation system, and the reward and punishment system (Kern and Willcocks, 2000). By performance measurement evaluation scheme, I mean the metrics that will be used to evaluate vendor performance. The reward and punishment system refers to the compensation agreement and the incentive and penalty clauses that determine the level of vendor compensation. It is reasonable to conclude that contract terms are the single-most important determinant of vendor behavior.

To the extent possible, the contract must attempt to account for future business conditions and technology trends, and specify the terms of the relationship in these scenarios. Given the uncertainties inherent in future business and technological environments, it is impossible to accurately predict the demand

---

[7]   While it is impossible to empirically demonstrate that the outsourcing option is cost minimizing—and indeed some companies do choose to source these services internally—assuming cost minimization predicts that the contract will focus on minimizing transaction costs.

for information services, the technologies with which to deliver these services and the associated costs over the course of a long-term outsourcing deal. Yet, the contract must specify service provisions and the corresponding price structure over the life of the contract. The challenge is twofold: to define the terms of the relationship for predicted future states and to provide a mechanism to manage the relationship when unexpected events occur related to either the business or the technology. The contract must therefore be simultaneously explicit and general, providing an overarching operating philosophy while detailing specifics.

6.2. Implications of Transaction Cost Economics for Information Systems Outsourcing Contracts

Once a company has decided to source IS services externally, the parties will negotiate a supply arrangement that attempts to address both parties' concerns with respect to anticipated transaction costs. From the perspective of economic efficiency (for a specified set of services), one can predict several desirable or normative features in a contractual arrangement.[8] Clearly, the provider should produce IS services efficiently, and should supply the agreed upon quantity and quality of services. The client should continue to procure services from an external provider as long as it is cost effective. If the service provider is not able to maintain its efficiency relative to other suppliers, the agreement should allow a shift to other suppliers. The agreement should allow supply and demand to adjust to changes in business conditions. The agreement should seek to minimize frequent negotiation over price and production levels, and should minimize the likelihood of litigation and its associated costs.

A contract addresses these issues through a variety of provisions. These provisions, or clauses, can be considered in two categories—pricing provisions and other (non-price) provisions. We know that the unit costs of providing information services typically decline over time due mainly to technological change manifested in the rapid decline in the costs of hardware. In addition to the direct benefits of the cost decline, there is also a capital-deepening effect (Gurbaxani and Mendelson, 1987), in that sophisticated IS managers substitute hardware for labor to achieve lower costs of production for most IS services. I assume that the contract specifies the price at which services will be provided over the duration of the contract. These prices may be specified in advance, or the methodology by which prices will be computed will be specified in advance. Of course, consistent with transaction cost economics, either party may attempt to engage in post-contractual opportunistic behavior to alter the prices in their favor.

---

[8] This set of desirable features is adapted from Joskow (1988) to reflect the IS context.

Before getting into a discussion of contractual provisions, we consider how a company chooses its IS services provider.[9] Milgrom and Roberts (1992) point out that even when needed services are specialized and unavailable through simple competitive market transactions, many of the advantages of competitive markets can be obtained by soliciting competing bids. Indeed, this is what is observed in this industry. A large proportion of outsourcing contracts result from a competitive bidding process. A typical process begins with a request for information with numerous providers responding. Based on their responses, a request for proposals is sent to a small set of vendors. Usually, two vendors are selected from these responses and asked to provide their best and final offers. In some cases, the internal services provider is asked to compete against the vendors. This competitive process drives prices down to the best-predicted state at the time of contracting. While there is uncertainty about future costs, the result of a competitive process is that a provider firm is not able to exploit any information advantage that it possesses regarding future technology trends relative to the customer.

Next, we consider the role of non-price provisions in economizing on transaction costs in IS outsourcing contracts.

6.2.1. **Non-price provisions** We argued that it is the existence of a durable transaction-specific asset that results in high transaction costs. Is it possible then that the client firm makes the investment in the assets—indeed they already own the assets—and the provider firm manages these assets?[10] For a variety of reasons, this is likely to be sub-optimal. We know that residual control and residual return ought to be aligned. Given that the focus of IS outsourcing is to improve the service offering relative to internal provision by reducing costs or improving quality, external providers will need to improve the quality of the assets. They do this by upgrading hardware systems, providing advanced training to the human asset and investing in preventive maintenance of software assets. External providers do not possess the incentive to improve assets that they do not own, since the residual return will accrue to others. Moreover, many of these assets are co-specialized and common ownership yields synergies that would not accrue otherwise. Thus:

---

[9] In contrast with some other sourcing decisions where the decision is made in advance of implementation, all companies have an internal IS department prior to the outsourcing decision. Even after the outsourcing decision is made, most companies retain responsibility for the provision of some IS services.

[10] This type of contractual arrangement is often seen in the hotel industry where the property is owned by a real estate company, and management services are provided by a hotel management company.

Proposition 1: The external provider will own the assets necessary to deliver services to the client.

In our case, it is the provider's ownership of the assets that becomes the major source of transaction costs. Note that the client's primary concern is not a durable transaction-specific investment, but rather the critical nature of the services provided; a significant failure to deliver the required services could have catastrophic implications for the client.

Next, if the vendor is going to make a significant investment in durable transaction-specific assets, then it will want a *long-term contract* (to avoid being held up) and *specified purchase obligations* on the part of the client. That is, it will require the client to commit to purchasing a certain volume of services. Given the rapid rate of technological obsolescence, seven years would be considered long-term in this industry. Moreover, I expect to see variation in duration based on the specificity of an asset. When an asset is more commodity-like, the contract can be shorter. Accordingly:

Proposition 2a: When a vendor firm makes a sizable investment in transaction-specific assets, it will seek a long-term contract, the duration of which will vary with the specificity of the assets.

Proposition 2b: When a vendor firm makes a sizable investment in transaction-specific assets, it will seek guaranteed purchase obligations.

Similarly, the client, concerned about its own potential hold-up, will want to ensure reliable delivery of services in the quantity and quality that it needs via a *supply obligation* provision, and *service level agreements*. Accordingly, I expect that provisions that ensure that the client will continue to purchase services over the duration of the contract, and that the supplier will continue to provide services that meet or exceed a prescribed quality level will be features of an outsourcing contract. This results in:

Proposition 3: When a client firm enters into a long-term contract, it will seek guaranteed supply obligations from the vendor to commit to supply a specified volume of services at or above a quality threshold.

Recall that human capital specificity is an important source of transaction costs in an IS outsourcing arrangement. As discussed above, providers are likely to acquire human capital from the client. A client, being concerned about the diversion of key employees to other customers of the provider, is therefore likely to require that these employees continue to provide services to the client for a period of time. As discussed earlier, human capital specificity is higher in application services, and it is more likely that this clause will occur in contracts where applications are an outsourced service. Accordingly:

Proposition 4: An outsourcing contract will include a key people provision when human capital specificity is high.

Uncertain demand and input price trends suggest that a client will not want to commit to price and quantity levels for the duration of a long-term contract. Yet, recognizing that the business and technology environments will change, a buyer would like to have the option to renegotiate prices within the framework of the contract with a minimum of haggling. So while prices may be specified at contract inception for the duration of the contract, the client will require *scheduled renegotiation* to account for unforeseen circumstances.

Proposition 5: A long-term outsourcing contract will include a provision for scheduled renegotiations.

Moreover, given rapidly changing input prices, and the uncertainty of knowing what a fair price will be in the future, large clients are likely to require an assurance that the price they are receiving is consistent with that received by comparable clients. Accordingly, they will request a *most favored customer* clause in order to ensure that they are indeed receiving a competitive price resulting in:

Proposition 6: A long-term outsourcing contract will include a most favored customer provision for large clients.

Unlike many tangible input goods, the definition of IS services and service levels is less precise. Moreover, the production and delivery of IS services is extremely complex and dynamic, and requires considerable interactions with a client's retained IS staff and with its end users. That is, from an operational perspective, outsourced service provision requires extensive coordination. In the face of this complexity and the importance of the service, these relationships will require management mechanisms to ensure effective functioning thereby economizing on these transaction costs. One governance mechanism to achieve a successful relationship is a senior management committee that meets periodically to assess the supply relationship. This leads to the following proposition:

Proposition 7: A long-term outsourcing contract will include provisions for governance structure that improves coordination between client and vendor.

In addition, if a relationship were failing, both parties would prefer a dispute resolution system such as arbitration that is lower cost than litigation, though litigation can remain an option, resulting in:

Proposition 8: A long-term outsourcing contract will include provisions for arbitration to reduce the costs of dispute resolution.

Given the difficulty in formally specifying and measuring the outputs and quality of IS services reasons, a client may not always be able to provide clear evidence of inadequate performance on the part of the vendor. Moreover, a client may want to reduce the potential of hold-up by a vendor firm by having the right to terminate the relationship without specifying a reason. Therefore, a client will want to be able to terminate a provider *for convenience*. To protect its transaction-specific investment in dedicated assets, a provider will require a monetary payoff which will depend on the time at which this clause is exercised; that is the payoff declines over time. A provider, on the other hand, cannot be given the option to terminate a client for convenience given the potential that such a provision would confer for hold-up of the client. On the other hand, both parties will seek to allow for *termination for cause*, which is non-performance in the case of the provider and non-payment on the part of the client. Thus:

Proposition 9: A long-term outsourcing contract will include provisions for the conditions by which an outsourcing arrangement can be terminated for cause.

Proposition 10: A long-term outsourcing contract will include provisions for conditions by which an outsourcing arrangement can be terminated for convenience by a client.

The contract must also deal with unforeseen contingencies that are unrelated to the supply relationship for IS services (such as acts of God, wars, or terrorist actions) that were not anticipated during contract negotiations. Both the client and the provider should anticipate that events can occur beyond the scope of any provisions for changes that have been incorporated in the contract. In these cases, both the client and provider will want to specify a mechanism by which the impacts of such events can be addressed. Correspondingly, we have:

Proposition 11: Long term outsourcing contracts will include a force majeure clause.

Finally, if the services provided are the source of competitive advantage, I would expect to see a clause that deals with *competitive issues*, placing restrictions on the work that the provider can perform for the client's competitors. On the other hand, if the services that are outsourced are commodity-like, this clause is not necessary. In a transaction cost sense, when the human capital or software assets are highly specific to a client, and are highly valuable, the vendor firm has the opportunity to exploit these assets at competing clients.

6.2.2. **Pricing provisions** The objective of any pricing provisions should meet two economic goals. It should attempt to eliminate incentives for opportunistic behavior, and it should promote efficient supply and demand decisions on the parts of the provider and client respectively.

There are two main elements to a pricing arrangement—the structure of the pricing provisions, and the magnitude of the prices. In our context, pricing arrangements for long term IS services contracts are quite difficult to specify given technological change, rapid price declines in some inputs, and unpredictability of the technology and business environments. In addition, macroeconomic variables such as inflation, taxes, and regulation can also have an impact on costs.

In general, there are several commonly observed approaches to the structuring of pricing provisions. The price could be set as a function of a *market price*, which would require the availability of a price on a similar service offering in a market. In this context, given the idiosyncratic nature of services—each client has different scale, geography etc.—such a market price does not exist. An alternative approach is that of a fixed price, either as a total (\$$x$ for each year of the contract) or per unit of service (\$$y$ per unit of service for each year of the contract). In the face of declining input prices, this scheme is inefficient in that the price will be below the cost of provision (including normal profits) in the early years of the contract giving the provider the incentive to renege.[11] In later years, the price will be above the cost of provision giving the client the incentive to breach the contract. Therefore, such a clause is appropriate only when the costs of supply are fixed over the duration of the contract, which is unlikely in our context.

Another approach is what I term a *futures price*. A futures pricing scheme is one where the pricing is specified in advance but the magnitude can vary over time. This too can be specified as a total (\$$x_t$ in year t for the entire service offering) or per unit of service (\$$y_t$ in year t per unit of service). For example, in the case of application systems maintenance, a futures price could be specified either as \$10 million in year one, \$9 million in year two and so

---

[11] Note that reneging does not mean that a supplier will quit, but given imperfect monitoring, may reduce the quality or quantity of a service.

on, or be specified as $125 per hour for a programmer in year one, $135 per hour in year two and so on. In this case, in a competitive bidding environment, the magnitude of the service price is likely to reflect the best predictions of future input prices. This form of pricing is appropriate in our context, and it is likely to be observed. However, given uncertain business conditions, and to the extent that prices are based on service volumes, this scheme is unable to adjust to substantial changes in service volumes as may be caused by the acquisition or divestiture of divisions. There are at least two ways to address this: one by allowing for renegotiation when such events occur, and the other is by adopting a *cost plus* pricing scheme. Thus:

Proposition 12: The time pattern of the prices for services in outsourcing contracts will reflect the anticipated trends in the costs of service provision.

A cost plus pricing scheme has many advantages. It ensures that the price charged to the client reflects the actual costs of the arrangement, and allows a client to accrue the benefits from faster input price declines, as is often the case with information technology inputs. It also takes away all incentives for a provider to renege given that it is able to cover all its costs including unexpected ones. The main concern with this scheme is that the supplier has no incentive to minimize production costs, given that a client can switch providers only after incurring substantial switching costs. One way to address this is to provide for this in the contract by incorporating anticipated cost declines, and coupling this with specific incentives for achieving cost declines faster than those specified in a contract. This results in:

Proposition 13a: Outsourcing arrangements that anticipate significant demand shifts are likely to use cost plus pricing.

Proposition 13b: Cost plus pricing will be accompanied by incentive arrangements that encourage a vendor to continually cut costs.

Finally, to allow for changes in macroeconomic factors such as inflation, or regulation, a pricing scheme can be adjusted by using a price index. For example, a price could be described in terms of its component costs, say hardware and labor costs, and an index applied to each component. This scheme promotes production efficiencies on the part of the provider. Thus:

Proposition 14: Absolute levels of prices specified at contract signing will incorporate adjustments based on a price index.

Next, I describe the data that will be used to examine these propositions.

7. DATA AND METHODOLOGY

I was able to obtain access to 10 outsourcing contracts that were signed in the mid to late 1990s. I must point out that this is a convenience sample. Given the confidentiality that surrounds these contracts, it is extremely difficult to obtain access to this source of data. All contracts were commercial and ranged in value from $30 MM to over $1B. Six of them entailed total outsourcing and four were selective outsourcing of data center services only. In all cases, the clients and providers were commercial organizations. For reasons of confidentiality, I am not able to provide more information on the clients or the providers. I read each contract, and occasionally spoke with executives from provider organizations when necessary to seek clarifications. It is worth pointing out that the contracts are extremely long running, into thousands of pages. Given the scope of the data, I simply report the frequency with which a provision—non-pricing or pricing—appears in a contract. These findings are presented in the next section.

8. FINDINGS

In Table 2, I present a summary of the incidence of the non-price provisions. In all ten contracts, consistent with Proposition 1, assets were acquired by the provider. Coupled with the uncertainty and complexity of the environment, the acquisition of durable transaction-specific assets creates the potential for high transaction costs.

Consistent with Proposition 2a, seven of the ten contracts were for greater than seven years, including all six total outsourcing deals and one data center deal. Of the remaining three deals of shorter duration, all were data center deals. When asset specificity is higher, as is the case with total outsourcing since it includes application services which we have argued requires specific human capital, contract duration is longer. Of the three shorter deals, two were expecting significant business changes and one had a very clear objective of retiring the mainframe environment. In the case of the two companies that were expecting business changes, the impact of these anticipated but yet unknown business changes implied very high levels of demand uncertainty. The contractual solution to dealing with heightened uncertainty was a shortening in the duration of the contract which served to reduce uncertainty. In the third case where the client's goal was to retire its legacy assets and move to a new technology platform, its strategic intent substantially reduced its dependence on the provider. It is important to note that a provider can adjust to a shorter

Table 4-2. Observed Non-Price Provisions

Provisions	Observation	Comment
Asset ownership	10/10	
Long-term contracts → 7 years	7/10	Shorter deals are all data center deals
Specified purchase and supply obligations	10/10	
Service quality—Service level agreements	10/10	Varied sophistication
Key people provision	5/10	Primarily on total outsourcing, consistent with higher asset specificity of application services component of total outsourcing
Scheduled renegotiation	6/10	Most large deals
Most favored customer	7/10	All large deals
Termination for cause, convenience	6/10	Termination for convenience available only to client
Management committee	8/10	All but very small deals
Arbitration	6/10	Two suggested litigation, two did not address issue
Force majeure	9/10	
Competitive issues	2/10	Only two large total arrangements

duration by investing a lower amount in specific assets, or by charging a higher price.[12]

All ten deals had specified purchase obligations, suggesting that this is a key mechanism to mitigate the costs associated with the durable transaction-specific investment. This finding provides very strong support for Proposition 2b.[13] In all cases, clients assumed the demand side risk. That is, they undertook to buy a set of services within a pre-specified range of volume for the duration of the contract. This provides the vendor with reasonable assurance that their durable transaction-specific investment will be protected.

Likewise, the vendor assumed supply-side risk by committing to provide services within the range of purchase obligations. The provider usually offered a discount if the quantity of purchased services exceeded the volume range, but the client was required to pay for a minimum level of service regardless of whether they were used or not. Strongly consistent with Proposition 3, all ten of the contracts had service level agreements though they were

---

[12] I did not have any means of assessing the value of the provider's investment relative to that of the acquired assets.

[13] Contrast this finding with the recent trend toward utility outsourcing where the assets that form the basis of service delivery are less specific and can be shared, and where purchase obligations are less stringent.

of varied sophistication. Some included bonus and penalty clauses, some were very detailed, while others were loosely specified. This set of clauses is aimed at ensuring the client of the requisite quality of services, and serves to align the interests of the vendor with those of the client by providing incentives to meet these requirements.

Only five of the ten contracts included a key people provision—these were all large total outsourcing deals. This provision guaranteed the supply of specific individuals to the client for a fixed duration. None of the pure data center deals had a key people provision. Recall that it is optimal for the vendor to own assets for reasons of co-specialization and for providing incentives to invest in and improve the quality of the assets. Furthermore, the other services included in these deals were largely commodity-like. This finding is consistent with Proposition 4 premised on the notion that human asset specificity is high primarily in the case of application services.[14]

Six of the ten contracts had provisions for scheduled renegotiation. All six deals were large in terms of the aggregate annual fees paid to the providers; the smaller deals did not contain this clause. This is consistent with ex ante market power of the providers. It is also the case that the larger deals incorporated multiple service lines, and were more vulnerable to unforeseen changes in the business or technology environments. In the case of one data center deal as discussed above, the vendor acquired assets from the client and contracted to operate them until they were retired at the end of the contract. In such a case, the vendor's costs are highly predictable, future changes in technology and business are unlikely to affect this service relationship, and renegotiation becomes unnecessary. Overall, these findings provide reasonable support for Proposition 6.

The seven largest deals also included a most favored customer clause consistent with Proposition 6; the smaller ones did not. Eight of the ten contracts included a specification of shared governance approach—a management committee comprised of executives from both parties—as a mechanism to ensure smooth functioning of the arrangement and reduce the likelihood of service delivery issues escalating into significant disputes. The only ones that did not were the two smallest deals. This validates Proposition 7 and also suggests the importance of coordination in an outsourced environment. Six of the ten deals included an arbitration option (Proposition 8), two suggested litigation as a dispute resolution mechanism, and two did not address the issue. When arbitration is not specified in the contract, litigation is usually the default though parties can always choose to seek arbitration.

Consistent with Propositions 9 and 10, six of the larger deals included a termination clause, including termination for cause and convenience. It is

---

[14] I was unable to confirm the activities that these key individuals were responsible for.

noteworthy that not all deals explicitly specify a termination clause. The clause specifies the payment schedule based on the date at which termination becomes effective, and serves to compensate the vendor for its durable transaction-specific investment in case of early termination. Termination for convenience is available only to clients while termination for cause is available to both parties. In the case of termination by a client, the payment is lower in the case of cause relative to convenience and the magnitude of the payment decreases over time. This provision also specifies that the vendor will continue to provide services in all cases of early termination until alternative supply arrangements have been made which mitigates the effect of a potentially powerful source of hold-up of the client.

Unsurprisingly, nine of the ten included a force majeure clause (Proposition 11). Only two of the contracts restricted the provider from working with competitors in any way, suggesting that most clients saw the outsourced services as commodity-like.

Next, I discuss the incidence of pricing provisions (see Table 3), first for data center services and then for application management services. In the case of data center services, I did not observe any market or fixed price contracts. Consistent with Proposition 12, prices vary over time and appear to reflect predicted costs in all ten cases. Three of the ten contracts were cost plus and seven of the ten contracts were futures prices. Of the futures price contracts, four were total prices and three were unit prices.[15] In the case of unit pricing, the components of pricing were processing, disk, tape and printing services. Moreover, in the case of unit pricing, the prices were banded in that they were specified for a range of service volumes. Consumption above or below the volume band resulted in a discount or penalty respectively. In the case of futures total prices, the deals were either small or were dedicated solutions with a cost structure that was independent of volume. I was not able to determine if all cost-plus contracts were expecting substantial variation in demand (Proposition 13a). Consistent with Proposition 13b, all the cost-plus deals included significant incentives for additional cost reductions.

Finally, consistent with Proposition 14, eight of the ten contracts were indexed for inflation—usually via the consumer price index. Interestingly, prices were adjusted based either on the increase in CPI applied to a pre-specified component of the costs, or as a pre-specified fraction of the CPI increase on the total cost. That is, the contracts recognized explicitly that increases in inflation only impact certain components of costs.

In the case of application services, three of the six contracts are futures unit prices. The units of service were either labor hour per job category, labor hour

---

[15] While only three of the ten contracts in my sample use futures unit pricing, I am aware from my experience in the industry that this the dominant approach.

Table 4-3. Observed Pricing Provisions

	Provisions	Observation	Comment
Data Center	Time-varying	10/10	
	Cost plus	3/10	All included.
			Cost-reduction incentives
	Futures	7/10	Aggregate, 3 unit-based
Application Services	Time-varying	6/6	
	Cost plus	3/6	All included.
			Cost reduction incentives
	Futures	3/6	All unit-based

regardless of job category, or software units (function points). Note that while two schemes are based on labor effort in which there is no demand-side risk to the vendor, one is volume-based in which demand-side risk is borne by the vendor. Three of the six were cost plus contracts; as in the case of data center services, they all included incentives for cost reductions. All six contracts were indexed for inflation, largely reflecting the increased weighting of labor as a component of cost for this service offering.

A majority of the contracts for application services included a benchmarking clause that required periodic productivity comparisons in the client's industry, with a requirement to perform at the top end of the percentile distribution. As discussed earlier, the unit costs of application services also decrease over time as managers improve software development productivity through the use of hardware-intensive software tools and development methodologies and are therefore enabled by lower hardware costs. This approach provides a reasonable though not failsafe mechanism that tries to ensure that the price a client pays its provider reflects productivity improvements without actually specifying the rate of improvement.

9.   DISCUSSION

In aggregate, the results are consistent with the predictions of transaction cost economics suggesting that the theory provides a powerful lens with which to analyze IS outsourcing arrangements. Providers make a durable transaction-specific investment in order to provide services to a client. Co-specialized assets are owned by a provider. Contracts are written to minimize transaction costs, and to promote efficiency.

The primary contractual mechanisms by which managers attempt to minimize transaction costs include both pricing and non-price provisions. Pricing provisions appear to promote efficient behavior on the part of the client and the provider. The pricing scheme is either a futures price that anticipates future costs, or is cost plus with incentive clauses that promote efficient production. In all cases, the specified prices or pricing scheme reflect the anticipated cost trends and are the result of a competitive bidding process. The anticipatory nature of this competitively determined pricing scheme motivates suppliers to produce efficiently over the duration of the contract, and to the extent that prices reflect costs, motivate the client to consume services efficiently. It is also important to note that while prices are proposed in the contract, there is some flexibility in the realized price due to indexing, as well as benchmarking and renegotiation clauses built into the contract.

Among the most important of the non-price provisions are the guaranteed purchase and supply obligations, which commit a client to a range of pre-agreed upon purchase volumes, and commit a supplier to providing these volumes. The guaranteed purchase obligation addresses a provider's primary hold-up concern of its significant investment in dedicated assets. Likewise, a buyer's primary vulnerability of costly denial of service is addressed through a guaranteed supply obligation wherein a supplier cannot stop providing services except in a few tightly specified instances. Service quality is also addressed through service level agreements. Significant non-performance by the provider is handled through termination agreements, either for cause or for convenience. These findings are consistent with those of Kern and Willcocks (2000) who also find that these clauses form the critical core of governance of an outsourcing relationship.

The primary differences in contractual features based on the type of outsourced activities manifest themselves in contract duration and in the key people provision clause. Long-term contracts are the norm given the significant investment in dedicated assets. However, when the assets are less transaction-specific as is the case for selectively outsourced data center deals, the observed duration is shorter in some cases. The key-people provision clause was observed only in total outsourcing deals, consistent with the higher human-capital asset specificity associated with application services in particular, and the broader set of activities included in total outsourcing arrangements.

The motivation for outsourcing seems to be economically rational. Client companies seek to exploit economies of scale and specialization, and are able to mitigate the impact of transaction costs that may be incurred when contracts are incomplete through the use of sophisticated contract provisions. Transaction cost economics provides a useful means of conducting an empirical analysis of contracts in the IS outsourcing industry.

There continue to be many unanswered research questions. One particularly important avenue for research is developing an understanding of the differences between companies that have chosen to outsource versus those that continue to in-source. While this research has shown the validity of transaction cost economics as a framework for analyzing outsourcing contracts for companies that have made the decision to outsource, a significant number of companies continue to rely on internal service provision. Are these companies using information services more strategically, or is their operation more idiosyncratic? Also, it is important to relate the structure of the contract both to the specific features of the particular supply arrangement and ultimately to its success. Such an analysis would require primary data collection and I am currently engaged in such an effort. It would also be useful to study more closely the effectiveness of specific relational governance mechanisms and how they complement contractual features.

In closing, it is worth making some broad industry observations. I have observed that the number of contract terminations in the overall industry to date is a very small percentage of the overall number of outsourcing contracts. A frequent source of dispute is, not surprisingly, the perception that the price for a given service is high. While benchmarking clauses were intended to address this concern, the incomplete nature of many of these provisions has led to conflicts about the appropriate benchmarking sample and methodology. In general, given the fact that providers are very concerned about reputation effects, and clients face switching costs and a lack of continuity in their business operations, both parties have strong incentives to make their relationships work. When disputes occur, they are often resolved by arbitration and sometimes by litigation. On the other hand, many contracts have been renewed for additional periods, while some have added new services to the original agreement. Newer contracts take into account many of the weaknesses of the earlier contracts by revising the scope and detail of the pricing and non-pricing provisions.

Finally, it is worth noting that the trend toward the external sourcing of IS services should be analyzed in the context of what appears to be a trend towards outsourcing more broadly. Namely, IS outsourcing is just one instance of the larger phenomenon toward outsourcing in general. Ever since Hamel and Prahalad (1990) argued in a seminal article that firms should focus on their core competencies and outsource non-core activities, managers in a variety of functional areas have exercised this option with increasing frequency. While early examples of outsourcing focused on product interfaces such as tangible components of finished goods, the trend in today's information economy is towards sourcing at information interfaces. Information-based processes, such as accounting and human resources management, in addition to IS services, are increasingly sourced externally and often to offshore locations. I believe that this trend offers up a rich new domain for the study of the efficacy of outsourcing contracts for other information-based processes from a transaction cost perspective.

REFERENCES

Adler, P., 2001. "Market, Hierarchy and Trust: The Knowledge Economy and the Future of Capitalism." *Organization Science* 12 (2): 214–234.

Alpar, P. and A. Saharia, 1995. "Outsourcing Information Systems Functions: An Organizational Economics Perspective." *Journal of Organizational Computing* 5 (3): 197–217.

Ang, S. and C. Beath, 1993. "Hierarchical Elements in Software Contracts." *Journal of Organizational Computing* 3 (3): 329–361.

Ang, S. and L. Cummings, 1997. "Strategic Response to Institutional Influences on Information Systems Outsourcing." *Organization Science* 8 (3): 235–255.

Ang, S. and D. Straub, 1998. "Production and Transaction Economies and IS Outsourcing: A Study of the U.S. Banking Industry." *MIS Quarterly* 22 (4): 535–552.

Apte, U., 1990. "Global Outsourcing of Information Systems and Processing Services." *The Information Society* 7 (4): 287–303.

Banerjee, A. and E. Duflo, 2000. "Reputation Effects and the Limits of Contracting: A Study of the Indian Software Industry." *Quarterly Journal of Economics* 115 (3): 989–1017.

Boerner, C. and J. Macher, 2001. "Transaction Cost Economics: An Assessment of Empirical Research in the Social Sciences." Working Paper, University of California, Berkeley.

Coase, R., 1937. "The Nature of the Firm." *Economica* 4 (16): 386–405.

Coase, R., 1992. "The Institutional Structure of Production." *American Economic Review* 82 (4): 713–719.

Clemons, E., L. Hitt, and E. Snir, 2000. "A Risk Analysis Framework for IT Outsourcing." Working Paper, The Wharton School, University of Pennsylvania (October).

DiRomualdo, A. and V. Gurbaxani, 1998. "Strategic Intent for IT Outsourcing." *Sloan Management Review* 39 (4): 67–80.

Fitzgerald, G. and L. Willcocks, 1994. "Contracts and Partnerships in the Outsourcing of IT." *Proceedings of the International Conference on Information Systems*, Vancouver, BC, Canada: 91–98.

Gartner Dataquest, 2003. "Worldwide IT Services Market Definitions Guide, 2Q03." *Gartner Dataquest Guide*, Stamford, CT (August).

Goldberg, V. and J. Erickson, 1987. "Quantity and Price-Adjustment in Long-Term Contracts: A Case Study of Petroleum Coke." *Journal of Law and Economics* 30 (2): 369–398.

Gopal, A., K. Sivaramakrishnan, M. Krishnan, and T. Mukhopadhyay, 2003. "Contracts in Offshore Software Development: An Empirical Analysis." *Management Science* 49 (12): 1671–1683.

Grover, V., M. Cheon, and J. Teng, 1996. "The Effect of Service Quality and Partnership on the Outsourcing of Information Systems Functions." *Journal of MIS* 12 (4): 89–116.

Gurbaxani, V., 1990. *Software-Hardware Tradeoffs and Information Systems Budgets.* Washington DC: ICIT Press.

Gurbaxani, V. and H. Mendelson, 1987. "Software-Hardware Tradeoffs and Data Processing Budgets." *IEEE Transactions on Software Engineering* SE-13 (September): 1010–1017.

Gurbaxani, V. and S. Whang, 1991. "The Impact of Information Systems on Organizations and Markets." *Communications of the ACM* 34 (1): 59–73.

Hamel, G. and C. Prahalad, 1990. "The Core Competence of the Corporation." *Harvard Business Review* 68 (3): 79–91.

Hart, O. and J. Moore, 1999. "Foundations of Incomplete Contracts." *The Review of Economic Studies* 66 (1): 115–138.

Huber, R., 1993. "How Continental Bank Outsourced its Crown Jewels." *Harvard Business Review* (January–February) 71 (1): 121–129.

Joskow, P., 1985. "Vertical Integration and Long-term Contracts: The Case of Coal-burning Electric Generating Plants." *Journal of Law, Economics, and Organization* 1 (1): 33–80.

Joskow, P., 1987. "Contract Duration and Relationship-Specific Investments: Empirical Evidence from Coal Markets." *American Economic Review* 77 (1): 168–185.

Joskow, P., 1988. "Asset Specificity and the Structure of Vertical Relationships: Empirical Evidence." *Journal of Law, Economics, and Organization* 4 (1): 95–117.

Kalnins, A. and K. Mayer, YEAR. "Relationships and Hybrid Contracts: An Analysis of Contract Choice in Information Technology." *Journal of Law, Economics, and Organization* 20 (1): 207–229.

Kern, T. and L. Willcocks, 1996. "*The Enabling and Determining Environment: Neglected issues in an IT/IS Outsourcing Strategy.*" European Conference on Information Systems, Lisbon, Portugal.

Kern, T. and L. Willcocks, 2000. "Contracts, Control and 'Presentation' in IT Outsourcing: Research in Thirteen UK Organizations." *Journal of Global Information Management* (October–December) 8 (4): 15–39.

Kern, T. and L. Willcocks, 2001. "*The Relationship Advantage: Information Technologies, Sourcing, and Management.*" Oxford, United Kingdom: Oxford University Press.

Klein, B., R. Crawford, and A. Alchian, 1978. "Vertical Integration, Appropriable Rents, and the Competitive Contracting Process." *Journal of Law and Economics* 21 (2): 297–326.

Lacity, M. and R. Hirscheim, 1993. *Information Systems Outsourcing: Myths, Metaphors and Realities.* New York, NY: John Wiley and Sons.

Lacity, M. and R. Hirscheim, 1995. *Beyond the Information Systems Outsourcing Bandwagon: The Insourcing Response.* New York, NY: John Wiley and Sons.

Lacity, M., L. Willcocks, and D. Feeny, 1995. "IT Outsourcing: Maximize Flexibility and Control." *Harvard Business Review* 73 (3): 84–93.

Lacity, M., 2002. "Lessons in Global Information Technology Sourcing." *Computer* 35 (8): 26–33.

Loh, L. and N. Venkatraman, 1992. "Determinants of Information Technology Outsourcing: A Cross-Sectional Analysis." *Journal of Management Information Systems* 9 (1): 7–24.

Lyons, B., 1994. "Contracts and Specific Investment." *Journal of Economics and Management Strategy* 3 (2): 257–278.

Masten, S. and K. Crocker, 1985. "Efficient Adaptation in Long-Term Contracts: Take-or-Pay Provisions for Natural Gas." *American Economic Review* 75 (5): 1083–1093.

Masten, S., 1996. "Empirical Research in Transaction Cost Economics: Challenges, Progress, Directions." In Groenewegen, J. (ed.), *Transaction Cost Economics and Beyond.* Boston, MA: Kluwer Academic Press, 43–64.

Milgrom, P. and J. Roberts, 1992. *Economics, Organizations, and Management.* Englewood Cliffs, NJ: Prentice Hall.

Nam, K., S. Rajagopalan, H. Rao, and A. Chaudhury, 1996. "A Two-Level Investigation of Information Systems Outsourcing." *Communications of the ACM* 39 (7): 36–44.

Poppo, L. and T. Zenger, 2002. "Do Formal Contracts and Relational Governance Function as Substitutes or Complements?" *Strategic Management Journal* 23 (8): 707–725.

"Professional Services, First, Kill the Consultants." *BusinessWeek Online*, 2002. www.businessweek.com (14 January).

Saunders, C., M. Gebelt, and Q. Hu, 1997. "Achieving Success in Information Systems Outsourcing." *California Management Review* 39 (2): 63–79.

Shelanski, H. and P. Klein, 1995. "Empirical Research in Transaction Cost Economics: a Review and Assessment." *Journal of Law, Economics and Organization* 11 (2): 335–361.

Strassmann, P., 1995. "Outsourcing: A Game for Losers." *Computerworld* (21 August).

Strassmann, P., 2004. "Most Outsourcing is still a Game for Losers." *Computerworld* (2 February).

Tapper, D., 2004. "Worldwide and U.S. IT Outsourcing Services 2004–2008 Forecast: A Potential Perfect Storm." Report #31089, Framingham, MA: International Data Corporation (April).

Wholey, D., R. Padman, R. Hamer, and S. Schwartz, 2001. "Determinants of Information Technology Outsourcing." *Health Care Management Science* 4 (3): 229–239.

Williamson, O., 1985. *The Economic Institutions of Capitalism.* New York, NY: Free Press.

Young, A., 2004. "Outsourcing Market View: What the Future Holds." Presentation at *Gartner IT Services and Sourcing Summit*, Las Vegas, NV (May).

ACKNOWLEDGEMENTS

This research has been supported by a grant from the U.S. National Science Foundation's Industry-University Cooperative Research Program to the CRITO Consortium and by its industry sponsors. I gratefully acknowledge the constructive comments made by Laura Poppo and two anonymous reviewers. The author is responsible for any remaining errors or omissions.

Chapter 5

MANAGING NETWORK ORGANIZATIONS IN THE KNOWLEDGE ECONOMY: LEARNING FROM SUCCESS AND FAILURE

Hamid R. Ekbia

School of Library and Information Science, Indiana University, 1320 E. 10th St., Bloomington, IN 47405-3907, e-mail: hekbia@indiana.edu

Abstract   The current economy has brought the network model of organization to the forefront of management theory and practice. The network model is often presented in organization and ICT literature with an air of enthusiasm that underscores the advantages of this model as flexible, cooperative, innovative, and knowledge and technology intensive. Such themes are normally based on a networking logic that assumes the trustful cooperation of large and small production firms in favor of competitive advantage in a rapidly changing and volatile environment. This chapter challenges both the logic and the themes based upon it. Using Enron as a case study, the chapter seeks to enrich the logic, to broaden the themes, and to finally arrive at a more realistic picture of the network enterprise. This is made possible by extending the unit of analysis beyond the production firm, to include, among others, subsidiaries, banks, investors, auditors, and government agencies. The managerial implications of these shifts will be discussed.

1.   INTRODUCTION

The information economy seems to favor the network model of organization. This is what various authors with various perspectives have argued for at least twenty years. Writing about a borderless world, Ohmae (1990) warned managers in this manner: "In a complex, uncertain world filled with dangerous opponents, it is best not to go it alone." Introducing the knowledge links within strategic alliances, Badaracco (1991) enumerated the basic conditions that need to be met in order for such alliances to succeed. More recently, Castells (2001) features the network enterprise as the human engine and the centerpiece of an informational economy. Similar accounts, albeit with a narrower scope, have been proposed in the organization and business literature (Powell, 1990, Miles, Snow, and Coleman, 1992, Miles and Snow, 1995, Nohria and Eccles, 1992, Grandori and Soda, 1995, Polodny and Page, 1998, Symon, 2000) as well as information and communication systems writings (Ching, Holsapple, and Whinston, 1996, Van Alstyne, 1997, Fulk and Desanctis, 1998, Fulk, 2001). These studies emanate from different perspectives but converge on a number of themes—most importantly, inter-firm cooperation, trust, and voluntarism, intra-firm team working, empowerment, and innovation, organizational flexibility, adaptability, and decentralization, and, most often, a close relation with information and communication technologies (ICT) (Van Alstyne, 1997).

Most of these accounts of the network enterprise rely on what it is called a "networking logic." Castells, for instance, asserts that this logic "seems to be well adapted to increasing complexity of interaction and to unpredictable patterns of development arising from the creative power of such interaction" (Castells, 1996, p. 70). The core intuition in Castells' account seems to be that such interactions "can now be materially implemented, in all kinds of processes and organizations, by newly available information technologies" (Castells, 1996, pp. 61–62). Castells discusses and promotes the network enterprise as one that uses the Internet and other computer networks to carry out its variegated operations—from management, financing, and innovation, to production, distribution, sales, and employee relations. The picture is one of a multiply nested organization in which divisions of large multinational corporations of yesteryears cooperate on a project-by-project basis with small and medium firms, which, taking advantage of the new ICT, are now able to leapfrog the limits of economies of scale (Kraak, 2000). The default assumption is that these entities would often cooperate on the basis of trust, transparency, and voluntarism.

It turns out that these assumptions and the logic on which they are based need significant enhancements in order to account for the full complexity of networking practices in the current economy. The goal of this chapter is to develop an extended model of network organizations that would account for such complexities. To this end, it is going to use the case of Enron as the main vehicle of discussion (and the case of Cisco as a point of reference). Both firms, as we shall see, represent faithful implementations of the network form of organization. Cisco is featured as the prime example of a successful network enterprise in Castells (2001). Before its collapse in December of 2001, Enron was also the subject of admiration in business and management literature for, among other things, its acquisition and networking strategy (Sherman, 2002). Therefore, the two companies provide useful cases for the study of network organizations.

The paper continues in Section 2 with a discussion of the method adopted in the current study and in Section 3 with a brief history of Enron. Section 4 outlines the dominant views of the network enterprise, and Section 5 examines these views against the Enron case and draws some broad lessons from the comparison. In light of these findings, Section 6 introduces a set of features that provide a more realistic picture of networking in the current economy, and Section 7 draws some general conclusions.

2. METHOD: LEARNING FROM FAILURE

The goal of this study is to analyze the different dimension of the management of network organizations in the current economy. The particular choice of Enron (and Cisco as a reference point) is motivated by the availability of vast amounts of data about them, which make a longitudinal study possible. My concern, as such, is not so much to understand the causes of the failure of Enron, nor is it only or even primarily the character of corporate crime. It is rather to use the case to achieve a better understanding of the dynamics of networking in the current situation. This approach fits the general category of "building theory from case study research" (Eisenhardt, 1989).

The study has adopted the approach of "learning from failure" (Petroski, 1992, Polodny and Page, 1998): Trying to discern the possible causes of failure, and drawing lessons to refine the situation. In this context, the terms "success" and "failure" should be understood properly. Not everything about Enron was fake and false, and not all aspects of Cisco's activity and strategy are probably pristine and pure. Our task is to tease out these cases, beyond the smokes and mirror of the media and the Wall Street (whether in times of prosperity or in days of stagnation), to get at a more realistic picture of the network enterprise and, hopefully, to draw useful lessons for the management of such networks. With this goal in mind, the main question for the study is, what pitfalls and potentials do network organizations provide and how is it possible to avoid the pitfalls and utilize the potentials?

In its attempt to address this question, the study has had to look beyond the boundaries of the Enron Corporation (again assuming that these boundaries are definable at all). Current accounts of network organization tend to focus on the *production* firm at the expense of other parts of the network, which on the surface seem to be peripheral or ancillary to the network but are as critical to its understanding as the production firm. As Polodny and Page (1998) have suggested, this is due to a naïve functionalism that is biased in its treatment of success and failure of network enterprises. Miles, Snow, and Coleman (1992), for instance, discuss three different types of network model (see Figure 1). Internal networks are intra-firm linkages operating on market principles (e.g., GM's component divisions), stable networks are formed by a large core

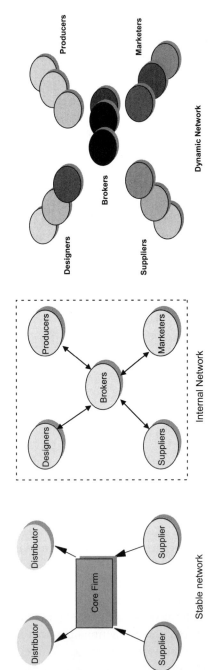

Figure 5-1. Common Network Types (Miles, Snow, and Coleman, 1992).

firm outsourcing parts of its business to external suppliers (e.g., BMW subsidiaries), and dynamic networks are temporary alliances organized around a lead or brokering firm, with each unit operating its own independent assets (e.g., Motorola, Reebok, and Dell Computers). The common feature among these varieties is that they all take the production firm as the unit of analysis. Castells, on the other hand, emphasizes the network character of the enterprise, but, in the final analysis, characterizes it as "an intermediary of supply and demand." This, as we shall see later (Section 4 below) leads him to take the "project" as the unit of analysis (1996).

I believe that neither the production firm nor the project provide the right level of analysis for understanding network organizations. Following Powell (2000), I would like to suggest the extended network that includes, among others, the partnerships, banks, brokerage firms, auditors, and government agencies as the appropriate unit of analysis. Powell also employs the notion of the "new logic of organizing" in discussing the network form, but portrays this new logic as involving three key interrelated developments:

1. a shift in the social organization of work from "jobs to projects";
2. a shift at the organizational level to flattened hierarchies and inter-firm networks;
3. a shift at the industry level to cross-fertilization across industries.

The focus of the current study is on the second development—namely, on the shift to a form of organization that seems to fit "neither market, nor hierarchy" (Powell, 1990). On this point, I strongly confer with Powell (2000) that, "The boundaries of many firms have become so porous that to focus on boundaries means only to see trees in a forest of interorganizational relations." Hence, this study follows the proposed mandate of taking "the interorganizational network as the basic unit of analysis" (ibid).

3. ENRON: A BRIEF HISTORY

Founded in 1984 as the merger of Houston Natural Gas and Internorth (which carried out the exploration, production, and transfer of oil and gas), Enron Corporation morphed into one of the largest U.S. corporations—$100 billion in revenue, $60 billion market value, and twenty thousand employees around the globe circa 2001. According to dominant accounts, this happened in the 1990s by the adoption of a new market strategy that leaned toward knowledge and "innovation," rather than the traditional ownership of physical assets. The central vision in Enron's enterprise was to fully use the financial and derivatives markets: to buy a commodity that somebody wanted to sell, and then sell it for a profit to someone who wanted to buy it. It began with oil and natural gas, and expanded to "pulp, paper, lumber, coal, steel, and weather" (Rubenstein, 2001). Weather, for instance, was traded in *swap* contracts, where a manufacturer (of, say, snowmobiles) or a power company agreed to pay Enron if there is a cold winter (and a tremendous amount of snow), and to get paid if otherwise. The same idea could be applied to a variety of derivatives, from electric power generation and pipeline capacity to broadband communication and the freight capacity of modular containers.

3.1. A Success Story

The central concept in 1990s Enron, in other words, was to sell capacity (Rubenstein, 2001). As a company executive had put it, Enron's "core business is not energy or market-making, but risk management," (ibid). It was this approach to the derivatives market that allowed Enron to diversify its activities over a broad range of products and services, branching out its organization accordingly—a key feature of a *networking strategy*. According to some accounts, in 2001 Enron Wholesale Services (EWS) traded over 1,000 kinds of products (ibid). According to others, Enron had added 1,700 (derivate) products in twenty markets (Maselli, 2001). In the meantime, Enron had created more than 870 off-balance-sheet subsidiaries as the legal and organizational vehicles for carrying out these activities (Dallas Observer, 2002).

In the 1990s, the overall trend in Enron's strategy changed from purchasing physical assets such as NGL (liquid natural gas) and petrochemical plants to one of an "asset-light" company that aimed to reduce physical property in favor of "innovative policies." Thus, it sold some of its assets—e.g., Enron Oil and Gas Co.—in 1999 in return for cash (Power Economics, 1999). While such moves surprised some analysts, Enron executives and a majority of analysts touted this as a healthy move toward a "knowledge organization." According to these groups of people, the key to Enron's success was its speed of operations, which was made possible by "wiring up" the company and by its extensive use of IT. The computerized standardization of the company's long-term derivatives contracts, for instance, resulted in the shortening of the time spent in closing a deal from hours to seconds (Beritano, 2002). Consequently, trading volume increased exponentially, a feature that is directly attributed to Enron's extensive use of IT. The speeding up was manifest in many other aspects of company life as well. Beritano (2002), for instance, claims that projects were completed in one-third the time that they would take at other companies. A project to integrate sales information with wireless devices, he reports, went from conception to deployment in 12 weeks. Analysts considered this speedup in operations as the main source of increase in revenues, which, a according to Enron's 2000 annual report, reached 59 percent in EWS (Enron Wholesale Services).

For these (and other) reasons, the business media credited Enron and its executives with various honors: *Fortune* labeled Enron's chairperson as a "revolutionary," and ranked the company as the most "admired" and most "innovative" in the U.S. for six consecutive years. *Business 2.0* and *Red Herring*, as late as August and September 2001, respectively, revered Enron with flashy titles and covers. *Fortune* (2000), building on analyst forecasts, had declared that Enron's latest adventure "to make bandwidth a commodity" was destined to succeed "absolutely." Some ICT specialists advertised Enron's "leap of faith" in deploying an "All-IP backbone" as the validation of their "conception of the New Network Architecture" (Communications Today, 1998). Others, who were more skeptical for mainly technical reasons—e.g., problems of connectivity (of various networks), provisioning (of bandwidth requirements on a real-time basis), and the "last-mile question"—maintained their optimism until the collapse of Enron (Bryce, 2001).

In short, a visible consensus of Enron executives, financial analysts, IT specialists, and business media portrayed in their stories a very flamboyant picture of Enron. This enthusiasm started to fall off around October 2001, and came to a halt with the collapse of Enron on December 2, 2001.

3.2.   A Failure Story

Despite all the cheer, the picture behind the scene was much more uneven. Enron had its share of failed business projects, especially on the international scene, from the very beginning[1]. One of the first failures was a "take or pay" contract (a form of derivative for the actual delivery of the commodity), in which TGT, an Enron subsidiary, agreed to take 260 million cubic feet of gas per day for ten years from the North Sea to the Great Britain. With the fall of gas price to half of the contract figure, Enron lost $537 million as early as 1997 (Dallas Observer, 2002). The most controversial contract, however, was LJM2 Co-Investment LP. Although critics consider entities such as these little more than shells, LJM2 was indeed more than a paper company (Bilodeau, 2002). Formed in 1999, LJM2 was regarded as an "alternative, optional source of private equity for Enron to manage its investment portfolio risk, funds flow, and financial flexibility" (ibid). Its limited partners included a wide spectrum of individuals and institutions—from financial entities such as Merrill Lynch and Co., JP Morgan Partners, American International Group Inc., and Leon Levy,

---

[1] Some analysts have argued that Enron's failures on the international scene had begun much earlier, and were widespread. They were, however, ignored by both the U.S. government and international bodies such as the World Bank, because of their low impact at home, and the perception that they were a source of income for the U.S. economy (see Wysham and Vallette, 2002).

the former chairman of Oppenheimer Funds Inc. to Arkansas Teacher Retirement System, Princeton University's Institute for Advanced Study (of which Levy is vice-chairman), and John Friedenrich, a former chairman of the board of Stanford University. The investments of these investors ranged anywhere from $500,000 to $30 million, but their diversity speaks to the complexity of the networks that were woven inside and outside of Enron.

3.3.   Networking Strategy

A close examination reveals that Enron epitomizes a network form of organization on various dimensions. Organizationally, Enron was divided into many different parts and activities—e.g., Enron Wholesale Services (EWS), Enron Energy Services (EES), Enron Transportation Services (ETS), Enron Broadband Services (EBS), and so on. On the outside, Enron had links with a huge number of organizations, which consisted of subsidiaries—e.g., Enron Communications (ENE), Azurix Corp. (water unit), etc.—as well as partnerships and alliances—e.g., LJM1/2, JEDI partnership with Calpers (California State-employees' Pension Fund), Raptors (a partnership with Ciena Corp. and Cisco Systems to implement Enron Intelligent Network, and partnerships with Global Crossing and Qwest for trading bandwidth, etc.). Enron was surrounded by a huge network of special purpose entities (SPE), many of which were accounting or legal artifacts with unique and innovative relationships with the company. Swartz and Watkins (2003) report and portray the complexity of these networks in great detail.

Technologically, Enron was among the most heavily wired companies of the 1990s. Many years after its ascendance, the up-to-date quality of Enron technology can still be a point of envy for many firms in the U.S. and around the world. Enron operated on a global scale. Its operations extended throughout the Americas, Europe, Africa, and many parts of Asia (Share, 1999). The Internet was the main medium for these operations. It is reported that 60% of Enron trades were done over the Internet by Enron Online (EOL), which was able to provide real-time prices for as many as 30 trades per minute, increasing the average number of trades for each trader to five per day instead of the traditional three per week (Maselli, 2001).

Financially, a large group of major and minor banks and investments firms were linked to Enron in various ways. The multiplicity and variety of these links provides a complex picture of the financial networks surrounding the company. Very briefly, while the security firms (J. P. Morgan Chase, Merrill Lynch, Citigroup, and others) were trading Enron's stocks through their brokerage divisions, their analysts were involved in evaluating the company's performance, and their managers, sometimes having personally invested in Enron, provided consultation advice to its executives. These multiple, often conflicting, links generated a complex web of inconsistent relationships the implications of which has become the subject of much legal inquiry and criminal investigation (Chaffin, 2002, Creswell, 2002, Greider, 2002, Oppel, 2002, Wayne, 2002b). What was often portrayed as a lender-borrower relationship was, indeed, a multivalent relationship that, on the one hand, forced Enron to meet Wall Street expectations and, on the other, turned the banks into promotional agents and propaganda mouthpieces of Enron.

To make this picture even more complicated, there were major differences in the relations of Enron with different classes of investors and creditors. While big creditors had at least partial access to insider information, minor creditors did not enjoy that privileged status. These relationships followed different developmental paths during the years. Big creditors, having become heavily involved with Enron's finances (mainly through inflated interest rates), had much at stake to maintain the status quo by promoting Enron's reputation. Thus, when the situation started to deteriorate, the big creditors basically collaborated in false image making with Enron. "If they stopped pedaling," to use the apt analogy suggested in Greider (2002), "the bicycle would fall over." One aspect of this accelerating dynamics was an increased consolidation between the banks and Enron, a point of significance in later accusations of insider trading for banks (ibid). Minor investors' relationship with Enron, on the other hand, followed an almost opposite tack. Although they were likewise lured into cooperative investment by the promise of grand profits, their links with Enron gradually degenerated into deception and victimization, as manifested in the pursuing legal investigations.

In sum, according to various criteria, Enron can be justifiably deemed as a paradigmatic example of a network organization. In fact, a comparison with Cisco, which is featured as the prime example of a successful network enterprise in Castells (2001), would demonstrate that Enron is no less exemplary than Cisco of a network organization (see Table 1).

3.4. Enron versus Cisco

Castells (2001) highlights Cisco Systems as exemplary of the transformation toward the network enterprise described earlier (Section 1). This assessment is based on the information about the kinds of networks that support Cisco's activities in production, manufacturing, supply, accounting, etc. It may be instructive, therefore, to compare this data with similar data about Enron (see Table 1; the features of comparison are selected according to what Castells has considered significant in the Cisco case; all the data about Cisco is from Castells (2001), and about Enron is from various sources listed as reference).

The information in this table is not exhaustive, nor are the comparisons unique in terms of the items mapped between the two companies. The point

Table 5-1. Comparison between Cisco Systems and Enron in Terms of Networking

Feature	Cisco	Enron
Activity	Making of Internet backbone equipment (85% of global market of routers)	Trading of commodities in the derivative market
Internet Sales	Cisco Connection Online (CCO)	Enron Online (EOL)
Online sales	90% of orders: $40 mil. /day (first half of 2000)	60% of trade: $\sim$ \$10,000 mil. /day (1999)
Extranet	Manufact. Connection Online (MCO) 90% outsourced	EnronCredit.com
Inventory System	Dynamic Info System	Clickpaper.com
Employee Intranet	Cisco Employee Connection (instant communication across the globe)	1. SAP 2. Dealbench.com 3. eHROnline: human resources 4. Web portal for company lawyers
Accounting Intranet	Procedures streamlined (allows up-to-date books)	Part of SAP e.g. CATS (cross-application time sheet)
Infrastructure	?	Enron's Intelligent Network (EIN) (All-IP backbone)
Partnerships	Merged 70 companies between 1993 and 2000	Had more than 870 partnerships

is to demonstrate that Enron is no less exemplary than Cisco of a networked e-business enterprise, for what counts as the essence of e-business, according to Castells, is "the Internet-based, interactive, networked connection between producers, consumers, and service providers" (Castells, 2001). And Enron fits this picture very faithfully.

4.   PREVALENT NETWORK THINKING

As I mentioned earlier, various authors from various perspectives have written about the network model. Among them, Castells' account stands out as a grand narrative of a new mode of production based on the network form of social organization and empowered by new ICT. This narrative, as we suggested, provides the background assumptions and the logic behind most other accounts of network organization. According to Castells, we live in a new economy, characterized by three fundamental features—namely, its being (2000):

1. Informational: the capacity of generating knowledge and processing/ managing information determine the productivity and competitiveness of firms;
2. Global: its core, strategic activities (finance, R&D, trade, services, etc.) have the capacity to work as a unit on a global scale;
3. Networked: it is based on a new form of economic organization, the network enterprise.

What is new about this economy, according to Castells, is the emergence of new ICT, especially the recent shift from computer-centered to networked-diffused technologies, which gives rise to a "virtuous circle" where the use of knowledge-based, information technologies leads to an increasing generation of knowledge that, in turn, calls for further employment of those technologies. These technologies have also brought about serious transformations in the nature of work toward flexible schedules, of a culture organized around electronic media, of a politics that is media-centered and very expensive (hence, corruptible), and of a nation-state whose legitimacy is undermined, turning it into a "network state" that shares power with other local, national, and international institutions. Most prominent among these various networks, however, is the network enterprise, characterized by Castells in the following manner (see Figure 2):

> This is not a network of enterprises. It is a network made from either firms or segments of firms, and/or from internal segmentation of firms. Large corporations are internally decentralized as networks. Small and medium businesses are connected in networks. These networks connect among themselves on specific business projects, and switch to another network as soon as the project is finished. Major corporations work in a strategy of changing alliances and partnerships, specific to a given product, process, time, and space. Furthermore, these cooperations are based increasingly on sharing of information. These are information networks, which, in the limit, link up suppliers and customers through one firm, with this firm being essentially an intermediary of supply and demand, collecting a fee for its ability to process information (2000: 10–11).

This characterization leads Castells to postulates that, "The unit of this production process is not the firm but the business project" (ibid). Furthermore, he bequeaths the network with "an unprecedented combination of flexibility and task implementation, of coordinated decision making, and decentralized execution..." (2000: p. 15). Finally, having suggested that networks work on a binary logic of inclusion/exclusion, he predicts that "information networks, through competition, gradually eliminate other organizational forms, rooted in a different social logic" (p. 16).

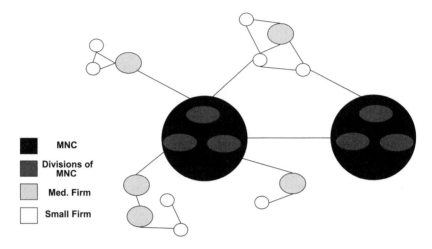

Figure 5-2. Castells' picture of the network enterprise.

Table 5-2. Common background assumptions among accounts of network organizations

1. Market orientation in economic philosophy
2. Trust as the dominant relational modality
3. Flexibility in response to market demands
4. Adaptability in dealing with changing environment
5. Informationalism in terms of mode of production
6. Deregulation in legal approach
7. Internationalism in scope

In short, Castells' account is provides a set of elements that often play the role of background assumptions in most other accounts of the network organization (see Table 2).

Organization theorists have also written extensively about network organizations. Although this notion is far from being agreed upon among different authors, the core intuitions converge on a set of common features. Baker (1992) describes the network organization as one that "can flexibly construct a unique set of internal and external linkages for each unique project." Miles and Snow (1995) portray the "voluntary, cooperative network" as one that is "de-layered, highly flexible, and controlled by market mechanisms rather than administrative procedures." Van Alstyne (1997), comparing and contrasting the computational, economic, and societal metaphors of network organizations, finds "collective purpose" as a distinguishing design element of networks from centralized organization, and emphasizes the role of "reputations, commitments, and trust" in their functioning. In short, as Fulk (2001) has summed up,

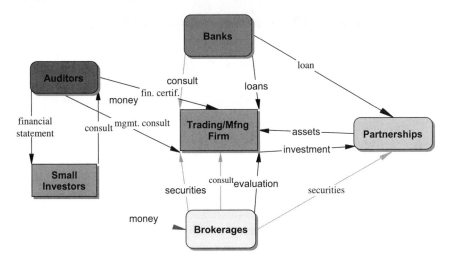

Figure 5-3. A multivalent negotiated network.

Table 5-3. Common themes among accounts of network organizations

1. Cooperation in inter-firm connections
2. Voluntarism as the dominant inter-firm relationships
3. Team spirit in intra-firm relations
4. Decentralization in organizational structure
5. Empowerment in management style
6. Transparency of operational mechanisms

a burst of theory and analysis has established "the network as the most important emergent organizational structure and the pre-eminent metaphor for sense making by academics and practitioners alike." The common focus among these views is the *flexible*, *voluntary*, and *cooperative* character of network organizations due to their extensive internal and external linkages (cf. Grandori and Soda, 1995, for a review; see Table 3).

5. THE MANAGERIAL DIMENSIONS OF NETWORKING

The themes and assumptions listed in Tables 2 and 3 provide the dominant framework for thinking about network organizations. In this section, I would like to examine those themes and assumptions against facts about Enron. The purpose, as I mentioned earlier, is to discern the potentials and pitfalls presented by a networking strategy, and to draw appropriate lessons for the management of network organizations.

5.1. Managing Alliances: Trust or Antagonism?

[N]etworks are evolving that possess characteristics similar in part to the Japanese *keiretsu*—an organizational collective based on cooperation and mutual shareholding among a group of manufacturers, suppliers, and trading and finance companies. (Miles and Snow, 1992)

Cooperation among firms in different forms and capacities—asset, technology, expertise, information, etc.—is the cornerstone of the network enterprise and what has motivated its creation in the first place. To be sure, a company like Enron depends for its functioning on close cooperation with a huge number of partnerships, investment banks, creditors, analysts, auditors, and so on. These functional links would presumably lend support to the validity of the central theme of inter-firm cooperation and trust. There is, in other words, a certain degree of truth to the above assertion by Miles and Snow. But to conclude from this that cooperation is the only mode of inter-firm relationship is rather simplistic. In fact, Miles and Snow (1992) consider the possibility of non-cooperative behavior, but underplay it with optimism: "Of course, the fact that network linkages are external does not guarantee that they will always be efficacious to each of the parties, but it does push the parties toward performance-based equity." This "push" does not seem to have prevailed in the case of Enron.

There is compelling evidence in favor of persistent non-cooperative and even antagonistic links between Enron and its affiliates. A famous example of this antagonism is the case of JEDI, Enron's partnership with Calper (California Pension and Retirement Fund), in which Enron invested $500 million in JEDI2 by first cashing $383 millions worth of JEDI1, and used Chewco Investments as an "outsider" to pay $383 million and take the place of Calper. In light of this, the multiple relationships between Enron and Calper could be depicted as one where cooperation constitutes only one link, and others of which can be characterized as manipulation, deception, game playing, and so on (see Figure 4). Similarly, the relationship between Enron and the auditing firm Arthur Anderson had multiple links such as auditing, consulting, and management advice (Figure 5). Interestingly, all of these could be characterized as "cooperation" but, as it has become increasingly clear, they involve contradictory senses of cooperation based on a conflict of interest (Barboza, 2002). Thus, any story that takes cooperation as the only mode will be pregnant with contradiction.

Finally, and most complicated, is the relation between Enron, investment banks, and brokerage firms. Here the inter-firm links take a truly multivalent, nuanced, and dynamic character. The multiplicity of links between Enron and various bodies in the investment banks could only be understood through a fine-grained analysis that exposes the details of the internal structure of the

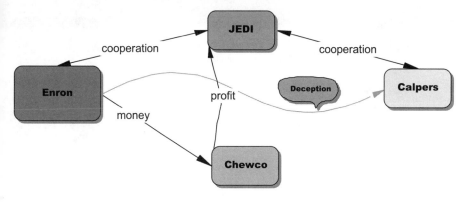

Figure 5-4. Deceptive links with partners.

firms. Very briefly, while the security firms (J. P. Morgan Chase, Merrill Lynch, Citigroup, and others) were trading Enron's stocks through their brokerage divisions, their analysts were involved in evaluating the company's performance, and their managers, sometimes having personally invested in Enron, provided consultation advice to its executives (Figure 5c). These multiple, often conflicting, links generated a complex web of inconsistent relationships the implications of which has become the subject of much legal inquiry and investigation (Barboza, 2002, Chaffin, 2002, Creswell, 2002, Greider, 2002, New York Department of Law, 2002, Oppel, 2002, Wayne, 2002a, 2002b). What was often portrayed as a lender-borrower relationship was, indeed, a complicated link that forced Enron to meet Wall Street expectations, on the one hand, and turned the banks into promotional agents and propaganda mouthpieces of Enron, on the other.

A prominent example of such relationships is the deal made between Enron and Merrill Lynch in December of 1999, according to which Merrill Lynch allowed Enron to book a $60 million profit. This made it possible for Enron to report $259 million 4th-quarter profit, or 31 cents a share, and to meet analysts' forecasts, as a result of which its share price climbed 27 percent. Enron executives benefited tremendously (besides bonuses, twenty top executives sold $82.6 million in stock after January's earning announcement). Merrill Lynch reportedly received $8 million for its role in this deal (for the cancellation of the contract in April 2000) (Barboza, 2002). At the same time, Merrill Lynch's sales force was promoting Enron's stock, and the bank's private equity group was asking investors to contribute over $250 mil to one of Enron's off-balance partnerships. Arthur Anderson auditors were also aware of these transactions all along, and despite consideration of the possibility of a restatement, did not ask for it after the cancellation of the contract.

The above analysis lends support to our suspicion about the dominantly cooperative character of the links as the modus operandi of network organiza-

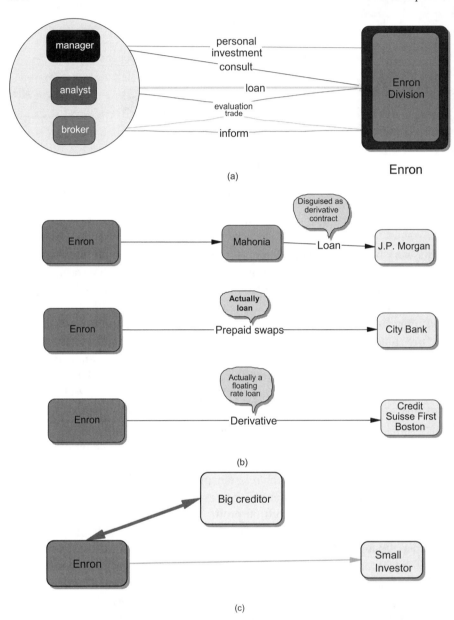

Figure 5-5. (a) Multivalent links with brokerage firms; (b) Complex contracts with banks; (c) Nuances links with investors and creditors.

tions (Whetten, 1981; cf. Van Alstyne, 1997). The links of a network are often multivalent, nuanced, and asymmetric in nature, and as such have the potential to be used by partners dominantly for cooperative and trustful purposes or for antagonistic and deceptive intentions.

5.2. Managing the Stakeholders: Transparency or Secrecy?

Even when a network's components are commonly owned, the essential structure of the organization is external—an exoskeleton of clearly specified, objectively structured contracts any buy-and-sell agreements that guide interactions rather than internal schedules, procedures, and routines. (Miles and Snow, 1992)

Transparency of operations and practices is another aspect of the network organization highlighted in the cooperative model. Miles and Snow (1992) consider transparency and voluntarism, as "two unique characteristics of the network form." They assert that "the essential relationships among components are external (and thus highly visible to all parties)." While considering the possibility that "attempts at personal gain may be made," therefore, they postulate that "the behavior will be much more transparent." The authors contrast this situation with that of older organizational forms where, for example, "cost data and/or performance measures may be manipulated by simply changing accounting conventions—such as the way in which overhead expenses are accumulated and assigned."

This assessment, again, is only partially true. The externality of the relations among firms can contribute to the transparency of transactions, but they do not guarantee it. And nowhere is the lack of guarantee better demonstrated than the notorious accounting practices of organizations such as Enron—practices that, despite Miles and Snow's hypothesis, are much more open-ended and manipulable in the network context, and were at the heart of Enron's networking strategy. In partnerships, for example, the common practice in Enron consisted of two rather orthogonal cycles, as follows: In one of them, Enron shifted failed businesses onto the partnership's accounts, and moved some assets, such as a water plant or a broadband unit, into the partnership. In the other, it borrowed loans, funded by investors such as J. P. Morgan, and booked them as earnings on assets. Accounting procedures and rules played a critical role in making these possible.

False accounting practices seem to be not rare in American business—a fact that has recently become the topic of wide public debate and policy-making (Altman, 2002a, Coffee, 2002, Gosselin, 2002, Morgensen, 2002). In fact, as Mulford and Comiskey (2002) have shown, the possibility for carrying out such practices is built into the accounting standards, providing corporations a leeway to play "financial numbers game" without breaching legal limits. What makes these undetectable is the so-called "impenetrability" of the numbers (Altman, 2002a). More seriously, however, the transactions in the derivatives market are of such a sophisticated nature that they make it difficult for people to understand them, let alone detect possible flaws in them. It was the blurry character of such transactions, some analysts suggest, that allowed Enron to post in its balance sheets banks' loans as "asset from price risk management" and their repayments as "liabilities from price risk management"—potentially misleading terms that can only attract the attention of a very alert expert. Enron, as some experts suggest, "certainly used complexity to its advantage," but the complexity was of such a nature that it finally imperiled the system (Altman, 2002b, Sloan et al., 2001).

Discussing the current accounting rules, Coffee (2002) says: "Enron was ingenious about trying ways to exploit the ambiguities and the limitations of those rules. They in particular tried to treat the partnerships as independent entities, even though they might have liability for it." He then explains how Enron took advantage of the rules "by finding third parties that would buy a 5 percent equity interest in Enron affiliates, thereby allowing the liabilities of those affiliates to be kept off the balance sheets." This reveals that a certain degree of independence on the part of the affiliates was not only real, it was also desirable for Enron.

In view of these facts, it would be fair to conclude that not only the network form of enterprise does not guarantee visibility and transparency, it creates new possibilities for hidden and covert, albeit "legal," transactions that are much more difficult to detect due to their complexity. Therefore, the proper managing of such networks calls for an explicit effort to implement mechanisms that promote visibility and minimize secrecy.

5.3. Managing the Employees: Empowerment or Coercion?

The organization itself has changed it organizational model, to adapt to the conditions of unpredictability ushered in by rapid economic and technological change. *The main shift can be characterized as the shift from vertical bureaucracies to the horizontal corporation.* (Castells, 1996, p. 164)

Network organizations are often described as lean or flat hierarchies, where management's major role is "to create learning-oriented partnerships within the firm and among network members," and leadership is viewed as "a shared responsibility among colleagues, not as a superior-subordinate relationship" (Miles and Snow, 1995). Advocating a "human investment philosophy"—to be opposed to the "human relations" and "human resources" views of earlier decades—these authors mention as a prime example of its real implementation a small computer graphics company. But they believe that the same approach would work in large companies, "though, of course, ... (it) poses a considerable challenge." Cases such as Enron, however, suggest that, more than a challenge, this might to be a dilemma.

The dilemma has to do with the dual aspects of decentralization as an organizational principle—namely, the balance between participation/flexibility and coordination/stability. Different authors have pointed this out, albeit from different perspectives. Murray and Wilmott (1997), for instance, discuss the possibility that "the establishment of quasi-autonomous profit centers... may have the unintended effect of fragmenting and unbalancing established structures" (p. 169). (Foss, 2001), on the other hand, has invoked the problem of "selective intervention" to discuss the organizational and psychological barriers that lie on the road to full-fledged decentralization. Benveniste (1994, p. 74) discusses the difficulty of avoiding what he calls "articulation errors" (roughly, the mismatch between goals and potentials) in decentralized environments. Castells (1996, p. 166) also mentions this difficulty, but nevertheless prescribes the "horizontal corporation" as "a dynamic and strategically planned network of self-programmed, self-directed units based on decentralization, participation, and coordination." This prescription seems not to have worked in Enron.

Enron is often described as a highly decentralized corporation, with its executives pushing decentralization to an extreme, encouraging business units to compete rather than cooperate (Beritano, 2002). But this policy had its flip side, and that was the segmentation of the organization into non-cooperative units set up as "silos" or "islands." An expert once described Enron as a "compartmentalized structure like the CIA," where each department does its own job without knowledge of others (PBS News Hour, Feb. 8, 2002).

In correlation with the above, Enron is reported to have "a go-go corporate culture," with traditional business controls cast away (Banerjee et al., 2002). This culture—"from top officers who insisted they were unaware of financial details to a relaxed attitude about conflicts that let executives sit on both sides of multimillion-dollar deals"—figure heavily in many accounts of Enron's collapse (ibid). Some experts suggest that the "go-go culture" of the late 1990s created a "casino atmosphere" inside many corporations, in which people tended to disregard the issues of accountability for fraudulent behavior (Johnson, 2002). A notorious example of this behavior is the LJM deals in which Enron's CFO is reported to have personally profited $30 millions in a matter of a few weeks (Barboza and Schwartz, 2002). Examples such as these, according to reports, abound to tens and hundreds.

In regards to employee empowerment, Murray and Wilmott (1997) have observed that:

> While the rhetoric of empowerment is used liberally by commentators and practitioners, there is also a good deal of coercion in companies experimenting with networking. This may be of the 'cooperate or else' form of coercion; or it may be more subtle and insidious but no less coercive. At the heart of the matter is the employment relationship. (p. 175)

In addition to Cruver's autobiographical account (2002) of direct coercion in Enron, signs of more subtle kinds of forbidding behavior have become public. For example, reports by employees about instances of fake floor activity during visits by analysts (Corn, 2002) could be interpreted as such, if we grant that an employee will not normally volunteer for such behavior unless there is some positive or negative incentive (reward or coercion). A more commonplace instance of coercion, however, could be traced in the daily activities of traders who were made to engage in false, circular trades, known variably as Fat Boy, Death Star, and so on with other energy trading companies, in order to show a high volume of trading in the market (Barboza, 2002, Ekbia, 2004).

In sum, these observations lead to the conclusion that there are flip sides to decentralization, team spirit, and empowerment the potential for which is built into the very structure of the network organizations. A network form, in and of itself, does not bring about team working and employee empowerment.

5.4.   Managing the Market: Competition or Manipulation?

Financial markets, by and large, are outside anyone's control. They have become a sort of automaton, with sudden movements that do not follow a strict economic logic, but a logic of chaotic complexity, resulting from the interaction of millions of decisions reacting in real time, in a global span, to information turbulences from various origins—including economic news concerning profits and earnings. Or their anticipation. Or the reversal of what was expected. (Castells, 2001, p. 87)

A key background assumption in theories of "new economy" is the shift from mass production to flexible production based on competitiveness and productivity (Castells, 1996, p. 154–156). According to theorists of this economy, the resilient presence of small and medium firms, as "agents of innovation and sources of job creation," has given rise to a market that is pretty much out of anyone's control. In other words, the behavior of the market emerges from numerous interactions among millions of "factors"—decisions, news, gossip, expectations, etc.—turning it into an "automaton" that works on the principle of "Darwinian correction" (Castells, 2001, p. 88).

This account of the new market, while partially true, suffers from two major problems. First, it does not address what Castells himself considers "the real questions"—namely, "when, how much, and why" market values go up or down (ibid, p. 79). Second, and more importantly, it invests too much hope and optimism in the efficacy of the Darwinian mechanisms of the market. Both problems found violent expressions in Enron's activities in the energy and bandwidth markets.

The involvement of Enron, and other energy trading companies, in the California energy crisis of 2000 has become increasingly evident (Krugman, 2002a, 2002b, Oppel, 2002; see Ekbia in press for a detailed account), and seems to be the tip of an economic iceberg whose full scope is yet to be determined by the possible unraveling of further information. It is reported that these companies were heavily involved in circular transactions where they bought electric power—in fact, the derivative or "capacity"—from suppliers for putative consumption outside California, creating an environment of artificial shortage, and selling back the same commodity at a much higher price in the California energy market. A similar pattern of activity is discerned in the bandwidth trading market, but for the sheer purpose of creating the false image of high trading volume in the market and affecting stock values (Barboza, 2002)[2].

While the legal aspects of such activities might still be debated, their implications for the present topic are rather obvious—namely, despite the optimism about the autonomy of the market, instances such as these reveal that the prevailing complexities of network enterprises have created ample opportunities for intrusion and meddling in the market. The Darwinian correction mechanism, likewise, has limited efficacy in dealing with deviant behavior, especially if we do not discount, as is usually done, the significance of timely correction. In the volatile markets of today, as some analysts and experts have noticed, the timing of response is of essence, although not the whole issue (Morgenson, 2002).

In short, as Castells and others have emphasized, current market mechanisms have played a key role in the creation of the network enterprise. A good understanding of the former, therefore, is a crucial prerequisite for analyzing the latter. However, invoking vague terms such as "information turbulence," which put agency in the hands of unknown market elements, does not seem to carry us too far in that direction. A more appropriate and useful concept in this context, I believe, is "information asymmetry," which is extensively discussed by market economists, but sociological and information-theoretic accounts of which are still in the waiting. The managerial lesson, however, is rather obvious: It is as much wrong (and in the long run fruitless) to try to manipulate the market through network-type collusions as it is to rely totally on the Darwinian mechanisms of the market to guide the enterprise.

5.5.   Managing the Regulators: Social Engagement or Political Pressure?

Essentially, deregulation unleashes entrepreneurial behavior, which in turn raises the level of competition. Often deregulation creates new outsourcing

---

2   Energy trading companies such as Enron are not featured in Castells' (2001) account of the "new economy" and network organizations, except in a passing comment when, discussing the 2001 downturn, he says: "Only a few companies escaped devaluation in the stock market, particularly utility companies, well known to Californians for their impeccable business practices" (p. 89).

opportunities—as seen, for example, in the increased privatization of public corporations and agencies in many countries. Most important, deregulation reduces margins, and this requires companies to maximize returns on all assets. (Miles, Snow, and Coleman, 1992)

Closely related to the theme of market competition are issues of deregulation and privatization, which are usually brought up in the context of developed and developing economies, respectively, as effective mechanisms for enhancing productivity and competitiveness in the global market. The dominant trend is to demote the role of the state in the economic arena. Castells shares with this trend the conviction about the important role of deregulation in the current economy, but differs from it in giving the state a decisive economic role at the same time (Castells, 1996, p. 90). He justifies this by the interdependence and the openness, on an international scale, of markets, which necessitates the close engagement of governments as the strategic planners of national economies. On the other hand, he argues that the power of nation-state is dispersed among many other organizations that undermine the central role of the government (2000).

It is now public knowledge that Enron had established a strong web of political influence in all branches of the government (Institute for Policy Studies, 2002, Lobby Watch, 2002, Salant, 2001) as well as the media (Sherman, 2002), mainly aimed at deregulating the energy market. It is also known that energy trading companies used the deregulated market to raise margins and prices. This network of influence did not, ironically, work for Enron under critical circumstances (Naím, 2002), confirming Castells' assessment that the current economy "is indeed a highly politicized economy" (ibid). But, more significantly, it also nullified optimistic expectations such as expressed in the above excerpt that deregulation raises the level of competition, reduces margins, etc.

In light of this, it would be fair to expect network enterprises to play an increasing role in broader social issues and to accordingly accept more responsibility. On the other hand, political pressure, of the kind exercised by Enron, does not necessarily serve the long-term interests of a network enterprise.

5.6.   Managing IT and Information: Potential or Panacea?

The new economy, spearheaded by e-business, is not an on-line economy, but an economy powered by information technology, dependent on self-programmable labor, and organized around computer networks. (Castells, 2001, p. 99)

Information and knowledge, according to many accounts, is the hallmark of the current economy (Castells, 1996, 2001), and information and communication technology is featured as having more than one role in today's business and organization (Fulk and Desanctis, 1998)—namely, as:

- The medium of coordination, communication, and interaction among network components
- The infrastructure or the nervous system of the network that makes possible fast and vast response to market demands, permitting economies of scale and scope
- A means for the storage, processing, and transfer of data
- A vehicle of innovation and competitiveness
- A tool for strategic planning via simulation and modeling[3]

Enron, as we have seen, took full advantage of these capacities in almost all aspects of its business and organizational practice. The interesting question to ask is: What role, if any, does information technology, in each of the above capacities, play in the early success and late failure of a firm like Enron?

Expert opinions do not provide an accurate answer to this question. During the success period, almost everyone praised Enron for its innovative approach to IT application (Business Wire, 1992, Durgin, 1994, PR Newswire, 1997, Dow Jones News Service, 1998, Hanks, 1999, Kranhold, 1999, Wilson, 1999, Kirkpatrick, 2000, Maselli, 2001, Poruban, 2001), but opinions tend to diverge in the aftermath of Enron's collapse. Some IT experts point out the issues of incompatibility among different IT systems and applications, while others emphasize usability (e.g., of a $2 million software package called Quest Spotlight for database monitoring) and inconsistency—as one IT specialist put it: "Enron IT was as cutting edge as it was byzantine... They ran a $100 billion company on Access and Excel" (see Beritano, 2002). A more contextual view links the failure of the technology to a lack of planning on the part of management, which resulted in interruption of information processes or in disorganization of data ("islands of data"; ibid). The launching of the SAP project in 2000 seemed to have begun a policy reversal in the direction of a centralized management of IT, coming to partial fruition in 2001. Some specialists have suggested that this could have reversed the sequence of events had it been started earlier.

The common thread among these reports is that Enron's management had not planned its ICT, and this resulted in the depletion of resources, the interruption of information processes, and the disorganization of data ("islands of data"; ibid). To be sure, ICT contributed to Enron operations in terms of speed, scope, scale, and even pubic relations (Ekbia, in press), but they did not have a decisive impact on the company's direction. As Murray and Wilmott (1997, p. 167) have argued, "It is one thing to acknowledge the presence of ICT. It

---

[3] Castells (1996) discusses these aspects of information technology in different places, but emphasizes that the distinctive character of informationalism—the current socio-economic system that followed industrialism—is "its superior capacity to process symbols" (p. 92). This is a thesis a discussion of which would take us astray from the present topic. We hope to address it elsewhere.

is quite another to argue that they are radically transforming the structure of organizations and societies." The failure of Enron confirms once again the lesson that technology by itself does not drive organizational change (Kling and Lamb, 2000, Symon, 2000).

What's more, we argue that network organizations do not, in principle, depend upon computer networks or the Internet. Take, for example, Hollywood production companies or general contractors who remodel or renovate homes. Due to their project-oriented character, these enterprises have most of the characteristics outlined for the new network enterprise, but are in no serious way dependent upon digital information technologies. Castells correctly points out that the network model is a traditional form of organization with a long history in different industries and different parts of the world. However, he suggest, what is new about the emerging network enterprise is its informational character that closely binds it to the advances in ICT. We argue, to the contrary, that those network enterprises that extensively employ such technologies do not solely depend on the Internet for expediting communication. Rather, they depend upon proprietary networks, telephone networks as well as the Internet for this purpose. In short, the dependence of network enterprises, even in their recent emerging forms, on information technology and the Internet in particular is far from established.

5.7.   Managing Global Partners: Fairness versus Imposition

[A]llliances of various kinds have given rise to the "stateless" corporation in which people, assets, and transactions move freely across international borders. (Miles, Snow, and Coleman, 1992)

Last, but not least, among the central themes in accounts of network organization, is "globalization." This is a multifaceted theme that touches on many issues from social development and economic justice to world politics and multi-culturalism. Castells (1996) has, in fact, covered all of these topics, and we can only touch on issues relevant to present topic here. Castells' main hypothesis in this respect is that, "as the process of globalization progresses, organizational forms evolve from *multinational enterprises* to *international networks*, actually bypassing the so-called "transnationals" that belong more to the world of mythical representation..." (p. 192). Arguing against the idea that transnational corporations are "citizens of the world economy," Castells suggests that "networks are asymmetrical" in regards to the international distribution of wealth and power, but suggests that no single element can impose its diktat because of the "logic of the network" (pp. 192–193). Unfortunately, Castells does not explain how this "logic" overcomes (or even ameliorates) asymmetry and prevents imposition. The case of Enron, indeed, shows that this does not happen.

Documented reports are available that clearly show the one-sided and im-positional character of many projects carried out by Enron around the world, their adverse social and political impacts, and the role of U.S. and local gov-ernments as well as international agencies in implementing them (Wysham and Vallette, 2002). It is suggested further that many of these adversities were sim-ply ignored until their consequences began to be manifested in the American scene. All of these indicate the unfounded nature of the notion of a "stateless firm" invoked by Miles et al., and the impotence of the networking "logic," as invoked by Castells, in preventing power asymmetries in global relations.

The topic of globalization is too vast to be satisfactorily discussed here, but the case of Enron makes it clear that reckless behaviors of the kind mani-fested by Enron around the globe do not pass unheeded and come back to bite perpetuators.

6.   MANAGING THE NETWORK ENTERPRISE: POTENTIALS AND PITFALLS

What emerges from the above observations is a picture of network orga-nization that is much more complex and variegated than the prevalent SCN. While the themes outlined in Table 3 might be central in theorizing some as-pects of the network enterprise, they certainly are not the only conceivable ones. Similarly, the background assumptions outlined in Table 2 hold up in some cases, but not in others. In fact, as we see in the case of Enron, many of them are harshly and explicitly violated in practice, displaying a great deal of variability among cases. To be able to deal with this variability, we should consider the full range of possibilities provided by the network organization, such as outlined in Table 4. This table portrays the network enterprise, in the most general case, as a collection of heterogeneous entities (firms, inter- and intra-firm bodies) with multiple links, which can vary in terms of character and strength (see Figure 3). The character of the links could be anything from to-tal cooperation, trust, and voluntarism to outright antagonism, deception, and coercion.

This picture poses a huge challenge for the management of network en-terprises. It shows that this form of organization involves many different di-mensions, which vary in terms of nuance, balance, and strength, generating a spectrum of possibilities. According to this picture, the leaders of network enterprises should not only be aware of these dimensions and the potentials and pitfalls that they provide, they should have a well-defined strategy to po-sition their organizations on these various spectra. This means that the precise character of the network enterprise is up to its leadership. This is especially important because of the opportunity for greater leverage in a network econ-omy.

Table 5-4. Themes and Assumptions Characteristic of MNN

Themes		Background Assumptions	
Cooperation	Antagonism	Market orientation	Market manipulation
Voluntarism	Opportunism	Trust	Deception
Team Spirit	Individualism	Deregulation	Collusion
Decentralization	Centralization	Flexibility	Rigidity
Empowerment	Coercion	Adaptability	Gaming behavior
Transparency	Secrecy	Informationalism	Strategic misinformation
		Internationalism	Network protectionism

These observations are borne out by some of the prominent examples of network organization. Recent accounts of Cisco's acquisition policy, for instance, confirm the main premise of our analysis about the nuanced and multivalent character of the links in network organization, even in the most celebrated cases of success. In their detailed analysis of the implementation of this policy before and after acquisition, Mayer and Kenney (2002) emphasize the importance not only of due diligence in the acquisition process, but also of the many dimensions of socio-cultural similarity between the acquired firms (usually high-technology start-ups) and the acquiring firm (Cisco in this case). In a recent acquisition reported in the media (namely, that of Linksys), Cisco has adopted a novel strategy that gives a lot of autonomy to the acquired firm in order to inhibit, among other things, the "meddling" of Cisco employees in the affairs of the subsidiary (Wall Street Journal, 2003). Such examples show that the role of conflicts and mismatches goes way beyond day-to-day trivialities to attain strategic significance. Companies like Cisco implement effective networks, not because they neglect or streamline these aspects, but mainly because they incorporate them in their strategic planning. Likewise, companies like Enron structurally fail, mainly because of their meddling in the affairs of other network participants (e.g., partners, small investors, auditing firms) and the meddling of some other participants (e.g., large banks, analysts, etc.) in Enron affairs. This is not to say that there are not other differences between Enron and Cisco—e.g., in terms of organizational culture, strategy, ethics, industry, and so on. It is to say that the story of Enron is, among other things, a structural failure under the tensions generated by internal and external antagonism, mistrust, secrecy, and so on.

7.   CONCLUSION

In an interesting coincidence, a recent special issue of The Academy of Management Executive (2003) on "building effective networks" features both

Miles and Snow (Ketchen, 2003) and Sherron Watkins (Pearce, 2003), former Enron vice president. What is interesting about these reports is the sharp contrast of perspectives represented in them. Whereas, in harmony with their previous views, Miles and Snow reiterate "the use of 'dynamic networks' to expand reach and flexibility of the firm," Watkins is concerned about the widespread lack of trust in business leaders (which is at its lowest point in decades). It is this difference in perspectives that the present paper tries to highlight and accommodate.

Sociologists such as Castells have made network organizations the centerpiece of their theorizing about network societies. Castells' emphasis on network societies leads us to feel comfortable with networked organizations and multinational firms. While he points out conflicts (in markets, for instance), his overall portrayal of these organizations is one of "well-behaved" entities. From what we have learned about Enron, it is amazing to see simultaneously how much Enron fits Castells' characterization of the network enterprise "as an intermediary that collects a fee for its ability to process information" and how much it fails to show the other attributes suggested by Castells and taken for granted in the popular literature on this form of organization. Common among these are assumptions of cooperation between all nodes, together with normal forms of "due diligence" and honesty when participants are in a relationship such as auditing. Furthermore, there is usually a narrow focus on the "production organization," whereas the functioning network may also include partners such as venture capitalists, investment bankers, and even competitors.

The reality of network organizations is much more complex than the typical conceptions of network organizations. While the network form is an advance over post-bureaucratic organizations, it is more convoluted, complicated, and pregnant with paradoxes. It might be flat, flexible, and team-oriented, but the flip side of these, as Sennett (1998) has argued, is uncertainty, the absence of deeply rooted trust and commitment, and the superficiality of teamwork. "How can mutual loyalties and commitments be sustained," Sennett asks, "in institutions which are constantly breaking apart or continually being redesigned?" (ibid). By the same token, the new economy might thrive in an unregulated and decentralized environment but, as Sassen (1998, 2001) has shown, it has also brought about expanded central control and a concentration of power in certain metropolitan areas of the world. It is questions and paradoxes like these that we have tried to address here and to capture in the proposed model.

This broadened perspective leads to a much more realistic picture of the network enterprise. The inclusion of the contradictory aspects shown in Table 4 above is the major advantage of the present study. This analysis does not apply only or even primarily to organizational crime. It may be especially applicable to new organizations or to firms that are operating in new and ill-understood industries or with new or poorly defined business models and practices. Whether we consider cases such as Amazon, Cisco, Walmart, and big pharmaceuticals, or take large-scale corporate scandals and failures such as Dynergy, Enron, Tyco, Worldcom, and so on, the major results of the current analysis equally apply. On the present view, Cisco and Enron are different, not because one instantiates an ideal network organization and the other does not, but because they fall on opposite ends of the spectrum on a number of important dimensions. The managerial implications of this view are also notable. As Porter (1998, p. 87) has concluded from his study of "clusters," executives must extend their thinking beyond what goes on inside their own organizations; "strategy must also address what goes on outside." Our analysis leads to a similar conclusion. In addition, our study suggests that managers should pay specific attention to these various dimensions, making sure that their organizations fall on the proper point on the spectrum. Only then can an organization reap the fruits of having a network structure.

REFERENCES

Altman, D. (2002a). "Enron Had More Than One Way to Disguise Rapid Rise in Debt." The New York Times (Feb. 17).

Altman, D. (2002b). "Contacts So Complex They Imperial The System". The New York Times (Feb. 24).

Badaracco Jr., J. L. (1991). The Knowledge Link: How Firms Compete Through Strategic Alliances. Boston, MA: Harvard Business School Press.

Baker, W. (1992). "The Network Organization in Theory and Practice." In N. Nohria and R. Eccles (eds.), Networks and Organizations. Basingstoke, Macmillan: 142–162.

Banerjee, N., Barboza, D. and Warren, A. (2002). "At Enron, Lavish Excess Often Came Before Success," The New York Times (Feb. 26).

Barboza, D. (2002). "Ex-Executives Say Sham Deal Helped Enron". New York Times (August 8).

Barboza, D. and Schwartz, J. (2002). "The Finance Wizard Behind Enron's Deals." The New York Times (Feb. 6).

Bell, D. (1973). The Coming of Postindustrial Society: A Venture in Social Forecasting. New York: Basic Books.

Benveniste, G. (1994). The Twenty-First Century Organization. San Francisco: Jossey-Bass.

Beritano, S. (2002). "Enron IT: A Tale of Excess and Chaos," CIO, at http://www.cio.com/executive/edit/030502enron.html.

Bilodeau, O. (2002). "In Eye of Enron Storm, a Partnership Is Rocked," Legal Times, 02/21/02.

Bryce, R. (2001). "Fueling Bandwidth Trading: How energy companies plan to change telecom." Interactive Week, vol. 8(31): 20–23 (August 13).

Burns, T. and Stalker, G. (1961). The Management of Innovation. London: Tavistock.

Business Wire (1992). "D&B Software Launch Redefines Role of Software, Computers, Application Users and Software Vendors." (March 23).

Castells, M. (1996). The Rise of The Network Society. Malden, MA: Blackwell Publishers.

Castells, M. (2001). The Internet Galaxy: Reflections on the Internet, Business, and Society. Oxford, UK: Oxford University Press.

Chaffin, J. (2002). "Enron Complaint Cites 'Sham' Merrill Deal." Financial Times (Oct. 2).

Ching, C., Holsapple, C. W. and Whinston, A. B. (1996). "Toward IT Support for Coordination in Network Organizations." Information & Management 30: 179–199.

Coffee, J. (2002). "Accounting for Bad Accounting." An interview at: http://www.essential.org/monitor/enroncoffee.html.

Communications Today (1998). Nov. 19.

Corn, D. (2002). "Enron on the Hill." The Nation (24 January 2002).

Creswell, J. (2002). "Banks on the Hot Seat." Fortune Magazine 146(4): 79–82.

Cruver, B. (2002). The Anatomy of Greed: The Unshredded Truth from an Enron Insider, New York: Carroll and Graf Publishers.

Dallas Observer (2002). Feb. 07.

Dow Jones News Service (1998). "Power Shock-3: Enron Known As Sophisticated Risk Manager" (July 9).

Durgin, Hillary (1994). "Natural Gas Traders Inch into Computer Age." Houston Chronicle (July 31).

Eades, J. (2000). "The Information Age (Book Review)." Journal of the Royal Anthropological Institute 6(2): 340–341.

Eisenhardt, K. M. (1989). "Building Theories from Case Study Research." Academy of Management Review 14(4): 532–550.

Ekbia, H. R. (2004). "How IT Mediates Organizations: Enron and the California Energy Crisis." Journal of Digital Information 5(4). Available from: http://jodi.ecs.soton.ac.uk/Articles/v05/i04/Ekbia/.

Fortune (2000). 141(2): 127 (Jan. 24).

Foss, N. J. (2001). "Selective Intervention and Internal Hybrids: Interpreting and Learning from the Rise and Decline of the Oticon Spaghetti Organization." DRUID Working Paper No. 01-16.

Fulk, J. (2001). "Global Network Organizations: Emergence and Future Prospects." Human Relations 54(1): 91–99.

Fulk, J. and Desanctis, G. (1998). Articulation of Communication Technology and Organizational Form. Shaping organizational Form: Communication, Connection, and Community. G. D. J. Fulk.

Gosselin, Peter G. (2002): "Enron a Rerun of History." The L. A. Times (Feb. 22).

Grandori, A. and Soda, G. (1995). "Inter-Firm Networks: Antecedents, Mechanisms and Forms." Organization Studies 16(2): 183–214.

Greider, W. (2002). "The Enron Nine." The Nation (May 13).

Hanks, S. (1999). "This Intelligent Network Really is the Computer." Lightwave 16(7): 89–93.

Institute for Policy Studies (2002). "Enron's Pawns: How Public Institutions Bankrolled Enron's Globalization Game" (March 22).

Johnson, C. (2002). "Enron Case Shapes Up As Tough Legal Fight". Washington Post, A01 (Feb. 18).

Ketchen Jr., D. J. (2003). An Interview with Raymond E. Miles and Charles C. Snow. The Academy of Management Executive 17(4): 97–104.

Kirkpatrick, D. (2000). "Enron Takes Its Pipeline to The Net." Fortune 141(2): 127–131.

Kling, R. (ed.) (1997). Computerization and Controversy. San Diego, CA: Academic Press.

Kling, R. and Lamb, R. (2000). IT and Organizational Change in Digital Economics: A Socio-Technical Approach. Understanding the Digital Economy—Data, Tools and Research. B. K. E. Brynjolfsson. Cambridge, MA: The MIT Press.

Kraak, A. (2000). Debating Castells and Carnoy on the Network Society. The Gauteng Seminars. http://www.anc.org.za/ancdocs/pubs/umrabulo/umrabulo9c.html#f1 (accessed in Jan. 2004).

Kranhold, K. (1999). "Enron to Unveil Pact Involving Real Networks." The Wall Street Journal (Jan. 21).

Krugman, Paul (2002a). "Everyone Is Outraged." New York Times (July 2).

Krugman, Paul (2002b). "Clueless in Crawford." New York Times (August 13).

Lobby Watch (2002). "Houston Judges Got $200,550 From Enron and Its Law Firm." (March 21).

Maselli, Jennifer (2001). "Information: The Most Valuable Asset." Information Week, 852: 32–3 (August 27).

Mayer, D. and Kenney, M. F. (2002). "Economic Action Does Not Take Place in a Vacuum: Understanding Cisco's Acquisition and Development Strategy." BRIE Working Paper 148.

Miles, C. C. and Snow, R. E. (1992). "Causes of Failure in Network Organizations." California Management Review 34(4): 53–67.

Miles, C. C. and Snow, R. E. (1995). "The New Network Firm: A Spherical Structure Built on a Human Investment Philosophy." Organizational Dynamics 23(4): 5–20.

Miles, C. C., Snow, R. E. and Coleman Jr., H. J. (1992). "Managing 21st Century Network Organizations." Organizational Dynamics 20(3): 5–21.

Morgensen, G. (2002). "Information Sooner, Yes, but Make It Better, Too." The New York Times (May 5).

Mulford, C. W. and Comiskey, E. (2002). The Financial Numbers Game: Detecting Creative Accounting Practices. New York: John Wiley and Sons.

Murray, F. and Wilmott, H. (1997). Putting Information Technology in its Place: Towards Flexible Integration in Network Age? Information Technology and Organization: Strategies, Networks, and Integration. R. C. D. L. Brian P. Bloomfield. Oxford, UK: Oxford University Press: 160–180.

Naím, Moisés (2002). "The Creative Destruction of Enron." Financial Times (March 3). Republished on the Web by Carnegie Endowment for International Peace at http://www.ceip.org/files/Publications/2002-03-03-naim.asp?form=pubdate.

New York Department of Law (2002). "Merrill Lynch Stock Rating System Found Biased by Undisclosed Conflicts of Interest." Press Release (April 8).

Nohria, N. and Eccles, R. (eds.) (1992). Networks and Organizations. Boston: Harvard Business Press.

Ohmae, K. (1990). "The Borderless World: Power and Strategy in the Interlinked Economy." New York: Harper Business.

Oppel Jr., R. A. (2002). "Wall Street Analysts faulted on Enron." The New York Times (Feb. 28).

Pearce, J. L. (2003). "Former Enron vice president Sherron Watkins on the Enron collapse." The Academy of Management Executive 17(4): 119–125.

Petroski, H. (1992). "To Engineer is Human: The Role of Failure in Successful Design." New York: Vintage Books.

Polodny, J. M. and Page, K. L. (1998). "Network Forms of Organization." Annual Review of Sociology 24: 57–76.

Porter, M. (1998). "Clusters and the New Economics of Competition." Harvard Business Review, November–December: 77–90.

Poruban, Steven (2001). "Enron's Lay Sees More e-Commerce Changes for Industry." The Oil and Gas Journal 99(16): 32–33.

Powell, W. W. 1990. "Neither Market nor Hierarchy: Network Forms of Organization." Research in Organizational Behavior, 12: 295–336.

Powell, W. W. (2000). "The Capitalist Firm in the 21st Century: Emerging Patterns." In P. DiMaggio (ed.). "The Twenty-First Century Firm." Princeton: Princeton University Press.

Power Economics (1999). Vol. 3(7): 6–11. Wilmington Publishing Ltd.

PR Newswire (1990). Neither Market Nor Hierarchy: Network Forms of Organization. Research in Organizational Behavior. L. L. C. Barry M. Staw. Greenwich, Connecticut, JAI Press Inc. 12: 295–336.

PR Newswire (1997). "Enron Announces First Metering Systems Using Two-Way Wireless Communications and a Satellite-Enabled Network for All Electricity Consumers" (Dec. 15).

Rubenstein, D. (2001). "At Enron, A Decade of Transformation." Corporate Legal Times 11(119): 1–4.

Salant, J. (2001). "Bush-Backing Enron Makes Big Money off Crisis." The Associate Press. (Jan. 25).

Sassen, S. (1998). Globalization and Its Discontents. New York: The New Press.

Sassen, S. (2001). The Global City. 2nd edition. Princeton University Press.

Sennett, R. (1998). The Corrosion of Character: The Personal Consequences of Work in The New Capitalism. New York: W. W. Norton & Company.

Share, J. (1999). "Enron Executive Hopeful over Prospects in Africa, Asia." Pipeline and Gas Journal, 226(8): 20–24. Oildom Publishing Company of Texas, Inc.

Sherman, S. (2002). "Enron: Uncovering the Uncovered Story." Columbia Journalism Review, March/April, at http://www.cjr.org/year/02/2/shreman.asp.

Sloan, A., Rosenberg, D., and Gesalman, A. B. (2001). "Digging into The Deal that Broke Enron." Newsweek 138(25), 48–49 (Dec. 17).

Sonnentag, S. (2000). "Working in a Network Context—What Are We Talking About? Comment on Symon." Journal of Occupational and Organizational Psychology 73(4): 415–418.

Swartz, M. and Watkins, S. (2003). Power Failure: The Inside Story of the Collapse of Enron. New York: Doubleday.

Symon, G. (2000). "Information and Communication Technologies and Network Organization: A Critical Analysis." Journal of Occupational and Organizational Psychology: 398–414.

The Academy of Management Executive (2003). 17(4).

Van Alstyne, M. (1997). "The State of Network Organization: A Survey in Three Frameworks." Journal of Organizational Computing 7(3).

Wall Street Journal (2003). "While Some Companies Whisper, Others Crow." June 9.

Wayne, L. (2002a). "Enron, Preaching Deregulation, Worked the Statehouse Circuit." The New York Times (Feb. 9).

Wayne, L. (2002b). "Congress to Investigate Wall St.'s Ties With Enron." The New York Times (Feb. 19).

Whetten, D. A. (1981). "Sources, Responses and Effects of Organizational Decline." In: J. R. Kimberly and R. H. Miles (eds.), The Organizational Life Cycle. San Francisco.

Wilson, Carol (1999). "Building A Better Backbone—and Business Plan." Inter@ctive Week 6(36): 39–42 (Sept. 6).

Wysham, D. (2002): "Enron's Empire: How Government and International Agencies used Taxpayers Money to Bankroll the Energy Giant's International Investments." http://www.corpwatch.org/issues/PID.jsp?articleid=2279.

Wysham, D. and Valette, J. (2002). "Chronology of Enron's Empire," CorpWatch, April 11, 2002.

ACKNOWLEDGEMENTS

The author would like to thank James Pick for his thorough review of the manuscript and for his useful comments. He would also like to thank the editors for their persistence in organizing the seminar and all the ensuing efforts that led to the publication of this volume.

Chapter 6

UNDERSTANDING SOURCING AS A STRATEGIC BUSINESS: THE RISKS AND REWARDS OF STRATEGIC SOURCING AND INTER-FIRM ALLIANCES IN INDIA

Eric K. Clemons, Sashi Reddi, and Saleha Asif

Operations and Information Management Department, The Wharton School, University of Pennsylvania, Philadelphia, PA 19104

1. INTRODUCTION

The Jones Center at the Wharton School has been studying outsourcing, insourcing, and right-sourcing since 1991 [4–6]. Outsourcing, especially cross-border outsourcing, is increasing rapidly.[1] The research questions being addressed in this study include,

- How is outsourcing used most effectively?
- What areas within the business should next be considered as areas for outsourcing?
- What regions, and what technologies, will next become central to the increase in outsourcing?
- What are the limitations to outsourcing? What applications should not be targets for outsourcing, which should not be considered appropriate for cross border outsourcing? For those areas deemed appropriate for outsourcing, what limits are there to outsourcing and how much should be retained for internal processing, if any?
- What are the concerns of outsourcing clients and how can they be addressed when selling outsourcing services? How will these concerns affect profitability of vendors, and how will addressing them affect profitability?

---

[1] A recent Gartner Group study of outsourcing done with the Wharton School suggests that the global market for Business Process Outsourcing will be $110 billion in 2003, and will grow by more than 9% annually, reaching $173 billion by 2007. The same study suggests that the North American market will likewise grow by more than 9% annually, from $69 billion in 2003 to $97 billion by 2007.

The remainder of this brief paper will address the following issues:

- Examination of what is new and what is not in the rapid development of cross-border outsourcing.
- The risk-reward tradeoffs that motivate outsourcing, just as they motivate most or all business decisions.
- A detailed discussion of the risks, both strategic and operational. Strategic risks are defined here to be those that are caused by deliberate opportunism of the vendor, seeking to maximize profits by taking actions outside the contract and in direct contrast with the best interests of clients. Operational risks are those caused by an unintentional inability to perform, caused by a wide range of factors, from lack of familiarity with the client's operations to a failure of data transmission needed to perform essential tasks.
- A brief treatment of the rewards available from outsourcing.
- An introduction to organizational architecture, a form of micro-economic analysis that studies the design of organizations to get the best possible tradeoff between expected performance and expected risks.
- The risk-reward experience with organizational architecture, based on preliminary studies in India.
- A discussion of how much of this recent phenomenon is unique to India, and an examination of why the most rapid growth has been in Bangalore and Hyderabad.
- A framework for assessing which applications have been moved off shore and how they are best structured.
- Predictions for the future of cross-border outsourcing.

2.   WHAT IS NEW AND WHAT IS NOT?

Outsourcing of services in India is rapidly expanding. Some of this is very new, with call centers in India that could pass for those in Iowa, having operators with neutral English accents, using names like Sid and Martha, comfortably chatting about football and basketball playoffs while waiting for data to come up on their screens. Some of it is as old as contracting, with customers' concerns about strategic vulnerability, opportunistic repricing, and vendor extortion in later years of a multi-year sourcing contract: *"But what will it really cost me next year?"*

2.1.   The Risk Profile

The profile of risks encountered during business process outsourcing is largely the same as it would be for software development outsourcing or for physical component outsourcing. Strategic risk and operational risk can be further divided, as follows. Strategic risks include:

- **Shirking**, is deliberate under-performance while claiming full payment. This can take many forms, such as billing for more hours than were actually worked, or substituting more junior personnel for the senior staffers specified in the contract, or simply reducing effort and not trying as hard as possible to make a difficult sale or to debug a persistent problem. No matter what form it takes, shirking requires an information asymmetry; that is, the shirker does not want to be caught, and thus shirking requires that the client does not have sufficient information to monitor effort. This is called the principal agent problem or moral hazard in other contexts and has been extensively studied [1,7,13,17–20].
- **Poaching**, is the theft of data or intellectual property or the misuse of assets that were provided by the client to the vendor to allow the vendor to perform the contract. A vendor might be able to sell a list of great accounts, or some specialized pricing expertise, to the client's direct competitors. Poaching has only recently received attention as a form of strategic risk, probably because it is more significant in business process outsourcing contracts than it was in traditional industrial procurement [5,6].
- **Opportunistic repricing**, which occurs when a client enters into a contract and makes specific investments to facilitate the performance of the contract. Often, once the client has transferred operations or facilities to the vendor, the client will then have no alternative, or no way of re-internalizing operations. The client is then extremely vulnerable to the vendor choosing to increase prices in subsequent years. The phenomenon is enabled by "post-contractual small numbers bargaining," which is simply another way of saying that after the contract has begun, the client has very few viable options other than continuing with the vendor. This has been seen as central to the analysis of transactions costs and their impact on organizational governance [12,18–20]. Early empirical work demonstrated that ownership of assets is indeed consistent with their specificity and the risk that this creates [9–11].

Numerous authors have written about the relationship between transactions risks and strategies for IT outsourcing [8,14,15,21].

Unlike strategic risks, operational risks are not caused by intentional actions by the vendor. Rather, they occur when the vendor is unable to complete the task to the desired and promised level of performance. This can have numerous causes; there is no simple historical classification. These risks include poor decisions due to lack of skill and training; poor performance due to lack of data, especially when the vendor is remote from the client and the client's data; a set of cultural differences that may make it difficult for the vendor to interpret the client's requests or the client's customers' needs; and other problems caused by the history of interaction between the two organizations.

The cross-border sourcing phenomenon is driven by or newly enabled by IT for transfer of monitoring and operational data. It is possible to move the data needed for selling, support, and operations to any point in the world where it is needed, and it is possible to move data back to clients anywhere in the world so that they can assess performance. This is new.

In contrast, neither the availability of skilled workers, nor the presence of enormous wage-rate differences between the US and India are new. India did not start producing hundreds of thousands of college graduates beyond those required by its domestic labor market only in the late 1990s, nor did Indian workers suffer an 80% drop in wage rates in the late 1990s. For this reason it is safe to say that the possibility of cross-border wage rate arbitrage did not first originate in the late 1990s, and the sudden increase in cross-border outsourcing that we observe starting at this time must have another explanation.

The fundamental concerns of clients in process outsourcing are very similar to their concerns in component outsourcing:

- Fit and Integration.
  Processes have to couple tightly with the rest of business processes; tech support has to be based on the latest version of the code and the latest version of manuals.
  Fit and integration has long been an issue, irrespective of whether the outsourcing is for components or processes. Fiber optic wiring harnesses cannot be cut or spliced easily and they have to be consistent with the latest design of the aircraft wing or the automobile body and the positioning of all electronic sensors and activators.
- Monitoring of Effort and Commitment.
  It is difficult to monitor the effort put into service process outsourcing and hence it may be difficult for the client organization to assure that it is actually getting what it is paying for.
  Problems with vendor performance when monitoring is difficult, called principal-agent problems, are as old as commerce. The number of defects in components, or substitution of lower quality product for high quality product is as real a problem in component sourcing as in business process sourcing.
- Strategic vulnerability and opportunistic repricing.
  A client organization that outsources critical business processes like order entry, customer support, or data center management may become very vulnerable. Without a data center an entire organization will grind to a halt. Moreover, once control over a process is given up, and the personnel and physical resources needed for it have been disbursed, it can be very difficult to re-internalize the process later. The vendor may thus acquire enormous power and may use it in subsequent contract negotiations, or to demand payments outside the terms of the contract.

Likewise, exploitation of a vulnerable client is as old as commerce. Numerous examples can be found in the 1880s and 1890s when companies were forced to invest in unnecessary vertical integration to avoid the risks of strategic vulnerability. Meat packers like Armour owned their refrigerated rail cars to avoid exploitation by railroads. Brewers made their own kegs, had their own lumberyards, and even owned forests [2].

Even the allocation of effort across borders to capture the advantage of labor rate differentials is not new. The *captive* offshore processing centers of AOL, Dell, and GE are not very different from American automobile companies' production of truck parts in Mexico or electronics and toy manufacturers' location of production facilities in Hong Kong and elsewhere in the Far East.

3. TECHNOLOGY AND THE REDUCTION OF RISKS

Technology reduces the client's strategic risks. Faster, cheaper, and more reliable technology enables improved monitoring systems. It also facilitates switching vendors if necessary, to the extent that common platforms are employed and to the extent that the client retains ownership of data and software needed to implement service outsourcing. The presence of high speed, reliable, and nearly ubiquitous access to technology is new to Bangalore and Hyderabad, and dates back only to the late 1990s.

Likewise, technology has reduced the client's operational risks. Vendors' call center operators have access to the same operational data on products and services, or on the clients' customers, that the clients' own personnel would have. This is new not only to India but also more generally, and requires a combination of technology, security, and access to data.

4. ORGANIZATIONAL ARCHITECTURE

4.1. Components of Organizational Architecture

Organizational architecture *is* about risk-reward tradeoffs. More precisely, it is about the design of the firm to achieve the right balance between improving best-case performance and design of the firm to reduce worst-case risks. Because of the impacts of technology on risks and on performance, the design tradeoffs are changing.

Working with Brickley's concept of organizational architecture [2] and applying it to outsourcing decisions, we see it as having five principal components rather than the four he stresses:

- The *Allocation of Property Rights*—Who should own the resources needed for production and have the residual claims on their output, and why? In part this addresses questions of strategic risk and the decision to locate activities inside the firm or outside it. If monitoring is difficult or impossible, shirking may be a problem, unless the work is being done by an owner, who keeps the benefits of his efforts.

Historically, the allocation of property rights was a fundamental mechanism for the reduction of strategic risk, assuring that those activities with significant risk of opportunistic behavior were kept within the firm.

- The *Allocation of Decision Rights*—Where should decisions be made and why? Who has the right incentives to make decisions that are best for the firm? Who has access to the information needed to make the best decisions? This latter piece used to be a much more significant restriction on the allocation of decision rights.

  Historically, the allocation of decision rights was a fundamental mechanism for the reduction of operational risk, assuring that those activities with a high degree of operational risk were performed where those risks could best be managed.

- The *Design of Information Architecture*—Where should decision-related information reside and why? With improvements in data communications and data storage, firms have many more options than they used to. (We place greater emphasis on this than Brickley did and have elevated it to equal status with his four other criteria for our analysis of outsourcing decisions.)

- The *Design of Incentive Structures* — what behaviors do we want to reward?

- The *Design of Monitoring and Evaluation Systems*—how do we know whom to reward?

4.2. Organizational Architecture and Allocation of Work

Allocation of decision rights within the firm. The allocation of decision rights focuses on making decisions where the best results can be expected. Principally, this entails allocating decisions to those who have the information needed to make the correct decisions. Secondarily, the allocation of decision rights entails having decisions made by those who have incentives most closely aligned with the interests of the firm, although within organizational architecture the principal emphasis on this aspect of decision making is treated in incentives and monitoring. Where operational risks are highest the work would generally best be performed close to where it would be needed, and with tight and careful monitoring of performance within the firm itself. Where operational risks are highest, historically, the work was best performed closest to the areas most directly related to the operations, and where strategic risks were highest, historically, the work was best performed by those whose future behavior was most likely to be consistent with protecting the long term interests of the firm. Although the organizational architecture framework acknowledges that principal agent problems create strategic risk even within a single firm, the principal focus is on aligning decision making with possession of the necessary information. This is illustrated in Figure 1.

Allocation of work and sourcing decisions: Where strategic risks are highest, work is historically best done within the firm and where operational risks are highest the work is historically best done closest to those most directly affected by the quality of its performance. This is shown in Figure 2.

Our experience with the allocation of work and sourcing decisions: If our assessment of the impacts of technology on risks is correct, then we would expect to see more outsourcing today, even of those activities where outsourcing historically would have entailed unacceptable levels of strategic risk. This is indeed consistent with our experience, as shown in Figure 3. In particular, it is interesting to note the following:

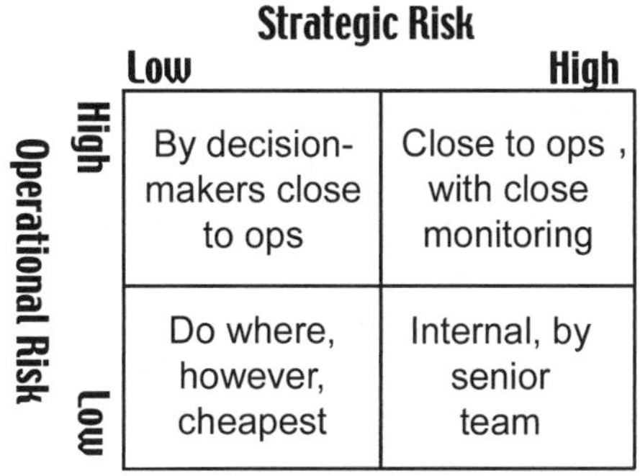

Strategic Risk

	Low	High
High	By decision-makers close to ops	Close to ops , with close monitoring
Low	Do where, however, cheapest	Internal, by senior team

Operational Risk

Figure 6-1. The design of work (allocation of decision rights) as predicted by organizational architecture in the presence of operational risk.

Strategic Risk

	Low	High
High	Outsource, but close to home	Internal, close to home base
Low	Do where, however, cheapest	Internal, where cheapest

Operational Risk

Figure 6-2. The allocation of work (property rights and decision rights) as predicted by organizational architecture in the presence of risk.

Figure 6-3. Examples of the allocation of work in the presence of various degrees of strategic and operational risk.

- Thames Water/Wipro: The entire communications network of Thames Water is managed remotely from Bangalore by Wipro. The outsourcing of full network management at Thames Water would until recently have been considered impossible due to the time lag in getting all data to Wipro, creating high levels of operational risk.

- Map Encoding at InfoTech: InfoTech in Hyderabad has a UK client who provides a trace of historical use of land. When a customer is considering buying a house or other building he can readily determine any and all previous uses of the property on which the building is located. If the location's history is questionable in any way—a history of sink-holes, or prior use as a munitions factory or a refinery or fuel storage depot—this information is immediately available to the prospective buyer. In order to accomplish this InfoTech, a Hyderabad outsourcing vendor, had to encode several centuries of land use maps for its client. This was originally considered to have high operational risk, since the vendor would need to recognize the previous function of a site from its name. The Iron Duke is safe—it is merely a pub. Duke's Iron Works is not safe, since a metal working facility produces toxic slag. However, training and the ease of coordinating with the client via jpg files attached to email messages can reduce operational risk.

- Capital One/MSource: Capital One is an extremely successful US-based credit card issuer that follows advanced and highly proprietary information-based strategies to identify, target, and retain highly profitable customers. Retention specialists are highly skilled professionals who negotiate via telephone with profitable customers whose recent charging behavior suggests they are being courted by other card issuers. It is the job of the retention specialists to work with these customers and determine an annual percentage interest rate (APR) that will retain their business for Capital One. The retention specialist is trained to offer them a rate that is profitable for Capital One and still likely to be among the most attractive that would be available to this customer in the marketplace. The retention specialists' compensation is tied to the "spread" between the lowest possible rate that could be offered to the customer and the rate that the customer ultimately accepts. This negotiation appears to require a deep understanding of Capital One's strategy, and of the culture of the U.S. credit card customer. It also requires understanding all other offers available in the U.S. market. Just as Thames Water outsourcing would until recently have been impossible due to operational risk, similarly, account retention specialists at Capital One would have been considered impossible to outsource because of high operational risks. However, with coaching available to them via software, retention specialists can be outsourced with acceptable levels of operational risk. With the proprietary pricing models embedded in "sealed black box" software, the transfer of expertise that could lead to poaching is managed well. Since the vendor never actually learns how Capital One makes its decisions, the high strategic risk of outsourcing is effectively mitigated. Consequently, Capital One has been able to outsource much of the retention specialist operation to MSource.

- Capital One has proprietary pricing models that are used to support retention specialists when negotiating with good customers who are considering transferring to competing card issuers. Outsourcing the development of software to support retention specialists has no operational risk, but the strategic risk from unintentionally sharing this proprietary expertise remains so high that it is considered impossible to outsource.
- Where both strategic and operational risks appear low, many designs may be considered. Merrill Lynch outsources small systems data processing from itself. That is, since its recovery from the September 11 World Trade Center Disaster, Merrill Lynch has operated a shared corporate data center for small systems operations previously managed by individual departmental users within Merrill Lynch. In a very real sense, Merrill Lynch is serving as an outsourcer, but one where all clients are internal to Merrill Lynch. If Merrill Lynch were not large enough to enjoy economies of scale in this operation, no doubt it would have outsourced to a true third party service provider. Cisco and other North American switch manufacturers outsource order entry and order processing from Infosys and Wipro. Dell and AOL use internal (captive) call centers in Bangalore for customer support. We note that all these client organizations are large enough not to require an outsourcing contract simply to achieve economies of scale. Since labor costs are not a critical component of their facilities management, Merrill Lynch works internally. Since labor costs are a significant expense in call center operations the others have chosen to exploit the gains from off-shore operations. Order entry is of course critical to the functioning of a business,

and it would thus appear that outsourcing this function would create significant strategic risk. However, Infosys in particular has taken actions to assure that the customer can readily reassume control over this function, assuring that the strategic risk is low. More technically, we would say that while the function is critical, the client does not face a "post contractual small numbers bargaining situation," meaning that it continues to have alternatives to continuing with its selected vendor. This reduces the vendor's power and the client's risk. Since strategic and operational risk are both low, these operations are outsourced. However, both Dell and AOL feel that a very high degree of specialized training is required for their call center help desk and member services operations in order to eliminate operational risk. AOL achieves this by retaining these operations within an internal (captive) off-shore unit. In contrast, Dell outsources at least some of these operations, but retains a monitoring function to ensure that quality service is provided to its customers.

4.3.   Assessment and Implications

Our assessment of the outsourcing operations to India that we have seen is that outsourcing as currently practiced is generally beneficial.

- We observe *allocative efficiency*, for both labor and capital. That is, investments are made and work is performed where it most cost-effective to do so.
- *Transactions costs* are manageable; that is, the costs of arranging work, supervising it, monitoring performance, and controlling risks are not creating excessive frictional losses.
- Total costs of providing services, the actual production costs of labor and capital as well as the frictional losses due to transactions costs, appear to be minimized.
- Moreover, we believe that *uneconomic vertical integration* is being reduced; that is, firms are outsourcing that which can and should be outsourced, to achieve economies of scale.

In short, the current status of off-shore outsourcing in India should be seen as an over-all improvement in economic efficiency.

5.   UNIQUELY INDIA?

Is there any reason why this outsourcing should be seen as a uniquely Indian phenomenon? Phrased differently, do other countries enjoy labor rate differentials relative to the US and the West, and have telecommunications advances more effectively integrated many nations into the global economy? It should be clear that progress in communications is occurring in many nations, reducing transactions costs associated with moving business processes there, and many countries enjoy highly skilled labor forces, fluent in English, with lower wage rates. Thus we see no reason that this should be a uniquely Indian phenomenon, and every reason to expect increasing competition from Manila, Kuala Lumpur, Shanghai, Lahore and other locations throughout Asia.

Although the factors that have led to an increase in outsourcing are not unique to India, the largest increase has indeed occurred in India. The explanation for this can largely be found in a series of actions taken by Karnataka and Andhra Pradesh, the states in India that have enjoyed the most dramatic increases.

Probably the greatest single change in India was a change in the nature of the relationships between the central government in Delhi and the local state governments, permitting much greater local control. In turn, the state governments in Karnataka (Bangalore) and Andhra Pradesh (Hyderabad) focused both on business development generally and on technology outsourcing as an industry opportunity more specifically. Import regulations were significantly liberalized, making it possible to acquire necessary technology. Both states made investments in technology infrastructure, especially satellite antenna farms for connection to the global broadband technology networks, with or without the cooperation of India's long distance telecommunications monopoly. Likewise, other investments were made in shared technology infrastructure, such as high speed microwave links to allow high speed local access to the points of global interconnection and technology parks ready for occupancy by small and medium sized technology firms.

We are led to conclude that the concerted actions of state governments allowed Bangalore and Hyderabad to exploit valuable resources—a large population of educated college grads in liberal arts and engineering. However, any region in the world that possesses comparable resources and is neither more remote nor more accessible than southern India could potentially replicate this; telecoms infrastructure made the growth of Indian outsourcing possible, and it can likewise make the growth of outsourcing possible elsewhere.

6.   FRAMEWORK FOR ANALYSIS

To review, the dimensions that we have considered relevant to characterize a sourcing decision include the following:

- Internal captive unit, or external outsourced operations.
- Close to or far from the other operations being supported.
- With decision-making residing with the operations being sourced, or with the operations that are supported by sourced operations.

We see a clear progression of applications being outsourced over time. Initially only the simplest applications were considered appropriate for outsourcing to remote locations, those with low strategic risk and limited operational risk. As firms became more experienced with outsourcing, vendors had a better sense of what could be done, and clients had a better sense of the risks that they were assuming.

We classify some activities as *highly data intensive*. These activities might require large amounts of market information, or of up-to-the second status reports from thousands of network sensors, or of appropriate styles of dress in dozens of American markets. Other activities are *highly subjective*, requiring a rapid assessment of what approach will work best with an angry customer. Those activities that were least data intensive and least subjective—order capture and order transcription, or custom software development, for example—have been easiest to outsource and were outsourced first. Next, as network technologies improved it became possible to outsource more data intensive activities, since the operational risk is significantly reduced. Cross-selling and remote facilities management are examples of more data intensive activities. Finally, highly subjective activities represent the next frontier, including activities like delinquent account collections or eCommerce website design.

7.   PREDICTIONS

We classify as simple applications those with limited expertise required and limited barriers to entry preventing new entrants from becoming competitors. A number of applications, including in-bound call centers for order capture and simple member support such as review of alternative pricing plans fall into this category. Not surprisingly, we would expect competition to increase for simple applications and today's profit margins to be significantly eroded.

There are numerous more complex applications that are currently being outsourced or that could be outsourced in the future. Some of these are more difficult because they require significant training and cross-cultural expertise, others because of the need for expensive infrastructure and secure facilities, still others because of limited access to complementary assets, like the personnel who actually did the original code development. This can include financial cross-selling and up-selling or delinquent account collections, remote network management, or tech support and code maintenance. These markets are more difficult to enter, and consequently we would expect to see them to remain more profitable for those firms able to compete in them.

Other predictions are more difficult to make. Captive units make sense for firms large enough not to need the economies of scale offered by outsourcing and able to avoid all strategic risk by internalizing remote operations; while outsourcing remains a viable alternative for most other firms in many instances. The future of joint ventures is less clear; they may, in some instances, provide a risk management mechanism for firms that wish to reduce strategic risk without investing in full ownership. They may be required for legal or regulatory markets in some environments. And they may provide a useful intermediate or transition stage, with full ownership eventually being transferred to one party or the other.

It is likewise difficult to predict the future of other markets, like China, the Philippines, Pakistan, or Kuala Lumpur. At present the profit margins available in India are large enough that firms have behaved with great integrity. Even as the provision of outsourcing services grows in other markets, India's advantage may not be under threat as long as India is able to maintain excellent service levels, continues to provide high degrees of customer satisfaction, and is able to meet demand. It is possible that competition could arise as a result of either of two trends: a) if increasing competition among Indian outsourcing vendors were to damage profitability to the point that firms felt the need to perform with lower standards in order to earn adequate profits, or b) clients experienced significant economic loss as a result of one or more Indian outsourcing vendors' exploiting strategic risks. Either one would surely be detrimental to the competitive standing of Indian vendors and could provide an opening for foreign competitors. This change in vendor behavior could occur for a variety of reasons, including a reduction in demand for outsourcing services. Alternatively, if demand were to increase beyond India's ability to meet it, this too could provide an incentive for the development of additional international alternatives.

8. NEXT STEPS FOR RESEARCH AND CONCLUSIONS TO DATE

8.1. Next Steps

We have a list of additional questions to address and data to get. All are aimed at a single issue: What applications work best for outsourcing?

- What can we learn from recent experience: How do different risk profiles map best into specific organizational architecture designs? That is, what motivates specific decisions concerning the allocation of decision rights, the decision to insource or outsource, and the decision to remain local or go off shore?
- What information systems for support of operations and for monitoring performance work best for each organizational design?
- How can processes be redesigned to facilitate outsourcing? Is it possible to split different tasks among different vendors, or to divide the work load of a single task among different vendors, to improve the risk profile of the outsourcing relationship?

- What are customers' perceptions of risks and how are they managed?
- What are customers' perceptions of benefits and are they indeed supported by the data?
- What cannot be outsourced, regardless of geographic location?
- What cannot be done remotely, regardless of whether or not it is done within a single firm?

8.2.   Preliminary Analysis

It is premature to offer firm conclusions, but our preliminary analysis of our field studies suggests the following:

- Improved telecommunications infrastructure has greatly reduced the operational risk associated with remote off-shore operations, allowing a great increase in off-shore captive units and off-shore outsourcing alike.
- Where strategic risks remain high, off-shore operations are more likely to be run through captive units, especially when the client is large enough not to require a vendor in order to achieve economies of scale.
- Where the gains from off-shore outsourcing are high enough, it may be possible to outsource even highly risky operations. However, the outsourcing of highly risky operations, such as retention specialist operations at Capital One, may require careful redesign of business processes before outsourcing, and the careful division of tasks among different firms.

REFERENCES

[1] Alchian, A. and H. Demsetz, "Production, Information Costs, and Economic Organization", *The American Economic Review*, Vol. 62, 1972, pp. 777–795.
[2] Brickley, J.A., C.W. Smith, and J.L. Zimmerman, Managerial Economics and Organizational Architecture, 2nd Edition, McGraw-Hill, 2000.
[3] Chandler, A.D., *The Visible Hand*, Cambridge, Mass; Belknap Press, 1977.
[4] Clemons, E.K., S.P. Reddi, and M.C. Row, "The Impact of Information Technology on the Organization of Economic Activity: 'The Move to the Middle Hypothesis' ", *Journal of Management Information Systems*, Fall 1993, vol. 10, no. 2, pp. 9–35.
[5] Clemons, E.K. and M.C. Row, "Information Technology and Industrial Cooperation: The Changing Economics of Coordination and Ownership", *Journal of Management Information Systems*, Vol. 9, No. 2, Fall 1992, pp. 9–28.
[6] Clemons, E.K. and M.C. Row, "Information Technology and Economic Reorganization" (E.K. Clemons and M.C. Row), *Proceedings, 10th International Conference on Information Systems*, December 1989, pp. 341–351.
[7] Grossman, S. and O. Hart, "The Costs and Benefits of Ownership: A Theory of Vertical and Lateral Integration", *Journal of Political Economy*, Vol. 94, 1986, pp. 691–719.

[8] Gurbaxani, V., "The New World of Information Technology Outsourcing", *Communications of the ACM*, Vol. 39, No. 7 (July 1996), pp. 45–46.

[9] Joskow, P., "Vertical Integration and the Long-Term Contracts: The Case of Coal-Burning Electric Generating Plants", *Journal of Law, Economics, and Organization*, Vol. 1, 1985, pp. 33–80.

[10] Joskow, P., "Contract Duration and Durable Transaction-Specific Investments: The Case of Coal", *American Economic Review*, Vol. 77, March 1987, pp. 168–185.

[11] Joskow, P., "Asset Specificity and the Structure of Vertical Relationships: Empirical Evidence", *Journal of Law, Economics, and Organization*, Vol. 4, 1988, pp. 95–117.

[12] Klein, B., R.G. Crawford, and A.A. Alchian, "Vertical Integration, Appropriable Rents, and the Competitive Contracting Process", *The Journal of Law and Economics*, Vol. 21, No. 2, October 1978, pp. 297–326.

[13] Holmstrom, B., "Moral Hazard and Observability", *Bell Journal of Economics*, Vol. 10, 1979, pp. 74–91.

[14] Lacity, M.C., L.P. Willcocks, and D.F. Feeny, "IT Outsourcing: Maximize Flexibility and Control", *Harvard Business Review*, May–June 1995, pp. 84–93.

[15] Lacity, M.C., L.P. Willcocks, and D.F. Feeny, "The Value of Selective IT Sourcing", *Sloan Management Review*, Spring 1996, pp. 13–25.

[16] Milgrom, P. and J. Roberts, *Economics, Organization, and Management*, Englewood Cliffs, NJ, Prentice Hall, 1992.

[17] Tirole, J., *The Theory of Industrial Organization*, MIT Press, Cambridge, 1988.

[18] Williamson, O.E., *Markets and Hierarchies: Analysis and Antitrust Implications*, The Free Press: New York, 1975.

[19] Williamson, O.E., "Transaction-Cost Economics: The Governance of Contractual Relations", *Journal of Law and Economics*, Vol. 22, 1979, pp. 297–326.

[20] Williamson, O.E., *The Mechanisms of Governance*, Oxford University Press, New York, 1997.

[21] Quinn, J.B. and F.G. Hilmer, "Strategic Outsourcing", *Sloan Management Review*, Summer 1994, pp. 43–55.

ACKNOWLEDGEMENTS

The authors gratefully acknowledge the financial support that they received from the Reginald H. Jones Center of the Wharton School, and its Sponsored Research Project on Information, Strategy, and Economics. We acknowledge the assistance of the Directorate of Information Technology in Bangalore and the cooperation of senior officers at InfoSys, Wipro, InfoTech, MSource, AOL, and Dell. Our colleague Ravi Aron at the Wharton School provided useful insights and provided the data on growth in outsourcing. It is always a pleasure to acknowledge the contributions of our friend and colleague Michael Row, whose early work inspired our interest in outsourcing of complex processes.

Chapter 7

PERSONALIZATION AND TECHNOLOGY-ENABLED MARKETING

Lee G. Cooper

UCLA Anderson Graduate School of Management, 110 Westwood Plaza, PO Box 951481, Los Angeles, CA 90095-1481

INTRODUCTION

Despite a few very heralded failures in 2000, online retail is a vital and growing sector. While the rest of the economy was sinking further into recession, on-line sales grew 21% to $51.3 billion in 2001, jumped 48% to $76 billion in 2002, and are expected to increase to $96 in 2003. Approximately 70% of on-line retailers showed positive operating margins in 2002, up from 56% the year before.[1] As we come out of recession the U.S. Commerce Department reports that the increase in online retailing is five times as great as the increase in the rest of the retail sector.[2] Most online retailers (63%) updated their inventory management systems to better manage their supply chain.[3] On-line retailing leads in Forrester's industry-by-industry analysis of Website usability.[4] Personalization leads this trend.

Personalization, One-to-One Marketing, and Technology-Enabled Marketing all refer to the basic process of using computer-mediated environments to create an experience for the consumer that seems tailored to his or her particular needs and interests. Anticipated, relevant, and timely are the criteria that Godin (1999) offers in his discussion of personalization in permission-based email and Web marketing. Jupiter Research (Foster, 2000) efers to the personalization chain as an iterative five-step business cycle: storage, access, mining, tuning, and targeting. The consumer's response to a targeted offer initiates a new cycle. Thus, we should think of personalization and technology-enabled marketing as the demand end of a dynamic merchandising system.

---

[1] *The State of Retailing Online 6.0: Performance Benchmark Report*, June 2003, Shop.org.
[2] Wall Street Journal, August 22, 2003.
[3] *The State of Retailing Online 6.0: Performance Benchmark Report*, June 2003, Shop.org.
[4] Forrester, "First Look: Research Highlights for Forrester Clients," August 7, 2003.

This chapter considers personalization in computer-mediated environments, and the algorithms that underlie it. It looks at the basics of modern marketing—segmenting, targeting, positioning, and purchase-event feedback —and relates how these basics are applied in computer-mediated environments. I begin with several fictionalized illustrations of personalization in action, I then discuss personalization in terms of the marketing fundamentals (i.e., segmenting, targeting, positioning, and purchase-event feedback). I follow this with a discussion of the basic approaches to developing a personalized approach to customers (i.e., clustering, artificial intelligence systems, collaborative filtering, profiling, and segment-based learning). How to address the basic business questions comes next (i.e., "Who are our best customers?" "What products do these customers purchase?" "What other products and services do we have that these customers might like?" and "How can we acquire more customers like these?"). The chapter concludes with a real-market test of the improvement in customer response that comes from segment-based learning, and a few expectations for future developments in personalization.

1.   AN ILLUSTRATION

Frank Stone points his browser to his favorite Web music store. Because he is a repeat customer, the site sees him coming. While the local bricks-and-mortar music store is stuck with the retail space that greets all customers and the low-wage personnel that makes customer memory almost impossible, this Web merchant, CD-Direct, recognizes Frank as a returning customer and designs the whole storefront on the fly to better appeal to his preferences. This is not science fiction. Such customization capability is off-the-shelf technology. What is new is the ability unobtrusively to connect learned customer preferences with this customization.

A Web merchant can have almost limitless inventory, but very limited visual opportunity to make the right offer. Display real estate is very scarce. Thus, taking advantage of what is known about the customer is essential. Frank is male, 25–34, in ZIP code 16611. Geographically, that is in western Pennsylvania (region: rural). Geo-demographically, that is the Lunch Pail Rural segment,[5] with average income $40,853 (from the U.S. Census), mostly blue-collar workers, with high-school education or less. So Frank is greeted with a screen that welcomes him back personally (an easy look-up). The homepage features the Bruce Springsteen "Greatest Hits" CD that is then the most popular in this segment, and the Nirvana "Nevermind" CD on which the store got a special deal. Both of these are filtered to ensure the store isn't offering Frank something he already bought there. If Frank has bought the Springsteen

---

5   The segmentation scheme is discussed later.

CD, a Tom Petty CD that is second on the chart for Lunch Pail Rural replaces Springsteen. On the top right are two banner ads: the first for Penn Pizza, a regional restaurant tagged to his ZIP code and segment; the second a Rusty "Jeans for your life" banner, the most popular banner for Frank's segment and gender. At the bottom left is a cross-sell box that features Springsteen's Tour 2000 tickets available on HOTTIX.com that is tagged by a manual rule to both ZIP code and segment. If Frank has bought any CDs that he hasn't rated for CD-Direct, a box shows up on the middle right asking for his feedback. The Web merchant keeps a list of all unrated CD purchases, requesting feedback after enough days for evaluation have past.

Mary Brennan clicks her Favorites link to CD-Direct. Mary is female, 55+, in ZIP code 10024—the New York Metro area (region: highly urban). Geo-demographically, that is the Downtown Elite segment, with average income $96,158, mostly executive jobs, with bachelor degrees and up. For Mary, the homepage comes up featuring Miles Davis' "Kind of Blue," the most popular CD in the Downtown Elite segment, and the Nirvana album highlighted for all customers, again filtered to ensure that CD-Direct doesn't waste scarce feature space on CDs Mary has already bought there. The two banner ads at the top right feature "Fly JFK to London"—a banner tagged to her segment and ZIP code—and "Time for a change," a Risot.com ad showing a woman's watch, one of the most-clicked banners for Mary's gender-segment combination. The cross-sell box at the lower left features "Uptown: Quality Real Estates since 1922," tagged to her segment and ZIP code. A music-genre ID in Mary's cookie could identify her as having made enough classical music purchases to be a known classical-music fan. The Web storefront could then present the most popular classical CDs in the Downtown Elite segment, filtered to ensure the store isn't offering something already bought there. Tabs to the left of the banner ads direct Mary deeper into the site, to sections devoted specifically to each of the music genres—classical, jazz, pop, rock, and hip-hop—where screens are personalized with the offers most popular for her segment and gender in that particular genre, as well as standard search functions for finding what she wants. Banner ads rotate to the next-most popular in her segment with each successive screen requested.

If a new customer arrives, the Web music store can configure the screen without genre preferences, but with the cross-genre picks of the most profitable or otherwise most desired segment. Or the site can experiment to find the offers that most likely lead to new customer acquisition across segments—exposing only a small number of new customers to what might be failing combinations. If the new customer arrives by clicking a banner ad from another site, specific agreements could send an otherwise anonymous segment tag along with the new user, so that the offers could be tailored to segment preferences even for first-time visitors. Similarly, targeted email campaigns for new customers can come with hot links that allow for traditional list-scoring as well as segment tags that help customize offers.

2.   THE BASICS OF TECHNOLOGY-ENABLED MARKETING

These illustrations highlight the roles of Segmenting, Targeting, Positioning, and Purchase-Event Feedback—the fundamentals of modern marketing. The Web doesn't change the fundamental principles, but it does create new opportunities for using these fundamentals.

2.1.   Segmenting

The foundations for modern approaches to market segmentation were codified in a special issue of the *Journal of Marketing Research* in 1978 (Wind, 1978). Behavioral segmentation dominated academic efforts at marketing-methods development for the subsequent 15 years. Following a traditional social-science, statistical approach, a sample of a firm's consumers would typically be intensely measured on attitudes, opinions, and interests; lifestyles and values; or other characteristics that the firm considered relevant to its marketing efforts. A multivariate statistical model (e.g., factor analysis, multidimensional scaling, cluster analysis, or discriminant analysis) would either classify or aid in classifying consumers into relatively homogeneous groups or *segments*. The firm would look for easily identifiable (i.e., actionable) keys that could tag the customers or potential customers in desired segments so that not every person had to be measured intensely. *Targeting* would involve a firm deciding which segments constituted its best market opportunity. Messages would be *positioned* to appeal to the known characteristics or preferences of the targeted segments.

The diffusion of checkout scanners in retail environments broadened the opportunity for behavioral segmentation. While scanner-based shopper panels started as small adjuncts to the retail tracking services, the rich record of frequent shopping choices enabled more powerful statistical approaches to segmentation (e.g., latent-class analysis, latent-mixture models, and choice-based individual differences models for multidimensional scaling). The ubiquitous loyalty-club cards for grocery shoppers enable point-of-purchase targeting at the segment or even individual level. But a major difference exists between the grocery shopper and the Internet shopper. While over 98% of customers who enter a grocery store end up purchasing, typically less than 2% of customers who show up at an e-commerce site end up purchasing.

Despite the paucity of *behavior* in the records of most e-commerce sites, behavioral approaches to segmentation still dominate. The analyticals favorite include:

- *Clustering* — Uses statistical techniques to group site visitors with similar characteristics into segments,
- *Artificial Intelligence*, or "AI" — A range of technologies, including natural language processing, expert systems, and neural networks,
- *Collaborative Filtering* — Uses algorithmic techniques to infer preferences based on similar behavior from others, and
- *Profiling* — Characterizes individual consumers based on their interaction with Web site elements.

Clustering methods are essentially an interchangeable collection of heuristic statistical techniques that work on rectangular arrays of site-visitor/customer data to classify groups or segments that are internally homogeneous, yet differ from segment to segment. The collection of variables used in behavioral approaches to clustering or profiling needs to be selected uniquely for each site. The analytical core of these methods considers all the selected variables as dependent measures—with the primary goal of grouping. The interpretation of what each group represents, is also a site-by-site heuristic process. The prediction of purchase (or some other like criterion) is typically external to the clustering or profiling system.

AI systems can work on irregular arrays, but still require site-by-site determination of the overall information space. AI systems are often criterion oriented—implicitly or explicitly attempting to predict a particular outcome, such as purchase. The "black-box" AI systems, such as neural nets, remove the need for site-by-site interpretation. The cost, however, comes potentially in not understanding the rules that determine management actions on one's Website. The expert-systems approaches often included in AI techniques are an exception to the black-box methods. Expert systems result in manual rules, which are discussed in Section 4.5.

Collaborative filtering is both least familiar and most representative of the first three approaches. There is a way of understanding collaborative filters that is very much like clustering—but with the criterion-related goal of determining a recommendation or offer for a customer. Think of a huge table of numbers that has a row for each individual who visits Amazon.com and a column for each book that has ever been bought on Amazon.com. A customer would have an entry of "1" in the column if that individual bought that particular book. A "0" would indicate no purchase. If you multiply the entries in the rows for any two customers, the resulting row for this pair of customers would have a "1" only where both individuals bought the same book. If you add the "1"s in that row, you would get a rough indication of how similar the book tastes of these two individuals were. Of course, you would also tend to have higher numbers for people who read more books, but there are ways of dealing with such issues. Now, think about two customers who have a relatively high similarity score. Most likely they have similar tastes, but have not read exactly the same books. Why not recommend to Customer A the books that Customer B has bought that Customer A has not, and vice versa? This is conceptually what collaborative filters help managers do—take the choices of individuals and use these choices as a basis for making recommendations to similar individuals.

A visual analog of the Table 1 described above would have a dimension for each book and position each individual according to which of the books that customer bought. This is simple to visualize with two books. All of the customers who bought neither book would be at the origin of the space, all of the people who bought only Book 1 would be grouped at [1,0], all of the people who bought only Book 2 would be grouped at [0,1], and all of the people who bought both books would be grouped at [1,1]. With two books, we could have four groups of individuals. As the number of books increases, the number of possible groups grows exponentially, but the number of actual groups doesn't, since not all possible combinations of books are bought. Tastes emerge from the overlapping patterns of books that similar people tend to read. Further, we know how close various subgroups are to each other using similarity metrics such as that described above or simple distance measures between the centers of different groups. If we look closely, we might find groups at proximal locations that all liked modern mystery novels, books on cooking, or high-technology management books. By drawing approximate boundaries around such groups, we could develop recommendation schemes that capitalize on the taste similarities in those *neighborhoods*.

Many open questions surround collaborative filtering. *How do you draw boundaries around a neighborhood?* This is a heuristic procedure that requires close inspection and detailed knowledge of the business domain. *How often do you update the neighborhood?* Ideally you would update the information in real time, but the requirement to reinterpret the boundaries makes even monthly or quarterly updating rarely practical. Much useful information is lost in the interim. *Can you develop a scalable business model if each e-commerce site must be filtered anew?* The management personnel who possess the domain expertise that aids interpretation are not the same as the personnel who understand the analytical techniques. *How many purchases are required before you can classify a customer as belonging to a particular neighborhood?* The conventional wisdom is that collaborative filters are most beneficial in *high-touch* e-commerce sites (i.e., sites where repeat visitation and frequent purchase is the rule). DVD rental services are good examples of high-touch sites. After a customer has made a dozen or more rental choices, collaborative filters do a better job of reflecting consumer preferences. The exception here concerns when household DVD rentals reflect the preferences of different people in the household. How does the site know if the recommendation is for a child or an adult, a man or a woman? *How do you account for whether or not buyers liked a product (i.e., purchase event feedback)?* Collaborative filters do not naturally accommodate customer satisfaction feedback. Recommending books or DVDs that similar customers chose, but did not like, is a bad idea. *What good are purchase records when visitors outnumber buyers 50-1?* The conventional wisdom also notes collaborative filters are relatively useless when dealing with new customers or when trying to convert visitors into customers.

Profiling is typified by Engage.com's approach. The company collected 800 supposedly anonymous pieces of information on each Internet user who received Engage.com ads. Just like wanting to know which of 800 books a person bought, you should realize that most of this huge table is empty. Knowing 800 things about an individual may be as useful as knowing nothing. The data are simply too sparse to reveal stable, interesting, and useable patterns in 800-dimensional space—particularly when behavioral response to a banner ad is so rare. Mining for patterns in 800-dimensional space is the kind of endeavor I would assiduously avoid. It reminds me of the full-page ad in the *Wall Street Journal* showing a very full-bodied mid-20s young man, arms folded, leaning up against a grocery-store wall, wearing only diapers:[6]

> DSS transaction no. 0095 11265: Loaded, Queried, Analyzed . . . At 6:32 PM Every Wednesday, Owen Bly Buys Diapers and Beer. Do Not Judge Owen. Accommodate Him.

I do not believe you can build a business around the 14 people for whom this ad rings true.

The other basic approach discussed in the *JMR Special Issue* on Segmentation involved geo-demographic segments. These approaches, which use U.S. Census data or geo-coded database information to segment neighborhoods, remain popular in the direct-mail niche of marketing. In direct mail, a 2% purchase rate can be quite profitable, unlike the grocery-shopping situation. This is more akin to what we see on the Internet.

In the not-too-distant past, a 2% click rate on a banner ad wasn't unusual, and converting 2% of the people who clicked through to your e-commerce site into purchasers was within normal expectation. Let's talk about purchases per million ads (PPMM). The old expectation was around 400 PPMM. With average click rates falling to .25% to .5%, the conversion rate is down to 50–100 PPMM. Further, while most grocery shoppers fill their market baskets with many items, the modal purchase on the Internet is one item. So, while behavioral segmentation has great potential in the behavior-rich grocery-shopping arena, behavior is rare in the e-commerce arena, and consequently the behavior-based approaches to segmentation are less applicable to the Internet.

---

[6]   Wall Street Journal, Ad for Tandem Computers Incorporated, May 15, 1997, page B3.

Geo-demographic segmentation can be a real asset in e-commerce. The basic information typically used includes ZIP code, age, and gender—called ZAG in the direct-marketing world. For the Internet, ZIP code is the key. It is the *action* key, in that many sites acquire ZIP codes by offering customizable services such as weather, local films, or cultural events. It is the *conceptual* key, in that ZIP code ties you into the mother of all secondary sources—the U.S. Census. While the individual census records contain very little information, and are kept secret for many decades, a sample within each census block is questioned much more extensively. The aggregate data are available within a couple of years after each decennial census.

The clusters used in the illustration at the beginning of this chapter came from a hierarchical clustering of selected geo-demographic variables from the U.S. Census. Particularly interpretable clustering patterns appeared in solutions with 68 clusters, 45 clusters, 22 clusters and 11 clusters. The particular illustration came from the 22-cluster solution. This number of clusters provided the data density (given the amount of traffic on a mid-to-large size e-commerce site) that allows statistically stable patterns of preference to be learned in short order. At the 22-cluster level, these segments range in size from Ethnic Elite, which constitutes over 10% of U.S. households, to Native Experience, which makes up less than .3% of households.

The U.S. Census is updated every 10 years, while, of course, neighborhoods undergo continuous change. This inevitable change is more of a problem for local retailers dealing with narrow product mixes and a few ZIP codes. For national merchandisers, the coarser classification into 22 segments means the overall cluster averages change much less. The negative of that inevitable change is outweighed by the advantages of having a single segmentation scheme that can transcend product categories (enabling cross-selling), and multiple communications media (enhancing new customer acquisition).

2.2.   Targeting

A tremendous advantage of an exogenous segmentation scheme, based on the U.S. Census such as this one, is that we do not need to re-segment for each web site. Firms can see the segment mix of their current customers, find out if certain segments are over- or under-represented in comparison to the U.S. population, and, by matching margin data with this segmentation, find out which segments are the most or least profitable. The segmentation system provides the ability to keep score in a way that aids targeting decisions. This kind of a segmentation tool levels the playing field between big and small firms.

The customization capability of Internet sites gives Web merchants the ability to target multiple segments with different appearances and offerings. Obviously, bricks-and-mortar businesses cannot reset display windows for each passing customer, but e-retailers can. They can try to attract their most desired segments and not appeal to the least-profitable ones. A single e-retailer can be a virtual mall, emphasizing service and high-end products in some segments while emphasizing costs and economy in others.

2.3.   Positioning

While I believe that the 68-cluster solution is most descriptive of the population, the 22-cluster system pushes the envelope for how articulated the system could be given the amount of traffic we could expect in practice. Data density is the important issue. Even ignoring age, which is often inaccurately reported, one needs to tract three levels of gender (i.e., male, female, and unknown). This implies tracking 66 groups for the 22 clusters. The more groups you have, the more data you need in order to be sure you know the most popular offering.

In each segment (or possibly each segment-gender-age combination), we have to position N offers. We need to know what are the most popular N offers and the order of their popularity, given only limited data from which we can learn this order. For a new offer, we need to know if it falls within the top N offers for a particular segment. We need to know this as quickly as possible.[7]

2.4.   Purchase-Event Feedback

We tend to forget this very important topic. Blockbuster clearly forgot purchase-event feedback in Take10—its initial experiment with recommendation systems (West et al., 1999). Take10 recommended 10 videos to customers based on their history of rentals. As pointed out above, a recommendation system may fail simply because it neglects to find out whether customers liked what it recommended. With profiling or collaborative filtering, one doesn't know how to incorporate customer satisfaction into recommendation systems. With a recommendation system that uses segment-based learning, coming up with weighting for recommendations is a straightforward, empirical matter. We accumulate some number of votes for each purchase by segment members and let positive feedback add to that count while negative feedback diminishes that count. Since most of the behavioral decision theory literature says that negatives have more impact than positives, we can give more weight to negative feedback than to positive feedback.

---

[7]   Eric Bradlow and I have worked on the statistical issues underlying these basic problems.

3. THE TRADITIONAL SWAP BETWEEN UNIVERSITY FACULTY AND BUSINESSES

In the scanner-data era, beginning in the early 1980s, the basic swap between university faculty and businesses involved *data* for *methods*: Data intermediaries such as A.C. Nielsen and IRI, either directly or through the Marketing Science Institute, provided store-tracking data and/or scanner-panel data to academics in major research universities around the world. Empirical marketing scientists developed methods for addressing basic management issues, putting these methods into the public domain through articles in top-tier journals such as *Management Science*, *Marketing Science*, and *The Journal of Marketing Research*. Manufacturers, and the data intermediaries themselves, could develop proprietary versions of the methods they found useful. Academics got to work on interesting problems, advance the state of knowledge, and advance their careers. Not a great deal of consulting resulted from this arrangement, basically because grocery retailers work on notoriously slim margins, and they don't have the management expertise to readily use the intellectual property resulting from the publications. Doctoral education benefited because PhD students were equipped and eager to handle the advanced statistical work. That was enough to sustain the model. Not very much of it filtered into the MBA classroom, because teaching advanced statistics to MBA students is a painful experience. Even when simulators were developed to eliminate the need to understand the statistical side, MBA students were not very enamored with the mundane complexities of tactical promotion planning and retail category or brand management. This is partly why grocery retailers find it hard to attract good MBAs.

I had been involved from the very beginning in setting up the university infrastructure to deal with the onslaught of scanner data. Because of my early work in market-share analysis (Nakanishi and Cooper, 1974), UCLA was one of the very first to receive such data. Gerry Eskin, one of the founders of IRI, heard me speak to a Procter-and-Gamble-sponsored invitational conference in the fall of 1982 (Cooper, Nakanishi, and Hanssens, 1982), thought my work could be applied to scanner data, and sent a tape full of scanner data out to UCLA with Penny Baron, another IRI founder, who began a stint as a visiting faculty member the following January.

Marketing academics were just as interested in trying to tame this newest data source, Internet data. What they tended to encounter were overworked and overstressed staffs of Internet companies that were unlikely to carry through on promises of data, or huge, raw Web site logs that required horrendous amounts of processing before even a glimmer of market intelligence would show. None-the-less, marketing researchers have persevered, developing methods for modeling log-file data from online content sites to estimate advertising exposure (Chatterjee, Hoffman, and Novak, 2003), panel-data models of purchase conversion (Ansari and Mela, 2003; Bucklin et al., 2002; Sismeiro and Bucklin, 2003; Moe, 2003; Moe and Fader, 2001, 2004; Bucklin and Sismeiro, 2003; Moe and Fader, 2002; Park and Fader, 2002; Moe et al., 2002), and navigational methods seeking to understand the antecedents of purcha se (Montgomery et al., 2002).

Since Internet data rapidly becomes massive, academics would benefit from other agencies or intermediaries doing the programming and most of the data handling. The Marketing Science Institute played a facilitating role with retail scanner data, and an analogous role would be helpful with Internet data. Most of the faculty contribution would be formalized in equations. Since you don't patent equations, the intellectual-property (IP) issues do not seem insurmountable. IP concerns should not be an inhibiting force.

4. A BUSINESS-INTELLIGENCE SUITE

Harnessing the demand end of the dynamic merchandising chain, as a personalization/recommendation engine inherently should, makes the development of business-intelligence suites relatively straightforward. The basic questions are: "Who are our best customers?" "What products do these customers purchase?" "What other products and services do we have that these customers might like?" and "How can we acquire more customers like these?"

4.1. Who Are Our Best Customers?

The easiest way to track this basic question is by a plot such as that in Figure 1, based on an analysis of data provided by eHobbies.com.[8] The X-axis shows profits per customer and the Y-axis show the dollar share of sales for each segment. For eHobbies.com, Ethnic Elite, Small Town Success, Wealthy Commuter, and Affluent Elite are the segments with above-average profits per customer and above-average dollar shares. In the spring of 2000, these were eHobbies.com's most valuable segments. Finding out what products they like, and using this knowledge for create up-selling and cross-selling opportunities, are basic elements of retail strategy. The "Margin Squeezers" are segments with above-average dollar share of sales, but below-average profits per customer. Is there a way to structure benefits such as free shipping that can increase the margins on these high-dollar segments? The "Underdeveloped Segments" have high profit per customer, but low dollar share. These segments

---

[8] I would like to thank Seth Greenberg, CEO of eHobbies.com, for allowing me to use these data.

are secondary candidates for cross selling aimed at increasing the dollar volume. Finally, the "Low Value Segments" buy little and have small profit per customer at current margins.

4.2.   What Products Do Our Best Customers Purchase?

To grow current customers, you must know their tastes. eHobbies.com has four major product groups: Models, Trains, Radio Controlled, and Die Cast. Models are most popular with ages 35–44, those in the Southeast region, and the Close-Knit Hispanic segment. The Close-Knit Hispanic segment contains households with average income and education, mostly Hispanics, and living in homes of average value. Many depend on public assistance. This is an Underdeveloped Segment in Figure 1. Trains are most popular with older (65–74) customers, male customers, and the Affluent-Elite segment—wealthy, highly educated, white-collar careerists who are mostly Caucasian and Asian-Americans who live in expensive homes in urban areas. Radio-Controlled products are most popular with the young (25–29) in the Urban-Challenge segment—low-income African Americans and Caucasians with higher unemployment rates, and who live in older, low-value, dense housing, mostly in industrial cities. Many tend to have below-average education, commute via mass transit, and receive public aid—a Low-Value Segment in Figure 1. Die-Cast products are favored by women, older age groups (55–64), those living in the Far-West region, and Diverse-City-Prime segment—above-average in-

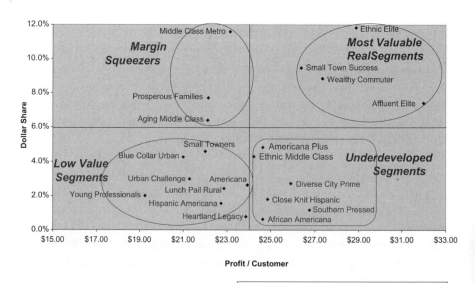

Figure 7-1. Crafting Segment-by Segment Marketing Strategies.

come, highly educated white-collar workers who are of diverse ethnicities including Hispanic, African American and Asian-American. Many live in urban areas, mostly in mid-Eastern states. This is an Underdeveloped segment for eHobbies.com.

When broken down by Most Valuable Segment, we find the Affluent Elite's favorite products are Traxxas Nitro 4-TEC RTR Car, Christmas Mixed Train Starter Set, JRS XP652 Helicopter Radio System, O-27 Lionel Santa Fe Special Train Set, and the G 2-8-0 Rio Grande C-16 #268-Bumble Bee. The Ethnic Elite favorites are 1/18 Porsche 911 GT1 '96 Street—Blue, Futaba 8UHPS PCM Radio System, Traxxas Nitro 4-TEC RTR Car, TTR RAPTOR 49BB PRO, Kyosho Dodge Ram QRC Combo, and the LGB's 30th Birthday Starter Set. Small-Town-Success segment's favorites are O-27 Lionel Santa Fe Special Train Set, Traxxas Nitro Rustler Truck w/Radio, Losi XXX-T 2 WD R/C Truck, and Hobbico Skyrunner R/C RTF EP Airplane. And the favorites for the Wealthy-Commuter segment are Traxxas Nitro 4-TEC RTR Car, O-27 Lionel Santa Fe Special Train Set, O-27 Lionel NYC Flyer Train Set, Hangar 9 Skypack Pilot Package, and the JR F400 with 4-517 Radio System.

These are simple answers to basic questions—easily obtained when the information systems are organized by a marketing-driven logic.

4.3.   What Other of Our Products and Services Might These Customers Like?

eHobbies.com had teams of veteran hobby-store owners coming up with manual rules for the complementary products to cross sell with each kit, but the empirical record provides an excellent substitute or complement for the hard-found expertise, and it's decomposable by segment. From the empirical record for the Affluent-Elite, Ethnic-Elite, and Wealthy-Commuter segments, we find the best cross sell for the Traxxas Nitro 4-TEC RTR Car is Dynamite BLUE THUNDER 20% high-performance fuel. For Small-Town Success it's the Futaba S148 Servo Precision J FM ("Genuine Futaba servos are the easiest and the most efficient way to upgrade your Futaba system").[9]

Looking at the cross-sell issue by product class gives you ideas that experts might not see. For dye-cast products, compliments are not popular. What sells in the same shopping cart are other dye-cast products. Multiple product discounts or other incentives to enhance the likelihood of larger shopping carts are indicated here.

For radio-controlled aircraft, the Hangar 9 Skypack Pilot Package is very popular at around $300 ("Hangar 9's Skypack package contains everything

---

[9]   This product description is from the eHobbies.com site.

Table 7-1. eHobbies.com's Experience Converting Browsers to Buyers

ZipSegment	Buyers	Browsers	Conversion
Ethnic Elite	1,680	2,07	37%
Small Town	1,580	698	69%
Wealthy Commuters	1,349	506	73%
Affluent Elite	992	428	70%
Diverse City Prime	488	292	63%

you need for takeoff. Convenient and comprehensive, the Skypack contains a JF F400 EX radio system, an MDS .40 FS Pro BB two stroke engine, one quart of Hangar 9's 'eroBlend fuel, a Master Airscrew 10 × 6 propeller and a Hangar 9 Start Up Field Pack which includes a glow igniter, fuel pump, chicken stick, four way wrench, two cycle glow plugs and starter tote.").[10] To an expert, putting this in your shopping cart is a sure sign that a beginning flyer is being set up. The empirical record and the expert would recommend a beginning trainer such as Hangar 9 Easy Fly 40 Trainer (Red or Blue).

The rules that generate these recommendations are simple *if–then* conditions. Rule-discovery algorithms, such as Cooper and Giuffrida (2000), Giuffrida et al. (1998), or specific ones as used here, easily capture the required evidence. They are readable and understandable by management with simple, empirical counts of the units, dollars, and margins involved. These are not the opaque results of collaborative filters or artificial-intelligence systems.

4.4. How Can We Acquire More Customers Like These?

The first step in acquiring new customers is trying to convert current browsers into customers. Offering something of value to convert a stranger into a registered browser enables customization that can increase the odds of converting browsers to buyers. eHobbies.com's experience converting browsers to buyers in their best segments is very good, as can be seen in Table 1.

Armed with registration information, eHobbies.com can *push* emails to browsers to try to convert them to buyers. A prototypical effort is shown in Figure 2.

In the online world, acquiring completely new customers has proven to be an expensive and uncertain proposition. If the same exogenously determined segmentation scheme was used independently by a number of Websites, then eHobbies.com's media buyers could indicate a willingness to pay some premium if eHobbies.com's banner ads are exposed only to eHobbies.com's best segments; in this case, Affluent Elite, Ethnic Elite, Small-Town Success, and

---

[10] This product description is from the eHobbies.com site.

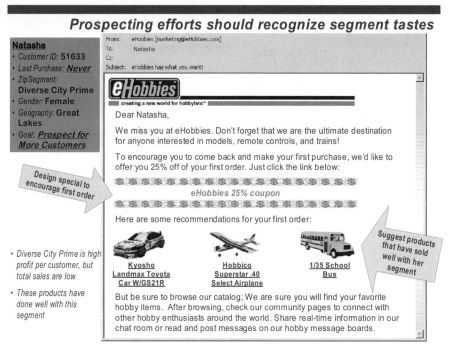

Figure 7-2. A prototypical effort.

Wealthy Commuter are the targets. This can be done anonymously, without the passing of customer identity, so that publisher sites don't violate their privacy policies.

Similar network benefits would accrue to email-list suppliers using the same exogenously determined segmentation scheme. Thus, emails could be crafted separately for each segment, with hot links that would cause recipients who chose to click through to be greeted at the site with segment-specific offerings. And finally, given that the action key is ZIP code, direct-mail lists can be bought for the ZIP codes in the desired segments. Thus, banner ads, emails, and direct mail can all be used to target the specific kinds of users that the site finds are its best customers. This is the benefit of a multi-channel segmentation system.

4.5. Improving Your e-Commerce Site

Putting the basics reported above into practice at an e-commerce site is straightforward, thanks to the standard capabilities of modern serve-side scripting languages. Figure 3 does this for eHobbies.com.

If management already knew all the things that the prior sections would help Websites learn, then the same benefits would accrue to Websites using

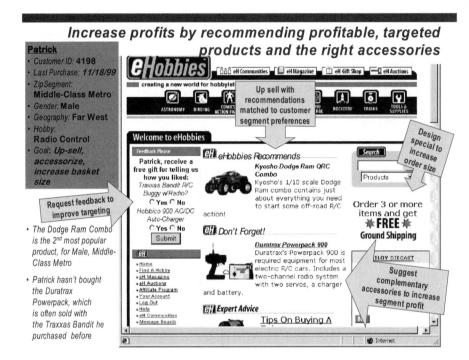

Figure 7-3. Increase profits by recommending profitable, targeted products and the right accessories.

manual-rules engines, such as BroadVision. Just as for the rules we learn with dataminers, manual rules are simple if-then statements that translate antecedent condition into actions (e.g., recommendations). If the Hangar 9 Skypack Pilot Package ends up in a shopping cart, then an expert would suspect a beginning R/C flyer is being set up, and consequently recommend a beginning training aircraft. As indicated above, eHobbies.com began by interviewing the veterans with years of hobby-shop experience to capture a set of such rules. While it is dangerous to assume you know all you need to know about your customers, many merchants moving from bricks-an-mortar operation to the web can use manual-rules engines to encapsulate the domain expertise they already have. I merely advocate that simple learning mechanisms, such as segment-based learning, be added to help the knowledge base grow. Manual rules and the rules from segment-based learning easily co-exist in personalization solutions.

5.   AD-OPTIMIZATION TEST

Personalization in computer-mediated environments will continue to grow. "Why? Because it works" (Foster, 2000).

A startup I worked with, which for the purposes of this chapter we will call Strategic Decision Corp., faced a compelling need to demonstrate that segment-based learning was a practical approach to Internet advertising optimizations problems. As with any Internet offer, we can learn how to target Internet banner ads more effectively using segment information. The special features of ad optimization do require fast learning, since the standard contract for a banner ad is only one month long, and budget constraints, since only a given number of exposures are paid for. As a condition of the C-Round venture funding the startup had to demonstrate that, for a consecutive, 30-day period, the segment-based learning and optimization produced at least 2X lift, including the time spent in learning, compared to a control group composed of these same campaigns. Some campaigns demanded so much traffic that optimization was nearly impossible. To satisfy the ad contract these banners had to be shown to too many segments for normal optimization. On the other hand, to insure that the optimization test was not just for cherry-picked campaigns, an additional condition require that, for the same 30-day period, the campaigns used to calculate the lift had to represent at least 50% of all paid traffic on the client site. The test criteria had to be satisfied before August 15, or the funding would be lost. This was a "bet the company" situation for the startup.

The startup began serving ads on the client site on May 19, 2000. Initially all ads were in a learning phase. But even by Day 2, some optimization was occurring. Figure 4 shows the cumulative performance. June 19th was the first day a full 30-day window of execution existed. By June 28th the criteria were satisfied. The startup had served approximately 153,000,000 banner ads on the client site without failure, and the Lift was 2.06.

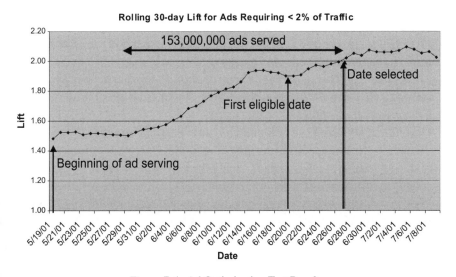

Figure 7-4. Ad Optimization Test Results.

The merchandizing side of personalization is much simpler to put into operation, than optimized ad serving. Product recommendations will rarely, if ever, require the 1,200 recommendations per second that can be demanded for banner ads. Products are typically not budgeted as to how many times they are to be shown in a month. And product life cycles are typically much longer that banner-ad life cycles, leaving much more time to benefit from what has been learned, before one item is replaced by another.

6. THE FUTURE OF PERSONALIZATION

Lately, managers are slowing down in their adoption of personalization techniques. Some have complained that, in the economic downswing that followed the Internet Bubble Burst, these techniques are too expensive and do not provide a big enough return on investment. One reason for this may be that we really do not know well enough consumers want from personalization. This is an area where marketing and behavioral scientists can add a lot of value—doing the research to uncover the *whys* so the techniques can work more efficiently at solving problems for which the consumers actually want answers. Lot of interesting research remains undone.

I am ever mindful of Alan Kay's famous slogan that the best way to predict the future is to invent it. Despite an alignment of agendas between marketing-science faculty at research universities and the most forward thinking Web merchants, I hesitate to forecast that faculty will invent the future of web merchandizing. I do, however, expect certain patterns to emerge:

1. Rule-based engines will grow at the expense of black-box systems. The basic tenet is that concerned management wants to know and understand the rules that are driving its marketing efforts. Whether rule-generating data-miners, manual rules, or some hybrid system will emerge is not clear. But I expect transparency to prevail. The exception to this lies in sensitive applications such as credit scoring, where not knowing the generating rules may have practical advantages for managers.
2. Despite the academic interest in behavioral segmentation, ZAG-based segmentation schemes will unite Web marketing with its natural brethren—direct marketing and database marketing. Multi-channel segmentation schemes that strengthen the ties between these allied fields will be favored.
3. Personalization engines will feed the demand component of integrated supply-chain systems.

As with any forecast, you are always on safer ground if the foundational elements are already positioned and operating. Such is the case with all three of these anticipated patterns.

REFERENCES

Ansari, Asim and Carl F. Mela (2003), "E-Customization," *Journal of Marketing Research*, 40, 2 (May), 131–145.

Bucklin, Randolph E., James M. Latin, Asim Ansari, Sunil Gupta, David Bell, Eloise Coupey, John D.C. Little, Carl Mela, Alan Montgomery, and Joel Steckel (2002), "Choice and the Internet: From Clickstream to Research Stream," *Marketing Letters*, 13, 3, 245–258.

Bucklin, Randolph E. and Catarina Sismeiro (2003), "A Model of Web Site Browsing Behavior Estimated on Clickstream Data," *Journal of Marketing Research*, (August), 249–267.

Chatterjee, Patrali, Donna L. Hoffman, and Thomas P. Novak (2003), "Modeling the Clickstream: Implications for Web-Based Advertising Efforts," *Marketing Science*, 22, 4, 520–541.

Cooper, Lee G. and Giovanni Giuffrida (2000), "Turning Datamining into a Management Science Tool," *Management Science*, 46, 2 (February), 249–264.

Cooper, Lee G., Masao Nakanishi, and Dominique M. Hanssens (1982), "Estimating Cross Competitive Influences on Market Share," The Procter and Gamble Invitational Psychometric Conference, October.

Foster, Cormac (2000), "The Personalization Chain: Demystifying Targeted Delivery," *Jupiter Vision Report, Site Operations Vol. 3*, New York: Jupiter Communications.

Giuffrida, Giovanni, Lee G. Cooper, and Wesley W. Chu (1998), "A Scalable Bottom-Up Data Mining Algorithm for Relational Databases." In *10th International Conference on Scientific and Statistical Database Management* (SSDBM '98), Capri, Italy, July 1998. IEEE Publisher.

Godin, Seth (1999), *Permission Marketing*, New York: Simon & Schuster.

Moe, Wendy W. (2003), "Buying, Searching, or Browsing: Differentiating between Online Shoppers Using In-Store Navigational Clickstream," *Journal of Consumer Psychology*, 13, 1&2, 29–40.

Moe, Wendy W. and Peter S. Fader (2001), "Uncovering Patterns in CyberShopping," *California Management Review*, 43, 4, 106–117.

Moe, Wendy W. and Peter S. Fader (2004), "Dynamic Conversion Behavior at e-Commerce Sites," *Management Science*, 50, 3, 326–335.

Montgomery, Alan L., Shibo Li, Kannan Srinivasan, and John C. Liechty (2002), "Predicting Online Purchase Conversion Using Web Path Analysis." Working Paper, Graduate School of Industrial Administration, Carnegie Mellon University.

Nakanishi, Masao and Cooper, Lee G. (1974), "Parameter Estimation for a Multiplicative Competitive Interaction Model-Least Squares Approach," *Journal of Marketing Research*, 11 (August), 303–311.

Sismeiro, Catarina and Randolph E. Bucklin (2003), "Modeling Purchase Behavior at an Ecommerce Website: A Conditional Probability Approach," *Journal of Marketing Research*, 40 (July), 249–267.

West, Patricia, Dan Ariely, Steve Bellman, Eric Bradlow, Joel Huber, Eric Johnson, Barbara Kahn, John Little, and David Schkade (1999), "Agents to the Rescue," *Marketing Letters*, 10, 3 (August), 285–300.

Wind, Yoram (1978), "Issues and Advances in Segmentation Research," *Journal of Marketing Research*, XV (August), 317–333.

Chapter 8

THE REAL VALUE OF B2B: FROM COMMERCE TOWARDS INTERACTION AND KNOWLEDGE SHARING

Mohanbir Sawhney[a] and Eleonora Di Maria[b]

[a]*Kellogg Graduate School of Management, Northwestern University, Leverone Hall, 2001 Sheridan Road, Evanston, IL 60208-2001;* [b]*TeDIS Center, Venice International University, Island of S. Servolo, 30100 Venice, Italy*

Abstract   The paper analyzes the evolution of business-to-business e-commerce (B2B) and outlines the emerging framework for business networks where interactive relations between firms are empowered by ICT. The rise and decline of B2B have highlighted the weaknesses of its hypotheses, focused on the benefits for firms to gain in efficiency through electronic transactions (Transaction cost theory). The economic and financial problems in which B2B marketplaces occurred have stressed the difficulties of their transaction-based business models, while the low value of e-commerce over the years can be explained in terms of firms' indifference in using electronic networks as new commercial channels. Instead, such emphasis on emerging technology solutions, mainly based on the Web, to connect firms with its customers, suppliers and partners increases firm's opportunities of interaction within its value chain. From a knowledge-based perspective, firms are discovering a completely different scenario and new drivers for their competitiveness, based on a renovated use of ICT to manage distributed business processes. Opposite to the e-commerce value proposition focused on spot efficiency of electric transactions, firms refer to ICT to enhance their established networks of business-to-business relationships.

1.   INTRODUCTION

Certainly, e-commerce was put at the core of the new economy paradigm, as the flag of the deep transformation driven by network technologies that was supposed to open a completely new economic era. Specifically, opposite to business-to-consumer, analysts stressed how the real opportunities in terms of value generation based on ICT should have risen from business-to-business e-commerce (B2B) (AMR Research, 2004, Lief, 1999a, 1999b). However, as we all know, the rise and decline of B2B have highlighted the weaknesses of its hypotheses, focused on the benefits for firms to gain in efficiency through electronic transactions.

The enhancement of connectivity between enterprises has led to tremendous business model innovation in business-to-business e-commerce. B2B e-commerce has gone through several generations of business models evolution, from Electronic Data Interchange (EDI) to e-commerce to e-marketplaces to incumbent-sponsored consortia (Kaplan and Sawhney, 2000; Phillips, Meeker et al., 2000; Kalakota, Oliva, and Donath, 1999). However, the economic and financial problems in which marketplaces occurred have stressed the difficulties of their transaction-based business models, while the low value of e-commerce over the years can be explained in terms of firms' indifference in using electronic networks as new commercial channels (Day, Fein, and Ruppersberger, 2003).

On the contrary, the emphasis on technology solutions mainly based on the Web to connect firms with its customers, suppliers and partners increases firm's opportunities of interaction within its value chain (e.g. Sawhney and Zabin, 2001). From a knowledge-based perspective, firms are discovering a completely different scenario and new drivers for their competitiveness, based on a renovated use of ICT to manage distributed business processes (e.g. Nonaka, 1994; Davenport and Prusak, 1998). Opposite to the e-commerce value proposition focused on spot efficiency of electric transactions, firms refer to ICT to enhance their established networks of business-to-business relationships. While on the one hand, firms stress the inadequacy of e-commerce technology solutions to manage their business processes and products into electronic environment (i.e. fashion industry), on the other hand, firms find interesting chances in using ICT for interactive marketing and supply chain collaboration.

The paper analyzes the evolution of business-to-business e-commerce (B2B) and outlines the emerging framework for business networks where interactive relations between firms are empowered by ICT. We draw on Transaction Cost Theory, marketing channel theory, and the theory of networked organizations to delineate key evolutionary themes in B2B e-commerce. We propose that B2B e-commerce is evolving from transactions to collaboration, and from pure channel forms to hybrid channel forms. We propose that enterprises will gradually evolve their connectivity with suppliers and trading partners into robust networks anchored by the enterprise as the hub, and connected to trading partners through shared business processes. We outline the structure, the scope, and the governance issues that arise in the formation of such networks. We also offer perspectives on where value may migrate and the new value extraction points that might emerge in the new scenario.

2. KNOWLEDGE ECONOMY, NETWORK OF FIRMS AND THE CRISIS OF THE *NEW ECONOMY*

As we know, the *new economy* has not maintained its promises of extraordinary economic growth and value generation that everybody expected to see just few years ago. Following the gains in business-to-business e-commerce, players at all levels—suppliers, manufacturers, customers, sales networks, etc.—should have been able to achieve interesting portions of the value created by the use of Information and Communication Technologies in economic processes (Merrill Lynch, 2000; Kelly, 1998; Schwartz, 1999).

The paper intends to explore the reasons for such a huge failure in expectations through an analysis of the hypotheses at the basis of B2B. Specifically, the idea proposed in this paper regards the fact that most of the mistakes in that vision were related to weak assumptions on the relationship between ICT and the economic sphere in B2B. Shifting the focus from the transaction to a wider perspective of processes at the basis of value generation offers a better comprehension of the real dynamics of the knowledge economy designed by ICT, where value lies in networks (e.g. Sawhney and Parikh, 2001; Gulati, Nohria, and Zaheer, 2000).

2.1. Transaction vs. Knowledge Focus?

Firms' competitive advantage can be enhanced dramatically by information technology, by transforming business activities and potentialities remarkably (Venkatraman, 1994). In particular, we refer to the development of information and communication technology as worldwide network technologies able to stock, elaborate, diffuse information (information functions) and to support people communication and interaction at distance (communication functions) rapidly and economically. Specifically, the Internet as a global open network is changing social and economic relationships in a relevant way. From an electronic network that enables social interaction as in the case of virtual communities, these technology infrastructures are becoming more and more strategic supports for business processes.

In the *new economy*, the most common way to look at the impact of ICT on firms and economic process was suggested by the prevalent theoretical approach of transaction costs (Williamson, 1985; Malone, Yates, and Benjamin, 1989; Bakos, 1997). According to such perspective, in fact, studies focused their attention on transactions and on the need for their cost reductions, and by this, many scholars emphasized the relevant advantages in the efficient allocation of resources brought to firms by electronic markets. Such new mechanisms of transaction management based on electronic solutions should increase players' benefits in managing exchanges with respect to more limited "old markets" in terms of time and space.

However, such revolution in exchanges did not occur. We argue that among the most important reasons we can be put the strong links existing between exchanges carried out in the markets and manufacturing and consumption processes related to such exchanges (e.g. Porter, 1985; Hagel and Singer, 1999). The enthusiastic perspective of cheap, speed and frictionless transactions (e.g. Brynjolfsson and Smith, 1999) stressed firms' opportunities in the short run, opposite to the required change in the domain of production and consumption, a wider but slower process with respect to exchange update. In particular, ICT were considered as the drivers to overcome market failures and reach an efficient allocation of resources rapidly (Baley and Bakos, 1997).

It is properly the ambiguity of the role that ICT could play in the process of value generation that nurtured the growth of the *new economy*. Following the transaction cost perspective, such technology solutions should offer a different (better) organization of exchanges. Instead, if we consider such scenario from a knowledge-based perspective—from *new* to *knowledge* economy—such network technologies are but an important source in innovation processes, in which the role of network is emphasized (e.g. Leonard-Barton, 1995; Chesbrough and Teece, 1996; Hagel and Armstrong, 1997). ICT could generate value by stimulating innovative dynamics in the domain of manufacturing activities, in the production of new meanings and new forms of consumption, in a framework of interactive and knowledge-intensive supplier (firm)–buyer (customer) relationships.

Stressing the transactional aspect of business relations, the focus is on the single exchange, based on the fulfillment of goods and on the related payment (price). Therefore, ICT were interesting tools able to increase the efficiency of such a spot activity, easily obtainable in the short period. However, in contrast to such point of view, many studies highlighted how the links between buyer and supplier go far beyond the simple transaction step to include also design activities (i.e. lead-users), post-sales services, interactive processes based on sharing experience (i.e. communities), and so on (Brown and Duguid, 2000; Dyer and Singh, 1998; Quinn and Hilmer, 1994). Above all, to extract the greatest value as possible, those connections should refer to rich, stable and trustable fabrics of relationships, where players can perceive to enter into profitable networks.

Those linkages between the sphere of buyers and suppliers, of consumption and production are properly the ones that were underestimated by *new economy*, specifically in the domain of B2B. ICT can be very useful to support such communication networks whenever they are not simply exchange platform, but technological infrastructures for interactive electronic contexts where players can share knowledge, projects, processes and risks. The transaction cost approach does not offer a complete understanding of the real effects of the digital revolution: the value does not lie in advantages of efficiency, rather in the enlargement of the network of players with whom the firm can dialogue as well as in the potentialities of interaction. It is not simply a problem of profitable exchanges carried out electronically. Instead of chasing ephemeral gaining of efficiency, firms could exploit ICT to access to the variety of contexts and contributions of many players, nearby and far from the organization, on the basis of innovative forms of sharing through organizational and technological networks.

In the present era, the real focus of competitive advantage is the ability to collaborate with suppliers, customers and partners within a network-based environment, in which network technologies are the backbone and the key enablers of this transformation. ICT is not simply used to obtain exchange automation between firms, but more generally it is a fundamental tool to support value creation based on distributed processes of innovation and knowledge sharing carried out within an online (and off line) collaborative framework.

2.2.   Beyond e-Commerce: The Relevance of Networks

The shift in considering ICT not only a tool for managing information but most of all a communication medium points out the great opportunity it gives to re-design and create the economic place for organizations in a different manner. On the one hand, innovations in network technologies and on the other hand the growing importance of immaterial activities (services, dematerialization) give centrality to knowledge, as the focus of business competitive advantage (Davenport and Prusak, 1998). The opportunity to codify, manage, stock and exchange knowledge made possible by ICT becomes the starting point to separate it from its material support (its local context) and diffuse it everywhere. From this point of view, network technologies assume a relevant role as important mediums to share knowledge inside the organization as well as among them (Hansen, Nohria, and Tierney, 1999). Consequently, innovative processes have known a rapid and wide evolution, through a path of knowledge management strictly related with technologies and multiple interactive contributions distributed in time and space.

The reduction of costs to generate knowledge is assured by mass production and scale economies, coupled with standard products and a rigid control of final markets. This specific organization model has soon had to face changes in the world of consumers and the imposition of new technologies that modify time and costs to create and share knowledge in depth (e.g. Sawhney and Prandelli, 2000). Information and communication technology enlarges also knowledge sources, and connects contexts in which firms can pick up and store knowledge, while increasing the opportunity to combine and replicate it. This means thinking a wider framework to create learning and innovation that is not constrained in one organization; on the contrary we can argue a mechanism which stimulates high specialization among economic actors, each one able to offer specific units of knowledge (Arora, Gambardella, and Rullani, 1998; Brown and Duguid, 2000).

The net becomes a new powerful tool to extend firm's collaboration towards new partners, where the system of relationships is not restricted only to the actors within firm's value chain. Suppliers, distributors, complementors and customers can rapidly get in touch through Internet, where new intermediaries offer firms coordination to support a dynamic design of business relationships and exchanges on the Web.

From the vertically integrated firm, which manages the supply chain hierarchically, network technology plays an important role in the process of opening of firm's value chain (Evans and Wurster, 1997; Sawhney and Parikh, 2001). The improvement in information and partners' searching potentialities offered by network technologies (*reach*) gives firms an interesting opportunities to enlarge the focus outside the organization (hierarchy) and to find new specialized actors with whom to build new business ties. The supply chain can be redesigned according to new strategies, where the internal processes are managed through outsourcing towards new partners and the global coordination and control are carried out mainly electronically.

The supply chain is transformed in a value network (Andrews and Hahn, 1998), where firm's opportunities to find new players to carry out a specialized activity in the different steps of the supply chain increase because of ICT. From transaction support, electronic network and emerging technological solutions drive firms to the redesign of the basis of their competitive advantages (expertise) in terms of business network redesign (Venkatraman, 1994). Electronic integration among the members of the network is carried out in order to facilitate the increase of expertise: from EDI system oriented to support transactions automatically, nowadays electronic networks are able to sustain new forms of collaboration and extend the access to knowledge through a growing and dynamic network. Firms have interesting choices in enlarging and enhancing their expertise by the exploitation of others' capabilities connected through the Web (March, 1991). Electronic networks allow the firm to enlarge the number of its partners and to create a network-based system at the basis of its competition.

According to the level of power in the firm at the central position in the web (the *architect*, Sawhney and Zabin, 2001), firms are able to design their own value chains exploiting modularity and communication and collaborative advantages of electronic networks. From a knowledge perspective, the value chain is no more just within organizations, but it can be reorganized, fragmented and reconfigured by the firm with the involvement of multiple business actors, each of them with a specific role in the process of value creation and as a source for competitive advantage.

Players that arrange, coordinate, and optimize the network of business-to-business relationships play a fundamental role, especially as regards the definition and management of new electronic environments to support these new innovative forms of organizations (Evans and Wurster, 1997; Hagel and Singer, 1999). Specifically, the sources of value embedded in the network may vary according to the role played by those third parties, who can actually assume the strategic leadership of the network itself (Sawhney and Parikh, 2001). In fact, firms' opportunities to enlarge the systems of connections outside their traditional boundaries towards new partners not only depend on the use of ICT in terms of information searching and interaction, but also on firms' abilities to extend their webs of partners.

3. THE EVOLUTION OF BUSINESS-TO-BUSINESS E-COMMERCE: A RETROSPECTIVE ANALYSIS

The rapid evolution in network technologies has transformed the business-to-business e-commerce (B2B) deeply, where efficiency increasing as well as partners' searching and interaction have been the main goals for firms to achieve. The exceptional growth and the rapid dynamics of B2B exchanges over the Web stress the greater B2B economic impact with respect to business-to-consumer (B2C). However, despite favorable forecasts provided by analysts about B2B trends, troubles suffered by many new comers during the end of 2000 and the beginning of the new millennium highlight that the competitive framework is still difficult to predict.

3.1. From the Myth of Disintermediation to Reintermediation Processes

Despite market advantages in terms of information aggregation, transaction support (logistics, settlement), exchange regulation and government (Bakos, 1998), the existence of market failures in the management of transactions (Williamson, 1985) justifies the hierarchy as the optimal mechanism of governance, under specific circumstances. The renaissance of the market as an efficient mechanism is described by Malone, Yates, and Benjamin (1987, 1989) who identify in the network technology the key system to eliminate market failures. Those technologies are able to provide wide information access to economic players, reducing searching costs and information asymmetry dramatically. Moreover, they increase communication efficiency and control and thereby benefits in terms of automation of transactions and risk reductions. According to this perspective, independent agents can manage economic transactions directly through the market, by exploiting electronic communication and information advantages (Bakos, 1991; Benjamin and Wigand, 1995).

An immediate consequence of firms' ability to find easily and rapidly their transactions partners is the disintermediation process, where existing middlemen are substituted by direct interactions among economic players in the electronic markets. Disintermediation is the process of replacement of traditional trading mechanisms with alternative ones (Davidow and Malone, 1992; Bakos, 1997). From the physical environment buyer-seller relationships shift towards the new marketspace, where information becomes the critical element to gain and sustain firm's competitive advantage (Rayport and Sviokla, 1994). In this perspective, network technology and the Internet specifically reduce transaction costs (electronic brokerage effect) in direct relationships between buyer and seller (manufacturer and customer), and so referring to the intermediary becomes more expensive (Malone, Yates, and Benjamin, 1987, 1989).

Despite these simplified forecasts, the elimination of middlemen is not a general trend in all kinds of transactions. Rather, these processes stimulate a remarkable transformation in the intermediary sphere, where new intermediaries arise and old middlemen change their functions. The term 'reintermediation' properly describes this phenomenon, where the disintermediated player can re-enter into the buyer–supplier chain, providing new value in transactions. On the one hand, traditional intermediaries decide to use information technology and transform their organizations in order to provide the same or new offering to their clients. On the other hand, completely new intermediaries emerge, providing their services only through the Net. In particular, they exploit the advantages of the electronic context, where marginal cost of information production and distribution (i.e. digital goods) is quite near to zero (Bakos, 1998).

Together with information intermediaries, linking middlemen were considered the most important ones in the new economy scenario as they add value in the transaction by connecting buyers and sellers and offering guarantees to both sides of the market. Brokers allowed the matching between buyers and sellers, generally through a catalog-based aggregation (fees) (Spulber, 1998). Auctioneers not only should have sustained the information process in transactions, but they should also have played an active part in their conclusion, in terms of new electronic channel or the creation of completely new markets (dynamic pricing) (Sawhney, 1999; Wimmer et al., 2000). Exchanges should have supported the matching between buyers and sellers especially for commodity or near-commodity markets. These intermediaries build up mechanisms of certification and guarantee (i.e. clearing), rules for trading and price definitions on a centralized basis. Finally, dealers were also involved in the ownership of the goods exchanged in the transaction, by offering a double service for buyers (ask prices) and sellers (bid).

To sum up, the idea of Internet frictionless commerce (Brynjolfsson and Smith, 1999) had to face a more complex scenario. Intermediaries add relevant value to business relationships, by coupling old functions and new business opportunities, also by trying to develop trust-based relationships (e.g. Bakos, 1998).

3.2. Taxonomy and Evolution of Business-to-Business Exchange Models

At its beginning the history of B2B is essentially firm-centric (Figure 1). Through proprietary systems (Electronic Data Interchange) firms manage transactions directly by point-to-point connections, to transfer codified information within closed infrastructures. Benefits of speed and automation in the transaction process are counterbalanced by negative problems mainly related to the low level of flexibility and opening of the EDI architecture, which requires high specific investments for each business-to-business relationship (Kalakota, Oliva, and Donath, 1999).

The second phase of the B2B arises from the Internet as an open worldwide network based on public standard and low costs of access. From mid-'90s, the emergence of the Internet increased firms' (and customers) possibilities dramatically. On the one hand, it is based on an open standard that avoids perils of asset-specific investments, by diminishing players' obstacles to enter into the network. On the other hand, Internet has a global dimension because of the possibility of connecting different (sub)networks into the web. Moreover, there is no central unit that rules the whole system, which is able to evolve according to unpredictable paths.

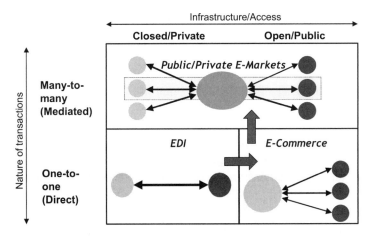

Figure 8-1. The History of B2B Evolution.

From a business-to-business point of view, the complete conclusion of economic transactions through the Internet, the electronic commerce process, involved players in the sell-side of the market as primary protagonists. From the simple exchange of data, network technology allows to carrying out complete online transactions in real time, while e-commerce relationships are still built by the firm with its customers in terms of one-to-one connections. A firm's Web site becomes the point to attract the demand and give open access to the firm's offering (Merrill Lynch, 2000).

However, the third and most important era of the B2B e-commerce is that of neutral market makers (hubs) as dominant focus in the scenario of *new economy* (Kaplan and Sawhney, 2000; Mahadevan, 2000; Phillips, Meeker et al., 2000). One of the most important advantages of the Internet as a worldwide network is, in fact, that it allows the development of many-to-many interactions where more players can be involved simultaneously. Hubs developed as third-party intermediaries that exploit Internet infrastructure to provide buyer-seller matching, within a specific industry (vertical) or a specific business function (horizontal) in a public marketplace (Sawhney and Kaplan, 1999). These electronic markets are managed by third parties, which occupy a central position between supply and demand, and aggregate both buyers and sellers in a neutral exchange environment. Specifically, hubs provide a many-to-many infrastructure able to sustain business-to-business relationships either within the boundaries of closed and private networks as EDI or in public environments as open online markets.

The development of these kinds of intermediaries was justified by the high value added to transactions in terms of aggregation of buyers and sellers, providing advantages of liquidity, and reducing transaction costs (Sawhney and Kaplan, 1999). Their central position in business-to-business relationships allowed them to influence both sides of the market to carry out e-commerce transactions within their Internet-based marketplace. Moreover, especially as regards vertical hubs, they are not generic electronic markets as those described by Malone et al. but are industry-focused. They should solve industry fragmentation problems, providing a unique central point of exchange for the players of the supply chain. Furthermore, those firms could find specialized and customized services and exchange mechanisms, tailored on the industry process characteristics of manufacturing and distribution. Their deep focus on a specific industry domain should have improved the e-commerce values for players in terms of content and relationships, while other economic agents have access to a well-targeted audience, increasing the effectiveness of their offering (Sawhney and Kaplan, 1999). Instead, horizontal hubs were specialized in specific processes or functions (i.e. MRO.com) and offer them across vertical markets, with high advantages under the scale perspective. Efficiency and process automation are the main goals and benefits provided by those intermediaries.

The category scope (vertical/horizontal) is one of the criteria to classify electronic hubs (Kaplan and Sawhney, 2000). The second one is related to the methods of purchasing carried out by firms, in terms of frequency of transactions, which is systematic or spot sourcing. With the catalog model, electronic hub provides aggregation among many buyers and sellers in stable and well-defined conditions of transactions as prices. Instead, the matching function in the electronic environment occurs through the dynamic market models that work specifically for non-standard (auction) or near-commodity (exchange) products (Sawhney and Kaplan, 1999).

Broadly speaking, these intermediaries promised to redesign the framework of business-to-business relationships by creating an actual alternative to the traditional context in which firms used to compete and interact. These marketplaces identify and offer firms best practices related to a specific industry (vertical marketplace) as a tool for benchmarking and consequently they increase the value achieved by firms in participating in that hub (Kerrigan et al., 2001). Especially in the past two years, due to initial success of these new neutral intermediaries such as e-Steel or PlasticsNet, firms observed which relevant benefits and fundamental sources for their competitive advantages could lie in the B2B e-commerce. Apparently, the well-established framework based on hubs eliminated doubts about what should have been the future for business-to-business transactions.

4. B2B E-COMMERCE AND THE THREE MISTAKES OF MARKETPLACES

Despite the raising number of these net market makers during the end of '90 and 2000, firms have approached these electronic marketplaces and the advantages they offer carefully, especially considering firm's embeddedness in established networks of business relations. Moreover, business-to-business e-commerce is far more complex than that on the consumer side. Basically, transactions among firms require the definitions of many different critical conditions (i.e. logistics, product specifications, or terms of payments) as well as the involvement of multiple decision-makers for the order approval (Phillips, Meeker et al., 2000). The number of participants may also be relevant (companies, employees, or professionals), especially when a transaction refers to complex processes, which require the collaboration among many players (engineering, creativity industries such as fashion, etc.). Above all, rules for exchange, communication and interaction procedures as fundamental infrastructures in B2B can vary not only among industries but also among firms specialized in the same industry. Negotiation processes as well as previous interactions among firms are critical factors that have to be taken into careful account. At the same time firms could face a lot of risks and disadvantages in going on line directly: potential channel conflict, increase in direct competition, organizational change, and coordination needs (e.g. Kalakota, Oliva, and Donath, 1999; Gulati and Garino, 2000).

As remarked for the business-to-consumer e-commerce, the business-to-business domain hubs focused on supporting exchanges of commodity (or near commodity) goods (Bakos, 1991). However, even hub intermediaries specialized in industries such as paper (i.e. Paperexchange.com), steel (eSteel.com), plastics (PlasticsNet.com) or energy (Altra.com) showed to encounter many problems in sustaining their business models. These intermediaries faced the critical problem of liquidity, related to the critical mass of players to attract and consequently the volume of transactions they can manage.

In fact the hub's growth is based on the number of participants and so because of its neutral position in the market it needs to involve both buyers and sellers (Bakos, 1991; Sawhney and Kaplan, 1999). Liquidity is a "chicken-and-egg" problem (Sawhney and Kaplan, 1999): demand enters into the market when a sufficient level of offer is available online, while sellers are interested in transacting through the electronic marketplace only when a relevant audience on the buy-side is ensured. No matter which side of the market obtains the main benefits, the hub has to convince as many industry players as possible in order to develop and sustain its market mechanisms (auction particularly), a difficult task especially with respect to high-fragmented industries.

One of the main problems that was evident to analysts and new players in the *new economy* very soon was that the low rate of e-commerce carrying out into through marketplace platforms was reducing the sustainability of hubs' models. The less the number of electronic transactions concluded on line, the lower hubs' fees and incomes related to such amount of transacted value. Focusing on transactions as the primary source of value for new intermediaries (revenue model) became the first driver of their flops.

4.1. The Three Reasons for Marketplaces' Failures

Morgan Stanley Dean Witter registered an exponential growth in marketplaces from 1995 to 1999, and AMR research registered more than 600 B2B electronic markets. Against general expectation, the take off of marketplaces did not occur (Day, Fein, and Ruppersberger, 2003). On the one hand, the overall amount of transactions through electronic markets has never reached the fabulous promises of 1999 (Forrester Research, Business 2.0). On the other hand, studies on buyers' behaviors concerning such form of transaction management confirms their low interests for hubs, especially when considering small and mediums enterprises (SMEs).

Actually, despite the pressures of emerging intermediaries (Porter, 2001), firms changed slowly their established networks of business relationships towards the opportunities of new technologies. Those intermediaries have experimented completely new technological solutions and were able to offer codes, standards and shared interfaces not available before (Roddy, Obrst, and Cheyer, 2000). However, the focus of such innovative service offering remained on transactions, by figuring out speed standardized exchanges, with a limited involvement of the players. In such a way, the importance of the buyer–supplier relationship has been underestimated, in contrast to what the Japanese model have suggested for years (few selected suppliers, long-term scenario) (Cusumano and Takeishi, 1991).

Hence, in high-concentrated industries, value generated by hubs not only appeared to be derisory, but also the role of new intermediaries has been reduced by emerging sponsored and private exchanges (see below), where leaders managed established business relationships controlled by themselves electronically (Berryman and Heck, 2001; Porter, 2001). Moreover, deep resistance to marketplaces has been put in place by firms—as many SMEs— embedded into a rich fabric of business relationships and specialized in products where the core of the firm's offer is determined collaboratively between buyer and supplier and mutual trust rises from rich interaction in the context (Porter, 1998).

To sum up, three are the key unsolved problems related to the model of B2B marketplaces, as we knew them during the *new economy*, which lead them to failure (Table 1):

1. From a *strategic* point of view, there was a relevant gap between the market-based B2B relationship offered by hubs (focused on price and standard conditions) and the richer fabric of long-standing specific relations already existent in different industries, places and supply chains. Hubs were simply not able to understand the potentialities in ICT with respect to such specificity and the variety of business situations and needs across industries. A price shown through an on line Web page may not be sufficient to describe a firm potentiality in terms of quality of its products or its ability to innovate. Suppliers may not be interested in competing through on line platforms that squeeze their proposals, while they may obtain better results through cooperative relations with their customers. These are just two examples confirming the fact that the hypotheses at the basis of hub model overestimated firms' interests in gaining efficiency and reducing transaction costs over time.

2. From a *technological* point of view, hub's solutions did not reflect the complexity of information domain and the dynamics of relationships and transactions to be supported by them. It is not enough to develop secure and

Table 8-1. The Three Mistakes of Marketplaces

	New economy perspective	Knowledge economy perspective
Strategy	Focus on *efficiency*	Focus on *innovation*
Technology	Technology platforms for managing *standardized spot exchanges*	Technology platforms for managing *interactive collaborative relationships*
Business model	Short term (value drivers: *finance*)	Long term (value drivers: *manufacture/industry*)

speed platforms (managing "the exit from the transaction"), if the main problem for firms concerns the management of a complexity that goes beyond transactions. As it is easy to understand, the business-to-business relation goes too far the transactional elements, to embrace deep relationships with customers or suppliers in many directions (design, quality certification, innovation activities, etc.). However, it should recognize the enormous effort carried out by hubs during the *new economy* bubble in experimenting technological solutions to face such a complicate scenario—and in this competence their renaissance could lie as solution providers (see below).

3. From a *financial* point of view, the revenue model based on transaction fees demonstrated to be unsustainable, by increasing the difficulties of financiers, who expected returns on the short term. In the growing financial bubble of the *new economy*, hubs promised to develop considerable sources of profits through transaction-based business models. Instead, there was a *mismatch* between the short term of the financial perspective and the long term required for the transformation in manufacturing processes and consumption models consistently with the new economic paradigm that should have followed the old economy.

Despite great advantages of automation capability in managing business-to-business relationships online, we think that satisfying firm's need of network coordination will be one of the most compelling challenges for the evolution of the hub. Companies within supply chains could think of marketplaces as principal supporters in competition and for business design. Electronic hubs have the necessary qualifications to become new dynamic and innovative environments where to gather information, collect and share knowledge, coordinate and manage complexity to help firms formulate their strategic decisions better (e.g. Wise and Morrison, 2000; Berryman and Heck, 2001).

According to those turbulent transformations, we believe that a new generation of B2B framework is emerging and is explained by the network economy picture. After the great attention given to increased efficiency provided by hubs, now the focus must come back to the network. Definitively, the principal

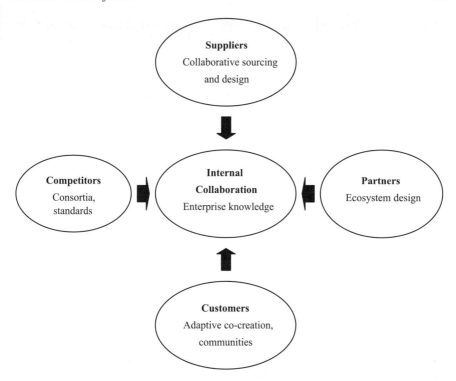

Figure 8-2. The Five Forces of Collaboration.

source of a firm's value and competitive advantage is linked with its capability to build and consolidate a wide partnership network (Gulati, Nohria, and Zaheer, 2000). Developing and sustaining relationships with suppliers, collaborators, customers, and complementors can be improved successfully through network technology (Figure 2). Hence, connections deployed through electronic hubs represent profitable investments.

5.   FROM TRANSACTION TO SHARING

With respect to the approach that emphases the transaction as the core of different technology platform proposals, the recent failure of marketplaces highlights the need for shifting the attention to the mechanisms at the basis of resource and risk sharing among firms in business-to-business relations. In business networks players depend on one another in the knowledge creation, access and diffusion related to specific contexts. Many are the evolutionary paths following the crisis of electronic markets that stress the vision of ICT as innovative tools for knowledge sharing.

Networks allow enlarging the division of cognitive labor (Arora, Gambardella, and Rullani, 1998; Brown and Duguid, 2000), by offering a strategic support to firms in a scenario of network-based organizational forms. Even in the case of electronic (digital) networks, drivers for knowledge management such as shared languages, systems of guarantees, communication, and cooperation still remain relevant.

In such perspective, a first path of evolution after hubs is related to industry leaders, who transform themselves into emerging managers of on line environment to rule established relationships in their specialized supply chains (Hoffman, Keedy, and Roberts, 2002; Berryman et al., 1998). Through sponsored and private marketplaces, those firms obtain again a central role in the dynamics of knowledge management, by subordinating the development of sophisticate technology platforms to their competitive strategies.

Another path of evolution refers to the transformation of marketplaces into collaborative business-to-business environment (collaborative marketplaces). The exploitation of opportunities related to network technologies could be perceived in terms of electronic places to share ideas, projects, experiences and knowledge within the network. Moreover, new opportunities for the neutral intermediaries are related to their roles as partners of firms in their value chains (focus on service) or more generally as a new player able to connect different contexts and sources of innovation (Sawhney, Prandelli, and Verona, 2003). Such players could have an extraordinary importance in generating value for firms by supporting firms' connection as well as by offering distinctive services.

5.1. The Rise of Industry Sponsored Exchanges

From February 2000 the B2B scenario changed dramatically, as many big leader companies in different industries announced the creation of consortia in order to develop proprietary industry marketplaces. After the announce of the Big Three in the automotive industry—their consortium (named Covisint) has been built for the management of procurement and suppliers' relationships—other leaders in different industries (airlines, energy, metal, or computer) are implementing new strategies in the business-to-business e-commerce domain. These new intermediaries, known as Industry Sponsored Exchanges (Phillips, Meeker et al., 2000) should offer leaders the opportunity to achieve supply chain efficiency, cost savings and increase time-to-market. The emergence of ISE highlights the persistent attention to the supply chain management.

On exploiting leaders' positions and power, these marketplaces can immediately benefit from the injection of liquidity provided by those firms, but with negative consequences in terms of transparency and equity management of the market exchange. More generally, they refer to biased hubs as an expression of one side of the market (either sellers or buyers), focused on the protection and satisfaction of its interests (Kaplan and Sawhney, 2000). Biased hubs do not have to face the liquidity problem because of their direct connection with players' wishes and goals. Above all, biased hubs offer greater benefits when fragmentation characterizes only one of the two sides of the market.

By breaking the supply chain into its essential entities (manufacturers, distributors, and buyers) as described in Figure 3, all these players show great attention towards the creation of their own marketplaces. Consequently, competition shifts from the neutral hub to the ISE level. Leaders are well aware of their important contribution in solving the liquidity issue neutral intermediaries had to face. Most important of all, private and sponsored exchanges stressed the role of leading firms in organizing and managing the web of relationships within and among value chains through on line environment, on the basis of rules and procedures defined by leaders. The constitution of consortia among leaders can have significant implications for the structure and operation of market exchanges (Sawhney and Acer, 2000; Goldman Sachs, 2000). An unfair competitive behavior could arise as a result of self-interest positions (Bakos and Nault, 1997; Johnson, 2000). However, those firms are also aware of the potentialities of such technology tools as collaborative platforms (i.e. Covisint), where the focus gradually shifts from efficient transactions to a deeper management of all the aspects of sourcing, manufacturing and commercial activities.

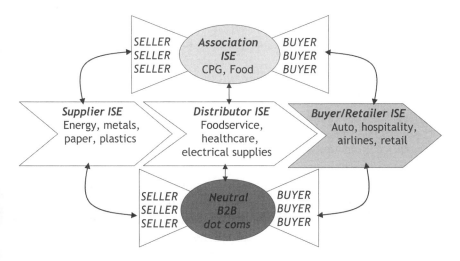

Figure 8-3. The Emergence of Industry Consortia.

5.2. From Transaction Management to Solution Providers and on Line Collaboration

The relevant experience of the new intermediaries in developing technology solutions for on line transaction management can lead them to new business opportunities.

VerticalNet, a pioneer in the scenario of B2B, has promoted such strategic path of evolution. Near the support to its vertical communities (industry marketplaces), VerticalNet acquired Atlas Commerce and became a provider of technological solutions for the management of the extended enterprise (*eXtended Enterprise Management*, XEM). By exploiting Atlas' competencies, a former company specialized in software solution for the management of private exchanges, VerticalNet was able to extend its technological offering considerably. Nowadays, VerticalNet offers one of the most complete suites for the management of sourcing, by coupling applications focused on collaboration between supplier and customer with platforms for managing many-to-many business relations.

By leveraging XEM characteristics of visibility and transparency, such solution allow enterprises managing processes of information search and exchange as well as multi-partner collaboration in an open environment, through just one universal standard-based tool for the whole network of business relations already existing. Platforms for *collaborative sourcing* support the management of *strategic sourcing* as well as firm's collaborative dynamics based on shared resources and processes. VerticalNet business model has progressively shifted from B2B content and community management towards technological services and has increased its revenues with respect to the low source of revenues related to marketplaces (Girishankar, 2001). Such *service specialists* may hence become interesting partners for firms in helping them using ICT for their strategic aims as the management of their networks of relations (Wise and Morrison, 2000).

From a knowledge-based perspective, such transformation stresses a more awareness of intermediaries in what could be their roles in the framework of firms' value webs, within the competitive scenario designed by ICT. In particular, it must recognize their contributions in the definition of innovative technological solutions to face complex problems of collaboration among players in electronic environment. The capacity to offer targeted and effective solutions in such domain (*problem solving*) requires more effort, knowledge and competencies than those needed for the management of efficient matching between demand and supply (Wise and Morrison, 2000). It means giving value and supporting firms' capacity and creativity to re-design their value ecosystems as a source of value, by providing them with solutions and services those firms are not able to develop by their own (*solution provider*).

6.   THE MISSING LINK FOR HUBS: MANAGING KNOWLEDGE-BASED NETWORKS

In the scenario drawn by network technologies, enlarging the circuit of knowledge means access to a greater number of ideas on the one hand and cost reduction of use on the other hand through the multiplication of occasions of knowledge use within the network. In a context where innovation is not just carried out within firms—by following a closed innovation paradigm—but by exploiting internal as well external knowledge (open innovation paradigm), the approach to ICT in business-to-business relationships has to be different from a pure e-commerce vision.

For decades, large firms have been able to settle the conditions (communication standards, guarantees, languages) required for an efficient management of innovative process within their value chains in relation to proprietary knowledge processes. In the same way, through the experimentation within industry sponsored marketplaces, industry leaders have remarked their central role in designing new electronic environment for knowledge generation and diffusion, where rules of behavior were defined by leaders.

On the contrary, in distributed manufacturing contexts, firms' ability and the capacity to define and to carry out network infrastructures able to guarantee a sustainable and reliable knowledge management system are less taken for granted. Such difficulties are even higher whenever it should shift from physical to electronic forms of interaction. Problems related to the definition of such rules refer to the nature of public goods of those infrastructures (Porter, 2001), where none of the firms (especially small ones) has the convenience to set up and manage them because of the externality effects. Hence, with respect to the initial enthusiastic hypotheses, promoters of e-commerce found more difficulties than those they expected, where the value generated from efficiency gaining and electronic market management tends to decrease over time (Porter, 2001). Opposite to the expectation, it is clear that managing B2B relationships is not a pure technology problem (i.e. e-commerce security). Instead, it is related to the promotion of public goods that is in the promotion of standard languages and codes of communication, able to support the extension of division of labor among firms beyond their specific organizational and territorial contexts.

Obstacles in communication—even in electronic markets—depend more on a linguistic gap than on a technological gap between firms. In highly structured industries, such as automotive, the reduction of such gap was made possible by the effort of big leading companies, which imposed their standards to suppliers and commercial networks. Instead, where there is not a clear leader, firm organizational practices are almost always incompatible (i.e. standard for quality definition, such as in the fashion industry) and therefore increasing difficulties in a process of convergence. Network standards, going beyond the EDI experience, do not help firms in managing efficient business relationships, but also in starting processes of knowledge sharing, where communication standards (languages) have a primary role. Standards increase flexibility on the one hand and increase supply chain differentiation, where players have different roles. Hence, in the network economy, from marketplace management, the intermediaries born with the new economy could renovate their offering by connecting firms within valuable business networks (Sawhney and Parikh, 2001).

The critical element for the sustainability of value networks managed electronically and their capabilities to support value creation over time is both in the ability to configure, coordinate and synchronize nodes dynamically and efficiently, and in the integration of the multiple contributions and activities within the whole network (Sawhney and Zabin, 2001). However, in this process of alternative solutions a trade-off exists for firms. On the one side, firms can set up new interactive connections with a growing number of firms rapidly, in order to establish business relationships and carry out exchanges with the support of electronic networks (Evans and Wurster, 1997). On the other side, firms must take into account where the real sources of value are in this rising system of partners. In fact, with respect to the large number of potential business connections that can be built up, only in a small portion of them lies the value created by the firm and its competitive advantage. Firms should have interests in sustaining specifically the strategic connections with suppliers, distributions and the market (customers), centered on the exchange of specialized knowledge at the basis for innovation and new potential value, where the balance between internal activities and outsourcing is strategically relevant for a sustainable competitive advantage (Chesbrough and Teece, 1996).

Innovation is a distributed process, where knowledge rises because of reciprocal contamination, shared language and practice. Value lies in the openness of the system that supports innovation (interaction), where players are not interested in protecting their own innovative activities and results (interdependent community of members). Value capture regards the transformation of the firm towards an open network of connections with multiple partners. In the second phase instead, firms could be interested in defining the rules of the game, that is standards or other mechanisms of control (ownership, interface, etc.). Value capture is related to the firm's ability in creating and acquiring those control systems (i.e. a privileged relationships with customers). The third phase of value maximization coming from innovation is the real step where firms can achieve value. In that step, customers are at the center of firm's strategy because they are important owners of knowledge related to the experience of offering. The value capture lies in the leverage of rich connections with customers, where they become part of the innovation system (Germany and Muralidharan, 2001).

By shifting the focus from electronic commerce to knowledge sharing, ICT reveal their important roles in the business-to-business scenario. Opposite to the emphasis on price, the crisis of marketplace and the selective use of technology solutions by firms (specifically SMEs) stress the fact that firms have recourse to more interactive and richer mechanisms for managing B2B relations. From such perspective, the value is built on dynamics of sharing, which support new innovation processes. In the coming years, an urgent strategic issue for firms will not be to solve the problem of efficiency in a static context (efficient allocation of limited resources), rather to have access to stimulating contexts where to acquire new occasions for innovating actively.

REFERENCES

Amit R. and Zott C. (2001), "Value creation in e-business", *Strategic Management Journal*, n. 22.

AMR Research (2004), *B2B Commerce Forecast: $5.7T By 2004*, www.amrresearch.com.

Andrews, P.P. and Hahn, J. (1998), "Transforming supply chains into value webs", *Strategy & Leadership*, July–August.

Arora A., Gambardella A., and Rullani E. (1998), "Division of Labour and the Locus of Inventive Activity", *Journal of Management and Governance*, n. 1, Fall.

Bakos Y. (1991), "A Strategic Analysis of Electronic Marketplaces", *MIS Quarterly*, vol. 18, n. 3, September.

Bakos Y. (1997), "Reducing buyer search costs: implications for electronic marketplaces", *Management Science*, vol. 43, n. 12.

Bakos Y. (1998), "The Emerging Role of Electronic Marketplaces on the Internet", *Communications of the ACM*, n. 8.

Bakos Y. and Nault B. (1997), "Ownership and Investment in Electronic Networks", *Information System Research*, vol. 8, n. 4, December.

Baley J.P. and Bakos Y. (1997), "An exploratory study of the emerging role of electronic intermediaries", *International Journal of Electronic Commerce*, vol. 1, n. 3.

Benjamin R. and Wigand R. (1995), "Electronic markets and virtual value chains on the information superhighways", *Sloan Management Review*, vol. 36, n. 2.

Berryman K., Harrington L., Layton-Rodin D., and Rerolle V. (1998), "Electronic Commerce: Three Emerging Strategies", *McKinsey Quarterly*, n. 1.

Berryman K. and Heck S. (2001), "Is the Third Time the Charm of B2B?", *McKinsey Quarterly*, n. 2.

Brown J.S. and Duguid P. (2000), *The Social Life of Information*, Harvard Business School Press, Cambridge, Mass.

Brynjolfsson E. and Smith M.D. (1999), "Frictionless commerce? A comparison of Internet and conventional retailers", *Management Science*, vol. 46, n. 4.

Chesbrough H.W. and Teece D.J. (1996), "When is Virtual Virtuous?", *Harvard Business Review*, January–February.

Das T.K. and Teng B.S. (2000), "Instabilities of Strategic Alliances: An Internal Tensions Perspective", *Organization Science*, vol. 11, n. 1, January–February.

Davenport T.H. and Prusak L. (1998), *Working Knowledge. How Organizations Manage What They Know*, Harvard Business School Press, Boston.

Davidow W.H. and Malone M.S. (1992), *The Virtual Corporation*, Harper Collins, NY.

Day G.S., Fein A.J., and Ruppersberger G. (2003), "Shakeouts in Digital Markets: Lessons from B2B Exchanges", *California Management Review*, vol. 45, n. 2, Winter.

Dyer J.H. and Singh H. (1998), "The relational view: cooperative strategy and sources of interorganizational competitive advantage", *Academy of Management Review*, vol. 23, n. 4.

Evans, P.B. and Wurster, T.S. (1997), "Strategy and the new economics of information", *Harvard Business Review*, September–October.

Germany R. and Muralidharan R. (2001), "The Three Phases of Value Capture", *Strategy & Business*, n. 22, First Quarterly.

Girishankar S. (2001), "Vertical Marketplaces Pioneers Reinvent Their Roles", *InformationWeek.com*, February 12.

Goldman Sachs (2000), *The Consortium Report: Businesses of the World, Unite?*, May 8.

Gulati R. and Garino J. (2000), "Get the Right Mix of Bricks and Clicks", *Harvard Business Review*, May–June.

Gulati R., Nohria N., and Zaheer A. (2000), "Strategic networks", *Strategic Management Journal*, vol. 21, n. 3.

Hagel J. and Armstrong A.G. (1997), *Net Gain*, HBS Press, Cambridge, Mass.

Hagel J. and Singer M. (1999), *Net Worth: Shaping Markets when Customers Make the Rules*, Harvard Business School Press, Boston, Mass.

Hansen M.T., Nohria N., and Tierney T. (1999). "What's Your Strategy for Managing Knowledge?", *Harvard Business Review*, March–April.

Hoffman W., Keedy J., and Roberts K. (2002), "The unexpected return of B2B", *The McKinsey Quarterly*, n. 3.

Johnson B. (2000), *B2B Exchanges: Making Customer Ownership Work*, Unpublished Paper, Stanford University, May, www.netmarketmakers.com

Kalakota R., Oliva R.A., and Donath B. (1999), "Move over, e-commerce", *Marketing Management*, vol. 3, n. 8, Fall.

Kaplan S. and Sawhney M. (2000), "E-Hubs: The New B2B Marketplaces", *Harvard Business Review*, May–June.

Kelly K. (1998), *New Rules for the New Economy: 10 Ways the Network Economy is Changing Everything*, Fourth Estate, London.

Kerrigan R., Roegner E.V., Swinford D.D., and Zawada C.C. (2001), "B2Basics", *McKinsey Quarterly*, n. 1.

Leonard-Barton D. (1995), *Wellsprings of Knowledge: Building and Sustaining the Source of Innovation*, Harvard Business School Press, Cambridge, Mass.

Lief V. (1999a), *Anatomy of New Market Models*, Forrester Report, February.

Lief V. (1999b), *New Marketplaces Grow Up*, Forrester Report, December.

Mahadevan B. (2000), "Business Models for Internet-Based E-Commerce: an Anatomy", *California Management Review*, vol. 42, n. 4, Summer.

Malone T.W., Yates J., and Benjamin R.J. (1987), "Electronic Markets and Electronic Hierarchies", *Communication of the ACM*, XXX, 6.

Malone T.W., Yates J., and Benjamin R.J. (1989), "The Logic of Electronic Markets", *Harvard Business Review*, May–June.

March J.G. (1991), "Exploration and Exploitation in Organizational Learning", *Organization Science*, vol. 2, n. 1.

Merrill Lynch (2000), *The B2B Market Maker Book*, Report, February.

Nonaka I. (1994), "A Dynamic Theory of Organizational Knowledge Creation", *Organization Science*, vol. 5, n.1.

Phillips C., Meeker M. *et al.* (2000), *The B2B Internet Report. Collaborative Commerce*, Morgan Stanley Dean Witter Report, April.

Porter M.E. (1985), *Competitive Advantage*, The Free Press, New York.

Porter M.E. (1998), "Clusters and the New Economics of Competition", *Harvard Business Review*, November–December.

Porter M.E. (2001), "Strategy and the Internet", *Harvard Business Review*, March.

Quinn J.B. and Hilmer F.G. (1994), "Strategic Outsourcing", *Sloan Management Review*, Summer.

Rayport J.F. and Sviokla J.J. (1994), "Managing in the Marketspace", *Harvard Business Review*, November–December.

Roddy D., Obrst L., and Cheyer A. (2000), "Competing in the Evolving Landscape of B2B Digital Markets", *Tradeum White Paper*, June 15.

Sawhney M. (1999), "Making New Markets", *Business 2.0*, May.

Sawhney M. and Acer J. (2000), "Dangerous Liasons", *Business 2.0*, October, 24.

Sawhney M. and Kaplan S. (1999), "Let's Get Vertical", *Business 2.0*, September.

Sawhney M. and Parikh D. (2001), "Where value lives in a networked world", *Harvard Business Review*, January.

Sawhney M. and Prandelli E. (2000), "Communities of Creation: Managing Distributed Innovation in Turbulent Markets", *California Management Review*, n. 4, Summer.

Sawhney M., Prandelli E., and Verona G. (2003), "The Power of Innomediation", *MIT Sloan Management Review*, Winter.

Sawhney M. and Zabin J. (2001), *The Seven Steps to Nirvana. Strategic Insights into eBusiness Transformation*, McGraw-Hill, New York.

Schwartz E.I. (1999), *Digital Darwinism: 7 Breakthrough Business Strategies for Surviving in the Cutthroat Web Economy*, Penguin, London.

Shapiro C. and Varian H.R. (1999a), *Information Rules. A Strategic Guide to the Network Economy*, Harvard Business School Press, Boston, MA.

Spulber D.F. (1998), *The Market Makers: How Leading Companies Create and Win Markets*, McGraw-Hill, New York.

Venkatraman N. (1994), "IT-enabled business transformation: from automation to business scope redefinition", *Sloan Management Review*, n. 2, 73–88.

Williamson O.E. (1985), *The Economic Institutions of Capitalism: Firms, Markets, Relational Contracting*, Free Press, New York.

Wimmer B.S., Townsend A.M., and Chezum B.E. (2000), "Information technologies and the role of middlemen: the changing role of information intermediaries in an information-rich economy", *Journal of Labor Research*, vol. 21, n. 3.

Wise R. and Morrison D. (2000), "Beyond the Exchange. The Future of B2B", *Harvard Business Review*, November–December.

Chapter 9

BUSINESS-TO-BUSINESS ELECTRONIC MARKETS: DOES TRADING ON NEW INFORMATION CREATE VALUE, AND FOR WHOM?

Haim Mendelson and Tunay I. Tunca

Graduate School of Business, Stanford University, Stanford, CA 94305-5015

Abstract   This paper studies the impact of a Business-to-Business electronic market on an environment where manufacturers used fixed-term contracts to purchase materials from suppliers. We focus on the effects of private information and consider the interaction between fixed-term contracting and the electronic market. We study the effects of the electronic market on the participants using four factors: changes in industry structure, information effects, volatility and price flexibility. We find that the effects of Business-to-Business electronic markets on industry performance are subtle, and that it can make the supply chain as a whole less profitable, with the benefits accruing largely to consumers.

1.   INTRODUCTION

This paper analyzes how a Business-to-Business (B2B) electronic market (or *exchange)* affects industry performance and what determines the benefits and costs created by the exchange for industry participants. We focus on the role of the electronic market as an enabler of trading on new information about demand and supply (cost) conditions and as an aggregator of market information. While one might naively assume that the ability to act on new information should make industry participants better off, the effects of introducing an exchange require a careful analysis of competing factors whose net effect on any given participant may be positive or negative. In this paper we identify, and quantify, these factors.

We believe the recent confusion about the value of B2B exchanges is partly the result of substituting wishful thinking and hyperbolae for a careful analysis of the issues. In February 2000, Forrester Research estimated that about $400 billion of trades would flow through B2B exchanges in the United States in 2000, and projected their growth to \$2.7 trillion (or 53% of all electronic supply chain transactions) by 2004 (Kafka et al., 2000). The investment community followed suit, investing more than \$5 billion in 363 companies that undertook such B2B efforts. An Ariba White Paper proclaimed: "Ultimately, all businesses will buy on a marketplace, sell on a marketplace, host a marketplace, or be marginalized by a marketplace," consulting firms advised companies to change their business processes so they could take advantage of the new capabilities, and some companies proceeded with implementations. Indeed, the logic of B2B exchanges seems compelling: the ability to trade in almost real time at low cost must surely result in significant value creation for supply chain participants, and could—in the long run—change the way supply chain transactions are conducted. This logic, however, fails to take into account the subtle effects of B2B exchanges on industry structure, information advantage, volatility and price flexibility, and the reallocation of profits that they entail, which are the subject of this paper.

With the bubble bursting, the investment and business communities lost much of their enthusiasm for B2B exchanges. And yet, some managers continue to believe in the value of these exchanges, and a recent survey conducted by the Institute for Supply Management and Forrester Research found that the use of such markets increased from 23% of companies surveyed in the third quarter of 2001 to 33% in the third quarter of 2003 (Bartels et al., 2003). The popular press followed suit, writing about B2B trading coming "back from the dead" and "enjoying a healthy renaissance" (Hellweg, 2002, Weinberg, 2003).

Some observers argue that B2B electronic markets failed to catch on as quickly as initially anticipated due the required *transition* to a new way of doing business, including adoption difficulties, uncertainties and the need to change business processes to take advantage of the capabilities of the new technology. But this leaves open a fundamental question: assuming all of these transitory difficulties have been overcome and B2B exchanges can be successfully implemented and adopted, what would their long-term impact be? Will they create value, and if so—for whom?

Resolving some of this confusion calls a theory to help explain participants' incentives and the equilibrium results obtained under the new market structure. In this paper we study the impact of introducing a B2B exchange to an industry that was characterized by fixed-price procurement. We focus on the effects of being able to utilize new information and on the supply chain participants' decisions how much (and whether) to buy (sell) in the contracting stage and how much to leave for exchange trading, when better demand and cost information are available. Our framework enables us to evaluate how and when a B2B exchange can create or destroy value, and for whom. It enables an examination of the effects of a B2B exchange on the use of traditional fixed-term contracting, and of factors that affect the operation and viability of the exchange itself.

We model a two-level supply chain with multiple suppliers and manufacturers who contract for an intermediate good. There are three periods in our model. In the first period, the suppliers contract with the manufacturers, setting the terms (price and quantity) of the contracts among them. Then, both the manufacturers and the suppliers receive new, private information. If there is a B2B exchange for the intermediate good, the participants can trade on the exchange in the second period, taking advantage of their updated information. In the third period, the consumer market (modeled as a Cournot oligopoly) clears. Thus, the manufacturers can purchase the intermediate good from the suppliers either via fixed-price contracts (in period 1) or on the exchange (in period 2).

In the contracting stage, there is no informational asymmetry among the participants. At the beginning of the second period, each manufacturer obtains a noisy signal about the realization of demand, and each supplier obtains a noisy signal about the realization of the unit production cost of the intermediate product. The B2B exchange (when it exists) enables the participants to trade the intermediate good based on their updated information. When trading on the exchange, both the suppliers and the manufacturers can be either sellers or buyers. For instance, if a manufacturer gets a signal indicating a lower than expected consumer demand and she already committed to a large contracted purchase level, she may be better off selling some of that quantity on the exchange.

The alternative structures we study in this paper are quite flexible. For example, manufacturers have the choice between contracting with suppliers in the first period, selling in the second period some of the quantity they bought in the first period to other manufacturers, or buying on the exchange from suppliers or other manufacturers. We find that in spite of the option to wait for the second period after new information has been realized, manufacturers in fact find it optimal to buy a positive quantity from the suppliers in the first period. Thus, our results explain how different modes of transactions can be formed endogenously in equilibrium. In particular, the manufacturers never postpone all of their purchases until the second period, when they can make decisions based on new information because of the cost of illiquidity on the exchange, which is pervasive.

We use the results of Mendelson and Tunca (2004) and Tunca (2004) to analyze the equilibrium of this game, which enables us to focus on the subject of this paper: the stakeholders' gains and losses due to the introduction of a

B2B exchange. We find that the effects of introducing a B2B exchange on the participants are subtle. We classify them into four main categories.[1]

1. *Effect on industry structure.* The introduction of the exchange changes the bargaining power among suppliers and manufacturers. Under the contracting scheme we study, the suppliers have a first-mover advantage that tends to increase their bargaining power. We find that the exchange levels the playing field, reducing the suppliers' advantage. More broadly, the exchange, being a neutral trading arena, reduces the advantage of the party who has greater power at the contracting stage.
2. *Information effects.* The participants in the B2B exchange can act on both their own signals, which are not available in the contracting stage, and the information available to *other* market participants, which is reflected in the market price. The B2B exchange thus serves as an effective (albeit imperfect) mechanism to aggregate information from all market participants.
3. *Volatility effects.* The ability to trade on up-to-date information increases quantity volatility, which in general harms both suppliers and manufacturers and results, in effect, in a wealth transfer from supply chain participants to consumers.
4. *Price flexibility.* Because suppliers and manufacturers can condition the quantities they trade on the B2B exchange on its price, they gain additional flexibility to "buy low or sell high," which can increase their profits.

Several recent papers examine the effect of B2B exchanges in different settings (see Kleindorfer and Wu, 2003 for a survey). Lee and Whang (2002) model a two layer supply chain with one upstream firm and a very large number of downstream firms. The market operates in two consecutive periods in each of which an independent demand (idiosyncratic for each downstream firm) is realized in the newsvendor fashion. In between the two periods, a horizontal exchange among the downstream firms takes place where these firms can trade their excess inventory. The model predicts that the exchange increases the allocational efficiency but may or may not increase supplier profits and the performance of the supply chain. Wu, Kleindorfer, and Zhang (2002) examine the effect of a spot market on capacity-intensive intermediate goods contracting, where the parties decide on both capacity and production. The spot price is determined exogenously, and contracting takes place in a Stackelberg fashion. The suppliers set separate prices for capacity and usage, and the buyers, after setting the maximum capacity in the contracting stage, choose how much to use from the capacity they acquired and how much to buy on the spot market. They find that if the suppliers are likely to access the spot

---

[1] A fifth effect is the secondary price impact of noise on manufacturers' profits (see Section 3). This effect is small.

market, then no contracting takes place. Unlike our model, in these models the exchange price is set exogenously rather than being determined by the private cost and demand information available to the parties. Tunca and Zenios (2006) study the trade-off between cost and quality when procurement can take place using relational contracts or exchange-based supply auctions. They find that an exchange can result in a quality increase in the consumer market.

Another related branch of the literature is on forward markets. Allaz and Vila (1993) (see also the references therein) examine the role of selling forward in a Cournot duopoly. They show that if a market exists that allows the duopolists to sell forward for delivery in the period when demand is realized, the firms will choose to do so in every period prior to the last one, making them worse-off while making consumers better-off. In a sense, the existence of the forward market creates a situation similar to a prisoners' dilemma for the duopolists. In our model, we find that firms tend to use both trading mechanisms (contracting and B2B exchange) rather than focus on one. This is a result of the trade-off between the inherent illiquidity of the exchange (Mendelson and Tunca, 2004) and the benefits of trading on up-to-date information.

The rest of this paper is organized as follows. Section 2 presents the model and introduces the equilibrium concept. Section 3 analyzes the costs and benefits of using the exchange, and Section 4 illustrates the impact of the exchanges on the supply chain. Section 5 offers our concluding remarks.

2. THE MODEL

There are M suppliers and N manufacturers ($M, N \geq 2$) in a two-level supply chain that serves a consumer market. There are three time periods in the model indexed $t = 1, 2, 3$. At $t = 1$, contracting takes place between the suppliers and the manufacturers, taking into account all participants' actions in periods 2 and 3. The contracts specify the quantity of the intermediate product that will be delivered from each supplier to each manufacturer at time $t = 3$, and the unit price that each manufacturer will pay each supplier per unit. Before period 2 begins, the parties get additional information: The suppliers get private information about the production costs that they will incur for producing one unit of the intermediate good, and the manufacturers get private information about the state of demand in the consumer market. Without a B2B exchange, the parties are unable to readjust their contractually-committed positions according to their updated information. However, if an exchange is available, then the participants can trade the intermediate good on the exchange using their information and readjust their positions at $t = 2$. At $t = 3$, the consumer market clears with the quantities produced by the manufacturers, who compete as a Cournot oligopoly. Figure 1 summarizes the timeline.

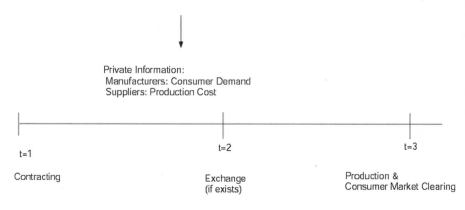

Figure 9-1. Model Timeline.

The consumer demand curve at $t = 3$ is assumed to be linear with slope normalized to unity. That is, the demand in the consumer market is given by

$$P_d = K + d - \sum_{i=1}^{N} Q_i, \tag{1}$$

where P_d is the clearing price in the consumer market, and Q_i is the quantity of the end product that is produced by manufacturer i for the consumer market. In (1), K represents the known component of the demand intercept and d represents the uncertain component. In a similar fashion, we denote $c = c_0 + h$ where h is the unknown component of the common production cost for all suppliers. Right before period 2, the manufacturers receive a noisy signal about d and the suppliers receive a noisy signal about h. Following Tunca (2004) and Mendelson and Tunca (2004), we assume that d is normally distributed with mean 0 and variance σ_d^2. The suppliers' unit production cost, denoted by c, is normally distributed with mean c_0 and variance σ_h^2. That is, $c = c_0 + h$ where h is normally distributed with mean 0 and variance σ_h^2. Before trading on the exchange, manufacturer i receives the signal $s_i^d = d + \varepsilon_i$, where ε_i are i.i.d. normal random variables with mean 0 and variance σ_ε^2. Similarly, supplier j receives the signal $s_j^h = h + u_j$, where u_j are i.i.d. normal random variables with mean 0 and variance σ_u^2. The noise terms are independent of d and h and the quantities contracted are common knowledge. Equilibrium conditions in the exchange are more formally given in the Appendix. Tunca (2004) derives a complex solution procedure for finding the equilibrium. In this article, we apply that solution procedure, focusing on the impact of introducing the exchange on supply chain participants.

When there is no exchange, denote the quantity contracted by each manufacturer by w_{ne}, the quantity contracted by each supplier by q_{ne} and the contract price per unit by p_{ne}. When there is an exchange, let w_i denote the quantity purchased by manufacturer i at $t = 1$ and let $w = (w_1, \ldots, w_N)$. Also denote the total quantity sold by supplier j at $t = 1$ by q_i and the contract price per unit by p_c. On the exchange, denote the quantity bought by manufacturer i by x_i, the quantity sold by supplier j by y_j, and the exchange price by p_e.

We study quantity competition among the suppliers in the contracting stage. The price set at $t = 1$ is the market clearing price under which the total quantity demanded by the manufacturers is equal to the total quantity committed by the suppliers. Thus, an equilibrium at this stage has to satisfy:

1. Given its competitors' quantities, each supplier chooses the quantity that maximizes his expected profit.
2. Given the market clearing price and the quantities selected by its competitors, each manufacturer chooses the order quantity that maximizes her expected profit.
3. The market clearing price is set so that the total quantity committed by the suppliers equals the total quantity committed by the manufacturers.

The equilibrium conditions are formally specified in the Appendix. Under this contracting scheme, the suppliers set their quantities before the market clearing price is determined, hence suppliers have considerable bargaining power compared to the exchange, which is a more neutral trading venue.

3. IMPACT OF THE EXCHANGE ON STAKEHOLDERS' SURPLUS

In this section, we address the effects of the B2B exchange on the surplus of the manufacturers, suppliers and consumers. We denote the total final payoffs for the manufacturers and the suppliers with the exchange by the random variables Π^m and Π^s respectively. For a specific manufacturer, given the structure and notation in Section 2, we have

$$\Pi_i^m = (w_i + x_i)\left(K + d - \sum_{k=1}^{N}(w_k + x_k) \right) - p_e x_i - p_c w_i, \tag{2}$$

and

$$\Pi_j^s = y_j(p_e - c_0 - h) + q_j(p_c - c_0), \tag{3}$$

for $i = 1, \ldots, N$ and $j = 1, \ldots, M$. Define the profits for the manufacturers and the suppliers without the exchange by Π_{ne}^m and Π_{ne}^s respectively. Finally denote the consumer surplus with the exchange by Π^c and without the exchange by Π_{ne}^c.

We focus on a linear equilibrium, i.e., an equilibrium where the participants' trading quantities are linear in the price and their signals. In a linear equilibrium, the quantity traded by manufacturer i on the exchange has the form

$$x_i = \alpha_0 + \alpha_s s_i^d + \alpha_p p_e, \tag{4}$$

where p_e is the market clearing price on the exchange. Similarly, the quantity traded by supplier j has the form

$$y_j = \beta_0 + \beta_s s_j^h + \beta_p p_e. \tag{5}$$

Our analysis focuses on symmetric linear equilibria and normal distributions. This is necessary for tractability and is common in the analysis of markets with information asymmetry with agents having correlated signals and multi-unit demands.[2] The in-depth analysis of such markets under private information is nearly impossible under more general conditions.

We start the analysis by considering how the manufacturers' profit functions change as a result of the introduction of the exchange. Using standard arguments, we can derive manufacturer i's expected increase in profit due to the exchange:

$$\Delta_i^m \triangleq E[\Pi_i^m] - \Pi_{ne}^m$$

$$= \left(E\left[(w_i + x_i)\left(K + d - \sum_{k=1}^{N}(w_k + x_k) \right) - p_e x_i \right] - p_c w_i \right) - \left(w_{ne}(K - N w_{ne}) - p_{ne} w_{ne} \right)$$

$$= \left(E[(w_i + x_i(s_i^d, p_e))(K + d)] - \sum_{k=1}^{N} E[(w_i + x_i(s_i^d, p_e))(w_k + x_k(s_k^d, p_e))] \right.$$

$$\left. - E[p_e(x_i)x_i(s_i^d, p_e)] - p_c w_i \right) - \left(w_{ne}(K - N w_{ne}) - p_{ne} w_{ne} \right)$$

$$= \left(K(w_i + E[x_i]) + \text{Cov}[x_i, d] - \sum_{k=1}^{N}(w_i + E[x_i])\left(w_k + E[x_k] - \sum_{k=1}^{N}\text{Cov}[x_i, x_k] \right. \right.$$

$$\left. \left. - E[x_i]E[p_e] - \text{Cov}[x_i, p_e] - p_c w_i \right) - \left(w_{ne}(K - N w_{ne}) - p_{ne} w_{ne} \right)$$

$$= \underbrace{\left(w_i + E[x_i] \right)\left(K - \sum_{k=1}^{N}(w_k + E[x_k]) \right) - \left(w_i p_c + E[x_i]E[p_e] \right) - \left(w_{ne}(K - N w_{ne}) - p_{ne} w_{ne} \right)}_{MB_i}$$

$$+ \underbrace{\text{Cov}[x_i, d]}_{MI_i} - \underbrace{\left(N \text{Var}[\alpha_s d + \alpha_p p_e] + \sigma_\varepsilon^2 + \alpha_s E[s_i^d p_e] \right)}_{MV_i} - \underbrace{\alpha_p \text{Var}[p_e]}_{MF_i} - \underbrace{2N\alpha_p\alpha_s \text{Cov}[p_e, \varepsilon_i]}_{MS_i}. \tag{6}$$

---

[2]   See, e.g., Novshek and Sonnenschein (1982), Vives (1984), Gal-Or (1985), (1986), Li (1985), Shapiro (1986), Raith (1996) and Jin (2000) for a sequence of papers that utilize similar structures to analyze the information sharing problem in oligopoly as well as O'Hara (1997) for such models relating to financial markets.

Similarly, supplier j's expected increase in profit due to the introduction of the exchange is

$$\Delta_j^s \triangleq E[\Pi_j^s] - \Pi_{ne}^s$$

$$= E[y_j(p_e - c_0 - h)] + q_j(p_c - c_0) - q_{ne}(p_{ne} - c_0)$$

$$= \underbrace{E[y_j]E[p_e] + q_j p_c - c_0(E[y_j] + q_j) - q_{ne}(p_{ne} - c_0)}_{SB_j}$$

$$\underbrace{- \text{Cov}[y_j, h]}_{SI_j} + \underbrace{\beta_s E[s_j^h p_e]}_{SV_j} + \underbrace{\beta_p \text{Var}[p_e]}_{SF_j}. \qquad (7)$$

Finally, the expected increase in consumer surplus is given by

$$\Delta_{CS} \triangleq E[\Pi^c] - \Pi_{ne}^c$$

$$= \frac{1}{2} E\left[\left(\sum_{i=1}^N w_i + x_i \right)^2 \right] - \frac{1}{2} \left(\sum_{i=1}^N w_{ne} \right)^2$$

$$= \frac{1}{2} \left(\underbrace{\left(E\left[\sum_{i=1}^N w_i + x_i \right] \right)^2 - \left(\sum_{i=1}^N w_{ne} \right)^2}_{CB} + \underbrace{\text{Var}\left[\sum_{i=1}^N w_i + x_i \right]}_{CV} \right). \qquad (8)$$

We define $\Delta^m = \sum_{i=1}^N \Delta_i^m$ and $\Delta^s = \sum_{j=1}^M \Delta_j^s$ as the increase in total manufacturer and supplier expected profits, respectively. We also define $\Delta_{SC} = \Delta^m + \Delta^s$ as the total increase in expected supply chain profits and $\Delta_{SS} = \Delta_{SC} + \Delta_{CS}$.

The decompositions in (6)–(8) show how the B2B exchange affects the profits of the manufacturers and suppliers as well as the consumer surplus. We classify these effects into five categories: *(i)* the effect of the exchange on industry structure, *(ii)* information effects, *(iii)* volatility effects, *(iv)* price flexibility, and *(v)* second-order price-impact effect. We discuss each of these effects below.

3.1. Industry Structure

The first terms in (6), (7) and (8) (labelled MB_i for manufacturer i, SB_j for supplier j, and CB for the consumers) reflect the changes in surplus due to the effects of the B2B exchange on industry structure. First, the new opportunity to trade on the exchange following the contracting stage tends to "level the playing field" and reduce the bargaining power the suppliers had in the contracting stage. In particular, the exchange creates a more neutral trading environment compared to contracting (where the suppliers were the first movers). Giving the manufacturers the option to trade on a neutral exchange reduces the bargaining power of the suppliers. As a result, we should expect this factor to benefit the manufacturers, with the term MB_i being positive (see Figure 2) and the term SB_j being negative.

3.2.   Information Effects

The ability to trade on the B2B exchange after the signals were observed by market participants can give them an advantage. The option of having postponed trades on the exchange enables the participants to better adjust the quantities they produce to more up-to-date demand and cost information. This has a positive impact on their expected profits.

There are two types of information that the exchange enables supply chain participants to utilize: Their *own* information and the information of *other market participants*, which is aggregated in the market price. The second terms in (6) and (7) (labelled *MI* and *SI*, respectively) reflect gains from utilizing information and they are positive. Hence, there is a positive correlation between x_i and d and negative correlation between y_j and h, showing that the ability to utilize better information has a positive effect on both the manufacturers' and the suppliers' profits.

The exchange improves the participants' profits not only by allowing them to use their own information, but also by enabling them to learn from the information observed by other market participants. Both the manufacturers and the suppliers obtain an aggregate summary of all market participants' signals by observing the clearing price on the exchange. The B2B exchange aggregates information in a *credible* way because participants ultimately transact at the equilibrium price (rather than just float information or misinformation that they don't have to act on). This improves both the quality of demand estimates for the manufacturers and the quality of cost estimates for the suppliers. Further, the price also contains information about *other* manufacturers' *production plans*, which can significantly improve decision making and profits for the manufacturers.

However, the transmission of information via the exchange price is not perfect. The reason is that the market price aggregates signals from both sides of the market. From the manufacturers' point of view, the impact of the suppliers' orders on the market price is noise; a symmetric argument applies when observing from to the suppliers' point of view. The higher this "noise", the lower the value of the information contained in the market price to the participants.

3.3. Volatility Effects

Even though all agents are risk neutral in our model, the exchange creates *quantity uncertainty* that adversely affects the participants' profits. This is shown in expressions (6), (7) and (8) by the terms labeled MV_i, SV_j and CV, respectively. Consider the manufacturers first. There is a positive correlation between manufacturer i's quantity and those of her competitors. This reduces manufacturer i's expected profits, because the positive correlation implies that manufacturer i will produce less for high-price outcomes and more for low-price outcomes. The last term in MV_i corresponds to another type of undesirable volatility: when a manufacturer gets a high demand signal, this should increase both the quantity she buys on the exchange and the exchange price—hence her costs. Again, this has a negative effect on the manufacturer's expected profits.

As for the suppliers, since they do not face a consumer market following trading on the exchange, the first effect does not exist, and the effect of volatility on their profits is limited to the second one, which is, again, always negative.

Contrary to the supply chain participants, the consumers benefit from volatility. Essentially, consumers' payoff resembles to that of a put option, making their gains from lower prices exceed their losses from higher prices. As the price variability increases, this "option" value increases, implying that the B2B exchange can improve consumer surplus.

In sum, the B2B exchange increases volatility, which has a negative effect on both manufacturer and supplier profits but a positive effect on expected consumer surplus.

3.4. Price Flexibility

The terms labeled MF_i and SF_j reflect a positive effect of the B2B exchange on all supply chain participants. On the exchange, both the manufacturers and the suppliers adjust their quantities to the market price, albeit in different directions. All else equal, if the exchange price is higher, the manufacturers decrease the quantity they purchase on the exchange while the suppliers increase the quantity they sell. This makes both sides better off. The expected magnitude of these benefits which result from the ability to act on the market price is increasing in the market price variance. Thus, unlike quantity variability which creates a harmful volatility effect (see Section 3.3), price flexibility increases the expected profits of both the manufacturers and the suppliers.

3.5. Secondary Price Impact of Noise

In addition to the above factors, the noise in the signals has a subtle effect on the manufacturers' profits, which is captured by MS_i in (6). If a manufacturer obtains a high noise term, this increases her trading quantity *and* the exchange price at the same time. A higher price for the intermediate good reduces all the manufacturers' production quantities and increases the consumer market price. It follows that a high noise term (ε_i) in a manufacturer's signal increases both her quantity produced and the consumer price, thereby increasing her profits.

Because of the additive structure of equations (6)–(8), we can decompose a market participant's surplus using the five factors discussed above. Note, however, that the factors interact indirectly, since each participant takes into account the performance of the exchange before deciding on how to allocate quantities between fixed-term contracting and the exchange.

4.   WHO GAINS AND WHO LOSES: A NUMERICAL DEMONSTRATION

In this section, we numerically examine a tractable setting to obtain further insights on the different stakeholders' gains and losses due to the introduction of the exchange. To that end, we apply the surplus decomposition of Section 3.

Figure 2 illustrates how changing the quality of *supplier* information affects the *manufacturers'* profits. In figure 2 Δ_i^m is the expected profit difference for a manufacturer. MB_i is the component of the change due to the change in industry structure, MI_i is the component due to information usage, MV_i is the change due to volatility, MF_i is the change due to price flexibility and MS_i is the change due to the secondary impact of noise (see Section 3). The parameter values are $M = N = 3$, $\sigma_d^2 = 5$, $\sigma_\varepsilon^2 = 1$, $\sigma_u^2 = 5$, $K = 20$ and $c_0 = 10$.

As discussed in Section 3, the suppliers' trades in response to the cost signals they observe act as noise from the manufacturers' point of view, as they make it more difficult for the manufacturers to infer the state of demand from the price observed on the exchange. Naturally, this noise is larger when the suppliers' signals are more informative, e.g., when σ_h^2 (the variance of the suppliers' marginal costs) increases keeping σ_u^2 (the noise variance of the suppliers' signals) constant. This tends to decrease Δ_i^m as the suppliers' signals get more informative (i.e., as σ_h^2 increases), as we observe in the first (left) part of Figure 2. The increasing right part of the curve demonstrates the benefit of trading price variability. As the suppliers' signals get more informative, the market price variability increases and MF_i correspondingly increases as seen in Figure 2. When the suppliers' signals are very informative (i.e., for large values of the variance of suppliers' marginal costs, σ_h^2), this effect is strong, leading to an increase in the manufacturers' profits.

In Table 1 the operator δ denotes the percentage increase in a performance measure due to the introduction of the B2B exchange. Specifically, $\delta p_c = p_c / p_{ne}$, is the percentage change in the contracting price; $\delta E[p_c] =$

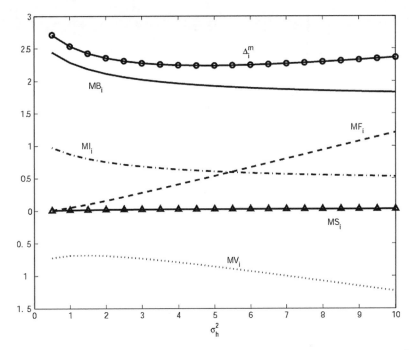

Figure 9-2. Sample Decomposition of Manufacturer Profit Difference with Varying σ_h^2.

$E[p_e]/p_{ne}$, is the difference between the expected exchange price and the contracting price with no exchange as a percentage of the contracting price with no exchange; $\delta TQ = (\sum_{i=1}^{N} Q_i)/q_{ne}$, is the percentage change in expected total production quantity; $\delta_s = \Delta^s/\Pi_{ne}^s$ is the percentage change in the expected supplier profit; $\delta_m = \Delta^m/\Pi_{ne}^m$, is the percentage change in the expected manufacturer profit; $\delta_{SC} = \Delta_{SC}/(\Pi_{ne}^m + \Pi_{ne}^s)$, is the percentage change in the expected supply chain surplus; $\delta_c = \Delta_{CS}/\Pi_{ne}^c$, is the percentage change in the expected consumer surplus; and $\delta_{SS} = \Delta_{SS}/(\Pi_{ne}^m + \Pi_{ne}^s + \Pi_{ne}^c)$, is the percentage change in expected social welfare (see Section 3). The parameter values in Table 1 span a range of discrete possibilities. The range is chosen so that the equilibrium outcome stabilizes at each dimension. For each margin level, the range covers 40,000 data points. For each margin level, the equilibrium outcome for 40,000 parameter combinations are calculated. For each case, N and M varied between 2 to 50, σ_d^2 and σ_h^2 varied between 5% to 75% of K and σ_ε^2 and σ_u^2 varied between 0.1% to 25% of K.

Table 1 shows how the B2B exchange affects the different components of surplus, studied in Section 3, for different "margin" levels defined as the percentage profit with sales at the highest willingness-to-pay consumer less the expected marginal cost divided by the former, i.e., $(K - c_0)/K$. In general, we can see that the B2B exchange increases quantities and reduces the prices for

Table 9-1. Percentage Change in Expected Prices, Quantities and Welfare Measures

Margin $(1 - c_0/K)$	% Change	δp_c	$\delta E[p_e]$	δTQ	δ_s	δ_m	δ_{SC}	δ_c	δ_{SS}
20%	Max	0	0.77	24.65	442.16	302.48	194.35	203.31	136.95
	Min	-3.92	-7.36	-0.67	-85.99	-68.97	-62.48	0	0
	Mean	-1.85	-2.17	6.92	-1.81	93.39	22.52	67.88	55.22
	Median	-1.18	-1.91	4.85	-31.61	88.73	18.27	65.41	48.23
40%	Max	0	0	21.07	94.13	120.18	16.94	82.85	39.63
	Min	-9.78	-12.93	0	-94.72	-59.22	-76.7	0	0
	Mean	-4.68	-5.24	9.04	-61.56	27.04	-30.45	32.52	15.47
	Median	-3.08	-4.27	8.87	-75.74	23.63	-27.77	29.62	15.48
60%	Max	0	0	20.08	34.58	67.38	0	61.11	21.7
	Min	-19.55	-22.21	0	-96.59	-59.84	-80.79	0	0
	Mean	-9.67	-10.66	9.74	-73.52	10.73	-41.86	26.7	8.15
	Median	-6.66	-8.73	9.8	-84.67	7.94	-40.38	24.03	8.06
80%	Max	0	0	30.97	11.92	53.41	0	71.77	15.46
	Min	-39.09	-41.25	0	-97.49	-60.88	-82.53	0	0
	Mean	-21.02	-23.03	10.1	-78.02	3.66	-46.41	24.91	5.61
	Median	-15.99	-20.43	9.99	-87.78	1.38	-45.59	22.94	5.34

the intermediate good. On average, manufacturers gain from the introduction of the exchange and the suppliers lose. The total change in supply chain surplus is generally negative. On the other hand, consumers are the ones who reap the benefits of the exchange, obtaining larger quantities (at a lower price) and benefiting from the variability in consumer prices that the exchange creates and hence extracting a larger consumer surplus. Table 1 suggests that the total surplus (which includes the consumer surplus) is higher due to the implementation of the exchange.

Figure 3 illustrates the effect of the exchange on the performance measures with varying margins $(1 - c_0/K)$. Panel (a) shows the median percentage changes in expected prices in the exchange and the contracting stages compared to the contracting case. Panel (b) shows the percentage change in total production quantity. Panel (c) shows percentage change in the surpluses of the suppliers, manufacturers and the consumers. Panel (d) shows the percentage change in the supply chain and social surplus. In panel (a), $\delta p_c = p_c/p_{ne}$, refers to the ratio of the change in the contracting price; and $\delta E[p_e] = E[p_e]/p_{ne}$, refers to the difference between the expected exchange price and the contracting price with no exchange as a ratio of the contracting

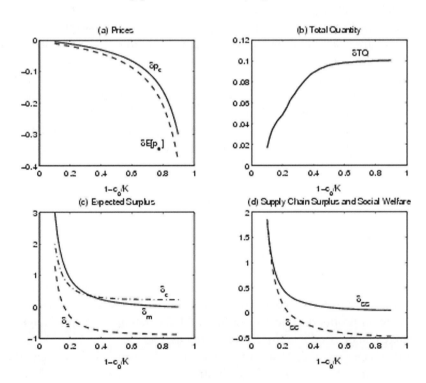

Figure 9-3. The Effect of the Exchange on the Performance Measures with Varying Margins $(1 - c_0/K)$.

price with no exchange. In panel (b) $\delta T Q = (\sum_{i=1}^{N} Q_i)/q_{ne}$, refers to the ratio of change in expected total production quantity. In panel (c), $\delta_s = \Delta^s/\Pi_{ne}^s$ refers to the ratio of the change in the expected supplier profits; $\delta_m = \Delta^m/\Pi_{ne}^m$, refers to the ratio of the change in the expected manufacturer profits; and $\delta_c = \Delta CS/\Pi_{ne}^c$, refers to the ratio, of the change in the expected consumer surplus. In panel (d), $\delta_{SC} = \Delta_{SC}/(\Pi_{ne}^m + \Pi_{ne}^s)$, refers to the ratio of the change in the expected supply chain surplus; and $\delta_{SS} = \Delta_{SS}/(\Pi_{ne}^m + \Pi_{ne}^s + \Pi_{ne}^c)$, is the ratio of the change in expected social welfare (see Section 3). For each margin level, the equilibrium outcome for 40,000 parameter combinations are calculated. For each case, N and M varied between 2 to 50, σ_d^2 and σ_h^2 varied between 5% to 75% of K and σ_ε^2 and σ_u^2 varied between 0.1% to 25% of K.

Figure 3 shows the median changes in the eight performance measures we consider with the introduction of the exchange as ratios. As seen in panel (a), the prices fall significantly when the exchange is introduced. The fall is most dramatic when the margins are high. The decrease in prices brings about an increase in the total quantity produced as seen in panel (b), and, again, the highest increase in total quantity takes place when the margins are the highest. As panel (c) demonstrates, decreased wholesale prices and increased quantities benefit the manufacturers and especially the consumers. Suppliers, on the other hand, suffer from the decreased prices which are a consequence of their loss of relative bargaining power with the introduction of the exchange. The sharp increase in the parties' surplus for lower margin levels is due to the benefits of information utilization and the fact that the magnitude of benefits from up to date information is highest relative to pure contracting surplus when the margins are low. Finally, panel (d) shows that the exchange can actually make the supply chain worse-off on average, especially when the margins are high. However, the large benefits accrued to consumers make the overall contribution of the exchange to social welfare positive.

5.   CONCLUDING REMARKS

In this paper, we analyzed the effects of Business to Business electronic markets on the supply chain. We demonstrated that the exchange shifts surplus across the participants and can hurt the supply chain as a whole. However, it can decrease the expected wholesale and consumer prices, thereby increasing the total quantities produced and the consumer surplus. As a result, even when supply chain profits decline due to the implementation of the exchange, the exchange can be beneficial for the economy as a whole.

In this paper we took a long-run perspective, focusing on the effects of the informational and transactional capabilities of the exchange once it has been adopted. In addition to its direct, well-known costs and benefits, we identified four effects of the exchange on supply chain participants. First, the B2B exchange levels the playing field among the suppliers and the manufacturers, resulting in a wealth transfer from the more powerful side at the contracting stage to the less powerful one, and a change in overall supply chain profits (which may be positive or negative). Second, the exchange benefits the participants by enabling them to utilize up-to-date information, potentially improving their decision making. This includes both their own information and information from other market participants, which is aggregated and transmitted via the market price. Third, the exchange creates price volatility and quantity uncertainty compared to the case when there is no exchange. This hurts the suppliers and manufacturers, while benefiting consumers. Fourth, the exchange increases the profits of supply chain participants by giving them the opportunity to adapt to the ex-ante variable exchange price before making their final trading decisions.

B2B exchanges have a number of well-known costs and potential benefits that were not covered in this paper. On the benefit side, an exchange can serve as a shared transaction utility that (in the long run) reduces both the transaction and software development costs for all market participants. Further, it can reduce the participants' search cost and contribute to collaboration and business process integration. On the cost side, reaping these benefits is difficult as it requires a significant upfront technology investment, a business process change, and a degree of trust which cannot be easily achieved. Further, the adoption of B2B exchanges is difficult because they are characterized by network effects that lead to the well-known "chicken and egg" problem.

Our results show that the introduction of a B2B exchange changes the market in subtle ways that can dramatically affect the profitability of suppliers and manufacturers. The performance and impact of B2B exchanges is thus expected to vary widely across markets and industries, and we believe a careful analysis of the four effects we identified is called for before an industry, and its participants, embark on a B2B effort.

REFERENCES

Allaz, B. and J.-L. Vila (1993). Cournot competition, forward markets and efficiency. *Journal of Economic Theory* 59(1), 1–16.

Bartels, A., R. Hudson, and T. Pohlmann (2003). Report on technology in supply management: Q3 2003. Technical report, ISM/Forrester.

Corrbett, C. J. and U. S. Karmarkar (2001). Competition and structure in serial supply chains with deterministic demand. *Management Science* 47(7), 966–978.

Gal-Or, E. (1985). Information sharing in oligopoly. *Econometrica* 53(2), 329–343.

Gal-Or, E. (1986). Information transmission-Cournot and Bertrand equilibria. *Review of Economic Studies* 53, 85–92.

Hellweg, E. (2002, April). B2B is back from the dead. Business 2.0.

Jin, J. (2000). A comment on "A general model of information sharing in oligopoly". *Journal of Economic Theory* 93, 144–145.

Kafka, S. J., B. D. Temkin, M. R. Sanders, J. Sharrard, and T. O. Brown (2000, February). E-marketplaces boost B2B trade. Technical report, Forrester Research.

Kleindorfer, P. R. and D. Wu (2003). Integrating long- and short-term contracting via business-to-business exchanges for capital-intensive industries. *Management Science* 49(11), 1597–1615.

Lee, H. and S. Whang (2002). The impact of the secondary market on the supply chain. *Management Science* 48(6), 719–731.

Li, L. (1985). Cournot oligopoly with information sharing. *RAND Journal of Economics* 16(4), 521–536.

Mendelson, H. and T. I. Tunca (2004). Strategic spot trading in supply chains. *Management Science* (Forthcoming).

Novshek, W. and H. Sonnenschein (1982). Fullfilled expectations Cournot duopoly with information acquisition and release. *Bell Journal of Economics* 13, 214–218.

O'Hara, M. (1997). *Market Microstructure Theory*. Cambridge, MA: Blackwell Publishers.

Raith, M. (1996). A general model of information sharing in oligopoly. *Journal of Economic Theory* 71, 260–288.

Shapiro, C. (1986). Exchange of cost information in oligopoly. *Review of Economic Studies* 53, 433–446.

Tunca, T. I. (2004). Information precision and asymptotic efficiency of industrial markets. Working paper, Stanford University.

Tunca, T. I. and S. A. Zenios (2006). Supply auctions and relational contracts for procurement. *M&SOM* 8(1), 43–67.

Vives, X. (1984). Duopoly information equilibrium: Cournot and Bertrand. *Journal of Economic Theory* 34, 71–94.

Weinberg, N. (2003, October 2). Quieter revolution. Forbes.

Wu, D., P. R. Kleindorfer, and J. E. Zhang (2002). Optimal bidding and contracting strategies for capital-intensive goods. *European Journal of Operational Research* 137(3), 657–676.

ACKNOWLEDGEMENTS

The authors gratefully acknowledge financial support by the Center for Electronic Business and Commerce at the Graduate School of Business, Stanford University.

APPENDIX: THEORETICAL BACKGROUND

The solution of the model starts with finding an equilibrium in the exchange. Basing on this equilibrium, we can find an equilibrium for the whole game.

Equilibrium on the Exchange

An equilibrium in the exchange satisfies the following properties:

- Given her signal, the equilibrium price and the vector of contracted quantities, each manufacturer maximizes her expected profit:

$$E\left[\Pi^m(x_i)\big|s_i^d, p_e, w\right] \geq E\left[\Pi^m(x)\big|s_{di}^d, p_e, w\right]$$
for all $x \in \mathfrak{R}$, $1 \leqslant i \leqslant N$.

$$(A.1)$$

- Given her signal, the equilibrium price and the vector of contracted quantities, each supplier maximizes her expected profit:

$$E\left[\Pi^s(y_j)\big|s_i^h, p_e, w\right] \geq E\left[\Pi^s(y)\big|s_i^h, p_e, w\right]$$
for all $y \in \mathfrak{R}$, $1 \leq j \leq M$.

$$(A.2)$$

- The market clears:

$$\sum_{i=1}^{N} x_i - \sum_{j=1}^{M} y_j = 0.$$

$$(A.3)$$

Using the technique given in Tunca (2004), we can find the linear symmetric equilibrium outcome corresponding to any given set of market parameters and the corresponding surplus. We refer the interested readers to that paper for details of that analysis. With that given, we examine the sample contracting scheme discussed in Section 2 on which our numerical results will based.

Before moving on to finding the equilibrium in the contracting stage, we first have to derive the structural forms of the value functions in the first stage. This is given by the following proposition.[3]

Proposition 1: $1 \leq j \leq M$, $E[\Pi_j^s]$ is a quadratic function of $\sum_{i=1}^{N} w_i$ and for $1 \leq i \leq N$, $E[\Pi_i^m]$ is a quadratic function of $\sum_{k \neq i} w_k$ and w_i.

For future reference, define

$$E\left[\Pi_j^s\left(\sum_{i=1}^{N} w_i\right)\right] = \pi_0^s + \pi_1^s \sum_{i=1}^{N} w_i + \pi_2^s \left(\sum_{i=1}^{N} w_i\right)^2$$

$$(A.4)$$

---

[3] See Mendelson and Tunca (2004) for a sketch of the proof for this proposition.

and

$$E\left[\Pi_i^m\left(\sum_{k\neq i} w_k, w_i\right)\right] = \pi_{00}^m + \pi_{0s}^m \sum_{k\neq i} w_k + \pi_{0w}^m w_i + \pi_{sw}^m\left(\sum_{k\neq i} w_k\right)$$

$$w_i + \pi_{ss}^m\left(\sum_{k\neq 1} w_k\right)^2 + \pi_{sw}^m w_i^2 \tag{A.5}$$

for all $1 \leq j \leq M$ and $1 \leq i \leq N$.

Equilibrium at the Contracting Stage

The equilibrium at the contracting stage satisfies the following conditions:

- The quantity that each manufacturer orders (w_i for manufacturer i) maximizes her total expected profits given p_c, the other manufacturers' demanded quantities and her information at the contracting stage:

$$E\left[\Pi_i^m\left(\sum_{k\neq i} w_k, w_i, p_c\right)\right] \geq E\left[\Pi_i^m\left(\sum_{k\neq i} w_k, w, p_c\right)\right] \tag{A.6}$$

for all $w \in \Re$ and $1 \leq i \leq N$.
- Each supplier's chosen production quantity (q_j for supplier j) maximizes her total expected profit given the aggregate demand schedule of the suppliers, the total quantity produced by the other suppliers and her information at the contracting stage:

$$E\left[\Pi_j^s\left(\sum_{i=1}^N w_i(q_j, q_{-j})\right)\right] \geq E\left[\Pi_j^s\left(\sum_{i=1}^N w_i(q, q_{-j})\right)\right] \tag{A.7}$$

for all $q \in \Re$ and $1 \leq j \leq M$, where $q_{-j} = (q_1, \ldots, q_{j-1}, q_{j+1}, \ldots, q_M)$.
- Total demand equals total supply at the contracting stage:

$$\sum_{i=1}^N w_i = \sum_{j=1}^M q_j. \tag{A.8}$$

When there is no exchange, it is straightforward to show that the equilibrium contract price satisfies

$$p_c = \frac{K + Mc_0}{M + 1}$$

and the contractually-committed quantity for supplier

$$j, \ j = 1, \ldots, M, \quad \text{will be } q_j = \frac{N(K - c_0)}{(N + 1)(M + 1)}.$$

And the ordered quantity for manufacturer

$$i, \ i = 1, \ldots, N \quad \text{will be } w_i = \frac{M(K - c_0)}{(N + 1)(M + 1)}.$$

The following proposition summarizes the outcome at $t = 1$ *with* the exchange:

Proposition 2: Given a linear symmetric equilibrium in the exchange, an equilibrium exists in the contracting stage. In equilibrium:

- If $\pi_2^s + (N - 1)\pi_{sw}^m + 2\pi_{ww}^m < 0$ and $c_0 - \pi_{0w}^m - \pi_1^s < 0$ then positive quantities are traded in the first stage. The equilibrium outcome is given by

$$q_j = \frac{N(c_0 - \pi_{0w}^m - \pi_1^s)}{2MN\pi_2^s + (M + 1)((N - 1)\pi_{sw}^m + 2\pi_{ww}^m)}, \quad j = 1, \ldots, M, \quad \text{(A.9)}$$

$$w_i = \sum_{j=1}^{M} q_j / N, \quad i = 1, \ldots, N, \quad \text{(A.10)}$$

and

$$p_c = \pi_{0w}^m + \frac{M((N - 1)\pi_{sw}^m + 2\pi_{ww}^m)(c_0 - \pi_{0w}^m - \pi_1^s)}{2MN\pi_2^s + (M + 1)((N - 1)\pi_{sw}^m + 2\pi_{ww}^m)}. \quad \text{(A.11)}$$

- *Otherwise, $q_j = w_i = 0$, $j = 1, \ldots, M$ and $i = 1, \ldots, N$.*

PROOF. By Proposition 1, for a given contracting price p_c, and the contracted quantities for manufacturers $k \neq 1$, the manufacturer i's problem at time $t = 1$ is

$$\max_{w_i} \left\{ \pi_{00}^m + \pi_{0s}^m \sum_{k \neq i} w_k + \pi_{0w}^m w_i + \pi_{sw}^m \left(\sum_{k \neq i} w_k \right) w_i \right.$$

$$\left. + \pi_{ss}^m \left(\sum_{k \neq i} w_k \right)^2 + \pi_{ww}^m w_i^2 - p_c w_i \right\}. \quad \text{(A.12)}$$

The first order condition is

$$\pi_{0w}^m + \pi_{sw}^m \left(\sum_{k \neq i} w_k \right) + 2\pi_{ww}^m w_i - p_c = 0. \tag{A.13}$$

It is easy to see that the second order condition, $\pi_{ww}^m < 0$, is satisfied. From (A.13), the aggregate demand curve follows as

$$\sum_{k=1}^N w_k = \frac{N(p_c - \pi_{0w}^m)}{(N-1)\pi_{sw}^m + 2\pi_{ww}^m}. \tag{A.14}$$

Given (A.14), and considering the market clearing condition $\sum_{j=1}^M q_j = \sum_{i=1}^N w_1$ the problem for the supplier j at $t = 1$ can be written as

$$\max_{q_j} \left\{ \pi_0^s + \pi_1^s \left(\sum_{k \neq j} q_k + q_j \right) + \pi_2^s \left(\sum_{k \neq j} q_k + q_j \right)^2 \right.$$

$$\left. + q_j \left(\pi_{0w}^m + \frac{1}{N}((N-1)\pi_{sw}^m + 2\pi_{ww}^m) \left(\sum_{k \neq j} q_{k+q_j} \right) - c_0 \right) \right\}. \tag{A.15}$$

The first order condition leads to

$$q_j = \frac{N(c_0 - \pi_{0w}^m - \pi_1^s)}{2MN\pi_2^s + (M+1)((N-1)\pi_{sw}^m + 2\pi_{ww}^m)} \tag{A.16}$$

for $j = 1, \ldots, M$ and the second order condition is

$$2N\pi_2^s + (N-1)\pi_{sw}^m + 2\pi_{ww}^m < 0.$$

It is straightforward to show that $\pi_2^s > 0$, from which the positive trading conditions follow.

Finally (A.10) and (A.11) follow from (A.16) as desired.   □

Chapter 10

INTER-ORGANIZATIONAL KNOWLEDGE TRANSFER AS A SOURCE OF INNOVATION: THE ROLE OF ABSORPTIVE CAPACITY AND INFORMATION MANAGEMENT SYSTEMS

Stephen S. Cohen[a] and Cinzia Dal Zotto[b]

[a]*Berkeley Roundtable on the International Economy (BRIE), University of California at Berkeley, Berkeley, CA 94720;* [b]*Jönköping International Business School, P.O. Box 1026, SE-551 11, Jönköping, Sweden*

1. INTRODUCTION: THE STRUCTURE OF THE PROBLEM

The radical improvements and massive diffusion of information and communication technologies within the last decade have fostered the development and exchange of new knowledge. Firms realize that they now compete in their abilities to access, acquire and appraise new information in order to enhance their innovation capacity by applying it. Davenport and Prusak (1998) note that though spontaneous and unstructured transfers of knowledge routinely take place across organizational and geographical boundaries, independently from the management of the process, companies are now expected to have well defined systems of knowledge management. A substantial literature addressing the competitive dimensions of information management is, therefore, developing. The important and not yet solved questions concern the conditions needed for effective information and knowledge transfer and how to establish them (Zahra and George, 2002). The exploration of these conditions is the principal concern of this essay which studies three very different kinds of firms: new, venture firms (our principal focus); serial acquirers (Cisco), operating at scale in world markets but rooted in a local ecology of venture firms, and Japanese majors, such as Toshiba, NEC and Fujitsu operating, in their rapid growth period, far from such an environment.

The effectiveness of organizational knowledge transfers is, of course, facilitated by the capabilities of the transferring and the recipient organizations to use what are, by now, more or less institutionalized transfer mechanisms such as licensing agreements, strategic alliances, mergers and acquisitions (Bahgat,

Kedia, Harveston and Triandis, 2002). If the existence of such mechanisms is the first condition to facilitate knowledge transfer, an even more important condition for the recipient organization is to possess appropriate absorptive capacity in order to locate, obtain, assimilate and apply such knowledge (Cohen and Levinthal, 1990, Leonard, 1995, Dyer and Singh, 1998). In particular, the ability to accumulate new knowledge constitutes a driving force in the development and growth of young firms (Penrose, 1959, Spender, 1996, Grant, 1996). Knowledge acquisition, if the knowledge is new for the recipient, opens new "productive opportunities" (Penrose, 1959) and enhances the firm's ability to exploit these opportunities (Yli-Renko, Autio and Sapienza, 2001). As young firms usually are resource constrained their development and growth is especially dependent upon innovatively combining their own specific knowledge with that of external partners (McDougall, Shane and Oviatt, 1994, Yli-Renko, Autio and Sapienza, 2001). Through inter-organizational relationships firms can get access to external knowledge and combine it with existing knowledge (Yli-Renko, Autio and Sapienza, 2001). The firm needs partners and an important potential partner to start with could be a Venture Capital firm.

In this paper we first focus on the relationship between the Venture Capital firm and it's Portfolio Companies. Our premise is that the more absorptive capacity both of the partners develop, the more likely it is that knowledge is transferred, assimilated and utilized as a basis of competitive advantage for both partners within the relationship—as absorptive capacity allows information to be assimilated, networked, transformed into knowledge and applied. Absorptive capacity and therefore knowledge transfer is enhanced by a suitable information system to manage demand, supply and application of existing information within the entrepreneurial network. Furthermore knowledge transfer depends upon the motivation of the Venture Capital firm to invest tangible and intangible resources in its portfolio companies and the motivation of the young firms to cooperate with their investors. This motivation stimulates the development of absorptive capacity. Prerequisites to enhance both motivation and absorptive capacity are the existence of a similar knowledge base, experience in the relevant field, and trust in the truth of exchanged information between the partners.

Analysing the relationship between a VC firm and its Portfolio Companies allows us to focus on the phenomenon of absorptive capacity, to tune its precision as an instrument and link it to the concepts of information management and knowledge transfer. However, this is insufficient to develop a more generalized concept. One way to advance towards that end is to study the more general cooperation and merger & acquisition activities and especially the premises and techniques of information management in M&A processes. The structure of the problems arising from these activities appears sufficiently similar to those existing within the relationship between the VC firm and its

Portfolio Companies to bound, and thereby clarify the concept. A comparison with the very successful experience of the major Japanese firms during the period 1960–80 in acquiring critical technologies from distant "partners", who faced rather limited "upside" benefits from the transfers, provides a check on generalizing from the VC based model, which we take through to its most powerful instance in the case of Cisco Systems. It also disciplines the structure of researchable propositions with which we conclude.

After defining information management and absorptive capacity we develop a set of propositions to structure and explain the concepts within the relationship between the VC firm and its Portfolio Companies. In order to describe the motives at the very base of knowledge transfer between VC firms and its financed new ventures Porter and Lawler's motivational theory is presented. The propositions derived are then further explored through two case studies. The paper finally presents a theoretical approach to the applicability of general information management and absorptive capacity models to explain and enhance cooperative relations involving knowledge transfer.

2.   INFORMATION MANAGEMENT

The concept of information has first to be defined. Even if the content of the concept is still the subject of debate, the most common definitions depict information as object oriented knowledge (Wittman, 1959, Strassmann, 1997, Picot and Franck, 1988, Krcmar, 2000). This means that only knowledge that contributes to taking decisions or actions can be defined as information. Consequently information can be seen as a production factor within the value chain process of a firm and, therefore, as an economic good (Witte, 1972, Gutenberg, 1983, Martiny and Klotz, 1989, Bode, 1993, Krcmar, 2000).

Management can be interpreted in different ways and its meaning varies in the practical and scientific literature. We agree with Leontiades (1982) and Krcmar (2000) in seeing the essence of management as creating and coping with change, risks and chances. Information management, therefore, represents efficient and effective "treatment" of information. It means creating and adapting information to the changing needs of the firm and transforming information potential into firm success/performance (Cash, McFarlan, McKenney, 1992, Heinrich, 2002). Major information management tasks are the management of the information economy, the management of information systems and the management of information and communication technology. For the purpose of this paper we will concentrate on the first management task, which refers to decisions on information needs and information supply that is, on information use/application.

A principal goal in the information economy is balancing information demand and supply, to provide decision makers with relevant information, to guarantee information quality, and to optimize the timing of information flow according to the economic principles (Witte, 1972, Eschenröder, 1985, Gemünden, 1993). Today the decision maker disposes of an enormous amount of information to fulfill his information needs. The real issue for future information management systems and, therefore, for future technology doesn't appear to be production of information and certainly not transmission. As early as 1997 Noam conceded that the difficult question had become how to reduce information and develop at the same time a "human friendly" usage culture of information and communication technology.

An information management system has therefore to bring the needed information to the decision maker at the right time and in the right form through a suitable information infrastructure (Österle, 1987, Horvath and Fulk, 1994, Krcmar, 2000). The search and the delivery process of needed information can be described through the lifecycle of the resource information, which is constituted of the three phases information need, demand and application: if the information application causes an information need pointing out a gap between information demand and offer, then a new cycle will be started with the objective to search for new information and cover the information need. Every new cycle moves towards a higher knowledge level if the existing information—considered a resource—is enriched with new information and if no information is forgotten. This implies the existence of a minimum level of absorptive capacity and of an ongoing learning process within the firm.

A first step to explore absorptive capacity is to identify an information gap within the individual or organizational frame of reference. A second step is to close this gap searching for and introducing the information needed to fill the information gap. Absorptive capacity grows with the quantity of information that can be assimilated and structured: this leads to the widening of the frame of reference. Absorptive capacity and learning processes allow information to be understood, assimilated, applied and transformed into knowledge. This knowledge will be updated through subsequent information search processes according to the changing needs of a firm that tries not only to respond to but also to foresee turbulent environments. An updated knowledge base allows the firm to lower its information needs and to specify its information demand. As a consequence the information search process is optimized and information overload can be reduced. A suitable information management system must be able to support these processes. In the next two sections the concept of absorptive capacity will be explained more precisely.

3.   THE ENTREPRENEURIAL NETWORK AND ITS EFFECTIVENESS

In order to explore the effects of absorptive capacity within the relationship existing between VC firms and their Portfolio Companies we first need to describe this relationship. Then, in Section 4, we will discuss the theoretical concept of absorptive capacity.

The aim of Venture Capital firms is to make returns through investing in a lot of different, risky new ventures, at least one of which should be successful. Therefore an important target of the VC firm's information policy is to reduce its risks and to improve its chances. Apart from financing the new company, venture capital firms usually bring in their experience in the field and a network of relations—social capital. Such a network is extremely useful for quickly finding the professional resources and competencies a new venture needs to grow. Additionally it can provide a start-up with reputation. This kind of support originates from knowledge transfer within the relationship network established between venture capital firms, their portfolio companies and their other partners—for example lawyers, other venture capital firms, business angels. The cooperation between the above mentioned partners can be named as an entrepreneurial network and constitutes a learning alliance (Berg, Duncan and Friedman, 1982, Arora and Gambardella, 1990, Mitchell and Singh, 1996). The effectiveness of knowledge transfer within the entrepreneurial network depends upon the absorptive capacity of each partner in the network, that is on their ability to assimilate and replicate the transferred knowledge. In this way a portfolio company's linkages with a venture capital firm provide it with access not just to the knowledge held by its partners but also to the knowledge held by its partner's partners (Gulati and Gargiulo, 1999). In addition, we assume that knowledge transfer between VC firms and their partners is influenced by the presence of different cultural patterns within the entrepreneurial network. This influence is supposed positive if the organizational culture of the network members is similar, and negative in case of different cultural patterns. Cultural influences can further explain why VC firms are "local". **Our hypothesis** is, therefore, that an entrepreneurial network can enhance more innovations and achieve a better standard of performance if it is characterized by its members' high absorptive capacity and similar cultural patterns: both facilitate understanding and allow access to and application of the new knowledge being transferred within the entrepreneurial network.

4.   THE CONCEPT OF ABSORPTIVE CAPACITY
WITHIN THE ENTREPRENEURIAL NETWORK

Cohen and Levinthal (1990) view absorptive capacity as a firm-level construct, an ability the firm develops over time by accumulating a relevant base
of knowledge which can improve understanding and, therefore, contribute to
innovation. This strictly depends on an individual's frame of reference which
enables the individual to learn. Organizational units with a high level of absorptive capacity are likely to harness new knowledge from other units and
apply it to help their innovative activities. Without such capacity organizational units cannot learn or transfer knowledge from one unit to another (Cohen and Levinthal, 1990, Tsai, 2001). Absorptive capacity is supported (1)
by systematic knowledge accumulation and (2) by a prolonged process of investment: an organizational unit's absorptive capacity for learning depends on
its endowment of relevant technology-based capabilities (Mowery, Oxley and
Silverman, 1996). R&D investment is therefore a necessary condition for the
creation of absorptive capacity. Organizational units with a high level of absorptive capacity and aware of the above mentioned condition invest more in
their own R&D and have the ability to produce more innovations (Nicholls-
Nixon, 1993, Tsai, 2001). As a general result we can say that permanent learning processes are necessary conditions to develop absorptive capacity.

Absorptive capacity involves not only the ability to assimilate new external knowledge, thus broadening the individuals' frame of reference, but also
the ability to apply such knowledge to commercial ends and thus create the
opportunity for profit (Cohen and Levinthal, 1990, Tsai, 2001). As a consequence, the development of absorptive capacity is an interesting strategy for
reducing managerial and technical risk. However, knowledge generated by individual organizations does not come to bear on an organization independently
(Crossan and Lane, 1999). Knowledge is socially constructed and organizational learning involves a complex social process in which different units interact with each other (Berger and Luckmann, 1966, Huber, 1991). As we are interested in a general concept of absorptive capacity on an inter-organizational
level we shift the unit of analysis of the Cohen and Levinthal's construct from
the firm to the learning alliance (the learning dyad—Lane and Lubatkin, 1998)
existing between Venture Capital firm and its Portfolio Companies. Learning
alliances can be seen as networks which promote social learning and therefore
make linked organizations more astute collectively than they are individually
(Kraatz, 1998).

We argue with Lane and Lubatkin (1998) that the ability of a firm to learn
from another is jointly determined by the relative characteristics of the partners
in the learning alliance. According to Lane and Lubatkin a firm's absorptive
capacity, that is its ability to value, assimilate and apply new knowledge from

a learning alliance partner depends upon (a) the specified type of new knowledge offered by the partner, (b) the similarity between the partner firms' organizational practices/structures and (c) one firm's familiarity with the partner's set of organizational problems (Lane and Lubatkin, 1998). An individual's learning is greater when the new knowledge to be assimilated is related to the individual's existing knowledge structure (Ellis, 1965, Estes, 1970, Bower and Hilgard, 1981, Grant, 1996) that means its frame of reference. Similarly, in order to recognize and value new knowledge a firm's prior scientific or technological knowledge must possess some amount of prior knowledge basic to the new knowledge. In this way prior knowledge will be relevant enough to facilitate understanding (Cohen and Levinthal, 1990) and therefore learning processes. A firm's ability to internalize knowledge is greater when the learning alliance partners' knowledge-processing systems—or the more readily observable organizational practices—are similar. Finally the more familiar a firm is with the types of projects and problems that the partner handles, the more readily it will be able to commercially apply new knowledge acquired from the partner (Lane and Lubatkin, 1998). Therefore we can state that the amount and structure of prior knowledge as a firm's frame of reference must be similar between the partners within the learning alliance. As absorptive capacity is dynamic and should be developed, we add that its level depends also upon the partner firms' motivation to foster the learning alliance. Through learning alliances firms can speed capability development and minimize their exposure to technological and environmental uncertainties by acquiring and exploiting knowledge developed by the alliance partners (Grant and Baden-Fuller, 1995, Gulati and Gargiulo, 1999, Lechner, 2001).

If we analyze the learning alliance between the Venture Capital firm and it's Portfolio Companies according to the above theoretical assumptions, we can identically state that also in such a specific relationship the absorptive capacity of both partners improves with

1. increasing similarity of content and structure of the learning alliance partners' knowledge base,
2. increasing similarity of the learning alliance partners' information management systems,
3. increasing familiarity of the partners with the problems and projects handled by the other partners,
4. the motivation to foster the learning alliance and knowledge transfer between the partners and
5. the existence of a suitable information management in order to balance information demand and offer according to the information needs within the learning alliance.

A small example can help understand these statements. Mondo Media is a graphic production studio founded in 1988. In 1998 the company turned from outsourcing provider to an original "film" studio. Unfortunately most of the Internet related start ups faded away and together with them the market that Mondo Media was hoping to serve. The strategic change of the company was financed by technology oriented Venture Capital firms which over the past 20 to 30 years have been mainly dealing with software companies. These VC firms were therefore not acquainted with the media and entertainment business and couldn't provide any relevant information or knowledge to Mondo Media. As the company's customers were famous brands and blessed it with a good reputation, the VC firms were though motivated to invest in the company. This is a typical case where the VC firms have a completely different knowledge base compared to the Portfolio Company, are not familiar with the projects handled by it and can't therefore contribute to develop absorptive capacity within the cooperative relationship.

At this point it is clear that not only information management contributes to the improvement of absorptive capacity by balancing information demand and offer within the entrepreneurial network. Evidently an increasing absorptive capacity contributes to move the information life cycles to upper levels: information previously acquired and recognized as relevant becomes an available knowledge resource for the alliance partners, their subsequent information demand is more selective and as a consequence the search processes are optimized. Further, in order to confirm the importance of motivation for the improvement of absorptive capacity, we need to specify the nature of motivation.

As a first result we can formulate the following three conceptual propositions:

Proposition 1a: The more similar the knowledge base of the Venture Capital firm and its Portfolio Companies—the alliance partners—the higher the level of their absorptive capacity.

Proposition 1b: The more familiar the partners of the entrepreneurial network are with the problems and projects handled by the other partners, the higher the level of their absorptive capacity.

Proposition 1c: The greater a partner's ability to learn, the higher is its level of absorptive capacity.

Proposition 1d: The higher the level of the partners' absorptive capacity, the more balanced and specific information demand and offer within the entrepreneurial network and the lower the information overload.

5. ABSORPTIVE CAPACITY AND MOTIVATION THEORY WITHIN THE ENTREPRENEURIAL NETWORK

There is a general agreement on defining behaviour as a product of the interaction between person and situation. The same can be said for motivation, the process at the very base of behaviour. In this sense motivation at work is defined as a series of forces originating both from inside and outside of a person in order to activate a work oriented behaviour and to determine its form, direction, strength and duration (Weinert, 1992, Heckhausen, 1989). According to Bühner (1997) the interaction between rewards, satisfaction and performance generates mechanisms that activate the motives needed to guide behaviour towards the firm's objectives. Motives originate from individual needs. Rewards or incentives can be introduced to activate motives and give them the desired direction. Motives generate the motivation process which in turn leads to performance and satisfaction. A famous example of a motivation theory, which can be linked to the concept of absorptive capacity, is given by Porter and Lawler.

Porter and Lawler's (1968) motivation theory bases on the fact that performance is followed by a reward, later evaluated by the satisfaction that the reward itself has generated. Performance represents the result of a working effort. Motivation to work depends on that effort as well as on the value of rewards and on the probability of their entrance. The variables included in the theory are the following:

- Value of rewards: subjective and depends on the situation in which a person finds him/herself. It also depends upon the satisfaction of needs that a reward produces.
- There is a subjective probability of a reward as consequence of an effort towards the desired behavior. This probability originates from the expectancy that rewards depend on performance and that performance comes out of efforts.
- The effort represents the willingness of a person to execute a task and therefore to give a certain performance. Motivation is generated from the combination of the value and the probability of rewards after an effort. For Porter and Lawler the effort and not performance is the central variable of the process.
- Abilities and traits are seen as a constant input that contributes to performance together with the effort.
- Role perception helps to give direction to the effort in order to reach performance and success.

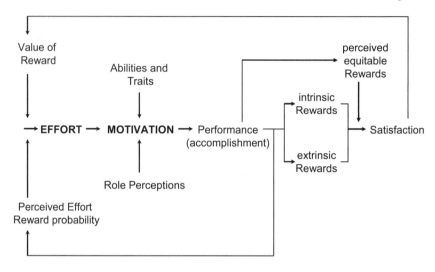

Figure 10-1. Porter and Lawler's (1968) motivation theory.

- Performance is measured by the role reached through a certain behavior. How successful an individual executes his/her tasks therefore depend on effort, abilities and role perception.
- An individual expects rewards in order to satisfy his/her needs. Rewards can be intrinsic or extrinsic, that is the result of thinking or given by a third party.
- The perception of the equity of rewards depends on individual expectations.
- Satisfaction originates from a comparison between individual expectations on and realized rewards.

The relationship between the different variables can be seen in Figure 1.

According to Porter and Lawler motivation theoretically increases if effort rises. This function can be influenced by qualification and role perception as intervening variables (Vroom, 1964). The relationship between performance and rewards is not very clear. On one hand it sets the premise of being able to measure performance and efforts. On the other hand rewards expectations depend on performance too, so that satisfaction is a multi-dependent variable. The feedback process between satisfaction and value as well as probability of rewards implies a learning process: the more effort a partner puts in executing a task, the more he/she will be rewarded and vice-versa (Porter and Lawler, 1968, Drumm, 2000).

If we apply this theory to the relationship between Venture Capital Firm and its Portfolio Companies we can deduce interesting assumptions. Porter and Lawler's motivation theory is based on intra-organizational work relationships. In order to apply it to the inter-organizational relation existing between the Venture Capital firm and its Portfolio Companies we need to adapt the theory considering motives and goals of the different partners within the entrepreneurial network. A firm can motivate an employee to perform according to its goals introducing a system of incentives. The same doesn't hold true when considering an inter-organizational relationship such as the entrepreneurial network, where the partners cooperate but are independent actors with independent goals. Only a commonality of interest, such as the success of the portfolio company, can activate a motivation process which leads the partners in the entrepreneurial network to pursue a mutual final objective (Larsson, Bengtsson, Henriksson and Sparks, 1998). The task to be executed in this context would be knowledge transfer. From the Venture Capital (VC) firm perspective, its effort in transferring knowledge to the Portfolio Companies (PC) depends on the value and the probability of the reward, which in this case is represented by the PC's success. This effort, together with abilities and role perception—if the VC firm thinks to have the appropriate abilities and is aware of the role it could play in helping the PC to have success—determines the Venture Capital firm's motivation to transfer its relevant knowledge to the PC firm. Depending on the success of the knowledge transfer, which in turn depends on the relevance of the transferred knowledge and on the absorptive capacity of both partners, intrinsic and/or extrinsic rewards are generated: an intrinsic reward could be represented by a good relationship with the portfolio company which contributes to build social capital (Cohen and Fields, 2000, Yli-Renko, Autio and Sapienza, 2001), while the extrinsic reward is mainly constituted by the success of the PC. Both rewards lead to the satisfaction of the VC firm with its investment in knowledge transfer (see Figure 2). The VC firm knows that if it uses the same strategy with another Portfolio Company under the same conditions—transfer of relevant knowledge to the PC, understanding of its role in the VC-PC relationship, absorptive capacity of both parties—the probability of another satisfying reward—success of the venture firm—increases. The success of knowledge transfer from the VC firm to the portfolio company cannot be achieved if the portfolio company is not motivated to absorb the transferred knowledge. From the portfolio company point of view, its effort to absorb knowledge from the VC firm depends on the value and the probability of the reward too, which is always the PC's success. If the transferred knowledge is relevant, then the PC firm knows that its probability of having success increases the more relevant knowledge it absorbs from the VC firm. The success of knowledge transfer generates intrinsic rewards such as a good relationship with the VC firm and extrinsic rewards represented by the PC's success. These common rewards lead to the satisfaction of both partners within the entrepreneurial network, motivating them to future knowledge transfer processes (see Figure 2).

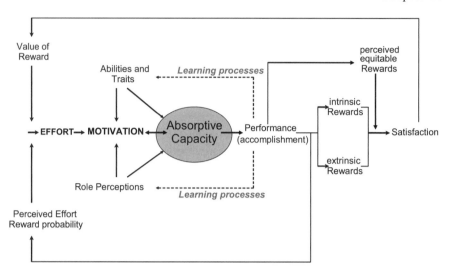

Figure 10-2. The combination of Porter and Lawler's motivation theory with the concept of absorptive capacity.

The process of developing absorptive capacity can now be defined more precisely. Absorptive capacity depends on motivation but also directly on relevant qualification and traits, as well as role perception. If between the VC firm and its PC there is similarity of knowledge base, similarity of organizational practices as well as information management systems and familiarity with the handled projects then the capacity to value, assimilate and apply the transferred knowledge increases. As a consequence the performance outcome and therefore rewards and satisfaction improve too. Improved performance increases rewards probability, which in turn enhances effort and motivation to learn and transfer additional relevant knowledge. Furthermore performance stimulates learning processes. Performance is represented in our case by successful knowledge transfer. If knowledge has been assimilated and successfully applied by the Portfolio Company, as a consequence the VC firm is more motivated to help the Portfolio Company also in the future and therefore to foster the learning alliance. Each knowledge transfer process represents also a knowledge creating process: if the VC firm is receptive, from one knowledge transfer process it can absorb knowledge which in turn can constitute new knowledge, and therefore a source of information, in another knowledge transfer process involving different portfolio companies. Inter-organizational learning is therefore the outcome of the interacting partners' abilities and choices to be more or less transparent and receptive (Larsson, Bengtsson, Henriksson and Sparks, 1998). Learning processes improve the relevant abilities and the role perception of both VC firms and PC companies. Improved abilities and role perception contribute finally to improve the absorptive capacity of all partners within an entrepreneurial network. As a consequence the knowledge base of the alliance partners' increases, information needs and demand become more selective and information overload can be reduced. This leads again to the optimization of the information search process.

Another small example can clarify these relations. In 2000 Mobileway was founded with the idea to build a global network for the international exchange of SMS all over the world. The business idea was backed by prominent Venture Capital firms which provided Mobileway not only with their own expertise in the wireless business and market but also with the typical high level introduction to further investors and customers. By balancing technology development with its financial needs the company is now successfully growing. Indeed the similarity of knowledge base between the main investors and their customer has enhanced the development of absorptive capacity and knowledge transfer within the entrepreneurial relationship. This has positively influenced the VC firms' satisfaction with their investment as well as perception of value and probability of rewards for their investment of tangible and intangible resources in the company. Consequently the VC firms' motivation to further invest in the company and to look for other investors as well as Mobileway's motivation to cooperate with them has been increased. This (1) further improves absorptive capacity within the entrepreneurial network and (2) allows the VC firms to transfer the newly absorbed knowledge as relevant information to other PC companies within their network. Here emerges the role of the VC firm as teacher or "knowledge-to-information" transformer and therefore as central linking pin who promotes learning within the entrepreneurial network.

As a second result we can add to the propositions 1a, 1b, 1c and 1d the following four propositions:

Proposition 2a: The higher the satisfaction of the VC firm with knowledge transfer in previously supported ventures, the higher its motivation to further knowledge transfer.

Proposition 2b: The higher the VC firm's perception and value of its future rewards (represented by the PCs' expected success, which increases with the similarity of conditions which brought to success previous PCs), the higher its motivation to further knowledge transfer within the learning alliance.

Proposition 2c: The higher the VC firm's and PCs' absorptive capacity, the higher the VC firm's motivation to further knowledge transfer.

Proposition 2d: The higher the motivation to further knowledge transfer between the learning alliance partners, the higher their absorptive capacity and the lower information demand and overload within the alliance.

As an intermediate important result we can state that (1) all partners in an entrepreneurial network should develop absorptive capacity; (2) investment risk and new ventures' failure can be reduced if VCs not only invest financial capital but also develop abilities and competencies to support their portfolio companies which are usually only typical of consultancy firms. Last but not least a successful knowledge exchange can only take place if a suitable information management is available and optimized by the development of absorptive capacity and by the role of the VC firm as promoter of knowledge/information exchange—and therefore of learning processes—within the entrepreneurial network.

However, these theoretical findings refer to the relationships existing between VC firms and their portfolio companies. This is a very specific case. In order to generalize them we now need to apply the concepts of absorptive capacity and information management to a more general cooperation activity which is, to some extent, similar to a VC–PC relationship. This can be represented by (1) import of foreign technology through cooperation by the Japanese corporations and (2) the acquisition strategy used by Cisco System as core competence. We can then see if the concepts of absorptive capacity and information management have been important to enhance knowledge transfer within these knowledge and/or firm acquisition processes and if we can give further heuristic insight to this problem.

6.   TWO CASE STUDIES

6.1.   An Introduction

A good information management system that facilitates information assimilation and application by structuring not only information but also knowledge can be called a knowledge management system. Knowledge management systems are not general, all-purpose, tools effective equally for any task from quantum leap technology invention through incremental process improvements. They also are specific to differing environments: what works well for technology firms embedded in an ecology of multiple personal contacts with a large number of innovative technology firms will not work as well for large, traditional manufacturing firms, remote from a dense innovative environment, that are trying to move into new technologies. Knowledge management systems, to the extent they are both managed and systems, must be designed and optimized to achieve a primary purpose in a specified institutional context. In general, this is easy to accept in the abstract, but difficult for management to do in the operational. After all, a firm must be good at many things, especially if it is big: excellence in one aspect of its business is generally not sufficient for survival, let alone success. So selecting what you intend to do less well, and then designing a knowledge management system that sacrifices strength in important aspects of the business, in order to be especially strong in others, is often more troubling than challenging for management. Despite their difficulty, such strategic decisions are often made and implemented down through corporate architecture, processes and culture. For a young, or a small firm, the necessity to create and optimize a knowledge management system is all the more astringent. As knowledge is particularly scarce in young firms, a first task for them is to access knowledge: entering cooperation activities with other firms and therefore starting inter-organizational learning can lead to knowledge creation and exchange processes. In this context cooperation can be represented by relationships with VC firms, as already described in the paper, by licensing agreements or by mergers and acquisitions activities.

In this section, we look at two of the most successful of such knowledge management systems, each optimized for scanning and accessing external technology. Beyond that strategic focus, they differ in every other way. The first is the Japanese corporations, during the high growth period ranging roughly from 1960 through 1980; the second we might call the Silicon Valley/local ecology model as exemplified by its ablest practitioner, Cisco, and what it explicitly calls its "ecology" during the 1980s and 1990s. Both case studies in our context have an explorative function in order to detect the conditions that allowed a successful knowledge transfer between the involved partners and see if these conditions can be applied to the VCs–PCs relationship.

6.2.   The Case of the Japanese Corporations

The major Japanese corporations developed their knowledge management systems for the purpose of scanning, accessing, incorporating, localizing and, incrementally improving technology obtained from outside the firm, and outside its local environment, where the company from which the technology was obtained could not be assumed to play a very active, hands on, positive role in supporting the incorporation of that technology into the competencies of the Japanese firm. Imported technology, localized and subject to constant marginal improvements in product and process was the basis of the rapid transition of the large Japanese companies into rich, world competitive power-houses. In the words of the Japanese Economic Planning Agency reporting in 1980, "Japan's technological progress has been achieved so far through the introduction of foreign technologies" (129). Its sister agency, the Ministry of Science and Technology declared that same year, 1980, to be "the first year of the era of Japan's technological independence", thus defining and bounding the period quite neatly. The vast majority of U.S.–Japan corporate ventures from the 1950s until the mid-1980s involved licensing agreements that entailed the straight-out sale of U.S. patents, directly transferring basic research and development knowledge to Japanese manufacturers. From 1951 through 1983, Japanese companies entered into some 42.000 contracts for technology imports, paying a cumulative price of $17 billion. The Japanese expense to acquire this advances technology, about $500 million per year, was far lower than it would have cost to develop the same technology domestically (Taylor, 1995). "The massive transfer of technology from the United States and Western Europe in fact provided the technological basis for nearly all of Japan's modern industries. Without this critical technology transfer, no amount of capital and labor could have moved Japanese companies to their present competitive position so rapidly" (Abegglen and Stalk, 1985). And that does not include major and many minor technologies for which there was no signed agreement, or even any agreement at all on the part of the providing firm.

Our focus is on the knowledge management system that converted foreign technology into Japanese corporate competence, and it is clear and well defined. That system was completely optimized for localizing, accessing, mastering and incrementally improving the technologies and, especially, the processes of their production. Mansfield (1988) provides the basic numbers that distinguish the Japanese knowledge management system from those of their competitors and define its optimization: "U.S. firms take almost as long, and spend almost as much money, to carry out an innovation based on external technology as one based on internal technology. In Japan on the other hand, firms take about 25% less time, and spend about 50% less money, to carry out an innovation based on external technology than one based on internal technology". One could add that Mansfield's data probably underestimate the Japanese advantage in "carrying out" an innovation based on external technology because much of their spending is for production process improvement that extends the innovation beyond merely carrying it out. Big Japanese firms, during this period, spent very heavily on R&D. Japanese R&D expenditures rose steadily and more rapidly than their U.S. and German competitors throughout this period. The top twenty Japanese companies ranked by R&D total expenditures when compared with twenty U.S. companies similarly ranked, show the Japanese companies spending 20% more than their U.S. counterparts when R&D is measured as a percent of sales, and (Abegglen and Stalk, 1985).

Rosenberg and Steinmueller (1988) report further that Japanese firms devote about two-thirds of R&D to process improvement and one-third to product; U.S. firms display the opposite ratio. He explains the famously tight linkages in Japanese firms between product innovation, process improvement and the integration of personnel as, to a substantial degree, a function of the focus on developing "technology imitation strengths". By contrast, Rosenberg finds that, American firms have often "compartmentalized research and manufacturing functions". (We might note that it is nearly impossible, in the English language literature on the period that deals with Japanese corporate organization, knowledge management and technology development to find a paragraph without comparisons with American practice, and almost as rare without lessons for Americans to learn quickly or else!)

The Japanese knowledge management system has fostered continuous learning processes allowing the small Japanese firms started in the 1950s to become big, successful and worldwide competitive companies. Their characteristics are well known and repeatedly presented as including:

1. A concentration on accessing technology from outside the firm and outside its local environment.
2. A disciplined focus on improvement of acquired technologies and not the invention of new ones.
3. Improvement focuses on production processes.
4. Production is, therefore, intimately involved in R&D not separated organizationally, physically or socially.
5. Heavy and sustained investment in R&D, in licenses, in equipment and in people.
6. A focus on work force education and the use of educated workers.
7. A focus on extending participation throughout the organization in the permanent quest for marginal improvements down into the organization.
8. Retention and public valuing of personnel in whom knowledge is embedded.
9. Growth in volumes and market share, not just for competitive reasons afforded by cheaper and longer-term capital, but also because growth permits new production lines that embody, the one after the other, the latest marginal improvements.

Discussion

During the 1950s Japanese companies were still small, technologically weak and, generally, specialized (Rocha, 1997). Japan was a catch-up country. According to the technology gap approach, catching-up countries have the possibility of growing at a faster rate than leaders countries because they can exploit a backlog of existing knowledge developed elsewhere. As Abramovitz (1986) points out, a country's potential for catching-up can only be realized under the existence of three conditions: endowment of natural resources, an adequate national social capacity and technological congruence. Japanese companies met the first condition as they focused on work force education, fostering human resource development, and R&D. Moreover many observers find the Japanese banking and finance system well suited for long term and risky ventures, able to mitigate possible liquidity constraints (Fransman, 1990, Mahlich, 2000). One of the economic characteristics of social capacity is the ability of a country to identify and absorb technological knowledge generated outside the country, i.e. absorptive capacity (Temple and Johnson, 1998). In house scientific research helps companies to exploit external knowledge more efficiently since it generates the absorptive capacity (Cohen and Levinthal, 1990) that allows firms to plug into outside information networks (Mahlich, 2000). To avoid deterioration in a catch-up country's absorptive capacity as it closes the gap with the leader investment in R&D has to be carried out along the converging path (Criscuolo and Narula, 2001). Considering the growth and success of the big Japanese corporations as well as their huge investments in R&D combined with the acquisition of external knowledge—technology—holds the importance of enhancing absorptive capacity. Importing technology mostly through licensing agreements or patent acquisitions the Japanese corporations didn't have to face problems created by cultural distance. Such problems, which might occur when acquiring foreign firms, threaten understanding, learning processes and therefore the necessary absorptive capacity to assimilate and replicate the newly acquired knowledge.

6.3.   The Cisco Case[1]

Every aspect of an acquisition process has organizational considerations that cannot be separated from strategy and economics. In fast changing, high-technology fields, very often the capabilities of the employees of the acquired firm are a very significant component of a firm's value, thus their retention is vital for the preservation of the acquisition's value (Mayer and Kenney, 2002). This means that if these employees leave or their practice is so disrupted that their motivation at work disappears, then the technology that has been acquired won't be transferred from the acquired firm to the acquirer and the whole acquisition process will end up in a failure. We have already stated that technology—which is a kind of knowledge—transfer takes place when the parties have a similar knowledge base and are both familiar with the projects they handle so that they can understand each other, learn from each other, assimilate and then use the new transferred knowledge. Cisco is an ideal case within this frame as it has developed a successful process for using acquisitions as a central component in its overall competitive strategy: doubting their cost-effectiveness the company has substituted the high-powered R&D laboratories as owned by its major competitors with acquisitions. Nonetheless, being in a research-intensive industry, Cisco internal R&D was 17.6% of sales in fiscal year 2001 (Mayer and Kenney, 2002). When with a firm a product line has been acquired, it is still necessary to continue R&D for the later generations. Cisco's success is especially remarkable as acquisitions in the information technology industries have a long history of failure. Comparing Cisco

---

[1] This case was drawn from the excellent paper by David Mayer and Martin Kenney.

with competitors such as Nortel, Ericsson and Lucent, which are also aggressive acquirers, the company stands out as the only firm with solid finances continuing to make acquisitions. Cisco's story suggests that variables such as price alone cannot explain success, as the prices paid for its acquisitions were comparable to the market. The important questions seem to be not simply what to acquire but also how to acquire. To describe the Cisco case we follow the excellent and detailed analysis by Mayer and Kenney (2002).

First of all some data. As of January 2001 Cisco has made 71 acquisitions and effectively leveraged them to become an industry leader. The company maintained a compounded annual growth rate in revenues and profits of over 30% from 1987 through 2000 and without those acquisitions it would have likely been out-flanked by start ups. 68% of the acquisitions had one hundred or fewer employees and 34% had fewer than 50 employees. In terms of ownership 86% were private owned firms while the rest were public firms or divisions of public firms. 43% of the firms were shipping prior to being acquired while the others we still developing their products. Spatial proximity resulted to be determinant in the acquisition strategy: 44% of the acquired firms were located in Northern California. This percentage is higher in the early years when the company was probably learning how to acquire. Another significant percentage of acquired firms were located in the Boston area and in Israel, where there is a major concentration of venture capital financed, high technology start ups resembling the entrepreneurial environment of Silicon Valley. The main indicators for acquisition success are retention and market share, according to Cisco. Because of the high costs of an acquisition, the revenues from the existing product generation cannot provide a sufficient return to justify the acquisition, so the success of the follow-on product generation is vital. For this reason the retention of the engineers that developed the current generation is key to the future generations. We may here recall that 100% of the acquisitions had an overall annual turnover rate under 10%, which is significantly better than the average in Silicon Valley. Further, as of January 2001, 67% of CEOs of Cisco acquisitions were still in the company, while former CEOs led two of Cisco's three lines of business. Rapid market share growth, especially when the market is also growing quickly, results in enormous returns and can justify high acquisition prices. Cisco gained dominant market positions in seven industry categories, while in other three—DSL/ISDN, Optical Platforms and Wireless, all industries with entrenched competitors and which differed from Cisco's competency in electronics and software—Cisco has failed to capture 20% of the market. This means that 21 acquisitions out of 71 have not met Cisco's self stated criteria of success yet.

When Cisco first begun making acquisitions retention was thought to be desirable but did not appear to be a salient concern. The first acquisition, Crescendo Communications, was part of a larger process of reorienting Cisco toward switching. Located in Sunnyvale, California, Crescendo had just begun shipping a switch that could immediately be integrated into Cisco's product line. This acquisition cost $97 million in 1993 and by the fiscal year 2000 generated more than $7.4 billion in revenues (Wachovia Securities, 2000). This critical first transaction was embedded in a social network. Donald Valentine of Sequoia Capital, which was Cisco's first investor, was a lead investor in Crescendo. Moreover, one of Cisco's largest customers, Boing Corporation, was considering to buy Crescendo switches (Bunnell, 2000). Considering that Sequoia Capital had investments in 12 of the 71 acquisitions (Venture Economics, 2001) we can understand how the ecosystem could provide the needed information on the product and the management team. Given that all of the major data communications equipment firms acquired switching expertise, market success would be based upon the quality of the firm purchased, successful integration and rapid next generation product introduction. At the time Cisco had a very good asset in the channel to sell, install and service products for the global market that could be leveraged to make the acquisition a success. The strength of the sales and support functions affects the acquisition candidate in two ways: To the engineers in a start up these strengths constitute an incentive as they can speed the adoption of the product they have created. This is not only gratifying, the target firms' personnel will also benefit from the sales growth as they receive significant amounts of Cisco stock options. Should on the contrary the target firm refuse to be acquired at a fair price, Cisco will certainly acquire a rival hose product will then benefit from Cisco sales and service strength. In other words, Cisco would become a competitor.

Cisco methodology was not fully formed at the time of the 1993 Crescendo acquisition; the success of this deal prompted the company to make acquisitions an integral part of its strategy (Mayer and Kenney, 2002). In 1994 a manager was hired to focus exclusively upon acquisitions as a business process. In late 1998 a business integration unit was established and by 2001 the Human Resource team devoted to acquisitions had grown to 21 persons. Already in 1997 the Cisco CEO described five guidelines to define the desirability of potential acquisitions (Rifkin, 1997):

a) Both firms must share similar visions about where the industry is going and what role each company wants to play in the industry.
b) The acquisitions must produce quick wins for the shareholders.
c) There must be long-term wins for all four constituencies (shareholders, employees, customers, business partners).
d) The chemistry between the companies has to be right.
e) Geographic proximity is important to make interaction easier.

Cisco tried to make sure that every company acquired became part of Cisco, the main attention given to assess the cultural fit early on. Cisco's management saw managers and executives brought in by acquisitions as contributors who could help build the firm. These leaders were usually charged with ensuring the development of later product generations. Moreover by retaining the leaders Cisco was able to retain the other personnel. Further the retained executives illustrated to the management teams at later target firms that there were opportunities for newly integrated managers without being subordinated to current employees. In this way acquisitions came to be understood as a business process—not as an event—and it was routinized. The appearance of organization, routine and "professionality" reassures the target firm contributing to a smooth process (Zollo and Singh, 2002, Mayer and Kenney, 2002). This was extremely important as acquisitions became the mechanism that provided Cisco with the future products. Cisco decided that these could be found in the local start up ecosystem from which it had once emerged. Cisco developed a portfolio of tactics to tap knowledge and capabilities that are constantly emerging in the ecosystem. First of all a business development group was created. Then, in order to participate to the development of the ecosystem, Cisco allowed its executives and managers to remain actively embedded in their previous networks of relations. As former entrepreneurs and Cisco executives they have great credibility and are often contacted as references, advisors, investors in start-ups. A lot of Cisco executives serve on the firms' board of directors of start ups or venture capital: this embeds them in a rich flow of information about new firms and technologies that might become future acquisitions.

After a target firm has been identified an executive sponsor who will be responsible for assuring that the acquisition and subsequent integration process receives executive level attention is recruited. He is usually the individual that recognized the technology as significant and has already had informal contacts with the potential target firm and in some cases know the key personnel, at least professionally. In order to assess culture, management qualities, leadership styles informal meetings between senior management are started. Only after the Business Development manager is satisfied with the informal dialogue more formal due diligence begins. 6–8 weeks prior to the announcement integration preparations start. Emphasis is given to frequent interactions with the target firm in order to create a shared understanding and trust. A team including public relations, sales, HR, and marketing personnel from both Cisco and the target firm is formed to ensure interaction. The team meets weekly to discuss progress. The Business Development unit maintains a web site cataloguing the progress in ten areas such as HR, product marketing, finance etc. Next to each aspect of integration a sign indicates the degree of completion. These web sites constitute the central source of information and include an event timeline, on-site visit log, fact sheets. The integration plan must be competed prior to announcing the deal. The announcement is a critical moment as at this time employees experience the maximum uncertainty. The prior discussion, the clear plan and the organized professionalism of the acquisition team dampen though the apprehension of acquisitions. This is reinforced by the fact that leaders of the acquired firm already know their positions within Cisco and thus are able to reassure their employees. An early and complete due diligence assures the cultural fit while the continuous interaction mitigate uncertainty and confusion. Cisco orchestrates acquisition and integration processes to retain the employees and not interrupt the acquired firms' product development. This is an important insurance for the success of Cisco's acquisitions.

Discussion

Comparing the acquisition success to effective knowledge transfer, from the analysis of this case study we can draw some interesting conclusions. Experiencing acquisitions failures when targeting firms with different knowledge and competencies, Cisco tried to later target firms with similar knowledge bases: in this way the company exploited the target firm's and its own existing absorptive capacity. In order to further develop the existing absorptive capacity and enhance knowledge transfer Cisco promoted continuous interactions and therefore information exchange within the team responsible for preparing the integration. Cisco also introduced implicit incentives to motivate employees to foster learning and therefore knowledge transfer processes. We may recall here the fact that for the engineers of the target firm joining Cisco could mean accelerating the adoption of the product they developed, while receiving Cisco's stock option they would also financially benefit form a growth in sales. These incentives though work only if there is a socio-cultural similarity between the acquirer and target firm. In fact the target firm's employees would probably leave Cisco if their values would seriously differ from the values of the current employees. The bigger the difference between values, the higher the cultural distance between the acquirer's and the target firm's employees. Values allow or impede communication, understanding and therefore cooperation as well as knowledge transfer. Sharing the same values means cultural similarity and improves the ability to assimilate and replicate new knowledge—that is absorptive capacity. Different values can coexist if the intensity of the values preference is weak. A weak intensity of the values preference means that one cooperating partner can accept a change of order in his preference list, if this helps to find a compromise with the counterpart. This behavior reveals the willingness to overcome the remaining cultural distance through mutual understanding and learning processes. Cisco tried to acquire only firms that shared the same values. If the values differed the company tried to check that at least the intensity of the values preference wasn't high. After recognizing that the exploration of cultural distance is vital for the effectiveness of acquisition processes—and therefore for knowledge transfer—the company gave extreme importance to the informal mechanism by which it could gain access to relevant information. Information management proved therefore to be determinant in the identification of the target firm but also later during the integration process: leaders of the target firm had to reassure their employees providing them with relevant information, while the Business Development team within Cisco had to continuously update the web page with information on progress.

7.   CROSS CONCLUSIONS AND RESULTS

Both the Japanese corporations and Cisco achieved high growth through the acquisition of external knowledge. The strategies followed, and the institutional organizations are different, but oriented toward the same final goal: acquire technology instead of developing it internally. In order to be able to apply and improve the acquired technology the Japanese corporations quickly understood that investments in human resource development and in R&D were necessary conditions. Indeed developing employees allows firms to build the relevant knowledge base—that is a minimum level of absorptive capacity—in order to assimilate and apply the acquired technology. Through R&D investments the absorptive capacity of firms can be increased and the acquired technology improved. Cisco's strategy consisted in acquiring firms that seemed to be entering emerging markets and have a similar knowledge base and culture. Knowledge base and culture similarity improve understanding and therefore the ability to assimilate and apply the acquired technology. Further, retaining the personnel of the acquired firm enhances the odd for success in later generation products. Compared to the case of the Japanese corporations, which enhanced their own receptivity without giving any transparency and, therefore, developing a competitive learning strategy (Rohlen, 1992, Larsson, Bengtsson, Henriksson and Sparks, 1998), Cisco understood that—in order to develop a collaborative learning strategy and ensure the success of future product development—both the ability as well as the motivation to be receptive and transparent were required within the "acquisition alliance". For this reason Cisco gave space and responsibility within the company to the management of the acquired firms. Further, in the Cisco case the successful role of the VC firm as knowledge exchange promoter is recognizable.

The analysis of the differing case studies disciplines the concepts of absorptive capacity and knowledge management. More general assumptions regarding a learning alliance between firms could be built on the following researchable propositions, most of which derive from the VC network analyses developed in Sections 4 and 5:

1. The more similar the knowledge base and the information management systems between the partners in a cooperation process which stimulates interorganizational learning—that is within a learning alliance—the higher the level of their absorptive capacity and therefore the higher the effectiveness of knowledge transfer.
2. The more similar the knowledge structure between the partners within the learning alliance, the higher the level of their absorptive capacity.
3. The more motivated the alliance partners are to foster learning and knowledge transfer within the alliance, the higher their level of absorptive capacity.
4. The lower the cultural distance between the partners within the learning alliance, the higher their level of absorptive capacity.
5. The higher the level of the alliance partners' absorptive capacity, the more balanced and selective information demand and offer within the learning alliance, the lower the information overload and therefore the more effective the knowledge transfer.
6. The higher the satisfaction of the firm with knowledge transfer in a previous cooperation, the higher its motivation to further knowledge transfer (and therefore to acquire another firm or another technology).
7. The higher the firm's perception and value of its future rewards, the higher its motivation to further knowledge transfer within a learning alliance.
8. The higher the cooperation partners' absorptive capacity, the higher their motivation to further knowledge transfer and the more effective the knowledge transfer within the established learning alliance.

The Japanese case points in a different direction or, at minimum, bounds the general applicability of the individual, "gain–gain" motivational dynamic of the VC ecology model and the importance of the various factors needed to create momentum in gain–gain transfers. It shares with the VC model, the importance of absorptive capacity in the absorbing firm, and the various forms of investment and human capital valuing needed to develop that capacity. But the case shifts attention from the role of trust in gain'/gain propositions to the more general idea of the role of some powerful lever, to generate the transfer. That lever could take any of various forms ranging from the expectation of mutual gain, down through the minimization of alternative sources of gain for the transferring company. Absent such a powerful lever—and the presence of such a lever is exceptional—the propositions apply to the general case, if we take general as most common, rather than inclusive.

The most important finding of this paper is that the general model of absorptive capacity can be successfully applied to explain knowledge transfer not only to the specific situation of the entrepreneurial network existing between VC firms and their Portfolio Companies, but also to the learning alliance that can arise from a more general cooperation activity. A successful application needs only the adaptation of the general model to the specific conditions of each "cooperation network", i.e. size and industry. A second important result is that absorptive capacity is based on permanent organizational learning processes of all partners in the cooperation network which, therefore, can be considered a learning alliance. The third important result relies on the combination of process motivation theory with the concept of absorptive capacity. This combination improves the explanation of not only the existence, but also the development, of effective absorptive capacity much better than before. Last, but not least, cultural similarity emerges as a strong favourable condition for building up absorptive capacity, stimulating learning processes and, therefore, allowing knowledge transfer. This process, in order to be effective, must be further sustained by a suitable knowledge management system. An instrumental concept of absorptive capacity must be part of the conceptual basis of inter-organizational coordinated learning. However the concept itself, and especially its instruments, need further research.

REFERENCES

Abegglen, James C. and Stalk, George Jr. (1985). Kaisha, The Japanese Corporation, Basic Books, New York.

Abramovitz, M. (1986). Catching up, forging ahead, and falling behind. Journal of Economic History, June 1986, 46(2): 385–406.

Arora, A., Gambardella, A. (1990). Complementarity and external linkages: The strategies of the large firms in biotechnology. The Journal of Industrial Economics, 38(4): 361–379.

Bhagat, R.S., Kedia, B.L., Harveston, P.D. and Triandis, H.C. (2002). Cultural variations in the cross-border transfer of organizational knowledge: An integrative framework. Academy of Management Review, 27: 204–221.

Berg, S., Duncan, J., Friedman, P. (1982). Joint Venture Strategies and Corporate Innovation. Cambridge, MA. Olegeschlager, Gunn & Hain.

Berger, P. and Luckmann, T. (1966). The Social Construction of Reality: A Treatise in the Sociology of Knowledge, Garden City, New York.

Bode, J. (1993). Betriebliche Production von Information, Wiesbaden.

Bower, G.H. and Hilgard, E.R. (1981). Theories of Learning, Prentice-Hall, Englewood Cliffs, NJ.

Bühner, R. (1997). Betriebswirtschaftliche Organisationslehre, 8. Auflage, Oldenburg.

Bunnell, David (2000). Making the Cisco Connection, New York.

Cash, J.I., McFarlan, F.W., McKenney, J.L. (1992). Corporate Information Systems Management: Text and Cases, 3rd edition.

Cohen, S.S. and Fields, G. (2000). Social capital and social gains: An examination of social capital in Silicon Valley. In: Kenney, M., Understanding Silicon Valley, Stanford University Press.

Cohen, Stephen S. and Zysman, John (1987). Manufacturing Matters, Basic Books, New York.

Cohen, W. and Levinthal, D. (1990). Absorptive capacity: A new perspective on learning and innovation. Administrative Science Quarterly, 35: 128–152.

Criscuolo, Paola and Narula, Rajneesh (2001). National absorptive capacity and the stage of development. Paper presented at the "Innovation, Learning and Technological Dynamism of Developing Countries" Conference, Maastricht 2001.

Crossan, M.M. and Lane, H.W. (1999). An organizational learning framework: From intuition to institution. Academy of Management Review, 24: 522–537.

Davenport, T.H. and Prusak, L. (1998). Working Knowledge. Harvard Business School press.

Drumm, H.J. (2000). Personalwirtschaft, 4. Auflage, Berlin/Heidelberg.

Dyer, J. and Singh, H. (1998). The relational view: cooperative strategy and sources of interorganizational competitive strategy. Academy of Management Review, 23: 660–679.

Ellis, H.C. (1965). The transfer of learning. Macmillan, New York.

Eschenröder, G. (1985). Planungsaspekte einer ressourcen-orientierten Informationswirtschaft. Eul, Bergisch Gladbach 1985.

Estes, W.K. (1970). Learning Theory and Mental Development, Academic Press, New York.

Fransman, Maratin (1990). The Market and Beyond: Cooperation and Competition in Information Technology Development in the Japanese System (sic), Cambridge University Press.

Gemünden, H.G. (1993). Informationsverhalten. In: Frese, E. (Hrsg.): Handwörterbuch der Organisation, 3. Aufl., C.E. Poeschel, Stuttgart.

Grant, R.M. and Baden-Fuller, C. (1995). A knowledge-based theory of inter-firm collaboration, Academy of Management Best Paper Proceedings, 17–21.

Grant, R.M. (1996). Toward a knowledge-based theories of the firm. Strategic Management Journal, 17 (Winter Special Issue): 109–122.

Gulati, R., Gargiulo, M. (1999). Where do interorganizational networks come from? American Journal of Sociology, 104(5): 1439–1493.

Gutenberg, E. (1983). Grundlagen der Betriebswirtschaftslehre, Bd. 1: Die Produktion. 24. Auflage, Berlin/Heidelberg/New York.

Heckhausen, H. (1989). Motivation und Handel, 2. Auflage, Berlin/Heidelberg.

Heinrich, L. (2002). Informationsmanagement—Planung, Überwachung und Steuerung der Informationsinfrastruktur, 7. Aufl., Oldenbourg, München.

Horvath, A.T., Fulk, J. (1994). Information technology and the prospects for organizational transformation. In: B. Kovacic (Ed.), New Aapproaches to Organizational Communication. State University of New York Press, Albany, NY.

Huber, G.P. (1991). Organizational Learning: The contributing process and the literatures. Organization Science, 2: 88–125.

Kraatz, M.S. (1998). Learning by association? Interorganizational networks and adaptation to environmental change. Academy of Management Journal, 41: 621–643.

Krcmar, H. (2000). Informationsmanagement. Springer, Berlin.

Lane, P.J. and Lubatkin, M. (1998). Relative absorptive capacity and interorganizational learning. Strategic Management Journal, 19: 461–477.

Larsson, R., Bengtsson, L., Henriksson, K., Sparks, J. (1998). The interorganizational learning dilemma. Collective knowledge development in strategic alliances. Organization Science, 9(3): 285–305.

Lechner, C. (2001). The competitiveness of firm networks, Peter Lang, Frankfur/Main.

Leontiades, M. (1982). Choosing the right manager to fit the strategy. Journal of Business Strategy, 3: 58–69.

Leonard, D. (1995). Wellsprings of Knowledge: Building and Sustaining the Source of Innovation. Harvard Business School, Boston.

Mahlich, Joerg C. (2000). Innovation in the Japanese Pharmaceutical Industry, Wien.

Mansfield, Edwin (1988). Industrial innovation in Japan and the United States. Science, Sept. 30.

Martiny, L., Klotz, M. (1989). Strategisches Informationsmanagement—Bedeutung und organisatorische Umsetzung. Handbuch der Informatik, Bd. 12.1, Oldenbourg, München Wien.

Mayer, David and Kenney, Martin (2002). Economic action does not take place in a vacuum: understanding Cisco's acquisition and development strategy. BRIE working paper 148, September 16.

McDougall, P., Shane, S. and Oviatt, B.M. (1994). Explaining the formation of international new ventures: The limits of theories from international business research. Journal of Business Venturing, 9: 469–487.

Mitchell, W., Singh, K. (1996). Survival of businesses using collaborative relationships to commercialize complex goods. Strategic Management Journal, 17: 169–196.

Mowery, D.C., Oxley, J.E. and Silverman, B.S. (1996). Strategic alliances and inter-firm knowledge transfer. Strategic Management Journal, 17: 77–91.

Nicholls-Nixon, C. (1993). Absorptive capacity and technological sourcing: Implications for the responsiveness of established firms. Unpublished Ph.D. dissertation, Purdue University.

Österle, H. (1987). Erfolgsfaktor Informatik—Umsetzung der Informationstechnik in Unternehmensführung. Information Management, 3: 24ff.

Penrose, E. (1959). The Growth of the Firm, Oxford University Press.

Picot, A., Franck, E. (1988). Die Planung der Unternehmensressource Information (I)+(II). WISU, 17. Jg., pp. 544–549, and pp. 608–618.

Porter, L.W. and Lawler, E.E. (1968). Managerial attitudes and performance, Richard D. Irwin, Inc., Homewood, Illinois.

Rifkin, Glenn (1997). Growth by acquisition: The case of Cisco Systems. In: Strategy and Business, Booz Allen and Hamilton.

Rocha, Federico (1997). Interfirm technological cooperation: Effects of absorptive capacity, firm size and specialization, Discussion paper #9707, INTECH, The United Nation University, Maastricht.

Rohlen, Thomas P. (1992). Learning. In: Kumon, Shumpei and Rosovsky, Henry, The Political Economy of Japan, Vol. 3, Stanford Univ. Press.

Rosenberg, Nathan and Steinmueller, W.E. (1988). Why are Americans such poor imitators? American Economic Review, 78: 2.

Spender, J.-C. (1996). Making knowledge the basis of a dynamic theory of the firm. Strategic Management Journal, 17: 45–62.

Strassmann, P. (1997). The Squandered Computer. The Information Economics Press, New Canaan (Connecticut).

Taylor, Mark (1995). Dominance through technology: Is Japan creating a Yen bloc in Southeast Asia? Foreign Affairs, November/December.

Temple and Johnson (1998). Social capability and economic growth. Quarterly Journal of Economics, 113(3): 965–990.

Tsai, W. (2001). Knowledge transfer in intraorganizational networks: Effects of network position and absorptive capacity on business unit innovation and performance. Academy of Management Journal, 44: 996–1004.

Venture Economics (2001).

Vroom, V.M. (1964). Work and Motivation, Wiley, New York.

Wachovia Securities, Hunt, George, Strauss, Robert and Barre, Bert (2000). IJL Financial Center, 201 North Tryon St., Charlotte, NC, 28202 (November 16).

Weinert, A.B. (1992). Motivation. In: Gaugler, E., Handwörterbuch des Personalwesens, 2. Auflage, Stuttgart, pp. 1429–1442.

Witte, E. (1972). Field research on complex decision-making precesses—The phase theorem. International Studies of Management and Organization. Fall, pp. 156–182.

Wittman, W. (1959). Unternehmung und unvollkommene Information, Köln/Opladen.

Yli-Renko, H., Autio, E. and Sapienza, H.J. (2001). Social capital, knowledge acquisition, and competitive advantage in technology based young firms. Strategic Management Journal, 22: 587–613.

Zahra, S.A. and George, G. (2002). Absorptive capacity: A review, reconceptualization, and extension. Academy of Management Review, 27: 185–203.

Zollo, Maurizio and Harbir, Singh (2002). Post acquisition strategies, Integration capability and the economic performance of corporate acquisition. In: Strategic Management Review.

Chapter 11

RESEARCH ISSUES CONCERNING ETHICS AND THE INTERNET: HOW CAN WE LIVE WELL IN CYBERSPACE?

Richard O. Mason

Edwin L. Cox School of Business, Southern Methodist University, Dallas, TX 75275-0333

1. CYBERSPACE: NEW POSSIBILITIES, MORAL CHALLENGES

In cyberspace humankind is creating a new world. Telecommunications, computers, the Internet, and its vibrant offspring, E-commerce—all parts of the vaunted National Information Infrastructure, NII—are among the latest of a long line of information technologies that are changing the way people relate to one another, the ways they communicate, live, work, do business, and entertain themselves. Novelist William Gibson coined the term "cyberspace," in Neuromancer, to describe the virtual, digital world these technologies have made possible. He also sought to distinguish this new electronic bit realm from a physical world characterized by atoms and more traditional relationships [1].

Cyberspace opens up an infinitude of opportunities and possibilities. "Our minds are finite," Alfred North Whitehead observed at the dawn of the information age, "and yet even in these circumstances of finitude, we are surrounded by possibilities that are infinite, and the purpose of human life is to grasp as much as we can out of that infinitude" [2]. Cyberspace reaches toward that infinitude. It is fundamentally a source for many new and different human behaviors, a great augmentation to human freedom. The purpose of human life, however, must not only be to grasp these new possibilities, it must also be to direct them toward the right and the good. Cyberspace is a new moral domain. By expanding freedom it opens up more possibilities for evil as well as good, for tyranny as well as democracy. Since cyberspace is being created by human beings to be inhabited by human beings it is essential that it be created to promote human well-being. History suggests that this is a significant challenge.

2. THE ASYNCHRONOUS PRINCIPLE: SCIENCE AND TECHNOLOGY OUTPACE ETHICS

A study of history reveals that each innovation in science and technology, when it is accompanied by enabling changes in the social organization, confronts society with new social and ethical issues to be resolved. Issues are created because the application of new knowledge or technologies expands the range of behaviors available for people to take. Developments in atomic power, nanotechnology, cloning, and human genetics are rather recent cases in point. Essentially science and technology are liberating. They add to the freedom of choice of those who have access to them by enhancing the range of possibilities and opportunities open to them. But, science and technology do not come equipped with a moral compass. They are morally variable. Their ethical dimensions depend on how they are used. They are, consequently, morally malleable. That is, they can be used to produce either good or harm. Any of these new behaviors may be judged either good or evil, right or wrong, just or unjust, or virtuous or despicable. In short, new technologies enlarge the moral domain. And, this poses new problems for society.

In an ideal society the application of science and technology is aligned and synchronized with the purposes and functioning of the social system. Innovations, thereby, produce human well being and promote the common good. Experience indicates, however, that actually reaching such a state of moral equilibrium is a rare occurrence. Instead, history favors an asynchronous principle: the rate of change of technology out paces the rate of effective adaptation of ethical reflection. Thus, the development of values, strategies and policies for achieving the common good tend to lag behind, often well behind, innovations in science and technology. As a corollary, the faster the pace of technological development the greater the gap between the current state of technological use and our conception of the common good.

In this cyber-era technology is expanding exponentially. In particular the conversion of data of all sorts into digital symbols (or "bits") and the ability to move, store, process and display these symbols in large volumes, rapidly and at low cost is growing at a stunning pace. Indicators abound. Microprocessor giant Intel forecasts that it will outpace one of its founder's seemingly over optimistic law of exponential growth. Gordon Moore stated that processing power doubles every 18 to 24 months for about the same cost. From 1971, the birth of chips, until about 1997 Moore's Law essentially held. Since then the pace as picked up. Circa 2000 an Intel chip holds about 30 million transistors. Processor density is expected to reach 600 million by 2010 [3]. Kurzweil, for example, forecasts that, whereas $1000 purchases about 1 billion calculations per second in 2000, $1000 will purchase about a trillion calculations per second in 2010 [4]. The ability to store and retrieve symbols is also growing at a similar pace. IBM, for example, forecasts that today's massive 36.2 gigabit (GB)—approximately a billion bit—storage devices will be superseded by 1000 GB disk drives by 2005 [5]. The advent and extensive adoption of packet switching and the Internet Protocol (IP) has extended the range, flexibility, and ultimately the bandwidth of telecommunications. Combined with Transmission Control Protocol (TCP), IP provides a virtually guaranteed reliable, error free symbol transmission between a source and a destination on a network. IP not only undergirds the Internet it is also rapidly becoming the means for diverse public and private networks to communicate. Voice, data, images, videos, music and the like flow gracefully intermingled on this pipeline. Improved compression techniques and more powerful servers, routers and digital signal processors are enhancing the speed and efficiency. Optical networking—carrying symbols across networks in the form of light pulses—increases the capacity of the telecommunications system to move symbols by an order of magnitude. For example, a single strand of glass fiber with a capacity of 40 gigabits per second can handle either 600,000 simultaneous voice telephone calls, 1.4 million Internet connections using 28.8 kbps modems, 4,000 full-motion video streams, or 200,000 high-quality audio feeds. Wireless is rapidly becoming an alternative communication source to twisted copper pairs and fiber optics. The conclusion is clear: the technology that supports cyberspace will continue to expand its capability for at least the next decade or so and likely well beyond.

Internet usage is also growing rapidly. At year end 1999 there were approximately 110,000,000 users in the U.S. and 259,000,000 globally. By February 2004, Neilson survey revealed that an estimated 204,300,000 people, or 74.9 percent of the population above the age of 2 and living in households equipped with fixed-line phones, had Internet access. This was up from 66 percent in February, 2003, and indicates that an earlier forecast that by 2005 Internet usage would grow to 206,550,000 in the U.S. and a jarring 765,000,000 globally is pessimistic. Moreover, usage will continue to grow after that time [6]. E-commerce on the Internet is also growing, creating a new economic foundation for society. A recent report by the University of Texas' Center for Research in Electronic Commerce found that:

- The Internet Economy generated an estimated $830 billion in revenues in 2000, a 58% increase over 1999, and 156% increase over 1998.
- The Internet Economy now directly supports more than 3,088 million workers, including an additional 600,000 in the first half of 2000.
- Whereas non-Internet related jobs grew at a rate of 6.9% for the six month period fourth quarter 1999 and first quarter 2000, total employment at Internet Economy companies grew 10% and Internet-related jobs grew 29%.
- Thus, the Internet Economy revenue is growing about twice as fast as Internet Economy employment.

- Internet Economy employees are increasingly productive employees. Revenue per employee increased 11.5% in the first half of 2000.

The authors concluded:

"The Internet is increasingly becoming part of the basic business model for many companies, laying the groundwork for even more impressive growth during strong economic conditions. The Internet is rapidly becoming an integral part of the traditional economy—like telephones, elevators, and personal computers over the years—leading to the day when there will be no separate measure of the Internet Economy" [7].

Cyberspace, with its almost ubiquitous global reach, its virtual nature, its interactivity, its mobility, and its increased speed and flexibility of information exchange, is making possible many new behaviors that have not yet been fully evaluated morally. Current scientific research into the attributes of cyberspace and the new economy is focused on what new behaviors are feasible, how they are constructed, and what their technical, economic and other properties are. Science seeks to grasp as much as it can out of the Whiteheadian infinitude of possibilities. Ethics research, or more accurately moral reflection, places human values on each of the possibilities. It examines new behavioral choices in light of moral principles, or "what ought to be," in an effort of determine which choices will lead toward a good society and which will not.

3. CYBERSPACE EXPANDS THE MORAL DOMAIN

The range of new behaviors available in cyberspace is enormous. Over a decade ago consultant Stan Davis summarized the ways that cyber-related technologies would affect the new economy. Business and other activities, he forecasted, could take place: any time, any place, with no (or little) physical matter involved, and featuring mass customizing to meet each person's individual needs [8]. A.T. Kearney Managing Director Douglas Aldrich believes that this new cyber economy is substantially here—as the University of Texas report suggests—and is already having a profound effect on the way work is done and value is created. He observes that several important social drivers are responsible for this: increased communication and computational capabilities (as summarized above), a faster pace of life, a greater need for information assimilation, and a stronger demand for control over one's time are. These forces are inexorably pushing our society toward a digital economy operating largely in cyberspace. In this new economy customers have unprecedented economic power [9].

In *Blown to Bits* Evans and Wurster, of the Boston Consulting Group, argue that the Internet Economy is redefining the information channels that link people together due to the spread of connectivity and of common information standards. People are now forming new relationships among themselves. New connections are also springing up between and among businesses including their customers, suppliers and employees. The information flowing in these relationships is, moreover, qualitatively different. Eliminated is a presupposed trade-off between the richness of information and the extensiveness of its reach—a kind of received doctrinal assumption that previously served as the informational foundation upon which all relationships such as customer franchises, vertical integration, and horizontal integration, were formerly based. In cyberspace, digitized information can simultaneously have a broad "reach"—because it allows a large number of people to exchange it freely—and still be "rich"—available by means of wide bandwidth, customized, interactive, reliable, trusted, secure and timely. One consequence is that traditional business structures are being dismantled and reformulated. Entire industries are being eliminated, severely modified or reconstructed as intermediaries.

Furthermore, the digitization of information, supported by advances in computing and communications, is changing how networks of all types work. Networks are becoming more intelligent. In these "smart" networks the ability to store, distribute, assemble and modify information is greatly enhanced. This makes the intelligence floating in them dynamic, able to be moved quickly to where it is requested or needed. Intelligence is distributable throughout the network. Small units of requisite intelligence may be coalesced into bundles on demand and sent to where they are needed to solve a problem.

All of this information flexibility, however, comes at a price. Users are frequently overwhelmed by the hordes of information and possibilities available to them. In an information affluent environment people need tools that help them to cope with "information anxiety"—that stupefying feeling produced by the ever-widening gap between what people understand and what they think they *should* understand [10]. Humans want to be able to assimilate information quickly and to make decisions easily. Echoing this point, Evans and Wurster note that a premium is being placed on one's ability to navigate effectively through the massive informational labyrinth that resides in cyberspace [11].

Human being's lives are also changed by their experience in cyberspace. Sociologist qua psychologist Sherry Turkle summarizes the effects of operating in cyberspace on people and their sense of identity:

> "In cyberspace, we can talk, exchange ideas, and assume personae of our own creation. We have the opportunity to build new kinds of communities, virtual communities, in which we participate with people from all over the world, people with whom we converse daily, people with whom we may have fairly intimate relationships but whom we may never physically meet." (pages 9–10) [12]

Cyberspace is being molded by our actions every day. It is affecting the ways in which we act toward one another as human beings. It is creating new relationships. In *Electronic Commerce Relationships: Trust by Design* a respected cyber pundit, Peter Keen, argues that the value in relationship comes from personalization, collaboration, community, and, central in his view, the design of trust [13]. These are all moral considerations. The advent of cyberspace is an ethical as well as a technical phenomenon. The overarching ethical questions are at least three:

- What do we want cyberspace to be?
- How is it to be constructed?
- And, importantly, how is it to be governed?

The answers to these questions center on human values. Needed is a form of social contract—an agreement between current and potential members of cyberspace to behave with reciprocal responsibility in their relationships with one another. Such a contract will serve as a basis for governance in cyberspace. Time, however, is of the essence. The new global network architecture that forms cyberspace is already being constructed. If social priorities are not articulated and enforced soon, they may be precluded in the future. Needed is a plan for the ethical governance and regulation of cyberspace.

4.   FOUR TOOLS FOR ETHICAL REGULATION

In a provocative book *Code and Other Laws of Cyberspace* law professor Lawrence Lessig considers the tools available for regulating the plethora of possibilities for human action that are being created in cyberspace. Essentially we have four approaches available to us to define and enforce social priorities in cyberspace [14]: design, markets, the law and social norms. These tools may be used singly or, more usually, in combination.

4.1.   Social Norms and Customs

Norms are mental models or guidelines by which members of cyberspace voluntarily control and evaluate their actions and those of others. Normative order is necessary to insure mutual co-operation and to avoid dysfunctional breakdowns or conflicts. The sociologist Emile Durkheim once called norms the "internal" environment of human behavior because norms are cultural, social and psychological. In a functional society people generally conform to its norms. They are usually accepted voluntarily as being legitimate, although they are often enforced by social coercion. When norms are the basis of social control persuasion is the primary control mechanism employed. Many of the early users of the Internet believe that norms are the only tools that should ever be used to govern cyberspace.

"In cyberspace," John Perry Barlow observed early on, "the First Amend-ment is a local ordinance." Barlow, along with Mitch Kapor, founded The Electronic Frontier Foundation (EFF) to keep cyberspace free from govern-ment and other powerful influences. Barlow proclaims in his "Declaration of Independence of Cyberspace":

"Governments of the Industrial World, you weary giants of flesh and steel, I come from Cyberspace, the home of Mind. On behalf of the future, I ask you of the past to leave us alone. You are not welcome among us. You have no sovereignty where we gather" [15].

In line with this view, the EFF has called for "open platforms."

Such a free and open world is primarily controlled by norms, often, as in the wild West, enforced by violence. When individual members are given this much liberty other members will act to control untoward behavior. The process is well documented. For example, in the path breaking Bank Wiring Room group of the Hawthorne Works studies, conducted at the Western Elec-tric Company during 1931–1932, production output norms set "freely" by the workers were, in fact, maintained by means of informal social control mecha-nisms such as "binging." Binging refers to the delivery of sharp punches to the arm of a person deemed to be a "rate buster" [16].

Inhabitants of cyberspace have developed analogs too. Lessing provides examples. "Talk about democratic politics in the alt. knitting news group, and you open yourself to flaming; "spoof" someone's identity in a MUD, and you may find yourself 'toadied,' talk too much in a discussion list, and you are likely to be placed on a common bozo filter. In each case, a set of under-standings constrain behavior, again through the threat of *ex post* sanctions imposed by community" [17] (page 89). A new vocabulary of cybernorms has been spawned. *Netiquette* refers to the accepted way to behave in e-mail, news groups and the like. *Flaming* is sending strong, argumentative, abusive, even incendiary messages to express a difference of opinion. *Trolling* entails writing outrageous messages designed to provoke a response, usually just for fun. *Spamming* (also called *cross-posting*) involves sending and reproducing multiple copies of a message to hundreds, even thousands, of others whose e-mail addresses have been obtained by various means. And, *toading* means turning a member into a virtual toad by wiping out his or her description and attributes from a server, game or MUD (and also perhaps replacing them with those of a slithering amphibian or other disgusting animal). Toading effectively annihilates the person's cyberspace character. Social norms, consciously and unconsciously applied, are—and will continue to be—important regulators in cyberspace; but, as Hobbes observed at the beginning of the Industrial Age, they are not adequate for the entire task. Hobbes envisioned the need for a state of some sort with rules and laws. Cyberspace will require some struc-tured controls as well.

4.2.   Positive Law

Law consists, in general, of a body of written or generally agreed upon rules and principles that govern the affairs of a community and that are enforced by political authority. Under the rule of law a member should choose an action only if it agrees with and does not violate the laws or regulations established by legitimate authorities for those parts of the system (jurisdictions or communities) in which the he or she is a member. Thus, in legal systems political authority rather than persuasion serves as the primary control mechanism. Legal systems include civil law—e.g. rules concerning contracts and torts, liability, property rights, privacy rights, defamation, obscenity and standing (the legal right to initiate a suit usually guaranteed by a territorial sovereign). They also include, of course, criminal law, and administrative law such as regulations, rules, or orders. In general legislatures enact laws, prosecutors work to enforce them, and the courts adjudicate conflicts and convict violators.

Cyberlaw is in its infancy, although the courts are beginning to be flooded with new cases [18]. A recent survey of global cybercrime laws supports this. It found that the legal systems of 33 out of 52 developed countries did not address any type of cybercrime, although about half of the deficient countries indicated that they were in the process of amending their legislation. Nevertheless, at this writing no complete legal framework has been developed to govern the use of the Internet and other aspects of cyberspace. If commerce and other aspects of social order are to prevail in cyberspace, however, a more comprehensive and cyber-sensitive legal system will be required. Once established, emerging legal institutions may compete with some of the social norms that have already been embodied in the technology or assumed by its current users. They will certainly influence future behavior in cyberspace. This is one of the reasons that avid libertarians like Barlow, Kapor and Ester Dyson argue against the need for law. In their view cyberspace is and should be a free and open frontier. But, socially responsible investment in cyberspace is likely to be stifled in the absence of a reliable legal framework. Moreover, the lack of an applicable legal system opens up many options for unprincipled actors to behave in dishonest, dysfunctional or even dangerous ways. In the modern world law is an important part of the social framework that shapes technological innovation. According to former SMU law professor Jane Winn "law can support the development of open public standards, or the creation of proprietary interests in technology." Thus, well crafted laws can stimulate development as well as protect many basic human rights in cyberspace [19].

Nevertheless, USC law professor Christopher Stone points out that despite the fact that it is a powerful control mechanism; the law has several severe limitations. One is the time lag problem. It takes a long time from the felt need for a law until an effective law is passed. The law is primarily a reactive institution. A second limitation centers on the political process by which laws are made. Powerful forces the control of whose behavior may be the intended object of a law often find ways to insure that laws that restrict their activities are not passed. Finally, there are problems with implementing and applying the law. For the law to work the damaged party must (1) know the fact that he or she has been injured, (2) know who caused the injury, (3) be able to access the nature and extent of the injuries, and (4) determine the cause of the injury (usually in a common sense interpretation that a jury or judge can understand). Legal systems assume further that if the responsible parties are found guilty of violating the law they will change their behavior in the future [20]. Given these limitations to social control by means of positive law some people recommend that markets be established to govern behavior in cyberspace.

4.3.   Markets

History has demonstrated that the "invisible hand" is one of the most effective social forces available for keeping human behavior within socially desirable bounds. By setting up "virtual economies" markets can be created within some aspects of cyberspace. These markets, operated by a freely functioning "invisible hand," then regulate user behavior. Activities, events and streams of bits in cyberspace are converted into commodities so that they can be produced, exchanged and distributed and, consequently, a value can be placed on them. In a market, or "free," economy economic units—e.g. private individuals or companies—conduct business by making autonomous decisions rather than following laws, government regulations or other externally derived plans. The primary control mechanism in a market is the balancing effect of competing self-interests as each unit makes its autonomous decisions in the marketplace. Two economic processes govern user's behavior: (1) exchange—a transfer of values between two economic units in cyberspace, and (2) allocation—a transfer of values to alternative ends within a given economic unit. In an economy a given commodity, such as a property right, has a plurality of uses to which it can be allocated. Therefore, a choice must be made as to the particular use to which it will be put. Moreover, these commodities are relatively scarce. Broadly available or free goods are at a minimum. Consequently, a value measurement scheme such as a pricing mechanism is used to determine a commodity's value and, hence, direct it toward its most economical use. Usually there are multiple economic units participating and these units normally have a different ranking of values for any given commodity based in part on its scarcity. In a market each economic unit measures its performance by determining its profit—the difference between its income and outgo or costs incurred as measured by the price or values system. The conventional liberal argument holds that fragmenting property into commodities and decentralizing decision making into individual units are required to insure a fair and just allocation of commodities. It claims further that a pricing scheme provides the incentives necessary to encourage the production of needed goods and services. Beyond their economic results these outcomes are also deemed necessary for political freedom and democracy [21].

Lessig cites cyberspace examples. "Pricing structures constrain access, and if they do not, busy signals do. . . . Areas of the Web are beginning to charge for access, as online services have for some time. Advertisers reward popular sites; online services drop low-population forums. These behaviors are all a function of market constraints and market opportunity." Nevertheless, markets have limitations. The desirability of their outcomes rests on some crucial, and sometimes unsupportable, assumptions.

Speaking in a corporate context Stone summarizes some of the limitations of markets: "One ought to be clear that those who have faith that profit orientation is an adequate guarantee of corporations realizing socially desirable consumer goals are implicitly assuming: (1) that the persons who are going to withdraw patronage know the *fact* that they are being "injured" (where injury refers to a whole range of possible grievances, from getting a worse deal than might be gotten elsewhere, to purchasing a product that is defective or below warranted standards, to getting something that produces actual injury); (2) that they know *where* to apply pressure of some sort; (3) that they are in a *position* to apply pressure of some sort; and (4) that their pressure will be *translated* into warranted changes in the institution's behavior" [22] (pages 88–89). In cyberspace these assumptions are not always well founded. Consequently, creating market mechanisms, while a powerful tool, can not be the only method used to regulate cyberspace.

4.4.   Architectural Design or *Code*

On the occasion of reconstructing the House of Commons in 1943 Winston Churchill opined: "We shape our buildings, and afterwards they shape us" [23] (page 1). As more people devote larger portions of their lives to cyberspace it is indeed cyberspace that is "shaping" us. Anything that shapes and molds human behavior a fortiori carries moral significance. The words we normally use to describe this shaping are "design" and "architecture." The art and science of designing and erecting buildings, dwellings and other physical things is the common idea of architecture. Its application assumes that some significant aspects of our world, both concrete and intangible, are not inevitable but are rather "conventional." They are the result of human choice guided by the exercise of human values. Churchman describes: ". . . design is thinking behavior which conceptually selects among a set of alternatives in order to figure out which alternative leads to the desired goal or set of goals" [24] (page 5). Thus, design requires a conscious choice of artifacts and structures so that they satisfy our practical and aesthetic needs.

The history of human development is, in part, also a story of design, beginning with cave dwellings, which reflected a minimum of human influence, and extending up to the modern megaopolis which is substantially human made. Since at least 3500 B.C. when the Sumerians developed cuneiform writing using a stylus to etch wedge-shaped symbols into soft clay information technology has played a significant role in shaping human affairs [25]. The pace has quickened since these humble beginnings as information technologies have played a more prominent role in our lives. Today society is moving into another new world that is almost entirely the product of human design: cyberspace. The "real world" or physical world, as Nicholas Negroponte points out, is comprised of atoms, those exceedingly small units of matter [26]. Design and architecture in this world have focused on rearranging atoms so that they better served human purposes. Humankind has become pretty good at doing this, although some critics question the social outcomes have been entirely beneficial. Our designed physical world, Karl Marx argues, is an act of self-creation in which humankind "starts, regulates and controls the material reactions between [itself] and nature ... by thus acting on the external world and changing it, [humankind] at the same time changes [its] own nature. [Society] develops [its] slumbering powers and compels them to act in obedience to [its] sway" [27]. Today, cyberspace is having the same kind of modifying effects on human beings and their lives.

In cyberspace the fundamental unit is "bits," strings of 0's and 1's reflecting off or on, no or yes, and the like. Expanded use of these binary digits is driving the digital revolution. As discussed earlier the use of bits is creating a digital economy and marketplace under girded by digital products, digital value chains and digital value networks [28]. In the digital world of cyberspace, design entails rearranging and controlling access to and the flow of bits. As a society we don't know as much as we should about what this means and how to manage it.

Lessig calls the architecture that regulates behavior in cyberspace *code*. "The software and hardware that make cyberspace what it is constitute a set of constraints on how you behave. The substance of these constraints may vary, but they are experienced as conditions on your access to cyberspace. In some places (online services such as AOL, for instance) you must enter a password before you gain access; in other places you can enter whether identified or not. In some places the transactions you engage in produce traces that link the transactions (the "mouse droppings") back to you [as for example Double Click's "cookie" did]; in other places this link is achieved only if you want it to be. In some places you can choose to speak a language that only the recipient can hear (through encryption); in other places encryption is not an option. The code or software or architecture or protocols set these features; they are features selected by code writers; they constrain some behavior by making other behaviors possible, or impossible. The code embeds certain values or makes certain values impossible. In this sense, it too is regulation, just as the architectures of real-space codes are regulations" [29] (page 89).

Thus, in cyberspace code is a significant regulator of human behavior and joins social norms, law and market forces as means for implementing ethics.

5.   THE CHALLENGE OF DESIGNING CYBERSPACE

A formidable task we face is to design cyberspace so that it truly serves human purposes. Time is of the essence. The asynchronous principle is relentlessly at work. Partial designs are being created everyday and used to grab part of the space in Oklahoma land rush style, as Cisco Systems consultants Hartman and Sifonis claim [30]. Left to its own devices this frenzy may result in a digital society that we don't want or are unable to control.

Architects and urban planners know that different elements of design are needed to satisfy different human needs. Reflect on your experience with various buildings—library, factory, shopping mall, school, post office, theater, train station, museum, concert hall, jazz club, your home. Each serves a different function in life. Each accordingly takes a different physical form. The layout and structure of a library, for example, facilitates interaction with books and other materials; whereas, a concert hall is designed to enhance the experience of listening to music. Rarely, at least without remodeling, does a building constructed for one purpose work well for another. Yet, every person's life involves numerous encounters with many, if not all, of these buildings. So, one needs to be able to flow easily and gracefully from one to another. The better the community design, that is, the better one structure is articulated with another, the better people's lives are experienced. Thus, human purposes, for specific needs and for life clusters of needs, play an all-important role in designing buildings and communities.

The discipline of architecture rests on this ethical function. It expresses our values, our ethos. And, it gives us a sense of place in the world. But, importantly, it also is used to constrain and channel our behavior. The caves of Cro-Magnon, for example, were essentially inseparable from the primitive society that emerged around them. The cave dweller's life and living possibilities were shaped by the nature of these places and, perhaps, by the simple instruments made from stone, bone and ivory they used for hunting and gathering. From this humble beginning innovations in technology and social organization led to new kinds of structures and artifacts, thereby, greatly increasing the options and possibilities for living that were open to human beings. In the process these innovations also added new constraints and abuses. Innovations made both good and bad behaviors possible.

The skyscraper, that great symbol of 20th century economic progress, was made possible by developments in steel fabrication and vertical transportation. These large urban structures were required to house the offices of an expanding bureaucracy created by modern industry. The thousands of people who worked, say, in the Chrysler or Empire State buildings inevitably have different life experiences than those who worked, to cite a comparative extreme, in Henry Ford's River Rouge automobile manufacturing plant near Detroit. These buildings were built to serve different purposes. They have different structures. They relate differently to their environment. They express different values. Consequently, they shape a different kind of person.

We must keep this relationship between form, function and values firmly in mind as we set out to design cyberspace. Each basic human need should be served as effectively and efficiently as possible while at the same time cyberspace should serve the entire cluster of human needs together so that they each are met comfortably. Moreover, just as in a well designed community people flow easily from one facility to another, in cyberspace people should be able to move with ease from one information function to another. This is a crucial requirement for design.

5.1. Two Theories of Design

The design of cyberspace may be guided by one of two general philosophical approaches. Cyberspace can be designed either as a *machine for living* in the manner of the modernist, functionalist architect Le Corbusier, or it can be viewed as a home for human *dwelling* in the spirit of Martin Heidegger, the German philosopher who pioneered existential phenomenology.

5.1.1. Cyberspace as a Machine
Le Corbusier sketched out massive, comprehensive plans for entire cities such as Plan Voisin for Paris, the "business city" of Buenos Aires, and a master plan for Rio de Janeiro. Architecture for Corbusier "is the art above all others which achieves a state of platonic grandeur, mathematical order, speculation, the perception of harmony that lies in emotional relationships." The straight line, the right angle, and the imposition of international building standards were all part of an approach he called "the principle of functional separation." "The poverty, the inadequacy of traditional techniques have brought in their wake a confusion of powers, *an artificial mingling of functions*, only indifferently related to one another," Le Corbusier wrote with his brother Pierre. "We must find and apply new methods ... lending themselves naturally to standardization, industrialization, Taylorization," a reference to Frederick Winslow Taylor the noted turn-of-the-century efficiency expert [31]. The segregation of functions allows planners to think clearly and more easily about efficiency. Le Corbusier further argued that clear decisions must be made between an artifice's structure and the circulation and

movement it allowed. Choices also must be made between arrangement and furnishing, on the one hand, and construction approaches on the other. If these functions were co-mingled or interrelated architecture would never reach its great promise. Urban zones may be planned more readily if they each serve only one purpose. Pedestrians should not compete with automobiles or trains. Functionally segregated units are united in a hierarchy. For Le Corbusier skyscrapers are the command centers and brains of the city. *"Human happiness already exists,"* he wrote, it is "expressed in terms of numbers, of mathematics, of properly calculated designs, plans in which the cities can already be seen" [32].

5.1.2.   Cyberspace as a Dwelling Many people, however, view Le Corbusier's rigid design approach as sterile. Jane Jacobs in her heartfelt critique—*The Death and Life of Great American Cities*—urges designers to envision a messier, perhaps fuzzier, kind of order, one based on each individual's and the community's personal experiences. Observing daily life from her Greenwich Village apartment window Jacobs found that personal belonging, identity, and social cohesiveness developed best in traditional, well-defined neighborhoods and along narrow, crowded, multi-use streets. Living in these conditions engendered a form of personal expression—and art form—as each inhabitant participated in a "street ballet," largely of his or her own making. Planners like Le Corbusier, she complains, substitute slick surface regularity and generic form for the gritty substance of real life. Instead we must tease out the underlying "secret order" in human affairs and build complex, cross-use places and facilities.

Jacobs' plea aligns with Heidegger's philosophy. Heidegger posited that a fundamental triadic relation exists between the mode of being of objects, of humanity, and of the structure of time. In his view, individuals are constantly in danger of being submerged in the world of objects, everyday routine, and the conventional crowd. Modern technological society, he argued, has deprived human life of meaning, a condition he called nihilism. His most influential work, *Being and Time* (1927), deals with the question, "What is it to be?" To stay afloat in a designed world a person must exercise his freedom and be authentic, true to him or herself. Heidegger stresses the significance of the concrete individual in contrast to rational abstractions and general principles and advocates human freedom and choice, focusing on the centrality of individual decision-making. He forms an imperative: human beings must be free to move freely and flexibly among the objects and structures they inhabit if they are to become fully human. People must be able to "dwell" in the material world as their original, authentic selves. Otherwise they sink into nothingness. In contrast to Le Corbusier's rational hierarchical model, an architecture based on Heidegger's philosophy is very organic, interrelated and "bottom up." Yet, each function must be designed and implemented so that a human being's dignity, decision-making ability and opportunity to flourish are preserved.

6. CHOOSING A DESIGN STRATEGY

What do these theories imply for the design of cyberspace? Whereas the architects of history have placed atoms in the world either according to a rational design—à la Le Corbusier—or let them evolve in the manner of Jacobs and Heidegger, the architects of cyberspace must manage bits. The new design calls for a balancing and positioning between the two: atoms interacting with bits and vice-versa. Yet, few people are currently addressing these broad issues. Instead cyberspace is emerging somewhat willy-nilly affording neither the geometric solidarity of rational planning nor the graceful flow of human experience from function to function. To paraphrase Jacobs we have yet to experience a cyber ballet.

Cyberspace can satisfy several important human needs. The possibilities and needs do reach toward infinity. The need for knowledge and truth, to point to one need, can be fulfilled by the digital library. The need for community and conversation by digital communications, notably multi-media e-mail and instant messaging. The need for leisure and entertainment by digital music, games and films. The need for economic exchange for goods and services of all types by e-commerce. The need for public goods by e-government. And, the need for adventure and discovery by the fantastic experience of digital worlds. Each of these functions requires its own digital form. A well conceived cyber-community provides all of these functions and more. It facilitates a user's (a citizen's or "netizen's") movement in and out of each of these functions on an as needed or desired basis. Herein lies a great design challenge. For the most part, to date, most programmers have worked diligently to develop an optimal set of code and procedures for just one of these functions. They have not tried to construct a society of functions, each function being separate and sound. Each function has claims on the others for information and resources and yet it also is a member of a greater cooperative system. A design for cyberspace that emphasizes just one function to the exclusion of others is lop-sided. Nevertheless, each function must be designed with its own integrity and be trustworthy, complete and efficient in its operations. Likely neither Le Corbusier's long straight streets with right-angled intersections nor Jacobs' intimate undulating Hudson Street will serve as proper metaphors. These represent two ends of a continuum within which we must find a meeting ground. How might we begin this searching process?

6.1.   A Proposed Charette

We are faced with two crucial issues. We must insure the integrity of each function performed in cyberspace and we must also insure that people can flow gracefully from one function to another as their life needs require. A monolithic approach will not work. The requirements for one function may be in considerable conflict with the requirements for another. Avatars and some types of chat rooms, for example, require anonymity; whereas, e-commerce and e-government can only function effectively if the system can identify and authenticate specifically and precisely who the parties are. Yet, collectively all of these and other functions are wanted by citizens of cyberspace. Needed is a method for prioritizing and coordinating the many possibilities.

One method for exploring relationships among the possibilities in cyberspace is to conduct a "charette"—an intense, on-the-spot design effort in which stakeholders representing various interest groups come together to discuss, workout, negotiate and decide on a master plan. In French charette means "cart." This particular usage for the term charette evolved during the second half of the 19th century in Paris and was used to describe a practice at the Ecole Des Beaux-Arts. During the semester architecture students worked intensively in project groups to develop their final drawings, fervently attempting to get them completed on time. When the due date arrived their professor strolled by picking up their portfolios in a cart. This led to the practice of calling any intense, short term design effort with a prescribed deliverable a charette. Architects now use the term to describe a short—usually 2–3 day—workshop in which a variety of different stakeholders from a community or user group discuss and debate alternative design options or approaches. The purpose is to find a synthesis from among the differing points of view, one that addresses as many different values, needs and concerns as possible.

Cyberspace needs a research charette. It is time for people from various walks of life in the physical world to come together and share their perspectives on inhabiting the virtual world. This collection of points-of-view must be global in scope, represent the technical philosophies that guide current hardware and software design, and include cultural, social, economic and moral perspectives. Essential are people who have a deep understanding of the evolving role of information in society. In the physical world people relate to atoms; in cyberspace they must relate to bits. In both of these relationships they seek meaning and identity. An effective charette—or a series of charettes conducted throughout the world—is also one method for closing the gap created by the asynchronous principle. That is, the results of the charette should help provide guidance for the ongoing, well nigh relentless, development of cyberspace.

How might the charette proceed? One possibility is for a small group of thought leaders to meet and develop a preliminary manifesto in the form of an exposure draft. It would include a proposed design and constitution. The draft would be posted on the web and its availability would be widely publicized. An on-line forum would be designed for soliciting comments on each major section of the draft and for overall comments. The comment form would be submitted via e-mail. Chat rooms would be encouraged. A period of approximately 90 days would be established during which comments could be received. At this point, the thought leaders would distill the comments and post a revision together with supporting and contrary opinions. A series of on-line town hall discussion sessions would be held. Finally, the thought leaders would post a final recommended version of the cyberspace design and constitution.

6.1.1.   Issues to Be Addressed During a Research Charette   Since cyberspace is rapidly affecting all aspects of human life on this planet there are many issues to be addressed during the charette. The goal is to identify, clarify, discuss and, if possible, resolve as many issues as possible by applying the tools of norms, positive law, markets and architectural design or code. The outcome will be a social philosophy for cyberspace. The initial result will, however, likely look more like the *Federalist Papers* than Barlow's dogmatic "Declaration." Yet, it is essential that Barlow's voice also be heard among others.

Among the closely related areas to be addressed are:

- Open Source Software (OSS) or Proprietary? OSS is software made available in source code form at no cost to developers. The Linux operating system—named for its creator Linus Torvalds—is an example. Many of the most widely used programs on the Internet—those used for delivering e-mail, distributing discussion groups, serving domain name systems' queries, and serving Web pages—already are OSS. At an extreme is Richard Stallman who since the mid-1980's has pushed GNU (Gnu's Not UNIX) through his Free Software Foundation. Stillman believes that proprietary software is the problem and free software is the solution because it serves to liberate people rather than dominate them. Should institutions such as general public licenses (GPL) be generalized? Traditional IT organizations found in major companies and governments tend to favor more pay-for-product, restricted software like Microsoft and IBM while many Internet-based startups gravitate towards systems like Linux. These movements seem to be on a collision course.
- Property. Who Owns Intellectual Property? How are property rights— copyright, patents, trade secrets, brands—to be determined and protected in cyberspace? Is there a difference between owning atoms and owning bits? How can fair exchanges of property—especially bits—be determined? How

can peer-to-peer systems such as Napester be regulated? Should for example cyberspace be designed to support the "trusted systems" proposed by Mark Strefik [33].

- Privacy. What areas of cyberspace can a citizen inhabit in private? Which must be open? Do citizens in cyberspace have a right to a private space or anonymity? What requirements for authentication—revealing aspects of one's identity—should be established? What rights do governments, economic units, or others have to know the real world identity of people acting in cyberspace? What can they know about them? How is confidentially enforced? Under what conditions can one's right to privacy be subjugated? How should policies for fair use of personal information be established and enforced? Discussion groups and avatars often rely on anonymity, even the ability to assume multiple personalities. To the contrary e-commence and e-government applications usually require a precise identification of the parties involved.
- Taxation. Governments operate by means of taxing policies predicated on the stock or flow of atoms within identifiable geographical spaces in the physical world. No such constraint is present in cyberspace, unless it is built in. Taxation requires that transactions are traceable to parties operating in cyberspace.
- Borders and Zones. How should cyberspace be partitioned? Even, should it be partitioned? How should cyber-partitions be articulated with physical space partitions? How are real world people related to partitions for voting, taxation, and other purposes? How is sovereignty established in each partition? How is behavior regulated within each partition? How are conflicts among sovereigns to be resolved?
- Free Speech. How free can speech be in cyberspace? From its beginning cyberspace has been rather open in its freedom of speech. Virtually anybody could post anything they wanted to. How should concerns for censorship, libel, slander, defamation be implemented in cyberspace?
- Accuracy and Validity. Who is responsible for the validity and accuracy of the information that circulates in cyberspace? How should it be vetted?
- Digital Divide. Who gets access to cyberspace and the information it contains? Full participation in cyberspace requires access to appropriate transducer and processing technology, access to information on the net, and adequate education to understand and use the information effectively in society.
- Contracts. How are contracts in cyberspace established and enforced?
- Security and Encryption. What information flowing in cyberspace may be encrypted? Who can hold the keys? Under what conditions can a key be used to decode? Where can and should firewalls be used? How are passwords, verification "cookies," digital certificates, and digital signatures to be assigned, protected, verified and used?

- Payment Systems and Clearing. How are financial transactions to be made and controlled in cyberspace? How are accuracy, reliability, and liquidity to be established?
- Governance. How will differences among parties be adjudicated in cyberspace? How are regulations and rules to be established and enforced in cyberspace?

7.   CONCLUSION

The most important overarching research issue with respect to the Internet, electronic commerce, networks and other aspects of cyberspace is to develop a set of institutions for governing their use. Today, virtually every facet of human endeavor is affected by network technologies. Commerce, government, libraries, education, science, politics, communications, entertainment, recreation, investment, health care and law are among the social functions that are being shaped by cyberspace. But, the asynchronous principle is at work. Cyberspace is being constructed faster than society is developing its moral guidance. The available tools for guidance are social norms, positive law, markets and architectural design or code. A research charette is proposed during which representatives of real world society come together to discuss and debate issues to be resolved about the functions and their operation in cyberspace. The results of the charette will serve as a policy framework for guiding research into the moral issues entailed in the development and governance in cyberspace.

REFERENCES

[1] Gibson, William, *Neuromancer*, New York: Ace, 1984.
[2] Whitehead, Alfred North, *Dialogues of Alfred North Whitehead*, Boston: Little Brown, 1954, page 16.
[3] See "Intel Products and Museum" Visited Sept. 2000 http://www.intel.com/pressroom/navigation.htm.
[4] Kurzweil, Ray, *The Age of Spiritual Machines*, New York: Penguin, 1999, page 277.
[5] See http://www.storage.ibm.com/technolo/grochows/gol.htm.
[6] Computer Industry Almanac, 1999, and http://www.wired.com/news/print/0,1294,62712,00.html.
[7] Cited in "Measuring the Internet Economy" Center for Research in Electronic Commerce, Graduate School of Business, University of Texas at Austin, January 2001, http://www.internetindicators.com.
[8] Davis, Stanley M., *Future Perfect*, Reading, Mass.: Addison-Wesley, 1987.
[9] Aldrich, Douglas F., *Mastering the Digital Marketplace*, New York: John Wiley & Sons, 1999.

[10] See Wurman, Richard Saul, *Information Anxiety*, New York: Bantam Books, 1989.

[11] Evans, Philip and Wurster Thomas, *Blown to Bits*, Boston, Mass.: Harvard Business School Press, 2000.

[12] Turkle, Sherry, *Life on the Screen*, New York: Touchstone, 1997.

[13] Keen, Peter, Balance, Craigg, Chan, Sally, and Schrump, Steve, *Electronic Commerce Relationships: Trust by Design*, Upper Saddle River, NJ: Prentice Hall, 2000.

[14] I am influenced by reading Lessig's book and personal conversations with Jane Kaufman Winn on these tools. See Lessig, Lawrence, *Code and other Laws of Cyberspace*, New York: Basic Books, 1999.

[15] Barlow, John Parry, "Declaration of the Independence of Cyberspace," http://www.eff.org/~barlow/Declaration-Final.html.

[16] See Roethlisberger, Fritz J. and Dickson, William J., *Management and the Worker*, Cambridge, Mass.: Harvard University Press, 1939.

[17] Lesing, Lawrence, *Code and other Laws of Cyberspace*, New York: Basic Books, 1999.

[18] See, for example, Johnson, David, Handra, Sunny, and Morgan, Charles, *Cyberlaw: What You Need to Know About Doing Business Online*, Toronto, Canada: Stoddart, 1997, and Cavazos, Edward and Morin, Gavino, *Cyberspace and the Law: Your Rights and Duties in the On-Line World*, Cambridge, Mass.: The MIT Press, 1996.

[19] Winn, Jane Kaufman, unpublished manuscript entitled "eCommerce: Legal Issues," Dated Wednesday, May 10, 2000.

[20] Stone, Christopher D., *Where the Law Ends: The Social Control of Corporate Behavior*, New York: Harper Torchbooks, 1975. See especially Chapter 11, pages 93–110.

[21] For a development of this argument see Lindblom, Charles E., *Politics and Markets: The World's Political–Economic Systems*, New York: Basic Books, 1977.

[22] Stone, Christopher D., *Where the Law Ends*, New York: Harper & Row, 1975.

[23] Cited in Wasserman, Barry, Sullivan, Patrick, and Palermo, Gregory, *Ethics and the Practice of Architecture*, New York: John Willey & Sons, 2000 (page 1).

[24] Churchman, C. West, *Design of Inquiry Systems*, New York: Basic Books, 1971 (page 5).

[25] See, for example, Lucky, Robert, "The Quicking of Science Communication", *Science*, Vol. 289, 14 July 2000, pages 259–264.

[26] Negroponte, Nicholas, *Being Digital*, New York: Alfred Knopf, 1995.

[27] Quoted in Risebero, Bill, *The Story of Western Architecture*, New York: Charles Schribner's Sons, 1979, page 7.

[28] See, for example, Aldrich, Douglas F., *Mastering the Digital Marketplace*, New York: John Wiley & Sons, 1999.

[29] Lesing, Lawrence, *Code and other Laws of Cyberspace*, New York: Basic Books, 1999.

[30] Hartman, Amir and Sifonis, John, *Net Ready: Strategies for Success in the Economy*, New York: McGraw-Hill, 2000.

[31] Le Corbusier (1964), *The Radiant City: Elements of a Doctrine of Urbanism to Be Used as the Basis of Our Machine-Age Civilization*, trans. Pamela Knight, New York: Orion Press, pages 29–30.

[32] Ibid., page 93.

[33] See "Trusted Systems: Devices that enforce machine-readable rights to use the work of a musician or author may create secure ways to publish over the Internet." *Scientific American*, March 1997, pages 78–81.

Chapter 12

STATUS SEEKING AND THE DESIGN OF ONLINE ENTERTAINMENT COMMUNITIES

De Liu[a], Xianjun Geng[b], and Andrew B. Whinston[a]

[a]McCombs School of Business, The University of Texas at Austin, 1 University Sta B6000, Austin, TX 78712-0201; [b]Management Science, Mackenzie 370, Box 353200, Business School University of Washington, Seattle, WA 98195-3200

Abstract   The main purpose of this chapter is to offer an overview of status seeking in online entertainment communities (OECs) and design issues associated with status seeking. *Status* refers to one's standing in a social hierarchy as determined by respect, deference, and social influence (Ridgeway and Walker 1995). The value of status is demonstrated in the *status-seeking* behavior among participants of OECs. Status seeking is a particularly strong motivating force used by entertainment providers to promote the usage of online entertainment. It is therefore interesting to study the implications of status seeking for the design of OECs. In this chapter, we lay out the theoretical and empirical foundation for status seeking in OECs and provide a game-theoretic framework for analyzing it. We discuss a handful of design issues associated with status seeking in the context of OECs. We also identify several open issues for future research.[1]

INTRODUCTION

"The online experience, the ability to create virtual communities online, is going to be a much bigger part of the industry going forward."

Robbie Bach, Microsoft Xbox Chief Office[2]

The development of new information and communication technologies has initiated a radical transformation in the entertainment industry, characterized

---

[1] We want to thank Matti Hämäläinen from CodeToys for helpful comments to our chapter and for providing numerous insights on online gaming. We also thank Herb Kelleher, Center for Entrepreneurship, for providing financial support for this research.
[2] Originally quoted in Lewis (2003).

by the decline of passive entertainment and the rise of interactive online entertainment. On the one hand, the traditional model of selling packaged content to customers met serious challenges from disruptive technologies. Amid the proliferation of digital music and peer-to-peer file sharing on the Internet, global music sales dropped by 5% in 2001, then 7% in 2002 (BBC News, 2003). The television industry also suffered accelerating loss of audience, partially attributable to digital video recorder technology such as TiVo, which enables users to record shows and play them back on their own time, often without commercials. According to a recent report (Nelson, 2003), young adult viewers of prime-time television dropped sharply by 7% last year. On the other hand, the new interactive online entertainment, represented by electronic gaming, enjoyed double-digit growth rates in the past decade despite the technology slump. The 2002 sales for game software, hardware, and accessories increased by 8% to $10.3 billion, surpassing Hollywood record box-office sales of $9.27 billion (Black, 2003). The top sports game title, Madden NFL 2004 by Electronic Arts, reaped $200 million in sales and attracted more eyeball hours than HBO's hit show The Sopranos.

Online entertainment communities (OECs) played a vital role in fueling the growth of the electronic gaming industry. In 2002, the Big Three game console makers—Sony, Nintendo, and Microsoft—supplemented their game consoles with Internet connections. This move was heartily welcomed by players: according to an analyst in GartnerG2, in just three months some 400,000 gamers adapted their game consoles for playing online (Lewis, 2003). Microsoft recently launched XSN, the Xbox Sports Network, which allows Xbox users to connect to the Xbox Live service to play in online communities. Microsoft contended that the creation of online communities rather than content will become the biggest part of the online entertainment industry.

The importance of OECs to online entertainment providers (OEPs) is best reflected in new and fast-growing Massively Multiplayer Online Games (MMOGs). MMOGs, such as EverQuest, are originated from text-based multiuser dungeons (MUD) but have the same graphics as the state-of-the-art video games. The first true MMOG, Ultima Online, was launched in 1997 and has since built a subscriber base of about 250,000 players. Currently there are more than six million people who pay $10–20 a month to take part in MMOGs. The global market for MMOGs is expected to reach $2.7 billion in revenue by 2006 (Staehlin, 2003). MMOGs usually allow thousands of players, at the same time, to inhabit a virtual game world and experience adventures there. Each player in a MMOG can have one or more virtual persona, which are called *avatars*. Avatars can have different clothing, height, hair color, weapons, etc. Players maneuver their avatars to perform a variety of activities such as traveling, fighting monsters, building their skills and, of course, talking to others' avatars. The ability to socialize, including communicating, competing, and collaborating with others, is the most attractive feature of MMOGs.

Online communities are also essential to the fast-growing mobile gaming industry. The idea of using wireless gaming to hook up users has gained a lot of attention among telecom companies. They have spent billions of dollars in the transition to the new generation of wireless networks, called 3G, but so far have not come up with sufficient traffic to cover their investments. Mobile gaming, or more generally mobile entertainment, holds a promise for the telecom industry. Mobile games utilize wireless data technologies, such as text messages or WAP, to enable real-time interaction among users and between users and service providers. By 2002, mobile gaming had become the top wireless data traffic in Europe. The global mobile game industry is estimated to generate $12.8 billion in revenue by 2008 (Frost & Sullivan Report, 2002).

While content is still important for online entertainment, social values such as the sense of belonging and status have become noticeable and sometimes even vital. Status is such a pervasive social value in almost all OECs. For example,

- **Mobile Millionaire.** Mobile Millionaire is a text-message-based mobile game that has recently gained popularity in Europe. The game is based on the popular TV show "Who Wants To Be a Millionaire." Players of Mobile Millionaire answer trivia questions stored on a game server. The game is designed so that players can retrieve and answer trivia questions using their mobile phone through the text-message or WAP service. Users are billed according to the number of messages they send and receive. In countries like Japan they are also charged a monthly subscription. The game ranks users on a monthly basis. Halls of fame are used to give special recognition to the best players of the month. In countries such as Britain and Finland, mobile network providers also give monetary prizes, including cash and cell phones, to winners. The following figure shows an example of a hall of fame.

It is not surprising to see status-seeking behavior in OECs. In fact, sociologists have concluded that status seeking is pervasive in virtually all societies (Ball et al., 2001). What's new in this chapter is examining status seeking from the business perspective and explicitly dealing with design issues under the objective of maximizing profits. We are especially interested in the normative aspects of status seeking: how to shape status seeking to reinforce the revenue of OECs.

Sociology has a long tradition of studying the emergence and the evolution of status seeking. At least three theories dealt with the emergence of status in group settings—functionalism (Bales, 1953), exchange theory (Blau,

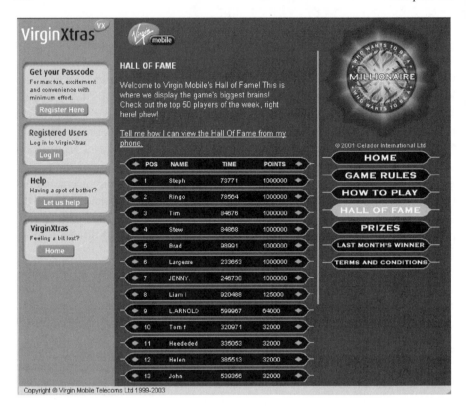

Figure 12-1. The hall of fame for Mobile Millionaire.

1964), and dominance-conflict theory (Ridgeway and Walker, 1995). While these theories offer extensive knowledge on the group processes that enable the emergence of status structure, they have largely focused on interpreting status formation in general social settings and haven't explicitly dealt with the design issues from the business point of view.

This research is important for three reasons. First, status is an important value provided by OECs. From gamers craving halls of fame in wireless gaming to racing to higher levels in MMOGs, it is impressive how concerned people are with their status in OECs. Second, this research is particularly important because of the unparalleled opportunities for OEPs to influence status seeking. OEPs can choose not only what status criteria to use and what the status symbols look like but also they can literally create the whole virtual environment (how it feels, what people can do in it, etc.). Many OEPs have introduced various kinds of competitions to induce status seeking, such as halls of fame, rankings, tournaments, and ladders. However, there are few theoretical guidelines on what is the most effective design of these competitions. Finally, the advantages of doing research in this area lie in the uniqueness of the online entertainment industry as a source of data on user behavior and as a field for experimenting with different designs. Due to the digital nature of OECs, it is often easier to collect information on user behavior and manipulate design features.

We provide a game-theoretic framework for analyzing the impact of status seeking on total profits and design issues associated with status seeking. Status seeking boils down to a contest in which each individual chooses the amount of effort to expend in competing for status. We draw upon the economics literature on contests and study the decisions of choosing design parameters, including prize allocation, segmentation of the population, etc. The main advantage of using the game-theoretic framework is to deal with the complex effects of different design features, especially when the users differ in their skills.

This research is related to the research on online communities. The value of online communities to firms has received increasing attention in recent years (e.g., Armstrong and Hagel, 1996, Nambisan, 2002). Research on online communities has examined the motive for users to participate in online communities from different perspectives, including social exchange (Fulk et al. 1996, Butler, 2001, Wasko and Faraj, 2000), social identity (Hogg and Terry, 2000), and economic incentives (Wasko and Faraj, 2000, Gu and Jarvenpaa, 2003). Wasko and Faraj (2000) reported that people participate in online forums because it enhances their standing in their profession. However, status seeking has not received systematic treatment, especially from the perspective of online community design.

The rest of the chapter is organized as follows. The next section reviews the behavioral foundation of status seeking, drawing upon the literatures in psychology and sociology. We follow by discussing the business consequence of status seeking in online communities. In Section 3, we introduce a game-theoretic approach to study status seeking. Section 4 discusses current research results on the design issues. In Section 5, we identify several open issues for future research. The last section concludes the chapter.

1. WHY DO PEOPLE STRIVE FOR STATUS?

The desire for status is one of the basic human needs in taxonomies developed by psychologists such as Abraham Moslow (1968, 1971). Csikszentmihalyi (2000) wrote on the relationship between consumption and the need for status, or self-esteem:

The need for self-esteem—to feel competent, respected, and superior—is present already in children, and is presumably active even when the lower-order needs are not entirely met. But they become fully active after survival, safety, and belongingness needs are more or less taken care of. At that point we can indulge in purchasing goods that show our uniqueness and separate us from the rest of the crowd.

Many sociology researchers view status as a means to obtain resources (e.g., Lin, 1990, 1994) or power (e.g., Thye, 2000). Thus, status is pursued as a "rational" tool. In line with this view, Ball and his colleagues found in experimental settings that individuals with higher status were conceded higher benefits in negotiations (Ball and Eckel, 1996) and markets exchange (Ball et al., 2001). Status also leads to power (Lovalgia, 1994, 1997). This view is consistent with the fact that many social and economic resources, such as tenure positions and salesperson compensation, are allocated based on relative rankings.

Another view holds that status is not only a means to an end but also an emotional end in itself. Evolutionary anthropologists have long identified status seeking as an ancient emotional tendency in primates (Barkow, 1975). Biological experiments on monkeys connected the gaining of status to high blood serotonin levels (blood serotonin level is associated with pleasure) (McGuire and Raleigh, 1985). Therefore, people may pursue status for emotional reasons rather than external benefits. In a recent study, Loch et al. (2000) showed that people valued status even when status was nothing but applause from an audience. Indeed, in online gaming examples, people show interests in pursuing a hall of fame or rankings, even without prizes or other immediate extrinsic rewards.

Whether status is pursued as a rational goal or an emotional end, status seems to signal individuals' competence. Although above-mentioned arguments and evidence are developed in the offline community context, they apply to OECs as well. In online gaming communities, status oftentimes sends signals about the competence of players; it may also lead to more resources and power (e.g., prizes, game credits, privileges).

2.   WHY SHOULD ONLINE ENTERTAINMENT PROVIDERS BE CONCERNED ABOUT STATUS SEEKING?

The role of status seeking in OECs mainly lies in its motivating power: the desire for status can motivate users to take actions to influence their status, which in turn enhances providers' profits. The status-building actions, which we call *status-seeking activities*, normally involve spending time, effort, and money to improve one's performance. For instance, in mobile gaming, users are willing to spend more hours for the sake of entering the top-10 players

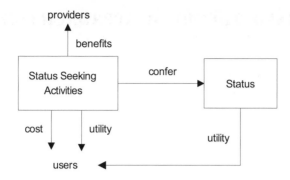

Figure 12-2. The role of status seeking in online communities.

of the week. In this regard, status seeking is a potentially valuable tool for providers of the online entertainment community to promote usage.

The value of status may not be the only outcome of status-seeking activities. Status-seeking activities can be intrinsically valuable as well, as they are in OECs. Studies in psychology (e.g., Csikszentmihalyi, 1975) show that the use of skills itself can be a source of enjoyment. We postulate that the participation in online communities is affected both by the intrinsic enjoyment and the motive of status seeking. Figure 2 characterizes the relationship among status, status-seeking activities, and users' and providers' benefits.

The consumption of online entertainment is in some sense analogous to Frank's (1985) notion of positional goods. Participating in online entertainment (especially those that require skill and creativity) not only produces intrinsic utility of enjoyment but also helps one achieve status in the online communities. Frank's theory of positional goods predicts that when people are concerned about relative positions, they tend to overspend on positional goods. Similarly, status-seeking users also tend to spend more time in online entertainment than those who do not care about status.

Status-seeking activities in online communities can be multidimensional and may not be always beneficial to community providers. For instance, one of the controversial issues in massively multiplayer online gaming is macroing, using macros to simulate keyboard and mouse movements so that one can collect game credits without playing in person. While macroing enhances one's status (assuming it is not detected or punished), it reduces the player's lifetime with the game and so eventually undermines the OEP's profits. A similar argument is also made by Loch et al. (2000) in a teamwork setting. Loch et al. contend that people may undertake politicking, which does not contribute to the productivity of the group.

3. A GAME-THEORETIC APPROACH FOR STUDYING STATUS SEEKING

Status seeking in OECs is analogous to the race by business schools to get good rankings, except that prizes for business school rankings are high-quality students (Schatz, 1993), and prizes for high ranking in online games are psychological rewards. Status seeking falls into the generalized notion of *contests* in economics literature, which encompasses various economic and social activities such as rent seeking, patent racing, R&D tournaments, salesperson competition, and so on. A common element of these different activities is that the allocation of the resources—monopoly rents, patents, prizes, funding, and student quality—are based on the relative performance of participating parties. In economic terms, "contests are situations where agents spend resources to compete for one or more prizes" (Moldovanu and Sela, 2001).

The game-theoretic approach is widely adopted in the economic literature in studying contests. For instance, in the seminal work by Lazear and Rosen (1981), contests are formulated as a competition among agents, each of whom invests unobservable effort to produce an output valued by a principal. We also adopt a game-theoretic approach to study status-seeking contests. A status-seeking contest is viewed as a game played by individual users, where usage is their investment and status is their prize. The game-theoretic approach enables us to obtain theoretical insights on how design variables such as prize allocation and segmentation of the population can affect profits of OEPs.

We start with a somewhat general framework that accommodates different specifications of status-seeking contests. We present its use in the next section with a particular model specification. It is useful to start by describing the key variables captured in the generalized model.

- **Usage.** We assume the main status-seeking activity in online entertainment communities is using the service provided by the OEP, denoted by the variable *usage* (measured in hours). Usage plays three roles in our context. First, usage of the service provides the intrinsic value of entertainment. Second, usage costs money, in the form of payments made to the OEPs. Third, usage improves a user's performance and enhances the user's status.
- **Ability.** Ability reflects a user's talent or skills. In our framework, one's performance is not only affected by usage levels but also by ability. Heterogeneity in user ability levels is virtually inevitable in OECs. Such heterogeneity may arise either because users are different in their talents per se (e.g., the eye-hand coordination skill or the accuracy of recall) or because they have gained different levels of experience. Because most status-seeking contests in online communities are skill-based, we preserve the ability factor as an important variable in our framework. Note that skill-based contests

are different from games of luck such as lotteries or sweepstakes. In the latter, only the number of entries (corresponding to usage) affects one's chance of winning.

Following conventions in the economic literature, we assume that ability is *private information*, i.e. users know their own ability,[3] but do not know the level of ability others may have. This assumption is consistent with the fact that in online communities it is more difficult to assess others' true ability, given that individuals can easily hide behind their IDs or avatars. We assume ability factors are drawn from a common distribution, referred to as the *ability distribution*, and this distribution is *common knowledge* to all the users and the OEP. In reality, users may gain such knowledge from their previous observations or indirectly from their peers. Note that the ability distribution is ex ante knowledge and the realized ability profiles of the population are not known to the user.

- **Random factor.** Sometimes to win a status-seeking game, one needs not only usage and ability but also a bit of "luck." We model such luck as the random factor in a user's performance. Note that the magnitude of the randomness can sometimes be controlled by the designers of online communities, e.g., by introducing randomness into the outcome of a fight with monsters.

We consider that there are n *potential* users of the online entertainment service, indexed by $i = 1, \ldots, n$. A user's *performance* (x_i) is affected by *usage* (t_i), *ability* (μ_i), and a *random factor* (ε_i). We let the performance function be $f(t_i, \mu_i, \varepsilon_i)$. f increases in all three arguments. We assume each ability parameter is an independent draw from a common distribution F and each random factor in performance is an independent draw from a common distribution G. We assume that F, G and n are known by all the users and the OEP (note that actually the number of participating users may be less than n).

Status is allocated according to rank-order performance of participating users. We also call status a *prize* due to their common nature. All users agree upon the value of status. Denote the value of ranking the first as v_1, the value of ranking the second as v_2, and so on ($v_1 \geq v_2 \geq \cdots \geq v_n$).

A user's overall utility consists of the utility from winning a status, the intrinsic utility of using the online entertainment service, and the disutility of payment to the OEP pt_i. Let ρ_{ij} denote the user i's probability of being jth in

---

[3] However, the assumption that users know their own ability may be questionable because some studies suggest individuals may misjudge their own abilities or lack knowledge about themselves (Tversky and Kahneman, 1974). More research is needed to account for these considerations.

the contest, given the user's ability μ_i and usage t_i. The user's expected utility from status is

$$\sum_{j=1}^{n} \rho_{ij} v_j.$$

We assume the user's intrinsic utility from usage is $\theta_i \cdot t_i$ and payment to the OEP is $p \cdot t_i$. The overall user utility is given by

$$U_i(t_i) = \sum_{j=1}^{n} \rho_{ij} v_j - p t_i + \theta_i t_i.$$

Note that not only ρ_{ij} is affected by x_i (hence t_i, μ_i and ε_i), it is also affected by x_j ($j \neq i$) (hence μ_j, t_j, and ε_j). But since a user does not know others' ability parameters or their choice of usage level, the user can form an estimation of others' performance based on his knowledge about the common distribution F and G as well as his belief about other users' strategy as discussed below.

A user's *strategy* is defined as a mapping from the user's ability parameter to his choice of usage level, denoted as $t_i(\mu_i)$. A strategy profile of all users forms a *Nash equilibrium* if it satisfies an *incentive compatibility* (IC) condition, which requires that no one can be better off by deviating from his strategy given others' strategy, and an *individual rationality* (IR) condition, which requires that each participant's expected utility of participating is non-negative.

We assume the marginal cost of providing online entertainment service is a constant, which we normalize to zero without loss of generality. In addition, the OEP also incurs a fixed fee for organizing the contest which may include the cost for prizes, hiring judges, advertising fees, etc. Since these costs are sunk, we can drop them from consideration in the provider's profit function without affecting the study of the design issues.

We assume online entertainment charges a fixed subscription fee p_e and a usage fee p for using online entertainment service. When $p_e = 0$, the OEP purely relies upon usage fee for profits. When $p = 0$, the OEP only charges a subscription fee, and usage is free of charge. In the former case, the OEP maximizes the aggregate usage of all users. In the latter case, the OEP maximizes the number of users who participate in OECs. An intermediate case is that the OEP charges a subscription fee plus a certain usage fee. All three cases are seen in real world applications.

The expected profit of the OEP therefore writes

$$E\left[\sum_{i=1}^{n}(p_e\delta_i + p_s t_i)\right], \quad \text{where } \delta_i = \begin{cases} 1, & \text{if } i \text{ participates,} \\ 0, & \text{else.} \end{cases}$$

Note that at the time of design the online entertainment community, the OEP does not know the exact ability parameters of users. As a result, δ_i and t_i, which depends on μ_i, are random variables to the OEP.

This framework captures main features of status seeking in OECs. First, it reflects that the usage of online entertainment service not only generates intrinsic value of entertainment, but also gives rise to the value of status. Second, it captures the fact that users differ in ability, which can explain the variation in the level of status-seeking activities. Third, and important, the design objective of the OECs is to maximize the total "input" of all users rather than their "outcome."

In terms of methodology, this framework is related to other models of contests. For instance, Kalra and Shi (2001) studied a salesperson contest model where they restricted agents to identical abilities. Moldovanu and Sela (2001) studied an all-pay auction model of contests in which the designer maximizes total output of all contestants. Our framework is similar to that of Singh and Witman (2001). Alternative ways of modeling contests exist, including a rent-seeking model by Tullock (1980), a model of consumption by Frank (1985), and an R&D tournament model by Fullerton and McAfee (1999) and Bolton and Ockenfels (2000).

4. DESIGN ISSUES

Although striving for status is "built into us," the criteria on which status rests as well as the symbols of status are, to some extent, selectable by the community (Barkow, 1989). The possibility of shaping status seeking is the most important aspect examined in this chapter. As we have argued earlier, the design issues for online communities are even more important than for off-line communities, given the abundant opportunities to manipulate features of online communities. We explore these possibilities in this section.

The results discussed below are based on a particular case of the general framework presented in the previous section (Liu, Geng, and Whinston, 2004). In particular, we maintain that users differ in their ability levels, but their performance is a deterministic function of usage and ability. We also assume the intrinsic utility from online entertainment service is the same for all users so that we can concentrate on studying how the ability factor affects the amount of status seeking. In addition, we assume that the OEP charges only a usage fee so that it maximizes the aggregate usage of all users.

4.1.   Structuring Status-Seeking Contests

4.1.1.   Optimal Prize Structure   In some cases, monetary or fantasy prizes are used by OEPs to enhance competition. For example, Madden NFL 2004 offers a trip to Las Vegas worth $4,000 to the winner of a national tournament. Mobile Millionaire offered monthly prizes in some countries, for instance, a $2,915 first prize and cell phones for second to fifth winners in UK. How should the total prize money be allocated in order to attract and stimulate usage?

Given a limited prize budget, OEPs need to determine the optimal number and sizes of prizes to achieve maximal profits. In general, a high-ranked prize appeals more to the high-ability segment than a low-ranked prize. On the other hand, a low-ranked prize appeals more to the low-ability segment of the population than a high-ranked prize. In general, the optimal number of prizes is determined by several factors including the shape of the ability distribution and the number of users. We found that a *winner-take-all* prize structure is optimal for the monotone hazard-rate[4] ability distributions. We also found that a winner-take-all prize structure is optimal for a sufficiently large population. A winner-take-all prize structure is favored in a larger community: as the community grows, each user's chance of winning drops. But low-ability users' chance of winning drops more quickly than those high-ability users'. As a result, a winner-take-all prize structure, which appeals to high-ability users the most, is most affective. These findings suggest that in status-seeking contests it is usually costly to motivate the low-ability segment.

4.1.2.   Optimal Entry Fee   Entry fee is another instrument that can be used to shape the status-seeking activities. Charging an entry fee affects the total profits of OEPs in three ways (illustrated in the following figure): (1) it excludes low-ability contestants whose expected utility of participation is low; (2) it decreases the usage levels of participating contestants, but (3) it also generates an entry fee revenue from participating users (the following figure demonstrates the loss from excluded users and the overall gain from participating users). We show that by charging a small entry fee, the total gain from participating users offsets the loss from excluded users. This is because by charging a fee the OEP loses usage from a small segment of low-ability users whose usage is very low, but increases profits among participating users.[5] Therefore, an entry fee should be charged.

---

[4]   Monotone hazard-rate distributions include normal, exponential, logistic, uniform, and any distribution with non-decreasing density (Bagnoli and Bergstrom, 1989).

[5]   See Liu, Geng, and Whinston (2004) for details.

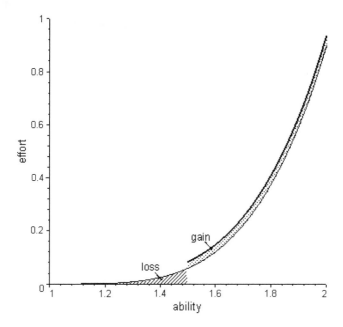

Figure 12-3. Entry fee.

4.1.3.   Criteria for Status   Providers of online communities often have the flexibility to choose the criteria on which status is determined. For example, when designing an MMOG game, designers can determine the set of skills that are required to advance a game character. Different status criteria trigger different sets of status-seeking activities. Even when the set of status-seeking activities is the same, the choice of status criteria may affect the weights of the usage and the ability factors and therefore the incentives for status seeking.

Our analysis suggested the following guidelines in choosing status criteria: (1) when choosing status criteria, the anticipated status-seeking activities triggered by the criteria should be in line with the business objective of the online communities; (2) if the providers are able to choose the weight of usage (or ability) in determining status, giving more weight to usage helps promote status seeking. By deemphasizing the ability factor, the providers create a de facto more homogenous population, thus intensifying competition.

4.2.   Structuring Status-Seeking Communities

One design issue involves segmenting the population into multiple groups. Community designers may want to segment the population for a variety of reasons, e.g. because individuals have distinct interests or the group is too large to manage. Here we focus on how status seeking affects segmenting decisions.

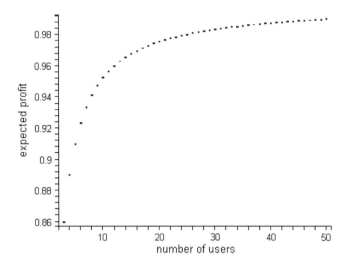

Figure 12-4. Impact of the group size.

Our conclusions can be combined with other considerations in making segmenting decisions.

Depending on the way the population is segmented, community designers can potentially control the size and the composition of segments. So our discussion of segmenting decisions starts with these two variables.

4.2.1.   Impact of the Group Size   We considered altering the size of the group but not changing the ability distribution of the community or the value of status (an example of this is splitting a population based on geographic locations). We found that the total usage spent on status seeking increases with the group size. However, this trend reaches a limit as the group size goes to infinity. The following figure (based on a numerical example) demonstrates this trend.

To see the intuition, consider the effect of adding an additional user to the community. This additional user contributes a certain amount of usage but reduces others' usage because additional participation decreases others' chances of being at the top. As the size of the community grows, both effects decline, but the former effect declines faster than the second effect. This is because the positive effect is from a single user whereas the negative effect is an aggregate effect and has a factor of n, which helps to slow down the speed of decline as n increases. Both effects converge to zero as n grows large; the two effects balance each other in the end.

4.2.2.   Impact of the ability distribution   Which of the two communities with the same size but different ability distributions generates more total profits? We found that the answer to this question is connected to the notion of "*homogeneity*"—a population is more homogeneous if the ability ratio between any two percentiles in the ability distribution is closer to 1. For example, a uniform distribution on $[1, 2]$ is more homogenous than a uniform distribution on $[1, 4]$, since the highest ability level is two times of the lowest ability level in the former distribution, compared to four times in the latter. Homogeneity is different from variance because, for instance, a uniform distribution on $[1, 2]$ has lower variance than a uniform distribution on $[10, 20]$ but the two distributions are equally homogenous. We found that the more homogenous a group's ability distribution, the higher equilibrium usage the users will devote. This finding is consistent with the common sense that competition will intensify in a close match. The implication for OEPs is that if they can manage to create a more homogenous community, they can expect more usage and profits.

4.2.3.   Impact of Segmentation   Based on analysis of the impact of size and ability distribution, we reach the following conclusions regarding segmentations: (1) a *horizontal segmentation* (the segmentation that reduces group sizes but does not change the ability distribution) reduces the overall level of status-seeking activities, and (2) a vertical segmentation (a segmentation based on ability levels) *may* increase the total level of status-seeking activities. The first result immediately follows from our result regarding the impact of community size. The second result holds because segmenting a community based on ability levels generates two opposite effects: on the one hand, segmentation reduces the size of groups, thus negatively affecting the total level of status-seeking activities; on the other hand, segmentation may increase homogeneity in each segment, thus increasing the total level of status-seeking activities.

5.   FUTURE RESEARCH DIRECTIONS

5.1.   Some Extensions of Theoretical Research

- **Dual goals of OEPs.** OEPs may have dual goals: attracting more users and retaining them longer. These two goals may not always be compatible. For example, by attracting more customers, one could decrease incumbent users' chances of being at the top and thereby reduce their willingness to compete in OECs. One practical question is how to trade off these goals to achieve maximal profits? What are the implications to setting the price for entry (p_e) and the price for usage (p)?
- **Multiple-period status seeking.** One way of extending the current research is to study multiple-period status seeking. Status seeking in OECs often

proceeds in a repeated fashion. When the timeline for contests extends beyond just one period, some of the competition mechanics may change. First, there might be a learning effect; users can gradually gain skills over time. Second, the entertainment value could also fluctuate, as users may become more curious or bored. One interesting issue in this multiple-period context is whether the OEP should maximize usage of customers in their early stages or try to maximize the length of each user's lifetime in the online community. There is also an issue of how to allocate prizes over the lifetime of users.

- **Overlapping generations.** In the proposed framework, we have assumed that users participate in the contest at the same time. However, in the real world, users may join online communities at different times, which creates a natural disadvantage for latecomers. In addition, in MMOGs, some customers may decide to replay the game using a different avatar. In such a case, the user may also face disadvantages in competing. Should OEPs account for the time of arrival in setting rules of competition, such as handicapping the veterans? Should OEPs segment users by their time of arrival? The answers to those issues are important for designing a more profitable online entertainment community.

- **Information and uncertainty.** How much should OEPs let users know about their peers (their current and past performance, usage, abilities, etc.)? When should they be given such information? How much randomness should be built into the ranked outcome? Both information and uncertainty affect the users' assessment of their probability of winning—therefore their motives to seek status. A total transparency of information or early release of information may discourage disadvantaged users from competing. Similarly, if a high-level player can beat a low-level player for sure, the game becomes uninteresting for both. On the other hand, lack of transparency and total randomness may impair the value of status, since users cannot effectively communicate their high status to their peers. Further investigation is required with regard to how much uncertainty should be introduced into status seeking in online communities.

- **Status seeking and the competition of online communities.** We are concerned about how status seeking affects the competition among OEPs. As more entertainment providers resort to online communities to attract and retain customers, the competition among online communities will become acute. The willingness to remain in one community will be affected by how the rule of status seeking is set up. A user could abandon an online community for another if the user feels unfairly treated or hopeless in getting a reputable status. On the other hand, a user who has invested in status seeking and has established status in one online community may be inclined to stay, even when another online community charges a lower usage-fee. Thus, status in online communities has become a critical factor in a community's success. Yet it is not yet understood how status seeking changes the climate of competition among OEPs.

- **Status seeking and markets for virtual goods.** Markets for virtual goods emerged not long after OECs were established. For instance, EverQuest players once traded virtual game properties—spells, houses, game currency, and even avatars—on eBay. Although Sony pressed eBay to ban such auctions, black markets for EverQuest game properties are still popular. Using the exchange rate between Norrathian Platinum Pieces (the currency used in EverQuest), Castronova (2001) estimated that the per capita gross national product for Norrath is $2,266, making Norrath the seventy-seventh richest country in the world. Not restricted to EverQuest, trading virtual game properties are active among the MMOGs. For instance, a rare "Jedi knight" in the Star Wars Galaxies recently sold on eBay for $1,900. The popularity of markets for virtual items raises the question of the ownership of the virtual property: who owns the virtual properties created in an online community? While this issue can be studied on the level of economy, (e.g., how to tax and regulate the trading of virtual properties), it is certainly interesting to study how such trading can affect the game providers. Status seeking provides useful insights into this issue.

From the perspective of status seeking, the introduction of an external market for virtual properties boils down to an additional dimension of status-seeking activities, i.e. money, besides usage and ability. The money-rich but time-constrained users are the ones who are willing to shortcut by buying game items to enhance their status. We refer to them as *short-cutters*, individuals who haven't gone through the process and may not have the ability or skills of those who have achieved their status through usage and talent. As more and more short-cutters join the status-seeking communities, the status is increasingly less informative about the competence of its owners, and so the value of status will decline. Correspondingly, the incentive for status-seeking is undermined.

However, the analysis does not stop here. Those time-rich players may choose to become professional gamers who earn game credits, accumulate game properties, and advance avatars, not for themselves but for sales. Incentives for these players increase as a consequence of the external market for virtual game properties. In summary, OEPs need to trade-off the negative effect (diluting the value of status) against the positive effect (attracting additional user segments including professional gamers and short-cutters). As short-cutters flood the online game communities, the coordination value of status is undermined as well. For instance, it may be difficult to coordinate team activities in a situation where a short-cutter assumes a leadership position in a guild war but does not have the appropriate knowledge to lead one.

5.2.   Empirical and Experimental Research on Status Seeking

A notable advantage of studying status seeking in the context of online entertainment is the opportunity to conduct empirical and experimental research. Secondary data on user activities may be obtained through analyzing community archives publicly available or privately provided by OEPs. These data often contain detailed information on the type and duration of activities of users and their profile snapshots (e.g., rank, credits, and number of winnings). Usage information can be easily obtained by looking at the usage pattern of online entertainment users. However, no measurement of the latent variable *ability* is immediately available. It is possible for researchers to estimate users' skills by looking at their past performance, such as scores in past games. Another latent variable is the intrinsic value of entertainment, which can vary from one user to another. Research in psychology, e.g. by Csikszentmihalyi (1975), has looked into what constitutes the fun factor in various contexts. As it is no simple matter to proxy the fun factor through secondary data, the above theory may offer a clue on when users might be having fun.

An alternative way of collecting data on online entertainment users is through surveys. A web-based study (Yee, 2002) on online entertainment has attracted thousands of participants. Survey data is usually able to measure latent variables, such as ability and fun, by asking people about their perceptions.

Two important issues regard empirical testing of the status seeking in OECs. The first is how ability and the fun factor affect status-seeking activities. Are they consistent with the equilibrium predictions provided by the theoretical framework? To isolate the effect of status seeking remains a major challenge because the effect of status seeking is often compounded with other motivations, such as intrinsic enjoyment and just killing time.

Another interesting empirical issue is whether the theoretical predictions on optimal design are consistent with real-world data. This chapter discusses several empirically testable propositions with regard to the optimal design of status-seeking contests. For instance, the optimality of winner-take-all prize structures, the impact of segmentation on levels of status seeking and overall profits, the impact of optimal entry fees, etc. However, an obstacle exists to testing these results using secondary or survey data. There may not be enough variations in design features for us to draw statistical conclusions. Even if there are enough samples with design variations, they may be polluted with other variations (e.g., size and composition of communities and cultural differences) whose impact is hard to determine. For these reasons, we consider lab experiments or field experiments, which offer researchers more control over the design variables, as a better way to test theoretical results on optimal design issues.

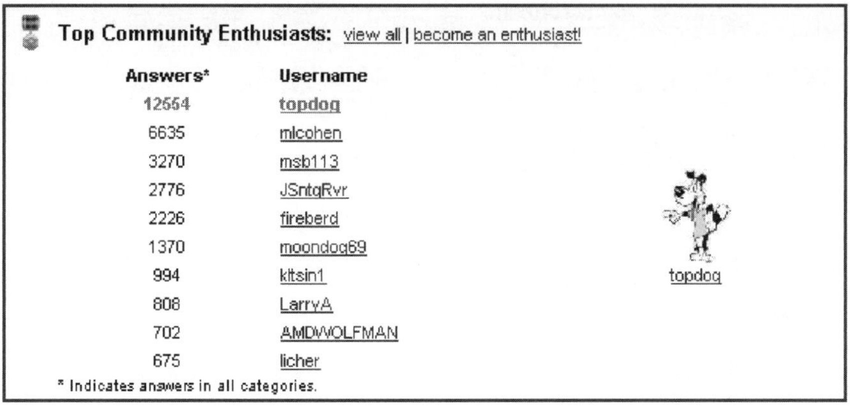
Top Community Enthusiasts: view all | become an enthusiast!
Answers*
Username
12554 topdog
6635 mlcohen
3270 msb113
2776 JSntgRvr
2226 fireberd
1370 moondog69
994 kitsin1
808 LarryA
702 AMDWOLFMAN
675 licher
topdog
* Indicates answers in all categories.

Figure 12-5. The rankings of customer contributors in HP user community.

5.3. Beyond Online Entertainment Communities

Though we mainly study status seeking in the context of online entertainment, research outcomes in this particular type of online community may have general implications. In fact, status seeking is pervasive in all types of online communities. Here are a few examples that status seeking is leveraged by other online community designers.

- **Peer-to-peer customer-support communities.** Internet-based customer-support communities not only bring together novice and experts, but also allow customers to share their knowledge with peers. A rationale behind peer-to-peer support is that customers, provided with appropriate incentives, can become effective contributors of knowledge in online communities. Rewards and token recognitions based on certain rankings are among the commonly used strategies by community providers (Gu and Jarvenpaa, 2003). One example is Hewlett Packard (HP), which operates 35 discussion boards for its entire product categories including imaging, printing, PCs, and software. Those customer communities allow novices and (internal or external) technical experts alike to share their knowledge, information, and assistance, and encourage learning. As of October 2002, HP boasts some two million postings in its 35 discussion boards. An active user could answer as many as a few hundred questions. The following figure shows the recognitions of frequent contributors on the first page of HP's customer community.
- **Customer-supplied reviews.** Customer reviews are crucial for online retailers such as Amazon.com. Customer-written reviews provide important information on quality of products and services and enables buyers to purchase with confidence. To avoid conflicts of interests, financial incentives

Figure 12-6. Amazon's top reviewers.

are often not appropriate for rewarding voluntary reviewers. In such circumstances, status recognitions are almost an exclusive tool for encouraging customers to write quality reviews. Amazon.com recognizes quality reviewers using electronic tokens such as "top-10" or "top-500" reviewers. Anecdotal stories from newspapers suggest that a little token saying "top-500 reviewers" or "top-100 reviewers" serves as a powerful reward to volunteer customer reviewers. The following screen shot captures the recognitions of top-ranked customer reviewers at Amazon.com.

In both the above-mentioned online communities and OECs, the competition for status serves to encourage more inputs from users. Therefore, the discussion in this chapter can be extended to other types of online communities. However, there are also a few notable differences between these online communities and OECs, which might require caution in adapting research results obtained in the context of OECs to other contexts.

First, different online communities have different purposes. The customer-support community and Amazon's reviewer community belong to *production-oriented online communities* because providers of these communities maximize total outcome, i.e., reviews and peer advice. On the other hand, online entertainment provides the basis for *consumption-oriented communities* because OEPs maximize total input, i.e., usage. This suggests that design principles of production-oriented online communities should favor inputs from high-skilled users over low-skilled users, whereas in OECs they are treated as equal.

Second, users have different roles. In customer-support communities, users can help and be helped by others. Similarly, in Amazon reviewer communities, users can benefit others (by writing a review) or benefit from others (by reading a review). In online entertainment communities, however, users are not classified as contributors and beneficiaries. In MMOGs, for example, users are likely to be achievers, explorers, killers, and socializers (Bartle, 1996). For different roles in online communities, status seeking is likely to have different impacts.

Last, designers of other online communities may not enjoy the same freedoms as the online entertainment communities. For example, in online entertainment the designer can choose to what extent the outcome of a combat is subject to uncertainty, while designers of other online communities may not be able to do that. Therefore, some of the design principles obtained in the online entertainment context may not be implementable in other online communities.

6. CONCLUDING REMARKS

In conclusion, this chapter identifies status seeking as a pervasive phenomenon in OECs. The importance of status seeking for firms lies in its power to direct users' attention to status-seeking activities. Driven by the desire for status, users are willing to invest more usage, time, or even financial resources in OECs. This motivating force as a source of profits for OEPs is highlighted in this chapter. This chapter focuses on the design issues involved in status seeking in OECs. In OECs, providers have more control over the status criteria, symbols for status, and even the whole virtual environment. These opportunities give rise to the managerial importance of studying status seeking in OECs.

The grand prospect of interactive entertainment over the network has made the management of online communities unprecedentedly important for business providers. Historically, consumers have accounted for only about 25 to 30 percent of total spending on information technology. However, recent signs show that this share looks certain to rise (Foremski et al., 2003). Thanks to the digitization of music, video, photography, and mobile telephony, individual users are able to record, replay, and edit entertainment content at home. High-speed home network and mobile data technologies have pushed the boundary of home digital entertainment to the online communities. In a recent event, an air force sergeant at an air base in Germany was able to play video games with his son in the United States using the Xbox Live service (Jainchill, 2004). Currently, cable providers, TiVo-like specialized digital devices, game console makers, and PC makers are racing to become the centerpiece of future digital home entertainment. Perhaps the one who successfully creates an online community of users will prosper, rather than those who control the hardware, software, or content.

REFERENCES

Armstrong, A. and J. Hagel (1996). The real value of online communities. *Harvard Business Review* 74: 127–141.

Bagnoli, M. and T. Bergstrom (1989). Log-concave probability and its applications. University of Michigan Center for Research on Economic and Social Theory Working Paper: 89-23.

Bales, R. (1953). The equilibrium problem in small groups. In T. Parsons, R. F. Bales, E. A. Shils (eds.), *Working Papers in the Theory of Action*, Glecoe, Free Press: 111–161.

Ball, S. B. and C. C. Eckel (1996). Buying status: experimental evidence on status in negotiation. *Psychology & Marketing* 13: 381–405.

Ball, S. B., C. C. Eckel, P. J. Grossman and W. Zame (2001). Status in markets. *Quarterly Journal of Economics* 116: 161–188.

Bartle, R. (1996). Hearts, Clubs, Diamonds, Spades: Players Who Suit MUDs. http://www.brandeis.edu/pubs/jove/HTML/v1/bartle.html.

Barkow, J. H. (1975). Strategies for self esteem and prestige in Maradi, Niger Republic. In Williams, T. R. (ed.), *Psychological Anthropology*, The Hague: Mouton, pp. 373–388.

BBC News (2003). http://news.bbc.co.uk/1/hi/entertainment/music/2931589.stm.

Berger, J. R., C. L. Fisek, M. H. Norman, Z. Robert (1998). The legitimation and delegitimation of power and prestige orders. *American Sociological Review* 63: 379.

Black, J. (2003). EA gets its game on: the video-game maker has a load of hit titles under its belt, including the Harry Potter series. And it may be about to hit the next level. *Business Week Online*, March 24, 2003.

Blau, P. (1964). *Exchange and Power in Social Life*, New York: Wiley.

Bolton, G. E. and A. Ockenfels (2000). ERC: A theory of equity, reciprocity, and competition. *American Economic Review* 90(1): 166–93.

Butler, B. (2001) Membership size, communication activity, and sustainability: a resource-based model of online social structures. *Information Systems Research* 12(4): 346–362.

Castronova, E. (2001). Virtual worlds: A first-hand account of market and society on the cyberian frontier. CESifo Working Paper No. 618.

Csikszentmihalyi, M. (1975). *Beyond Boredom and Anxiety: Experiencing Flow in Work and Play*. San Francisco, CA: Jossey-Bass Publishers.

Csikszentmihalyi, M. (2000). The costs and benefits of consuming. *Journal of Consumer Research* 27: 267–272.

Foremski, T. London, S. S. Morrison, and R. Waters (2003). The two-speed tech sector: As corporate spending stays flat, the industry sets its sights on users. *Financial Times* (London), December 2, p. 12.

Frost & Sullivan (2002). European global mobile gaming markets. Research Report.

Frank, R. H. (1985). The demand for unobservable and other nonpositional goods. *American Economic Review* 75(1): 101–16.

Fulk, J., A. J. Flanagin, M. E. Kalman, P. R. Monge, and T. Ryan (1996). Connective and communal public goods in interactive communication systems. *Communication Theory* 6(1): 60–87.

Fullerton, R. L. and R. P. McAfee (1999). Auctioning entry into tournaments. *Journal of Political Economy* 107(3): 573–605.

Gu, B. and S. Jarvenpaa (2003). Online Discussion Boards for Technical Support: the Effect of Token Recognition on Customer Contributions. *Workshop on Information Systems and Economics (WISE) 2003*, December.

Huberman, B. A., C. H. Loch, et al. (2003). Status as a valued resource. *Social Psychology Quarterly*, forthcoming.

Hogg, M. A. and D. J. Terry (2000) Social identity and self-categorization processes in organizational contexts. *Academy of Management Review* 25(1): 121–140.

Jainchill, J. (2004). Gaming with an opponent who's 'over there'. *The New York Times* January 15, p. E7.

Kalra, A. and M. Shi (2001). Designing optimal sales contests: A theoretical perspective. *Marketing Science* 20(2): 170–193.

Kanan, P. K., A. Chang, and A. B. Whinston (1998). Marketing information on the I-way. *Communications of the ACM* 41: 35–43.

Lazear, E. P. and S. Rosen (1981). Rank-order tournaments as optimum labor contracts. *Journal of Political Economy* 89(5): 841–864.

Lewis, P. (2003). The biggest game in town: Music? Sales down. Hollywood? Hit or miss. Tech? Flat. No wonder everyone wants to be in video game. *Fortune*, September 15.

Lin, N. (1990). Social Resources and Social Mobility: A Structural Theory of Status Attainment., In Ronald Breiger (ed.), *Social Mobility and Social Structure*, Cambridge University Press, pp. 247–271.

Lin, N. (1994). Action, social resources and the emergence of social structure. In Barry Markovsky, Jodi O'Brien, and Karen Heimer (eds.), *Advances in Group Processes*, vol. 11, pp. 67–85.

Liu, D., X. Geng, A. B. Whinston (2004). Optimal design of consumer contests. Working paper, University of Texas at Austin.

Loch, C. H. H., A. Bernardo, and S. Stout (2000). Status competition and performance in work groups. *Journal of Economic Behavior and Organization* 43(1): 35–55.

Lovaglia, M. J. (1994). Relating power to status. *Advances in Group Processes* 11: 87–111.

Lovaglia, M. J. (1997). Power and influence: A theoretical bridge. *Social Forces* 76: 571–603.

Moldovanu, B. and A. Sela (2001). The optimal allocation of prizes in contests. *American Economic Review* 91(3): 542–558.

Maslow, A. (1968). *Toward a Psychology of Being*, New York: Van Nostrand.

Maslow, A. (1971). *The Farther Reaches of Human Nature*, New York: Viking.

McGuire, M. T. and M. J. Raleigh (1985). Serotonin—behavior interactions in vervet monkeys. *Psychopharmacology Bulletin*, 21: 458–463.

Nambisan, S. (2002). Designing virtual customer environments for new product developments for new product development: toward a theory. *Academy of Management Review* 27(3): 392–413.

Nelson, E. (2003). Advertising: Nielson ratings come under fire—television networks blame agency as number decline for young male viewers. *The Wall Street Journal* November 17: B10.

Ridgeway, C. L. and H. A. Walker (1995). Status structures. In Cook, K. S., Fine, G. A., and House, J. S. (eds.), *Sociological Perspectives in Social Psychology*. Needham Heights, MA: Allyn and Bacon: pp. 281–310.

Ridgeway, C. L. and K. G. Erickson (2000). Creating and spreading status beliefs. *American Journal of Sociology* 106: 579–615.

Singh, N. and D. Witman (2001). Contests where there is variation in the marginal productivity of effort. *Economic Theory* 18(3): 711–744.

Shatz, M. (1993). What's wrong with MBA ranking surveys? *Management Research News* 16(7) 304–328.

Staehlin, C. (2003). Making MMOGs: Redefining "product development". *Austin Game Conference 2003*.

Thye, S. R. (2000). A status value theory of power in exchange relations. *American Sociological Review* 65: 407–432.

Tullock, G. (1980). Efficient rent-seeking. In J. B. et al. (eds.), *Towards a Theory of the Rent-Seeking Society*. College Station, TX: A&M University Press.

Tversky, A. and D. Kahneman (1974). Judgment under uncertainty: Heuristics and biases. *Science*, 185: 1124–1131.

Tyrrell, P. (2003). Realities of a virtual economy. *The Financial Times*, September 28.

Wasko, M. M. and S. Faraj (2000). It is what one does: Why people participate and help others in electronic communities of practice. *Journal of Strategic Information Systems* 9(2–3): 155–173.

Yee, N. (2002). Facets: 5 Motivation Factors for Why People Play MMORPG's, http://www.nickyee.com/facets/home.html.

Chapter 13

SERVICE DESIGN, COMPETITION AND MARKET SEGMENTATION IN BUSINESS INFORMATION SERVICES WITH DATA UPDATES

Bashyam Anant[a] and Uday S. Karmarkar[b]

[a]*Macrovision Corporation, 4301 Norwalk Drive, San Jose, CA 95129;* [b]*UCLA Anderson Graduate School of Management, 110 Westwood Plaza, Los Angeles, CA 90095-1481*

Abstract   Business information services are intermediaries that collect, collate, package and distribute information of value to professional users. We consider two technologies that such intermediaries may use for delivering information. First, a packaged design that uses physical media like CD-ROMs to distribute information. Second, an online service that delivers such information via the Internet or other online networks. We model a market where subscribers may choose between "self-service", where they collect and collate information directly from sources, and a third party service provider who provides either a packaged design or an online service. Subscribers are indexed by their volume of usage for the service. In a duopoly, we show that providers with online or package technologies will serve different market segments. The package provider's limited ability to provide current information, combined with decreasing search costs in an online service will make a package provider increasingly vulnerable to being driven out of the market by the online provider.

Keywords: Industrial marketing, pricing, segmentation, competitive strategy, computers, databases, Internet, non-cooperative games, competition in information goods

1.   INTRODUCTION

Many professionals rely on current information relevant to their work. Some firms/subscribers may obtain information directly from source—what we refer to as the "self-service" option in the rest of the paper. In other cases, a third party intermediary, referred to as a Business Information Service provider, may undertake to collect and collate the information, and deliver it to subscribers either in the form of a database "packaged" as a CD-ROM (or other physical media) or as an online service. Thus, a Business Information Service provider is an intermediary between information sources and firms or subscribers that have a use for that information.

Examples of such services include: Reuters and Bloomberg for foreign currency price information delivered to currency traders; the Lexis/Nexis online service for legal, regulatory and company information; Jeppesen (a Times Mirror Company) for aeronautical maps in CD-ROM and paper formats targeting pilots and flight controllers and Component Information Services, described below, to motivate our research questions and modeling assumptions (Bashyam and Karmarkar, 2000).

Component Information Services provide engineering information on semiconductor components for electronic design engineers. These services are essentially catalogs of electronic components with detailed technical descriptions of parts, engineering drawings and usage tips. Design engineers use this information to choose between alternative components for products they are developing. Even today, many such component catalogs are printed books or loose-leaf publications in binders.

Design engineers in this market always have the "self service" option, which refers to firms (and design engineers therein) collecting components information in whatever format (paper, CD-ROMs, websites, online downloads) their vendors make them available in and patching together an index or even a rudimentary database to this information, if possible. While this approach is cheap, it is more than likely to miss out the latest parts (because the search process is neither complete nor focused on current information) and does not simplify a design engineer's task of comparing components across vendors. Users will likely experience a large search cost to get to the component they are looking for, may give up and make sub-optimal component choices as a result.

Two Component Information Services were launched in the nineties to provide a components catalog for design engineers to alleviate the problem they faced searching for and comparing components from different vendors—i.e., lowering their search costs for component selection. The two services, Aspect Development and EnGenius (a Motorola division), took very different approaches to designing their service offering, and have evolved differently.

EnGenius, an online service (Electronic Engineering Times, 1993) launched in 1993 was the first online catalog of semiconductor components. Catalog information was stored in standardized form, in the SGML (Standard Generalized Markup Language) format. Component vendors, who wished to have their product information contained in the database, transmitted data in the SGML format to EnGenius over an online network which EnGenius' software normalized to a common parts description hierarchy to allow comparisons. A subscriber of the service could connect to the database through the Internet. They could then search for, compare, view, edit and print (but not store) information about components that met requirements. Besides raw product data sheets, EnGenius provided images and technical comparisons of components. EnGenius charged subscribers a fixed fee ($39/month) plus a marginal price, which could be a fee per download or a fee per online session, or an hourly fee.

EnGenius ceased operations in 1994. Its failure was attributed to a catalog database that had too few components (only 5000) to be of use to engineers and high online search costs (because accessing the service's rich mix of graphical, textual and parametric information was too slow over available networks).

Aspect Development launched its service around the same time as EnGenius. Aspect provides a "packaged" service that consists of a database on CD-ROMs bundled with a software search engine to query and compare components information in the database. The CD-ROM and search software are shipped to a subscriber firm every 3–4 weeks—this update cycle is necessary to enter enough new data (between updates), manufacture CD-ROMs and send them to customers. Aspect originally created its database by collecting raw data from semiconductor companies in paper, CD-ROM and online files and entering data manually into its database. It uses the same process for capturing on going updates. Aspect's approach costs it more per record to update and maintain its database—a cost that was largely borne by component vendors in EnGenius' approach. Nonetheless, Aspect's database today has a stable size of 5 million components from 931 vendors that collectively account for 85% of such components sold worldwide. Its customers include most of the 200 largest electronic manufacturers in the world who on an average pay a fixed annual subscription fee of about $500,000.

These case studies reveal several tradeoffs in the Business Information Services market that drive its evolution and help formulate the research agenda for this paper. First, online (e.g. EnGenius) and packaged (e.g. Aspect) services differ in their ability to deliver current information—specifically, longer update cycles for package versus online services. Second, search costs for users differ in the technologies. It is likely to be lower in the package versus online service because of online network delays in retrieving information. Third, pricing mechanisms for a package provider are less flexible than for an online provider. An online provider can charge a "pay per use" marginal charge, in addition to a fixed charge, as the EnGenius example demonstrates. A package provider is obviously more constrained in pricing because pay per use metering is not possible—in our model, we abstract this limitation into a simple fixed price charged by the package provider. Fourth, online providers like EnGenius can lower their database creation and update costs relative to package providers because they can have information sources submit information in a standard and normalized format and avoid or minimize costly data entry. Fifth, the database size is a critical determinant of the value of the service to subscribers as well as costs for building and maintaining a database (regardless of who bears the cost) as the failure of EnGenius demonstrates. Sixth, database size and pricing are two crucial service design parameters under the control of providers. Other services attributes such as the update frequency and minimum search costs are largely "frozen" by technology choice. Seventh, service providers have to ensure greater value for their service compared to the "self service" option, where subscribers collect and collate information directly from sources, in order for them to use a third party provider.

Given the above dynamics between online and package providers, our intent in this paper is to examine the following questions:

- How do technology choices impact service design and performance?
- How do service design characteristics, such as search costs, update frequency, pricing and database sizes affect the value of third party information services?
- Given the above relationships, how would online versus package providers position their service if they compete?
- What technology (online versus packaged) should a service provider choose given the inherent tradeoffs in the technology? When would both approaches be used and how?
- Was a service like EnGenius doomed to fail given its high search costs and sparse database? If not, under what conditions could they have survived?

To answer these questions, we model the Business Information Services market as a duopoly where subscribers may choose between their "self service" option or one of the third party services—an online service or a package provider. Subscribers are indexed by their annual usage of such services. To capture a subscriber with a given usage volume, a service provider must exceed the value provided by that subscriber's self service option. The value provided by a service provider is a function of their service design, which is driven by their technology choice (online or packaged) and choice of service design parameters, specifically database size and pricing (fixed and marginal prices). A service provider's technology choice automatically "freezes" certain aspects of service design, such as (the minimum possible) update frequency and search costs, while aspects such as database sizes and pricing are under the control of the service provider. Our models for self service, online and package provider options relate a subscriber's value for each option to their usage volume, update cycles, search costs, database size and pricing. Subscribers pick whichever option (online, package or "self service") provides maximum value, allowing us to determine market segments for different options. In a duopoly, two third party providers, having chosen their technology (online or packaged), compete for subscribers who also have a "self service" option, by choosing their profit maximizing service design parameters, namely database sizes and fixed and marginal (for the online provider only) prices.

Our results are as follows. In a duopoly with an online and package provider, we show that providers will differentiate their service design by choosing different database sizes and prices, and serve different subscriber segments (i.e. different usage volume segments). Two cases are possible in a duopoly. First, when the update interval for the package provider is high enough and/or when the search costs in the online service are low enough, we show that the package provider will serve low usage volume subscribers, if they enter the market at all, while the online provider serves high usage volume subscribers. Second, when search costs are high enough in the online service and/or the package service's lower search costs compensates for its longer update interval, we show that the online provider will always enter (as long as they can be profitable), but serve low usage volume subscribers, while the package provider will server high usage volume subscribers. We also show that package providers are increasingly vulnerable to being driven out by online providers as online search costs improve. These results allow us to draw insightful conclusions about the questions we set out to answer.

2.   LITERATURE REVIEW

As a representative work from the information sciences literature, Westland (1989) describes the determinants of market structure in online information services. Using a statistical model, he shows that high acquisition rates for data, coupled with low obsolescence rates, increase total marginal costs of maintaining an online database, resulting in a concentrated market with few firms. This observation, in part, supports the restricted market structure assumptions (i.e. duopoly) made in this paper. We also model how acquisition rates and obsolescence rates relate to database size.

The market segmentation effects described in this paper are most closely related to Moorthy (1988), which provides a duopoly model for understanding pricing and product design strategies. Potential consumers evaluate a product on its price and quality when choosing between the duopolists and a substitute producer. He shows that the duopolists differentiate their product, the higher quality being chosen by the higher margin firm. The marginal utility of a subscriber to an information service provider is similar in its economic effects to the product's quality attribute in Moorthy's work. Our paper however, explicitly relates the tradeoffs in technology (update cycles, search costs, pricing models, fixed and variable costs for providers) and choice of service design

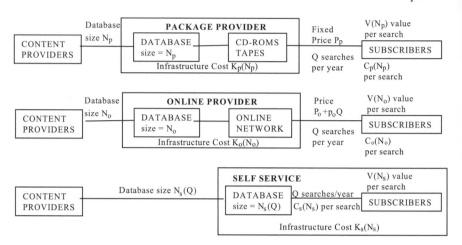

Figure 13-1. Packaged and online services compared with the self-service option.

parameters (database sizes, pricing) to the value to customers for different information delivery options and to market segmentation and market structure.

The rest of the paper is organized as follows. Section 3 details the model. In Section 4, we analyze the self service option for a given subscriber with a certain usage volume which determines the threshold benefit level that a service provider must meet or exceed to capture that subscriber. In Section 5, we analyze a market where two service providers compete for subscribers who have a self service option by picking their database size and pricing, to describe market segmentation results. A final section concludes this work.

3. THE MODEL

The model structure and notation is depicted in Figure 1. Subscribers to business information services are indexed by their annual volume of usage of the service denoted by Q (searches/year). Subscribers may choose between an online or a package provider or may prefer "self service", where in they collect, collate and assemble a database of their own directly from source.

Subscribers pay an annual fixed charge P_p if they use a packaged provider. For the online service, subscribers pay both a fixed charge P_o and a marginal charge per search p_o, since usage can be monitored. We use the subscript "p" to denote a "packaged" and "o" to denote an online service in the rest of the paper. In reality, pricing for a package service is somewhat more complex than a simple fixed price described here. Aspect Development (Bashyam and Karmarkar, 2000), for example, uses a tiered pricing arrangement based on the number of subscribers that simultaneously access their database (within their own environments, not online)—it is easy to see that Aspect is effectively us-

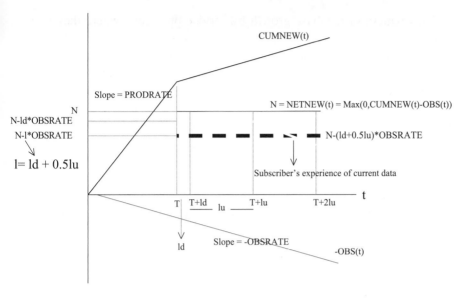

Figure 13-2. Growth pattern for new information in a service. Service providers grow their database to a size N, after which they "ship" it to subscribers at an update interval lu. Subscribers may experience an additional lag time ld, between when an update is ready and when they receive the database.

ing a menu of marginal prices from which subscribers can choose. We assume in our model that the package provider charges a simple fixed charge, primarily to reflect a package provider's limitation of not being able to use "pay per use" schemes available to online providers. Our models will still be applicable if we were to assume a marginal price for the package provider as well.

Service providers create a database and allow subscribers to access it, either in-house (for the package service) or online. The service provider's process for building their database is shown in Figure 2. In the figure, the provider starts building a database at time $t = 0$. $CUMNEW(t)$ represents the cumulative records in the service provider's database at time t. The slope $dCUMNEW(t)/dt$ is the service provider's production rate for new records, denoted as $PRODRATE$ in Figure 2 for the case where $CUMNEW(t)$ is linear. $OBS(t)$ represents obsolete records at time t. The slope $dOBS(t))/dt$ is the rate at which records obsolesce in the database, denoted as $OBSRATE$ in Figure 2 for the case where $OBS(t)$ is linear. The difference between the two curves $(CUMNEW(t) - OBS(t))$ is equal to the net new records in the database at time t, denoted by $NETNEW(t)$. At $t = T$, the service provider decides to alter their production rate to match the obsolescence rate. Consequently, the net new records in the database stabilizes at $NETNEW(t) = N$ for all $t \geq T$. N is referred to as database size in the rest of the paper.

This pattern of database growth by service providers, where they reach a "steady state" database size over time, is supported by current practice in the business information services industry. Aspect Development, for example, began by rapidly adding components to its database in the initial years. When a large percentage of new components in the electronics industry had already been captured in the database, Aspect was able to reduce its production rate to more or less the rate at which components obsolesced. Aspect's "steady state" database size today stands at over 5 million parts from 921 manufacturers that collectively account for over 85% of the worldwide electronic components produced.

We assume that once service providers reach their steady state database size N, they allow subscribers to begin using the service. As in Figure 2, the provider "ships" a database of size N at an update interval lu, after entering new records since the last update, cleansed of obsolete records. Subscribers also experience a delay ld between when a service provider finishes an update and when the subscriber receives it—this is the time it takes, say for a package provider to manufacture CD-ROMs and ship them to customers. Effectively, the subscriber "experiences" a database with fewer new records because the data in the database becomes obsolete between updates and during the delay between when an update is completed and when the subscriber receives it. The subscriber's view of the net new records in the database at time t is represented by the serrated line in Figure 2. In the case where $CUMNEW(t)$ and $OBS(t)$ are both linear as in Figure 2, it is easy to show that the average database size "experienced" by a subscriber in steady state is $N - l * OBSRATE$, where $OBSRATE = \mathrm{d}OBS(t)/\mathrm{d}t$ and $l = ld + lu/2$, denotes the effective update interval. In other words, the subscriber experiences a database that is smaller than the provider's steady state database size N by as many records as become obsolete during the provider's effective update interval. We assume for simplicity that the effective update interval ($l = ld + lu/2$) is not a service design parameter for providers, mainly because it is largely governed by the choice of technology (packaged versus online). For example, a package provider may find that shipping daily updates may be cumbersome for subscribers because of change over and version control problems, even if distribution costs were not an issue for the provider.

Service providers incur two types of costs for building and maintaining their service. First, they incur fixed costs relating to R&D costs for creating a normalized data hierarchy, software for cleansing and normalizing raw data, search software for the database and user interface software. Fixed costs also include cost for the hardware used for performing data entry and connecting the provider to an online service (in the online case). Second, they incur variable costs that depend on the size of the database created.

These pertain to the actual cost of data acquisition (e.g. copyrighted information), reconciling format differences, data entry and indexing (Bashyam and Karmarkar, 2000). Boeri and Hensel (1995) estimate a cost of \$4.70 per record for data entry, formatting and indexing in the SGML (Standard Generalized Markup Language) format for the legal publishing industry. Up to the time the database reaches steady state ($t \leq T$) the service provider incurs these variable costs at the rate of $dCUMNEW(t)/dt$ (see Figure 2). After that, these costs are incurred at the rate of $dOBS(t)/dt$. If $CUMNEW(t)$ and $OBS(t)$ are linear, then the total variable cost incurred to build and maintain a database can be expressed as $kN + k * OBSRATE * t$ $(t \geq T)$, where k is the variable cost per record. On an annualized basis, the fixed and variable costs can be abstracted into a cost function $K_i(N_i)$, where i indicates the underlying service delivery technology, the subscripts s, p, and o denoting "self service", packaged, and online information service options respectively. When $CUMNEW(t)$ and $OBS(t)$ are linear, $K_i(N_i) =$ (1 year) $*$ ((fixed costs $+ k_i N_i$)/(useful life of service) $+ k_i * OBSRATE$). Let $K_i(0) =$ (fixed costs)/(useful life of service) $+ k_i * OBSRATE$. Thus, $K_i(N_i) = K_i(0) + k_i N_i$/(useful life of service). As formulated, the steady state database size, N, is a crucial variable in the design of the service.

We assume that $K_o(N) < K_p(N)$ because an online provider can drive down their marginal production costs per record (i.e. $k_o < k_p$) by having content sources submit updates in a standard format. The online provider lowers their cost by transferring the cost of cleansing, normalizing and entering data to the source, practiced, for example, by EnGenius. The package provider takes on these costs which is why we assume $K_o(N) < K_p(N)$. Of course, this also implies that the fixed costs are more or less comparable, which is a reasonable assumption in practice because most of the fixed costs are common to both types of providers.

For the package service, there may be additional costs for duplicating the database on CD-ROMs for each subscriber. However, these costs do not depend on the database size and are negligible compared to the costs for data entry. Specifically, manufacturing costs for CD-ROMs are independent of the amount of data they contain. Unit manufacturing costs for standard CD-ROMs are about \$1 in lots of 1000, with mastering charges adding \$700 to the total, bringing the manufacturing cost per CD to less than \$2 (Weidemer and Boelio, 1995).

An online provider may incur costs for data transmission to subscribers if they are on a private wide area network. For ease of exposition, we assume that these costs are subtracted from the marginal price per search (p_o) that the online provider charges. An online provider's fixed costs may also be impacted by their market share because database queuing delays in a successful service may result in additional infrastructure costs to support an acceptable

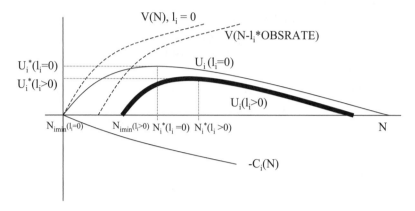

Figure 13-3. Net benefit U_i for a subscriber in technology i as a function of database size, and effective update interval.

level of service for a large subscriber base. For simplicity, we assume that these costs are factored into the fixed costs by determining the costs associated with the upper bound on market share for the online provider (for example, by determining the fixed costs for the provider to support their monopoly market share). Note that database queuing delays also impact the package provider, except that the resulting fixed cost increases would be borne by the subscriber.

Subscribers incur a search cost for each record accessed. The search costs depend on several characteristics of the database including its size (in number of records), depth of information capture per record (e.g. how many fields describe a record), access technology (whether packaged or online), quality of indexing, degree of specialization of the service (e.g. a database customized for particular segment of users) and queuing delays (particularly, in an online service). Online data transfer rates can be 100 times slower than the transfer rate for a CD-ROM. Even today, many small and mid-sized businesses do not have high speed online access. Queuing delays in an online service further add to the search costs for online subscribers. Queuing delays in the online case depend on the number of subscribers connecting to the service simultaneously, which is driven in part by the service's market share. For simplicity, we assume that the online provider spends additional fixed costs to deliver an acceptable response time (i.e. acceptable search costs) based on an upper bound of their market share. We assume that the essence of the search cost for a query may be captured in a cost function $C_i(N_i)$, $C_i(0) = 0$, which accounts only for its technology and database size dimensions. Factors such as the quality of indexing, degree of specialization and depth of information capture per record are not modeled into the search costs because they apply equally to online and packaged services, while our interest in this paper is study the impact of their differences. Naturally, we expect the search cost to increase with database size for a given technology. Because of data transfer and queuing delay limitations, it is reasonable to assume that $C_p(N) < C_o(N)$ for a database size N. In addition, we should expect (though we do not assume) that $C_o(N) < C_s(N)$ because typically a self-service database is often less functional than a third party service. For example, in the components information service example, the self-service database used by many firms is a collection of free paper databooks and CD-ROMs provided by component manufacturers (Bashyam and Karmarkar, 2000). Such databases have little or no search capabilities, as a result, self-service searches are likely to be more costly than an online (third party) service for a given database size N. In rare cases, it is conceivable that a subscriber firm may actually be able to build a "self-service" database that is as sophisticated as a third party service—in such cases, it is conceivable that such firms may enter the service provider market themselves. This was the case with Motorola with its EnGenius Components Information Service—as a large user of components information, they were able to build their own database and provide third party access to it as a service. In summary, we assume that $C_p(N) < C_o(N)$, but make no assumptions about where $C_s(N)$ falls in this ordering.

Subscribers derive an intrinsic value of information, regardless of how it is delivered, which is abstracted into $V(N)$, $V(0) = 0$, common to all subscribers. Because of the update interval in delivering the service to a subscriber, they effectively experience a database of size $N - l * OBSRATE$, where l is the effective update interval and $OBSRATE$ is the rate of obsolescence of information, as discussed in Figure 2. Thus, a subscriber's net value for each search in an information service is $U_i(N) = V(N - l_i * OBSRATE) - C_i(N)$; let $U_i(0) = 0$, $U_i(N) \geq 0$ for $N \geq N_{i\,\min}$, where the subscripts i (s, o, or p) relate value to the underlying service technology. We assume that for $N \geq N_{i\,\min}$, $U_i(N)$ is a concave function of N, with a unique maximum at N_i^* (see Figure 3). This assumption captures the notion that, for a given search, more information is valuable, but after a certain number of alternatives, the search costs become significant and lower the net benefit from the search. To summarize, we assume:

Assumption 1: $V(N)$ and $C_i(N)$ are both monotonically increasing functions of the database size, for an information delivery technology i. In addition, the net benefit function, $U_i(N) = V(N) - C_i(N)$ is concave for $N_i > N_{i\,\min}$ with a unique maximum N_i^* as in Figure 3. If $V(N)$ is more "concave" than $C(N)$, this assumption would hold.

N_i^* is the maximum database size that a provider would build—anything more than N_i^* will not add value to subscribers given their search costs. Note that N_i^* depends on the effective update interval l_i ($i = s, p, o$) for the service provider as a shown in Figure 3. The effect of the update interval is to increase the maximum database size (N_i^* ($l_i > 0$) > N_i^* ($l_i = 0$)) and decrease the corresponding maximum net benefit (U_i^* ($l_i > 0$) > U_i^* ($l_i > 0$)) for subscribers. It is reasonable to expect that $l_s < l_o < l_p$, because of the longer update cycles in a packaged service compared to online or self service options. Clearly, the package provider will not be viable in certain industries (e.g. in industries with $OBSRATE > N_p^*/l_p$), which is why package providers are absent in markets such as financial information services.

In sum, this section provided us with the essential ingredients of the cost structure of information service providers and cost and benefits for their subscribers. In the next section, we explore the subscriber's self service option. By characterizing a subscriber's self-service benefit, we establish the lower bound on the benefit that a third party provider (online or package) must exceed to capture that subscriber. In Section 5, we first derive the subscriber's benefit function for online and packaged options. Then, we analyze a duopoly with two providers that compete for subscribers indexed by their usage volume Q and have the option of self service. Though the market structure assumptions appear restrictive, they are actually quite representative of many information services markets. For example, Aspect is a monopolist in the Components Information Services (though it may seem that component distributors with their websites may compete with Aspect, in reality such websites are of little use to design engineers that Aspect targets. Distributor web sites are oriented towards procurement professionals who need to check price and availability of specific components). Reuters, Bloomberg and Jeppesen monopolize their markets. We believe that such concentration arises because of the specialized nature of content, high liability costs associated with incorrect information, high data entry and update costs, service branding and long lead times to create a valuable service—factors that lead to high entry barriers.

4. THE SELF SERVICE OPTION

Potential subscribers to information services are characterized by the number of searches they undertake per year, denoted by Q; $0 \leq Q \leq Q_{\max}$. Given their level of usage, a firm opting for self service must decide its preferred database size N_s, by trading the benefits of a large database against the costs of building and maintaining it. For simplicity, we assume the lag time for self service $l_s = 0$. The net benefit per search is given by $U_s(N) = V(N) - C_s(N)$, for a database of size N.

The problem solved by a subscriber firm with annual usage of Q searches is:

$$N_s(Q) = \arg \text{Max}\big(V(N_s) - C_s(N)\big)Q - K_s(N_s), \quad N_s \geq 0,$$

$$W_s^*(Q) = \text{Max}\big(V(N_s) - C_s(N_s)\big)Q - K_s(N_s), \quad N_s \geq 0,$$

where

N_s = the size of the self service database; we will treat N as continuous for convenience;

$V(N)$ = the value to the firm from searching a database of size N; $V(0) = 0$;

$C_s(N)$ = the firm's cost of searching in its in-house database of size N; $C_s(0) = 0$;

$U_s(N)$ = the firm's net marginal benefit;

$K_s(N)$ = the firm's annual cost of creating and maintaining a database of size N;

$W_s^*(Q)$ = the net benefit from self service for a subscriber with annual usage Q.

The self service benefit function $W_s^*(Q)$ is characterized below. Proofs are given in Appendix A.

Proposition 1:

(a) $W_s^*(Q)$ is convex, non-decreasing in Q, $W_s^*(Q) \geq 0$. See Figure 4.

(b) $W_s^*(Q) \geq U_s^* Q - K_s(N_s^*)$, where $N_s^* = \arg\sup_{N \geq 0} U_s(N) = \sup_{N \geq 0} U_s(N)$.

(c) The linear bound of (b) is approached asymptotically as Q becomes large. If U_s^* is positive then $W_s^*(Q)$ is eventually increasing.

$W_s^*(Q)$ represents the minimum benefit that a third party information service provider must ensure in order for a potential subscriber firm with annual usage Q to join the third party service. U_s^* is the maximum possible benefit under self service (see Figure 3), and is driven by the self service search costs traded against the value of a self service database.

5. MODELS OF COMPETITION

Here, we develop duopoly models where two information service providers compete with the self-service option. Service providers choose their profit maximizing service design parameters, their database size N_i, and price parameters (fixed price for package, fixed and marginal price for online). As a first step, we characterize the benefit functions for subscribers under online and packaged technology below.

5.1. Subscriber Benefit Functions for Package and Online Services

5.1.1. Package Provider's Benefit Function In the package service, the number of searches made by a subscriber cannot be monitored, and the subscriber can only be charged a fixed price $P_p \geq 0$ for the service. The value from the package service for a subscriber making Q searches/year can be written as:

$$\big(V(N_p - OBSRATE * l_p) - C_p(N_p)\big)Q - P_p$$
$$= U_p(N_p - OBSRATE * l_p)Q - P_p,$$

where N_p, $OBSRATE$, l_p are the packaged database size, obsolescence rate and effective update interval for the package provider. Notice that the benefit function is linear.

5.1.2.   Online Provider's Benefit Function   In the case of an online service, a subscriber's search activity can be monitored, and a charge p_o made for each search. The value from the online service for a subscriber making Q searches/year can be written as:

$$\big(V(N_o - OBSRATE * l_o) - C_o(N_o) - p_o\big)Q - P_p$$
$$= \big(U_o(N_o - OBSRATE * l_o) - p_o\big)Q - P_o,$$

where $U_o(N_o - OBSRATE * l_o) = V(N_o - OBSRATE * l_o) - C_o(N_o)$ and N_o, $OBSRATE$, l_o are the online database size, obsolescence rate and effective update interval for the online provider.

Figure 4 displays these benefit functions along with the self-service benefit function $W_s^*(Q)$. In the figure, it is easy to visualize market segments for online and package providers by having subscribers choose whichever option (self service, online or package) maximizes their benefit. Importantly, Figure 4 reveals that the market segment for package and online providers is a contiguous interval of the form (Q_1, Q_2), since the subscriber's benefit function is convex for self service and linear with an information service provider. These market segments can be described by:

$$M_p = \Big\{ Q \,\Big|\, \max\big(W_s^*(Q), \big(U_o(N_o - OBSRATE * l_o) - p_o\big)Q - P_o\big)$$
$$< U_p(N_p - OBSRATE * l_p)Q - P_p \Big\}$$
$$M_o = \Big\{ Q \,\Big|\, \max\big(W_s^*(Q), \big(U_p(N_p - OBSRATE * l_p)Q - P_p\big)\big)$$
$$< \big(U_o(N_o - OBSRATE * l_o) - p_o\big)Q - P_o \Big\},$$

where M_p and M_o are to the market segments for the package and online providers, respectively.

5.2. Models of Duopoly

In this section, we consider a duopoly where potential subscribers choose between self-service and one of the two third party providers, whichever maximizes their net annual benefit. An illustrative segmentation is shown in Figure 4. Two cases can occur. In one case, the segments are adjacent; in the other, the segments are separated by a group of subscribers that select self service. For a given set of price and size decisions, these cases can be detected by finding the breakeven point between the two information service providers, and checking to see whether the value of self service at this point is higher or lower than that for the information services. This observation is summarized in Proposition 2, and is used to determine the market shares for the duopolists.

Proposition 2: Define $Q_{po} = (P_p - P_o)/(U_p - U_o + p_o)$. If $W_s^*(Q) \leq U_p Q_{po} - P_p$, then the market segments of the duopolist are adjacent, otherwise a group of self service subscribers separate the two segments. Visualize this by manipulating the benefit lines in Figure 4.

When Proposition 2 holds, the market share for the packaged provider is given by $MS_p(N_p, P_p, N_o, P_o, p_o) = G(Q_{po}) - G(Q_{p2})$ if $U_p > U_o - p_o$ and by $G(Q_{p1}) - G(Q_{po})$ if $U_p < U_o - p_o$, where Q_{pi}, are as in Figure 4, and $G(Q)$ is the proportion of subscribers whose annual usage volume exceeds Q.

Consider the case where one firm provides a packaged database, and the other an online one. Define A and B as the strategy spaces for the packaged and online information service providers respectively. We characterize them below:

$$A = \left\{ (N_p, P_p) \big| N_{p\min} \leq N_p \leq N_p^*, \ 0 \leq P_p \leq P_p^{\max} \right\} \subseteq R_+^2$$

$$B = \left\{ (N_o, P_o, p_o) \big| N_{o\min} \leq N_o \leq N_o^*, \ 0 \leq P_o \leq P_o^{\max}, \right.$$
$$\left. 0 \leq p_o \leq U_o^* \right\} \subseteq R_+^3$$

where for $i = s, p, o$

$U_i^* = \max_{N \geq 0} U_i(N - OBSRATE * l_i)$ is the maximun benefit per search for provider i;

$N_i^* = \arg \sup_{N \geq 0} U_i(N - OBSRATE * l_i)$, is the benefit maximizing database size for provider i.

Let a and b denote strategies of the two players, with $PR_i(a, b)$ denoting the profits for firm i, and should be interpreted as the profit that the package provider makes given strategy vector b for the online provider and vice-versa. The upper bound $P_{i\max}$ on fixed price is clearly provider i's fixed price as a

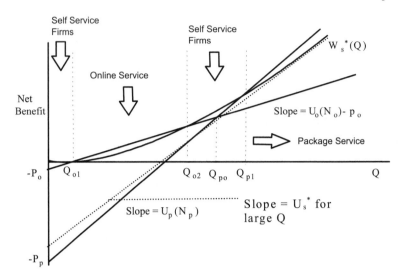

Figure 13-4. Disjoint market segments in heterogeneous duopoly, see Proposition 4.

monopolist. The upper bound on database size N_i^* arises because U is concave (Figure 3), and exceeding N^*, costs more without capturing a larger market, as can be seen by manipulating the slope of either provider's benefit line in Figure 4.

Firms play a one shot game in which they choose the service design parameters in their control (for package provider (N_p, P_p), for online service (N_o, P_o, p_o) simultaneously. We assume that the technology choice decision (online or package) is made before the game is played.

We define a Nash equilibrium for that game as follows (Friedman, 1977):

Definition 1: A Nash equilibrium is a combination $(a^*, b^*) \in A \times B$ that satisfies $PR_a(a^*, b^*) \geq PR_a(a, b^*)$ for $a \in A$ and $PR_b(a^*, b^*) \geq PR_b(a^*, b)$ for $b \in B$.

A Nash equilibrium is essentially a pair of strategy vectors (database size and prices) for the package and online providers such that the package provider, taking the online provider's equilibrium strategy for granted, has no incentive to change their equilibrium strategy and vice versa for the online provider. Equivalently, each player's strategy is really their combination of slope (U_i, which is governed by database size and marginal charge) and intercept (P_i, fixed price) of their benefit functions as in Figure 4.

A necessary and sufficient condition for an equilibrium to exist is for the profit function $PR_i(N_p, P_p, N_o, P_o, p_o)$, $i = p, o$ to be quasi-concave (Friedman, 1977) and for the strategy spaces (A and B) for the two players to be compact. In general, it is not possible to derive analytical expressions for the profit functions formulated earlier for the package and online providers, primarily because we cannot derive analytical expressions for the breakeven points for the providers (see Figure 4). As a result, concavity of the profit functions cannot be established. However, we are able to derive conditions that characterize the equilibrium in a duopoly, which allows us to drive interesting conclusions about market structure and segmentation effects. This is discussed next.

5.2.1. **Duopoly with Homogenous Service Providers** Suppose that there are two providers of packaged (or online) databases, with similar technologies and capabilities, so that they have the same cost structure for creating and maintaining databases, and provide customers with the same search capabilities, implying the same search cost functions. Index the two firms as 1 and 2. We assume that customers will pick the service that delivers the maximum benefit to them. Then the following holds:

> **Proposition 3:** Consider a market with two identical service providers, indexed 1 and 2. If both providers survive in equilibrium, they will employ different database sizes and prices, such that $P_1 > P_2$ and $U(N_1) - p_1 > U(N_2) - p_2$, make identical equilibrium profits and have disjoint market segments—an example of disjoint market segments is depicted in Figure 4. Note that if there are two online providers, the result holds with $p_{1,2} \equiv 0$

It is useful to visualize the disjoint market segments result for the case when $F(Q)$ is a Binomial distribution. Suppose the usage volume is either $q1$ or $q2$ ($q2 > q1$), with $x\%$ of the subscriber base having usage volume $q1$ and $(1 - x)\%$ with volume $q2$. By definition, the market segments will be disjoint. It is easy to see that if both providers survive, one provider will opt for subscribers with volume $q1$ and the other will serve subscribers with volume $q2$. In addition, both have to make equal profits, otherwise, the lower profit firm has an incentive to mimic and undercut the higher profit firm.

> **Corollary 3.1:** Consider a market with more than two identical service providers. If all providers survive in equilibrium, they will employ different database sizes and prices, such that $P_i > P_j$ and $N_i > N_j$, for any i and $j, i \neq j$, make identical equilibrium profits and have disjoint market segments.

5.2.2. **Duopoly with Heterogeneous Service Providers** Consider a market with one package and one online provider.

Let $M_p = \{Q | U_p Q - P_p > \max(W_s^*(Q), (U_o - p_o)Q - P_o)\}$ denote the market segment for the package provider. Then, the package service provider's problem may be stated as:

$$\max PR_p(N_p, P_p, N_o, P_o, p_o) = P_p m MS_p(N_p, P_p, N_o, P_o, p_o) - K_p(N_p),$$
$$a \in \{P_p, N_p\} \subseteq A,$$

where

> m = the total number of potential subscribers;
> P_p = fixed charge (annualized) for purchasing the packaged information service;
> $MS_p = G(\min\{M_p\}) - G(\max\{M_p\})$ is the provider's market share;
> PR_p = is the net profit for a given database size and fixed price;
> $F(Q)$ = is the proportion of subscribers with less than Q searches per year;
> $G(Q) = 1 - F(Q)$, is the proportion of subscribers with more than Q searches per year;
> $A = \{(N_p, P_p)|N_{p\min} \leq N_p \leq N_p^*, 0 \leq P_p \leq P_p^{\max}\} \subseteq R_+^2;$
> $U_p^* = \max_{N \geq 0} U_i(N - OBSRATE * l_p);$
> $N_p^* = \arg\sup_{N \geq 0} U_i(N - OBSRATE * l_p).$

The online provider's problem can be stated as:

$$\max PR_o(N_p, P_p, N_o, P_o, p_o)$$
$$= P_o m MS_o(N_p, P_p, N_o, P_o, p_o) + m p_o S(N_o, P_o, p_o) - K_o(N_o),$$
$$b \in \{P_o, p_o, N_o\} \subseteq B,$$

where

> $MS_o(N_p, P_p, N_o, P_o, p_o) = G(\min\{M_o\}) - G(\max\{M_o\})$
> is the provider's market share,
> $M_o = \{Q|(U_o - p_o)Q - P_o > \max(W_s^*(Q), U_p Q - P_p)\},$
> $S(N_o, P_o, p_o) = E(Q_o 1) - E(Q_o 2),$ where $E(Q) = \int_Q^{Q_{\max}} Q f(Q) dQ,$
> $B = \{(N_o, P_o, p_o)|N_{o\min} \leq N_o \leq N_o^*, 0 \leq P_o \leq P_o^{\max}, 0 \leq p_o \leq U_o^*\},$
> $U_o^* = \max_{N \geq 0} U_o(N - OBSRATE * l_o),$
> $N_o^* = \arg\sup_{N \geq 0} U_o(N - OBSRATE * l_o).$

Two possibilities can arise in this market. First, when $U_o^* > U_p^*$, which may happen if higher search costs for the online service are overcome by that providers shorter update cycles (because $l_o \ll l_p$) or if search costs in the online service drop below that of the packaged service. Second, when $U_o^* \leq U_p^*$, which may happen if search costs for the package service are so low that they overcome that provider's longer update intervals (because $l_p \gg l_o$).

In the first case, we can show that if the package provider enters the market at all, they will have to serve low end (low Q) subscribers and make smaller profits in equilibrium than the online provider. In the second case, the situation is reversed with the package provider serving high volume subscribers while the online provider serves low volume subscribers. These are summarized below:

Proposition 4: Consider a market with one online and one package provider. When $U_o^* > U_p^*$, if the package provider enters the market, they will serve low volume subscribers and make less profits than the online provider. The online provider will make higher profits than the package provider and serve high volume subscribers with a database size and marginal price such that $U_o > U_p^*$. The online provider's profits by imitating the package provider's low end strategy (slope of the benefit line and fixed price), has to be lower than what the online provider makes by serving high volume subscribers. If not, the online provider will monopolize the market.

Proposition 5: Consider a market with one online and one package provider. When $U_o^* \leq U_p^*$, the online provider enters the market as long as they make a profit, but will serve low volume subscribers. If the package provider enters the market, they will serve high volume subscribers with a database size such that $U_p > U_o^*$. The online provider will pick a low end strategy (slope of the benefit line and fixed price), which if imitated by the package provider would result in lower profits for the package provider compared to their high end strategy.

A key insight from Proposition 4 and 5 is that the online provider always enters the market as long they can make a profit and will try to drive out the package provider if possible. Using a numerical example to simulate the above models, we are able to show that a package provider would be driven from the market as search costs in the online service decrease. The simulation starts with $U_o^* \leq U_p^*$, then U_o^* is increased by reducing search costs. We are able to show that profits for both providers decrease because of price competition. Eventually, when the search costs are equal, the package provider stays out of the market, and the online provider becomes a monopolist. As more subscriber firms connect to high bandwidth online access, package providers will struggle to survive given their larger costs for database creation and updates. Providing online access may be the only strategic option for the package providers in the future. By going online, such a firm would capture high end users through the packaged design and low end users through an online service.

Table 13-1. Payoff matrix for Period 1 game

		Player 1 Choice in Period 1 (Profit = first term in each pair)	
		Package	Online
Player 2 Choice in Period 1	Package	$(-PR, -PR)$ or (PR_{p0}, PR_{p0})	(PR_{o1}, PR_{p1})
	Online	(PR_{p1}, PR_{o1})	$(-PR, -PR)$ or (PR_{o0}, PR_{o0})

5.2.3.   **The Two Stage Duopoly Game**   What technology should a service provider choose, based on their knowledge of competition and profits in the market? Consider a market where there are two identical providers, indexed 1 and 2. They play a two stage game as follows. In Period 1, each provider picks a technology (either online or package). In Period 2, knowing each other's technology choice they pick their service design parameters (database sizes and prices) in a one shot game as described in Sections 5.2.1–2. The Period 2 game is a sub-game of the overall game—its equilibrium has been characterized in Propositions 3–5. The payoff matrix for the Period 1 game is shown in Table 1.

The profit pairs in Table 1 correspond to what each firm would make in equilibrium in the Period 2 sub-game. When both firms pick identical technologies, we know from Proposition 3 that either they will drive each other out and make negative profits (denoted by $-PR$ in Table 1) or if they both survive, they will make equal profits (denoted by PR_{p0} when both firms pick a package design and survive and by PR_{o0} when both pick an online service and survive). When one picks online and the other package, the equilibrium profits for the package firm is denoted as PR_{p1} and by PR_{o1} for the online provider—these values will have to calculated using the heterogeneous duopoly results of Propositions 4 and 5.

If there is no equilibrium in the Period 2 sub-game where both providers survive with identical technologies (i.e. according to Proposition 3, there is no choice of strategies where profits are equal and segments disjoint), we can show that the overall equilibrium in Period 1 will result in one firm picking the package design and the other will pick the online service. If there is an equilibrium in the Period 2 sub-game where both firms survive (i.e. according to Proposition 3, there exists a choice of strategies where profits are equal and segments disjoint), then three possibilities can arise in the overall game in Period 1. First, both providers choose a package design in Period 1—this will happen if $PR_{p0} > PR_{o1}$ in Table 1. Second, both providers choose an online service in Period 1—this happens if the Period 2 sub-game results in $PR_{p0} < PR_{o1}$ and $PR_{p1} > PR_{o0}$. Third, one provider chooses an online service and the other picks package design in Period 1—this happens if the Period 2 sub-game results in $PR_{p0} < PR_{o1}$ but $PR_{p1} < PR_{o0}$.

The preceding discussion reveals that in the general case all possible patterns of market evolution can happen depending on the distribution of usage volumes ($F(Q)$) and service design trade offs (pricing, database sizes, update intervals, search costs) inherent in the technologies.

6. NUMERICAL RESULTS

In this section, we provide numerical results for the equilibrium model where we assume that firms play a single period game and choose their service design parameters (database sizes and prices) simultaneously. We use the Component Information Services market to exemplify cost and benefit functions described earlier.

6.1. Cost and Benefit Functions

Assume that the query volume of the subscriber population has a triangular distribution on $[0, Q_{\max}]$ with a given mode m_f. The value function is taken to be exponential. Database building and update costs are assumed to be linear in the database size. The search cost function is also assumed to be linear. Thus, $C_i(N) = c_i N$, $K_i(N) = K_i(0) + k_i N$, $V(N) = d(1 - \exp(-bN))$, $i = s, p, o$, denoting self service, packaged and online options. With these assumptions, we find the following:

Proposition 6: For the above cost and benefit functions and a triangular $F(Q)$, the subscriber's self service net benefit is given by

$$W_s^*(Q) = \begin{cases} 0, & Q \le k_s/(db - c_s), \\ QU_s(N_s(Q)) - K_s(N_s(Q)), & Q > k_s/(db - c_s), \end{cases}$$

where

$$N_s(Q) = -\ln\left(\frac{c + (k/Q)}{db}\right)\Big/b, \quad Q > \frac{k_s}{db - c_s}.$$

The upper bound on the fixed price for a service provider is obtained by solving the monopolist's problem for that firm. For service provider i, $i = p, o$ this turns out be as below:

Proposition 7: For any N_i, the maximum price that a monopolist provider would charge is

$$U_i(N_i)\max\left\{Q_{\max}/3, \sqrt{m_f Q_{\max}/3}\right\},$$

where m_f is the mode of the triangular distribution. The upper bound for the fixed price is given by

$$p_i \max = U_i^* \max\{Q_{\max}/3, \sqrt{m_f Q_{\max}/3}\}.$$

The lower bound on all price parameters is, of course, zero. Even with these simplifying assumptions, it is not possible to establish the concavity of $PR_i(N_p, P_p, N_o, P_o, p_o)$, $i = o, p$, necessary and sufficient conditions for the existence of an equilibrium (Friedman, 1977). Thus, we solve the duopoly game numerically.

6.2. Component Information Services Example

Consider the following example from the electronic component information services industry. A typical electronic design for a product (say a notebook computer) priced in the range \$1000–\$2000 might have approximately 30 discrete components. Suppose potential subscribers to the information service look for exactly one particular component for their designs, say an 8-bit comparator or a floppy disk controller. N (database size) is interpreted as the number of alternatives that are contained in the database for that component. Judicious component selection for a product priced in the given range could reduce the cost of the design or increase its selling price in the market by, perhaps, \$150, or roughly \$5 (=150/30) per component in the design. For example, by reducing the power consumption of a notebook computer, a firm could increase its battery life, which could translate into a higher selling price for the product. Thus, for each search, subscribers stand to gain a maximum of \$5, if they searched exhaustively for the ideal component. We assume that the value function for search is given as $V(N) = 5(1 - \exp(-N/5))$, that is, $d = \$5$, and $b = 0.2$. This implies that the first 5 alternatives generated by a search deliver 63% of the maximum value, which is realistic.

The maximum usage volume, $Q_{\max}$, is related to such factors as the size of the subscriber firm, the number of design engineers, the number of concurrent product development teams, and its rate of introduction of new products. The largest of the subscriber firms is assumed to contain 100 concurrent design teams, each developing one product per year, each of which requires one search for the particular component. Thus, we set $Q_{\max} = 100$. As before, we assume that $K_p(N) > K_o(N)$, for a given database size N, since the packaged service incurs higher marginal costs for digitizing data from data books, whereas the online service has semiconductor manufacturers perform this activity. The remaining cost parameters are displayed in Table 2, for which we solve each of the market models described previously.

Table 13-2. Test matrix for market model

Parameter	Value
Q_{max}	100
Q_{min}	0
Mode	10
m	700
b	0.2
d	5
$K(0)$: $(Ks(0), Kp(0), Ko(0))$	(0, 30000, 3000)
k: (cs, cp, co)	(0, 3, 1)
a: (as, ap, ao)	(0.9, x, y)
OBSRATE	0

Table 13-3. Database size, pricing, market share and profits for information service providers for Table 1 with $c_p = 0.0075$, $c_o = 0.2$

Market	Duopoly		Monopoly		Monopolist with Both Service Designs	
Parameter	Packaged	Online	Packaged	Online	Packaged	Online
N	24.28	8.05	24.28	5.65	10.57	
P	122.34	8.61	158.66	0.00	218.88	0.00
P_o	–	1.19	–	2.23	–	2.26
PR	14,267.91	6,421.57	24,695.70	54,179.78	40,369.26	
MS	0.52	0.43	0.49	1.00	0.27	0.73

6.3. Results

The pricing, profit and market penetration under different service designs and market structures are shown in Table 3. We see that the lower search cost package service is able to command a higher fixed price in a duopoly, and serves the high end of the market. Conversely, the online provider covers the lower end subscribers. The packaged service's choice of database size is very close to $N_p^* = 24.46$ because of its high fixed costs of building the database. For that reason, its database size is same when the service is a monopolist. As the packaged design reduces only its fixed price when moving from a monopoly to a duopoly, its profits certainly decline, but not to the same extent as the online service provider. The online provider's profits drop from \$54,179 to \$6,421 when the market structure changes from monopoly to duopoly, because of a corresponding increase in database size and a decrease in marginal price.

Market coverage in the duopoly is 95%, whereas it is 100% when the on-line provider is a monopolist and when the packaged service provider offers both technologies. The online provider is unable to serve the lower 5% in the former case because the average usage level in the lower 48% ($= 100\%$–52%) of the market is too low to support a zero fixed price for online usage. When the online provider is a monopolist, the high end 52% of the market effectively subsidize the low end users, making a zero fixed price viable. Likewise, when the package provider offers both technologies, the upper 27% of the market subsidizes the remaining 73%, as seen by the \$60 ($=\$218$–\$158, see Table 2) premium they pay compared to the case when the provider has only the packaged technology.

Low end subscribers covered by the online provider derive greater surplus (measured by the gap between $W_s^*(Q)$ and $U_o(N_o)Q - P_o$)) when the online service competes with the packaged provider. In fact, in the duopoly, $N_o = N_o^* = 8.05$. Choosing a lower size would limit the fixed price that provider could charge, making it impossible to recover their fixed costs. In a monopolistic market, the online provider barely exceeds the benefit for the self service case, though his search cost is less than one-fourth that of self service. Note that the size of the database, 5.65, is also well below $N_o^* = 8.05$. As a monopolist, the provider covers the entire market with a zero fixed price, but revenues from marginal usage of the database more than recover their fixed costs.

6.4.   Effect of Online Search Costs

In the component information services industry, subscriber search costs played a crucial role in the evolution of the industry. Apparently, these charges were very significant for subscribers to EnGenius, which took 45 seconds to download a datasheet image through a 9600 baud modem. As search costs for online access improve, profits for the package service provider (Figure 5) drop steadily because while fixed costs remain the same, the price that the market is willing to support drops. The profits for the online provider first increase because low volume firms switch from self service to the online service. Profits decrease because of price competition erodes profits. In the limit, when the search costs are equal, the packaged service provider stays out of the market, and the online provider becomes a monopolist.

Improvements in online technology have serious consequences for the package service provider, given their larger costs for database creation and updates. This is likely to happen in the near future, as more subscriber firms connect to high bandwidth online access. Providing online access may be the only strategic options for the packaged service provider in the future. By going online, such a firm would capture high end users through the packaged design and low end users through an online service.

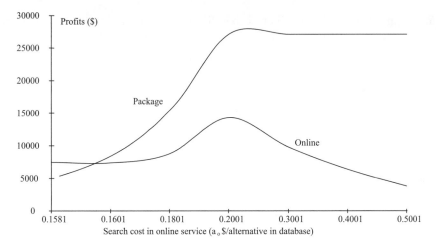

Figure 13-5. Effect of online search costs on profits for package and online providers in a duopoly. Search costs are linear: $C_i(N) = a_i N$, with $a_p = 0.0001$. All other parameters are given in Table 1.

7. CONCLUSIONS AND FUTURE RESEARCH DIRECTIONS

We have examined how technology choice (online versus package) and service design parameters (database sizes, pricing) impact market segmentation and structure in information services markets by relating tradeoffs in the different options (search costs, update intervals, pricing mechanisms) to benefits for subscribers. We showed that package providers will serve high volume subscribers if they are able to ensure a low search cost that overcomes their longer update intervals compared to online services. Where the update intervals in the package design are longer and are compounded by declining online search costs, we showed that the package provider will be increasingly vulnerable to being driven out of the market by the online provider. Relative to the questions we set out to answer in our Introduction, our results for the two stage game (technology choice followed by selection of database sizes and pricing) show that both package and online can be feasible options for providers as long as they are positioned in the appropriate market segments. As for the failure of EnGenius, our results would argue that they could have been a successful business but were brought down by their service design (high price compounded by a small database), incorrect positioning (they could perhaps have targeted low volume users who could tolerate the high search costs) and premature market entry (specifically, before they had a significant-size database).

Several extensions of the present model are possible. Some hint at survival strategies for package providers faced with declining online search costs.

First, markets where subscribers value different information—that is, they are indexed by both their usage volume Q, and the type of information they desire. In this case, it should be possible to show that providers will create smaller databases tailored for each type of customer segment. For a package provider, in particular, this strategy will result in higher revenues than a "one database size fits all approach". Using Figure 4, it is easy to see that a package provider may miss out low volume subscribers with a "one database size fits all approach"—this may be remedied by choosing a set of smaller database sizes (a set of lower slopes for the benefit line, with lower prices to match), effectively increasing market coverage. This is a revenue maximizing tactic Aspect Development has used—they sell several databases tailored for vertical markets such as medical instruments companies, military users and telecommunications—subscribers in these segments have specific component categories that they are interested in searching for. Second, the self-service search cost may itself be a function of subscriber characteristics. For example, $C_s \sim C_s(Q, N)$, where in the self service search costs depend on the usage volume. This may reflect the fact that large volume users may be able to create a fully functional database in-house, such as the example of Motorola in the Component Information Services example. It is possible to show that the self service benefit function will remain convex as long as $C_s(Q, N)$, is decreasing and concave in Q, which is a reasonable assumption. Of course, in this case, the package and online provider's benefit functions are also convex (not linear as before) but we expect segmentation results to hold largely unchanged. Third, database queuing delays impact a subscriber's response time (i.e. search costs). Queuing delays can be expected to be proportional to the market share for the provider and impact online subscribers more. As such, this extension would be intractable, but for simple assumptions on usage volume distribution $(F(Q))$ interesting results may be derived. For example, with a Binomial distribution ($x\%$ of the subscriber base with usage volume $q1$, $1 - x\%$ with volume $q2$), it would be possible to show cases where the online provider may avoid high volume users because of high search costs and increase in their fixed costs. Finally, in Bashyam and Karmarkar (2004) we have analyzed a similar setting to that of this paper, but where consumers can be indexed based on two segmentation variables: the volume (number of searches) and the value associated with each search.

REFERENCES

Bashyam, T.C.A. and U.S. Karmarkar (2000), "Aspect Development Inc (A)", *Managing the Global Corporation: Case Studies in Strategy and Management*, J. De La Torre, Y. Doz and T. Devinney (Eds.), 2nd Edition, pp. 335–348, McGraw Hill, New York.

Bashyam, T.C.A and U.S. Karmarkar (2004), "Usage Volume and Value Segmentation in Business Information Services", in *Managing Business Interfaces: Marketing, Engineering, and Manufacturing Perspectives*, Chakravarty, A. and J. Eliashberg (Eds.), Kluwer Academic Publishers.

Boeri, R. and M. Hensel (1995), "What Good is SGML?", *CD-ROM Professional* 8(4), 108–110.

Electronic Engineering Times (1993), "Two launch component information services", n770, November 1, pp. 16–18.

Friedman, J. (1977), *Oligopoly and the Theory of Games*, North-Holland, Amsterdam.

Moorthy, K.S. (1988), "Product and Price Competition in a Duopoly", *Marketing Science* 7(2), 141–168.

Rockafellar, R.T. (1970), *Convex Analysis*, Princeton University Press, Princeton, New Jersey.

Weidemer, J.D. and D.B. Boelio (1995), "CD-ROM versus Online: An Economic Analysis for Publishers", *CD-ROM Professional* 8(4), 36–42.

Westland, J.C. (1989), "Topic Specific Market Concentration in the Information Services Industry: Evidence from the DIALOG Group of Databases", *The Information Society* 6, 127–138.

Appendix A: PROOFS OF PROPOSITIONS

PROOF OF PROPOSITION 1. (A). Observe that $W_s^*(Q)$ is the maximum over a set of functions linear in Q, and is therefore convex (Rockafellar, 1970). (B). $W_s^*(Q) = U_s(N_s)Q - K_s(N_s) \geq (U_s(N_s^*)Q - K_s(N_s^*)$, from the definition of $N_s(Q)$. (C). It is sufficient to show that $N_s(Q) \to N_s^*$ for large Q. The first order condition for $W_s^*(Q)$ may be written as

$$Q\left(\frac{\partial U_s(N)}{\partial N} - \frac{K_s'(N)}{Q}\right) = 0.$$

$K_s'(N)$ is bounded above since $N_s(Q)$ is.

Thus, the solution to the above first order condition approaches the solution to

$$Q\frac{\partial U_s(N)}{\partial N} = 0.$$

$\square$

PROOF OF PROPOSITION 2. Obvious from Figure 4. $\square$

PROOF OF PROPOSITION 3. Assume that if both suppliers use identical product design and pricing strategies, they split the market equally. Suppose both suppliers survive in the market, but $N_{a1} = N_{a2} = N$, $P_{a1} = P_{a2} = P$ in equilibrium. Keeping a database size of N, Firm 2 can then price at a level infinitesimally smaller than Firm 1, and capture the entire market. Firm 1 reacts likewise, and the two firms undercut each other till one firm charges the smallest price $P_0(N)$ such that $m P_0(N)MS(N, P_0(N)) - K_{ai}(N) = 0$. The other firm then stays out of the market, which reverts to a monopoly. A similar argument applies when both attempt to change their product designs while charging identical prices in equilibrium. Thus, if both firms survive, they utilize different pricing and design strategies. Clearly, the higher priced firm will then use a larger database, otherwise, it will be dominated. In addition, they must make identical profits, otherwise, the lower profit firm can mimic the size of the other firm, and undercut its price and do better. Next we need to establish that the market segments are non-adjacent/disjoint in equilibrium. Suppose an equilibrium exists where both providers make identical profits but use different database sizes and prices as described above and have adjacent market segments. Then, one provider can mimic the other's strategy (size and price), undercut price slightly and capture the entire market. Firms engage in this type of competition until both firms make zero profits. If they both make zero profits, it must be that $P_{a1} > P_{a2} > P_0(N_{a2})$, since $P_0(N_{a2})$ is the smallest price at which either firm makes a zero profit as the sole provider with a size N_{a2}. Then, Firm 1 can mimic Firm 2's size, undercut their price, and do better. When this happens, firms engage in intense price and size competition until one firm charges $P_0(N_a^*)$, while the other firm stays out, reverting the market to monopoly. Therefore, it must be that if both survive, they make identical profits, and occupy different and disjoint segments. In such a case, each provider, given the equilibrium strategy of the other firm, has no incentive to mimic the other provider because doing so will only reduce its profits.   □

PROOF OF COROLLARY 3.1. Take any providers two at a time and use Proposition 3.   □

PROOF OF PROPOSITION 4. Segment the strategy space of the online provider into

$$B' = \{(N_o, P_o, p_o) | N_{o\,\min} \le N_o \le U_o^{-1}(U_p^*),$$
$$0 \le P_o \le P_o^{\max}, \ 0 \le p_o \le U_o^*\}$$

and

$$B - B' = \{(N_o, P_o, p_o) | N_o > U_o^{-1}(N_p^*), \ 0 \le P_o \le P_o^{\max}, \ 0 \le p_o \le U_o^*\}.$$

For $b \in \mathbf{B}'$, the online provider will simply dominate the package provider because (1) the online provider has a better cost structure $K_o(N) < K_p(N)$ for all N and (2) the online provider can mimic whatever strategy (database size and price) the package provider uses, undercut them and do better because the online provider gets usage revenues while the package provider does not. So, if the package provider enters at all, it has to be the case that online provider chooses a strategy in $\mathbf{B} - \mathbf{B}'$. In this case the slope and intercept of the online provider's benefit line satisfies $U_o - p_o > U_p$ and $P_o > P_p$. Choosing that high end strategy should result in greater profits for the online provider compared to a strategy where they mimic the package provider, and undercut them. If not, the online provider will revert to dominating the package provider and returning the market to a monopoly. If the condition of online provider profits is satisfied, it has to be the case that online provider makes greater profits than the package provider when they serve the high end market because the online provider has lower costs than the package provider and gets additional usage revenues. □

PROOF OF PROPOSITION 5. Segment the strategy space of the package provider into

$$A' = \left\{ (N_p, P_p) \big| N_{p\,\text{min}} \le N_p \le U_p^{-1}(U_o^*),\ 0 \le P_p \le P_p^{\text{max}} \right\}$$

and

$$A - A' = \left\{ (N_p, P_p) \big| N_p > U_p^{-1}(U_o^*),\ 0 \le P_p \le P_p^{\text{max}} \right\}.$$

For $a \in A'$, the package provider will attempt to dominate the online provider by mimicking that provider's strategy (slope of the benefit line and fixed price). However, in the competition that ensues (both providers increase the slope of benefit line and drop fixed price), the package provider will be the first to drop out because (1) the online provider has a better cost structure $K_o(N) < K_p(N)$ for all N and (2) the online provider will always have larger revenues than the package provider because of their usage revenues. Thus, if the package provider enters at all, they will pick a strategy in $A - A'$. This leaves the low end market completely open to the online provider who will enter as long at they can make a profit. The slope and intercept of the package provider's benefit line will satisfy $U_p > U_o - p_o$ and $P_p > P_o$. Choosing this high end strategy should result in greater profits for the package provider compared to a strategy where they mimic the online provider's low end strategy, and undercut them. If not, the package provider will attempt to dominate the online provider, eventually lose and returning the market to a monopoly for the online provider. Thus, the online provider picks a strategy such that the package provider, if they were to mimic the online provider's strategy (benefit line slope and fixed price), will make less profits than if they stayed at the high end. Note that the online provider is guaranteed positive profits for this strategy since their costs are lower and revenue higher with any strategy that the package provider would imitate. ☐

PROOF OF PROPOSITION 6. With $V(N)$ concave, $C(N)$ and $K(N)$ linear in N, $QU_s(N) - K_s(N)$ is concave in N for each Q. Thus, the first order conditions are sufficient. When

$$Q \le \frac{c_s}{db - a_s}, \qquad N_s(Q) = -\ln\left(\frac{c+k}{Q/db}\right)/b < 0,$$

which being infeasible, we set $N_s(Q) = 0$.

Thus, $N_s(Q) = \max\{0, -\ln((c + k/Q)/db)/b\}$, which upon substitution into the benefit function gives the proposition. ☐

PROOF OF PROPOSITION 7. From Figures 4 and 5, it is enough to consider $U_i(N_i) \ge U_s^*$ to derive an upper bound for the fixed price. Then, for a given

$$U_s^*, MS_i(N_i, P_i) < MS_i\left(N_i, l - P_i/\left(U_i(N_i)Q_{\max}\right)\right).$$

Substitute that market share bound in the monopolist packaged service provider's objective function in Section 5.1.1 along with the formula for the triangular distribution. Differentiate it with respect to P_i to obtain

$$P_i^{\max}(N_i) = \max\left\{U_i(N_i)Q_{\max}/3, \ U_i(N_i)\sqrt{m_f Q_{\max}/3}\right\},$$

where m_f is the mode of the triangular distribution. Substituting $U_i(N_i) = U_i^*$ gives the bound in the proposition. ☐

Chapter 14

CHANNEL STRATEGY EVOLUTION IN RETAIL BANKING

Reynold E. Byers[a] and Phillip J. Lederer[b]

[a]*Graduate School of Management, University of California, Irvine, CA 92697;* [b]*William E. Simon Graduate School of Business Administration, University of Rochester, Rochester, NY 14627*

Abstract   Information and banking technology have combined to throw the retail banking business model into disarray. Many predicted that lower cost online-oriented services such as Citibank's Citi f/i venture would dominate the retail banking market and drive out high cost old technologies. The subsequent failure of Citi f/i and other virtual banks raises questions about how technology choice affects retail banking competition: Under what conditions would an online-only banking strategy be successful? When can a bank deploy both old and new technologies and still be competitive? Can an ATM network substitute for a branch network? Do customers' attitudes about technology affect banking strategy? We use an economic model of a competitive retail banking market to address those and other questions. Our model allows banks to choose their technology, including establishing separate branch and ATM networks or relying on third party ATM networks. We also include customers that have differing attitudes toward technology. Our analysis suggests that customer preferences, rather than technology cost structure, drive the evolution of banks' strategic technology choices. Also, banks in our model tend to deploy ATMs in the same numbers as branches, despite ATM's cost advantages. Finally we show that virtual banks will remain unprofitable until a much larger proportion of the population is comfortable with online bank transaction technology. These results suggest that banks should carefully study their customers' preferences to align major strategy shifts with customer attitudes.

1.   INTRODUCTION

The rise of the information economy with its associated technological developments radically altered the retail banking distribution model. New distribution technologies including PC banking, Electronic Bill Payment and Presentment, and remote wireless access have all contributed to changing the way that customers and banks interact with one another. Banks love the fact that new distribution technologies have drastically lower cost structures than old technologies. Further, the growth and development of information systems technology makes each distribution channel potentially more powerful. However, the banking industry has reacted to that growing power and technological sophistication with uncertainty and high profile failures. Even the largest banks that are considered savvy users of technology, such as Citibank, have made serious missteps resulting to millions of wasted dollars and alienated customers. Uncertainty and failure have led to many unanswered questions in the industry: Can a "virtual bank," originally predicted to dominate, even survive? Are branches really dead? Can ATMs serve as a primary point of physical customer contact? We seek to address these issues with an economic model of a competitive banking market. First we will discuss Citibank's experience to illustrate the problems the industry faces.

Citibank has long been among the largest five banks in the U.S. and among the most technologically advanced, but even they have had problems adjusting to the use of new technologies. While Citi was not the first to deploy a PC banking system, they were among the earliest, allowing customers to connect via modem using Citi's "Direct Access" banking product. Direct Access was considered one of the best PC banking products and as Internet technology came to the fore it morphed and grew to become a full-featured transactional website that was, again, considered one of the best in the business. Citibank was also the first major bank to eliminate *all* fees for its online banking channels. This move was seen as a major attempt to be highly customer-oriented, to drive transaction traffic to the cheaper online channels, and to set the bar for the entire industry. Despite these early successes, Citibank's desire to further leverage electronic channels led them into a major failed initiative called Citi f/i. The vision driving Citi f/i was to cater to technologically aware customers and minimize transaction costs by relying only on ATMs and the online banking channel. In fact, Citi f/i customers would not be allowed to use branches. Keeping transactions out of teller-staffed branches would mean very low costs. The hope was that customers that were comfortable with ATMs and the Internet would prefer the convenience, speed and self-service nature of electronic channels. Citi f/i was quietly launched in August of 1999 and less than a year later Citibank announced that Citi f/i would be discontinued and replaced with a "new service." It was clearly stated that the new service likely would not include a "ban on branch transactions" as Citi f/i had. While there were many questions about the viability of Internet-only banking strategies, Citi f/i had planned to overcome those doubts by using ATMs to serve as a physical presence. That physical presence, however, was not enough to sustain Citi f/i. Further, Citibank was not alone, as other banks made the same error and closed

Internet-based bank ventures; two prime examples are Bank One's Wingspan-Bank.com and Bank of Montreal's mbanx. What misunderstanding led these otherwise competent banks to be so mistaken? (Power, 2000).

We propose to examine this phenomenon with an economic model of banks that choose distribution technologies, serve varied customer segments, and compete against each other. We will also place particular interest in how separate ATM networks influence bank strategy and competitive marketplace results. We will allow the banks in our model to freely choose from a wide array of banking technologies. In particular, our model allows a branch to design separate ATM and branch networks. This is important as current estimates show that approximately 40% of all ATMs are "off-site," i.e., they are not collocated with a branch. Thus, a bank manages the branch and ATM distribution channels separately in practice and we seek it approximate that in our model. We will capture customer preferences through a simplified segmentation scheme based on customer attitudes toward technology. We also include competition between banks in our model. This inclusion is significant and representative of reality. If not for competition, banks could slowly experiment with new technologies and slowly deploy information technology effectively throughout their distribution system. With competition, the cost of a single misstep could be millions of dollars wasted, dominance foregone, and shattered customer confidence; as seen in the previously mentioned examples.

By structuring our model to approximate the industry we will address questions that shed light on the interaction of technology and competition. We include a rich array of relevant parameters including fixed and variable costs, customer preferences for technology, inconvenience and search costs for customers. We seek to address questions such as: Under what conditions can the old technologies simply be abandoned? When can the old and new technologies coexist, and in what mix? How is the equilibrium number of active banks affected by cost and consumer preference parameters? We formulate the competitive model and provide sufficient conditions for the existence and uniqueness of an equilibrium. We characterize the equilibrium using numerical analysis due to complexity of the model.

We answer our research questions by numerical sensitivity analysis on the model. We show that the equilibrium mix of banks is most sensitive to the *relative* size of consumer segments, and is not as sensitive to the absolute size of the market. We also examine how ATM networks figure in distribution strategies. Surprisingly, despite the significant lower cost of ATMs compared to branches, both are used in roughly equal quantities. Additionally, we find that network ATMs form a significant part of successful bank strategies when most customers prefer electronic transaction methods. Further analysis shows that the equilibrium results are relatively insensitive to the fixed and variable costs of technology. The results generally suggest that changing consumer behavior, rather than bank cost structure, drives changes in retail bank competitive strategies at equilibrium.

While there are some papers with related modeling techniques, our approach is unique in analyzing the banking distribution strategy question. For a full discussion of related literature we refer the reader to Byers, Freimer and Lederer (2004) and note that this model represents an extension of that paper. Byers, Freimer and Lederer (2004) demonstrate how to model a competitive retail banking market and how to guarantee the existence of an equilibrium, despite non-convexities in the banks' cost functions. We extend that work by allowing banks to create branch and ATM networks independently of one another and consider the existence of third-party, non-bank ATM networks. These extensions are significant as ATM networks, both proprietary and outsider-owned figure prominently in current banking industry strategy.

Our results create both a validation of bank strategy and a caution. Since the high-profile failures of Internet-only banks in 2000 and 2001 many banks have abandoned attempts to shunt customers into high-technology outlets. Instead, they have adopted a "full-service" strategy by installing all technology choices and allowing customers to pick their preferred methods of transacting. This attitude is consistent with some of our results. However, our analysis also suggests that if customer preferences shift significantly over time, banks should change their strategy to match; likely meaning a shift to online channels. The caution is then that banks should make sure that they learn their customers' preferences and attitudes and shift with them, rather than try to incite customers to change their behavior.

The presentation is organized as follows. Section 2 presents the model of the market for retail banking services, including consumers and banks. Section 3 presents sensitivity analysis, and Section 4 presents the conclusions and ideas for future research.

2.   MODEL OF RETAIL BANKING MARKET

We build our model with two differing customer segments and six different types of banks. Customers are spread throughout a geographic region and the banks compete for their services. Customers are distinguished by their attitude toward electronic transaction technology; i.e., those that embrace Internet banking and those that don't. Banks choose their distribution system according to both cost and considering the two types of customer segments. We consider six bank types that represent the primary strategies that have been seen in U.S. banking markets over the past 10 years. These six types include those that are hypothesized to endure in the future, e.g., Internet-only banking. Segmenting consumers and banks in this manner allows us to capture the main tradeoffs that banks and consumers face in order to examine a market equilibrium that can represent practical retail banking competition.

We begin by describing the customers, the banks and the competitive entry equilibrium. In defining the model in the rest of this section we will use the notation found in Table 1.

2.1.   Customers

We assume that there are two customer segments located in a geographical region. Specifically, we consider the segment that prefers branch transactions, the "b" segment, and the segment that prefers electronic transaction methods, the "e" segment. Effectively, we are assuming that all the customers in this region need to conduct the same types of transactions and their only differentiating point is the technology they would choose to use. We model these preferences by imposing an additional cost on the consumer for using a transaction method other than the "preferred" channel. For example, if a b customer uses an ATM, then that customer incurs some additional cost due to "disutility," denoted $h_{b\text{ATM}}$. We assume that the b segment prefers branches, followed by ATMs, and dislikes electronic methods the most. The e segment reverses that preference order, as in Table 2.

Customers also incur cost for travel. This cost can be considered both as a customer's value of time, but also a general cost of inconvenience of traveling or searching for a physical location. We assume that customers consider their average distance to a branch or ATM when choosing a bank. As we assume that customers travel and engage in banking transactions at random times, average distance to a branch or ATM is an appropriate convenience measure. We also assume that the e customer segment incurs a greater travel cost than the b segment. This assumption is in harmony with current industry wisdom that customers that are more willing to conduct electronic transactions have higher income and opportunities and thus would incur more inconvenience in travel.

Customers choose banks and transaction channels based on the total cost of a relationship with a bank. We call that total cost the *full price*. Full price consists of the actual price charged for the transaction (set by the bank), the disutility incurred at the point of transaction (due to customer preferences), and travel cost incurred by the customer, if applicable. For example, suppose a b customer conducts a transaction at an ATM; then the full price P_b would be the sum of the price that bank i charges to a customer of type b for using an ATM, the disutility that a customer of type b incurs by having to use an ATM, and the cost of having to travel $1/n_{i\text{ATM}}$ miles on average, where $n_{i\text{ATM}}$ is the

Table 14-1. Notation used in this model and defined in Section 2

Indices	
K, k	Set of distribution technologies K = {branch, ATM, PC, NATM} and technology choice index
J, j	Set of customer segments $J = \{b, e\}$ and segment index
I, i	Set of Bank types: $I = \{$Branch, Full, Kiosk, Virtual, Branch Only, PC Only$\}$ and bank-type index

Cost Parameters	
h_{jk}	Models customer preference for technology: Disutility imposed on customer segment j by a transaction through technology k ($ per transaction)
β_j	Customer cost of travel: Coefficient of segment j's disutility due to distance ($/mile)
F_k	Yearly fixed cost of placing an outlet using technology k in the market region
G_i	Overall fixed cost of a distribution channel: Yearly fixed cost of maintaining a network for bank type i ($/year)
c_k	Per-transaction cost to a bank: Coefficient of variable cost per transaction's linear term ($/transaction)
d_{jk}	System congestion cost: Coefficient of the variable cost per transaction's quadratic term ($/transactions2)

Decision Variables	
n_{ik}	Number of outlets of type k for bank type I
$p_{jk}; \vec{p} \in R^J$	Price per transaction charged to segment j ($) for a transaction through technology k
P_j	Full price per transaction to segment j: Full price includes price, travel costs and disutility due to technology type
$m_i; \vec{m} \in R^I$	Number of banks of type i. The vector bank-types
$\tau_{ijk} \in R$	Number of transactions supplied by bank type i, serving customer segment j with distribution technology k
$\vec{\tau} \in R^{JK}$	The vector of transactions for bank type i
$\vec{\tau} \in R^K$	The vector of production for segment j and strategy i by distribution channel

Demand Parameters	
$D_j(\vec{P}); \vec{D}(\vec{P})$	Demand by segment j given full price vector $\vec{P}$; vector of demand for each customer segment given price vector $\vec{P}$

Table 14-2. Ordering of customers' technology preferences, by customer segment

	Segment "*b*"	Segment "*e*"
Most Preferred	Branch	Online
	ATM	ATM
Least Preferred	Online	Branch

number of ATMs placed by bank i, and β_b is the cost per mile that a customer of type b incurs.[1] Specifically,

$$P_b = p_{ib\text{ATM}} + h_{b\text{ATM}} + \frac{\beta_b}{n_{i\text{ATM}}}. \tag{1}$$

We assume that customers will choose the bank that provides the least cost price and channel combination. Further, we assume that demand is a decreasing linear function of full price. Assume also that e customer demand is less price elastic than the b customer demand.

2.2.   Banks

Each bank seeks to maximize its profits by choosing a distribution infrastructure and setting transaction prices. The choice of a distribution system is complex. It requires evaluating multiple levels of differing cost structures and weighing the effect of the infrastructure itself on the two customer segments. For example, while Internet technology represents the lowest cost structure for a bank, can a bank with only an Internet presence compete with other banks offering a more varied distribution system?

We consider that banks choose from among six primary types, built upon four primary distribution technologies. The distribution technologies are branches, ATMs, Internet banking and Network (third-party owned) ATMs. The bank-types that we consider we will denote as the *Branch, Full, Kiosk, Virtual, Branch Only* and *PC Only*. The technology choices of each bank-type are summarized in Table 3. First, the *Branch* strategy represents the "classical" bank type that was the primary bank type until PC banking came along. This bank type relies primarily on a network of branches and mainly serves b customers as they prefer branch-based transactions. The *Branch* bank-type also maintains proprietary ATMs that it can use to serve either b or e customers. Second, the *Full* bank offers a complete selection of technologies to its customers; branches, ATMs, Internet banking and the use of third-party network ATMs. The benefit of this bank type is that it can serve customers using their preferred transaction methods. The drawback of this bank type is high fixed costs. Third, the *Kiosk* bank-type represents an attempt to remove the high costs of full-scale branches from the classical model by replacing them with less costly groups of ATMs and an Internet banking system. This bank type looks to serve b customers with the ATMs, despite the fact that those customers prefer branches, and e customers with Internet banking. This strategy

---

[1]   Note that the functional form for average distance, $(1/n_i)$, holds exactly for location using the ℓ^1 norm, but generalizations are possible for powers of $(1/n_i)^{k/2}$ for $k = 0, 1, 2$, etc. leading to general results.

Table 14-3. Technology choices for each bank-type in the model

	Branch	Full	Kiosk	Virtual	Branch only	Internet Only
Branches	✓	✓			✓	
ATMs	✓	✓	✓			
Online		✓	✓	✓		✓
3rd party ATMs		✓		✓	✓	

is influenced by Citibank's "Citibank f/i" banking strategy discussed in the Introduction. Fourth, the *Virtual* bank serves customers with an Internet banking system and allows its customers to use third-party ATM networks. This bank type focuses primarily on e customers but can serve b customers with the network ATMs if possible. Fifth, the *Branch Only* type relies on a branch network to serve b customers and third-party network ATMs to serve e customers. Finally, the Internet Only bank is simply an Internet banking system and allows no use of network ATMs; this bank type effectively ignores the b customer segment. These six cover the majority of actual bank types seen in the U.S. market. Table 3 shows the technology choices of each bank-type.

Upon choosing to enter the market, a bank then sets capacity in each of its distribution channels. That is, for each customer type $j = \{b, e\}$ and distribution channel $k = \{\text{branch, ATM, PC, NATM}\}$ the bank chooses a volume of transactions it expects to complete. In general notation, this volume decision is given by τ_{ijk}, where i indexes bank-type. We also assume that banks are free to choose whether to enter the market. Thus, the equilibrium mix of banks, both number and type is endogenous.

Each technology carries its own cost structure. We consider both variable and fixed costs in the model. The costs vary widely from system to system, with the Internet method generally accepted as least cost. Branches are considered to have both the highest fixed and variable costs. ATMs are cheaper than branches, but more costly than Internet banking systems. Network ATMs have no fixed cost for a bank as they are owned by third parties; however, the variable cost will be much higher than a regular ATM transaction due to network and interchange fees. These relationships are expressed as follows:

$$0 = F_{\text{NATM}} < F_{\text{PC}} < F_{\text{ATM}} < F_{\text{branch}},$$

$$c_{\text{PC}} < c_{\text{ATM}} < c_{\text{branch}} < c_{\text{NATM}}.$$

Further, we assume that each technology exhibits decreasing returns to scale in transaction volume, owing to system congestion. That is, for a given system, as the number of transactions processed through it increases, congestion increases in the system, thereby increasing the average transaction cost.

We model this congestion by adding a convex term to the bank's cost function with coefficient d_{jk}; for simplicity we make the convex term quadratic.

Bank-types that use branches or proprietary ATMs decide the optimal number of each to place in the market. A greater number of physical locations increases the convenience that a bank offers its customers, but increases the bank's overall distribution cost.

We allow banks in our model to set the number of branches and ATMs independently one from the other. This model construct reflects actual banking practice and allows for the possibility of a wide variety of bank behaviors. In practice, banks nearly always include at least one ATM at each branch location; however, the relatively low fixed cost of placing an ATM also leads some banks to place multiple ATMs off-site. In our model, given the large difference in cost structures between branch and ATM placement, it is reasonable to posit that active banks would create vastly different ATM and branch networks; specifically, a much larger network of ATMs than branches. It appears that a bank could save significant costs by using ATMs instead of branches and provide better service to customers by reducing total travel cost. While there may be many customers that prefer branches, the high cost of branches limits that size of a network that a bank could build and still be competitive. Following this reasoning an argument could be made that the *Kiosk* bank type could be a viable market competitor under a wide range of market conditions. This tension between the cost and service tradeoffs between branches and ATMs presents a compelling question that we will address with numerical examples in Section 3.

We use conditions of perfect competition in this market for banking services. Banks are Full-Price takers, that is, each bank considers itself small enough that its individual decisions do not affect the market full price.[2] Profit for bank i is denoted π_i and is given below in (2).

$$\pi_i = \sum_{j \in J} \sum_{k \in K} p_{ijk} \tau_{ijk} - \sum_{j \in J} \sum_{k \in K} c_k \tau_{ijk} - \sum_{j \in J} \sum_{k \in K} d_{jk} \tau_{ijk}^2 - \sum_{k \in K} G_k$$

$$- \sum_{k = \{b, \text{ATM}\}} n_{ik} F_{ik}. \tag{2}$$

The first term represents the revenue a bank makes, composed of prices charged to each customer-technology combination and the volume of the same. The rest of the equation represents the bank's cost function; specifically, linear variable cost, quadratic variable cost (to model the decreasing return to scale),

---

[2] Note that banks are *full-price* takers, that is to say that banks set prices for transactions, but the resulting full-price has to equal the market full-price.

the fixed cost of each distribution technology, and the fixed cost of placing branches and/or ATMs.

Our assumption that banks are full price-takers, P_j puts a limit on the price, p_{ijk}, that a bank can charge. That is, the most a bank can charge is the market full price, less disutility and travel costs. Using equation (1) as an example, algebraically solving to find the price a bank can charge a b customer at an ATM yields

$$p_{ib\text{ATM}} = P_b - h_{b\text{ATM}} - \frac{\beta_v}{n_{i\text{ATM}}}. \tag{3}$$

We will make this substitution into the profit equation (2) to create a profit function of full price and cost in order to solve for equilibrium. Having made the substitution, we can now solve for the optimal number of branches and ATMs by taking partial derivatives; the solution is given in (4) below:

$$n_{ik}^* = \sqrt{\frac{\sum_{j\in J} \beta_j \tau_{ijk}}{F_{ik}}} \quad \text{for } k \in \{b, \text{ATM}\}. \tag{4}$$

The optimal number of branches (or ATMs) depends on the total travel cost incurred by the customers that use them and the fixed cost of placing a branch (or ATM). Notice that the optimal number of outlets increases with total travel cost and decreases with fixed costs. Further note that, like the EOQ in inventory calculations, the optimal number of outlets exhibits economies of scale. Thus, the portion of bank cost that comes from location of facilities has economies of scale, while the portion of cost due to conducting transactions exhibits diseconomies of scale. This combination of economies of scale in some terms and diseconomies in other terms leads to a non-concave profit function as shown (after substitution of (4) into (2)) in the bank's objective in equation (5):

$$\pi_i^*(\vec{P}) = \max_{\tau_i} \pi_i\left(\vec{P}, \vec{\tau_i}\right)$$

$$= \max_{\tau_i} \sum_{j\in J} \sum_{k\in K} P_j \tau_{ijk} - 2 \sum_{k=\{b,\text{ATM}\}} \sqrt{F_{ik}} \sqrt{\sum_{j\in J} \beta_j \tau_{ijk}}$$

$$- \sum_{j\in J} \frac{\beta_j}{n_{NT}} \tau_{ijNT} - \sum_{j\in J} \sum_{k\in K} h_{jk} \tau_{ijk} - \sum_{j\in J} \sum_{k\in K} c_k \tau_{ijk}$$

$$- \sum_{j\in J} \sum_{k\in K} d_{jk} \tau_{ijk}^2 - \sum_{k\in K} G_k, \tag{5}$$

$$s.t. \quad \tau_{ijk} \geq 0, \quad \forall j \in J, \, k \in K. \tag{6}$$

Supply will equal demand in equilibrium. Thus, we define a bank's supply function as the transaction volume that maximizes a bank's profits. Formally, the supply function for bank-type i is given in equation (7):

$$\vec{s}_i(\vec{P}) = \left(\sum_{k \in K} \arg\max_{\vec{\tau}_i} \left(\pi_i(\vec{P}, \vec{\tau}_i) \right) \right)_{j \in J} \tag{7}$$

As all banks maximize their profit by choosing supply, the total supply of transactions in the market is noted as in equation (8):

$$\vec{S}(\vec{P}) = \left(\vec{S}_i(\vec{P}) \right)_{j \in J} = \left(\sum_{i \in I} m_i s_{ij}(\vec{P}) \right)_{j \in J} \tag{8}$$

Having defined consumers, banks, and demand and supply, we address the issue of equilibrium. Drawing on Arrow and Hahn's (1971) definition of equilibrium, a competitive equilibrium in this context must satisfy the following four conditions: each firm has decided whether or not to enter the market and each market entrant has chosen volumes to maximize individual profits. These two conditions signify that each firm has acted in its best interest and has no incentive to deviate. The third condition is that supply equals demand; standard for all competitive equilibrium models. Finally, no other bank can enter the market and earn a positive profit; i.e., no bank that has chosen not to enter has incentive to deviate. A formal definition follows.

Competitive Equilibrium with Free Entry: Let $\vec{D}(\vec{P})$ represent the vector of customer demands at full prices $\vec{P}$. A competitive equilibrium for a given vector of firm types $\vec{m}$ consists of a full price vector $\vec{P}^*$ and a vector of firms' transaction volume decisions, $\vec{\tau}^*$, such that $\vec{\tau}^* = \vec{s}_i(\vec{P}^*)$ for all $i \in I$,

$$\vec{S}(\vec{P}) = \left(\sum_{i \in I} m_i \tau_{ij} \right)_{j \in J} = \vec{D}(\vec{P}), \quad \text{and} \quad \pi_i(\vec{\tau}_i^*) = 0 \quad \text{for all } i \in I.$$

Existence and uniqueness of an equilibrium are accomplished by showing that a competitive equilibrium maximizes Social Welfare, the sum of firm profits and consumer surplus. We have constructed our model to fit the structure in Byers, Freimer and Lederer (2004) and refer the reader to that paper for a formal existence and uniqueness proofs. While equilibrium does exist and is unique, there is no closed form expression for the equilibrium outcome. As a result, we continue analysis of the model by conducting numerical tests with an efficient procedure.

3.   NUMERICAL EXAMPLE

This section presents sensitivity analysis that examines the effect of various parameters on the market equilibrium. The complexity of the model forces the sensitivity analysis to be done numerically. The analysis will examine the effect on equilibrium of changing customer demands, variable costs, and fixed costs of PC banking systems.

Values for the parameters in the analysis are estimates derived from industry publications. References include *American Banker Magazine* and the book *Distribution 2000: Developing and Implementing Strategies for Retail Financial Institutions*. Numbers gathered from those sources are representative of a wide range of banks and allow for a reasonable range for approximation. Note that the coefficients on the quadratic cost terms are not readily available from industry literature. The coefficients used in the analysis below are chosen empirically to represent the current number of banks in a market of about 500,000 people. Table 4 gives the point estimates and ranges for each of the parameters used in the analysis. We assume the diseconomy of scale for branch transactions is greater than that for ATM transactions, which is larger than that for PC banking. We assume that network ATMs exhibit the least diseconomy of scale effect due to the fact that those machines are owned by third parties and require neither maintenance nor marketing on behalf of the competing banks.

The sensitivity analysis uses the above parameters to examine the effects on the equilibrium mix of banks and transaction volumes of varying demand, variable costs and fixed cost. The solution procedure is written in *Mathematica*. The procedure finds the optimal quantities for a given vector of firms and then updates the vector of firms until KKT conditions are satisfied.

3.1.   Sensitivity Analysis and Relative Market Size

The first test examines the market outcome as demand shifts from the *b* segment to the *e* segment. The industry generally accepts that the number of those who are comfortable using PC technology will grow tremendously during the next several years. To conduct the test, the demand curve slopes are held constant while the intercepts are adjusted. The intercepts are varied as to maintain a constant total number of potential transactions (at zero price) of 28 million. The results are shown in Figures 1 and 2.

These results have interesting implications for an existing bank looking to survive in the market. Before electronic PC and Internet banking existed, all banks were, of necessity focused on branch delivery, corresponding to the first observation in Figure 1. As the *e* customer segment begins to grow (observation 2) all banks in the market keep their branch networks, and some of them add PC or Internet banking capabilities. Since the *e* segment is very small, PC banking overcapacity is an issue and not all banks add that channel. A bank

Table 14-4. Parameters

Parameters			
Variable Costs: linear		**Variable Costs: quadratic coefficients**	
c_{branch}	$0.55 per transaction	$d_{bbranch}$: b customer at Branch	6×10^{-7}
c_{ATM}	$0.30 per transaction	d_{bATM}: b customer at ATM (NATM)	9×10^{-7}
c_{PC}	$0.11 per transaction	$d_{ebranch}$: e customer at Branch	8×10^{-7}
c_{NATM}	$0.75 per transaction	d_{eATM}: e customer at ATM	7×10^{-7}
		d_{ePC}: e customer at Internet	6×10^{-7}
Customer travel costs			
β_b	$1.5 per mile	β_e	$2.25 per mile
Customer Disutility			
h_{bB}: b customer at Branch	0	h_{bATM}: b customer at ATM	2.5
h_{bATM}: b customer at PC	3.5	h_{eB}: e customer at Branch	1.75
h_{eATM}: e customer at ATM	0.75	h_{ePC}: e customer at PC	0
Fixed Costs (Annual fixed costs. One-time charges are amortized over 10 years.)			
Branch Placement: Cost Per Branch	$500,000 per branch	PC banking System	$50,000
Branch Network: Fixed Cost	$400,000	Overhead	$1,000,000
ATM/location	$100,000 per location	Start-up	$500,000
ATM network	$200,000		
Demand Coefficients			
a_1: Intercept	25	a_2: Intercept	10
b_1: Slope	1×10^{-6}	b_2: Slope	3.3×10^{-6}

that had been in the market previously could continue to function and compete successfully without electronic banking. On the other hand, as the e customer segment becomes a larger share of the market, our hypothetical bank will have to add Internet banking or be forced out of the market. Note also that there is market consolidation during the rise of the e customer segment, so some banks will be forced out of the market whether or not they adopt electronic banking, resulting in net exit. As total transaction volume tends to remain the same, the surviving banks will seek greater transaction volumes in both proprietary and third-party owned systems. This suggests that a bank that stays active in the market can rely on the third-party ATM networks as a strategy for serving higher volumes, as the bank incurs less cost due to congestion in that channel. Eventually, as the e customer segment becomes the dominant segment, most banks will convert to Internet only banks. Notice, however, that as long as there is some b customer demand, there will be at least one bank with a branch network active in the market.

We also chart the number of branches and proprietary ATMs that are used in the market, as shown in Figure 3. The total number of branches steadily

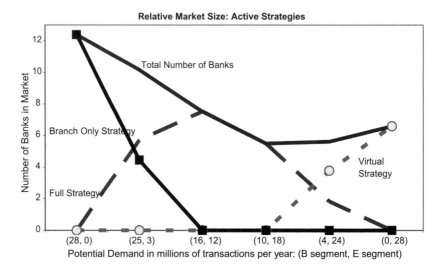

Figure 14-1. Number of banks resulting in market when relative size of the customer segments is varied.

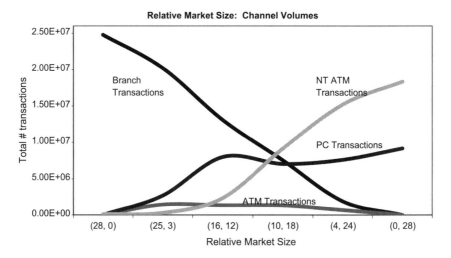

Figure 14-2. Total transaction volume through each technology as relative size of the customer segments is varied.

declines as the volume of *b* customers' transactions drops, and ATMs rise and fall with the Full strategy. The drop in branches is primarily due to the decline in the number of active banks, although individual Full Strategy banks do slowly remove branches. ATMs behave in the opposite way, however. When the number of ATMs (and total ATM transaction volume) in the market decreases, individual banks are actually *increasing* the size of their proprietary

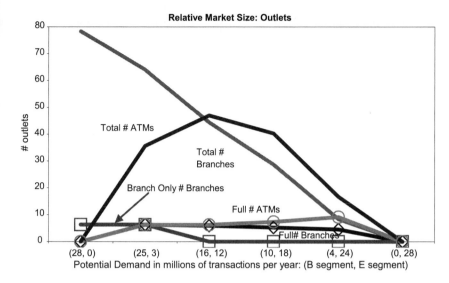

Figure 14-3. Number of branches and ATMs used by active banks as customer demand shifts from *b* customers to *e* customers.

ATM networks, by as much as 50%. As a bank alters its distribution system to meet changing market needs, it can avoid being forced out of the market by serving more of the growing *e* customer base with ATMs. Each bank grows their ATM network and ATM transaction volume, but consolidation leads to fewer total ATMs and transactions in the market.

Surprisingly, banks using both branches and ATMs place similar numbers of each. Banks in this model can choose the optimal number of branches and ATMs separately. Given that the fixed cost of each branch is 7.5 times the fixed cost of each ATM, one could expect that there would significant variability in the size of the branch network versus the bank's own ATM network. Figure 3 shows that this is not the case. While there is some difference—some growth in ATM network and some reduction of branches—in the penultimate observation, in most observations a bank keeps the same number of branches and proprietary ATMs. This result is driven by the consumer disutility for using an ATM. Both customer segments incur disutility and travel cost in using an ATM, thus limiting the profitability of that channel. As a result, banks tend to place fewer ATMs than one might expect.

Network ATMs figure prominently when *e* customers are the dominant segment. *e* customers experience less disutility at an ATM than do *b* customers; $0.75 versus $2.5. Further, while *e* customers have higher unit travel costs, the large number of available network ATMs limits the total travel cost incurred per transaction. Finally, as discussed previously, banks are able to place a high volume of *e* customers with the network ATMs since they incur little congestion cost in that channel. All of these factors combine to make network ATMs and important channel for serving the *e* customer segment.

3.2. Sensitivity Analysis on the Fixed Cost of PC Banking

This sensitivity test examines the effect of a range of fixed costs for PC banking systems. All other parameters are set to their base levels and the up front fixed cost of a PC banking system is varied. The results are presented in Figures 4 and 5.

As the fixed cost of PC banking falls, banks respond by adding PC and Internet systems. This result is expected; however, it is surprising that even though the mix of banks is changing, the total number of transactions served in the market remains constant for both customer segments. Thus, as PC banking systems become more affordable, the analysis shows that branch banks choose to become full banks, while roughly the same total number of transactions is served and the same number of competitors remains. Additionally, as PC banking systems become cheaper, transaction volume through PC banking and proprietary ATMs increases and Network ATM volume decreases. The shift from Branch Only banks to Full banks includes a transfer of *b* customers from Network ATMs to proprietary ATM systems. Thus, the affordability of PC banking systems also serves to boost the more "conventional" proprietary ATM channel. Some have suggested that as PC banking systems become ever cheaper, the *e* customer segment will be served by virtual banks, regardless of the relative size of the *e* segment. This analysis contradicts that supposition and suggests that banks can hold virtual competitors at bay by serving their customers in their preferred channel.

3.3. Sensitivity Analysis on the Density of Demand

This test varies the density of demand, i.e., the ratio of market sizes of the two customer segments is kept constant but the total market size is varied. This enables testing of the model in denser market regions. The results are presented in Figure 6.

This figure shows that when total demand is very small, only the branch only strategy is viable due to its low fixed cost and ability to serve *b* customers at their preferred channel. However, as demand grows, but the e customer segment remains relatively small, a bank doesn't need to radically alter strategy. A bank could be successful either using branches or both branches and Internet banking. That is to say that specialization in the *b* segment is a valid strategy. Notice that unlike the results from the analysis on the relative size of the customer segments (Figures 1 and 2) there is no specialization in the *e* segment. Some have suggested that one should expect to see virtual banks leveraging their low fixed costs to "steal" profitable *e* customers from the full banks. The

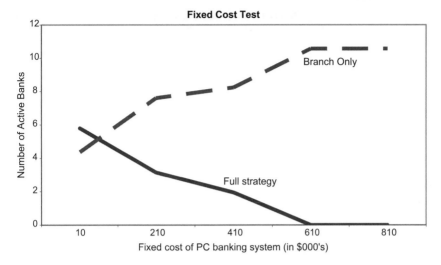

Figure 14-4. Number of banks in the market as the fixed cost of PC banking systems is varied.

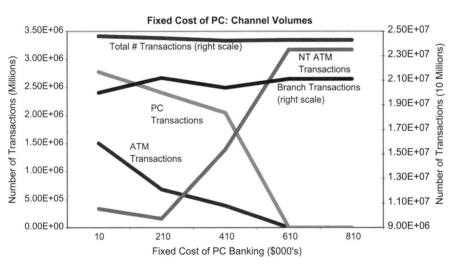

Figure 14-5. Transaction volumes in each channel as the fixed cost of PC Banking systems is varied.

sensitivity analysis supports the opposite. The full strategy is able to serve enough *e* customers through the lower-cost PC banking channel to prevent entry by virtual banks but leaves volume to be served by branch banks. This test suggests that unless the *e* customer segment grows relative to the *b* segment, the full strategy is the only one to serve *e* customers.

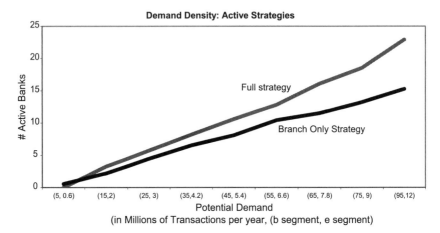

Figure 14-6. Number of banks in the market as total size of the market is increased.

Table 14-5. Number of banks, denoted (full, branch only), in the market as variable costs are varied

		Branch Variable Cost			
		$0.10	$0.55	$1.00	$3.00
PC Variable	$0.01	(5, 2.71)	(5.81, 1.32)	(6.67, 0)	(5.91, 0)
Cost	$0.10	(4.98, 4.76)	(5.18, 3.18)	(7.32, 0)	(6.24, 0)
	$0.25		(5.36, 4.23)	(6.39, 2.39)	(6.98, 0)
	$0.55		(4.42, 6.21)	(4.63, 5.8)	(7.09, 0)
	$1.00			(3.31, 7.34)	(7.24, 0)

3.4.   Variable Cost Parameters Example

This example considers the variable cost parameters for branch and PC transactions. The general industry wisdom is that a bank can respond to falling PC costs by migrating their customers to that system and, thus, there will be a rise in the number of full and virtual banks in the market. In the example, both variable cost parameters are tested at low, medium and high values. The variable cost of an ATM transaction is taken as the average of the branch and PC variable cost and the cost of a network ATM transaction is $2/3$ more than an ATM transaction. The results follow in Table 5.

The table shows that varying the variable cost parameter affects the outcome, but not as conventional wisdom would dictate. As branch costs increase to their highest level, though branch only banks exit the market, virtual strategies still do not enter. This result suggests that without a shift in customer preferences, variable cost alone does not imply widespread changes in how banks compete in the market.

4. CONCLUSION AND FUTURE RESEARCH FOR RETAIL BANKING MODEL

The rise of the information economy has had a profound impact on retail banking distribution strategy. New technologies, new information systems and their convergence have thrown much of the industry into confusion. The result has been a variety of banks attempting an array of distribution strategies, some apparently successful and some wildly disastrous. This paper sheds light on the choice of distributions strategy by banks taking into account the competitive market for retail banking services. The model is based on perfect competition and characterizes the equilibrium distribution strategy choice. It includes heterogeneous consumers and explores six bank strategies that are modeled after practical bank moves in the U.S. banking market. Finally, numerical examples shows how several parameters affect the equilibrium outcome and suggests how an existing bank can alter its distribution strategy under various market conditions.

Assuming two customer segments and six strategies, the examples demonstrate that a bank needs to focus on the relative size of the customer segments. Specifically, when the *e* customer segment is dominated by the *b* customer segment, some banks will add Internet capabilities, but a branch-focus is still a viable strategy. Then, as the number of consumers that prefer PC transactions increases *and* the number of customers that prefer branches decreases, a bank will need to add Internet capabilities and then make that channel the primary focus until, when there are only *e* customers extant, there are no more branches. This result contrasts with the analysis in which the relative size of the customer segments was kept constant while the overall size of the market was varied. That test demonstrated that even though the magnitude of the *e* customer segment increased, an existing bank could hold virtual banks at bay simply by incorporating Internet systems into their strategy. This move allows the existing bank to keep their *e* customers by giving them what they want and to keep their *b* customer base.

Additionally we examine both proprietary and network ATM use. The tests show that ATMs, despite their drastically lower cost structure are generally deployed in the same numbers as branches due to the disutility incurred at ATMs by both customer segments. We also show that network ATMs play a significant part of a bank's strategy when the *e* customer segment is the majority. Network ATMs are attractive to a bank despite their high variable cost because the bank incurs little congestion cost.

Further, the analysis demonstrates that the equilibrium is relatively insensitive to technology cost differences. Only when the difference between PC and branch transactions is at its greatest do all banks add PC systems. However, when the difference in costs is not as high, strategy choices in equilibrium are unaffected.

These results suggest that changing consumer behavior and attitudes, instead of banks' cost structure, effects significant changes in distribution strategy. If the segment of consumers that prefer PC banking remains small relative to the segment that prefers branches then there will still be a market for specialized branch banks and the full banks can prohibit successful entry of virtual banks. However, if the e segment grows at the expense of the b segment, as some have predicted, the model predicts that banks will first need to add Internet systems and then, eventually, make that the primary (or only) proprietary channel.

The current analysis is illuminating but leaves room for further work. For example, network externalities may well play a role in the type of banking competition that we have modeled. Thus, adding a component of network externalities could be a good extension of the current model. Further, we have limited ourselves to two customer segments for ease of exposition; a finer segmentation may also contribute to the effectiveness of this work.

REFERENCES

Arrow, Kenneth J. and Hahn, Frank H., *General Competitive Analysis*, North-Holland, 1971.

Bauer, James L. "Distribution 2000: Developing and Implementing Strategies for Retail Financial Institutions" *Lafferty Publications*, 1995.

Beato, Paulina, "The Existence of Marginal Cost Pricing Equilibria with Increasing Returns" *The Quarterly Journal of Economics*, Vol. 97, Iss. 4, November 1982.

Byers, Reynold, Freimer, Marshall, and Lederer, Phillip J., "Retail Banking Choice of Distribution Strategy in a Competitive Market", Working Paper, 2004.

Chelst, Schultz and Sanghvi, "Issues and Decision Aids for Designing Branch Networks" *Journal of Retail Banking*, Vol. 10, Iss. 2, Summer 1988.

Eliopoulis and Kouzelis, "Branch Planning Through Decentralized Marketing and Regional Analysis Studies," *European Journal of Operational Research*, Vol. 30, Iss. 1, June 1987.

Harker, Patrick, "Introduction: the Service Quality and Productivity Challenge," in: The Service Quality and Productivity Challenge, Patrick T. Harker (ed.), Kluwer Academic Publishers, 1995, 1–10.

Hopmans, "A Spatial Interaction Model for Branch Bank Accounts," *European Journal of Operational Research*, Vol. 27, Iss. 2, November 1986.

Power, Carol, "Citi f/I Closure Shows Branches Still Matter: Internet-only banks seems to be losing steam," *American Banker Magazine*, June 27, 2000.

Prasad, B. and Harker, P., "Pricing Online Banking Services Amid Network Externalities," Working Paper, 2000.

Stoneman, Bill, "Online Transactions Finally Reach Critical Mass," *American Banker Magazine*, July 23, 2002.

Chapter 15

A PROACTIVE DEMAND MANAGEMENT MODEL FOR CONTROLLING E-RETAILER INVENTORY

Uday M. Apte[a] and S. Viswanathan[b]

[a]*Graduate School of Business and Public Policy, Naval Postgraduate School, 555 Dyer Road, Monterey, CA 93943, e-mail: umapte@nps.edu;* [b]*Nanyang Business School, Nanyang Technological University, Singapore 639798, e-mail: vish@pmail.ntu.edu.sg*

Abstract   The web-based buying process requires the buyer to navigate through a series of web pages. Moreover, the web pages for a particular buyer can be customized based on his general profile and previous purchasing behavior. Hence, as compared to a traditional retailer, the e-retailer (who sells products directly to customers through the Internet) is able to exercise a much greater influence over the demand level for its products. This allows an e-retailer to proactively dampen the demand for a niche product and guide the customers to generic substitutes when the on-hand inventory level is low relative to the sales rate. Use of *proactive demand management* (PDM) can reduce inventory related costs and improve the overall profits.

In this paper, we develop a model for e-retailers exercising PDM by adjusting the display prominence of a product to control its supply chain inventory. The demand realized for the product is deterministic but dependant on the level of prominence with which the product is displayed on the web pages. The model considers two levels of prominence for the product's display. When the product is displayed prominently, all the potential demand is captured. When the product is displayed less prominently, part of the demand for the product is guided to a generic product which has better economies of scale. The price of the product is fixed and there are standard inventory costs such as holding cost, penalty cost and ordering cost. The objective is to maximize the long-run average profits per year. We derive closed form equations for the optimal parameter values for implementing PDM.

A numerical analysis is performed to estimate the benefits of PDM. The numerical analysis reveals that PDM can increase profits by as much as 12%. PDM is more beneficial when a larger proportion of the potential demand for the product can be guided to a generic substitute. PDM is a beneficial strategy to adopt when the inventory related costs per unit of demand are significant compared to the profit margin.

Keywords: Retail inventory management, e-retailing, retail supply chain management, inventory control, B2C ecommerce, marketing-operations interface, proactive demand management

1. INTRODUCTION

The spectacular rise and equally spectacular fall in the fortunes of many dotcom companies is a much-publicized phenomenon of the recent past. However, the fact remains that e-Commerce is transforming business processes of entire industries in the U.S. and elsewhere in the world, and few companies are likely to flourish long without consciously responding to the opportunities and challenges presented by Internet. *e-Retailing*, which involves sale of products directly to customers through the Internet, is a major component of the consumer-oriented activity in e-business. Since the Internet is an information-intensive environment that allows for greater interactivity with customers, e-retailing has the potential to dramatically transform the way the marketing and operations function are managed for achieving better business results.

One innovative action that the e-retailer can take lies at the intersection of marketing and operations. The web-based buying process requires a customer to navigate through a series of web pages. Moreover, the web pages for a particular buyer can be customized based on his general profile and previous purchasing behavior. Hence, by suitably designing the web pages, the e-retailer is able to control the navigation process, offer the customer a suitable set of products to choose from, and thereby appropriately manage the demand level. The e-retailer can thus proactively manage the demand for its products. In this paper, we focus on a specific type of *proactive demand management* (PDM) strategy, where the demand is proactively managed by adjusting the prominence of display of the product. We develop a model for e-retailers exercising PDM by adjusting the display prominence of a product to control its inventory.

The practice of prominent display tactics to promote greater demand for items has been common in traditional grocery stores and supermarkets. For instance, the shelf space in a regular store that is at the eye level, end of the aisles, or the entry or checkout area of the store carries a premium as it tends to attract the customer's attention more easily. But unlike in a traditional store, an e-retailer has the capability to both increase as well as dampen demand by adjusting the display prominence. Moreover, this can be done dynamically without any physical effort of moving the products.

The motivation for the PDM model and the related research addressed in this paper were triggered by the practices adopted by JCPenney.com, the Internet retailing arm of JCPenney, one of the largest U.S. retailer of apparel and other merchandize. A customer navigating the JCPenney web site can get a particular category of items displayed by choosing the appropriate category through the menu tree or through a search. Typically, a particular category of item is displayed in a sequence of web pages. For example, if one chose to view "Men's Polo Shirts", the possible choices would be displayed over three to four pages with about nine specific items displayed in a page. The customer would have to click to the next page to view the next set of items in the category. When JCPenney.com desires to prominently display a certain item, say a particular polo shirt for men, the company displays it in the first page under the category.

Upon reaching a sufficiently low inventory level relative to the ongoing sales rate for the item, the company attempts to reduce the expected stockout costs by dampening the item's demand by displaying it in the third or fourth page under the category. At the extreme, when the company is completely out of stock of an item, it simply stops displaying the item on the web page so that the buyer never even gets to order it. Thus, JCPenney proactively dampens the demand for a product when its on-hand inventory level is lower relative to the sales rate, and thereby attempts to reduce the stockout and other inventory related costs, and increase the average contribution margin. Based on interviews with the managers at JCPenney.com, we understand that they are able to decrease or increase demand significantly by adjusting the display prominence of an item. Their web site design and continual updating of product displays on the web site is based on this premise of proactively managing the demand.

The experience of JCPenney illustrates the opportunities available to e-retailers in selling fashion goods. However, given the general applicability of the PDM strategy, it can also be beneficially used by e-retailers that sell routinely purchased items such as the grocery goods, non-fashion apparel, or household goods. Consider for example a niche product such as a particular brand of Muselix breakfast cereal. One may reasonably assume that among those that buy Muselix, there exist two types of customers; those that are die hard loyalists of the cereal who will not substitute it with any other cereal in case of a stockout, and others who may be willing to consider purchasing a more widely used generic product, such as corn flakes. Given the fact that there is a set of loyal customers who will only buy the niche product, it is clearly worthwhile for the e-retailer to stock and offer this product. At the same time, the overall demand for the niche product is bound to be relatively smaller compared to a more widely used generic product. Therefore, the marginal inventory related cost for satisfying an additional unit of demand would be much lower for the generic product.[1] Therefore, if the profit margin

---

[1] This is assuming that the cost parameters for the generic product are equal to or of the same order as that for the niche product. Recall from the economic order quantity (EOQ) model that the total cost is a function of the square root of demand. Therefore, the total inventory

for the generic product is similar to that for the niche product, it would be cost effective to encourage the not-so-loyal customers of the niche product to substitute to the generic product, especially when the inventory level for the niche product is low. In this case, the e-retailer or e-grocer could display the Muselix cereal prominently during a certain fraction of the inventory replenishment cycle when the inventory level is high or when receipt of new supplies are imminent, and thereafter, upon reaching a sufficiently low inventory level, display the cereal less prominently while subtly guiding the customers to a generic product.

While we are not aware of the specifics of how PDM is implemented in companies other than JCPenney, we believe that virtually any e-retailer or e-grocer can benefit from the PDM strategy by suitably adjusting their product display tactics. Unlike the case of JCPenney.com, most e-groceries such as Peapod.com presently list all the items within a product-category in a certain order. The default in the case of Peapod.com is to list the items in alphabetic order. However, the customer has the option to sort the list according to attributes such as price, unit price, weight and popularity and specific product attributes such as calories, carbohydrate content, and cholesterol. Moreover, unlike JCPenney.com, e-groceries such as Peapod list all the items in a product-category in a single, scroll down page. For example under the category of "Breakfast cereals-cold grain", there are about forty five items and all are listed in a single page that one can scroll down. Therefore, all the items that are listed and displayed under a product-category have the same level of display prominence for a particular customer.

The web pages can however be customized for different categories of customers based on their individual demographics and previous purchase behavior. Hence, during prominent display, the product could be listed under its particular product-category to all customers, while during less prominent display the product is displayed only to certain groups of customers who are more loyal to the particular product.[2] This can be done by having a "display-flag" field for the item record in the product database. The information about each customer's loyalty [i.e., degree of willingness (or lack of it) to substitute to a more widely used generic product] to the particular product can be stored in the customer database based on the customer's past purchase behavior. When the display-flag for an item suggests less prominent display, and the customer's loyalty to the item is low, then the item is not displayed (nor listed under its

---

related cost is concave with respect to the demand, and the marginal cost decreases as the demand increases.

[2] We could in fact have different levels of displays depending on the categories or number of customers to whom the product is displayed during less prominent display. We only deal with two levels of displays in this paper. The multi-level display model is taken up in an extension to this paper.

product-category) to the particular customer. Instead the particular customer gets guided to a more widely used generic product that is always listed or displayed prominently.

The research presented in this paper addresses this potential application of managing the demand proactively for the niche product by adjusting the display prominence for the product. Specifically, we develop a model for e-retailers exercising proactive demand management of a product to control their inventory. The demand for the product is assumed to be deterministic, but dependent on the level of prominence of display of the product on the customers' web pages. The model considers two levels of prominence for the product's display. When the product is displayed prominently, all the potential demand is captured. When the product is not displayed prominently, a portion of the potential customers substitute to a more widely used generic product with a possibly different profit margin, and a certain proportion of the potential customers may leave the web site without buying any product. The price of the product is fixed and there are standard inventory costs such as holding cost, penalty cost and ordering cost. The objective is to maximize the long-run average profits per year. We derive closed form equations for the optimal parameter values for implementing PDM. The results we derive show that the proportion of time demand is proactively managed through less prominent display is directly proportional to the inventory holding cost, penalty cost, ordering cost and the extent to which the potential demand for the niche product can be guided successfully to a generic substitute. It is inversely proportional to the profit margin of the product.

A numerical analysis is performed to estimate the benefits of PDM. The numerical analysis reveals that PDM can increase profits by as much as 12%. PDM is more beneficial when a larger proportion of the potential demand for the niche product can be guided to a generic product. PDM is a beneficial strategy to adopt when the inventory related costs per unit of demand are significant compared to the profit margin.

The classical inventory models treat demand levels (or their distributions) as given, and then derive the inventory policies that minimize the total cost. In contrast, by proactively managing the demand, the e-retailer is able to simultaneously increase the total revenue from the niche and the generic products while keeping the inventory holding and stockout costs low. The principal contributions of this research are to (i) extend classical inventory models to deal with the PDM approach in e-retailing, (ii) develop model solutions, and (iii) generate managerial insights by identifying conditions under which the PDM approach can be beneficially used.

The rest of the paper is organized as follows. In the remainder of this section, we provide a survey of related research in the literature. In the next section, we explain the assumptions underlying the model and define the notation we use. In the two sections thereafter, we present two cases of the PDM model, with the former section dealing with a situation with no backlogging of demand allowed and the latter addressing a situation when backlogging is allowed. Thereafter, we present results of a numerical study including a sensitivity analysis, and identify conditions under which PDM approach can be beneficially implemented. Finally, we conclude the paper with a summary and a few closing remarks on the potential for future research.

1.1. Review of Related Research

There are three main bodies of specific research related to the work in this paper. One body of related research deals with models for management of product assortment and allocation of shelf space for traditional retailers. For a traditional retailer, the demand realized for the products depend on how they are displayed on the shelf. Therefore, the assortment of the products carried, the amount of shelf space allocated to them and their inventory levels have an impact on the demand. Papers addressing the issue of product assortment decisions include Urban (1969), Shugan (1989) and Mahajan and van Ryzin (2001). Papers dealing with shelf space allocation include Cairns (1962, 1963), Curhan (1972, 1973), Corstjens and Doyle (1981), Zufryden (1986), Bultez and Naert (1988), and Bultez et al. (1989). The problem of simultaneous determination of product assortments and shelf space allocation have been addressed by Anderson and Amato (1974), Borin et al. (1994) and Borin and Farris (1995).

A related problem area is inventory models with demand dependant on the inventory level. Papers dealing with this issue include Baker and Urban (1988a, 1988b) and Urban (1992). Urban (1998) addresses the problem of simultaneously determining the product assortments, shelf space and inventory control decisions. This body of research has some similarity to the problem addressed in this paper, since for a traditional retailer, demand can be manipulated by adjusting the shelf space allocation and inventory level. However, unlike an e-retailer practicing PDM, for a traditional retailer, demand cannot be adjusted dynamically as shelf space allocations remain fixed for a period of time. It would also be difficult for a traditional retailer to guide the consumers proactively to alternative products when the inventory level for the product is low but non-zero. Another body of literature that is related to the underlying problem studied in this paper is inventory models for substitutable products. Most of the research in this area study single period problems with probabilistic demand. Two of the earliest work on this problem was done by Veinott (1965) and Ignall and Veinott (1969). Subsequent analysis of the single period problem with substitutable products were carried out by McGillivray and Silver (1978), Parlar and Goyal (1984), and Pasternack and Drezner (1991).

More recent papers involving single period and multiple products include Bassok, Anupindi and Akella (1999), Smith and Agrawal (2000), and Mahajan and van Ryzin (2001). Inventory models for substitutable products, deterministic demand and infinite horizon were addressed by Drezner, Gurnani and Pasternack (1995) and Gurnani and Drezner (2000). In inventory models with substitution, the basic assumption is that a fraction of customers substitute demand to another product if their preferred product is out of stock. However, the demand is still generated externally and the retailer is just a passive demand taker. In the proposed paper, the e-retailer proactively manages demand and encourages substitution and in fact substitution takes place even before the product is out of stock.

The third body of related research looks at inventory models where demand is influenced by the pricing decision. Some of earlier research efforts in this area include those by Whitin (1955), Kunreuther and Schrage (1973) and Fershtman and Spiegel (1986). One recent paper that has looked at pricing and inventory decisions in the context of e-retailing is Bhargava, Sun and Xu (2006), who consider models for e-retailer for stock-less operation. Unlike in our paper, they assume that part of the demand can be lost during periods of stockouts as this will increase the delivery lead time for the customer. They look at how pricing can be used a strategy to encourage customers to place orders during periods of stockouts when the delivery lead time is higher. Thus pricing is used as a tool to reduce the inventory costs, but demand is still exogenously determined, albeit based on the pricing decision of the e-retailer.

2.   MODEL PRELIMINARIES AND NOTATION

As discussed earlier, the model we develop specifically addresses the needs of e-retailers who use their web site to display and sell products online. The proposed model is targeted at such items as grocery goods, non-fashion apparel, or household goods, that are routinely purchased and for which the as-

Table 15-1. Notation

D_H	High demand rate (units/year) resulting from a prominent display
D_L	Low demand rate (units/year) resulting from a less prominent display, $D_L < D_H$
T	Inventory replenishment cycle time (year)
α	Fraction of the cycle time during which D_H, the high demand rate, is realized, $(0 \le \alpha \le 1)$
K	Order cost ($/order)
h	Inventory holding cost ($/unit-year)
π	Profit contribution per unit excluding inventory costs ($/unit)
m	Profit adjustment factor for potential demand not satisfied directly by the product during less prominent display. The appendix provides details on how m can be calculated.

sumption of deterministic demand is reasonable. Further, the model is particularly useful to e-retailers selling a niche product to two types of customers: a core group of loyal customers who will not purchase an alternative product, and other customers who may be willing to buy a more widely used generic product when the niche product is not available or is displayed less prominently. The notation used in the model is defined in Table 1.

The inventory for the product is replenished on a fixed cycle and the main issues facing an e-retailer are determining the length of the inventory replenishment cycle, T, and the way demand is to be proactively managed. The level of prominence with which a product is displayed on the company's web site is the primary lever used by the retailer to influence, and proactively manage, the demand for the product. Thus, when the item is prominently displayed on the retailer's web site, demand at a (relatively) higher rate, D_H, is generated for the product. Such prominent display is used for a fraction α of the inventory cycle. During the remaining part of the inventory cycle, the item is displayed less prominently, resulting in a lower demand rate, D_L.

In this scenario, when the product is displayed less prominently, the lower demand rate, D_L, for the product is assumed to come from a set of loyal customers who strongly prefer the product under consideration and have a zero product substitution rate. The remaining potential customers, who represent a potential reduction of $(D_H - D_L)$ in demand for the product, are diverted to a generic (substitute) product. The profit margin realized during the period with less prominent display is therefore generated by the sales of both the niche product and as well as the generic product. However, not all the potential customers end up buying the generic product; a portion of the potential customers do purchase the generic product, while the remaining customers leave the e-retailer's Web site without purchasing any product. It is implicitly assumed that the inventory cost parameters (K and h) for the generic product are similar to (or of the same order as) that for the niche product. It is also assumed that the demand rate for the generic product is higher as it is a more widely used item.[3] The inventory related costs are concave with respect to demand (based on a straightforward application of the EOQ formula). Therefore, the marginal inventory related costs of satisfying a part of the demand difference

---

[3] As the generic product (such as corn flakes) is more widely used, the assumption of higher demand is not unreasonable. However, it is not necessary that the generic product has higher demand than the niche product. The only requirement is that the combination of revenue/profit margin, substitution loss and cost effects for the generic product should leave the profit adjustment factor m reasonably small. In other words, for the PDM strategy in our model to work, the generic product should either have higher demand rate or lower values of the inventory cost parameters (K, h&p). Also, the demand difference ($D_H - D_L$) could be diverted to more than one generic product. [See the discussion on the calculation of the profit adjustment factor m in the appendix].

$(D_H - D_L)$ through the generic product would be lower than if it was satisfied with the original, niche product. This is one of the motivations for the use of the PDM strategy.

We define a profit adjustment factor m ($0 \le m \le 1$) in the model to capture (i) the portion of the demand difference $(D_H - D_L)$ that is not substituted; (ii) the marginal inventory related costs incurred on the generic product and (iii) the difference in profit contribution if any between the original product and the generic substitute. Thus, during less prominent display, the profit contribution will be generated at a rate of $[\pi D_L + (1 - m)\pi(D_H - D_L)] = [\pi D_H - m\pi(D_H - D_L)]$. Additional discussion on how the profit adjustment factor m can be calculated is provided in the Appendix.

We assume that the lead time for replenishment of the product is zero, but non-zero lead time can be easily incorporated as the demand is deterministic.

3. PROACTIVE DEMAND MANAGEMENT WITH NO BACKLOGGING OF DEMAND

First, we consider the case where no backlogging of demand is allowed and formulate a profit-maximization model. Note that in every inventory cycle, for a given fraction α of prominent display, it is always better to have the prominent display (D_H) first, and the less prominent display (D_L) next, since this leads to lower average inventory level (and same average demand) as compared to the opposite sequence (first D_L and then D_H). Given this consideration, the inventory cycle will be as shown in Figure 1, where s is defined

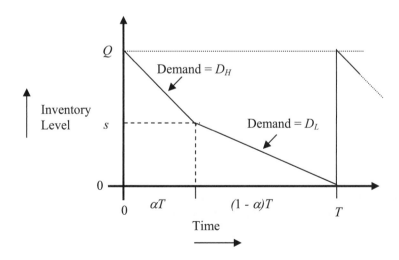

Figure 15-1. Inventory Diagram (with no backlogging of demand).

as the critical inventory level for switching from prominent to less prominent display.

The average inventory level

$$\bar{I} = \frac{1}{T}\left[\left(\frac{\alpha}{2}D_H T + (1-\alpha)D_L T\right)\alpha T + \left(\frac{(1-\alpha)}{2}D_L T\right)(1-\alpha)T\right]$$

$$= \frac{T}{2}\left[(D_H - D_L)\alpha^2 + D_L\right]$$

During high and low demand periods, the profit contribution, excluding inventory holding costs, will be generated respectively at the rates of πD_H and $[\pi D_L + (1-m)\pi(D_H - D_L)]$. The average profit contribution per year

$$R = \alpha\pi D_H + (1-\alpha)\left[\pi D_H - \pi m(D_H - D_L)\right]$$

$$= \pi D_H - \pi m(D_H - D_L) + \pi m\alpha(D_H - D_L)$$

Accounting for the ordering and inventory holding costs, we get the average annual profit,

$$Z = \pi m\alpha(D_H - D_L) + \pi\left[D_H - m(D_H - D_L)\right]$$
$$- \frac{K}{T} - \frac{hT}{2}\left[(D_H - D_L)\alpha^2 + D_L\right] \tag{1}$$

For any given α, the optimal value of T that minimizes Z is given by

$$T = \sqrt{\frac{2K}{h[(D_H - D_L)\alpha^2 + D_L]}} \tag{2}$$

Substituting equation (2) into (1), we can express Z as just a function of α as shown below.

$$Z(\alpha) = (D_H - D_L)\pi m\alpha + \pi\left(D_H - m(D_H - D_L)\right)$$
$$- \sqrt{2Kh[(D_H - D_L)\alpha^2 + D_L]} \tag{3}$$

Since the fraction of the inventory cycle time with high demand cannot be more than 1, we have the constraint $0 \leq \alpha \leq 1$. Therefore, the profit-maximizing model can be formally defined as

Maximize $Z(\alpha)$

s.t. $0 \leq \alpha \leq 1$

It can be shown that $Z(\alpha)$ is concave in the feasible region of α. From the first order condition with respect to α, we get

$$\frac{dZ}{d\alpha} = (D_H - D_L)\pi m - \frac{(\sqrt{2Kh})\alpha(D_H - D_L)}{\sqrt{(D_H - D_L)\alpha^2 + D_L}} = 0 \tag{4}$$

Simplifying equation (4) we get

$$\frac{(2Kh)\alpha^2}{(\pi m)^2} = (D_H - D_L)\alpha^2 + D_L$$

or

$$\alpha^2 \left[\frac{2Kh}{(\pi m)^2} - (D_H - D_L) \right] = D_L \tag{5}$$

Note that for $0 \le \alpha \le 1$,

$$\frac{dZ}{d\alpha} = (D_H - D_L)\pi m \left[1 - \sqrt{\frac{2Kh}{(\pi m)^2}} \sqrt{\frac{1}{[(D_H - D_L) + (D_L/\alpha^2)]}} \right]$$

$$\ge (D_H - D_L)\pi m \left[1 - \sqrt{\frac{2Kh}{(\pi m)^2}} \sqrt{\frac{1}{D_H}} \right]$$

Therefore, if $\frac{2Kh}{(\pi m)^2} \le D_H$, $\frac{dZ}{d\alpha} \ge 0$, for $0 \le \alpha < 1$. Hence, $\alpha = 1$ will maximize Z in that case. Otherwise equation (5) gives

$$\alpha = \sqrt{\frac{D_L}{\frac{2Kh}{(\pi m)^2} - (D_H - D_L)}} \tag{6}$$

The optimal value of α therefore is,

$$\alpha = \begin{cases} 1 & \text{if } \frac{2Kh}{(\pi m)^2} \le D_H \\ \sqrt{\frac{D_L}{\frac{2Kh}{(\pi m)^2} - (D_H - D_L)}} & \text{otherwise} \end{cases} \tag{7}$$

The closed form expression for the optimal value of α is given by equation (7). The optimal replenishment cycle T and the corresponding profit Z can be obtained by substituting for α into equations (2) and (3). Note from equation (7) above, that when $\pi m \ge (\sqrt{2KhD_H}/D_H)$, $\alpha = 1$. In other words, when the profit contribution per unit that is lost (by guiding part of the niche product demand to the generic product) is higher than the average per unit inventory related costs of the niche product, then it is best to display the niche product prominently all the time and not have PDM at all.

Proposition 1: *In the model for proactive demand management with no backlogging of demand, the optimal policy displays the following property:*

$$\alpha = \text{Min}\left\{1, \frac{\pi m}{hT}\right\}, \quad \textit{i.e., either } \alpha = 1 \textit{ or } \alpha = \frac{\pi m}{hT} \tag{8}$$

PROOF. Provided in the Appendix. □

Remarks and managerial insights Proposition 1 implies that the fraction of time the prominent display is used is (a) proportional to πm; (b) inversely proportional to the holding cost rate, h; and (c) inversely proportional to the optimal cycle time, and therefore inversely proportional to the order cost, K. This means that the optimal proportion of time in an inventory cycle when the demand is proactively managed through less prominent display, $(1 - \alpha)$, is directly proportional to the inventory holding cost, ordering cost and the extent to which the potential demand for the niche product can be guided successfully to a generic product. It is inversely proportional to the profit margin of the product.

Note that when $m = 0, \alpha = 0$. When the profit adjustment factor $m = 0$, it implies that during less prominent display, all the demand difference $(D_H - D_L)$ can be guided to a generic product and the same revenue $[\pi(D_H - D_L)]$ can be obtained without incurring any inventory cost for this demand. In this case, we would obviously want to have less prominent display all the time and guide all the potential demand that is substitutable to a generic product. While this is a theoretical possibility, it would be unlikely in practice. Even if the profit margin for the generic product were much higher, there would still be substitution loss (as there would be some customers who would just turn away from the web site especially if the price of the generic product is higher). If the profit margin for the generic product is much higher, m could be even be negative. The model developed will still work and the optimal $\alpha = 0$. The insights in this case are similar to the case for $m = 0$, and again this would be unlikely in practice.

4. PROACTIVE DEMAND MANAGEMENT WITH BACKLOGGING OF DEMAND ALLOWED

As discussed earlier, in the part of the cycle when the inventory level is positive, we will first have high demand and then low-demand, if any, as this

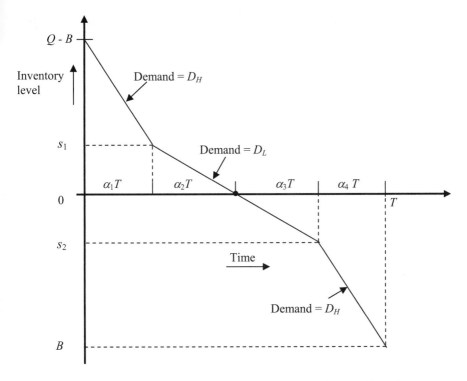

Figure 15-2. Inventory Diagram (with backlogging of demand allowed).

minimizes the inventory holding cost. By the same logic, in the part of the cycle when there is backlog (or negative inventory position), it is better to have low demand first and high demand next, as this generates the backlog at a slower rate and reduces the penalty cost. In other words, in a general situation for PDM with backlogging allowed, the inventory curve would be shaped as shown in Figure 2.

When the replenishment is just received, the inventory level is high, and therefore the item is prominently displayed on the web page to generate high demand. The prominent display is used for α_1 fraction of the inventory cycle. After the inventory drops to a certain critical level, s_1, the item is less prominently displayed leading to low demand. The inventory level reaches zero after α_2 fraction of the inventory cycle and the demand is backlogged thereafter for the α_3 fraction of the inventory cycle. It should be noted that before the next replenishment is received, at the critical inventory position, s_2, the item is prominently displayed again to take advantage of the imminent stock receipts and to generate higher demand. The prominent display is used for the remaining fraction, α_4, of the inventory cycle.

We develop a profit maximization model for the situation shown in Figure 2. We use the same notation as before. Additionally, we use p to represent penalty cost rate for backlogged demand (dollars per unit per year).

$$\text{The average inventory level} = \frac{D_H \alpha_1^2 T}{2} + D_L \alpha_1 \alpha_2 T + \frac{D_L \alpha_2^2 T}{2}$$

$$= \frac{T}{2}\left(D_H \alpha_1^2 + 2D_L \alpha_1 \alpha_2 + D_L \alpha_2^2\right)$$

$$\text{The average shortage/backlog level} = \frac{D_L \alpha_3^2 T}{2} + D_L \alpha_3 \alpha_4 T + \frac{D_H \alpha_4^2 T}{2}$$

$$= \frac{T}{2}\left(D_L \alpha_3^2 + 2D_L \alpha_3 \alpha_4 + D_H \alpha_4^2\right)$$

Hence, the average inventory related costs per year, or the total of average order, inventory holding, and back order costs per year, is given by

$$TC = \frac{K}{T} + \frac{hT}{2}\left(D_H \alpha_1^2 + 2D_L \alpha_1 \alpha_2 + D_L \alpha_2^2\right)$$

$$+ \frac{pT}{2}\left(D_L \alpha_3^2 + 2D_L \alpha_3 \alpha_4 + D_H \alpha_4^2\right)$$

The average annual profit contribution, excluding inventory related costs, is

$$R = \pi \left[D_H(\alpha_1 + \alpha_4) + D_L(\alpha_2 + \alpha_3) + (1 - m)(D_H - D_L)(\alpha_2 + \alpha_3)\right]$$

Since $\alpha_1 + \alpha_2 + \alpha_3 + \alpha_4 = 1$,

$$R = \pi D_H - \pi m(\alpha_2 + \alpha_3)(D_H - D_L)$$

Hence, average profit per year

$$Z = \pi D_H - \pi m(\alpha_2 + \alpha_3)(D_H - D_L)$$

$$- \frac{K}{T} - \frac{hT}{2}\left(D_H \alpha_1^2 + 2D_L \alpha_1 \alpha_2 + D_L \alpha_2^2\right)$$

$$- \frac{pT}{2}\left(D_L \alpha_3^2 + 2D_L \alpha_3 \alpha_4 + D_H \alpha_4^2\right) \tag{9}$$

For a given value of $\alpha = \{\alpha_1, \alpha_2, \alpha_3, \alpha_4\}$, the optimal value of T that maximizes Z is given by

$$T = \sqrt{\frac{2K}{[h(D_H\alpha_1^2 + 2D_L\alpha_1\alpha_2 + D_L\alpha_2^2) + p(D_L\alpha_3^2 + 2D_L\alpha_3\alpha_4 + D_H\alpha_4^2)]}}$$

(10)

Substituting (10) into (9), we get

$$Z(\alpha_1, \alpha_2, \alpha_3, \alpha_4) = \pi D_H - \pi m(\alpha_2 + \alpha_3)(D_H - D_L)$$

$$- \sqrt{2Kh(D_H\alpha_1^2 + 2D_L\alpha_1\alpha_2 + D_L\alpha_2^2) + 2Kp(D_L\alpha_3^2 + 2D_L\alpha_3\alpha_4 + D_H\alpha_4^2)}$$

(11)

The profit maximization model can be defined as

(P)   Maximize $Z(\alpha_1, \alpha_2, \alpha_3, \alpha_4)$

s.t. $\alpha_1 + \alpha_2 + \alpha_3 + \alpha_4 = 1$ (12)

and $0 \leq \alpha_1, \alpha_2, \alpha_3, \alpha_4$ (13)

It can be shown that Z as given in (11) is a jointly concave function of $\alpha_1, \alpha_2, \alpha_3$, and α_4 in the feasible region of α.

The Kuhn Tucker (KT) conditions for the problem (P) are

$$\frac{\partial Z}{\partial \alpha_i} + \lambda + u_i = 0, \quad i = 1, 2, 3, 4 \text{ and}$$

(14)

$$u_i\alpha_i = 0, \quad i = 1, 2, 3, 4$$

(15)

where λ is the dual variable corresponding to constraint (12), and u_i, $i = 1, \ldots, 4$, are the dual variables corresponding to constraint (13). Rewriting (14) for each i, the KT conditions corresponding to (14) can be written as

$$-\sqrt{\frac{2K}{\psi}}(hD_H\alpha_1 + hD_L\alpha_2) + \lambda + u_1 = 0$$

(16)

$$-\pi m(D_H - D_L) - \sqrt{\frac{2K}{\psi}}(hD_L\alpha_1 + hD_L\alpha_2) + \lambda + u_2 = 0$$

(17)

$$-\pi m(D_H - D_L) - \sqrt{\frac{2K}{\psi}}(pD_L\alpha_3 + pD_L\alpha_4) + \lambda + u_3 = 0$$

(18)

$$-\sqrt{\frac{2K}{\psi}}(pD_L\alpha_3 + pD_H\alpha_4) + \lambda + u_4 = 0 \tag{19}$$

where,

$$\psi = hD_H\alpha_1^2 + 2hD_L\alpha_1\alpha_2 + hD_L\alpha_2^2 + pD_L\alpha_3^2 + 2pD_L\alpha_3\alpha_4 + pD_H\alpha_4^2.$$

From expressions (16) to (19), it is clear that for $\alpha_i \geq 0$, $\frac{\partial Z}{\partial \alpha_i} \leq 0, i = 1, \ldots, 4$. Clearly, in the absence of constraint (12), the optimal solution to problem (P) is $\alpha_i = 0$, for all i. Therefore, the solution strategy would be to increase the α_is until constraint (12) is satisfied such that there is the least decrease in Z. This means, that the α_i with the largest gradient (or smallest absolute value of $\frac{\partial Z}{\partial \alpha_i}$) would be increased first, until its gradient is no longer the largest. The procedure would be continued until (12) is satisfied.

Lemma 1: *In the optimal solution to problem* (P), (i) *either* α_1, α_4 *are both greater than zero, or they are both equal to 0 (and therefore,* $u_1 = u_4$*), and* (ii) *either* α_2, α_3 *are both greater than zero, or they are both equal to 0 (and therefore,* $u_2 = u_3$*).*

PROOF. Provided in Appendix. □

Proposition 2: *In the optimal solution to the problem* (P),

(a) $(\alpha_1 + \alpha_2) = p/(h + p)$ *and correspondingly* $(\alpha_3 + \alpha_4) = h/(h + p)$
(b) $\alpha_4 = (h/p)\alpha_1$ *and* $\alpha_3 = (h/p)\alpha_2$.

PROOF. Due to Lemma 1, $u_2 = u_3$. Therefore, by comparing (17) and (18), we get $(\alpha_3 + \alpha_4)p = (\alpha_1 + \alpha_2)h$. Using (12), (a) is then straightforward. Result (b) can be proved by comparing (16) and (19), and some algebraic manipulations using the Lemma 1 result, $u_1 = u_4$, and the result (a). □

Proposition 2 implies that in the model for PDM with demand backlogging, the optimal policy displays the following properties:

1. As in the standard inventory models, the fraction of cycle time with positive inventory level $(\alpha_1 + \alpha_2)$ is equal to $p/(h + p)$. Correspondingly, the fraction of the cycle time with backlogged demand $(\alpha_3 + \alpha_4)$ is equal to $h/(h + p)$.
2. The time spent with low-demand (high-demand) operation during the part of the replenishment cycle with backlogged demand is equal to (h/p) times the time spent with low-demand (high-demand) operation during the part of the cycle with positive inventory level.

3. The proportion of time spent with low-demand operation during the part of the replenishment cycle with positive inventory level is same as the proportion of time spent with low-demand operation during part of the cycle with negative inventory level, i.e., $(\alpha_2/(\alpha_1 + \alpha_2)) = (\alpha_3/(\alpha_3 + \alpha_4))$. This also implies that if we have low-demand operation (or PDM) during the part of the replenishment cycle with positive inventory level, we will also have low-demand operation during the part of the replenishment cycle with backlogged demand.

Due to Proposition 2, α_2, α_3, and α_4 can be written in terms of α_1 as follows.

$$\alpha_2 = \left(\frac{p}{h+p} - \alpha_1\right), \qquad \alpha_3 = \frac{h}{p}\left(\frac{p}{h+p} - \alpha_1\right), \qquad \alpha_4 = \frac{h}{p}\alpha_1 \qquad (20)$$

Substituting (20) into (11) we get,

$$Z(\alpha_1) = \pi D_H - \pi m(D_H - D_L) + \pi m(D_H - D_L)\left(\frac{h+p}{p}\right)\alpha_1$$

$$- \sqrt{2K}\sqrt{\left(h(D_H - D_L)\alpha_1^2\left(\frac{h+p}{p}\right)\right) + \left(hD_L\frac{p}{h+p}\right)} \qquad (21)$$

It can be shown that $Z(\alpha_1)$ given by (21) above is concave. Differentiating (21) w.r.t. α_1, we get

$$\frac{dZ}{d\alpha_1} = \pi m(D_H - D_L)\left(\frac{h+p}{p}\right)$$

$$- \frac{(\sqrt{2K})h\left(\frac{h+p}{p}\right)(D_H - D_L)\alpha_1}{\sqrt{\left(h(D_H - D_L)\left(\frac{h+p}{p}\right)\alpha_1^2\right) + \left(hD_L\frac{p}{h+p}\right)}} \qquad (22)$$

It can be shown that, if $\frac{2Kh}{(\pi m)^2} \le D_H(1 + \frac{h}{p})$, $\frac{\partial Z}{\partial \alpha_1} > 0$, for $0 \le \alpha_1 \le \frac{p}{h+p}$. Hence, in this case it is optimal to set α_1 to its maximum possible value of $\frac{p}{h+p}$. When $\frac{2Kh}{(\pi m)^2} > D_H(1 + \frac{h}{p})$, the optimal value of α_1 is obtained by setting $\frac{\partial Z}{\partial \alpha_1}$ given by expression (22) equal to zero.

Therefore, we get the optimal value of α_1 as,

$$\alpha_1 = \begin{cases} \frac{p}{h+p} & \text{when } \frac{2Kh}{(\pi m)^2} \le D_H\left(1 + \frac{h}{p}\right) \\ \sqrt{\frac{D_L\left(\frac{p}{h+p}\right)}{\left[\frac{2Kh}{(\pi m)^2} - (D_H - D_L)(1 + \frac{h}{p})\right]}} & \text{otherwise} \end{cases} \qquad (23)$$

Explicit, closed form expressions (in terms of problem parameters $K, h, p,$ π, D_H and D_L) can now be written for T, α_2, α_3 and α_4 by using equation (23) along with equations (21) and (10).

It is optimal to use $\alpha_1 < p/(h + p)$ or $(\alpha_1 + \alpha_4) < 1$ (i.e., PDM is beneficial) when $\frac{2Kh}{(\pi m)^2} > D_H(1 + \frac{h}{p})$. We note that in the case with no backlogging of demand, the equivalent condition was $\frac{2Kh}{(\pi m)^2} > D_H$. In other words, if PDM is beneficial in the case with backlogging, it will certainly be beneficial in the case without backlogging, but not necessarily vice versa. The reason for this is as follows. In the backordering case, there is additional benefit from back-ordering itself. Therefore, to make PDM beneficial, the benefits have to be higher than in the case without backlogging. Therefore $\frac{2Kh}{(\pi m)^2}$ has to be greater than a larger value $D_H(1 + \frac{h}{p})$. Note that in the limiting case, as $p \to \infty$, the case with backlogging allowed and the corresponding formulas reduce to the case without backlogging.

Proposition 3: *In the model for proactive demand management with back-logging of demand allowed, the optimal policy displays the following properties.*

(i) $\alpha_1 = \min\left\{ \dfrac{\pi m}{hT}, \dfrac{p}{h+p} \right\}$

(ii) $\alpha_2 = \max\left\{ \left(\dfrac{p}{h+p} - \dfrac{\pi m}{hT} \right), 0 \right\}$

(iii) $\alpha_3 = \max\left\{ \left(\dfrac{h}{h+p} - \dfrac{\pi m}{pT} \right), 0 \right\}$

(iv) $\alpha_4 = \min\left\{ \dfrac{\pi m}{pT}, \dfrac{h}{h+p} \right\}$

PROOF. Provided in Appendix.   □

Remarks and managerial insights   Proposition 3 implies that the fraction of replenishment cycle time a product is prominently displayed (resulting in high demand) is given by, $\min\{ \frac{\pi m}{T}[\frac{1}{h} + \frac{1}{p}], 1 \}$ and this is (a) proportional to πm; (b) inversely proportional to the holding cost rate, h, for the time during part of the replenishment cycle with positive inventory level, and to the penalty cost rate, p, for the time during part of the replenishment cycle with backlogged demand; (c) inversely proportional to the optimal replenishment cycle time and therefore inversely proportional to the ordering cost, K. This again means that the optimal proportion of time in an inventory cycle when the demand is proactively managed through less prominent display is directly proportional to the inventory holding cost, penalty cost, ordering cost and the extent to which the potential demand for the product can be guided successfully to a generic product. It is inversely proportional to the profit margin of the product. Other remarks and insights discussed under Section 3 would be applicable here as well.

5. NUMERICAL EXAMPLE AND ANALYSIS

To better understand the dynamics of proactive demand management and its impact on profitability, we constructed a numerical example and performed sensitivity analysis using this example. For the base case in the numerical example, the parameter values used were as follows: $D_H = 2000$ units per year, $D_L = 1000$ units per year, $\pi = \$3$ per unit, $K = \$300$ per order, $h = \$2.5$ per unit per year, $p = \$10$ per unit per year for backlogged demand, and $m = 0.1$. With these parameter values, the optimal values of decision variables were found to be $\alpha_1 = 0.228, \alpha_2 = 0.572, \alpha_3 = 0.143, \alpha_4 = 0.057$ and $T = 0.527$. The values of profit with and without PDM, Z_{PDM} and Z_O respectively, were then computed to estimate the incremental benefit of PDM approach. The increase in profit from using PDM was found to be about 4.4%.

In conducting sensitivity analysis, we changed the value for one parameter at a time to determine impact of individual parameters on the optimal values of $\alpha_1, \alpha_2, \alpha_3, \alpha_4$ and the profit, Z. The results of the sensitivity analysis are summarized in the form of graphs presented in Exhibit 1. To simplify presentation, we added α_1 and α_4 to compute the total fraction of inventory cycle time, α, that the item is to be prominently displayed. When $\alpha = 1$, it implies that prominent display is used throughout the inventory replenishment cycle; i.e. PDM is not used. A lower value of α indicates that PDM is used for a large fraction of the inventory cycle time. Of course, $\alpha = 0$ implies that a less prominent display is used all the time. From equations (6) and (23), this is possible when either the profit margin per unit π, or the profit adjustment factor m is zero, or when the inventory cost parameters K or h are extremely large. The values of profit with and without PDM, Z_{PDM} and Z_O respectively, were also computed to estimate the incremental profit, ΔZ, resulting from the use of PDM approach. The results of this sensitivity analysis are discussed below.

- Graph 1 depicts the impact on changes in the niche demand rate during less prominent display, D_L, on α and the profit. For this purpose, the ratio of D_L/D_H was varied in the range 0.1 to 0.9, with the value of D_H kept fixed at 2000 per year. The graph shows that α increases and Z_{PDM}, profit with PDM, decreases as D_L increases. To better understand the incremental benefit of PDM, the graph also shows as a line of reference, the value of the profit without PDM, Z_O. It is interesting to note that at lower values of D_L, the use of PDM can lead to as much as 12.4% extra profit. The decrease

Exhibit 1: Sensitivity Analysis

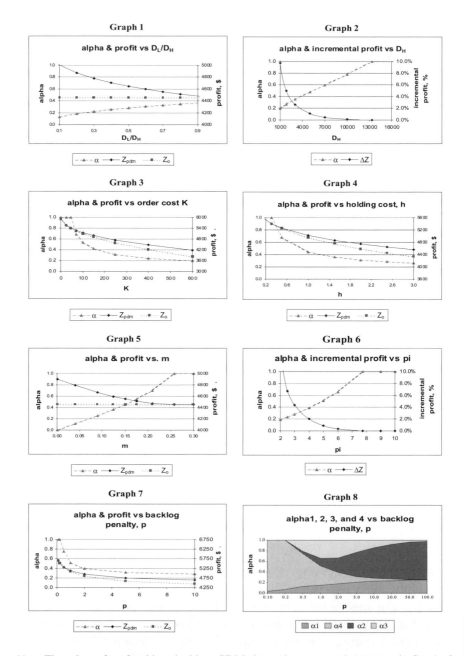

Note: The values of profit with and without PDM changed over a very large range in Graphs 2 and 6, and hence instead of showing Z_{PDM} and Z_O, we have chosen to show incremental profit, ΔZ, in these graphs.

in profit with an increase in D_L may seem counterintuitive, but the reason for this is as follows: D_L represents niche demand that can't be satisfied with a generic product. Thus, increased D_L reduces the retailer's ability to influence demand and thereby to profitably substitute demand. For the same reason, percentage of time PDM is practiced decreases (or α increases) with increase in the niche demand D_L.

- Graph 2 analyzes the impact of D_H on α and the incremental profit from PDM. For this analysis, both D_H and D_L were changed simultaneously with the ratio of D_L/D_H kept fixed at 0.5. It can be seen that as D_H increases, the value of α increases, and this value ultimately rises to one, when $D_H(1 + \frac{h}{p}) \geq \frac{2Kh}{(\pi m)^2}$. At low values of D_H, extra profit to the tune of 9.7% is realized by using PDM, but the incremental profits from PDM decreases as D_H increases. As discussed earlier, the primary benefit of PDM is the reduction in supply chain inventory costs. As D_H increases, the absolute value of profit increases and the inventory related costs (as a fraction of the revenue) become less significant. This, in turn, reduces the size of incremental benefits.

- Graphs 3 and 4 respectively capture the impact of order cost, K, and the inventory holding cost, h. These graphs show similarity in the nature of their impact. For very low values of K (or h), $D_H(1 + \frac{h}{p}) \geq \frac{2Kh}{(\pi m)^2}$; hence α equals one. In other words, when K (or h) is low, inventory costs are insignificant; therefore it is not worthwhile to practice PDM. But beyond a certain threshold level of K and h, the value of α monotonically decreases as the value of K (or h) increases. Furthermore, as intuition would suggest, profitability decreases with an increase in either K or h. However, it should also be noted that at large values of order cost and/or inventory holding cost, PDM plays a larger role in containing the total inventory related costs. Thus, the incremental benefit from using PDM is shown to be higher for higher values of K and h.

- Graph 5 shows the influence of m, the profit adjustment factor during less prominent display, on α and profits. A larger m implies that the benefit of proactively dampening demand is lower because either a lesser portion of the demand difference $(D_H - D_L)$ is substituted or marginal inventory costs for the generic product is higher or the profit margin for the generic product is lower. Therefore as the graph indicates, α increases and profit decreases with an increase in m. Beyond a certain value of m, PDM is not used as α attains the value of one, and thereafter the profit level remains constant at Z_O.

- Graph 6 illustrates the influence of π, the profit margin per unit of the product, on α and incremental profits. As π increases, the absolute value of profit increases and therefore the inventory costs become less significant. This, in turn, reduces the size of incremental benefits. Therefore, as π increases, α increases and attains the value of one beyond a certain value of π.

- Graph 7 depicts the influence of the penalty cost rate p on α and profit. Clearly, when p is very low, the inventory costs become insignificant as the demand can always be backlogged and satisfied without incurring any inventory holding or penalty costs. Therefore there is no benefit of PDM and α is close to one. As p becomes larger, inventory costs become significant and profits reduce, and by the same token α decreases and the benefit of PDM increases.

- Graph 8 represents the way optimal values of $\alpha_1, \alpha_2, \alpha_3$, and α_4 change as the penalty cost, p, increases. As in Graph 7, for low values of p, α $(= \alpha_1 + \alpha_4)$ attains a value of one. Beyond a certain value of p, the optimal action is to begin using PDM, and thus, all alphas attain non-zero values. At high values of p, clearly backlogging is not an attractive option and therefore only α_1 and α_2 attain positive values.

The sensitivity analysis shows that using PDM can lead to substantial increase in profit, and this profit increase can be as high as twelve percentage points or more when compared to the base case where no PDM is used. In general, using PDM is beneficial under the following conditions:

- When the non-substitutable niche demand, D_L, is relatively small compared to the demand level during prominent display, D_H. In other words, when a larger proportion of the potential demand for the product, D_H can be guided to a generic product.

- When the value of m, the profit adjustment factor during less prominent display, is small. In other words, when a large fraction of customers are willing to purchase a generic product, the profit margin of the generic product is comparable to the original product and the marginal inventory costs for the generic product are low.

- When the inventory related costs per unit of demand are significant and are comparable to the profit margin, π. That is, when π is of the same order as and comparable to h and when the order cost K is sufficiently large.

- When the penalty cost for backlogging is sufficiently large. However, at very large values of p, PDM is implemented with no backlogging of demand.

6. CONCLUSIONS AND FUTURE RESEARCH

The buying process in e-retailing requires the buyer to navigate through a series of web pages. Hence, by suitably designing the web pages, the e-retailer is able to exercise a much greater influence over the demand level for its products. In this paper, we have developed a model that enables an e-retailer to proactively manage demand for niche products and thereby increase overall profits. The classical inventory models treat demand level as given, and derive optimal policies that minimize total costs. We have extended the classical inventory models by considering demand that is dependent on the level of prominence with which a product is displayed on the web pages and obtained closed form solutions for the model. We believe that this paper is the first to address the proactive demand management approach for managing inventory for e-retailers. The main contributions of this paper are to (i) extend classical inventory models to deal with PDM approach, (ii) develop model solutions, and (iii) generate managerial insights by identifying conditions under which the PDM approach can be beneficially used.

The model solution provides guidance to an e-retailer on how to manage its inventory and product display for niche products. Specifically, the model solution provides the percentage of time for which PDM should be practiced by using a less prominent display. The optimal proportion of time in an inventory cycle when the demand is proactively managed through less prominent display is directly proportional to the inventory holding cost, penalty cost, ordering cost and the extent to which the potential demand for the niche product can be guided successfully to a substitute, generic product. It is inversely proportional to the profit margin of the niche product.

Numerical study using an example revealed that proactive demand management for a niche product can increase profits for an e-retailer by as much as 12%. The study also showed that in general, using PDM is beneficial when (i) niche demand (from very loyal customers) is relatively small compared to demand level during the prominent display, (ii) a significant proportion of the potential customers for the niche product are willing to purchase a substitute, generic product and (iii) inventory related (ordering, holding and penalty) costs as a percentage of the sales revenue are significant and comparable to the profit margin for the product.

One of the key insights of this paper is that, in e-retailing, one can attempt to direct most variety-insensitive customers to the Black-Model-T or the generic product with higher demand such as corn flakes. This is done by individually tracking the purchase behavior of the customers and determining whether they are variety-insensitive (i.e. willing to substitute to a generic product such as corn flakes). The rational for doing this is to reduce costs and increase profits by reaping economies of scale for the generic product. Considering the product proliferation that has occurred on the retail shelf space in the last twenty years, PDM is a very useful and worthwhile strategy for e-retailers to consider.

The extent to which PDM is practiced would depend on the model parameters. When the profit contribution per unit of the niche product (and/or when the profit contribution per unit lost by guiding part of the demand for niche product to the generic substitute) is sufficiently high, it is not worthwhile practicing PDM and therefore, the niche product would be displayed prominently all the time. On the other hand, when profit contribution per unit lost by guiding the part of the demand for the niche product to the generic product is very low or when the non-substitutable niche demand (D_L) is negligible, it is worthwhile to have PDM or less prominent display of the niche product all the time. In between these two extremes of the parameter values, PDM would be practiced for a part of the inventory cycle time. When the average inventory related costs per unit for the niche product ($\sqrt{2KhD_H}/D_H$) are higher than the profit contribution per unit lost by having less prominent display, it is worthwhile to have PDM or less prominent display for the niche product for at least part of the inventory cycle.

Given the fact that this is the first paper in this stream of research involving PDM, there are of course limitations to the model developed in the paper. On the face of it, it might seem that stochastic demand is more realistic, and it does not make sense to turn away demand when it is deterministic. But this is the somewhat counter-intuitive insight from the paper: Even in deterministic demand scenarios, there is case for proactive demand management. Stochastic demand for regularly consumed items will make the model more realistic but does not necessarily add more insights. However, while the assumption of deterministic demand is reasonable for regularly consumed grocery products, this might be unrealistic in other situations such as for fashion products. It should also be pointed out that we have only explored one possible approach to proactive demand management by adjusting the display of the product on the web site. There are possibly other ways to proactively manage demand; for example, by offer of price discounts for the generic product, special promotions etc. The model we developed has not considered these possibilities, but PDM through price discounts for the generic product can be handled by appropriately calculating the m. Other ways of proactively managing demand could possibly be explored in the future. Another key issue is the estimation of model parameters accurately in practice. While the PDM strategy can clearly bring benefits to the e-retailer, the precise estimation of the model parameters such as D_H, D_L and m is not a trivial issue in practice. The model we developed has also ignored the consumer behavior implications due to the PDM strategy: PDM generally implies lesser choice for the customer, and this might affect demand adversely; on the other hand, due to PDM, customers face stock out situations less often and this might impact the demand positively. The impact of the competitor's marketing strategy including pricing is also not considered in our model.

We hope to address some of these limitations in our future research. There are also several other avenues for future research. The inventory costs incurred and the revenue obtained due to potential customers substituting to a generic alternative is implicitly incorporated in the model through the profit adjustment factor, m. When the inherent demand for the generic product is large enough, this would be accurate. One could make the model richer and more precise by bringing the generic (substitute) product and its inventory cycle/costs explicitly in. Another possibility is to consider several related niche products and one or more widely used generic products together in a single model. Another possible research issue is to extend the present model to consider more than two levels of display or demand. Finally one could consider proactive demand management strategies for fashion goods such as apparel for which a newsboy framework would be more appropriate. The authors are currently working on some of these research issues.

REFERENCES

Anderson, E. E., & Amato, H. N. (1974) A Mathematical Model for Simultaneously Determining the Optimal Brand-Collection and Display Area Allocation. *Operations Research*, 22, 13–21.

Baker, R. C., & Urban, T. L. (1988a) A Deterministic Inventory System with an Inventory-Level-Dependent Demand Rate. *Journal of the Operational Research Society*, 39, 823–831.

Baker, R. C., & Urban, T. L. (1988b) Single Period Inventory Dependent Demand Models. *Omega*, 16, 605–607.

Bassok, Y., Anupindi, R., & Akella, R. (1999) Single-period Multi-product Inventory Models with Substitution. *Operations Research*, 47, 632–642.

Bharagava, H., Sun, D., & Xu, S. (2006) Stockout compensation: Joint Inventory and Price Optimization in Electronic Retailing. *INFORMS Journal of Computing*, Forthcoming.

Borin, N., & Farris, P. (1995) A Sensitivity Analysis of Retailer Shelf Management Models. *Journal of Retailing*, 71, 153–171.

Borin, N., Farris, P., & Freeland, J.R. (1994) A Model for Determining Retail Product Category Assortment and Shelf Space Allocation. *Decision Sciences*, 25, 359–384.

Bultez, A. & Naert, P. (1988) SH.A.R.P.: Shelf Allocation for Retailers' Profit. *Marketing Science*, 7, 211–231.

Bultez, A., Naert, P., Gijsbrechts, E. & Abelle, P.V. (1989) Asymmetric Cannibalism in Retail Assortments. *Journal of Retailing*, 65, 153–192.

Cairns, J. P. (1962) Suppliers, Retailers and Shelf Space. *Journal of Marketing*, 26, 34–36.

Cairns, J. P. (1963) Allocate Space for Maximum Profits. *Journal of Retailing*, 39, 43–55.

Corstjens, M., & Doyle, P. (1981) A Model for Optimizing Retail Space Allocations. *Management Science*, 27, 822–833.

Curhan, R. C. (1972) The Relationship between Shelf Space and Unit Sales in Supermarkets. *Journal of Marketing Research*, 9, 406–412.

Curhan, R. C. (1973) Shelf Space Allocation and Profit Maximization in Mass Retailing. *Journal of Marketing*, 37, 54–60.

Drezner, Z., Gurnani, H., & Pasternack, B.A (1995) An EOQ Model with Substitution Between Products. *Journal of the Operational Research Society*, 46, 887–891.

Fershtman, C., & Spiegel, U. (1986) Learning by Doing, Inventory and Optimal Pricing Policy. *Journal of Business and Economics*, 38, 19–27.

Gurnani, H. and Z. Drezner, Z. (2000) Deterministic Hierarchical Substitution Inventory Models. *Journal of the Operational Research Society*, 51, 129–133.

Ignall, E., & Veinott, A.F. Jr. (1969) Optimality of Myopic Inventory Policies for Several Substitutable Products. *Management Science*, 15, 284–304.

Kunreuther, H., & Schrage, L. (1973) Joint Pricing and Inventory Decisions for Constant Priced Items. *Management Science*, 19, 732–738.

Mahajan, S., & van Ryzin, G. (2001) Stocking retail assortments under dynamic consumer substitution. *Operations Research*, 49, 334–351.

McGillivray, A., & Silver, E.A. (1978) Some Concepts for Inventory Control Under Substitutable Demands. *INFOR*, 16, 47–63.

Parlar, M., & Goyal, S. (1984) Optimal Ordering Decisions for Two Substitutable Products with Stochastic Demands. *OPSEARCH*, 21, 1–15.

Pasternack, B., & Drezner, Z. (1991) Optimal Inventory Policies for Substitutable Commodities with Stochastic Demand. *Naval Research Logistics*, 38, 221–240.

Shugan, S.M. (1989) Product Assortment in a Triopoly. *Management Science*, 15, 304–320.

Smith, S., & Agrawal, N. (2000) Management of Multi-item Retail Inventory Systems with Demand Substitution. *Operations Research*, 48, 50–64.

Urban, G.L. (1969) A Mathematical Modeling Approach to Product Line Decisions. *Journal of Marketing Research*, 6, 40–47.

Urban, T.L. (1992) An Inventory Model with an Inventory-Level-Dependent Demand Rate and Relaxed Terminal Conditions. *Journal of the Operational Research Society*, 43, 721–724.

Urban, T.L. (1998) An Inventory-Theoretic Approach to Product Assortment and Shelf-Space Allocation. *Journal of Retailing*, 74, 15–35.

Veinott, A. Jr. (1965) Optimal Policy for a Multi-Product, Dynamic, Non-Stationary Inventory Problem. *Management Science*, 12, 206–222.

Whitin, T. (1955) Inventory Control and Price Theory. *Management Science*, 2, 61–68.

Zufryden, F.S. (1986) A Dynamic Programming Approach for Product Selection and Supermarket Shelf Space Allocation. *Journal of the Operational Research Society*, 37, 413–422.

Appendix
Calculation of Profit Adjustment Factor *m*

There are three elements to the calculation of the profit adjustment factor for the potential demand ($D_H - D_L$) that is guided to a generic (substitute) product. First is the difference in profit contribution excluding inventory costs between the original (niche) product and the generic product. Second is the substitution loss, since not all the potential demand is substituted. And finally the marginal inventory costs for the generic product for handling this additional demand.

Let the profit contribution excluding per unit inventory costs for the generic product be π_s. Let the effective substitution rate for the potential demand guided to the generic product be γ. In other words, the fractional rate of loss in demand due to lack of substitution is $(1 - \gamma)$. Therefore, the additional profit contribution obtained from guiding the potential demand difference $(D_H - D_L)$ to the generic product is

$$\Delta R_s = \pi_s (D_H - D_L)\gamma$$

Let the original demand for the generic product (excluding demand guided to it from the niche product) be $\tilde{D}$. Let the ordering cost and inventory holding cost rate for the generic product be $\tilde{K}$ and $\tilde{h}$ [Note that if the inventory model for the generic product allows for planned stock-outs and backlogging of demand, then we just need to redefine the holding cost as $\tilde{h}' = \tilde{h}(\frac{\tilde{p}}{\tilde{h}+\tilde{p}})$, where $\tilde{p}$ is the penalty cost rate for backlogged demand]. If the generic product only faces the demand $\tilde{D}$, then the optimal order quantity

$$\tilde{Q} = \sqrt{\frac{2\tilde{K}\tilde{D}}{\tilde{h}}}$$

and the cost incurred is

$$\tilde{Z} = \frac{\tilde{K}\tilde{D}}{\tilde{Q}} + \frac{1}{2}\tilde{Q}\tilde{h}$$

Let $\Delta D_s = (D_H - D_L)\gamma$

The increase in the average demand rate for the generic product from the niche product is ΔD_s. Note that the demand increase occurs only during less prominent display. Therefore with the increased demand, the demand rate for the generic product is not constant. The optimal policy and the cost for the generic product with the increased demand $\tilde{D} + \Delta D_s$ cannot be determined by the EOQ model. In fact, determining the true optimal policy and cost can be very complex as it depends on the duration of the inventory cycle for the generic product and timing of the less prominent display in relation to the inventory cycle for the generic product. The optimal policy in fact need not be stationary. However an approximate cost (which is an upper bound on the optimal cost) can be found by assuming that we continue with the same order quantity $\tilde{Q}$. The revised, average ordering cost would then be $\frac{\tilde{K}(\tilde{D}+\Delta D_s)}{\tilde{Q}}$. But as the inventory is consumed faster due to higher demand rate in some cycles, the average inventory holding cost will be lower than or equal to $\frac{1}{2}\tilde{Q}\tilde{h}$. Therefore the new total average inventory related cost

$$\tilde{C}_{new} \le \frac{\tilde{K}(\tilde{D} + \Delta D_s)}{\tilde{Q}} + \frac{1}{2}\tilde{Q}\tilde{h}$$

Therefore, the marginal inventory cost from guiding the potential demand difference $(D_H - D_L)$ to the generic product

$$\Delta C_s \le \frac{\tilde{K}\Delta D_s}{\tilde{Q}} = \Delta D_s \sqrt{\frac{\tilde{K}\tilde{h}}{2\tilde{D}}}$$

Hence a conservative estimate of the net profits from guiding the potential demand to the generic product is

$$Z_s = \pi_s(D_H - D_L)\gamma - \sqrt{\frac{\tilde{K}\tilde{h}}{2\tilde{D}}}(D_H - D_L)\gamma \tag{24}$$

For the PDM model for the niche product, we had used the profit adjustment factor m to define

$$Z_s = \pi(D_H - D_L)(1 - m) \tag{25}$$

Combining (24) and (25), we get

$$m = \frac{1}{\pi}\left(\pi - \pi_s\gamma + \gamma\sqrt{\tilde{K}\tilde{h}/2\tilde{D}}\right) \tag{26}$$

Rewriting (26),

$$m = (1 - \gamma) + \gamma\left(1 - \frac{\pi_s}{\pi}\right) + \frac{\gamma}{\pi}\sqrt{\tilde{K}\tilde{h}/2\tilde{D}} \tag{27}$$

The profit adjustment factor m as written in (27) has three terms. The first term is the effect of substitution loss (or lost sales), the second term is the revenue effect (due to the difference in profit margin for the niche and generic product) and third term is the effect of the marginal inventory cost. When the profit contribution for both the products are identical, the marginal inventory costs for the generic product is negligible, and almost all the demand difference $(D_H - D_L)$ is substituted, then $m \approx 0$.

If we assume that the marginal profits for the generic product were equal to the niche product (i.e. $\pi_s = \pi$), the second term or the revenue effect disappears and the profit adjustment factor m is just the sum of the substitution loss and the marginal inventory cost. For the PDM strategy to work, we want the profit adjustment factor m to be as low as possible. Therefore it is desirable that γ, the effective substitution rate to be is as large as possible, and the marginal inventory cost to be as small as possible. If the demand rate for the generic product $\tilde{D}$ is very large, the effect of the marginal inventory cost would be very small. Alternatively the inventory cost parameters $\tilde{K}$ and $\tilde{h}$ should be as small as possible. Realistically, the inventory cost parameters for the generic product would be of the same order as the niche product (i.e. $K \cong \tilde{K}$, and $h \cong \tilde{h}$), therefore for the PDM strategy to work, we would need the demand $\tilde{D}$ to be large or much larger than D. Note that, if $\pi_s > \pi$, then m could even take on negative values, but this again would be unrealistic in practice as the substitution rate γ would in that case be low as the customers would not want to switch to a product with higher price.

Note that the PDM model could be easily extended to a situation where the demand is guided to more than one generic product (so long as we are able to estimate the portion of the demand guided to a particular generic product). The profit adjustment factor m can then again be calculated along the lines discussed above but taking into account multiple generic products.

Proof of Proposition 1 We need to prove (8) only for the case $\alpha < 1$. When $\alpha < 1$, substituting (7) into (2), we get

$$
T = \sqrt{\frac{2K}{\left(\frac{h(D_H - D_L)D_L}{\left[\frac{2Kh}{(\pi m)^2} - (D_H - D_L)\right]} + hD_L\right)}}
$$

$$
= \sqrt{\frac{(2K/h)\left[\frac{2Kh}{(\pi m)^2} - (D_H - D_L)\right]}{D_L\left[(D_H - D_L) + \frac{2Kh}{(\pi m)^2} - (D_H - D_L)\right]}}
$$

$$
= \left(\frac{\pi m}{h}\right)\sqrt{\left(\frac{1}{D_L}\right)\left[\frac{2Kh}{(\pi m)^2} - (D_H - D_L)\right]} = \frac{\pi m}{h\alpha}
$$

Hence, $\alpha = \frac{\pi m}{hT}$.

Proof of Lemma 1 We only show the proof for (i). The proof for (ii) is similar. Assume the contrary, i.e. $\alpha_1 > 0$, and $\alpha_4 = 0$ in the optimal solution to problem (P). As $\sum_i \alpha_i = 1$, $\psi > 0$. Therefore, by comparing (16) and (19), it is clear that $\frac{\partial Z}{\partial \alpha_4} = 0 > \frac{\partial Z}{\partial \alpha_1}$. Therefore, an improved solution can be obtained by increasing α_4 by a small value δ and correspondingly decreasing α_1. Therefore, it is not possible that $\alpha_1 > 0$ and $\alpha_4 = 0$ in the optimal solution to (P). Similarly it can be argued that the optimal solution to problem (P) cannot have

$\alpha_1 = 0$, and $\alpha_4 > 0$. Therefore, either $\alpha_1 = \alpha_4 = 0$, or both $\alpha_1, \alpha_4 > 0$ in the optimal solution to (P). It is also easy to see from the above argument that, in the optimal solution to (P), $\frac{\partial Z}{\partial \alpha_1} = \frac{\partial \check{Z}}{\partial \alpha_4}$. Therefore by comparing (16) and (19), we get $u_1 = u_4$.

Proof of Proposition 3   Substituting (20) into (10) we get

$$T = \sqrt{\frac{2K}{\left(h(D_H - D_L)\left(1 + \frac{h}{p}\right)\alpha_1^2\right) + \left(hD_L\frac{p}{h+p}\right)}} \tag{28}$$

We need to prove (i) only for the case when $\alpha_1 < \frac{p}{h+p}$. Substituting (23) into (28), and after further manipulations we get

$$
\begin{aligned}
T &= \sqrt{\frac{2K}{\left(hD_L\frac{p}{h+p}\right) + \left(\frac{h(D_H-D_L)D_L}{\left[\frac{2Kh}{(\pi m)^2}-(D_H-D_L)\left(1+\frac{h}{p}\right)\right]}\right)}} \\[2mm]
&= \sqrt{\frac{(2K/h)\left(\frac{2Kh}{(\pi m)^2} - (D_H - D_L)\left(1 + \frac{h}{p}\right)\right)}{D_L\frac{2Kh}{(\pi m)^2}\frac{p}{(h+p)}}} \\[2mm]
&= \left(\frac{\pi m}{h}\right)\sqrt{\frac{\frac{2Kh}{(\pi m)^2} - (D_H - D_L)\left(1 + \frac{h}{p}\right)}{D_L\left(\frac{p}{h+p}\right)}} = \frac{\pi m}{h\alpha_1}
\end{aligned}
$$

Hence when $\alpha_1 < \frac{p}{h+p}$, $T = \frac{\pi m}{h\alpha_1}$ or $\alpha_1 = \frac{\pi m}{hT}$. Therefore,

$$\alpha_1 = \min\left\{\frac{\pi m}{hT}, \frac{p}{h + p}\right\} \tag{29}$$

The rest of the results can be obtained by substituting (29) into (20).

Chapter 16

INFORMATION TECHNOLOGY IMPACT ON BUSINESS PRACTICES: THE UCLA BIT PROJECT[1]

Uday S. Karmarkarand Vandana Mangal

UCLA Anderson Graduate School of Management, 110 Westwood Plaza, Los Angeles, CA 90095-1481

Abstract   The Business and Information Technologies (BIT) project at UCLA includes a survey aimed at providing a base line study of the impact of technology on business practice. The study documents the information technology driven changes that are occurring across a wide spectrum of industry sectors in the United States and Canada. Changes in the nature of the workplace, B2C relationships, the structure of business processes in terms of B2B relationships, technology adoption and globalization are observed. The results indicate that businesses are changing internally as well as in terms of their interactions with their customers and trading partners. As might be expected, the rate of change is perhaps not as rapid as might be suggested by the "high water mark" examples that are described in the popular business press. However, the changes are without question both pervasive and on-going.

1.   INTRODUCTION

Information has become the backbone of the economy in the United States. The study by Apte and Nath (2004) that follows earlier work by Machlup (1962, 1980) and Porat and Rubin (1977), puts the size of the information sector at over 55% of the value added to the GNP of the US in 1992 and at about 63% in 1997. Even a conservative extrapolation of the results of these studies would put the information sector at well over 65% of the GNP today

---

[1]   Support for BIT has come from CMIE, UCLA International Institute's Global Impact Research Program, the AT&T Foundation, UCLA Anderson School's Center for International Business Education and Research (CIBER), Applied Computer Research, and UCLA Anderson School's Entertainment Management Program. The authors would like to thank all these sponsors and supporters.

and growing steadily. In short, information technology has become a major part of the US economy, and can be expected to continue dominating it for the foreseeable future.

The BIT survey documents the changes brought about by IT deployment to business structure, organization, and practice across a wide spectrum of industry sectors in the United States and Canada. The Internet phenomenon was primarily a matter of a fundamental change in information logistics, with the protocols of the web superimposed on a deregulating and increasingly competitive telecommunications environment. With new technologies and systems on the horizon, a second slower wave of change based on infrastructure development, and then probably a third wave based on information processing, intelligent agents, and natural interfaces (as distinct from just the shipping and handling of information) is expected. It is expected that all these technological and infrastructure developments will change the structure of firms in terms of organization and work process, will change information chains and inter-organizational relationships, and alter the structure of industrial sectors, to the point that the traditional categories do not apply very well.

One basic change is in the nature of the workplace. Many office workers now face a screen for some significant period of time during work hours. The screen is a very different workplace from a desktop, since it is much better connected with places, people and processes outside the workplace. The screen (or interface) is also easily liberated physically from the desk and cubicle. It is apparent that the traditional notion of contemporaneous co-location as the core of an organization is ready to disappear. However it is not clear how and when this will happen, or what will take its place. It is also not clear how lines of authority, responsibility and communication will be established in the new firm. Perhaps the concepts of span of control and hierarchy will disappear in favor of some form of just-in-time and "only-when-needed" management.

Changes well beyond just the new phraseology are also occurring in the B2C relationships in firms. There is no question that sectors such as retailing, travel services and financial services have been transformed, not just in terms of new entrants, but for the incumbents as well. For many consumer goods and services, the web is now a growing carrier of brand equity and customer recognition; it has become a new face for a company. The changes in the B2C layer are beginning to ripple back into supply and service chains. The impact on logistics, freight and delivery services is most easily seen, but many other equally dramatic changes are occurring inside and between firms, that are invisible to the casual observer.

The reducing costs of information logistics suggests obvious changes in business practice. As transaction costs drop and large volumes of information can be reliably and quickly transported, there will be changes in the structure of business processes that exploit these advantages. Some of the consequences for B2B interactions have already been observed, although hype and overestimation have tended to distract from the very significant reality.

Perhaps the most important issue today is the overall impact of these technologies on the structure of industry sectors and the economy as a whole. Many sectors are coalescing and converging. For example, newspapers, magazines and broadcast organizations are all colliding on the web. Those sectors will fragment and reform into new alignments which exploit their core strengths. The position that newspapers have held because of the economics of delivering information bundles to the door, is seriously threatened by on-line channels. For example, newspapers are not now or in the future, the strongest suppliers of "breaking" news, especially in multi-media formats. The television networks have the best collection and packaging systems for that task. Newspapers may hold on to criticism, commentary and review, though magazines could easily start to compete for that role. In turn, TV broadcasts will face challenges from web casts. Magazines will have to contend with web based competitors, and go on the web themselves. Of course, these changes will not occur overnight. For a time, most media and publishing companies will have to think in terms of both sheets and screens.

Similar stories can be told for other sectors and for international trade. What is important is that these changes are significant, and deserve to be followed closely. It is relatively easy to make broad brush comments about the changes that are underway, as we have above. However, hard information about the extent and distribution of these effects is not easily found.

The next section contains a brief literature survey. Section 3 describes the research questions addressed in the survey. Results are summarized in Section 4 and detailed in Section 5. Section 6 discusses conclusions and offers recommendations for future research.

2.   LITERATURE REVIEW

The rapid growth of technology use has raised the visibility of Information Technology related expenditures to the point where long range IT spending growth rates range between 3–9% (survey of CIOs by Goldman Sachs). For most firms, technology ranks only behind compensation and occupancy in the overall budget. IT has become tightly woven into nearly all facets of office management and practice areas. Firms are spending over $316 billion (Judge et al., 1998) on Information Technology. Although several organizations are deploying IT to remain competitive and to be able to offer the products and services their competitors offer, it is critical for managers to be able to justify their large investments in IT especially with the falling costs of technology and steady transition to cheaper labor overseas.

As such, it is critical for researchers to understand and develop tools that will help managers determine whether their IT investments will result in positive impacts for their organizations. Even today, a large number of managers invest in IT without performing a comprehensive and conclusive analysis on the expected payoffs from IT investments. This can be attributed in large part to the lack of established tools for measuring IT impacts and to the difficulty and unreliability of using the tools that do exist.

Although information technology is a relatively new field, a large body of literature exists with significant studies that have tried to explain and measure the impacts of information technologies (Gurbaxani and Whang, 1991; Barua et al., 1995; Loveman, 1994; Hitt et al., 2002). These studies have included various measures of productivity (Mukhopadhyay et al., 1997; Lehr and Lichtenberg, 1999) and organizational performance (Sircar et al., 2000; Mahmood and Mann, 1993) to measure impacts. Theoretical (Gurbaxani and Whang, 1991), Analytical (Thatcher and Oliver, 2001) and empirical studies exist (Talon et al., 2000; Karmarkar et al., 1995). Studies have been performed at various levels including the economy and industry (Strassman, 1990), the firm (Brynjolfsson and Hitt, 1996) and the level of the application (Banker and Kauffman, 1991). Qualitative and Quantitative Studies have also been performed for various countries (Tam, 1998). More recent studies have also included corporate initiatives such as business process reengineering (Devaraj and Kohli, 2000) in the analyses.

In spite of the considerable literature in this field, an overall picture of technology impact has not emerged with clarity. Some early studies have found no significant impacts or even negative impacts from IT investments in organizations (Strassman, 1990; Roach, 1991). More recent work however has shown positive impacts from investments in information technologies (Lehr and Lichtenberg, 1999). There are new calls for studies to be conducted that employ large volumes of survey data that is cross sectional as well as longitudinal (Devaraj and Kohli, 2000).

3. RESEARCH QUESTIONS IN THE BIT SURVEY

The purpose of the BIT survey is to provide a baseline study of the effect of technologies on business practice. As such the study is quite broad in its scope. It is intended that the survey will be complemented by more detailed investigations at the sector and technology levels, and these are already underway. It is also intended that the survey will be repeated in multiple countries, so as to permit a general comparison of the similarities and differences in business practice across the world. Furthermore, the survey will be repeated annually so as to establish trends in technology adoption and practice effects.

The starting point in designing the survey was to list the major issues facing businesses as a consequence of technological change in information and communication tools. These issues were used to develop hypotheses about the nature of the changes that might occur in business practice. The survey questions were then constructed to address these changes. The questionnaire design was a joint effort between the US, Italy and India BIT teams; those other groups report on their initial studies elsewhere in this volume.

The questionnaire was divided into six major topics or segments. These topics and the questions in each are described below.

Technology Adoption/Infrastructure and Budget Trends

Question 1 – What technologies are organizations using currently or planning to use in the neat future? What technologies are organizations not using and not planning to use in the future?

Question 2 – What technologies have organizations invested in (and not invested in) over the last 3 years?

Internal Organization

Question 3 – How are organizations changing internally in terms of their workforce?

Question 4 – How are organizations changing internally in terms of their structure?

Question 5 – Are organizations outsourcing some of their business processes? Is Business Process Outsourcing (BPO) more popular for certain functions in the organization such as accounting, marketing, IT and finance?

Questions 6 & 7 – What is the outsourcing budget for organizations for IT and non IT functions? How much of the total outsourced business is offshore?

Customer Facing Interactions

Question 8 – Are relationships with customers developed and maintained using multiple touch points? What are the most popular touch points?

Questions 9 & 14 – How is Customer View integrated using certain technologies? What mechanisms are used by organizations to perform customer segmentation?

Questions 10, 11 & 12 – Are Promotion and Advertising budgets shifting towards online channels? Which online advertising methods have been adopted by organizations? In going online, are organizations creating a new face in terms of branding concept, slogan, logo and name?

Question 13 – For which functions is Customer Relationship Management (CRM) becoming automated?

Questions 15 & 16 – Is the number of organizations selling products and services online increasing? How is online business different from traditional business?

Trading Partner Relationships

Question 17 – What technologies are organizations using for communicating with their trading partners?

Question 18 – What IT-based channels and B2B mechanisms are organizations using for purchasing?

Business Results

Questions 19 & 20 – What Economic and Operational business results are being impacted by technologies? What Strategic areas are being impacted by information technologies?

Globalization

Questions 21 & 22 – Are organizations becoming more global? Is the geographic reach of organizations increasing?

The research methodology and data are discussed in the Appendix. Results are discussed in the next two sections.

4.   A SUMMARY OF THE RESULTS

The results indicate that businesses are changing internally as well as in terms of their interactions with their customers and trading partners. As might be expected, the rate of change is perhaps not as rapid as might be suggested by the "high water mark" examples that are described in the popular business press. However, the changes are without question both pervasive and on-going.

Some of the key results of the survey are as follows:

- The internal organization of companies is changing significantly in terms of both structure and workforce. Organizations are indeed becoming more flat, with a wider span of control, more geographically distributed, and more "virtual".
- The workplace and work requirements are changing. Many employees face screens; many are being monitored for performance. Technical capabilities

are becoming necessary. Executives are asking for more and better structured information.

- The degree to which outsourcing and off-shoring are being pursued is still quite limited. IT services, payroll and market research are the more widely outsourced business functions. It will be interesting to see if this changes dramatically in the next survey.
- The technologies and systems that are the most widely adopted are eCommerce tools and websites, wireless hardware and software, security tools, collaboration and portal tools, and groupware/productivity tools. Among these, wireless and collaboration/portal tools are also on budgets for near-term planned adoption.
- Biometrics and digital receipts are not being widely examined or adopted. This seems a bit at odds with the high interest in security. One might conclude that security with respect to communications, data protection, site intrusions and the like, is the major concern at present. Security and identification in the physical sense are less of an issue.
- Radio Frequency Identification (RFID) is another technology that companies have not widely adopted as yet; in fact adoption rates were surprisingly low. However, many firms do plan to purchase RFID related systems in the near future and it will again be interesting to see what the next survey shows.
- The adoption of on-line sales has not as yet had a major impact on marketing strategy. In particular, there has not been a significant change in branding or positioning (across all respondents). However, there is substantial interest in having customers perform more self-service tasks while purchasing online.
- Technology adoption has caused internal communications costs and production costs to decrease. However, the costs of technology acquisition and implementation and, of consultancy and collaboration have predictably increased.

The next section provides a complete account of the survey results.

5. DETAILED SURVEY RESULTS

Technology Adoption/Infrastructure and Budget Trends

Question 1 – What technologies are organizations using currently or planning to use in the near future? What technologies are organizations not using and not planning to use in the future?

An overwhelmingly large number of organizations (90.3%) either already have or plan to have Websites and E-commerce technologies within the next 3 years. 86.7% of the organizations have/plan to have Wireless Hardware and Software; 78.2% have/plan to have Collaboration and Portal Tools;

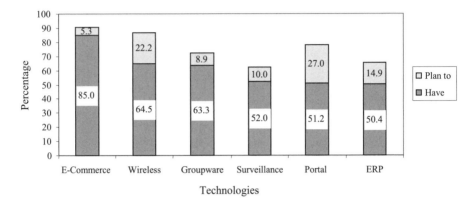

Figure 16-1. Technology Trends.

72.2% have/plan to have Groupware and Productivity tools such as Lotus Notes; 62% have/plan to have Surveillance tools and 65.3% of the organizations have/plan to have Enterprise Resource Planning (ERP). Among these technologies, Collaboration/Portal Tools (27%) and Wireless Technologies (22.2%) are the two most popular technologies on company budgets and slated for adoption in the next 3 years.

These trends are shown in Figure 1.

Technologies that fewer organizations plan to purchase in the next 3 years include Biometrics (21.8% have/plan to have while 43.9% of the organizations do not plan to have) and Digital Receipts (25.4% have/plan to have while 38.3% do not plan to have). Radio Frequency Identification (RFID) is currently adopted only by a very small percentage of organizations (6.9%). However, 21.8% organizations plan to purchase the technology in the next 3 years. These trends are shown in Figure 2.

Question 2 – What technologies have organizations invested in (and not invested in) over the last 3 years?

Security software (increased or increased significantly in 65.3% organizations) and Security hardware (increased or increased significantly in 62.5% organizations) top the list of technologies organizations have invested in over the past 3 years. Software applications (59.7%), Storage hardware (57.6%) and Wireless hardware and software (54.9%) budgets have also increased.

On the other hand, budgets for offshore outsourcing (10.5%) and on-demand computing (15.3%) have increased the least in the last 3 years. These trends are shown in Figure 3.

Question 2 – What technologies have organizations invested in (and not invested in) over the last 3 years?

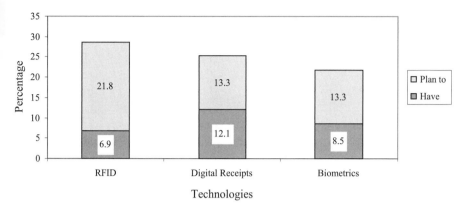

Figure 16-2. Technology Trends.

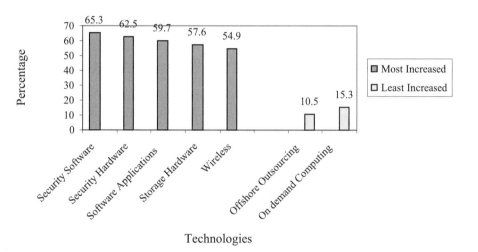

Figure 16-3. Budget Trends.

Security software (increased or increased significantly in 65.3% organizations) and Security hardware (increased or increased significantly in 62.5% organizations) top the list of technologies organizations have invested in over the past 3 years. Software applications (59.7%), Storage hardware (57.6%) and Wireless hardware and software (54.9%) budgets have also increased.

On the other hand, budgets for offshore outsourcing (10.5%) and on-demand computing (15.3%) have increased the least in the last 3 years. These trends are shown in Figure 4.

Codes for the trends are as follows:

1. Proportion of employees facing a screen is increasing
2. Demand for intelligence in information at executive levels is increasing

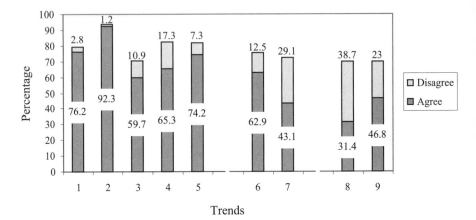

Figure 16-4. Internal Organization Workforce.

3. Collaboration between workers from use of Internet-based technologies is increasing
4. The need for IT skills at lower levels is going up
5. Workers need to retrain constantly to keep up with changing technologies
6. Use of teleconferencing is on the rise
7. More employees are telecommuting
8. Outsourcing is leading to workforce reductions
9. Automation of functions is leading to workforce reductions

Question 4 – How are organizations changing internally in terms of their structure?

The most significant trend is the increasing availability of new decision making and online technologies, as reported by almost three-quarter (74.6%) of the organizations.

Organizations are becoming flatter with fewer direct reports to each manager. Heterarchical organizations, widening the span of control of managers are becoming common. Organizations are becoming geographically dispersed with direct reports to a manager not located at the same location as the manager. Reduction in middle level management is somewhat observed.

Although a large number of organizations monitor customer facing interactions and, automated monitoring of workforce productivity is increasing, results do not indicate that organizations provide incentives to employees based on their productivity.

Support is not found for IT functions shifting from staff to line.

These trends are shown in Figure 5.

Codes for the trends are as follows:

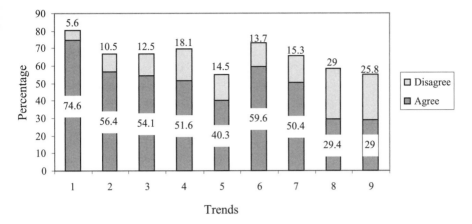

Figure 16-5. Internal Organization Structure.

1. New decision making tools and online technologies are increasingly becoming available
2. Span of control for most managers is widening
3. Organization is becoming flatter
4. Organization is becoming geographically dispersed
5. Number of middle level managers is decreasing
6. Service productivity is increasingly being monitored
7. Automated monitoring of workforce productivity is increasing
8. Incentives are based on monitoring of productivity
9. IT function is shifting from staff to line

Question 5 – Are organizations outsourcing some of their business processes? Is Business Process Outsourcing (BPO) more popular for certain functions in the organization such as accounting, marketing, IT and finance?

The most often outsourced business processes are Payroll, Market Research and IT Programming. 47.5% of the organizations outsource market research either significantly, partially or have plans to outsource in the next 3 years. Payroll is outsourced (partially or significantly or planned) by 43.1% of the organizations and IT Programming by 39.5% of the organizations. Finance, Accounting and Order Fulfillment are not outsourced with 78.6%, 76.6% and 60.9% of the organizations not currently outsourcing these business process functions respectively.

These are shown in Figure 6.

Questions 6 & 7 – What is the outsourcing budget for organizations for IT and non IT functions? How much of the total outsourced business is offshore?

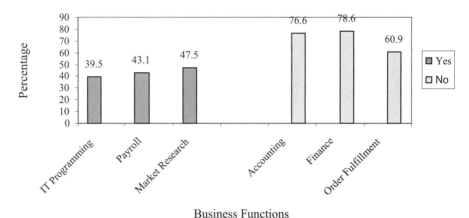

Figure 16-6. Internal Organization BPO.

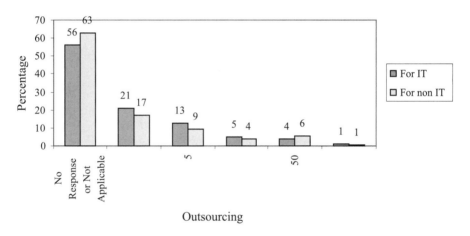

Figure 16-7. Outsourcing as a Percentage of Sales Revenues.

Organizations outsource about the same percentage of their IT functions as their non IT functions. Outsourcing patterns are shown in Figure 7. About a fifth (21%) of the organizations outsource up to 1% of their IT functions (as a percentage of total sales revenue), 13% outsource up to 5% of their IT functions (as a percentage of total sales revenue) and 5% outsource up to 10% of their IT functions (as a percentage of total sales revenue). In terms of non IT functions (as a percentage of total sales revenue), about 17% of the organizations outsource up to 1%, under 10% outsource up to 5% and, 4% outsource up to 10% of their non IT functions. These results are based on a smaller sample as more than half of the organizations did not respond or felt that it did not apply to them. This may also be interpreted that a large percentage of the organizations do not currently outsource.

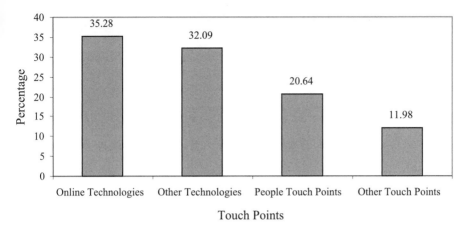

Figure 16-8. Customer Touch Points.

Although the survey instrument contained a question on offshore outsourcing (question 7), only a few responses were obtained hence, the results are not reliable. These results are therefore not documented in the current report.

Customer Facing Interactions

Question 8 – Are relationships with customers developed and maintained using multiple touch points? What are the most popular touch points?

Multiple touch points are used by organizations to interact with their customers. Phone (13.41%), email (13.15%), face-to-face (12.7%), company website – brochure-ware (12.17%) and regular mail (11.46%) are the most frequently used touch points. Screen pops (1.11%) and phone text messaging (1.69%) are the least used by organizations.

Touch points are grouped into the categories of Online Technologies, Other Technologies, People Touch Points and Other Touch Points. Their usage frequency is shown in Figure 8.

Touch points using Online Technologies are used by more than one-third (35.28%) of the organizations; touch points using Other Technologies are used by almost one-third (32.09%) of the organizations; over one-fifth (20.64%) of the organizations use People touch points and 11.98% of the organizations use Other touch points. Online Technologies include email, company website (brochure-ware), company website (transactional), screen pops and online intermediaries; Other Technologies include fax, phone, phone text messaging, phone (IVR – Interactive Voice Response) and phone (CTI - Computer Telephony Integration); People touch points include face-to-face interactions and referrals; and Other touch points include regular mail and any touch points that may not be in the list.

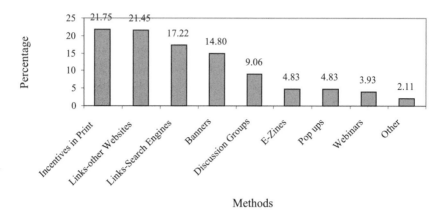

Methods

Figure 16-9. Online Advertising Methods.

Questions 9 & 14 – How are Customer Views integrated into the organiza-tion using certain technologies? What mechanisms are used by organiza-tions to perform customer segmentation?

Various technologies are used to integrate customer views into the organi-zation. Data Marts/Data Warehouses is the technology used by almost a fifth (19.58%) of organizations; Statistical Data Mining is used by 17.85% organi-zations and Customer Profiling is used by 15.16% organizations. Data mining with neural networks (1.73%) and Text Mining (2.11%) are the least used tech-nologies for customer view integration.

Almost a quarter (24.5%) of the organizations segment customers by geog-raphy and over one-fifth (21.19%) use portals for segmenting their customers. The least used methods for customer segmentation are automated cross-selling (e.g., using ATMs for banks) (5.96%) and developed user communities – in terms of channel management (8.94%).

Questions 10, 11 & 12 – Which online advertising methods have been adopted by organizations? Are organizations getting a new face in terms of branding concept, slogan, logo and name in going online? Are Promo-tion and Advertising budgets shifting towards online channels?

Organizations use various channels for online advertising. Incentives in printed material to drive customers to the company website are used by more than a fifth (21.75%) of the organizations; Advertisements or Links on other websites to drive traffic to the company website are used by 21.45% organi-zations, Advertisements or Placement in search engines to drive traffic to the company website are used by 17.22% organizations and Web Banners are used by 14.8% of the organizations. These and other trends are shown in Figure 9.

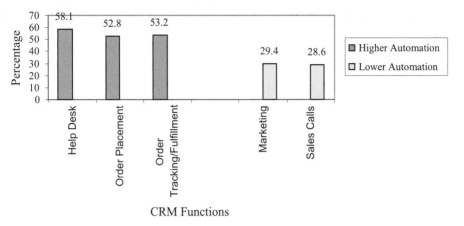

Figure 16-10. Automation of CRM Function.

Although a large number of organizations currently have websites, only a few organizations have changed their online image in terms of their slogan, logo, name or branding concept. Among the organizations that have a new/changed image in going online, branding concept (23%) and logo (23%) have been changed in most cases.

The survey instrument contained a question (question 11) on online advertising budgets. However, due to the few responses that were obtained for this question, data is not reported here.

Question 13 – Which Customer Relationship Management (CRM) functions have been automated?

CRM functions that are automated (either partially or completely) include Help Desk, Order Placement and Order Tracking and Fulfillment. CRM functions that have been automated the least include Sales Calls and Marketing. As shown in Figure 10, 58.1% of the organizations have automated Help Desk, 53.2% of the organizations have automated Order Fulfillment and Tracking and 52.8% of the organizations have automated Order Placement. Only about a quarter of the organizations have automated their Sales Calls (28.6%) and Marketing (29.4%) functions.

Questions 15 & 16 – Are the number of organizations selling products and services online increasing? How is online business different from traditional business?

More than half of the organizations (58.17%) offer Traditional as well as Online services and products. Although one-third (32.69%) of the organizations have only traditional stores, only 1.44% organizations have online stores only.

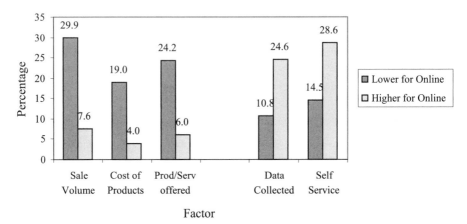

Figure 16-11. Online versus Traditional.

Online business is compared with Traditional business using several factors. Among these, Sales Volume, Cost of Products, Products/Services Offered, Data Collected and Self Service tasks performed by customers are found to be different between online and traditional businesses. Figure 11 shows these differences. Lower as well as Significantly Lower responses are combined under the category of Lower for Online; Higher as well as Significantly Higher responses are shown under Higher for Online. As seen in the figure, online sales volumes are lower than traditional sales volumes for almost one-third (29.9%) of the organizations, Products and Services offered are lower for online for 24.2% organizations and Cost of Products are lower for online for about one-fifth (19%) of the organizations. Data Collected and the number of Self Service tasks performed by customers are higher for online for 24.6% and 28.6% of the organizations respectively.

Trading Partner Relationships

Question 17 – What application technologies are organizations using for communicating with their trading partners?

The most popular technology applications for communicating with trading partners used by organizations include Electronic Data Interchange (EDI) (45.6% of the organizations either have or plan to have the application), XML (45.2% of the organizations either have or plan to have the application) and Web-enabled communications (45.2% of the organizations either have or plan to have the application). Among these applications, XML (25.8% have, 19.4% plan to purchase) and E-payment (24.6% have, 19.8% plan to purchase) although not used as often as EDI (38.7% have, 6.9% plan to purchase) currently, are applications organizations plan to purchase in the next 3 years.

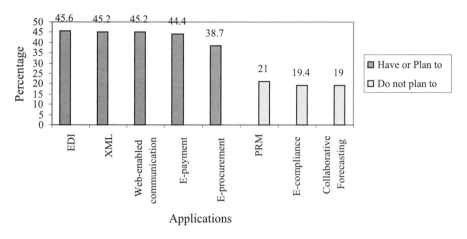

Figure 16-12. Communication with Trading Partners.

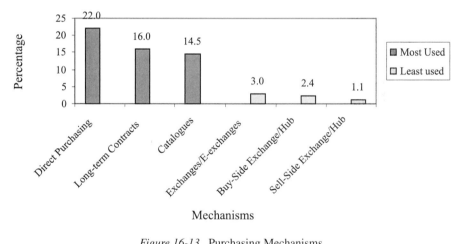

Figure 16-13. Purchasing Mechanisms.

Partner Relationship Management (PRM) (21%), E-compliance (19.4%), and Collaborative Forecasting (19%), are applications that many organizations do not have and do not plan to purchase in the next 3 years.

These trends are shown in Figure 12.

Question 18 – What IT-based channels and B2B mechanisms are organizations using for purchasing?

Organizations are using Direct Purchasing, Long-term Purchasing Contracts and Catalogues as B2B mechanisms for purchasing. Channels such as Exchanges/E-exchanges, Buy-side Exchanges/Hubs and Sell-side Exchanges/Hubs are the least used, as shown in Figure 13.

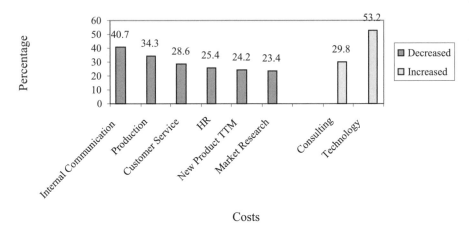

Costs

Figure 16-14. Business Results.

Business Results

Questions 19 & 20 – What Economic and Operational business results and Strategic areas are being impacted by technologies?

Various economic and operational results are impacted by technology. The highest cost reductions are in Internal Communications (decreased or decreased significantly in 40.7% organizations) and Production (decreased or decreased significantly in 34.3% organizations). Costs have also decreased for Customer Service, Human Resources (HR), New Product Time to Market (TTM) and Market Research.

However, Technology (increased or increased significantly in 53.2% organizations) and Consultancy and Communication (increased or increased significantly in 29.8% organizations) costs have gone up.

These business results are shown in Figure 14.

Technology has also impacted strategic areas in organizations. Understanding of Customer Satisfaction for Current Products and Services (51.2%) and Knowledge of Competitor's Products and Services (45.9%), Understanding of future product expectations (40.8%) and of customer buying behavior (40.7%) has improved due to technology.

These are shown in Figure 15.

Globalization

Questions 21 & 22 – Are organizations becoming more global? Is the geographic reach of organizations increasing?

Organizations are increasing their geographic reach in terms of Trade in Other Countries (increasing or somewhat increasing in 30.7% of the organiza-

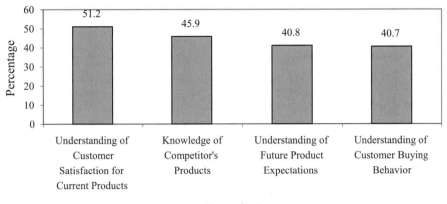

Figure 16-15. Strategic Areas Impacted by Technology.

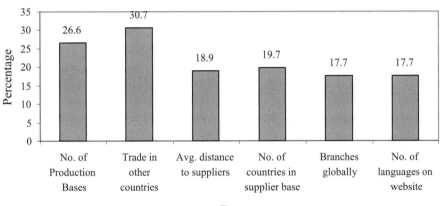

Figure 16-16. Globalization Trends.

tions), Number of Production or Service Bases in other countries (increasing or somewhat increasing in 26.6% of the organizations), and the Number of Countries in the Supplier Base (increasing or somewhat increasing in 19.7% of the organizations). Increased average distance to suppliers, increase in Branches/Distribution centers globally and the Number of languages on the website and in brochures are the other factors considered.

These are shown in Figure 16.

Globalization in terms of the regions to which organizations have expanded or are planning to expand to is shown in Figure 17. Over a third (35.5%) of the organizations currently have or plan to have operations in Canada and Mexico (NAFTA); over a quarter (27%) have/plan to have operations in Western

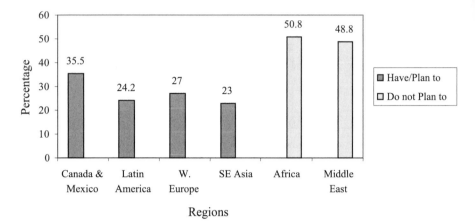

Figure 16-17. Globalization Regions.

Europe and about a quarter have/plan to have operations in Latin America (24.2%) and South-east Asia (23%). Close to half the organizations do not plan to have operations in Africa (50.8%) or the Middle East (48.8%).

6. CONCLUSIONS AND FUTURE RESEARCH

Major conclusions from the survey are as follows:

Technology Adoption/Infrastructure and Budget Trends

- Websites/E-commerce and Wireless hardware and software are the most used technologies.
- Biometrics, Digital Receipts and Radio Frequency Identification (RFIF) are not widely adopted by organizations. However, many plan to purchase RFID in the next 3 years.
- Budgets for Security software and hardware, Software Applications, Storage hardware and Wireless technologies have increased. Budgets for Offshore outsourcing and on-demand computing have not increased significantly.

Internal Organization: Workforce Trends

- The proportion of employees facing a screen has increased. There is a demand for decision support tools at executive levels, and for collaborative work tools. There is an increase in demand for IT skills at lower levels in the organization.
- Although Teleconferencing is becoming popular, Telecommuting is not as widely accepted by organizations.

- Automation is causing workforce reductions. However, respondents do not believe that outsourcing is causing reductions in the workforce.

Internal Organization Structure Trends

- The adoption of new decision making tools and online technologies has increased.
- Organizations are becoming flatter, have fewer levels of control and fewer middle level managers. Telecommuting though not extensively used today, is increasing and organizations are becoming geographically dispersed. As a result the use of Teleconferencing is increasing.
- More organizations are monitoring the productivity of customer facing employees and employing automated monitoring of workforce productivity. However, compensation is not based on these observations.
- Some organizations note a shift in the IT function from a staff role to line responsibilities, but this is not widespread as yet.

Internal Organization – Business Process Outsourcing (BPO)

- Market Research, Payroll and IT Programming are the most outsourced business functions and processes. Finance, Order Fulfillment and Accounting are the least outsourced business functions.
- Organizations outsource about the same percentage of their IT functions as their non IT functions.

Customer Touch Points

- More than one-third of the responding organizations use Online Technologies and Online Customer Touch Points and a little under one-third use Other Technologies (such as fax) as customer Touch Points.

Customer View Integration and Customer Segmentation

- Data Marts and Warehouses as well as Statistical Data Mining are the most popular tools for customer view integration.
- Almost a quarter of the respondents segment customers by geography. A fifth use portals.

Online Advertising and Selling

- Incentives in printed materials to drive customers to the company website are quite widely used. Advertisements or Links on other websites to drive traffic to the company website, Advertisements or Links on search engines to drive traffic to the company website and Web Banners are the most popular online advertising methods.
- Very few organizations have changed their online image in terms of product or company name, branding concept, logo or slogan.

Customer Relationship Management (CRM) Function Automation

- The CRM functions automated most often include Help Desks, Order Tracking and Fulfillment, and Order Placement. CRM functions with the lowest degree of automation are Sales Calls.

Traditional versus Online Selling

- The data collected and self service tasks performed by customers are higher for online selling while sales volumes, cost of products and the number of products offered are higher in traditional selling.

Trading Partner Relationships

- Electronic Data Interchange (EDI), XML and Web-enabled communications are the most popular communication technologies. XML and E-payment are two technologies that several organizations are planning to adopt and implement in the next 3 years.

Purchasing Mechanisms

- Direct Purchasing, Long-term Purchasing and Catalogs are the most used B2B mechanisms used for purchasing. Exchanges/E-exchanges, Buy-side Exchanges/Hubs and Sell-side Exchanges/Hubs are the least used purchasing mechanisms.

Business Results

- Internal Communication costs and Productions costs have decreased with technology adoption. Technology costs, Consultancy and Collaboration costs have increased.
- Technology has helped organizations obtain an understanding of their customer's satisfaction with current products and services and has improved the company's knowledge of their competitors' products and services.

Globalization

- Almost a third of the responding organizations are increasing globalization in terms of Trade with other Countries and more than a quarter are increasing the number of their production or service delivery bases in other countries.
- Organizations are expanding to Canada and Mexico (NAFTA), Western Europe, Latin America and South-east Asia. Very few organizations plan to establish operations in Africa or the Middle East.

The most striking outcome of the survey is perhaps the organizational impact of new technologies. It is clear that work life at the level of the individual, as well as firm wide organizational structures are changing. It is also clear that certain technologies and capabilities have been very widely adopted; eCommerce and active websites for internal and external communications are the most widespread. At the same time there are some rather negative results: organizations do not say that they have expanded their reach on the market side very dramatically. The adoption of hardware based technologies such as biometry and RFID appears to be slower than the software and communications side. Observation of these trends over several years will provide a more complete picture of the changes due to information technologies in businesses.

We note that since the survey is across all industry sectors, some finer analysis may reveal important local differences. Further research on specific industry sectors needs to be conducted. In addition, the firm level surveys do not easily reveal sector level changes. Industry and sector studies need to be conducted to understand those issues better.

Finally, the evolution to an information economy is a global phenomenon, though it may take time to diffuse to all countries. To understand the progress of this evolution, the BIT survey will be conducted in several countries across the world so that a complete picture of the global economy can be obtained.

REFERENCES

Apte and Nath (2004), The Size, Structure and Growth of the U.S. Information Economy, in U.M. Apte and U.S. Karmarkar (eds): Managing in the Information Economy: Current Research Issues, Kluwer Academic Publishing, forthcoming.

Banker, R.D. and Kauffman, R. (1991), Case Study of Electronic Banking at Meridian Bancorp, *Information and Software Technology*, Volume 33, Issue 3, pp. 200–204.

Barua, A., Kriebel, C.H. and Mukhopadhyay, T. (1995), Information Technologies and Business Value: An Analytical and Empirical Investigation, *Information Systems Research*, Volume 6, Issue 1, pp. 67–77.

Brynjolfsson, E. and Hitt, L. (1996), Paradox Lost? Firm Level Evidence on the Returns to Information Systems Spending, *Management Science*, Volume 42, Issue 4, pp. 541–558.

Devaraj, S. and Kohli, R. (2000), Information Technology Payoff in the Health-Care Industry: A Longitudinal Study, *Journal of Management Information Systems*, Volume 16, No. 4, pp. 41–67.

Gurbaxani, V. and Whang, S. (1991), The Impact of Information Systems on Organizations and Markets, *Communications of the ACM*, Volume 34, Issue 1, pp. 59–73.

Hitt, L.M., Wu, D.J. and Zhao, X. (2002), Investment in Enterprise Resource Planning: Business Impact and Productivity Measures, *Journal of Management Information Systems*, Volume 19, Issue 1, pp. 71–98.

Judge, P.C., Burrows, P. and Rheinhardt, A. (1998), Tech to the Rescue?, *Business Week*, pp. 30–31.

Karmarkar, U., Johansen, J., Nanda, D. and Seidman, A. (1995), Empirical Implications for Industrial Information Systems, *Journal of Management Information Systems*, Volume 12, pp. 59–82.

Lehr, B. and Lichtenberg, F. (1999), Information Technology and its Impact on Productivity: Firm-level Evidence from Government and Private Data Sources, 1977–1993, *Canadian Journal of Economics*, Volume 32, Issue 2, pp. 335–362.

Loveman, G.W. (1994), An Assessment of the Productivity Impact of Information Technologies. In T.J. Allen and M. Scott Morton (eds.), *Information Technology and the Corporation of the 90s*, Oxford University Press, Oxford, pp. 81–117.

Machlup, F. (1962), The Production and Distribution of Knowledge in the United States, Princeton University Press, Princeton, NJ.

Machlup, F. (1980), Knowledge: Its Creation, Distribution and Economic Significance, Volume 1: Knowledge and Knowledge Production, Princeton University Press, Princeton, NJ.

Mahmood, M.A. and Mann, G.J. (1993), Measuring the Organizational Impact of Information Technology Investments: An Exploratory Study, *Journal of Management Information Systems*, Volume 10, Issue 1, pp. 97–122.

Mukhopadhyay, T., Lerch, F.J. and Mangal, V. (1997), Assessing the Impact of Information Technology on Labor Productivity: A Field Study, *Decision Support Systems*, Special Issue on Economics of Information Systems, Volume 19, Issue 2, pp. 109–122.

Porat, M.U. and Rubin, M.R. (1977), The Information Economy (9 volumes), Office of Telecommunications Special Publication 77-12, US Department of Commerce, Washington, D.C.

Roach, S. (1991), Services Under Siege – The Restructuring Imperative, *Harvard Business Review*, Volume 69, Issue 5, pp. 82–91.

Sircar, S., Turnbow, J.L. and Bordoloi, B. (2000), A Framework for Assessing the Relationship between Information Technology Investments and Firm Performance, *Journal of Management Information Systems*, Volume 16, Issue 4, pp. 69–97.

Strassman, P. (1990), *The Business Value of Computers*, Information Economics Press, New Canaan, CT.

Talon, P., Kraemer, K. and Gurbaxani, V. (2000), Executives' Perceptions of the Business Value of Information Technology: A Process-Oriented Approach, *Journal of Management Information Systems*, Volume 16, Issue 4, pp. 145–173.

Tam, K.Y. (1998), The Impact of Information Technology Investments on Firm Performance and Evaluation: Evidence from Newly Industrialized Economies, *Information Systems Research*, Volume 9, Issue 1, pp. 85–98.

Thatcher, M. and Oliver, J. (2001), The Impact of Technology Investments on a Firm's Production Efficiency, Product Quality and Product Quality, *Journal of Management Information Systems*, Volume 18, Issue 2, pp. 17–45.

APPENDIX. RESEARCH METHODOLOGY

The Methodology

The study was conducted as a survey mailed to target organizations in multiple industry sectors. Each subject in the study was an independent organizational entity that controlled its own information technology and information policy, and had a Chief Information Officer (CIO) or similar management position within it. It is likely that since the subject organizations are able to make their own technology decisions (and investments), they also have profit and loss responsibility, although this is certainly not necessarily always the case. The surveys were addressed to the CIO (or similar position) as the person most likely to be knowledgeable about the subject.

The survey addressed a wide range of business practice, including technology adoption, internal organization, market facing activity, supplier and vendor relationships, and business results and performance consequences from the application of new technologies.

One of the reasons to use a survey (rather than interviews, case studies or direct data collection) was to be able to address a large number of industry sectors. Understanding the impact of technology on a large number of sectors was important so as to provide a more complete understanding of phenomena across the economy.

Major issues of interest were developed, which were then used to generate survey questions. The survey instrument was mailed to a database of over 24,000 individuals across all industry sectors in the United States and Canada. The data was acquired from an independent entity that collects corporate data. The CIOs (and related positions) were requested to complete the survey either by mail or on-line, where the survey instrument was also made available. Some face-to-face interviews were also conducted in the pilot phase of developing the survey.

The survey instrument (questionnaire) has seven major sections:

1. Technology Adoption/Infrastructure and Budget Trends – technologies adopted and budget trends
2. Internal Organization – changes in the internal organization's workforce, structure and in business process outsourcing due to technologies
3. Customer Facing Interactions – changes in advertising, image, relationship management and other customer facing interactions due to technologies
4. Trading Partner Relationships – changes in partner communications and purchasing mechanisms used due to technologies relationships
5. Business Results – operational and economic business results and strategic areas impacted by technologies
6. Globalization – globalization of the organization due to technologies
7. Organizational Profile – the basic "demographics" of the organization

The Data

The subject group of the survey consisted of organizations and sub-organizations that make independent decisions with respect to the acquisition, implementation and use of new technologies. The survey was sent to senior information systems managers as the individuals most likely to be able to respond to the survey.

About 250 responses were received. The sample characteristics were:

Titles of the respondents were as follows

CIO and other C Level Executives	30.24%
Directors	32.66%
Managers	18.55%
VPs	8.47%
Officers	4.44%
No Response	5.65%

Size of organization in terms of

Annual revenues

Up to 100 million dollars annual revenues	27.82%
100 million to 1 billion dollars	29.84%
Over 1 billion dollars	10.48%
No response or Not Applicable	31.85%

Number of employees

Up to 200 employees	12.10%
200 to 1000 employees	43.55%
Over 1000 employees	39.11%
No response or Not Applicable	5.24%

IT Characteristics of organization in terms of

IT Budget as a percentage of annual revenue

Up to 1%	22.89%
1% to 5%	32.93%
Over 5%	13.25%
No response or Not Applicable	30.52%

Number of IT employees

Up to 10 IT employees	31.05%
10 to 50 IT employees	39.92%
Over 50 IT employees	23.79%
No response or Not Applicable	5.24%

Sectors of organizations North American Industry Classification System (NAICS)

Wholesale Trade	21.91%
Educational Services	15.25%

Retail Trade	10.17%
Government	9.32%
Finance and Insurance	8.05%
Healthcare & Social Assistance	7.63%
Professional, Scientific & Technical Services	5.51%
Information	4.66%
Construction	3.81%
Manufacturing	3.81%
Utilities	2.97%
Administrative & support, Waste Management & Remediation Services	2.97%
Other Services	2.12%
Transportation & Warehouse	1.27%
Arts, Entertainment & Recreation	0.85%
Accommodation & Food Services	0.42%

Chapter 17

INFORMATION AND COMMUNICATION TECHNOLOGY IN INDIA AND ITS IMPACT ON BUSINESS SECTORS – A PILOT STUDY

Atanu Ghosh[a] and T.N. Seshadri[b]

[a]*Shailesh J Mehta School of Management, IIT Bombay, Powai, India;* [b]*Management Department, Birla Institute of Technology and Science, Pilani, Rajasthan, India*

1. INTRODUCTION

The Internet phenomenon was primarily a matter of a fundamental change in information logistics, with the protocols of the web superimposed on a deregulating and increasingly competitive telecommunications environment. It is expected that all the technological and infrastructure developments will change the structure of firms in terms of organization and work process, will change information chains and inter-organizational relationships, and alter the structure of industrial sectors, to the point that the traditional categories do not apply very well.

The Business and Information Technologies (BIT) Study, was initiated at the Center for Management in the Information Economy (CMIE)[1] at the UCLA Anderson School of Management. The main aim of the BIT project is to study the impact of new information technologies on business and industry structure and practice. The study will follow the changes that occur in firms and industry sectors over an extended time horizon. The first step in the process is to do a base line study that establishes the state of this universe, to provide hard information on what is really happening across the economic landscape because of changes in information technologies.

The research reported in this paper is the first pilot study that was conducted in 2003–2004 as part of the global BIT project. Other studies were conducted by SDA Bocconi in Italy, and the UCLA Anderson School. This research project had the primary aim of creating the appropriate survey instrument (questionnaire) and pre-testing it. Of course, the project also gained

---

[1] For more details on the Center of Management in the Information Economy visit http://www.anderson.ucla.edu/cmie.xml

insight into the present state of the adoption of these technologies in Indian industry.

2.   OBJECTIVES OF THE STUDY

The main objective of the research was to investigate the impact of the Internet and the new information technologies on the business organizations.

The study was divided into two phases:

Phase 1: Creating the Instrument

To study the existing set up of the Information Technology in the Industry and design the rough draft of the questionnaire.

Phase 2: Pre-testing the questionnaire

To assess the questionnaire and test its relevance, reliability and validity (keeping in mind the present Indian Business environment) by conducting a pilot (exploratory) study using the instrument designed.

To identify the critical problems that can arise for the respondents and the researcher through the course of conducting the final field study.

We summarize some salient features of the research project. The study is primarily *Descriptive* in that it does not test the causality of any phenomenon, though to a certain extent it attempts to seek explanation for some common questions. The primary purpose was to capture the present status of Indian corporate that uses these Technologies.

The initial phase (Phase 1) of the study consisted of unstructured in-depth interviews. This was used to determine the relevance of the underlying hypotheses and design the questionnaire for the pilot study. In the subsequent pilot survey, the questions were formalized.

The survey has used multiple types of variables and scales depending on the nature of the question. For example, the data pertaining to the use of different software packages were Nominal; the measurement of attitudes of the head of the IT departments of companies on the effectiveness of different systems was on a Likert (Interval) Scale. Except the first four respondents (where it was more of an unstructured interview), all the other respondents were given a questionnaire which was to be self administered and mailed back (or collected personally).

3.   SCOPE AND LIMITATIONS OF THE STUDY

Information systems in organizations are in a continual state of development. Increasingly, the Internet has become a vital tool for conducting businesses and a transition is taking place in the business application of these technologies. For example, more and more firms are making it easier for their personnel to have access to the firm's computing and information resources from remote sites. When the project was started technologies like VoIP had not yet had a large role in business applications, but it is already apparent that they will play a large part in the future.

Our limited sample size (30 companies, out of which 2 companies did not respond and one declined to participate in the study) did not permit the use of many statistical/econometric/multivariate analysis techniques that require larger data sets. Moreover the research being more descriptive than explanatory, does not attempt to investigate the causality of any phenomenon.

4. RESEARCH AND SURVEY METHODOLOGY

The research study entailed two major phases.

Pre-field Study

- Unstructured in-depth interviews were conducted to create the initial questionnaire (the instrument)
- Expert opinions on the questionnaire were collected and further improvements were made to the questionnaire.

Field Study

- A structured questionnaire was prepared and the survey was conducted by explaining the purpose of the research to the respondents and administering the questionnaire.
- A split panel test was also conducted to test certain questions that were felt to be inadequate in their design, to evoke responses from the respondents and to test the effect of changing the structure of these questions.

Most of the questions in the survey are not disguised; but to assess certain non-factual variables disguised questions are used. For example, there are some questions pertaining to the effectiveness of email, Internet etc. which measure the attitudes of the respondent and we take these data as the proxy for that of the organization as a whole. The rational behind this is that the respondents are typically top management personnel in the Information Technology department of the organization and they are in a position to assess the impact of these technologies on their organization. In some cases, to test the relevance of hypotheses and to assess the impact of the questionnaire on the respondent, personal interviews were combined with the completion of the questionnaire.

A small-scale split panel study was done by converting certain questions (rewording or changing the format to see the effect of the questionnaire). The objective of split panel test, done mid-way through the study, was to determine which version of a question or a set of questions was "better".

The split panel test was used to test

1. Alternative wordings of questions
2. The effect of changing the order of a set of questions
3. Alternative response options
4. Determining whether some other response options should be provided

Both the panels received identical treatment. The questionnaire version was changed but the mode of administration etc. remained the same to preserve the integrity of the comparisons. Evaluation of the split panel tests was done along with the analysis of the original questionnaire. The techniques included comparison of response distributions and examination of item non-response data.

Modifications in some questions/items used in the questions were made to increase the response rate and effectiveness of the questionnaire. Some of the respondents had reservations about some questions in the initial questionnaire, due to the sensitive nature of the topics addressed. This necessitated some changes in the later versions of the questionnaire.

References that were especially useful in preparing the questionnaire and for testing the quantitative reliability were "Essentials of Psychological Testing" by Lee Cronbach and "Questionnaire Design and Attitude Measurement" (by A.N. Oppenheim).

5. RESPONDENTS AND DATA COLLECTION

The population addressed by the survey consists of Indian firms or their division(s) having P&L (Profit and Loss) responsibility and autonomy, with most of their management staff in India. Since this study was of an exploratory nature, the sampling method employed was Purposive Sampling (judgmental). Ten industries were chosen with representatives from Service and Manufacturing sectors. Some of these industries, like banking, are advanced in the use of information technology, while many others area not. The Industries and the Companies involved in the survey are given in detail in Appendix I.

The main respondents targeted were the Chiefs or Heads of the Information Technology (Information System) Department; typically the CIO, CTO or the equivalent for division or subunits. However, the heads of the information technology function were not available to be surveyed for all respondents. In these cases the next official in the hierarchy was used as a proxy for the head of the Information Technology Department. Also in many cases, the respondent was recommended by the chief (head of the department), usually due to the higher involvement of the employee with the advanced technology projects of the company.

6. ANALYSIS OF THE QUESTIONNAIRE

The discrimination ability, validity and reliability of the questionnaire were examined. The instrument created was successful in discriminating between different characteristics of the development of information technology across different organizations. The main differentiators noted are:

- The maturity of the different industry sectors included, with respect to the use of information technologies. A sample of this analysis is shown in Appendix II, using Multidimensional Scaling Analysis done for the use of the different IT tools employed in the companies responding.

The following were found to be grouped as like technologies:

1. Videoconferencing, voice mail, mailing list, Internet, Intranet
2. EDI, newsgroup, teleconferencing, chat
3. Email
4. Extranet

The bases for discrimination were "usage pattern" and "the frequency of use". Detailed research on this with more observations in the sample might bear out some conclusive patterns in the comprehensive field studies. But the main point to be noted here is that, statistically the questionnaire discriminates between the different organizations in the sample under study.

- The evolution and the development of different industry sectors with respect to information technologies. Most Indian companies are still in the phase of using information technologies as an operational tool and do not employ IT as a strategic tool. This is indirectly reflected by the respondents not answering questions that are strategic in nature. Also the respondents answers to the question "What does e-Business mean to your company?" were as shown in Figure 1.

Most of the questions being factual, there is little concern about the reliability and validity of the questions. For the questions measuring the attitude of the CIO's/CTO's towards technologies that are present in their organizations, reliability tests were performed to ensure that the questions and the scales measured the attitudes effectively.

For example, the correlation between the responses to two questions related to "Age barrier of decision makers" and "Generation gap in using technology" is very high (0.937). One of the two items can be eliminated as they show high correlation and measure nearly the same construct, namely that "the age of the decision makers is affecting (is a barrier in) the implementation of new technologies".

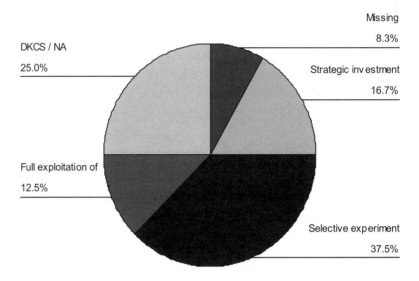

Figure 17-1. e-Commerce – Strategic vs Tactical tool.

7.   SURVEY RESULTS AND OBSERVATIONS

In the following pages, we summarize the results of the pilot survey. We do not address all the questions and subsections in detail (there are over 124 separate parts to the questionnaire). We have selected a few of the major issue areas and hypotheses for discussion.

Websites and brand/image adaptation on-line

All the companies had websites bearing their brand name and were mainly using the site for maintaining contacts with customers and other stakeholders. The main reasons cited for going online were to reach out and target well-informed consumers, to exploit the relatively favorable cost-benefit charac-teristics of the Internet as a medium, and to present a modern image in the competitive marketplace.

There were no radical changes in the brand characteristics; changes were mostly inconsequential and cosmetic in nature, if any. Firms in the banking industry, however, did change their brand features, logo or other characteristics on their sites.

Shifts in allocation of promotion and advertising expenditure across channels

Some of the highest spenders on advertising on the Internet media are ser-vice sector companies such as banks, insurance, and courier/transportation firms. The major spenders in the manufacturing sector are the FMCG[2] companies and the pharmaceutical companies. Among the key sectors:

Banking: Firms in this sector appear to spend the most on Internet advertising; close to 10% of the overall budget for advertising in a year.

Pharmaceuticals: An average of 5% of the annual budget is allocated to the Internet medium.

Courier: An average of 3% of the annual budget is allocated to Internet media.

Though the FMCG companies preferred not to answer this question, their advertising budget can be assumed to be relatively high for the Internet medium, with many of the major portals and websites running advertisements for these consumer goods companies.

Hotel industries do not advertise on portals, but most of the respondents claimed that they get indirect advertising without spending explicitly on advertisements, as many of the travel and hotel reservation portals refer their names and contain links to the hotel home pages.

Some industries like the pharmaceuticals were using media like email more extensively to communicate with their customers about new initiatives pertaining to their fields of specialization or to inform them about new publication and products. In case of pharmaceuticals the main mode of communication between the company and doctors was email.

The main advantages cited by most of the respondents for adopting digital media for advertising were:

- Relative cost-effectiveness of the channel
- Easy targeting of the segments using this medium
- Timeliness of messages
- Potential for interactivity and response

The main reasons that the respondents cited for Internet advertising to be less important than conventional advertising media were:

- In most cases, the target consumers are not Internet users or they are not often on-line
- It was difficult to gauge the impact of Internet advertising
- The lack of the penetration of the Internet in India

Also Internet advertising was thought to be more appropriate for ongoing campaigns, because it was seen as a channel for additional information. Banners and electronic magazines were the main type of advertising used intensively by companies.

---

[2]   Fast moving consumer goods

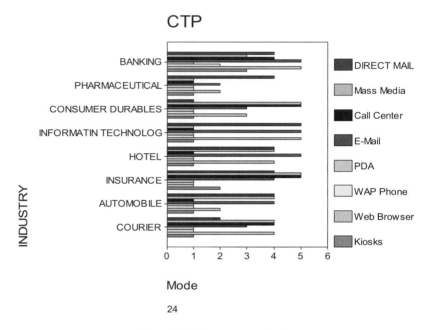

Figure 17-2. Customer touch points.

In the split panel test, the question pertaining to the "shift in allocation to the online media" was framed as a Likert scaled question. The response to this form was better than asking the percentage of advertising budget directly. This may be because most of the respondents did not know the exact allocation of budgets for the Internet medium and it was a cumbersome task for the respondent to search for the data within the organization for individual brands.

Customer touch points, Multiple touch points, Frequency of touch points

Usage of the Internet technologies has definitely increased the number of customer touch points and the frequency of contact. This is clearly visible through high usage rates of Internet based technologies like email, web-browsers etc. However, conventional media have not been sidelined.

The response rate on these questions was not high. Many of the companies were not monitoring touch points. They were also typically not monitoring web sites to study the behavior pattern of customers, but only for any security breaches or for counting the number of hits on their pages.

Increased investments in backroom for customer data base integration; use of data mining tools for customer analysis

Since databases are an essential part of the CRM implementation, the organizations that have implemented the CRM packages tend to be the ones who have invested heavily in these technologies and thus have their databases in-

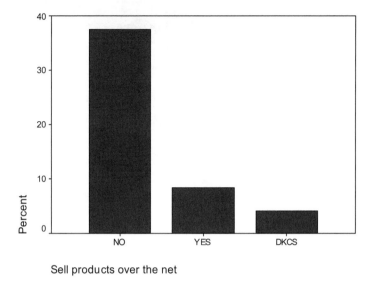

Figure 17-3. Retailing over the Internet.

tegrated to a large extent. And this segment typically consists of banks and hotels in our sample. Other industries do not feel the need to integrate their customer databases as the process is a costly one and difficult to implement. Some organizations like the SBI[3] have been facing the problem of database integration due to the geographic spread of branches, and the poor infrastructure available in many locations. Other industries with some degree of data base integration are the courier and insurance industries.

Retailing and Sales On-line

The use of Internet as a business transaction medium is still very low. There are many reasons for this and the major one quoted by many organizations was the poor penetration of the Internet in India, and consumers attitudes toward using the Internet as a medium of transaction.

Response rate on the question "What is the average number of times you communicate with your customers or vice versa?" was very low. The reason is apparently that data pertaining to customer contact are not either available easily or that contacts are not monitored.

CRM Implementation: the use of software packages, call centers, help desks, on-line support

Out of the 27 companies studied, only 5 had implemented CRM solutions, and only a few major modules were implemented. Many firms (like M&M) who had implemented ERP solutions are extending now to CRM modules.

---

[3]   State Bank of India

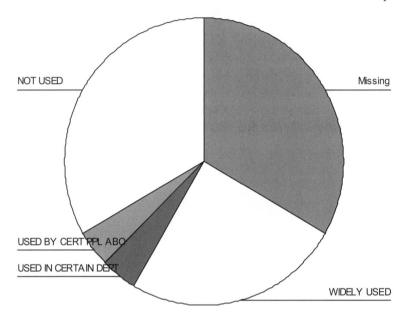

Figure 17-4. Utilization of Newsgroups and Bulletin Boards.

The main hindrances in the implementation of CRM solutions in India appear to be

- Cost factors: Complete third part CRM solutions (all modules) can be afforded only by very few companies
- Call center technology (used by many of the companies implementing CRM) is heavily dependent upon the penetration of telecommunications which is very low in India
- Lack of available databases of customers which form a crucial part of CRM solutions

Implementation in most companies is in a phased manner (if a standard package like Siebel or Talisma is implemented); or companies have chosen to build in-house customer management solutions.

Technology Use: Email

Email has become a vital tool and almost all the respondents stated that their organization used email extensively.

Technology Use: Bulletin Boards

The response to the question on use of bulletin boards and discussion tools, was moderate. The usage levels for respondents were quite high however.

Restrictions on Internet Access and Use

The main types of restrictions covered in this question were:

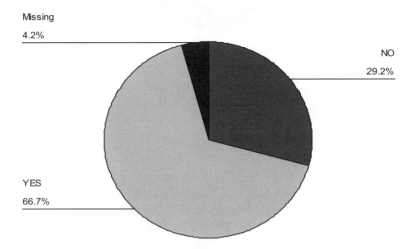

Figure 17-5. Restriction of Internet Access.

- Access to the Net only above a certain Cadre/Level
- Access to Internet for specific departments only
- Access to the Internet to employees only with special permissions or requirements.

Among these, there were multiple responses and the most common one was the special permission requirement.

Estimating what percentage of the executives on an average use Internet was found to be very difficult by the organizations and the response rate was very low. Most of the respondents marked "not monitored" as their response or attempted an estimate.

The preliminary findings suggest that most of the companies use the Internet as a medium of information disbursal. They are yet to mature into the stage of conducting business transactions over the Internet or to full fledged e-commerce.

Internal management: Use of ASP Models

None of the participants of the survey appeared to use ASP models. The main reasons cited were the lack of bandwidth and the lack of the required software within the company.

Productivity Increases

The respondents regarded on-line technologies as very effective in improving productivity. Figure 6 gives a summary of the responses on a scale of 1 to 5, where 5 represents strong agreement with respect to productivity increases.

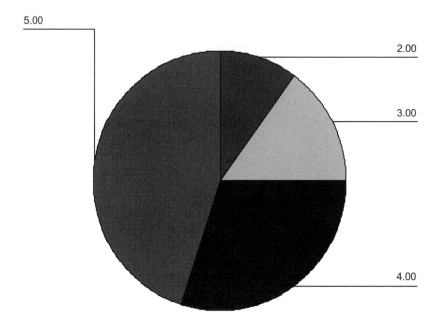

Figure 17-6. Effectiveness of the Internet.

8.   OUTSOURCING

The extent of outsourcing is increasing with "staff functions". But since the companies in the sample are from a broad range of industries, this trend is not universal. Banks, hotels and others outsourced much of their IT requirements.

9.   TECHNOLOGY: SUPPLY-SIDE PACKAGED SOLUTIONS

The overall response for this section was the lowest and was not suitable for any statistical or quantitative analysis. "The questions are not very relevant" was the common underlying message from the executives who filled out the questionnaire.

Implementation of SCM software was done only by a few cash rich companies. The implementation of i2 Technologies SCM solution by Asian Paints is one such example. Also e-procurement and online purchasing (e-sourcing) is being done by very few companies in India. Only a few companies like Telco and M&M have pursued such initiatives.

The lack of a real market is the main reason cited by these companies for not going the e-procurement route. Also cited are the reasons that most of the companies are satisfied with the present vendors and suppliers, who are domestic firms and the traditional telephone and fax channels are found to be the best way to communicate with them. Many of the suppliers are not very large volume players and they do not invest in modern information technologies as yet.

One initiative found in the FMCG industry of late is the use of ECR (Efficient Customer Response) systems. The companies that have joined efforts in this project are the FMCG giants – HLL (Hindustan Levers Limited), Proctor and Gamble, Nestlé, Colgate Palmolive, Johnson and Johnson, ITC, Godrej Consumer Product Limited, Karnataka Soaps – and major retail chains like Margin Free, FoodWorld and Subiksha. The technology enabler seen here includes the enterprise wide systems deployed in these companies and collaborative systems to be implemented among these companies to monitor SKU flow. Bar codes and scanners are to be deployed in a massive scale and EDI (Electronic Data Interchange) system are to be strengthened. Inter organizational interaction between the different participants has also increased as the result of sharing data pertaining to inventory and stock outs.

Digital hubs are not relevant in the Indian context and the use of e-market places is limited to a couple of industries like steel and automotive parts (examples of these include http://autopartsasia.com/ and http://www.steelchange.com).

The use of EDI was found to be restricted to the FMCG companies only, in the sample studied. Only two companies affirmed using XML (one in automotive and another in the banking sector).

10. SUMMARY

As a general observation, the main use of Internet technologies in most organizations was in utilizing the reach of the Internet to improve contacts with the customers and other stakeholders. Many respondent companies had elaborate plans to implement tools for establishing and maintaining their relations with their stakeholders and improve the performance of the organization. The facilities and the information available through the website were also oriented towards this. However, there were limits to the use on-line technologies in executing B2C transactions, primarily because of the low penetration rates of the Internet in the Indian population.

Other important applications were in the internal processes of the companies wherein the tools of modern information technologies were used quite extensively.

The use of supply side solutions is still very low in Indian companies, even among the largest and most sophisticated firms. Much of this can be attributed to the very fragmented nature of the supplier base and of the limited capabilities of second and third tier suppliers.

It is ironic that the implementation of advanced technologies for firms in many of the developed countries is done by Indian software companies, yet when it comes to the utilization of these technologies and the consumption of these technologies, Indian business houses and firms lag behind. Of course, the main reason for this as noted above, is the meager penetration of on-line technologies in both the consumer and industrial populations. We fully expect that as this survey is repeated, it will reveal the significant changes that occur due to economic progress within the country.

REFERENCES

Boyd, Harper W. Jr., Westfall, Ralph and Frasch, Stanley F., Marketing Research: Text and Cases, New Delhi: Irwin, 1999.

Cooper, Donald R. and Schindler, Pamela S., Business Research Methods, New York: McGraw Hill Higher Education, 2002.

Cronbach, Lee, Essentials of Psychological Testing, Third Edition, New York: Harper & Row, 1984.

Decenzo, David A. and Robbins, Stephen P., Human Resource Management, Sixth Edition, Singapore: John Wiley and Sons, 1999.

Galliers, R. D. and Land, F. F., "Choosing Appropriate Information Systems Research Methodologies." Communications of the ACM, 1987, November, 900–902.

Gurbaxani, V. and Whang, S., "The Impact of the Information Systems on Organizations and Markets." Communications of the ACM, 1991, January, 59–73.

Hair, J., R. Anderson, R. Tatham and W. Black, Multivariate Data Analysis with Readings, Fourth Edition, Prentice-Hall, 1995.

Hoque, Faisal, E-Enterprise – Business Models, Architecture and Components, Cambridge University Press, 2000.

Kaplan, Robert M. and Saccuzzo, Dennis P., Psychological Testing: Principles, Applications, and Issues, Pacific Grove, California: Brooks/Cole, 1997.

Koper, Steffano and Ellis, Juanita, The E-Commerce Book – Building the E-Empire, Academic Press, 2001.

Luck, David and Rubin, Ronald S., Marketing Research, Seventh Edition, New York: Simon and Shuster, 1987.

Miller, Irwin and Freund, John E., Probability and Statistics for Engineers, Third Edition, New Delhi: Prentice Hall of India Ltd, 1985.

Oppenheim, A. N., Questionnaire Design and Attitude Measurement, London: Heinemann, 1983.

REFERENCE WEBSITES

http://www.statsoft.com/textbook/stathome.html for statistics and Multivariate Analysis Research Techniques

http://trochim.human.cornell.edu/index.html for Research Methodologies http://www.ucalgary.ca/~newsted/ for research hints and links/references to doing research on MIS (Management Information System) Survey Instruments

http://edf5481-01.fa01.fsu.edu/Guide3.html on the reliability, validity and other tests

http://www.wip-j.net/survey2000.html World Internet Project – Japan

http://www.nasscom.org/NASSCOM's official site

http://asia.Internet.com/gives data pertaining to the trends in the technology

http://www.worldinternetproject.net/the official site of the World Internet Project

http://ecommerce.vanderbilt.edu/courses.html e-commerce research at e-labs, Vanderbilt University

http://www.ebrc.psu.edu/informs/e-businesscenter.html gives a list of e-business and centers of management of e-business at various universities

Appendix I

Table 17-1. List of Organizations (and the Personnel) Surveyed through the Course of the Research Project

	Industry	Name of the Organization
1	Banking	State Bank of India
		UTI Bank
		IDBI Bank
2	Pharmaceuticals	Wockhardt Ltd.
		Nicholas Piramal (I) Ltd.
		Pfizer Ltd.
3	Consumer Durables/	Philips Ltd.
	Home Appliances	Onida (MIRC Ltd.)
		Godrej Appliances Ltd.
4	IT – Hardware/Software/Services	Zenith Computers Ltd.
		Global TeleSystem Ltd.
5	Courier	Elbee Ltd.
		DHL
		Blue Dart
6	FMCG	Godrej Constrn. Prods. Ltd.
		Johnson and Johnson Ltd.
		Colgate Palmolive Ltd.
7	Hotel	Maratha Sheraton
		Holiday Inn
		Le Royal Meredien
8	Insurance	General Insurance Corp.
		Tata AIG
		New India Assurance Corp.
9	Automobile	Fiat Ltd.
		Mahindra&Mahindra Ltd.
10	Retail	Shoppers Stop
		Pantaloon Ltd.

Appendix II

Table 17-2. Results of MDS (Multi Dimensional Scaling) Analysis for Different Tools/Technologies Used in the Organizations

		Stimulus Coordinates Dimension	
Stimulus Number	Stimulus Name	1	2
1	Email	.5423	−.2137
2	Internet	.4878	−.0294
3	MLG_LST	.3838	−.0349
4	Chat	.4350	.0709
5	OLN_TELE	.3800	.0700
6	Voice	.3857	−.0558
7	NEWSGP	.3785	.0825
8	Intranet	.3802	−.0551
9	Extranet	−4.6771	−.0027
10	EDI	.5384	.1314
11	TELECONF	.3816	.0595
12	VDEOCONF	.3839	−.0227

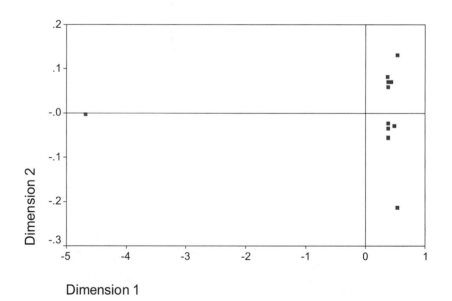

Figure 17-7. Euclidean distance model.

Chapter 18

FIRMS AND DIGITAL TECHNOLOGIES IN ITALY: THE NETWORK MOVES FORWARD

C. Demattè[a], A. Biffi[b], A. Mandelli[c] and C. Parolini[a]

[a]*Business Strategy Department, SDA Bocconi, Milan, Italy;* [b]*Information Systems Department, SDA Bocconi, Milan, Italy;* [c]*Marketing Department, SDA Bocconi, Milan, Italy*

Abstract   Implementation of new digital technologies in Italian firms has not been as rapid as might have been expected, even though they have started to change the way in which businesses are organized. After the disillusionment that followed the euphoria of the nineties, many firms have postponed their e-business investments as they look for more certain answers to their questions. We tried to find at least some of these answers in this study of the development of e-business in Italy by meta-analyzing relevant research studies (including the results of 16 case analyses developed at SDA Bocconi by colleagues working in different management disciplines), and by interviewing 56 e-business managers in firms of different sizes operating in various industries. The results of the study indicate that digital technologies and e-business have already changed the nature and organization of businesses, but perhaps in a different way from that originally expected. The use and impact of BtoC e-commerce is limited. Instead firms have mainly used digital networking technologies in order to reorganise their internal processes and relationships in the supply chain. The role of culture and of intangible resources has proved important.

1.   INTRODUCTION

The complex phenomenon of e-business has so far led to results that are generally difficult to assess. After the euphoric period between 1997 and the beginning of the year 2000, many firms have reconsidered their e-business investments (often including those already approved) because of the unsatisfactory results of the past. However, we believe that although the excessive optimism of some years ago encouraged some rash investments, the excessive scepticism characterizing the current economic phase is equally misplaced. The new information technologies have modified the information paradigm, and this has inevitably had a significant impact on the way in which firms compete, are managed, and communicate with their customers, suppliers and partners. One of the reasons for the apparently unsatisfactory results of past e-business initiatives is that during the initial development phase of the Internet, too much stress was placed on e-commerce. This overshadowed activities aimed at reorganizing internal and supply chain processes which, although they may be less striking from the outside, can lead to very interesting results if appropriately managed (as is demonstrated by many of the cases analysed in our research).

Far from the noise of front page news, many firms use networking technologies (hardware, software and communication systems) as they should be used: systems for managing relationships with key customers; systems for making back-end processes more efficient or effective; systems for improving their public image; and systems for improving the management of human resources.

For these reasons, we decided to consider the impact of digital technologies on the way enterprises do business, in the belief that:

- the Net has by now become an essential part of society and the economy;
- albeit at different times and in relation to their own particular applications, firms will have no alternative but to use the Net and web-based technologies as organizational development levers, and more simply, as a means of replacing their technological legacy systems when these become obsolete;
- in most economic sectors, the real potential of the Net (both from the business and the organizational point of view) has not yet been widely exploited;
- firms need to know how much of this potential they can realistically attain;
- many firms have developed functioning systems that are difficult to measure in terms of their performance.

Our study is based on empirical evidence collected using the following methodologies:

1. a meta-analysis of the available work produced by other authoritative research institutes;
2. a "multiple case-study" analysis of 16 case histories focussing on different company areas and functions;
3. a quantitative analysis of 56 interviews with e-business managers working in companies of different sizes operating in different industries (the first phase of our WIP-Bits project—see below).

2. THE BASIC PREMISE: SLOW IMPLEMENTATION IN ITALIAN FIRMS

In the period 1995–2001, e-business initiatives were set under way by a significant number of firms. According to the Net Impact Study USA,[1] the majority of US firms of all sizes had introduced Internet Business Solutions (IBS)[2] by 2001, and most had initiated their first IBS by the end of the 1990s. The picture in Italy is very different: only 11.4% of the firms with more than 20 employees have established IBS, against 61% in the USA and an average of 47% in Great Britain, Germany and France. Furthermore, the investments in Italy were made about three years later than those in the USA, and did not peak until 2001.

Although interesting, the data shown in Figure 1 do not fully reflect the real commitment of firms to e-business initiatives insofar as the Net Impact Studies only identify whether firms have invested in IBS and not how much they invested, thus giving equal weight to highly significant and totally marginal initiatives. Unfortunately, we do not have any data concerning the magnitudes of IBS investments, and therefore what follows is based on statistical data which, while not directly measuring the IBS phenomenon, are related to it in various ways.

Figure 2 shows the considerable growth of ICT investments in all Western countries over the last 20 years and, in particular, the higher level of investments in the USA.

However, the rapid growth of the ICT market seems to have come to an end in 2000, mainly because of the slower rates of investment in the USA and Japan (see Figure 3 and 4).

Other indicators of the orientation towards establishing IBS are firms' Internet access rates and the presence of web sites (necessary for any on-line initiative). Figure 5 shows these data for some Western countries, distinguishing internally and externally managed web sites. As can be seen, Italian firms have access rates that are comparable with those of other Western countries,

---

[1]   There are two Net Impact Studies. The first was undertaken in 2001 by Hal Varian, Robert Litan, Andrei Elder and Jay Shutter, and was based a sample of 2065 organizations in the USA and 634 in the three major European countries. The second was carried out in 2002 by Ferdinando Pennarola and Francesco Giavazzi, and was based on a sample of 1006 statistically representative production units in Italy. Both studies were financed by Cisco Systems.

[2]   In this paper, we shall use the definition of Internet Business Solutions (IBS) proposed in the Net Impact Study published in the USA in January 2002: "Any initiative that combines the Internet with networking, software and computer hardware technologies to enhance or improve existing business processes or create new business opportunities". IBS and e-business initiatives are considered to be synonymous.

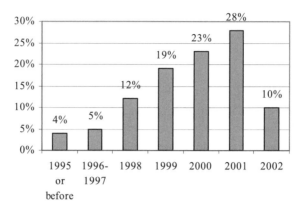

Year of starting first IBS

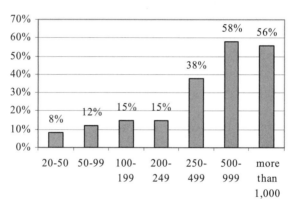

Company size (No. of employees)

Figure 18-1. Internet Business Solutions adoption rates and years of implementation in Italy.
Source: Net Impact Study Italy (2002).

but are characterized by a particularly small number of internally managed
web sites. Only Spain shows a similar pattern.

The immaturity of the on-line presence of Italian firms is confirmed by the
data shown in Figure 6, which indicate the very modest on-line presence of the
majority of them.

Another indicator of the sophistication of the implemented IBS is the number of firms with broadband connections. Figure 7 shows the percentages of
ISDN, xDSL or other broadband connections in some Western countries.

The most sophisticated IBS include on-line purchasing and sales initiatives.
As can be seen in Figure 8, the percentage penetration of such IBS among
Italian firms is one of the lowest in Western countries.

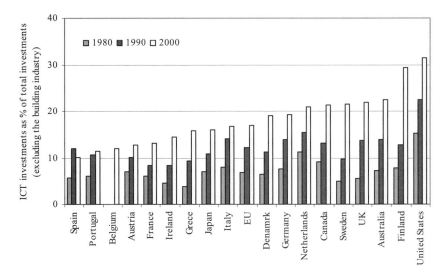

Figure 18-2. ICT investments (hardware and software) in OECD countries (1980, 1990, 2000). Source: Measuring the Information Economy, OECD 2002.

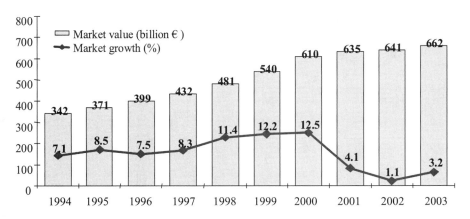

Figure 18-3. The ICT market in Western countries 1994–2003. Source: EITO 2002.

The position of Italian firms does not seem to be better if we consider the number of secure servers per million inhabitants: Italy is even behind countries such as Portugal and the Czech Republic (see Figure 9). This is particularly worrisome since the use of a secure server is a pre-requisite for any IBS initiative worthy of note.

The above picture clearly shows that while many firms in Western countries have implemented IBS over recent years, Italian firms have been particularly slow in establishing major e-business initiatives. The great majority of Italian firms thus find themselves having to decide on their first e-business initiative

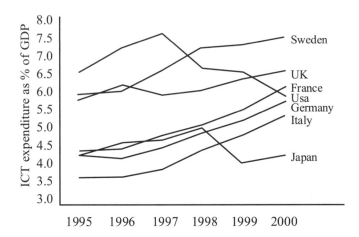

Figure 18-4. ICT expenditure as percentage of GDP. Source: EITO 2002.

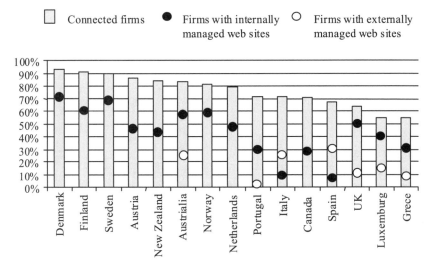

Figure 18-5. Internet access and the presence of web sites in firms with more than 10 employees. Source: Measuring the Information Economy, OECD 2002.

at a time in which even the most advanced countries are questioning the profitability of such investments. It is therefore more important than ever to analyse the results of what has happened in these years of experimentation.

From the point of view of online sales, results have been disappointing. B2C sales are much lower than anticipated and most of B2B sales are still transacted on old EDI systems. For comparative purposes, it is useful to note that on-line B2B sales in the USA in 2000 amounted to 213 billion dollars (as against about 29 billion dollars for B2C e-commerce), with an increase of

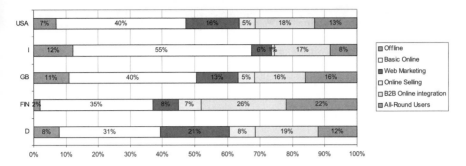

Figure 18-6. Types of on-line presence by country (2001). Source: Empirica/BMWI 2001.

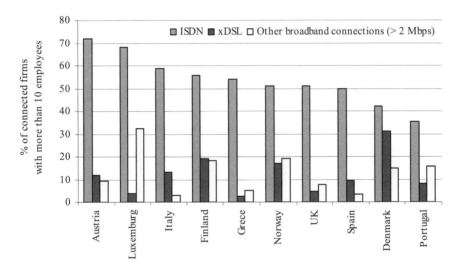

Figure 18-7. Broadband connections of firms with more than 10 employees. Source: Measuring the Information Economy, OECD 2002.

17% over the previous year. However, 88% of the B2B turnover was made using EDI systems and not the Internet. The same is true in Europe: for example, according to OECD data, B2B e-commerce in Great Britain in 2000 accounted for about 6% of total sales, but this goes down to 0.9% if we consider Internet commerce in its strict sense; and the corresponding figures for Italy were respectively 1.1% and 0.4%. Nevertheless, B2B transactions are increasing very rapidly: according to the CEI, for example, on-line B2B transactions in the USA in 2002 reached 793 billion dollars, and this was certainly due to a considerable increase in non-EDI transactions.

On the other hand, the results of IBS cannot be judged only on the basis of online sales: the impact on internal processes and overall productivity needs to be taken into account.

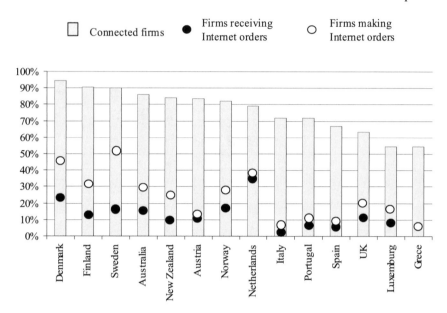

Figure 18-8. Internet access, and on-line purchasing and sales in some Western countries in 2001. Source: Measuring the Information Economy, OECD 2002.

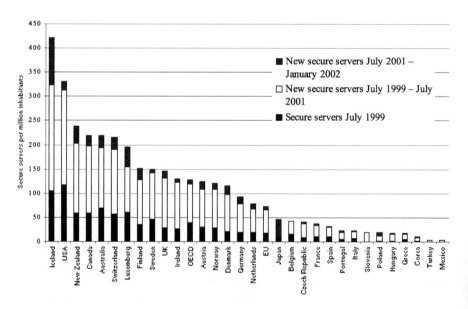

Figure 18-9. Number of secure servers per million inhabitants (2001). Source: Measuring the Information Economy, OECD 2002.

Table 18-1. Cost savings and impact on productivity of IBS investments. Source: Net Impact Studies

Data in percentages or billion of $ or €	USA 1996–2000	USA 2001–2010	UK-F-D 1996–2000	UK-F-D 2001–2010	Italy 1996–2001	Italy 2002–2006
Cost saving[a]	$72.8	$452.5	€5.2	€81.9	€9.17	€6.61
Cost saving as % of GDP in the considered period	0.88%	4.3%	0.09%	1.1%	0.89%	0.47%
Impact on annual productivity	+0.17%	+0.43%	+0.017%	+0.11%	+0.14%	+0.095%

[a]The cost saving shown in the table is the cumulative saving from the year of IBS implementation to 2000 or 2010, depending on the column. The impact is the estimated impact on the economies of the different countries of the organizations that have implemented IBS and declared that they have measured increased profits and/or decreased costs.

3. THE IMPACT OF E-BUSINESS: RESULTS FROM SECONDARY RESEARCH

A number of studies have tried to measure the impact of ICT technologies on productivity. Those that sustain the hypothesis of a positive impact include the Net Impact Studies carried out in the USA, Great Britain, Germany and France in 2001, and in Italy in 2002. Both found that IBS had a positive impact on company productivity, which (but only in the USA) is likely to become highly significant over the next few years. Table 1 summarizes some of the principal data presented in the two studies.

According to some studies, the differences in the impact of ICT technologies on productivity between the USA and European countries may be due to different levels of investment (see Figure 2 above). For example, in the period 1995–1999, ICT investments accounted for 30% of all company investments (excluding building) in the USA, but only about 15–20% of those in the four countries considered in the Net Impact Studies.

The results of the Net Impact Study relating to the USA indicate that Internet Business Solutions accounted for a significant proportion of the increase in productivity in comparison with the period 1974–1995, particularly if the forecasts for the period 2001–2011 are considered (see Figure 10).

There are many reasons for the widespread disappointment felt in relation to the Internet, most of which are unfounded in our opinion. The innovativeness of a system of universal connectivity such as the Internet cannot be anything but extremely important, even if it is more difficult to take advantage of this potential than many people imagined.

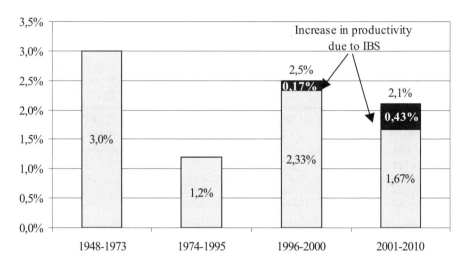

Figure 18-10. Impact of IBS on the increase in annual productivity rates. Source: Net Impact Study USA.

First of all, it is interesting to note that, as in the case of all great technological innovations, the attitude towards the Internet has passed from a phase of scepticism to one of exaggerated expectations and then to one of great disappointment. Studies of the diffusion of new technologies have shown that this alternation of negative and positive attitudes is typical, particularly when the new technologies are as systemic and all-pervasive as the Internet. After their initial scepticism, many firms saw the great potential of the Internet and launched major investment projects; however, the Internet and ICT technologies in general have a highly systemic nature. ICT innovations are essentially enabling: i.e. they allow the introduction of important strategic and organizational innovations, but do not *per se* increase a firm's efficiency and effectiveness. In order to be able to express their full potential, these technologies must be accompanied by profound changes not only in internal processes, but above all in the firm's relationships with its suppliers, customers and partners—and these changes take time and effort. We believe that it was precisely this systemic complexity that was underestimated during the phase of enthusiasm.

Another error made by many firms during the phase of euphoria was to invest in IBS in an indiscriminate manner, accepting everything that technology vendors had to offer without sufficiently considering the specificity of the firm's territory, industry and production pipeline, or its strategic and organizational profile. In this regard, it is also possible to criticise many vendors for having over-sold e-commerce platforms, thus often generating exaggerated expectations. The success of e-business initiatives and the choice of the most suitable type of IBS to adopt depend on many internal and external determinants that must be carefully evaluated and which may not be adequately addressed by pre-packaged solutions.

Furthermore, it must be remembered that positive results do not always have a direct and immediate effect in terms of reduced costs or increased profits, but may lead to less easily measurable advantages that have a positive but often unquantifiable impact on the firm's competitiveness.

In many cases, the investments made so far still need to be refined. The firms interviewed in the Net Impact Studies (excluding the Italian firms) believe that they have yet to see the most significant part of the cost savings related to the IBS investments they have already made. Finally, the average results obtained so far mask highly differentiated situations: the negative or disappointing results of some industries (and firms) need to be set against other situations in which the contribution of ICT technologies has been very positive.

It is important for the firms now having to decide whether to begin, extend or abandon e-business projects to pay close attention to the lessons emerging from empirical research studies and the reconsideration of the available data.

3.1. The Determinants of the Results of e-Business Initiatives

The question to which entrepreneurs and managers would like to find an answer is not whether e-business initiatives have been successful on the whole, but to what extent a given e-business project promises to be remunerative for their firms, at least in the medium-term. Unfortunately, there is no simple answer to this question: the success of an e-business initiative depends on a multiplicity of internal and external factors. Many firms were induced to make rash investments precisely because they underestimated the importance of their territorial, industrial and company specificities.

The main categories of the determinants of the results of e-business initiatives are described in Figure 11.

In this section, we shall try to outline the significance of each of the elements shown in Figure 11.

3.2. External Pre-conditions

A firm's technological investments are naturally related to the overall economic situation and the general expectations of economists, but also to the "readiness" of its business partners and customers. According to the findings of Forrester Research (2002) concerning a sample of 361 American firms of different sizes, the two main reasons hindering investments in e-business applications (particularly e-procurement) during 2001 were:

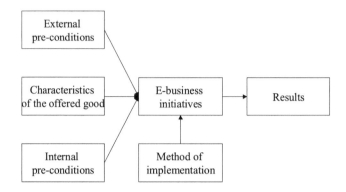

Figure 18-11. The determinants of the results of e-business initiatives.

1. the impact of the negative overall economic situation;
2. the lack of readiness of the firms (partners) with which the new applications would have allowed collaboration.

This second point largely overlaps what we have called external pre-conditions in Figure 11, the most important of which are the characteristics of the territory and the pipeline in which the e-business initiative is to be incorporated. In terms of territory, the success of such initiatives is above all tied to the degree of Internet penetration among end users (for B2C initiatives) and firms (for B2B initiatives).

Many research centres periodically monitor the end users that have access to the Internet and, although the percentages may vary depending on the definition of the user (e.g. only adults or all of the population), the majority of the statistics indicate that about 30% of the European population currently has access to the Internet as against 50% of the US population. According to Jupiter, for example, the European on-line population should increase from 31% in 2001 to 51% in 2007, whereas that of the USA should increase from 50% to 73% during the same period. The percentage penetration indicated for Italy is very similar to the European average (24% and 48%).

However, penetration rates are not very significant. Access to the Internet is now very widespread in all Western countries, and the between-country differences are quite rapidly decreasing. What really distinguishes the different geographical areas are the methods of access (Table 2) and the rate of use of sophisticated services (Figure 12).

As can be seen in Table 2 and Figure 12, what distinguishes Italy is not so much the rate of access, but the infrequent and basic use that Italians make of the Internet. There is a circular relationship between this situation and the unsophisticated presence of Italian firms on the Internet described above: the scarcity of sophisticated services does not encourage an intensive and evolved

Table 18-2. Methods of access to the Internet in some Western countries. Nielsen NetRatings 2001

July 2001	UK	France	Germany	Italy	Sweden	Netherlands	Japan	USA
No. of sessions per month	13	15	17	12	12	15	19	20
No. of individual sites visited	18	17	25	16	13	22	12	11
On-line time per month (hh:mm)	6:22	6:58	7:49	5:48	5:29	6:44	9:27	10:19
Universe of Internet users (millions)	23.9	11.1	27.9	18.7	5.5	8.7	46.7	165.2
Active users (millions)	13.1	5.5	15.1	8.3	3.0	4.5	20.1	102.1
Active users as % of users	55%	49%	54%	45%	55%	52%	43%	62%
Active users as % of the population	22%	9%	18%	14%	34%	29%	16%	37%

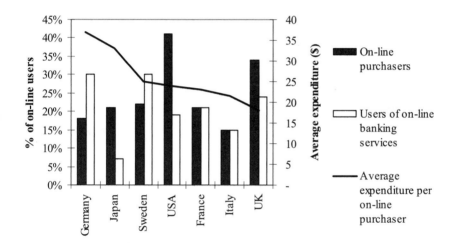

Figure 18-12. On-line purchases, on-line banking and average on-line expenditure of final users (2000). Source: Booz, Allen Hamilton (2002).

use of the network, just as the existence of unsophisticated users is not the best basis for an on-line initiative. However, to judge from a recent survey, the less sophisticated approach of Italian users seems to be due more to the limited offer than to any lack of experience with computers and the Internet (see Figure 13).

Moving on to the rate of penetration among firms, we can add some data concerning the difference in Internet access rates between small firms (see Figure 14) and the larger firms whose access rates are approaching 100%. We shall therefore try to give some indications of the methods of use of business users (see Figure 14 and Table 3 for the percentage of small firms that sell on line).

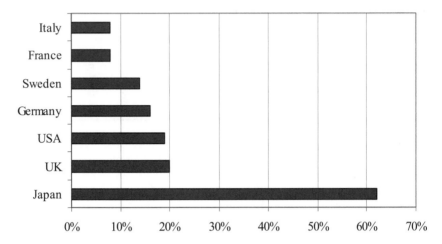

Figure 18-13. Percentage of users citing a lack of skill as a barrier to more sophisticated use.
Source: Booz, Allen Hamilton (2002).

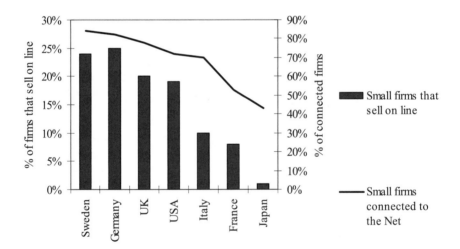

Figure 18-14. Internet access rates and the percentage of small firms (up to 50 employees) that
sell on line. Source: Adapted from DTI IBS 2001.

Once again, more than a difference in access rates, the data shown in Figure 14 and Table 3 highlight a difference in the methods of use. Furthermore,
the relative backwardness of small and medium-sized enterprises in comparison with their large counterparts is particularly worrying because of the high
degree of fragmentation of the Italian private sector.

However, regardless of size, we have previously pointed out that Italian
firms are little inclined to purchase on line. Figure 15 returns to this aspect
by showing the percentage of firms that purchased on line in 2000 and 2001

Table 18-3. Use of ICT technologies and e-commerce in Italy and Great Britain (2001). Source: Eurostat/European Commission (2001)

	Italy		Great Britain	
	SMEs	Large enterprises	SMEs	Large enterprises
Computers	86%	99%	92%	100%
Access to the Internet	72%	97%	62%	90%
Web site	9%	22%	49%	80%
On-line purchases	10%	21%	32%	50%
On-line sales	3%	8%	16%	35%

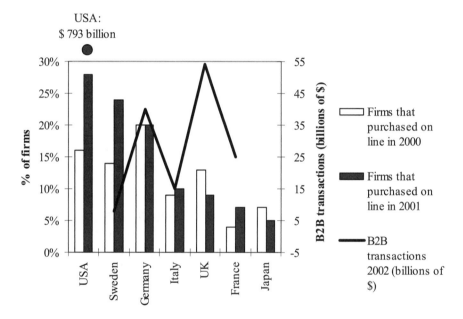

Figure 18-15. B2B purchases in some Western countries. Source: DTI IBS 2001 and CEI data for December 2002.

in some Western countries, as well as the total amount of B2B transactions in 2002.

In addition to customers, suppliers and partners, the government plays a significant role in determining territorial readiness and, in this regard, the Italian situation again seems to be particularly worrisome. According to an analysis by Booz Allen, the Italian government spent about 80 dollars per citizen on Information Technology in the period 2000–2001, against the more than 150 dollars spent in Germany, about 190 dollars in Great Britain and the USA, and as much as about 270 dollars in Sweden. This lack of public investment inevitably affects the quantity and quality of on-line public services. According

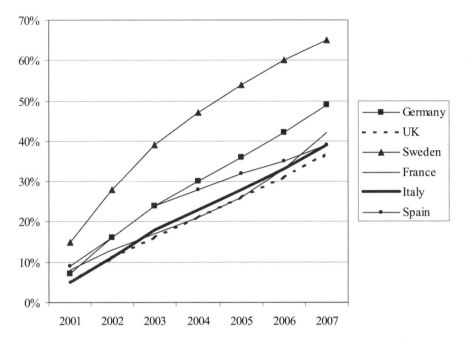

Figure 18-16. Percentage of on-line families with access to the fixed broadband network. Source: Jupiter 2002.

to Accenture's 2002 e-government report, the amount and sophistication of the on-line public services offered in Italy places it behind (in order) Canada, the USA, Australia, Great Britain, Germany, France and Japan.

Italy is characterized more by a lack of supply than a lack of demand for on-line public services. Despite their scarcity, the percentage of firms and individuals accessing them is in line with the average of the other countries, and higher than that in France and Germany. Furthermore, in the case of projects that involve the transmission of large amounts of data, an important determination of the territorial result is the diffusion of fixed and wireless broadband networks. Figure 16 shows the penetration rates of fixed broadband networks in some European countries. Although lagging behind Germany and Sweden, the forecast penetration rates in Italy are similar to those of the other major European countries.

In relation to access to broadband services in Italy, prices are a more significant negative factor than penetration rates. According to a Booz Allen analysis, in June 2002, the average monthly cost of a broadband connection in the retail segment was 60 dollars, against $20 in Japan, $29 in Sweden, $40 in Germany and Great Britain, and about $47 in the USA. The same study also found that the take-off level of subscriptions to broadband services is about $40.

All of the above territorial considerations must naturally be seen in the context of the firm's specific economic environment. What counts for Italian firms is therefore not so much the levels of readiness of Italy as a whole, but that of their own customers and suppliers, and the specific territorial framework in which the e-business initiative is to be set under way. It is therefore possible to speak of the level of readiness of the pipeline to which the firm belongs and, even more precisely, that of its individual suppliers, customers and partners. This level may be different from the average if, for example, the firm sells through particularly specialized channels or buys the majority of its purchases from particularly sophisticated large-scale suppliers.

3.3. Characteristics of the Offered Good

One of the mistakes most frequently made during the euphoric period of the Internet was the failure to consider whether on-line sales were compatible with the offered good. In the case of B2C e-commerce initiatives, the factors that should be considered when evaluating this compatibility can be summarized as follows:

- The possibility of digitalizing the good. Digitalized goods can not only be sold, but also delivered on line, thus leading to considerable savings in distribution costs.
- The importance of personalization. In the presence of personalization needs, on-line sales allow low-cost interactions with customers, thus reducing the costs of acquiring an order and the errors in making it up. Furthermore, in many cases, on-line configurers allow the price and composition of the personalized product to be immediately displayed, which facilitates the purchasing process for the customer.
- The difficulty of finding the good. In the absence of other advantages, it does not make much sense to think of selling a product on line that can easily be bought in a neighbourhood shop. Unique products (consider, for example, the success of eBay with collectible items) and difficult to find specialties are much more suitable for on-line selling.
- The impact of logistic costs on the delivered value and cost of the good. On-line sales are easier in the case of small and non-perishable goods of high value in relation to the cost of delivery. This does not exclude the possibility of selling goods with the opposite characteristics (as in the case of on-line supermarkets), but this requires setting up highly complex logistic structures that are difficult to amortize.
- Average prices and margins, and the frequency of purchase. The high costs of acquiring on-line customers, together with the high costs of home delivery, mean that e-commerce initiatives can only be self-sustaining if the acquired customers generate high levels of income and margins that are

preferably repeated over time. For example, the on-line sale of supermarket products involves very high logistics costs but also ensures high and continuous revenue levels per customer.

- The time or distance between purchase and consumption. At least until wireless terminals have become widepread, it will be easier to sell on line products that are purchased long before they are consumed (such as tourist services) than those bought on impulse.
- The possibility of digitalizing the information relating to the good. This must not be confused with the possibility of digitalizing the good itself because some digitalized goods are difficult to describe (such as ERP applications) and some physical goods are easy to describe (such as a branded packaged food product). It is more difficult to sell on line products that are difficult to describe in words or text (such as clothes or footwear).
- Frequency of interaction. Finally, the Net is an excellent channel when customer relationships are characterized by frequent purchases (or other interactions), as in the case of financial trading. In such cases, on-line supplies allow considerable advantages in terms of both customer and cost reductions insofar as repetitive operations can be automated and performed at low marginal costs.

The factors summarized above are reflected in the different success rates of e-commerce initiatives in different industries. In this regard, see Figures 17 and 18, which respectively show current European B2C sales, and the current and forecast importance of on-line sales by sector.

In order to complete what has been pointed out above, it needs to be added that what counts is not so much the sector to which a firm belongs, but its specific market segment and proposed supply system. For example, the book publishing sector includes segments that have many of the characteristics listed above (such as university publishing) and others that are much less suitable for taking advantage of the Internet's potential for innovation (such as best sellers). Furthermore, it is necessary to consider that the product sold on line does not necessarily have to be the same as that sold off line. In the case of university publishing for example, it is possible to think of on-line services and the sale of personalized printed and e-books that do not exist in the traditional supply systems.

Finally, it is necessary to point out that only some of the above comments about B2C apply to the B2B segment, including the possibility of digitalizing the good, the importance of personalization (customization), the difficulty of finding the good, the possibility of digitalizing the information relating to it, and the frequency of interactions or purchases. However, more relevant than the characteristics of the good are the readiness of the pipeline and the specific supply network, and the type of relationship between customer and supplier.

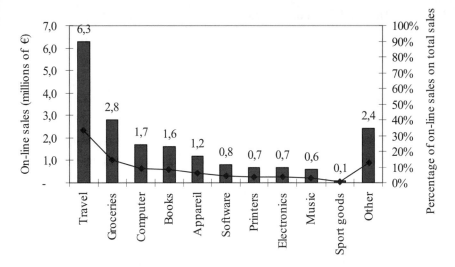

Figure 18-17. B2C sales in Western Europe by sector. Source: Jupiter 2002.

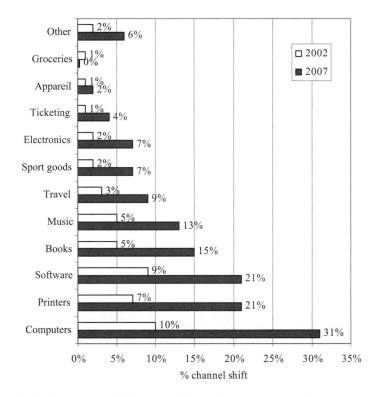

Figure 18-18. Importance of B2C sales in Western Europe by sector. Source: Jupiter 2002.

3.4.   Internal Pre-conditions

The internal pre-conditions for the success of e-business initiatives can be divided into three broad categories:

- social and organizational pre-conditions;
- the degree of control over the pipeline;
- strategic positioning.

Organizational pre-conditions. E-business initiatives express their full potential if they are incorporated in organizational contexts that are already used to digitalizing and sharing information. Such pre-conditions therefore include not only organizational pre-conditions in the strict sense, but also technological pre-conditions such as the presence of well-functioning ERP systems or, at least, systems that are sufficiently open and "interfaceable".

According to the results of a study conducted by MIT in 2002, investments in digital technologies increase productivity in general, but do so particularly if the firm has a considerable amount of organizational capital available. Organizational and technological capital are complementary. When a firm makes above-average investments in both organizational and technological capital, the results are more than proportionally better than when only one of the two levers is used. By organizational capital, we here mean the application and acceptability of the following initiatives:

1. free access to information;
2. distributed decision-making rights;
3. performance-related incentives;
4. investments in corporate culture;
5. the communication of strategic objectives;
6. recruitment excellence;
7. investments in human resources.

One particularly interesting result regards the synergy of these different organizational levers: the MIT researchers found that, when these changes are only partially introduced, the firm's results not only fail to improve but may actually worsen.

In the same study, what proved to be the most important variable in predicting the success of adopting digital applications was the strong support of senior management.

The concept of social capital is as relevant as that of organizational capital. Networks feed on relationships, but such relationships do not come out of the blue: they require investments and social capital, by which we mean the wealth of social relationships and the reputation of the economic player concerned. Social capital is the fundamental resource for building new social capital. A good reputation makes it easier to construct new relationships

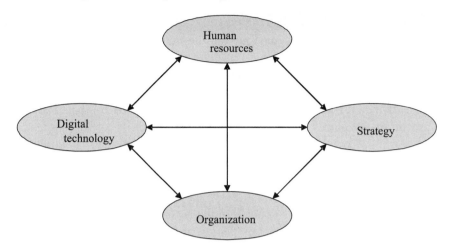

Figure 18-19. Management of a digital organization: technology is not enough. Source: Brynjolfsson (2002).

(above all in an environment as uncertain as the Net) because the perception of risk can only be diminished by the reassurance offered by the trust that has developed among the partners.

Trust is therefore both the input and output of digital relationships: without it, users do not have faith in on-line suppliers, and the informal organizational and inter-organizational networks made possible by the new technologies cannot be established. However, if the new activities generate satisfaction, they create new resources of trust for future relationships (Castaldo, 2002). Empirical research has shown that the decisions to entrust sensitive services (in this case, information) to a supplier are principally made on the basis of the trust inspired by firms with an established name and the trust built up as a result of off-line experiences. This attitude has been confirmed by many studies of the behaviour of on-line users, such as the results of SDA Bocconi's WIP 2001 study of the determinants of on-line trust when choosing information sources.

The majority of e-business initiatives go beyond the boundaries of individual firms, thus modifying the relationships between the different players in the pipeline (who are obliged to review their own relationships and operational processes) and, sometimes, even marginalizing traditional players by leading to the elimination of some categories of intermediaries. It is natural that such situations induce resistance or even trigger negative reactions that can only be neutralized by players with considerable bargaining power.

Furthermore, even in the absence of adverse reactions, the advantages of the Internet can only be fully acquired if the players involved manage to abolish the information barriers between them in order to share platforms, processes and the information itself. This is only possible in the simultaneous presence of trust (or social capital as defined above) and power. Pipeline leaders can often impose otherwise difficult behaviours on the other members of the pipeline. This can be clearly seen in the case of marketplaces. However well designed they may have been, none of the many independent marketplaces set up over the last few years has managed to take on a major role in its sector, but the decline of independent marketplaces has been paralleled by the emergence of private marketplaces or those managed by consortia of leading large-scale firms, such as Covisint, the automotive marketplace founded by Ford, GM, Daimler-Chrysler and GobalNetExchange, and promoted by Sears and Carrefour.

The possibilities of success and the most appropriate types of e-business initiatives to set up, not only depend on the sector and the offered product or service, but also on the strategic positioning of the individual firms. For example, a financial trading company whose customers are young and aggressive, but have medium-low assets, can obtain a considerable advantage by establishing initiatives that allow on-line interactions and the on-line transmission of orders to buy or sell. However, a company operating in the same sector whose generally older customers have considerably more assets and are more conservative in their investment choices could lose its competitive advantage if it were to switch the majority of its customer interactions on line. In this case, it may be much more appropriate to offer on-line information and managed portfolio consultation services, and to concentrate on using the new technologies to strengthen the service of the brokers who will continue to play a fundamental role in the management of customer relations.

Strategic positioning is due to a set of many factors, including:

- the type of competitive advantage being sought (cost or differentiation);
- the market segment(s) targeted by the firm, and the socio-demographic profile of its existing customers and those it would like to acquire;
- the location of the customers;
- competitive success, mainly measured in terms of market share and brand recognition.

When evaluating the possibilities of success of an e-business initiative, it is useful to compare the profile of on-line users with that of the firm's customers. Among other things, if the customers are final consumers, it is necessary to remember that their percentages of Internet accesses and methods of use vary in relation to factors such as average income, age, gender and geographical context (town/country, North/South, etc.). In order to give an idea of the impact of socio-demographic variables on access to the Internet, Figures 21 and 22 show the relationship between the percentages of Internet access and income/age.

In addition to considering the match between the profile of Internet users and the market segments supplied, it is also important to assess whether or

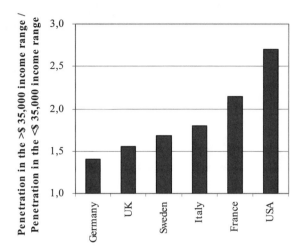

Figure 18-20. Income divide: ratio of Internet penetration between people in high and low income ranges in some countries. Sources: Jupiter 2002 and Booz Allen 2002.

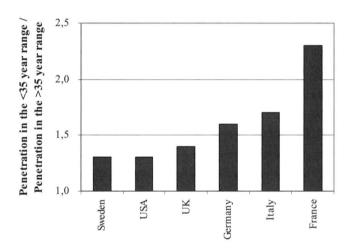

Figure 18-21. Age divide: ratio of Internet penetration between people aged up to 35 years and those aged more than 35 years in some countries. Sources: Jupiter 2002 and Booz Allen 2002.

not the off-line competitive strategy is compatible with the implications of an on-line presence. For example, a supermarket chain that has always counted on a cost strategy leading to the creation of an image of economy may find it difficult to attract on-line consumers willing to pay for the convenience of computer shopping with a home delivery service.

The analysis of Internet users must also take into account ongoing trends. According to the data on SDA Bocconi's World Internet Project, the number of

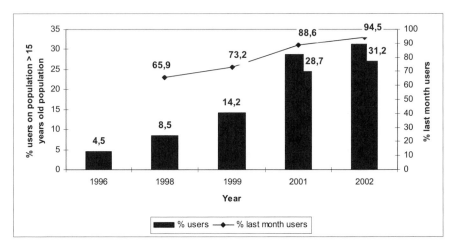

Figure 18-22. Internet users.

Internet users greatly increased between 1998 and 2001, but growth has been slower since 2002.

The on-line population consisted in 2002 of about 31% of Italians (considering the universe of people aged 16 years or more), and they are also becoming more regular users: only 66% of users declared using the Internet in the previous month in 1998, but the corresponding figure in 2002 was 94.5%. About 90% use e-mail, 45% use the Internet to make travelling arrangements, and 40% to listen to or download music: however, only 14.5% are involved in e-commerce.

The growing maturity of the Internet market is also demonstrated by the fact that almost half of the population have friends or relatives that can be reached via the Internet and that use of the Internet has become very widespread among the young (68% of people aged 18–24 years and 84% of university students).

3.5.   E-business Initiatives

E-business initiatives can support all company processes from internal processes to external relations, and from core to ancillary processes. The data shown in Figures 23 and 24 above provides an international comparison of the use of e-commerce, and interesting DTI IBS data show how ICT technologies are being used to transform support and core processes.

One interesting finding emerging from Figures 23 and 24 is that (with some exceptions) the level of use of ICT technologies for support functions is substantially similar in the different countries, whereas their use to transform core processes such as logistics, design and the management of re-orders seems to be much more related to the level of the countries' digital maturity.

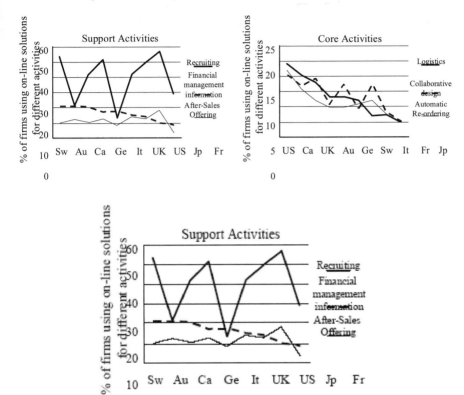

Figure 18-23. Use of ICT technologies to transform support and core functions in some Western countries. Source: DTI IBS 2001.

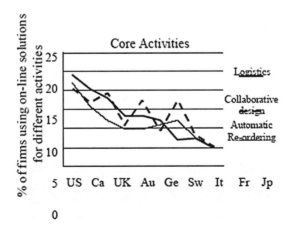

Figure 18-24. Use of ICT technologies to transform support and core functions in some Western countries. Source: DTI IBS 2001.

The ability to get the "network pieces" to "speak" to each other not only concerns aspects of internal organization, but also the various players in the value chain (or net). One particular difficulty in this regard arises from differences in the *readiness* of the collaborating players: this is especially critical in Italy because the majority of Italian firms are small. A recent IDC study (source: Sole 24Ore of 29 January 2003) found that, at the end of 2002, except for the managerial area, Italian SMEs made use of few and poorly integrated on-line applications at operational and business levels (automated Crm and Scm management, e-procurement, etc.), and concluded that this was also due to a "cultural bottle-neck".

A study carried out by Milan Polytechnic's Intranet Observatory in 2002 found that e-business initiatives aimed at improving internal processes were among the most widespread. This Observatory classifies intranets (divided into institutional, knowledge management and operation intranets) as follows, taking into account their different functions:

1. communications
2. service platforms
3. process supports
4. document management
5. collaborative work
6. communities

Among other things, the Observatory reported data showing that information (concerning benefits, company news, employees, departments and information from the personnel) occupy the lion's share of internal portals, and that greater use was made of static rather than dynamic applications, which usually indicates less sophistication and a loer service level. However, it is interesting to note the significant weight of the training applications made available through intranet portals. In its analysis of the reasons underlying the difficulties of developing intranets, the same study highlighted critical factors mainly related to the organizational and management resources necessary to support and govern these processes, thus confirming the results of Boston's MIT study of the relationship between organizational capital and investments in technology described above.

The decision-making process leading to the development of e-business applications is critical. There is often no consistency between the strategic objectives assigned to e-business initiatives and their real implementations: for example, the previously cited Intranet Observatory study found that knowledge building and sharing were among the most frequently declared objectives of intranets, whereas knowledge management applications are still rare in internal digital systems.

3.6.   E-business Results

Evaluating the results of an e-business initiative is a highly complex and delicate operation that can lead to mistaken conclusions and decisions if it is not done properly.

In the case of the intranets monitored by the Observatory of Milan Polytechnic, the firms were not very satisfied with the results. The study underlined the point that the factor which most clearly discriminated the successes from the partial failures seemed to be the care of the firm in managing and accompanying the introduction as a process of organizational change. In the unsuccessful cases, the firm limited itself to introducing community and document management technologies, without making any substantial organizational or managerial interventions, and paying little attention to communicating the initiative internally. In the most successful cases, the introduction of the technologies was accompanied by a deliberate strategy of communication and the management of change aimed at modifying interpersonal behaviors and relationships.

It is interesting to see that the ability to measure the results of e-business initiatives reasonably accurately is improving but cannot be taken for granted, and it is worth making some comments about the most frequently used measures of success:

- The number of visitors to a site is an imperfect measure of success insofar as what counts is the number of visitors belonging to the target and how many of these become new customers, how many buy, and to what extent they use the available on-line services.
- The number of new customers acquired is certainly significant, but needs to be compared with the unit cost of their acquisition. It is also important to evaluate the quality of the acquired customers: for example, if the site leads to the acquisition of customers who are more price conscious and less loyal than those acquired through other channels, the increase in the number of customers may give rise to pressure to reduce the firm's average margins.
- Reduced customer training and service costs are important, but it is also necessary to assess whether the automation of customer relations affects other aspects of the relationship, such as opportunities of cross-selling.
- A very small number of firms seem to calculate the return on investment (ROI); but when judging this finding, it must be borne in mind that such calculations can be very difficult whenever the aim of the e-business initiative is to improve quality rather than reduce costs, as better quality does not necessarily lead to an immediate increase in turnover. Furthermore, if a firm's main competitors introduce similar initiatives, strengthening on-line service may not lead to any incremental financials return, but simply represent a necessary step for maintaining previously acquired positions.

The above comments do not mean that such measures are useless. The number of visitors and new customers, reduced customer training and service costs, and ROI (if it can be calculated) only provide a partial picture of the results if considered individually, but if they are combined and considered together with other data, they can make an extremely significant contribution. We would simply like to stress that a correct evaluation implies a simultaneous and highly complex assessment of a large number of measurements.

Finally, it must be remembered that the ability to create value for customers does not necessarily lead to better financial results. In simplified terms, it can be said that the value created by a firm (or a network of firms) is the difference between the benefits created for its customers and the costs sustained in order to create them. It may happen that an innovation simultaneously leads to an increase in created value and a shift in the relative bargaining power of the players involved, with the result that the player creating the value may obtain only a small part of it for itself or even find that its own profitability decreases. For example, in the financial trading sector, the new technologies have certainly created the conditions for offering better customer service, but the advent of on-line trading has also reduced the level of differentiation perceived by customers and led to less flexible cost structures for the traders, thus triggering increased competitive pressures and a considerable reduction in the commissions that customers are prepared to pay. In this case, the greater created value has mainly benefited final customers, whereas the average profits of the traders have decreased. The negative impact that the Internet can have on sector attractiveness has been particularly underlined by Porter (2001).

4.   E-BUSINESS IN ITALY: EMPIRICAL FINDINGS FROM THE CASE ANALYSES

Doing business in the digital economy means materially participating in the development of the Net economy. The word "Net" seems to be the only one currently capable of describing the ongoing phenomenon because "new economy", "eBusiness", "Internet Business" and all of the words preceded by "e-" are too closely associated with a period of financial illusions that many also see as a period of substantial failure. The economy is based on (and will continue to grow in) a context characterized by the digitalization of products and services (above all those related to others whose tangible nature makes them impossible to convert into electronic form), and the digitalization of the working processes that support production, sales and distribution. The possibility of digitalizing products and services, and executing digitalized working processes, is based on two elements that are intrinsic to the network concept:

- the organization and establishment of *networked operations* as a set of internal and external cells,[3] which means seeing the network in terms of organizational logics and sensitivities;
- the full use of the technological and applicative infrastructure made available by the Internet in its intra- (intranets) and inter-organizational forms (the Internet in the strict sense and extranets).

In this perspective, individual firms have sought utility and value in their use of the Net in various ways:

- by developing new products and services in an attempt to increase turnover, broaden their customer base, enter new markets, and so on (what is meant by the strategic and commercial value of the Net economy[4]);
- by optimizing the execution of internal processes and functions in an attempt to increase efficiency and improve their internal image, motivation, etc. (organizational and economic value);
- by optimizing the execution of processes and functions involving third parties in an attempt to improve efficiency and establish more effective relationships with the environment (organizational, strategic and economic value).

Many firms considered the first as the best means of ensuring their development: their first and largest e-business projects were e-commerce projects, and were given precedence. The ongoing SDA Bocconi study and the present paper mainly concentrate on what seems to more hidden from the "public" (customers and the general press): i.e. the optimization actions which, although apparently having no strategic or commercial effect on company evolution, are often factors of profitability and the drivers of actions having a more strategic value insofar as they open up various positive perspectives:

- they improve margins by reducing costs;
- they generate useful internal knowledge and experience that can be used for more aggressive marketing and sales projects;

---

3   This element is well expressed by the concepts of cellular firms and value chains and constellations. See Landier H., *L'impresa policellulare*, Guerini e Associati, 1988; Norman R. – Ramirez R., *Le strategie interattive d'impresa. Dalla catena alla costellazione del valore*, Etaslibri; 1995.

4   In its strict sense, the Net economy can be defined as an economy founded on the intensive use of networking technologies within the context of the Internet, such as the use of the Web and its typical (browser) interfaces, TCP/IP communication protocols, etc. Although they allow network connections between different players (inside or outside an individual firm), traditional technologies such as EDI (electronic data interchange) solutions based on "proprietary" protocols should be excluded. In practice, the concept of an organizational and technological Net proposed here also includes technological solutions that, although destined to be replaced by extranet web-based logics, are still important elements of the Net itself.

- they allow people to adjust gradually to working in a network environment;
- they permit the development of a largely technology-based working culture;
- they make it possible to review or re-engineer functionally conceived working activities in a transversally integrated manner;
- they help to encourage the modernization of technological infrastructures that are no longer efficient and expensive to maintain.

It seems to be particularly interesting to analyze such projects in the contexts of traditional firms that were not directly founded as Internet-based startups but:

- were started in the pre-Net economy era and use the Net to carry out their usual business;
- or were set up by traditional firms in order to exploit the advantages of the Net and concentrate on different aspects of Net-based processes (such as Exiros of the Techint group[5]).

They operate in all economic sectors: public and private; profit and nonprofit; manufacturing; commercial; financial, personal and other services; and both the demand and supply side of technology. For the qualitative part of the survey, they were chosen on the basis of the following criteria:

- traditional firms;
- firms with completed Net economy projects, or projects that are being completed but whose results can already be evaluated;
- firms capable of measuring project results in a sufficiently objective manner by providing factors of evaluating and (if measurable) their related values.

Table 5 lists the firms on the basis of two variables: the company process involved in the organizational and technological investment; the type of project (Internet projects for e-commerce solutions and informative/promotional actions aimed at customers; intranet projects for internal use; extranet projects for investments in external processes involving privileged customers, suppliers, and partners).

Table 6 shows the most significant results individually declared by the firms for each of the processes on which they invested by purchasing and using web-based technology: the details of each case are given in Biffi and Dematte (2003).

Finally, Table 7 lists the principal factors allowing the success of the project and the good functioning of the involved process or processes.

An analysis of the set of cases and the considerations expressed in theoretical contributions lead to the following reflections:

---

5   See case below.

Table 18-4. Complete list of the cases studied, with information about the industries and the activities of the different firms

Firm	Industry	Product
USI – Unicredit servizi Informativi	IT services	Communication and IT services
Lyreco Italia	Direct distribution	Office stationery
Manuli Rubber Spa	Plastic manufacturing	Plastic components
Gavazza	Food manufacturing	Coffe
Linear Spa (gruppo Unipol)	Insurance services	Insurance products (car insurances)
BNL	Banking	Bank services for consumers and businesses
Nextra	Financial services	Financial investments
HP Italia	ICT	Computers and IT services
Comune di Modena	Local government	Local government
ACEA Spa	Local public utilities	Electrical power and water
Pirello Pneumatici	Plastic manufacturing	Tires
1city.biz (UniCredito)	Business services	Emarketplace BtoB
ABB Sace (Gruppo ABB)	Mechanical manufacturing	Electrical products
Techint/Tenaris	Engeneering	Plant construction
Dell Italia	ICT distribution	Distribution of computers
Nylstar	Textile manufacturing	Chemical textile fibers
Ducati	Automotive	Motorbykes

1. Firms tend to concentrate their efforts in certain areas of improvement and optimization:

   - provisioning, and the related functions of production, logistics and administration, by means of typical supply chain projects (ABB Sace, Techint, Dell and Nylstar, Manuli, Pirelli Pneumatici);
   - the management of human resources by means of intranet projects aimed at personnel (USI[6]; BNL; HP; Nextra);
   - B2B e-commerce using extranet applications (Unicredito, Manuli);

2. The multiple advantages and results must be precisely assessed and carefully evaluated. The most original include:

   - the creation of value in customer/supplier relationships when the supplier creates value for the customer by means of technologically governed outsourcing mechanisms (see the case of Lyreco);
   - the creation and use of image to increase customer loyalty (Ducati, Acea);

---

6 Example given in "Portali aziendali B2E in ambito bancario" *[B2E company portals in banking]*, in Biffi e Demattè, 2003.

Table 18-5. Areas of Net economy action and company experiences

Project Process	Internet	Intranet	Extranet
Internal/external production process planning and management		Dell	Manuli
Provisioning (purchasing, administration, logistics, monitoring)		HP Pirelli Pneumatici	ABB Sace, Techint2, Dell, Nylstar
Internal and external processes1	Lavazza (e-commerce)	Lavazza	Lavazza
Sales network automation		Lavazza	
Sales processes and customer management	Dell (e-commerce) Ducati Nylstar (e-commerce) Linear (information/ promotion) ACEA (e-services) Modena Council (civic network)		Dell (e-commerce) Ducati Manuli (e-commerce) Unicredito (e-marketplace) Lyreco (e-commerce) Linear (device) ACEA (e-services)
Financial management		Nextra	Nylstar, Unicredito (e-marketplace)
Information and communications management	Modena Council (civic network)	Nextra, HP, Modena Council	
Knowledge management		Lavazza, HP	
Human resources processes		Lavazza, Nextra, HP, BNL,USI	
Competence management		Nextra, BNL	

- improvements in administrative activities as such, and associated with core or support processes (Dell and Nylstar);
- the creation of value by means of product and service reconfiguration and extension (Linear, Acea).

Not all of the benefits are easily reproducible in different contexts, as is shown by the cases of Dell and Nylstar;

Table 18-6. Net economy actions and results

Process	Results
Improvements in provisioning process	Better index of stock rotation and warehouse value (ABB Sace, Techint, Dell)
	Reduced goods inward acceptance times (ABB Sace)
	Reduced purchasing costs (Techint, Dell, Nylstar, Pirelli Pneumatici)
	Reduced supplier management times (ABB Sace, Dell, Nylstar, Pirelli)
	Reduced purchasing times (Unicredito)
	Punctual deliveries (ABB Sace)
	Process transparency (Techint)
	Independence of cost items – logistics, purchasing, etc. (Techint)
	Greater control (Dell)
	Reduction in human resources (Techint)
	Awareness of responsibilities (Techint)
	Customer price savings (Unicredito)
	Rationalization of customer consumption (Acea)
	Selection of new opportunities/suppliers (Pirelli Pneumatici)
Improvements in administration process	Reduced resources and times for managing outgoing invoices (ABB Sace)
	Increased control (Dell)
	Flexible use of data (Dell)
	Timely data availability (Nylstar)
	Reduced error rate (Nylstar)
Improvements in managing production process	Better use of plant (Manuli)
	Reduced production planning resources (ABB Sace)
Customer management	Punctuality (Manuli)
	Reduced lead times (Manuli)
	Increased control (Dell)
	Invoicing transparency (Acea)
	Reduction in customer service personnel (Manuli)
	Greater loyalty (Ducati)
	More effective sales process (Manuli)
Management of human resources	Greater efficiency (Lavazza)
	Reduced operating costs and times (HP[1])
	Increased satisfaction of HR personnel (HP)
	More effective management of information and flows (BNL,USI)
Management of information and communications	Acquisition of a new culture (Nextra)
	More uniform communications systems (HP)
	Containment of resources dedicated to communications (HP)
	Greater timeliness and better quality (Dell, Acea)
Management of competences	More transparent assessment systems (Nextra)
	Greater perceived equity (Nextra)
	Reduced information overflow (Nextra)
	More widespread access to information (BNL)

Table 18-6. (Continued)

Process	Results
Company activities in general	More effective knowledge management (Lavazza)
	Better organizational climate (Lavazza)
Business development related to the core of the service	Acquisition of new customers for the management of purchasing processes (Techint, Unicredito)
	Greater facility in concluding contracts (Lyreco, Linear)
	Estension of range of services (Acea)
	Greater loyalty through the use of brand and community (Ducati)
Management and maintenance of technology and information system	Ease of updating new releases (BNL)
	Operational flexibility (BNL)

The company calculated the ROI of the investment, which was repaid in only 6 months.

Table 18-7. Success factors of the Net economy projects

Specific success factor of the action	Firm
Progressive process of acquisition and use	ABB Sace, HP[a]
Immediate search for information integration in the context of the value chain	Dell, Nylstar, Pirelli Pneumatici
Seeing the e-business not as a project but as rethinking the entrepreneurial formula	Manuli
Care over data normalization and the construction of databases	ABB Sace, Linear
Use of "layered" integration tools (middleware technologies and special interfaces) and not necessarily originally integrated tools	Lavazza, ABB Sace
Non-invasive approach to the change in working methods	Unicredito
Care and precision in designing the information support tool	Techint, Linear[b]
Strong sponsorship by company management	Techint, Unicredito
Valorization of the community concept	Ducati
Concentration of interfacing systems	HP
Redesign of processes and activities	Nylstar, Manuli, ACEA, Modena Council
Careful planning of the development of the personnel involved in using the electronic channel (knowledge and carreer paths)	Linear, ACEA, Modena Council
Careful planning of application management activities	USI

[a]The firm uses the concept of "evolving idea" to underline the basic aspect of the adopted implementation methodology.
[b]Prevalently in-house development.

- areas of improvement and optimization can be found in contexts of functional or horizontal process logic, but the latter seems to offer better results in terms of generated value[7];
- the spasmodic search for clearly measurable reasons (return on investment) is not necessarily a prerequisite for the action. In relation to projects for introducing e-mailing, the information systems manager of the Italian subsidiary of a multinational firm sustained in the mid-1990s that "in many cases, technology is not discussed but applied",[8] as a means of saying that so many applications are being created (who could now live and work without a telephone, even of the fixed type?). And this is demonstrated by a number of cases, such as Lavazza and the example of Usi concerning the contribution of banking portals. The problem is therefore not that of deciding whether to invest in a certain technology, but whether the obtained benefit can be pursued by means of a firm-specific success factor or is reproducible on the basis of the experience of others.

The overall picture that emerges from this study shows that the prospects of growth and development for Italian firms are interesting and capable of generating value for individual firms from different points of view. However, the main requirements for doing so are a sufficiently broad view of technological governance and a careful evaluation of the need to redesign work organizationally.

In brief, analysis of our cases confirms that the use of the e-business technologies can radically change the way of doing certain activities with substantial benefits of various kinds. But it also shows that the real advantages emerge when someone – who understands what the new technologies allow – reorganizes the way of designing products, managing purchases and interacting with suppliers, exchanging information with customers, and dialoguing and working with collaborators and peers involved in other processes. It is only if they are preceded by such rethinking and new organizational planning that the new technologies produce their expected effects. The renewal triggered by this work presupposes a clear identification of the way in which a firm wants to relate to its interlocutors (customers, suppliers, banks, shareholders and employees) in order to reap the various benefits of the more immediate and intense exchange that the new technologies allow.

---

[7] This seems to be particularly true in contexts in which vertical (functional) processes already have good levels of effectiveness and efficiency. In such cases, it seems to be possible to generate further value by integrating vertical processes in order to reduce redundancies and accelerating the passage of work from one process to another or between different phases of the same process managed by different functions.

[8] Teaching case "Sole Caldo" (unpublished), SDA Bocconi 1995.

These results have been, in the main points, confirmed by the quantitative analysis of the results of 56 interviews (mostly face-to-faces) to Italian firms of various industries and sizes.

5. E-BUSINESS IN ITALY: FIRST FINDINGS FROM THE BIT PROJECT

SDA Bocconi is participating with IIT Bombay and other research partners, in a project launched by the Center for Management in Information Economy of the UCLA's Anderson School of Management with the aim of studying the impact of digital technologies on the transformation of firms and economic sectors. The BIT project aims to collect data by means of surveys of samples of firms operating in different sectors in each country. One of its first phases involved conducting interviews in 56 firms of different sizes belonging to very different merceological sectors. Most of the interviews were conducted face-to-face by the researchers themselves. The first results of the project are summarized below.

5.1. Digital Firms

When asked which digital technologies/tool they use, the firms indicated (Figure 25) that e-mail has by now become a fundamental instrument of communication (widely used in almost all companies).

The data also show the growing importance of internal networks (used considerably more than the Internet). Some of the more sophisticated tools (e.g. mailing lists) are only used by specialized functions within the firms.

5.2. E-commerce and e-Procurement

Only a minority of the firms (Figure 26) have used e-commerce (electronic sales channels) and e-procurement (electronic purchasing channels). The e-commerce projects are often still experimental and mainly intended to improve service to existing customers.

5.3. E-business Results: Efficiency

The interviews also considered the business results made possible by the use of digital technologies. Although confirming that it is still difficult to make quantitative evaluations of the effects of using new digital technologies, and bearing in mind that we are still in a phase in which investments in technology often weigh negatively on the firms' profit and loss accounts, the examined cases made it possible to identify the first positive economic results above all in the areas of administrative efficiency and reduced internal communication costs.

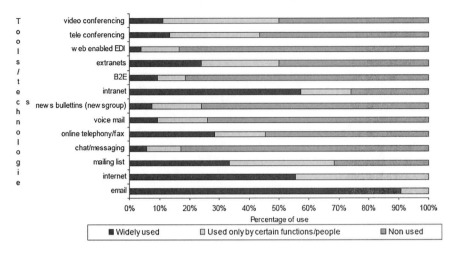

Figure 18-25. The use of technologies in different firms.

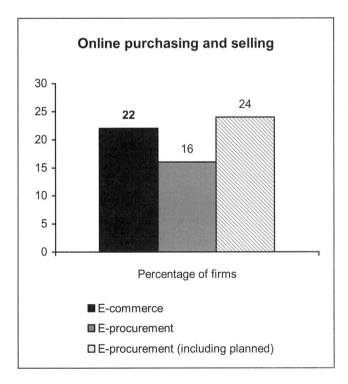

Figure 18-26. Purchasing and selling.

How has e-business influenced the operational and economic results of your firm?

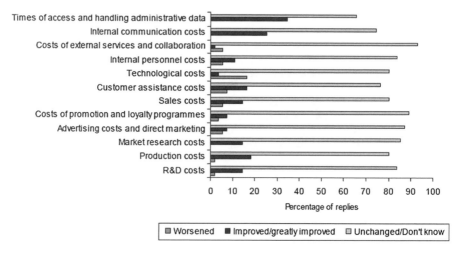

Figure 18-27. E-Business influence on your business.

5.4.   E-business Results: Creation of Intangible Resources

According to our analysis, E-business does not only lead to tangible economic results, but can also be measured in terms of the creation of strategic resources (Figure 28). The areas most frequently identified by the interviewees as showing the positive impact of e-business are those relating to the quality of knowledge supporting decision making and the area of relationships (satisfaction of employees, satisfaction and loyalty of customers, the strength of the brand among final customers and reputation in the business community).

5.5.   Network Firms

Digital technologies are already changing the face of company organization (Figure 28) by increasing the importance of remote communications and group work. Furthermore, work is becoming more flexible as a result of the use of outsourcing formulas.

The form of organization is changing. A network firm is not destructured and hierarchy-free, but it is no longer a traditional firm:

• E-business can increase managerial control instead of reducing organizational hierarchies.

• However, at the same time, the boundaries between different company functions become less clear cut and there is a radical change in communication models.

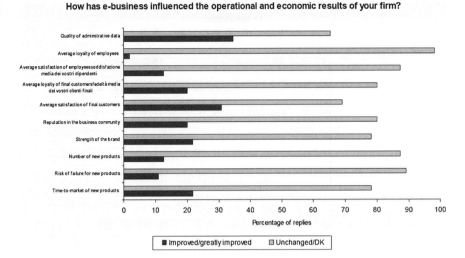

Figure 18-28. E-business influence in operational and economic results.

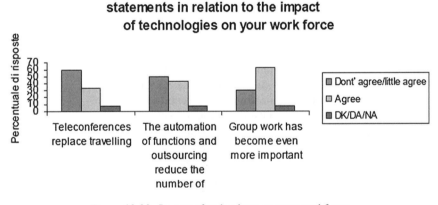

Figure 18-29. Impact of technology on your workforce.

The firms do not recognise themselves in the metaphor of "virtual firms" (see the importance of their physical nature and existing relationships), despite their high level of connectivity and flexibility.

5.6.   Networks of Firms

Outsourcing is increasing, but the number of partners with which the firms collaborate is not significantly increasing (Figure 30). Furthermore, the basis for the formation of new networks depends more on brand/reputation and the

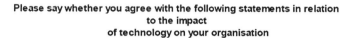

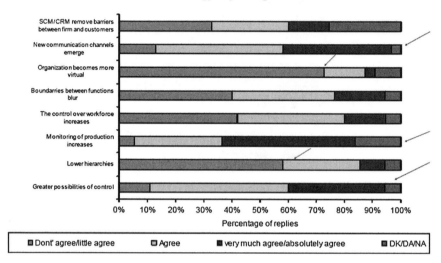

Figure 18-30. Network enterprise: control and flexibility.

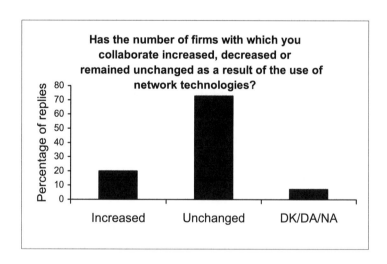

Figure 18-31. Result of the use of network technologies in the number of firms.

possibility of leveraging on existing relationships than on geographical proximity and the homogeneity of knowledge (Figure 31).

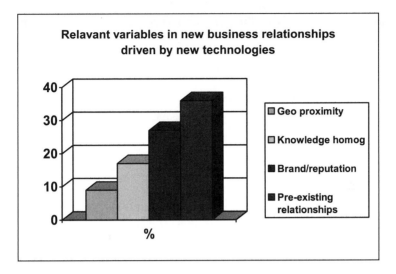

Figure 18-32. Relevant variables in new business relationships.

5.7. Summary of the Results of the Quantitative Analysis

Online and network technologies are diffusing in Italian firms and society, but the nature and characteristics of this transformation are complex and cannot be taken for granted. Summarizing our results we can say that:

1. firms digitalize relationships before transactions;
2. e-business requires technological investments, whose short-term results appear in the form of more efficient internal processes and the creation of strategic resources (quality and timeliness of knowledge, and quality of customer and employee relations), that we know are becoming the basis of sustainable competitive advantage in the knowledge economy;
3. the results of e-business depend on the invested tangible capital but also resources (culture and organizational capital);
4. firms are changing their organization, becoming more flexible and networked, inside and outside firm boundaries. This requires a major investment in rethinking the models (including cultural models) underlying their management practice.

6. CONCLUSIONS

The results of our study, summarized in this paper, show that e-business in Italy has reached a stage of development that makes it difficult to draw any simple and exhaustive conclusions. Analysis of the principal studies published over the last few years indicate a complex and ever-changing situation characterized by relatively little interest in direct e-commerce, and more investments in the automation and networking of internal processes and collaborations with customers and other partners in the value chain.

The available data highlight three phenomena whose particular relevance is due to their strategic impact:

1. the importance of cultural, social and organizational variables, not only as a pre-condition for the success of e-business projects, but also as a complementary "effect" of the projects themselves. This means that the existing intangible capital in the firms makes a competitive difference in the e-business scenario;
2. the "lateness" of the Italian companies in the digitalization of company *core processes* (logistics, purchasing, collaborative product development), which can create a country-level digital competitiveness gap;
3. the substantial difference in the rate of digitalization of company *core processes* between firms of different sizes. This can create a within-the-country digital competitive divide.

In order to network the organization, it is necessary to network knowledge and company relationships, which requires changing the idea of the firm, the idea of the market and the idea of organization. It is likely that who fails to invest in this new culture of firms and economic and organizational relationships, will find themselves at a considerable disadvantage that will be difficult to overcome in the future.

Furthermore, given that the automation of what we here call *core processes* is a relevant condition for the networking of firms and supply chains (which is in its turn a relevant condition for the development of efficiency-based and resource-based competitive advantages), we can expect that the *"e-business digital divide"* will redraw the map of economic power not only within countries, but also between countries in global markets. These changes are already profound even if not widely diffused; in order to be able to manage them, we have to accelerate our understanding and change capacities.

We are aware of the difficulty of measuring the results of e-business in Italy because of the short time since its introduction. However, we are also convinced that it is worth making an effort in this direction because it is already possible to see considerable changes in "digital organization" even if they have not yet led to better economic performances in all cases. The BIT project will study these strategic changes (which should not be ignored by the managements of firms operating in all economic sectors) by means of regular quantitative surveys based on interviews conducted in a significant sample of firms in the various countries involved. Analysis of these data over the next few years will allow us to give some additional answers to the questions that we and the managers of Italian firms are asking about the future of the Internet and other networks.

We believe that the work done so far will help the people who find themselves in the position of having to make complex decisions to capitalize both the positive and negative experiences of these highly experimental years. The time has come, for entrepreneurs and managers in manufacturing, service and public management spaces, to look at the real innovative potential that the Internet and ICT technologies can offer to their organizations in a more mature and balanced manner. They must not only carefully evaluate the presence or otherwise of the environmental, organizational and strategic pre-conditions necessary for the success of any e-business initiative, but must also be prepared to look with new eyes at their traditional ways of "doing things", by distinguishing those that are essential and indispensable elements of their company or industry business models from those that are related to an outdated information paradigm. Furthermore, in terms of management attitude, these managers must be aware that many e-business initiatives imply profound changes that require perseverance, flexibility and a clear strategic design.